Extraordinary Oregon!

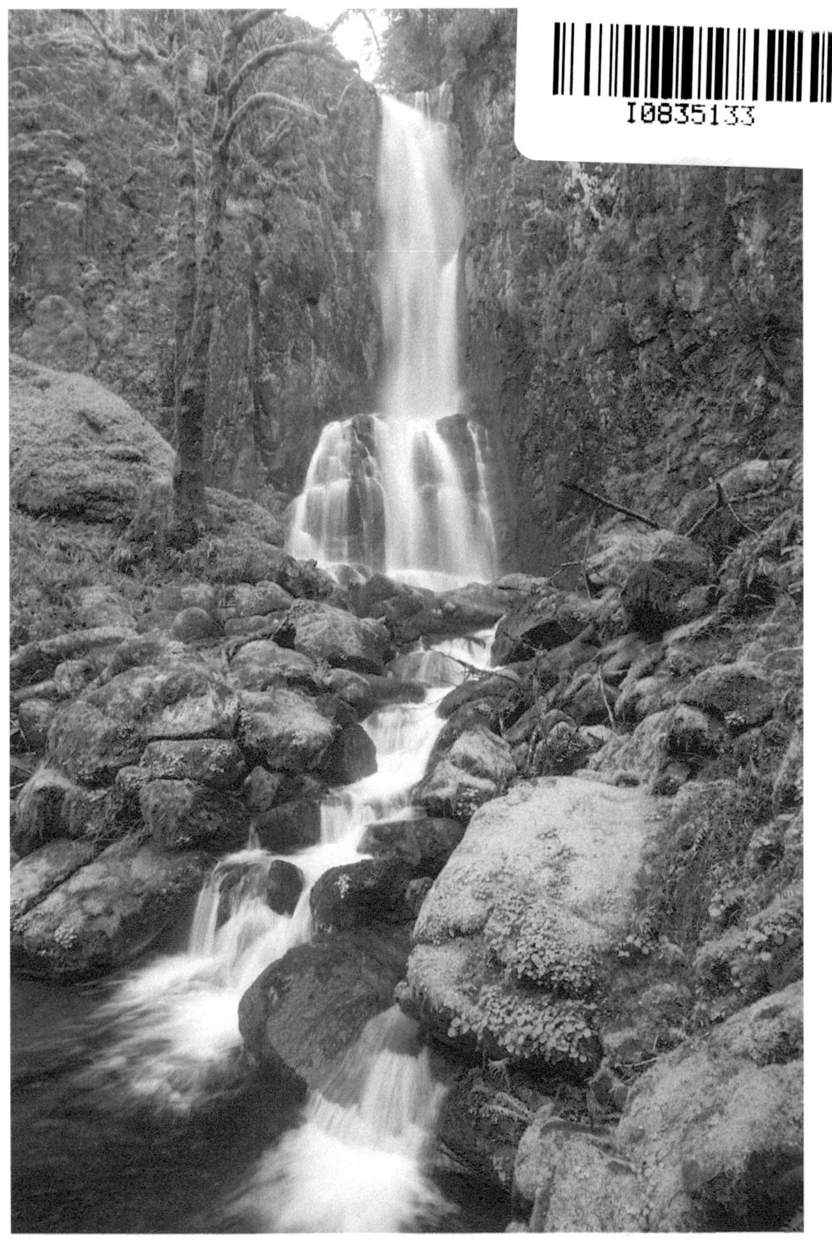

Matt Reeder

Printed in the United States of America
The Ruddy Hill Press

ISBN: 978-0-9889125-4-0
First edition, 2023

Written and designed by Matt Reeder. All photos and maps by Matt Reeder. Edited by Matt Reeder and Wendy Rodgers.

For more information about Matt Reeder, his books, his photos, and his adventures, see his website at: http://www.offthebeatentrailpdx.com

Maps in this book were generated with permission using CalTopo. For more information about CalTopo, see http://www.caltopo.com

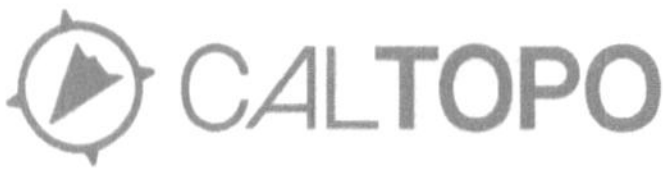

Cover photo: A small tarn with Eagle Cap in the distance (Hike 113)
Frontispiece photo: Kentucky Falls (Hike 10)
Back photo: Crater Lake from the trail to the Watchman (Hike 79)

Public land belongs to everyone. Do what you can to keep it that way.

Disclaimer: Countless hours were spent hiking, researching and writing the information found here. The author personally checked and verified all of the information here to the fullest extent of his abilities, and hiked every trail at least once - but in some cases as many as ten times. That being said, errors are always possible with a project as large as this. The author and the Ruddy Hill Press are not responsible for any mishaps that may occur while using this book. Furthermore, the landscape is constantly changing. Trail closures, road washouts, fire damage and land ownership changes can close hikes and alter the accuracy of the information found in this book. Last but not least, hiking is an inherently dangerous activity. Please prepare yourself before you head outside, make sure you check local conditions and know your limitations and those of everyone with whom you are hiking. Know before you go!

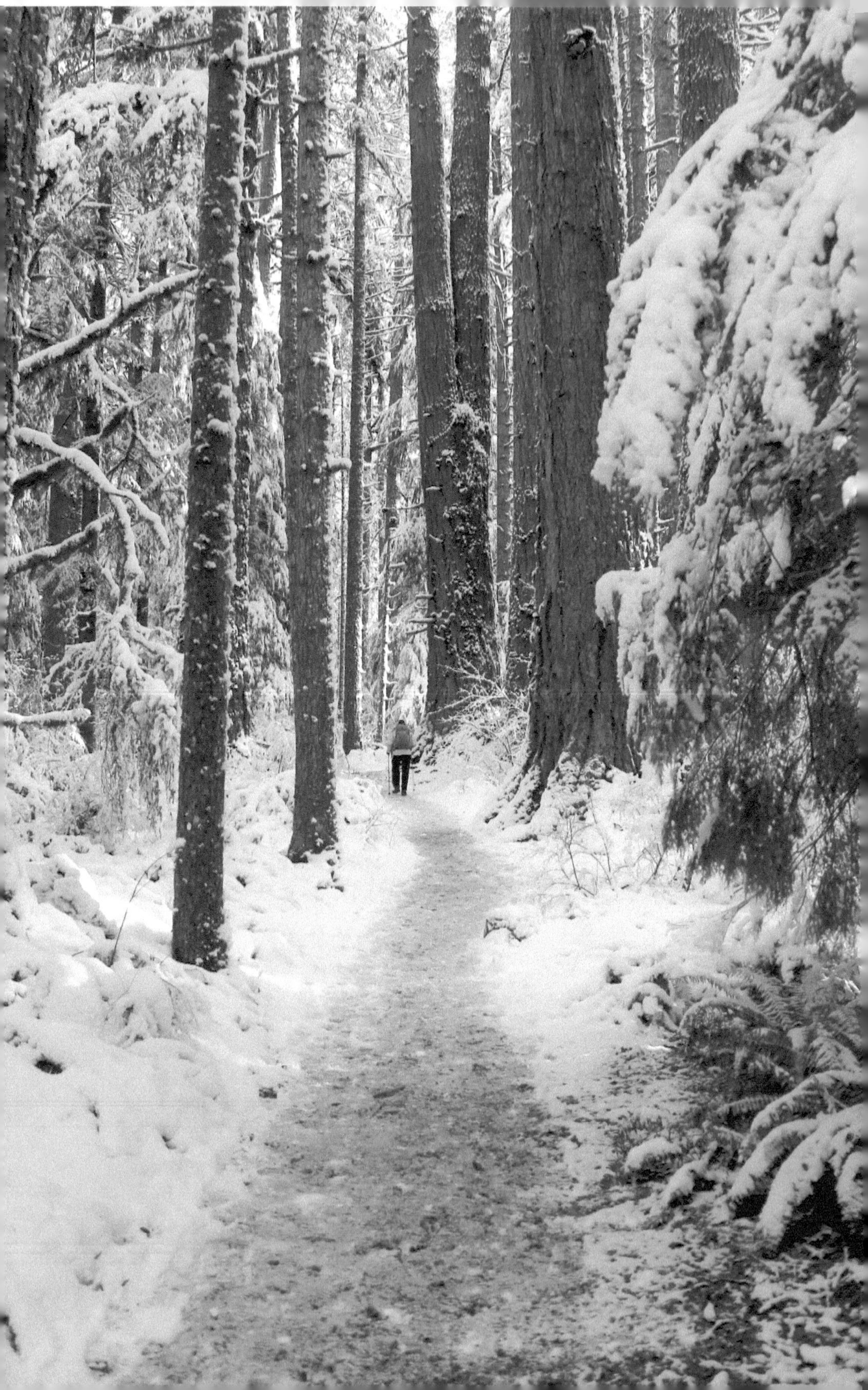

Acknowledgements!

As always, thank you most of all to Wendy, my partner on and off the trail. Thank you for your infinite patience during the writing of this book, and for enduring my many long trips away from home, far away from you. You always listen to my crazy ideas with a smile on your face, and respond with sarcasm and a kind suggestion. I'd be lost without you!

Thank you to all of my friends and family who have always supported me unconditionally through the long process of writing this and my other books. Your love means the world to me, and I couldn't do any of this without you.

I want to send a special thank you to my friends who joined me on hikes over the past few years of book research. I especially wish to thank Karl Langenwalter, Keith Dechant, Sarah Johnson, Zane Davidson, and Marcum Bell for joining me on some of my longer research trips for this book. Extra special thanks go to Karl Langenwalter for that night in Hells Canyon when I had a belly full of ouzo and a head full of hurt.

I want to thank Heather Polonsky and Silja Tobin for their friendship, kind suggestions, and constant encouragement during my work on this book. You're the coolest!

A special thanks goes to Franziska Weinheimer of Hike Oregon. Thank you friend for always listening to my crazy ideas, for helping me figure out the scope of my project, for giving me lots of helpful suggestions, and for being a friend for the past few years.

Thanks to the Mazamas, and especially the Adventurous Young Mazamas, for allowing me to lead hikes for all these years. You've helped me explore the Pacific Northwest, and I'm proud to be a Mazama. We climb high!

I also wish to thank my supporters who regularly contact me with ideas, suggestions, corrections, and inspiration. The internet can be a toxic and scary place, but I want to send my love and support to everyone who continues to inspire me. You are loved!

Finally, I wish to extend my endless love and gratitude to the musicians, artists, songwriters, and performers for giving me inspiration and helping me get through twelve years of long nights and endless road trips while researching this and my other books. My life would be empty without music.

Extraordinary Oregon!

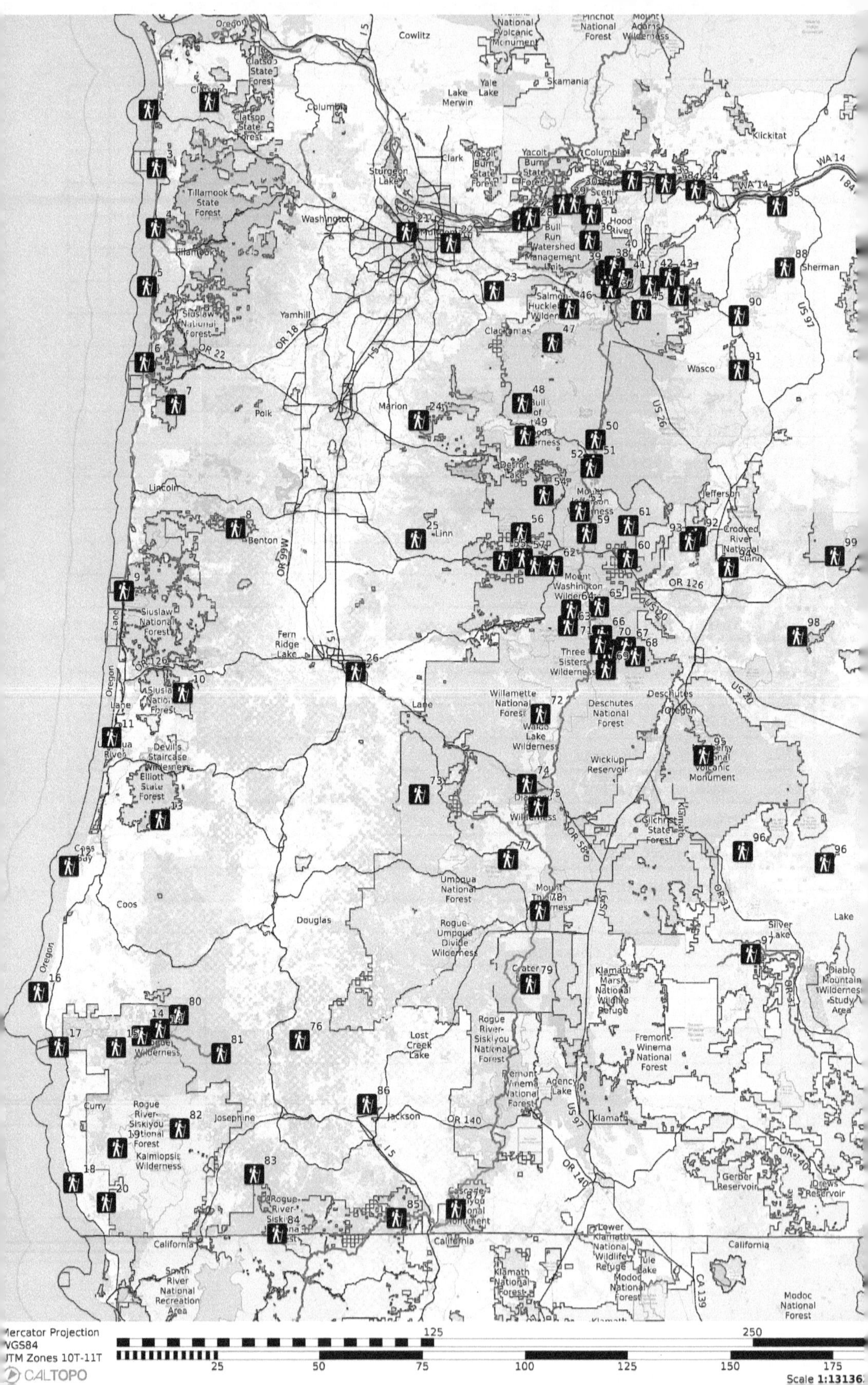

Mercator Projection
WGS84
UTM Zones 10T-11T
CALTOPO
Scale 1:13136

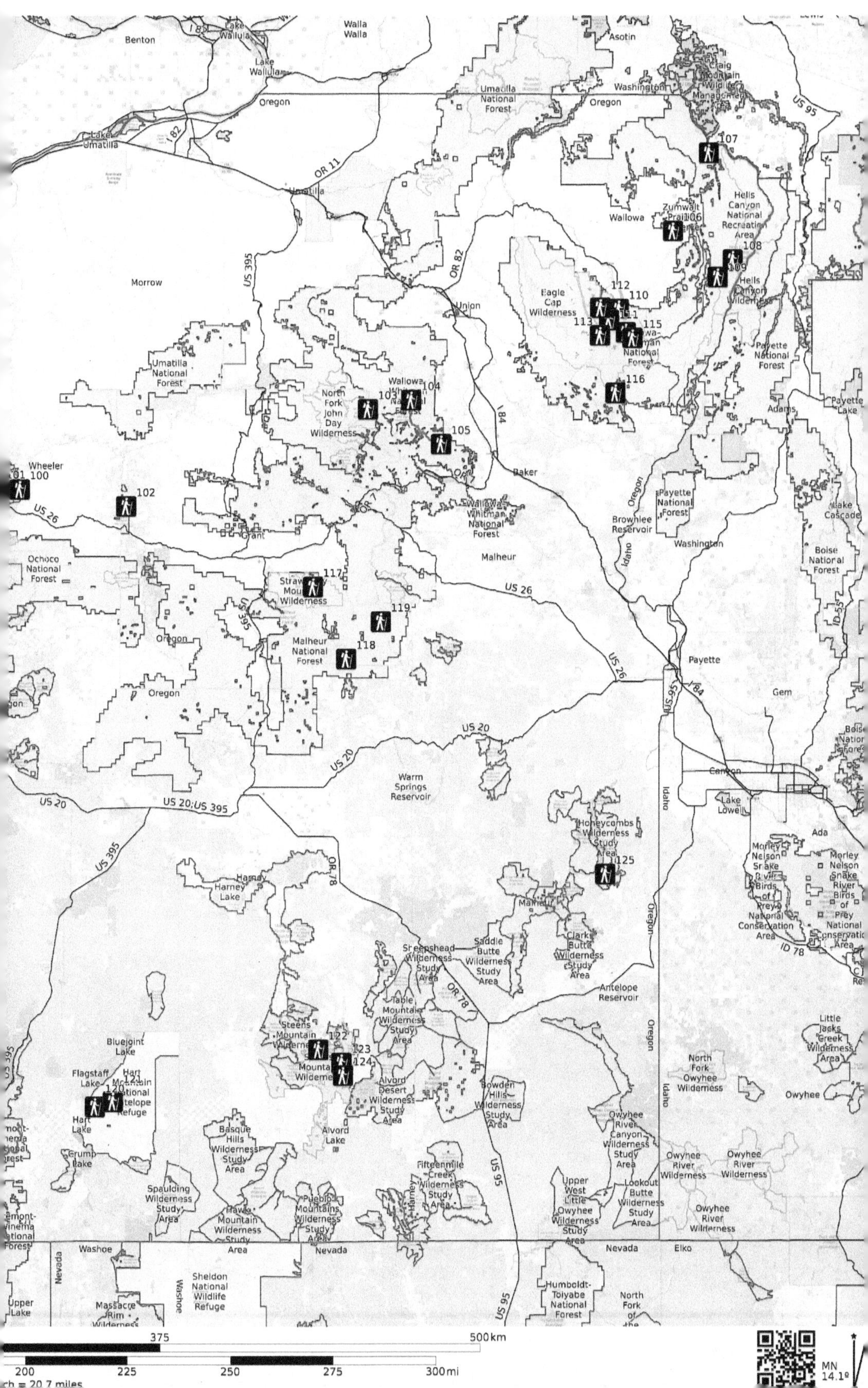

Benton
Lake Wallula
Walla Walla
Asotin
Oregon
Washington
Umatilla National Forest
Craig Mountain Wildlife Management
Lake Umatilla
OR 11
US 95
107
Wallowa
Zumwalt Prairie
106
Hells Canyon National Recreation Area
108
109
Hells Canyon Wilderness
Morrow
US 395
OR 82
Union
Eagle Cap Wilderness
112
110
113
115
Payette National Forest
116
Umatilla National Forest
Wallowa Whitman National Forest
104
103
North Fork John Day Wilderness
105
I 84
Adams
Payette Lake
Wheeler
101 100
102
US 26
Baker
Grant
OR 7
Wallowa-Whitman National Forest
Brownlee Reservoir
Washington
Lake Cascade
Ochoco National Forest
Malheur
Boise National Forest
117
Strawberry Mountain Wilderness
US 26
119
Malheur National Forest
118
Payette
Gem
US 20
Canyon
Warm Springs Reservoir
US 20
US 20;US 395
Lake Lowell
Idaho
Honeycombs Wilderness Study Area
125
Ada
Morley Nelson Snake River Birds of Prey National Conservation Area
ID 78
Harney
Harney Lake
OR 78
Malheur
Sheepshead Wilderness Study Area
Saddle Butte Wilderness Study Area
Clarks Butte Wilderness Study Area
Antelope Reservoir
Table Mountain Wilderness Study Area
Steens Mountain Wilderness
122
123
124
Little Jacks Creek Wilderness Area
Bluejoint Lake
Flagstaff Lake
Hart Mountain National Antelope Refuge
121
120
Hart Lake
Alvord Desert Wilderness Study Area
Bowden Hills Wilderness Study Area
North Fork Owyhee Wilderness
Owyhee
Owyhee River Canyon Wilderness Study Area
Basque Hills Wilderness Study Area
Alvord Lake
Crump Lake
Fifteenmile Creek Wilderness Study Area
US 95
Owyhee River Wilderness
Spaulding Wilderness Study Area
Pueblo Mountains Wilderness Study Area
Hawk Mountain Wilderness Study Area
Upper West Little Owyhee Wilderness Study Area
Lookout Butte Wilderness Study Area
Washoe
Nevada
Elko
Sheldon National Wildlife Refuge
Humboldt-Toiyabe National Forest
North Fork
Upper Lake
Massacre Rim Wilderness
375
500 km
200
225
250
275
300 mi
MN 14.1°

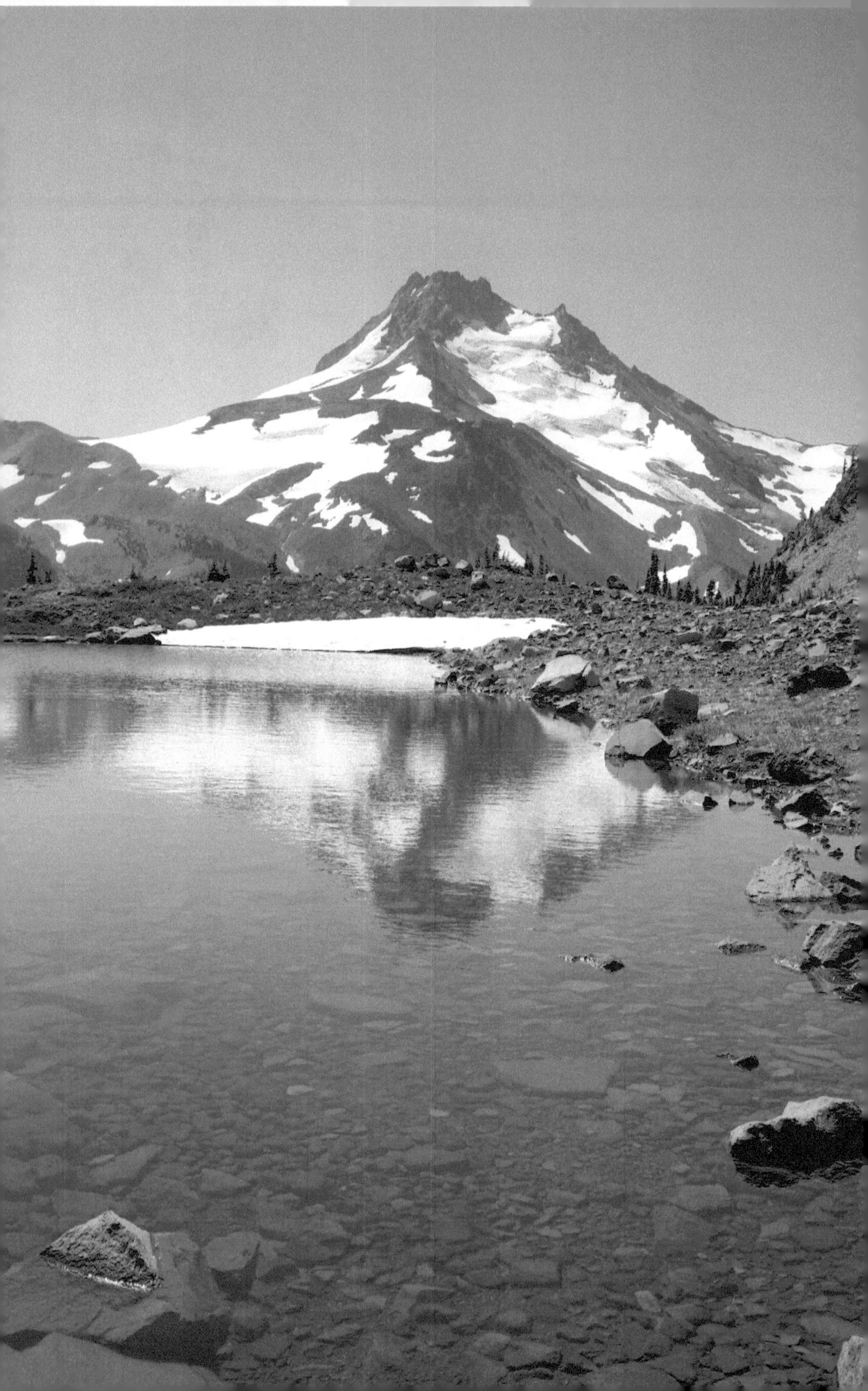

Extraordinary Oregon!

Some years ago I was on a hike in the Columbia River Gorge with friends when our conversation turned to the most beautiful states in the country. I'm not sure what led us to the subject, but it turned out that the four of us had each been to at least 35 of the 50 US states. So we decided to rank all fifty US states in order of scenic beauty. After some discussion, we decided that Alaska should be number 1. I argued for Oregon in the top spot, and I was outvoted. When the time came for the second spot, I managed to convince the rest of my friends that Oregon should be voted in at number 2 – over the suggestions of Hawaii, Utah, California, and Washington. Lofty praise indeed? I'm still not convinced that we chose our top spot correctly – I think Oregon should occupy the top spot.

I stand by my opinion. After all, what other American state can offer rugged coastline, jagged and glaciated volcanic peaks, expansive ancient forest, immensely deep canyons, and resplendently remote desert? Many of the states suggested in our discussion that day long ago can offer most of this – but none other than Oregon can offer them all. More than this, Oregon is a profoundly peaceful place. No matter where you are in the Beaver State, you will almost certainly find somewhere beautiful to explore. This is not something you can say about most other states.

I have spent most of my life in Oregon. When I was 7 years old, I moved from my family home in Central Illinois to Salem, where I would spend much of my childhood. My stepfather loved the outdoors, and he took me camping from a young age. I grew up hiking in the Cascades east of Salem, primarily in the Opal Creek canyon and on the west slopes of Mount Jefferson. We also went on extensive trips into the North Cascades and Olympic mountains in Washington, and into central and eastern Oregon. I climbed my first mountain, South Sister, at age 13. When I was 16, we moved back to Illinois to be closer to family. While I was happy to be closer to my family, I was very sad to leave the mountains I had grown to love so much. Oregon's scenic beauty remained on my mind until I moved back after finishing college in 2005. It has remained a central part of my life since then. I wrote three hiking guidebooks primarily centered in Oregon: *Off the Beaten Trail*, *101 Hikes in the Majestic Mount Jefferson Region*, and *PDX Hiking 365*. Much of my adult life has been spent exploring the near and far corners of the Beaver State. Simply put, I am in love with Oregon, and all that she has to offer.

This love sustained me through some of the darkest moments in the state's history. In 2020, I remained near home throughout the COVID-19 pandemic, and I spent my spare time exploring as many new and obscure trails as I could. I managed to find a lot of beautiful places that were new to me, places that helped me process the deadly plague spreading through the country and the world. And like so many of you, I watched in horror as the Labor Day Fires of 2020 tore through so much of the western half of the state, leveling some communities and consuming hundreds of thousands of acres of forest. I took these fires extremely hard, and in the aftermath I was left wondering what fresh hell could possibly be around the corner.

This book is a product of that anxiety. I decided to write this book sometime in early 2020, before the pandemic. I began to research the book during summer and fall of 2020. Over the next two years, I drove more than 20,000 miles across the state of Oregon and hiked something like 1,500 miles in Oregon alone. Over the course of this writing project, I saw much of what our state has to offer, and I came to love her even more. I did not get everywhere I wanted to go; most of this book was written on solo road trips on breaks from my day job, and there were some places that were simply impossible to get to. Fires, windstorms, snowstorms, and thunderstorms kept me away from places that I wanted to visit. For the most part, however, I managed to explore the state to the fullest extent possible, All of these adventures informed how I approached and created this project, and I emerged with the book you find in your hands right now. It was a labor of love, but I am very proud to present to you the most extraordinary hikes in Oregon.

How I chose each hike:
These are the most extraodinary hikes in Oregon. Every hike in this book - all 125 of them - is not only an excellent hike, but also offers a unique and fascinating experience that you are sure to love. Taste is subjective, of course; you may not like the drive to the trailhead, or you may not be as excited about wildflowers as I am, but there is much to love here for every Oregon hiker.

Hikes were chosen based on a number of factors: 1) all hikes must be easy to access and navigate (with some noteworthy exceptions); and 2) they must doable in one day (hikes that can be backpacked are also noted as such). For the former, I tried to avoid any hikes that require a jeep, truck, or high-clearance vehicle. There are some exceptions to this but for the most part, you should be able to drive a low-clearance vehicle to every trailhead in this book. I drove to all of these hikes in either a Subaru Impreza or a Subaru Outback. You should be able to do the same, although road conditions do sometimes change due to weather, logging operations, and changes in management.

Ease of hikes:
You may notice that I do not rate hikes by their difficulty. In my experience, the difficulty of a hike is based on so many subjective factors that any rating is completely pointless. Some people find hikes of 5 miles and no elevation gain to be difficult while others can hike as much as 30 miles with 6,000 or more feet of elevation in a single day. Complicating matters further are trail and weather conditions. For example, a hike with little shade and a moderate amount of elevation gain can become a very difficult hike on a hot day. The best strategy is to know your abilities, and plan for your hike accordingly.

If you simply must have difficulty ratings, here is a good guide:

- **Easy** – less than 7 miles and 1,000 feet of elevation gain
- **Moderate** – 6 – 10 miles with less than 2,000 feet of elevation gain
- **Difficult** – 8 or more miles with more than 2,000 feet of elevation gain
- **Very Difficult** – 12 or more miles with more than 3,000 feet of elevation gain
- **Hiking legend** – 15 or more miles with more than 4,000 feet of elevation gain

Hiking preparation - A disclaimer:
Before we get started, a disclaimer is necessary. Hiking is a joyous, wonderfully fun activity. Without taking proper precautions, it can also be very dangerous. Please be prepared wherever you go, whether it is to Powell Butte in Portland or Little Blitzen Gorge in the Steens Mountain Wilderness. Information and preparation can mean the difference between life and death. Furthermore, and I cannot stress this enough: **DO NOT** rely on your phone to get you out of an emergency! Many of the hikes in this book are within the range of cell phone service, but a great many hikes do not have any service at all.

The best line of defense against accidents and unfortunate circumstance is to go into each hike as prepared as possible. Bring a topographic map of each place you go. I have provided a map for most of the hikes in this book but you should still bring an additional map if possible. You should also check online or at your local ranger station to inquire about the most current conditions anywhere you go. This includes snow levels in the mountains during the winter and fire danger in summer. By preparing yourself before each outing, you can avoid becoming one of those people on the news.

Over the past dozen years, I have spent countless days on the trail and countless nights on my computer working on this book as well as my other three books. This does not mean that your experience will be the same as mine. Trail and road conditions change with every successive season. Wildfires, rainstorms, windstorms, heavy snowpack, avalanches and logging operations can cause great damage to roads and trails. You may find that something I have described is factually inaccurate as a result. If so, I would love to hear about it!

The Ten Essentials:
Many people go hiking with their phone, a water bottle, and a snack. You can get away with that one some hikes, but don't be one of those people! Being prepared for anything will help you enjoy the extraordinary hikes in this book to the fullest. You should always carry the Ten Essentials with you, no matter where you go.

These are the ten essentials:

1. A map of the area (preferably topographic and highly-detailed)
2. Compass and/or GPS (bring extra batteries or charge before you go)
3. Extra food
4. Extra water (especially in the summer)
5. Extra clothing (no cotton!)
6. A headlamp or flashlight
7. First Aid Kit (the more elaborate and stocked, the better)
8. Waterproof matches or a reliable lighter (or both)
9. Sunglasses and sunscreen
10. Knife and/or multitool with knife

There are six more items I highly recommend bringing to supplement the ten essentials:

11. A water filter or water purification tablets
12. An extra pair of warm socks wrapped in a waterproof plastic bag
13. Gloves, preferably waterproof
14. Duct tape (useful for repairing tears and emergency waterproofing)
15. A whistle
16. An emergency space blanket

While you should not need to bring your entire life with you on a hike, these sixteen items, most of them lightweight and easy to pack, will save your life in an emergency.

Last and perhaps most importantly, always let someone know where you are going and when you plan to return. This is a small and simple thing, but it will save your life! Many of the people you read about in the news do not do this, and Search and Rescue teams can waste valuable time trying to figure out where you are. Don't be one of those people!

Road access and directions:
I have made every effort to ensure the accuracy of my driving directions and clearly explain the road conditions where there might be a cause for concern. All directions start in the nearest major town, and are bullet-pointed at each important turn for maximum readability. US and state highways are labeled as US or OR (for example: US 26 and OR 214) while forest roads (which are maintained by the Forest Service, are labeled as FR (for example, FR 46 or FR 4690). While you can expect that paved roads listed in this book will be well-maintained and easy to drive on a yearly basis, the condition of gravel roads tends to change with each year and in some cases every season. Roads that do not receive regular maintenance are the ones most likely to be in rough shape.

Do NOT use your GPS to find road directions once you are out in remote areas – while they are frequently correct, the times they are not can lead you down roads that are no longer maintained, or in some cases, no longer exist. If you are unsure of directions or become lost, backtrack until you reach a well-traveled road. I also recommend purchasing a National Forest map or printing a general area map from topographic software to help you navigate the occasionally confusing backroads of our National Forests and BLM land.

I can highly recommend both the CalTopo and GaiaGPS services. I used both during the writing of this book, and both are very helpful for figuring out maps and trails. Be sure to download maps before you leave, and print them if you can. All maps in this book were created with CalTopo, and I used Gaia with pre-downloaded maps to help me navigate.

Land acknowledgements;
Last but absolutely not least, it is important to remember that all of these hikes are on native land. Hundreds of tribes called and still call Oregon their home, and we should acknowledge that we are on their land. I have made great effort to to acknowledge the tribes on whose land the hikes are located. For more information about traditional lands and land acknowledgements, see the Native Lands Project at https://native-land.ca/

I am also greatly indebted to the work of David G. Lewis, PhD, a historian and member of the Confederated Tribes of Grand Ronde. Lewis has spent much of his career researching and writing about the original peoples of Oregon and California, and his research has furthered my understanding and appreciation of the peoples who called and still call Oregon home.

For more information, see his blog here: https://ndnhistoryresearch.com/

Additional Resources:
These websites will give you a lot of useful additional information as you plan your hikes all over Extraordinary Oregon:

***Off the Beaten Trail (*www.offthebeatentrailpdx.com*):** This is my website, and I update it fairly often. Here you'll find more information on the hikes in this and my other books, color maps, blog posts, and photos...so many photos.

*** CalTopo (*www.caltopo.com*):** CalTopo is an exceptional resource for creating maps. I like to make maps of my trip before I go, so I have a paper map to reference while I hike. I strongly recommend purchasing a pro subscription to make the most of what CalTopo offers.

*** GaiaGPS (*https://www.gaiagps.com/*):** This service is an app you can download, but it is also available on web. I recommend a pro subscription so you can navigate offline, and I also recommend downloading maps on your phone before you go so you can follow your progress offline in the event you do not have cell service. I have made all of my tracks for this book public, so you can download them and use them to follow along with the hikes here.

*** Oregon Hikers (*www.oregonhikers.org*):** An online forum and field guide dedicated to hiking, snowshoeing and backpacking throughout Oregon, with a focus on the Portland area (the website used to be known as Portland Hikers). In the forums you can view trip reports for up-to-date information on hikes all across the region. Stop here before you leave the house for current information and browse the forums for great ideas!

*** Hike Oregon (*www.hikeoregon.net*):** Hiking guru Franziska Weinheimer has built Hike Oregon to help all levels of hikers, from newcomers to experienced trekkers. Here you will find write-ups of hikes from across Oregon, with a focus on Eugene and Bend. You will also find many videos and tutorials on how to prepare for hiking and backpacking trips. I cannot recommend this website enough.

*** Oregon Wildflowers (*http://oregonwildflowers.org/*)** – Similar to Portland Hikers but with a focus on wildflowers. You can view trip reports and see some of the webmaster Greg Lief's excellent wildflower photos.

*** Northwest Waterfall Survey (*http://www.waterfallsnorthwest.com/nws/*):** This website should be indispensable for those who love waterfalls. Every known waterfall in Oregon and Washington is catalogued and many are featured with full write-ups, great directions and absolutely spectacular photos.

With all that said, let's go hiking!

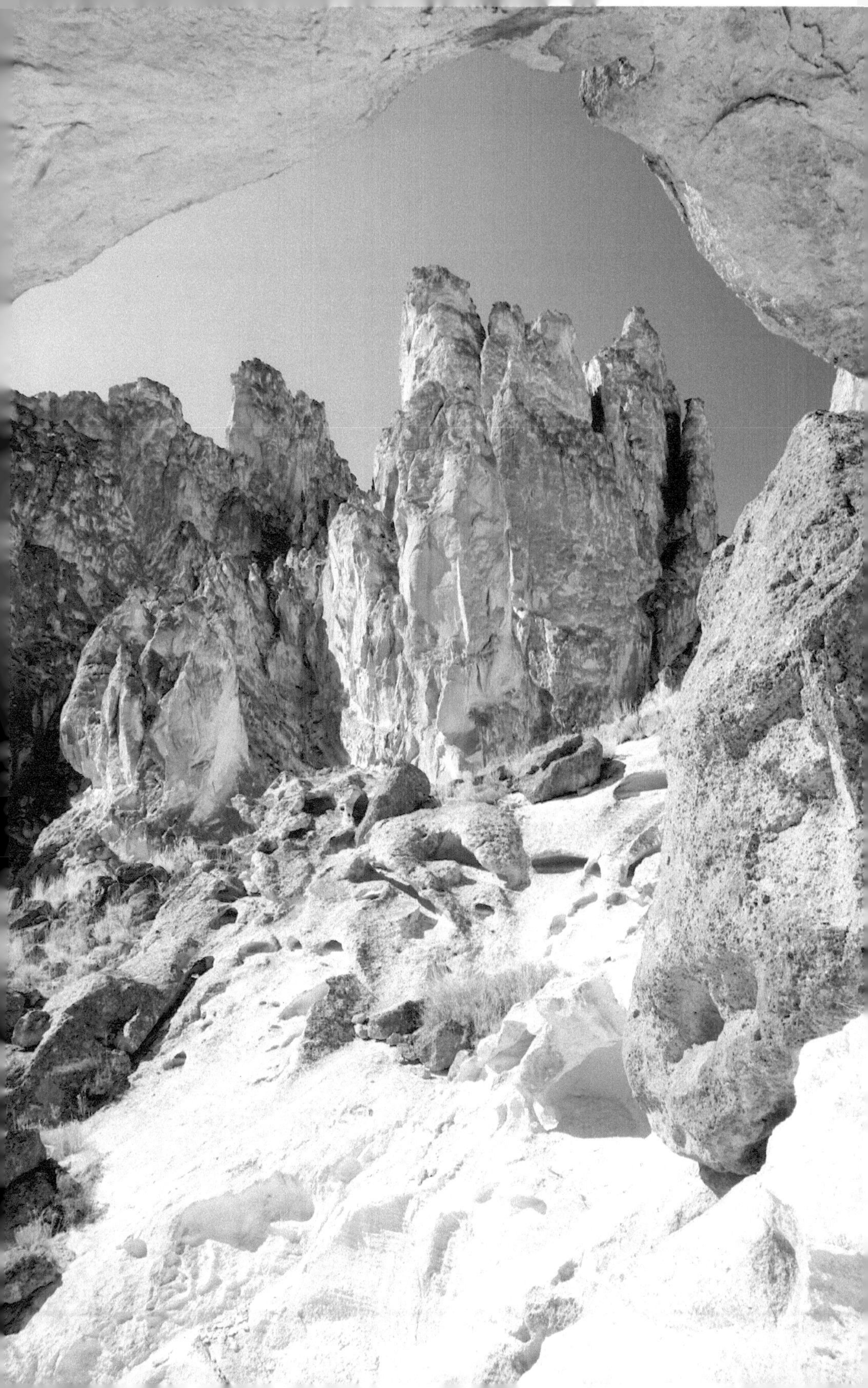

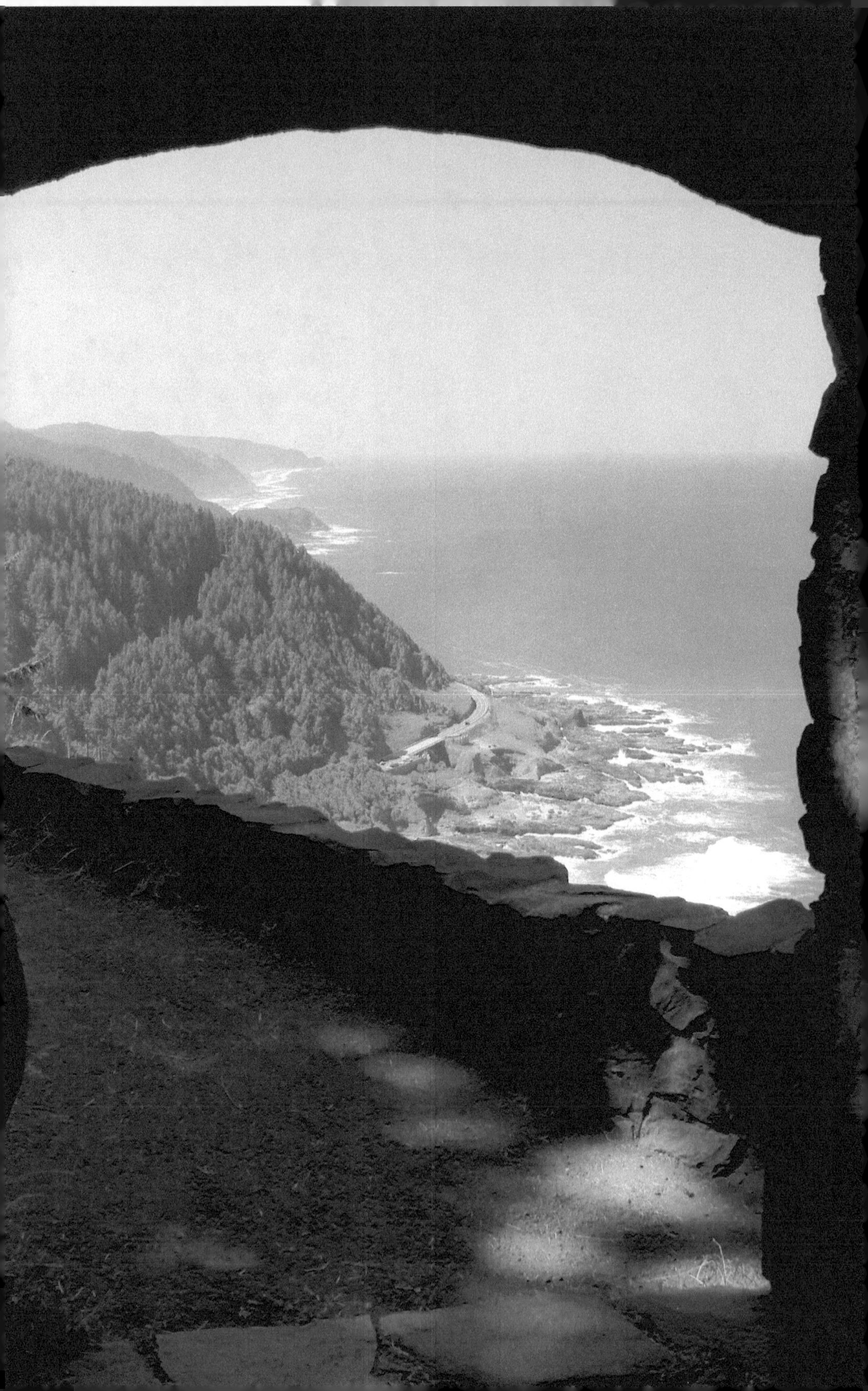

Coast and Coast Range

		Distance	EV Gain	Page
1.	Ecola State Park	7.7 miles	1,600 ft	20
2.	Saddle Mountain	5.2 miles	1,800 ft	22
3.	Oswald West State Park	8.7 miles	1,700 ft	24
4.	Bayocean Spit	8 miles	100 ft	26
5.	Cape Lookout	4.8 miles	700 ft	28
6.	Harts Cove	5.8 miles	1,100 ft	30
7.	Drift Creek Falls	3.6 miles	500 ft	32
8.	Marys Peak	9.6 miles	2,400 ft	34
9.	Cape Perpetua	6.5 miles	1,300 ft	36
10.	Kentucky Falls	4.8 miles	800 ft	38
11.	Threemile Lake	6.6 miles	600 ft	40
12.	Shore Acres State Park	5.2 miles	300 ft	42
13	Golden and Silver Falls	3.6 miles	800 ft	44
14.	Coquille River Falls and Hanging Rock	1.4 miles	500 ft	46
15.	Iron Mountain Botanical Area	1.8 miles	500 ft	48
16.	Blacklock Point	9.4 miles	400 ft	50
17.	Humbug Mountain	5.8 miles	1,700 ft	52
18.	Boardman State Park	7 miles	1,400 ft	54
19.	Windy Valley	4 miles	800 ft	56
20.	Oregon Redwoods Trail	1.2 miles	400 ft	58

There's nowhere quite like the Oregon Coast. It is 338 miles from Astoria to Brookings on US Highway 101, and yet you could spend an entire lifetime along the coast and never see everything there is to see. This is a world of rugged coves, hidden waterfalls, secret beaches, and misty coastal forest. Further inland you'll find rocky peaks, spectacular wildflower meadows, and viewpoints that stretch from the Pacific Ocean to the high peaks of the Oregon Cascades. Many guidebooks have been written on the Oregon Coast, and I could have devoted at least half this book to hikes along the coast and in the Oregon Coast Range. Presented here are my 20 favorite hikes from this area, from the Columbia River to the California border. In addition to the 20 hikes here, read through each entry closely for notes on other hikes in the area, suggestions on where to camp, and so much more!

Photo on left: Looking south from the stone house at Cape Perpetua's summit (Hike 9).

1. Ecola State Park

	Tillamook Head Loop	From Ecola Point
Distance:	3.3 mile loop	7.7 mile semi-loop
Elevation Gain:	800 feet	1,600 feet
Trailhead Elevation:	53 feet	197 feet
Trail High Point:	766 feet	766 feet
Seasons:	all year	all year
Best:	all year	all year
Pass:	$5 day use or $30 year pass	$5 day use or $30 year pass
On the traditional lands of:	the Chinook and Clatsop Peoples	the Chinook and Clatsop Peoples

Directions:

- From Portland, drive west on US 26 for approximately 74 miles to its end at US 101. Following signs for Cannon Beach, exit to the south on US 101 until you reach the first junction on your right for Cannon Beach
- From Cannon Beach, drive north on East 5th Street into Ecola State Park. Continue on this road 1.6 miles to a fee booth, where you pay the $5 day use to enter the park. Just after the booth, arrive at a junction. Left leads immediately to the Ecola Point Trailhead, while right leads to Indian Beach. Turn left and pull into the Ecola Point parking lot.
- If you'd rather skip the section through the woods and start at Indian Beach, keep right and drive 1.5 miles of narrow pavement to roads end at Indian Beach.
- **Drivetimes:** 5 minutes from Cannon Beach, 100 minutes from Portland

Hike: Oregon's coastline had already been inhabited by the Clatsop and Chinook peoples for millennia when Lewis and Clark arrived in 1805. The arrival of the Corps of Discovery, the first

Indian Beach in Ecola State Park.

European peoples to extensively explore what is now Oregon, ushered in the region's modern history. Lewis and Clark spent the winter of 1805-1806 along the stretch of coastline between what is now Astoria and Cannon Beach. In early 1806, Clatsop Indians led William Clark, Sacajawea, and other members of the Corps of Discovery across Tillamook Head to Indian Beach, where a beached whale offered the possibility of more meat and fuel oil. Upon reaching one of the many viewpoints looking south to the beach, Clark declared the view "... the grandest and most pleasing prospects which my eyes ever surveyed...". You can hike in the footsteps of history here at one of Oregon's most extraordinary hikes through the heart of Ecola State Park.

If you're planning on the shorter loop from Indian Beach, begin on the old road heading north into the woods from the beach. You'll follow this closed road uphill through ancient forest for 1.3 miles to a four-way junction just before Tillamook Head Camp. From this junction, continue straight a short distance to the shelters and campsites at Tillamook Head. Here, a trio of shelters and a pit toilet offer the possibility of staying overnight, should that pique your interest. Continue straight on a rougher trail another 0.2 mile to an obstructed viewpoint west to the Tillamook Rock Lighthouse, more than a mile out in the Pacific Ocean, The lighthouse, known as "Terrible Tilly", was operated between 1881 – 1957, The lighthouse still stands today but has gone through a series of owners and investors; today the primary occupants of the lighthouse are seabirds. You will also pass the remains of a World War II radar station just off the trail, which is off-limits to hikers. When you return to the hikers camp, turn right to continue the loop. The trail back down to Indian Beach is part of the Oregon Coast Trail. You'll pass through lovely forest and begin following switchbacks downhill. Along the way you'll have fantastic views south to Indian Beach, Ecola Point, and beyond that, Neahkahnie Mountain (Hike 3). After 1.3 miles of hiking downhill you'll arrive at a junction with the old road just before you reach Indian Beach.

If you're planning on the longer hike from Ecola Point, you'll need to hike 2.2 miles through deep and impressive ancient woods from Ecola Point to Indian Beach. This trail was rerouted after a series of storms destroyed the original trail that followed the sea cliffs between Ecola Point and Indian Beach. The new trail is delightful, passing under some truly huge trees and offering some nice views north to Tillamook Head and south to Ecola Point; that being said, I do miss the old trail, which featured magnificent views of the rugged coastline here. After 2.2 miles, you'll reach Indian Beach and its crowded parking lot. From here, follow the loop directions featured above, and then return the way you came.

If you still have a little energy upon returning to the parking lot, consider the short trails at Ecola Point, which feature more fantastic views.

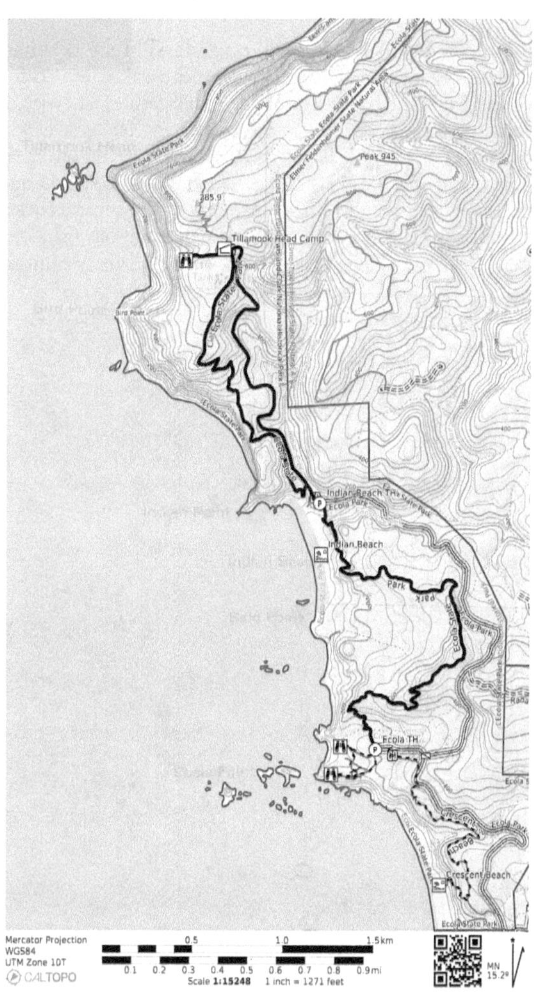

2. Saddle Mountain

Distance: 5.2 miles out and back
Elevation Gain: 1,800 feet
Trailhead elevation: 1,653 feet
Trail high point: 3,288 feet
Seasons: March - November
Best: May – June
Pass: None needed
On the traditional lands of: the Chinook and Clatsop Peoples

Directions from Portland:

- From Portland, drive US 26 approximately 63 miles northwest of Portland to a sign for Saddle Mountain State Park, not far beyond milepost 11. If you're driving here from Seaside or Cannon Beach, drive US 26 east for 11 miles to the turnoff for Saddle Mountain on the left side of the road.
- Turn right on this road and drive 6.9 of bumpy pavement, ignoring all side roads, to road's end at a large trailhead parking lot.
- **Drivetimes:** 100 minutes from Portland, 25 minutes from Cannon Beach and Seaside

Hike: Few places feel more like an island in the sky than Saddle Mountain, high in the northern Oregon coast range. Although a minor peak when compared to summits of the Cascades, Saddle Mountain is the highest point for many miles in every direction, and as you would expect, the views from the summit are extraordinary. The volcanoes of the Cascades rise to the east over the long and graceful course of the Columbia River, while the Pacific Ocean stretches out into the infinite arc of the earth's curve. The only major challenge with Saddle Mountain is finding a clear day to enjoy the view. I have done this hike several times and have had decent weather only once. If you come in the middle of summer you'll have the best views, but summer haze diminishes them somewhat. The best time to hike Saddle Mountain is in June, when the slopes are draped

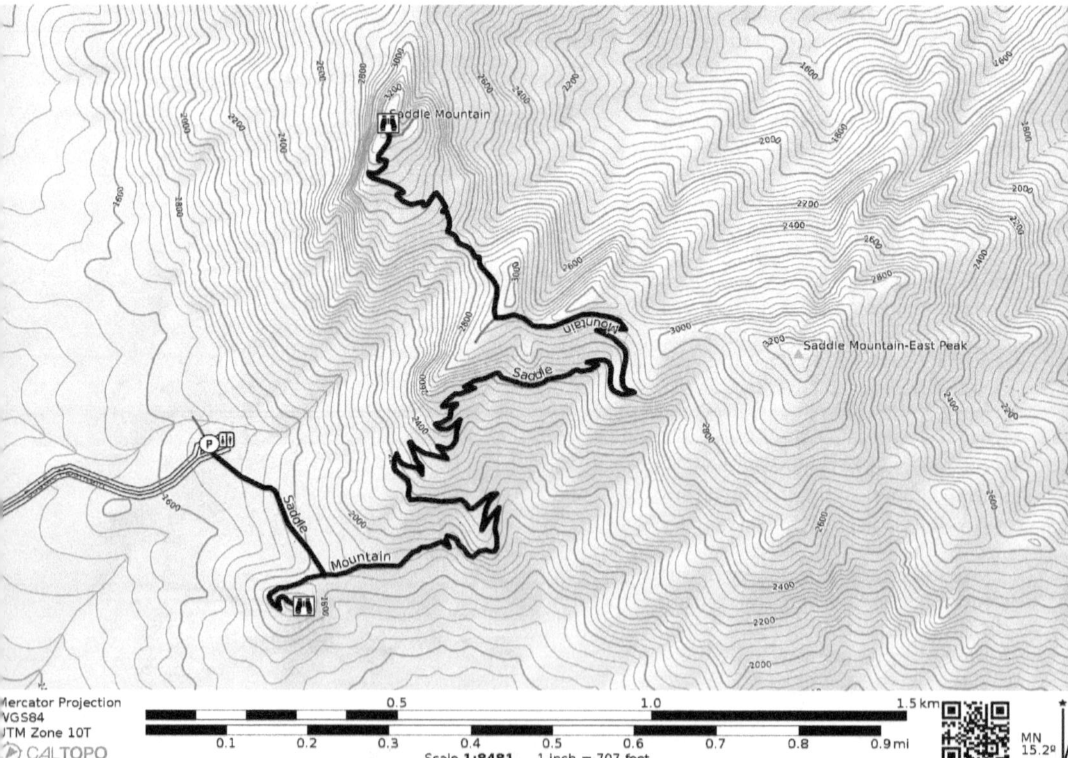

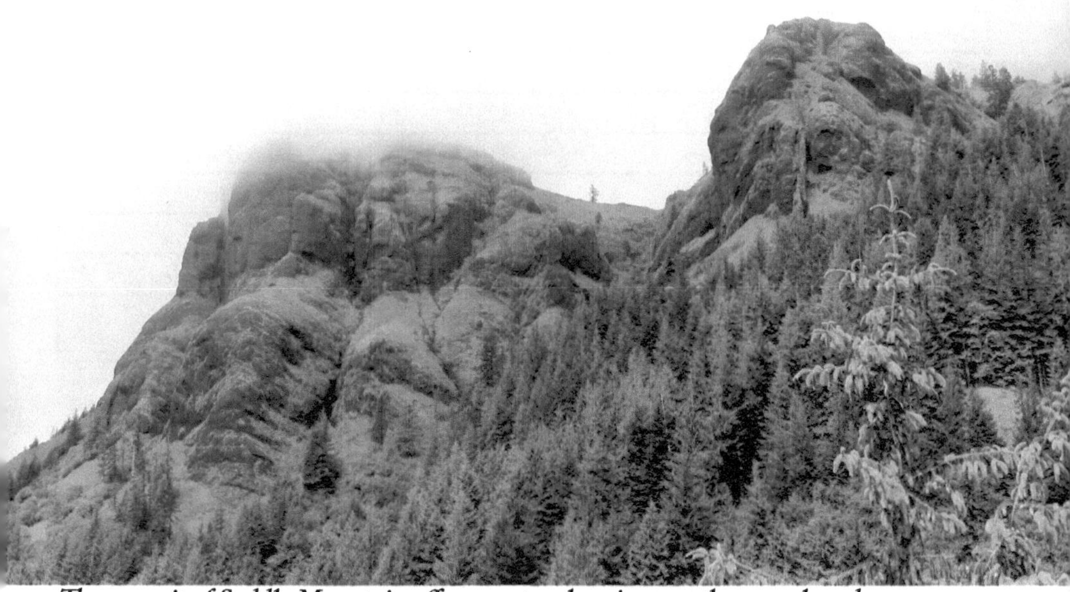

The summit of Saddle Mountain offers spectacular views on the rare clear day.

with some of the best wildflower displays in Oregon. One important note: Saddle Mountain State Park has been closed on and off since October 2021 due to a broken trail bridge and a missing bathroom. The trail is expected to reopen in Spring 2023.

From the trailhead, follow the Saddle Mountain Trail through a lush, mossy forest with a blanket of oxalis. The trail passes the state park's small campground and begins to climb at a steady grade. You will reach a junction with a side trail that offers a different perspective of Saddle Mountain, a worthwhile side trip. Beyond this junction, the trail climbs at a steady grade through a scenic forest of tall Douglas fir and overhanging vine maple. As you ascend, you'll find your progress slowed by a parade of spring and summer wildflowers. Look for red paintbrush and columbine, orange tiger lilies, yellow monkeyflower, blue larkspur, purple irises, brown chocolate lilies, and so many more. Being a wildflower enthusiast, I find this trail to be slow going as I stop to photograph the flowers here by the dozen. As the trail leaves the forest, the flower show is even more impressive. At 2 miles, the trail tops out at a false summit. From here, you'll round a bend and descend into the saddle for which the peak is named. The true summit of Saddle Mountain looms before you.

The trail descends into the saddle, offering views to Mount Rainier on the eastern horizon. From the saddle, you'll climb steeply the last 0.4 mile to the summit, much of it along fencing laid below the trail's tread to help control erosion on the rocky, muddy slopes below the summit. The trail reaches the summit at 2.6 miles, where the views astonish even on the frequent cloudy days here. Look for Astoria to the northwest, with the Astoria Column visible on a hilltop above the city. The Columbia River leads your eyes west to the vast sweep of the Pacific Ocean and east to the peaks of the Cascades from Rainier to Mount Jefferson. Marys Peak, the other monarch of Oregon's Coast Range, is visible on the southern horizon. It is said that the Olympic Mountains are visible on very clear days, but those are few and far between. On nice weather days there are few finer places in Oregon for a picnic, and there is ample room to spread out. Whenever you're ready, return the way you came.

3. Oswald West State Park

	Short Sand Beach	Cape Falcon	Neahkahnie Mtn
Distance:	1.6 miles out & back	4.9 miles out & back	8.7 miles out & back
Elevation Gain:	100 feet	700 feet	1,700 feet
TH Elevation:	82 feet	82 feet	82 feet
Trail High Point:	82 feet	236 feet	1,652 feet
Season:	all year	all year	all year
Best:	all year	July – October	April – June
Pass:	None needed	None needed	None needed
On the traditional lands of:	Chinook and Clatsop Peoples	Chinook and Clatsop Peoples	Chinook and Clatsop Peoples

Directions from Cannon Beach:

- From Cannon Beach, drive south on US 101 for 14 miles to Oswald West State Park.
- Pull into the day use parking lot on your left for Short Sand Beach, where US 101 crosses Short Sand Creek.
- If you're driving here from Portland, drive US 26 approximately 74 miles to its end just north of Cannon Beach, then merge onto southbound US 101 for 14 miles to the Short Sand Beach parking lot.
- **Drivetimes:** 20 minutes from Cannon Beach, 1 hour and 45 minutes from Portland.

Hike: Oswald West was love at first sight for me when I first visited sometime in the early 90s. Back in those days you could camp under the enormous trees above Short Sand Beach, and we made the most of an extremely rainy weekend in June as we explored the beach and the

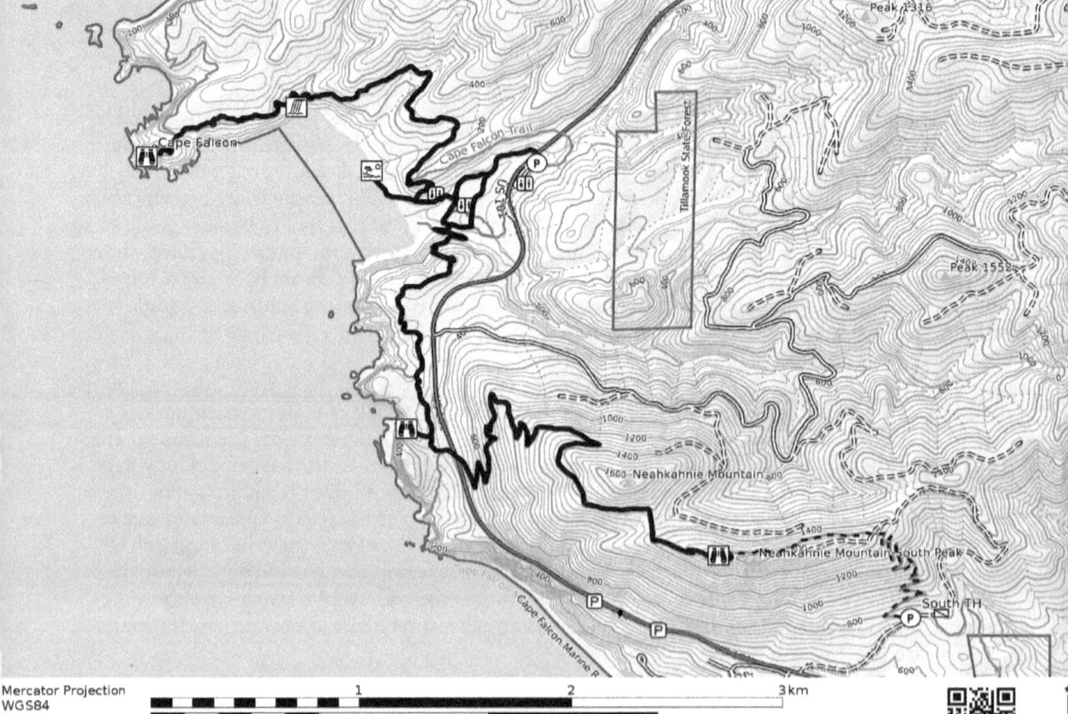

cloud forests on the slopes of Neahkahnie Mountain. This beloved state park, named after the early 20th-century governor who decreed that all beaches in Oregon should be public property, remains a favorite destination of many Oregonians – and my favorite place on this stretch of Oregon's extraordinary coastline. There are three excellent hikes in this park: an easy trail leads to gorgeous Short Sand Beach, one of the finest on the Oregon coast; a longer trail take you into the ancient forest above Short Sand Beach to Cape Falcon, which features a fantastic view across Short Sand to the slopes of Neahkahnie Mountain; and a trail to the summit of Neahkahnie Mountain, where you'll find one of the finest views on the entire Oregon coastline. What more could you possibly want?

Begin by hiking the wide trail downhill into a gorgeous coastal forest towards Short Sand Beach. You'll have a lot of competition for the trail with families, tourists, and surfers, all of whom love Short Sand Beach equally. The trail forks at 0.2 mile. Either way will take you to Short Sand, but for now, you should keep right and continue following Short Sand Creek through an impressive forest of massive Sitka spruce trees. You'll reach another junction at 0.3 mile. If you're hiking to Neahkahnie Mountain, turn left here (see directions below). For Short Sand Beach, keep right and follow the trail down to a bridge over Short Sand Creek. Cross the creek on a bridge and reach another junction at 0.5 mile with the trail to Cape Falcon. You'll turn right to hike to Cape Falcon, but for now, continue straight to an overlook of Short Sand Beach. Hikers with limited mobility should stop here, as the last few steps to the beach are rocky and steep. Once you reach the beach, prepare to be amazed! The beach is backed by huge cliffs and ancient forest on all sides, and a lovely waterfall tumbles onto northern end of the beach amid rocky tidepools that are only accessible during low tide. Even if you're planning on hiking to Cape Falcon or Neahkahnie Mountain, you may just decide to spend the rest of the day at the beach. You may therefore want to save the beach for the end of the day if you're planning on either longer hike.

If you are planning on hiking to Cape Falcon, return to the junction by the beach overlook and turn left at a sign for Cape Falcon. You'll follow the Oregon Coast Trail through impressive woods above Short Sand Beach. Expect lots of small ups and downs on this trail as it traverses the steep slopes above the beach. If you're visiting in winter or spring, you should also expect to hike one of the muddiest trails in all of Oregon. The trail passes above Blumenthal Falls, the waterfall that tumbles onto the north end of Short Sand Beach. You'll reach Cape Falcon's viewpoint at 2.4 miles, where various side trails lead to different views of the rocky coves below the cape. The view south to Short Sand Beach and Neahkahnie Mountain is particularly impressive. Return the way you came.

If you're hiking to the summit of Neahkahnie Mountain, you'll have to keep left at the junction before the bridge over Short Sand Creek described above. Follow the trail to a bridge over Necarney Creek, then hike uphill amid huge Sitka spruce for 1.3 miles to a trail junction. Left leads to Neahkahnie Mountain but first turn right to hike to a spectacular viewpoint of Devil's Cauldron's hidden cove. Return to the junction continue uphill to a crossing of US 101. Carefully cross the highway and locate the trail heading uphill into the woods. Massive amounts of trees fell along this stretch of trail during the September 2020 windstorm, closing the trail for two years. It is now open again. The trail switchbacks uphill on the western slopes of Neahkahnie Mountain, offering the occasional view of the coastline. At 4.2 miles, the trail passes through steep meadows just below the summit. The view south from here to Manzanita and its beaches is fantastic, but to reach the summit, you'll need to continue past the meadows back into the woods until you reach a junction on the left at a saddle. Turn left here and follow a steep trail to the rocky summit of Neahkahnie Mountain. The view down the coastline to the south is wonderful and worthy of the effort it takes to get there. Expect to share the summit with many admirers, as another, shorter trail reaches the summit from the south. Unless you set up a car shuttle to this southern trailhead, return the way you came.

Note: The campground I stayed at here in the 90s closed in 2009 after a giant Sitka Spruce fell across several campsites. The campground is greatly missed. If you're looking for a place to camp, you'll have to head south to Nehalem Bay State Park in Manzanita.

4. Bayocean Spit

Distance: 8 mile loop
Elevation Gain: 100 feet
Trailhead elevation: 22 feet
Trail high Point: 38 feet
Season: all year
Best: all year, but I like it best in winter
Pass: $10 day use fee
On the traditional lands of: The Tillamook and Siletz peoples.

Directions:

- From the junction of US 101 in downtown Tillamook, turn onto 3rd Street and drive west. This becomes the Three Capes Loop.
- Drive 5 miles to a junction with Bayocean Spit's gravel access road. Turn right here.
- Follow the lower road (the upper is the return road of this one-way loop) for 0.9 mile of very potholed gravel to the trailhead parking lot.
- **Drivetime from Tillamook:** 20 minutes

Hike: This delightful loop over Bayocean Spit follows a sandy beach with a somewhat sad history to the tip of the spit, where you can watch boats fight the current in the narrow inlet. From here, you'll follow a road along the forested interior of the spit, where you'll have views across to the low, logging-scarred mountains of the Coast Range. This hike packs a lot of variety and is worthwhile in every season. I especially enjoy visiting on the rare sunny day in winter where it's warmer here than at my Portland home. Whenever you come, you'll find much to love here.

The hike begins with a choice: do you follow trails across the sand dunes to the beach, or do you follow the obvious road along the inside of the spit? I prefer to do this loop in a clockwise

Bayocean Spit on a blustery, winter day. This is near the old town site.

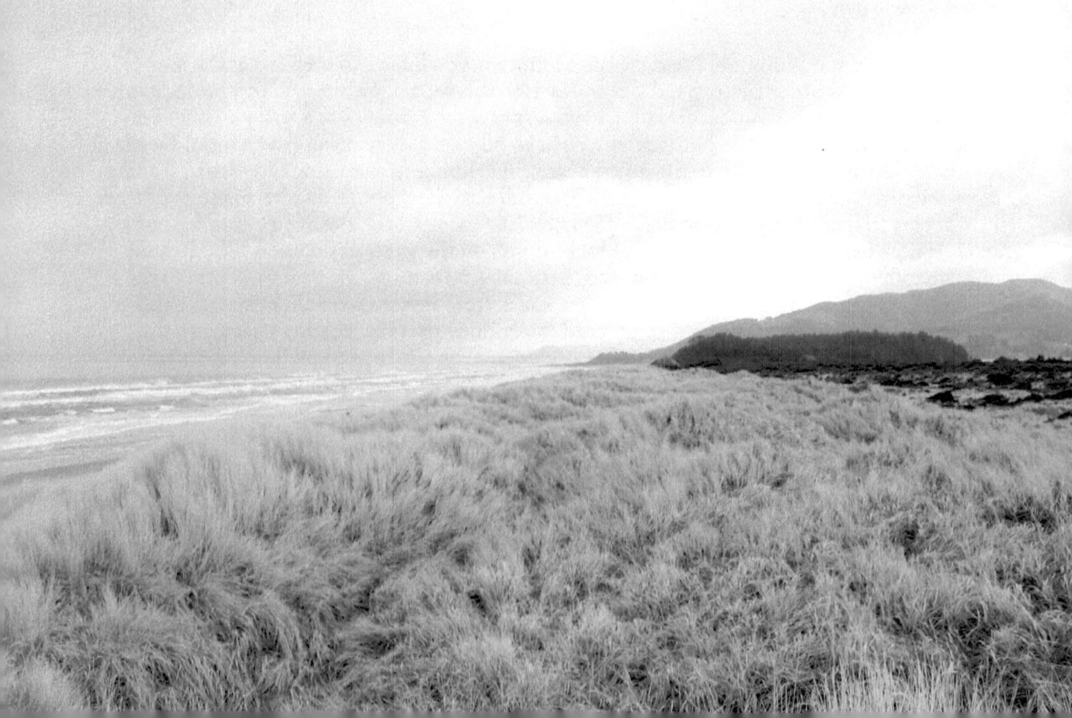

direction, starting with the beach. Locate the trail on the ocean side of the parking lot, and follow it for 0.4 mile across the sand dunes of Bayocean Spit. When you reach the ocean, rejoice! The hardest part of your hike is over. Turn right here to follow the spit north. You'll follow the tide for a little over 3 miles until you reach the jetty that marks the end of the spit. Although you are not quite halfway, the driftwood along the jetty is the best place to stop for a break. Note that it is not far to the other side of the bay; on the far side is another jetty, designed to make for the easiest possible entrance and exit to Tillamook Bay.

When you are ready to continue, follow an obvious trail across the sand and driftwood of the bay's tip until you locate the rocky road that follows the interior of the spit. This is your path for the rest of the hike. The road stays close to the bay, following the water's edge some ten to fifteen feet above the high tide line. Along the way back, you will notice the encroaching forest on the interior of the spit. Several trails pierce the dense greenery of this wild place, offering more chances for exploration.

Not far before you reach the trailhead, you will pass a sign noting the Bayocean Town Site. A plaque here explains the history of this spit, and the town that once stood here. The town was a planned community, founded in 1906 and built along the narrow strip of land on what was originally named Tillamook Spit. The town grew quickly, reaching a population as high as 2,000 by 1914. For many years the only way to access the town was via a rough boat trip around the coast. The town's citizens decided to have a jetty built at great cost to make the passage easier, but the resulting accumulation of sand accelerated the town's obsolescence. By 1953, the town was an island and the post office closed. Today there is nothing left of Bayocean, as much of the town washed into the sea during storms, and sand subsequently buried the rest. Take a moment to read the plaque and ponder how quickly nature can reclaim a town that once seemed so large.

From here, continue south on the gravel road until you reach the trailhead and the conclusion of your loop.

Note: Cape Meares is an excellent place to stop after you finish the hike. The road that links Bayocean Spit to Cape Meares has been closed due to a landslide since 2013, but construction will begin soon to reopen this connection. For now, you'll have to drive back towards Tillamook and follow signs to the lovely small town of Oceanside, and continue north towards Cape Meares. All of the beaches and short hikes on this little stretch of coastline are beautiful, and Cape Meares has a small trail network that includes a lighthouse, a massive and beloved tree known as the "Octopus tree", as well as tall trees and big views. This is a fun drive and the scenery is not to be missed.

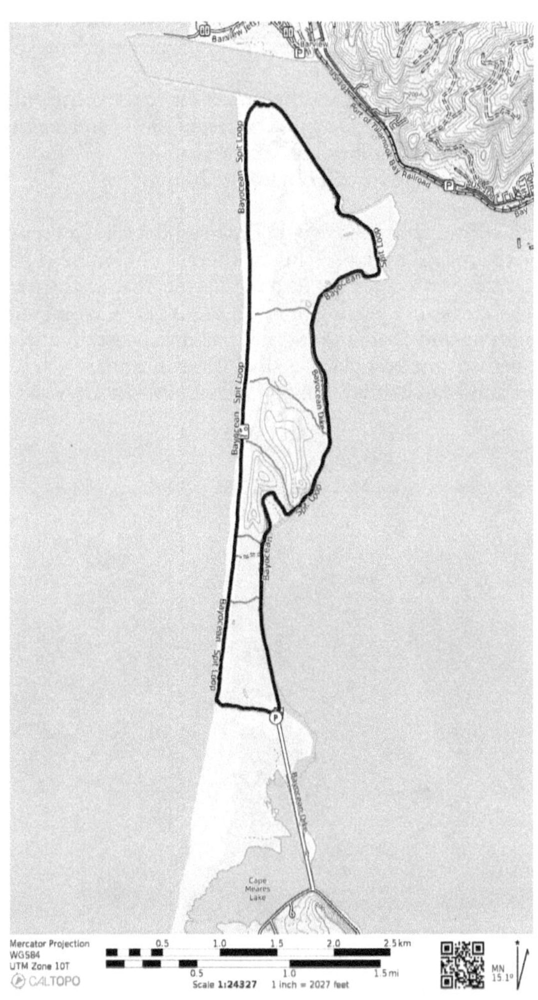

5. Cape Lookout

	Cape Lookout	South Beach
Distance:	4.8 miles out and back	3.8 miles out and back
Elevation Gain:	700 feet	850 feet (on return)
Trailhead Elevation:	866 feet	866 feet
Trail High Point:	866 feet	866 feet
Seasons:	all year	all year
Best:	all year	all year
Pass:	none needed	none needed
On the traditional lands of:	The Nestucca, Grand Ronde, and Siletz peoples.	The Nestucca, Grand Ronde, and Siletz peoples.

Directions from Tillamook:

- From downtown Tillamook, drive west on OR 131. Continue on 131 for 5 miles to a junction signed for Netarts. Continue south on OR 131, which is also known as the Three Capes Loop.
- Continue south another 5.2 miles to the south entrance of Cape Lookout State Park.
- Ignore the turnoff into the campground and continue south another 2.7 miles to the Cape Lookout Trailhead on your right.
- **Drivetime from Tillamook:** 20 minutes

Hike: Everywhere you go on the northern Oregon coast, Cape Lookout is visible somewhere on the coastal horizon. The cape, a relic of Columbia River Basalts from the Miocene Epoch, juts some two miles out into the Pacific Ocean. The trail that follows the cape to its end is an absolute beauty, passing through impressive Coastal rainforest and culminating in spectacular views up and down the rugged coastline. Most uniquely, the cape's geographic prominence makes it perhaps the best place in all of Oregon from which to watch gray whale migrations in December and March. If you simply cannot visit the Oregon coast without spending some time at the

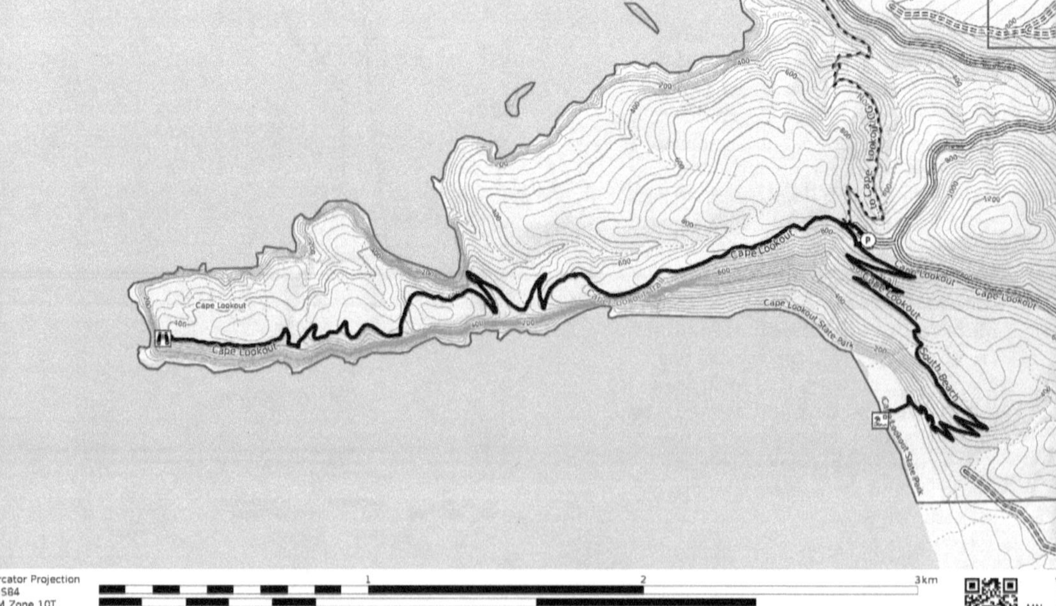

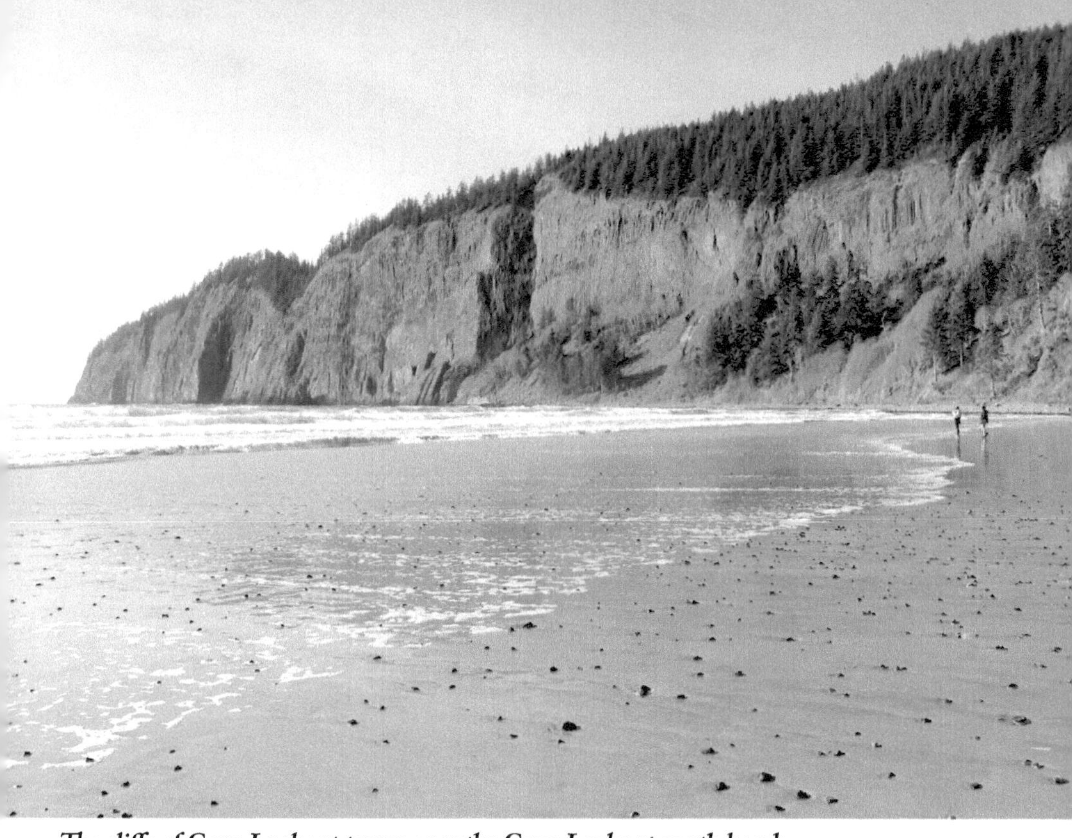

The cliffs of Cape Lookout tower over the Cape Lookout south beach.

beach, a trail leads downhill from the Cape Lookout Trailhead to Cape Lookout's south beach, a lovely slice of coastline beneath the huge cliffs of Cape Lookout. According to native historian David G. Lewis, Cape Lookout's original name is Nasitselz.

Both trails depart from the same trailhead but you should hike out to the end of Cape Lookout first. Begin by hiking the trail towards Cape Lookout. After 0.1 mile, the trail down to South Beach departs to the left. Ignore it for now and follow the Cape Lookout Trail west into the coastal rainforest that towers over the trail. If you're hiking this trail in the winter or spring, expect a muddy trail for much of the hike. You'll have occasional views north to the sandy expanse of Netarts Spit, another worthwhile hike if you're staying at Cape Lookout State Park. The trail drops into a saddle in the middle of the cape and then crosses over to the south side of Cape Lookout, where the trail opens up into the steep hanging meadows near the tip of the cape. Watch your step, as there are a few exposed places on the trail. At 2.4 miles, the trail reaches a fenced lookout at the tip of Cape Lookout. Truth be told, the fenced overlook can feel a bit crowded as there isn't much space to spread out, but the views and the scenery are so great you may not mind the crowds. If you're here in whale watching season, bring binoculars and be prepared to be amazed. When you're ready, return the way you came.

Many hikers will choose to return to the trailhead and finish their hike, but if you're in the need of some beach time, consider the hike downhill to South Beach. Return to the junction near the trailhead and turn right to hike downhill. The first mile descends gradually through open forest with a few looks down to the beach, but as you near the beach, views begin to open up back to Cape Lookout's huge cliffs. The forest here is as impressive as up on the cape, with huge Sitka spruce trees towering over a carpet of sword ferns. The trail passes above a Boy Scout camp and switchback down to the beach at 1.9 miles. South Beach is far less crowded than the trail to the end of Cape Lookout, and the cape's huge cliffs tower over the beach, making it feel almost like a refuge. The beach is fun to explore, but eventually you'll have to return the way you came.

6. Harts Cove

Distance: 5.8 miles out and back
Elevation Gain: 1,100 feet
Trailhead Elevation: 971 feet
Trail High Point: 971 feet
Season: July 16 - December 31 (closed to all hikers and vehicles January 1 - July 15)
Best: October - December
Pass: none needed
On the traditional lands of: the Salmon River, Grand Ronde, and Siletz peoples.

Directions:

- From McMinnville, drive southwest on OR 18 for approximately 52 miles to a junction with US 101 just north of Lincoln City.
- Turn right to drive north and begin watching your odometer closely.
- At exactly 3.7 miles from the merger of OR 18 and US 101, just as the road crests a hill, look very carefully for an unmarked road on the left side of the road at what first appears to be a pullout. If you miss the turnoff, you will need to continue to the next place where you can turn around and then return south until you find the road.
- Turn left onto FR 1861 and immediately pass a gate. Continue on this narrow and winding forest road for 3.1 miles to the upper Cascade Head Trailhead on the left. Continue 0.9 mile to the Harts Cove Trailhead at road's end.
- **Drivetime:** 20 minutes from Lincoln City

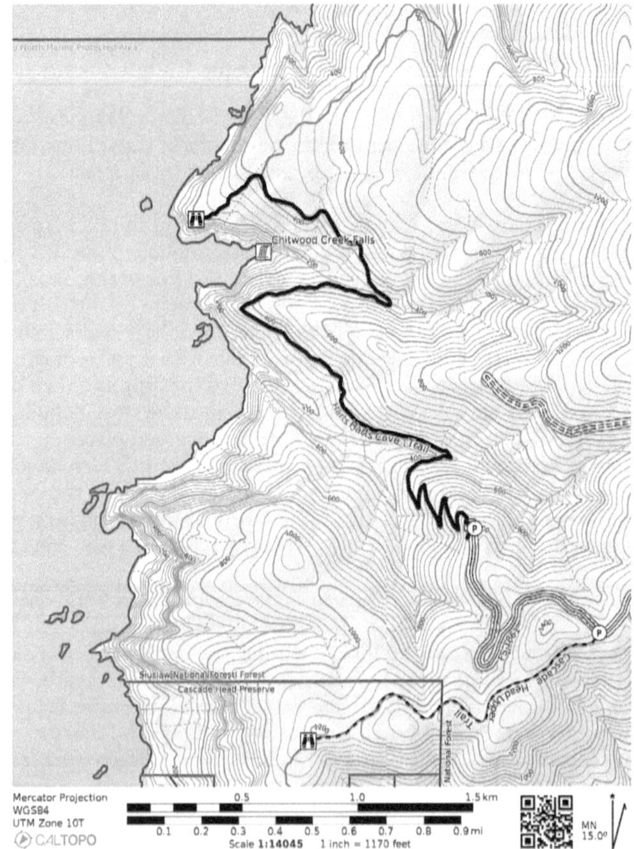

Hike: Sometimes it can be difficult to find the perfect coastal hike. In the summer many hikers hit the trails along the coast, hoping for some relief from Willamette Valley heat. In the winter, many of the trails are muddy and the weather borders on inhospitable, and hiking on the coast can seem less exciting. The trail to Harts Cove north of Lincoln City is quite crowded in the summer, and is definitely muddy in the winter, but it is a fantastic hike that features excellent views, some of the finest ancient forest on this part of the coast, and offers a peek at a rare sight: a waterfall tumbling directly into the Pacific Ocean. There's only one catch, and it's a big one: you can only do this hike starting on July 16. From January 1 to July 15, the trail and access road are closed to all vehicle and foot traffic to protect threatened species that live in the forest

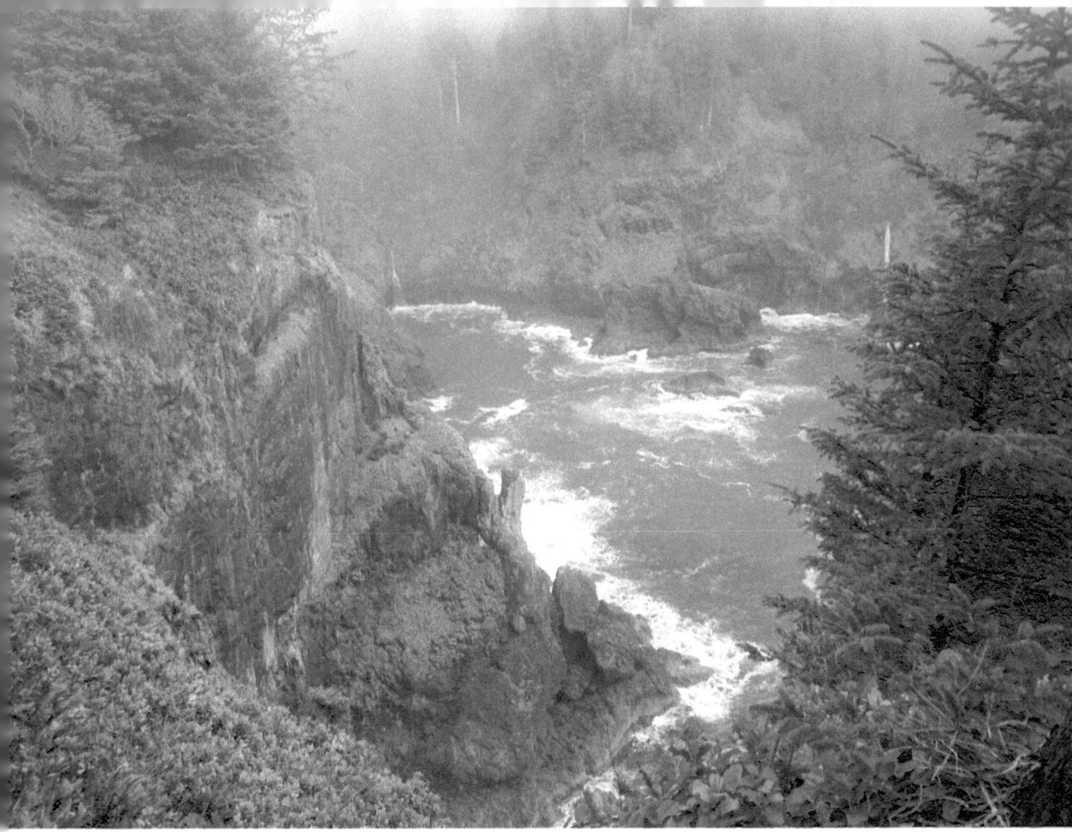

Harts Cove on a misty December day.

here. The best time to visit is in November and December, when the forest is shrouded in mist, the trail less crowded, and Chitwood Creek's waterfall runs at its fullest.

The Harts Cove Trail begins with a quick descent through a dark forest into Cliff Creek's canyon, losing 600 feet in the first 0.7 mile of hiking. The trail crosses Cliff Creek on a bridge and levels out, paralleling the creek at a distance for a while. Your eyes will soon be drawn upwards as the trail enters ancient woods. Although the ocean remains out of sight for most of the hike, its presence is always felt; for example, note that the huge trees you pass along the trail are almost all Sitka spruce, a species of tree that grows only in close proximity to the ocean. The cooling breezes of the Pacific are also a welcome antidote to late summer heat, and earlier in the morning it can feel almost cold on the trail once you've gotten used to the Willamette Valley's warm summer weather.

The trail descends a bit to an unbridged crossing of Chitwood Creek at 2 miles from the trailhead. The way is a little rougher beyond this point, as you climb back out of Chitwood Creek's canyon on a trail that can be muddy and rocky. At 2.6 miles, the Harts Cove Trail abruptly leaves the forest and commences a steep descent through the brushy meadows of Harts Cove's headland. The trail might be quite brushy if you come here right after the trail opens in mid-July. The tall brush hides a variety of flowers, from lupine to paintbrush to Checker mallow, a pink flower commonly found along the Oregon Coast. The brush also makes it difficult to find a good place to stop and rest, but with some patience, there are a number of spots that offer the views and flowers you seek. Perhaps the best spot on the headland here offers a view back into Harts Cove, where Chitwood Creek tumbles directly into the Pacific Ocean. South of the cove, arched rocks lurk just off the headland while the bark of the sea lion is always heard, even if only faintly. What a place!

Return the way you came.

7. Drift Creek Falls

Distance: 3.6 miles out and back
Elevation Gain: 500 feet
Trailhead elevation: 956 feet
Trail high point: 956 feet
Seasons: all year
Best: all year
Pass: None needed
On the traditional lands of: the Salmon River, Grand Ronde, and Siletz peoples.

Directions:

- From Salem drive west on OR 22 for 26 miles until it merges with OR 18. Continue on OR 18 / 22 and then OR 18 for another 21.8 miles to a junction on the left with FR 17 at a sign for Drift Creek Covered Bridge. If you're coming from Lincoln City, drive OR 18 for 4.9 miles east to the junction with Bear Creek Road on your right.
- Drive FR 17, known as the Bear Creek Road, for 8.8 winding, narrow miles to the Drift Creek Falls Trailhead on the left side of the road. Watch out for blind curves on your way in and out.
- **Drivetimes:** 1 hour and 20 minutes from Salem, 40 minutes from Lincoln City

Hike: This book is about extraodinary and unique destinations. Maybe it's a meadow of wildflowers, or maybe it's a hidden view out to the mountains; in the case of Drift Creek Falls near Lincoln City, it's a suspension bridge over Drift Creek's deep canyon, directly beside Drift Creek Falls, that transforms this otherwise fairly ordinary hike into something you simply cannot miss. Best of all, this is a fairly easy hike, one that almost anyone can enjoy without breaking too much of a sweat.

The trail departs from the large trailhead and immediately commences a gradual descent along

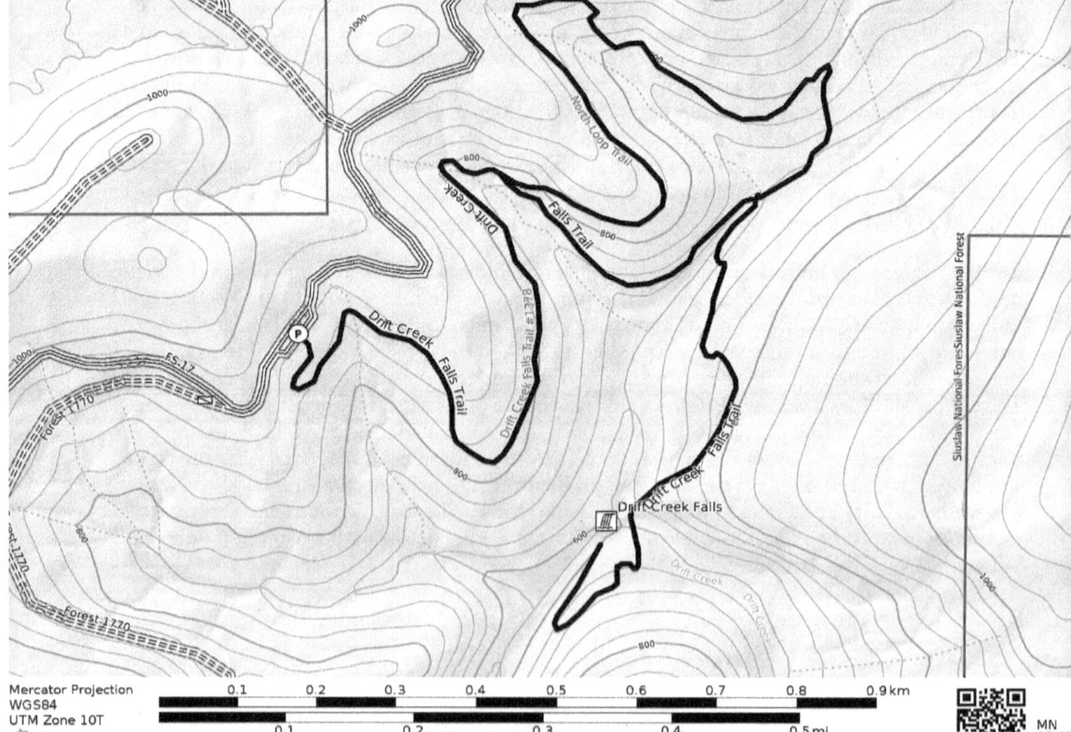

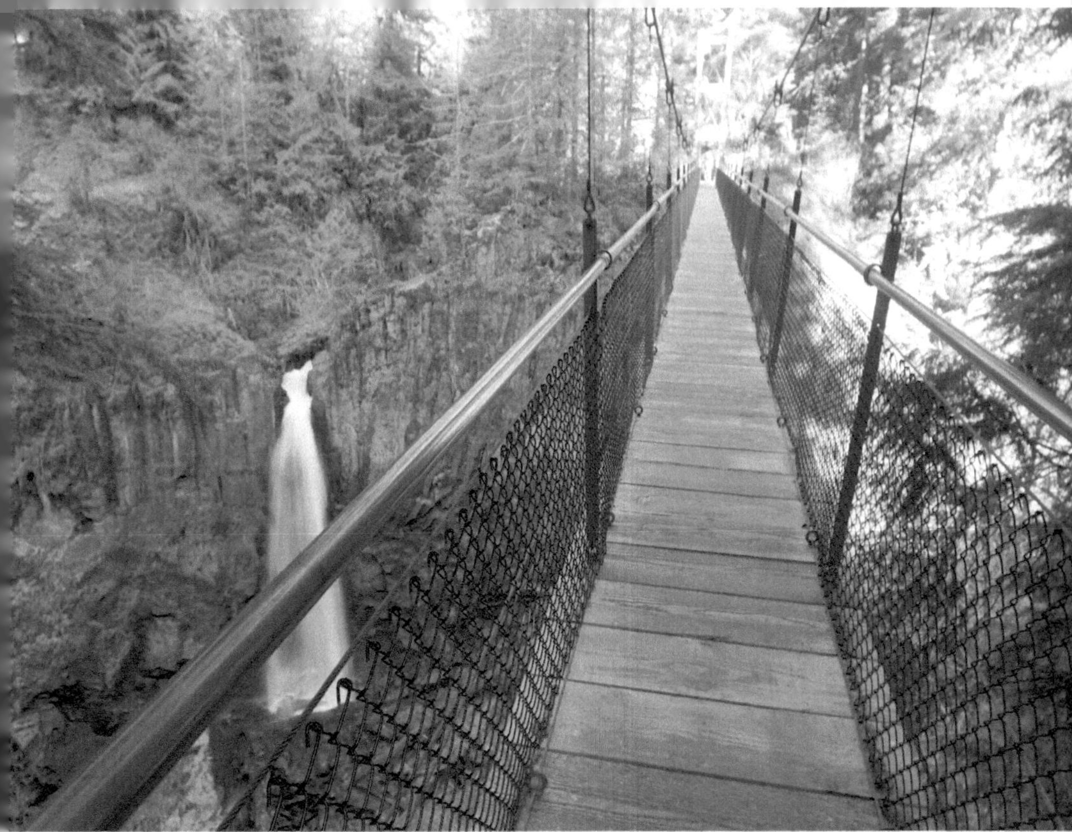

Drift Creek Falls and its surprising suspension bridge.

the forested slopes of Drift Creek's wide canyon. At 0.7 mile the trail arrives at a junction with the North Loop Trail, which will be your return route. For now, ignore this side trail and continue downhill on the wide Drift Creek Falls Trail. You will continue winding gradually downhill until the trail rounds a corner and arrives at the suspension bridge, at 1.3 miles from the trailhead. At 240 feet across and a height of 100 feet above Drift Creek, the bridge is a marvel. All credit goes to the Siuslaw National Forest for having the foresight and vision to install this bridge in such a scenic location. There is no risk of falling into the creek, but some eager hikers will jump on the bridge and delight in swaying the bridge back in forth. Once across the bridge, take a look down, at Drift Creek Falls below. The falls look different now than they used to; a landslide in 2010 changed the character of the canyon below the falls, and some say the canyon looks worse for the changes. Once across the bridge, you will arrive at a wide spot along the trail that is ideal for a break. Hikers who wish to hike on can continue on a rougher trail downhill to the base of Drift Creek Falls, below the bridge. The trail steepens and drops hikers downstream of the falls; from here you will need to pick your way around the boulders deposited in the canyon during the 2010 slide to the base of the falls. This is more fun in warmer weather, obviously, and many hikers wander down here looking for a place to cool off. From here, return the way you came back and over the bridge.

On your way back to the trailhead, I suggest making a loop following the North Loop Trail. Hike back uphill on the Drift Creek Falls Trail until you reach a junction with the North Loop Trail. Continue straight on this trail, which is narrower and brushier than its more popular sibling. The trail climbs gradually into an impressive forest of huge Douglas firs, which miraculously escaped the logging so common in this part of the Coast Range. Once you pass this small grove of ancient forest, the trail traverses the slopes below Bear Creek Road until it meets the Drift Creek Falls Trail again at 3 miles from the trailhead. Continue on the main trail here for 0.6 mile back to the Drift Creek Falls Trailhead.

8. Marys Peak

	Marys Peak Summit	Marys Peak via North Ridge
Distance:	1.2 miles out and back	9.6 miles out and back
Elevation Gain:	323 feet	2,400 feet
Trailhead Elevation:	3,776 feet	1,758 feet
Trail High Point:	4,097 feet	4,097 feet
Seasons:	May – November	May – November
Best:	May – July	May – July
Pass:	NW Forest Pass	none needed
On the traditional lands of:	The Chemapho and Kalapuya peoples.	The Chemapho and Kalapuya peoples.

Directions:

- From Corvallis, drive west on US 20 / OR 34 for approximately 7 miles to the far end of Philomath, where US 20 and OR 34 split.
- If you're planning on the longer hike via the North Ridge Trail, continue straight on US 20 for 1.8 miles to a junction with Woods Creek Road on the left.
- Turn left and drive 7.6 miles (the last 5.6 miles of which are gravel road; watch for potholes the last few miles) to the Woods Creek Trailhead.
- If you're just looking for the short but still satisfying hike to the top, you'll need to turn left on OR 34 at the split in Philomath.

Hiking up Marys Peak in the fog.

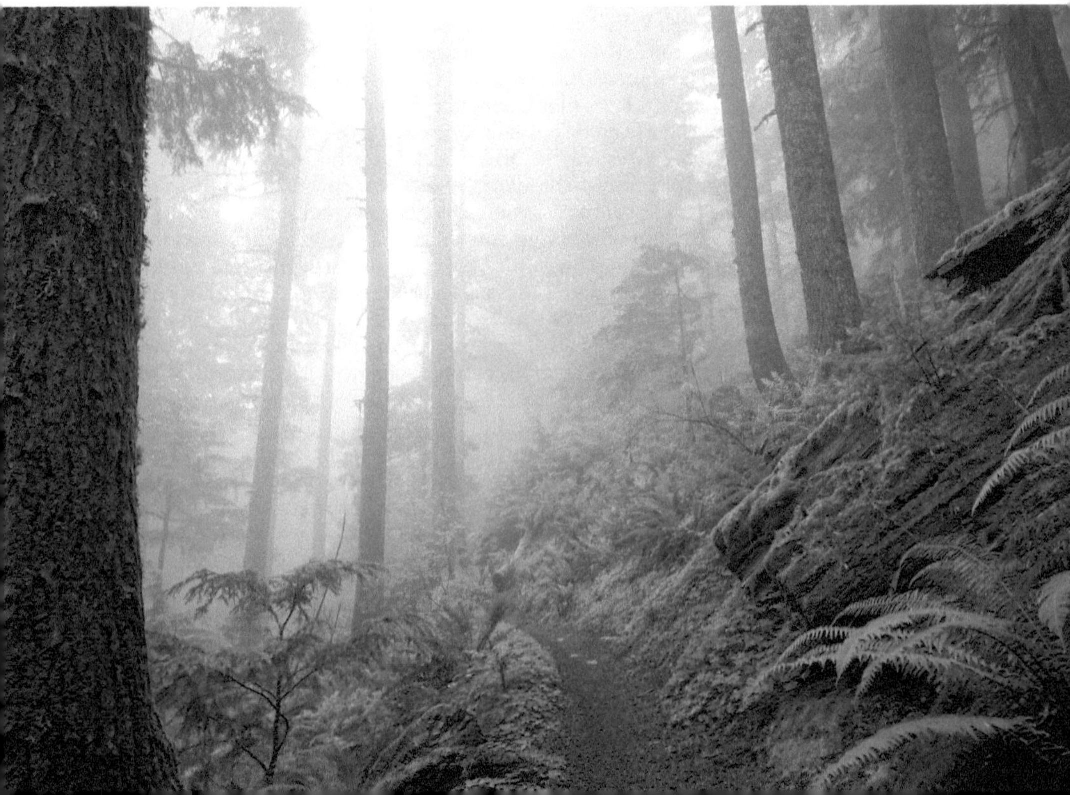

- Drive OR 34 southwest of Philomath for 8.9 miles to a junction on the right signed for Marys Peak.
- Turn right and drive 9.4 winding miles to the large parking lot below the summit.
- **Drivetimes from Corvallis:** 40 minutes for each trailhead

Hike: Marys Peak is the highest point in Oregon's Coast Range, and it feels like a world unto itself. From this high vantage point, you can see from the high peaks of the Cascades to the Pacific Ocean and nearly the entire Willamette Valley, as well as virtually everything else in between. There's more to see than just views here, thankfully; you'll also see masses of spring and summer flowers, ancient forest, vast and peaceful meadows, and surprisingly, smaller crowds than you would expect. Plan for any weather when you hike on Marys Peak, as fog and rain are common for much of the year.

If you're starting on the longer hike via the North Ridge Trail, you'll begin your hike with a gradual ascent through a lush, verdant forest. The trail settles into a series of long switchbacks in which you gain 1,700 feet over the first 3.5 miles. For much of the year fog hangs in the forest here below the summit, and you'll find yourself stopping to take in this magical realm. You may also encounter mountain bikers, who use these trails as much if not more than hikers. At 3.5 miles, you'll reach a junction with the Tie Trail which connects to the East Ridge Trail, offering hikers an option for an even longer hike. Continue straight and continue hiking uphill another 0.7 mile to the huge parking lot below the summit of Marys Peak. Expect to encounter many more people here. If you opted for the short hike, you'll start here.

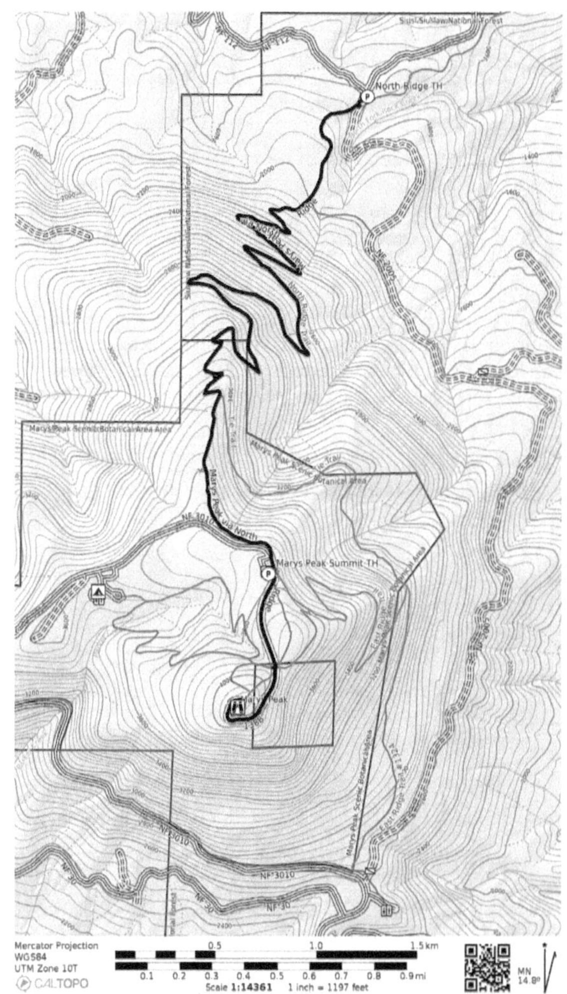

To continue to the summit, follow the gated road uphill through the vast summit meadows of Marys Peak. In June and July, the wildflower displays in these meadows are among the most extraordinary in the state of Oregon. Look for beargrass, paintbrush, lupine, and masses of orange tiger lilies, among many others. Reach the summit at 0.6 mile, or 4.8 miles from the Woods Creek Trailhead. Here the view is truly jaw-dropping! You'll look west to the Pacific Ocean, north and south to the rounded summits of the Coast Range, and east to the entire sweep of the Willamette Valley. Cascade high peaks from Mount Rainier to Diamond Peak line the eastern horizon. This is among the finest views in all of Oregon, and the only thing that detracts from it is the array of fenced-off communication towers and buildings on the summit. A number of trails leave from the summit plateau, offering the possibility of further exploration if you have the time. Otherwise, you should return the way you came.

9. Cape Perpetua

	Cape Perpetua short hikes	Gwynn Creek Loop
Distance:	2 miles out and back	6.5 mile loop
Elevation Gain:	200 feet	1,300 feet
Trailhead Elevation:	121 feet	157 feet
Trail High Point:	197 feet	1,146 feet
Seasons:	all year	all year
Best:	all year	all year
Pass:	NW Forest Pass	NW Forest Pass
On the traditional lands of:	Alsea, Siletz, and Grand Ronde peoples	Alsea, Siletz, and Grand Ronde peoples

Directions:

- From the Yachats River bridge just south of the town center, drive 2.5 miles to the signed turnoff for the visitor center on the left.
- Turn left and drive into the parking lot here.
- **Drivetime from Yachats:** 5 minutes

Hike: Located only a few minutes south of the town of Yachats (pronounced Yaa-Hots), Cape Perpetua is one of the most extraordinary places on the Oregon coast. I first visited when I was 10, at a time when few other than locals had ever heard of this area. Although we did not hike much, I fell in love with the ancient forest, churning seas, and huge views that have made this one of the most beloved spots on the Oregon coast. Cape Perpetua looks exactly the same as it did when I first visited all those years ago, a place out of time and one of Oregon's most extraordinary places. Many people who come here stop at the visitor center and then move on to Devils Churn and Thors Well, two of the most photogenic spots on the Oregon Coast, but hikers will also love a wild 6.5 mile loop up into the ancient forest in the lush canyon of nearby Gwynn Creek. There's something for everyone here.

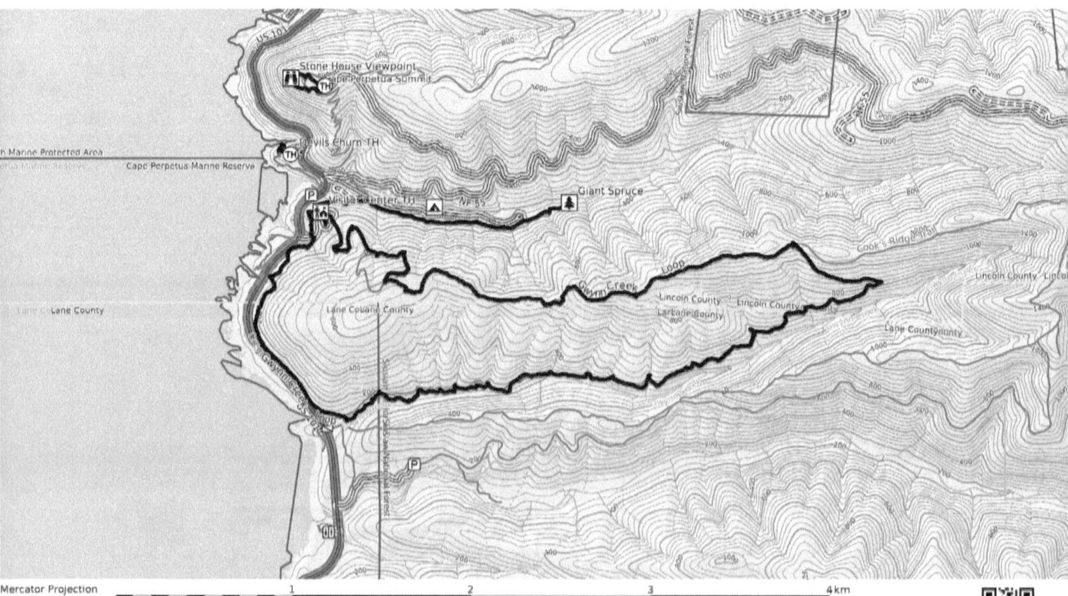

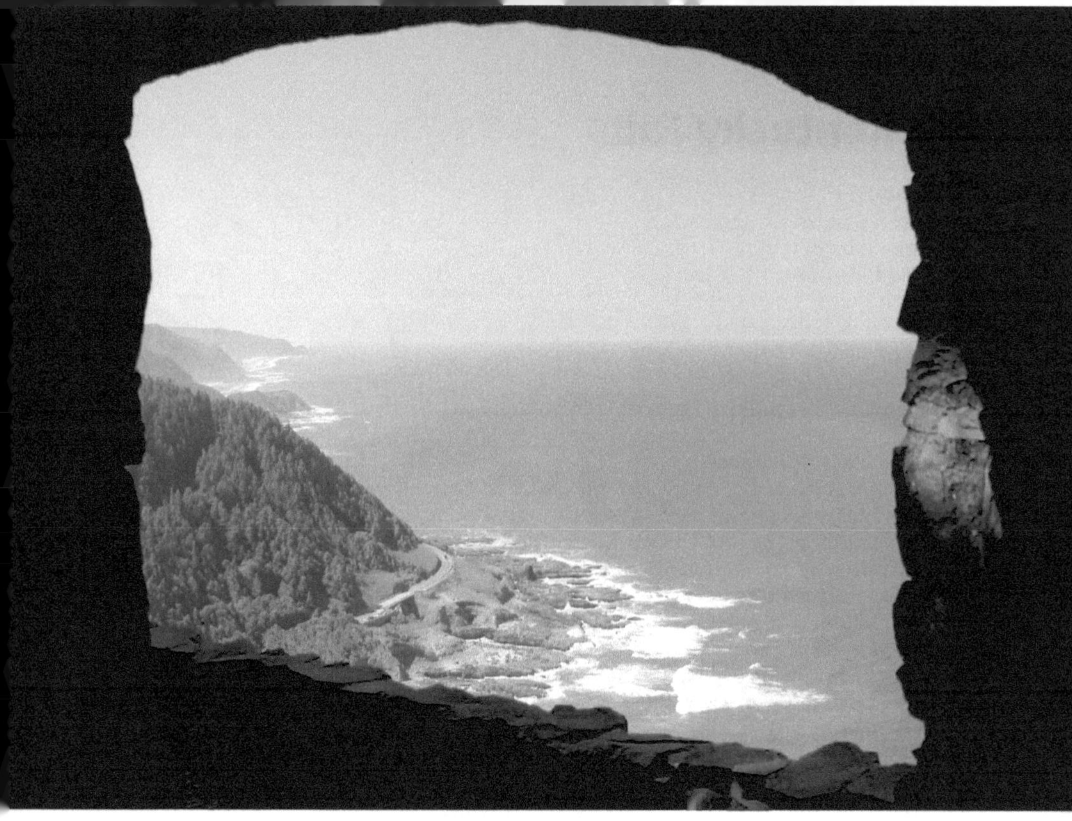

Looking south from the stone house at the summit of Cape Perpetua.

Before you plan on the longer loop, be sure to stop at the visitor center for any questions you may have, and to look over the map of this area. There is so much to do that you may want a plan before you decide to start your day. The easiest hike here is the short walk down to Devils Churn, a narrow cove where the pounding Pacific surf puts on a show, shooting out of cracks and spraying far up into the air. Although it only takes a few minutes to walk down here, you'll find yourself staring at the ocean far longer than expected. When you're ready for a longer hike, return to the visitor center. If you're not up for the Gwynn Creek Loop, consider hiking 2 miles round-trip to the Giant Spruce. Follow signs from the visitor center for 1 mile to this ancient tree, believed to be over 600 years old. Show the tree some respect and avoid climbing over its roots as so many visitors do. From here, return the way you came to the the visitor center.

Many hikers will want to end the day here, but for the longer Gwynn Creek Loop, look for the trail at the RV lot above the visitor center. Follow the trail for 0.3 mile to a junction, where you continue straight on the Discover Trail. You'll follow this trail uphill to a junction with the Cook's Ridge Trail, where you turn left. Follow this trail uphill through verdant forest for about 2 miles to a signed junction with the Gwynn Creek Trail at a saddle. Turn right here. Follow this trail downhill through spectacular ancient forest for about 3 miles. The predominant tree in this canyon is Sitka Spruce and there are some truly huge trees in Gwynn Creek's lush valley. When you reach a junction with the Oregon Coast Trail, turn right. Follow this trail for a mile back to the visitor center. Right before the visitor center, you'll cross the access road. From there, follow signs to the visitor center.

Before you leave the area, be sure to drive up to the summit of Cape Perpetua, where a stone house offers an extraordinary view of the gorgeous coastline of Cape Perpetua and points south. To find this upper trailhead, drive back to US 101 and turn right. In just 0.1 mile, you'll turn right at a sign for Cape Perpetua Campground. Follow this road for 0.8 mile, then turn left and drive 1 mile to the trailhead at road's end. A short trail leads to the stone shelter and its most extraordinary view.

10. Kentucky Falls

Distance: 4.8 miles out and back
Elevation Gain: 800 feet
Trailhead Elevation: 1,537 feet
Trail High Point: 1,570 feet
Season: March - November
Best: April - May
Pass: NW Forest Pass
On the traditional lands of: Quuiich (Lower Umpqua), Siuslaw, and Coos peoples

Directions from Reedsport:

- From the north end of Reedsport, turn right on Smith River Road.
- Drive 14.9 miles on this road (which becomes County Road 48) to a junction with North Fork Road (County 48A), immediately before a bridge. Turn left here.
- Drive this road for 7.4 miles to a bridge, where the road narrows to one lane and becomes FR 48. The road turns to gravel just after the bridge.
- Drive 2.7 miles of gravel and paved road to a fork in the road. Turn right on FR 23.
- Drive 4 miles of narrow paved road to the North Fork Smith Trailhead on the left. This is the lower Kentucky Falls trailhead.
- To continue to the upper trailhead (where this hike begins), drive uphill on winding FR 23 for 5.6 miles to a fork.
- Turn left onto FR 919 and drive 2.7 miles downhill to the Kentucky Falls Trailhead on the right side of the road.
- **Drivetime from Reedsport:** 1 hour and 15 minutes

Hike: Set deep in the Coast Range between Eugene and Reedsport, the North Fork Smith River Canyon has three of the nicest waterfalls you'll see in this part of Oregon. The hike there is an absolute delight too, passing through a green tunnel of ancient trees, mosses, and ferns, Far removed from the hustle and bustle of modern Oregon, this hike is a must for anyone who loves the best of what the Coast Range has to offer.

From the trailhead, locate the well-signed Kentucky Falls Trail on the opposite side of the road. You will begin hiking gradually downhill under huge and ancient Douglas firs in a deep canyon.

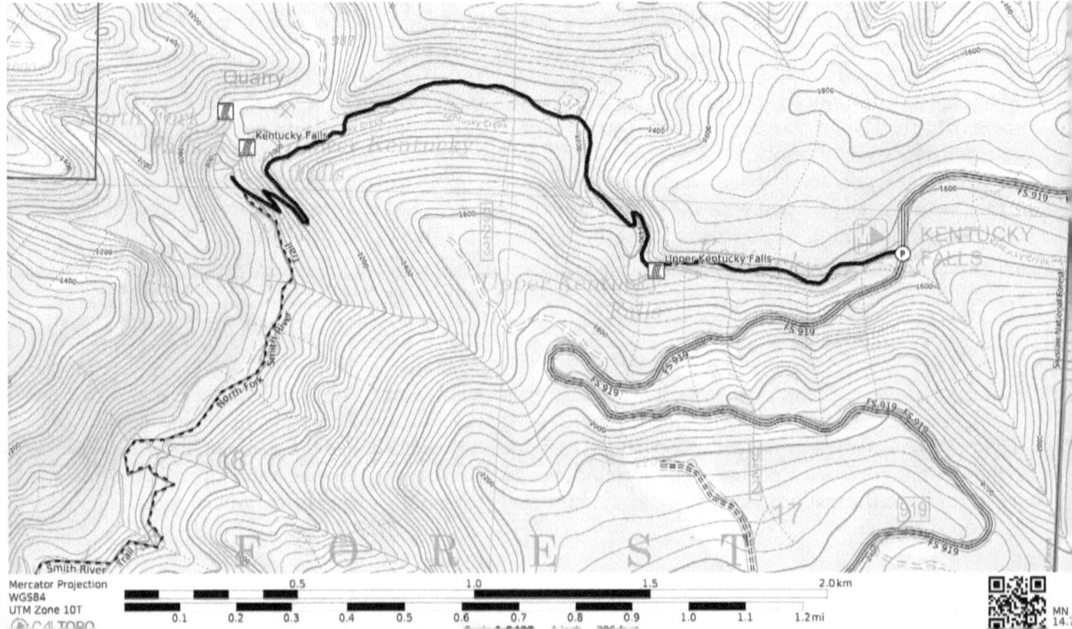

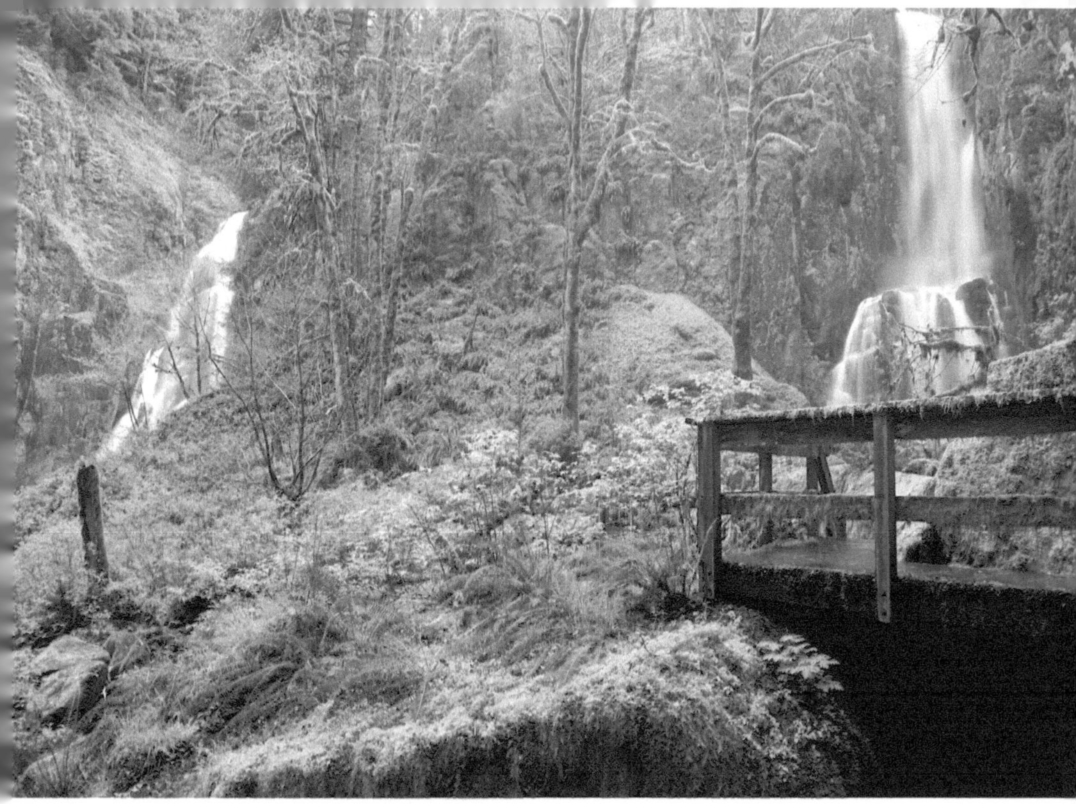

North Fork and Kentucky Falls, with the wooden viewing platform.

After 0.8 mile, the trail passes by the top of graceful Upper Kentucky Falls before descending to the base of the falls via series of switchbacks. Take a moment in this beautiful spot, deep in the mossy woods far from the worries of the world.From the upper falls, the trail passes by an unnamed falls and crosses the creek on a bridge. You will soon begin switchbacking gradually downhill. At a little over 2 miles from the trailhead, reach a junction with the North Fork Trail. Continue straight and you will arrive at a most wondrous view: North Fork Falls on your left, and Kentucky Falls on your right, falling side by side. Wow! Nowhere else in Oregon can you reach such a view with so little effort. The trail leads to a mossy boardwalk and ends at a viewing platform below Kentucky Falls. From this vantage North Fork Falls is somewhat obstructed; for a better view, you will have to hop off the trail, cross the creek, and climb up the banks of the North Fork Smith River - something I do not recommend. Most hikers will prefer to return the way they came.

Continuing your hike: Adventurous hikers may want to continue downstream along the north fork of the Smith River. The trail continues 6 miles downstream to the North Fork Smith Trailhead mentioned in the directions. There are no waterfalls but the scenery is wild and will satisfy the most adventurous souls. If you're coming from Reedsport and you're craving just a little more time on the trail, consider instead hiking the Nature Loop, which departs from the lower trailhead. This lovely ramble, less than a mile long, leads hikers through a grove of magnificent ancient forest amid a carpet of moss, ferns, and spring flowers. It is highly recommended!

Note: You can also drive here from Eugene. Drive west on OR 126 for 33 miles to a junction on the left with Siuslaw Road. Turn left and drive 1.6 miles to a junction on the right at a bridge with BLM 18-8-28. Turn right here and drive 1.5 miles to a junction on the left with Dunn Ridge Road. Turn left and drive 7.0 miles to a T-junction where the paved road ends. Turn left onto BLM 18-8-9, also known as Knowles Creek Road. Drive this road 1.1 miles to a 3-way fork just after a small pond. Stay on the center road and continue 1.7 miles to a junction with FR 23 on the right. Turn right and drive 1.6 miles to a junction on the right with FR 919. Turn right and drive 2.7 miles downhill to the Kentucky Falls Trailhead.

11. Threemile Lake

Distance: 6.6 mile loop
Elevation Gain: 600 feet
Trailhead Elevation: 39 feet
Trail High Point: 404 feet
Season: all year
Best: all year
Pass: NW Forest Pass
On the traditional lands of: Quuiich (Lower Umpqua), Siuslaw, and Coos peoples

Directions from Florence:
- From the junction of US 101 and OR 126 in Florence, drive south on US 101 for 13.2 miles to a signed turnoff for Tahkenitch Campground.
- Turn right here and follow signs for the trailhead.
- **Drivetime:** 20 minutes

Directions from Reedsport:
- From the junction of US 101 and OR 38 in Reedsport, drive north on US 101 for 8 miles to a signed turnoff for Tahkenitch Campground.
- Turn left here and follow signs for the trailhead.
- **Drivetime:** 10 minutes

Hike: The Oregon Dunes are a marvel of the natural world. In just a few minutes, you can step out of your car along a busy highway and lose yourself (both figuratively and literally) in a desert world that conjures images of the Sahara - except you'll have a cool ocean breeze to keep you company. In fact, the dunes here were the inspiration for Frank Herbert's classic science fiction novel ***Dune***. If the idea of hiking through this sandy wilderness intrigues you, there are several worthwhile hikes in the area. The best of these is the loop trek to Threemile Lake, which takes hikers to a beautiful lake just a short walk from the ocean.

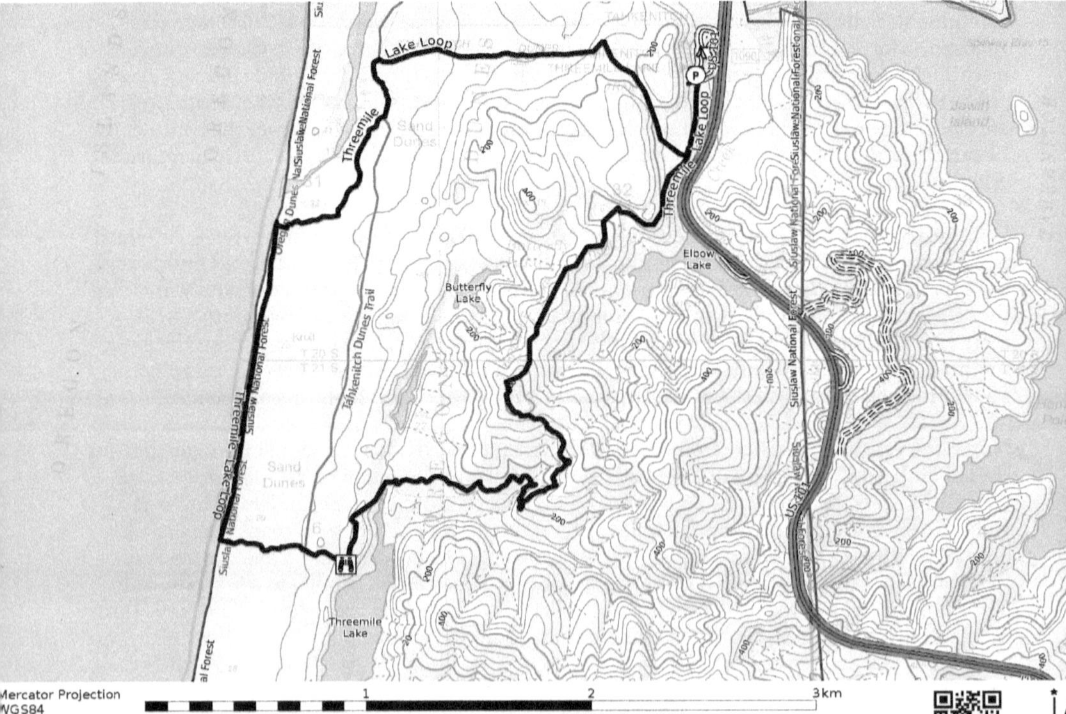

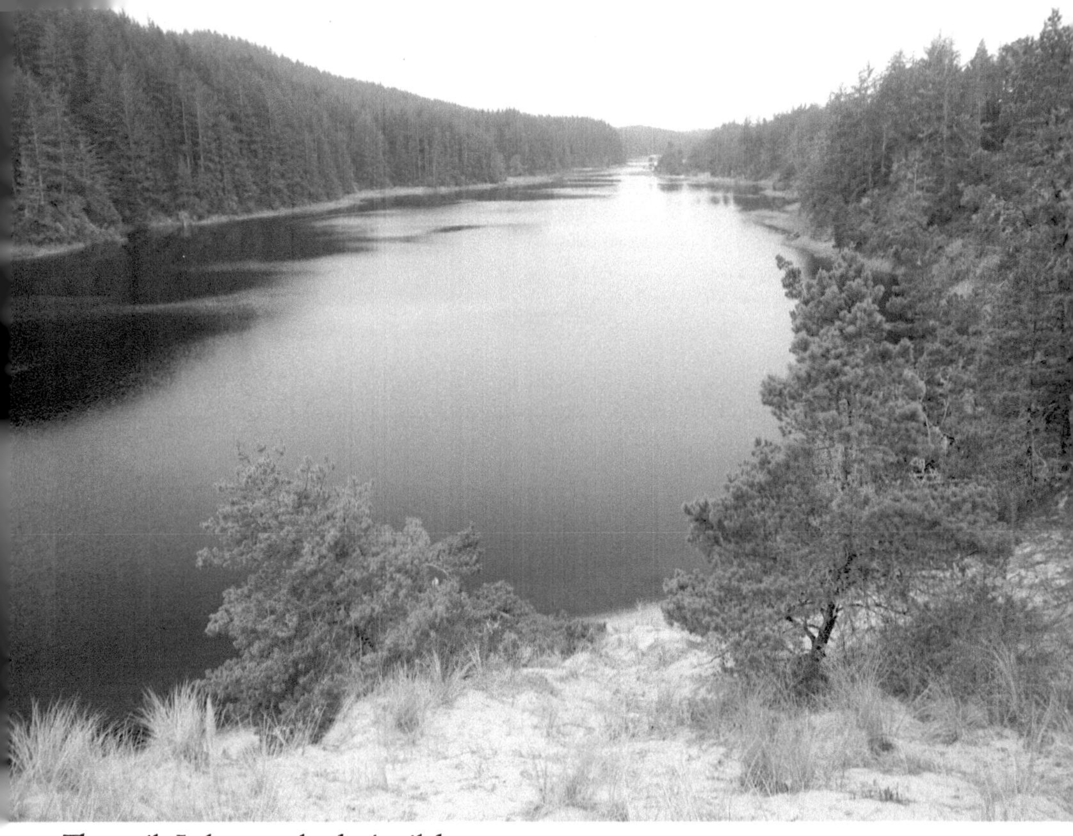

Threemile Lake on a cloudy April day.

From the signboard at the trailhead, follow the trail for 0.3 mile to a junction. Keep left at a sign for Threemile Lake to begin the loop. The trail meanders through a peaceful second-growth forest, occasionally passing over sandy stretches that remind you where exactly you are. The colorful understory here features tall rhododendrons, trilliums that bloom in April and huge specimens of skunk cabbage. Along the way you'll climb and descend into another green world, leaving the highway noise behind at last. At 2.5 miles from the trailhead, the trail crosses a long bridge at the head of Threemile Lake. Continue another 0.3 mile to a junction. Right leads to the ocean, but first turn left and follow a short trail to a bluff overlooking Threemile Lake. The lake is in fact 1.5 miles long (the name referring to the distance from the Umpqua River, which has over time become much longer), but appears to stretch out far into the distance. Steep sandy trails lead down to the lakeshore, but most hikers will prefer to stay on the bluff above, where the views are better and the sand inviting for a rest stop.

After you visit the lake, return to the junction and follow signs to the beach. You will pass a junction on your right with the Tahkenitch Dunes Trail, which is a way to shorten your loop that does not reach the beach. After just 0.5 mile from Threemile Lake, reach the ocean. From March 15th to September 15th, the dry sand along the beach here is closed to protect snowy plovers, an endangered seabird that nests in the sand above the high tide line. During this time, hikers will need to stay on wet sand near the shoreline for the next mile. You'll walk along the beach for one mile until you can see Tahkenitch Creek ahead of you. Do not cross the creek! The loop turns right here at a "115" sign located just above the beach. From here, you'll follow a trail along Tahkenitch Creek for a short distance, soon meeting the Tahkenitch Dunes Trail again. Turn right at a sign for Tahkenitch Campground and before long you'll at last be hiking across tall sand dunes. Follow posts across the dunes, and soon you'll enter a dark woods where the trees seem to form a tunnel over the trail corridor. When you come to the junction at trail's end, turn left and hike 0.3 mile back to the trailhead.

12. Shore Acres State Park

Distance: 5.2 mile semi-loop
Elevation Gain: 300 feet
Trailhead Elevation: 10 feet
Trail High Point: 87 feet
Season: all year
Best: all year
Pass: none needed
On the traditional lands of: the Miluk Coos people

Directions from North Bend:

- From North Bend, drive to the US 101 split. Turn right and follow signs for state parks and Charleston.
- Drive 0.8 mile to an intersection with Broadway Avenue. Turn left here and continue following signs for state parks.
- Continue following signs for state parks through Charleston to Sunset Bay State Park, a total of 11.4 miles from the US 101 split in North Bend.
- For the hike, park in the Sunset Bay South lot, by the restroom. As of Spring 2021, there is a basketball hoop at the trailhead. Bring a ball and play a game of HORSE after your hike! The trail departs to the right of the restrooms, at a signboard.
- **Drivetime from North Bend:** 20 minutes

Hike: The Oregon Coast is home to some spectacular hikes, but only this one features a classical English garden. This hike is no one-trick pony though, as it also features fantastic views up and down this stretch of coastline, ancient coastal forest, and the grounds of an early 20th century mansion and estate. This is a fun hike that everyone will enjoy!

Note: Dogs are prohibited on trails in Shore Acres State Park.

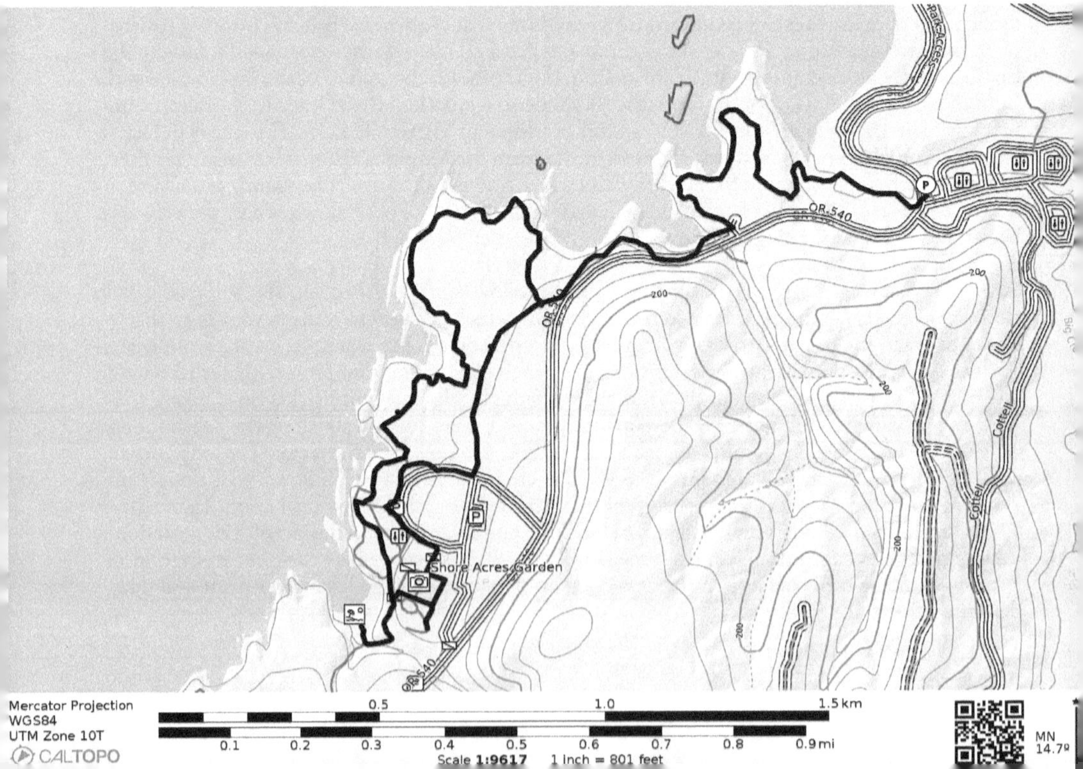

OR 540
Shore Acres Garden
Cottell
Mercator Projection
WGS84
UTM Zone 10T
CALTOPO
0.5 1.0 1.5 km
0.1 0.2 0.3 0.4 0.5 0.6 0.7 0.8 0.9 mi
Scale 1:9617 1 inch = 801 feet
MN 14.7º

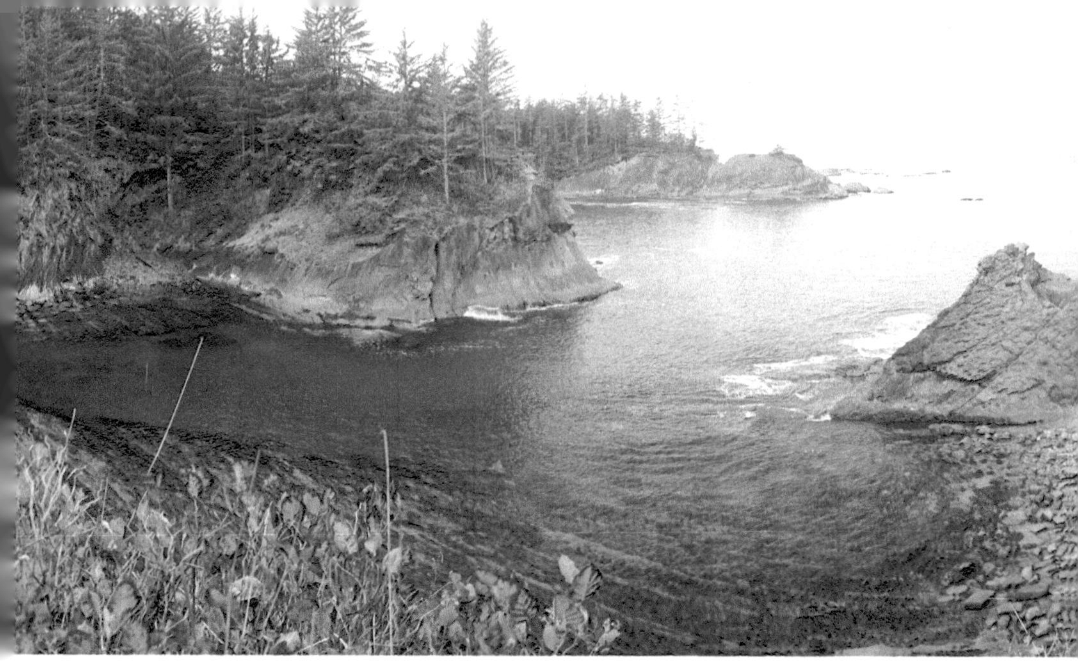

It is immensely fun to explore the coves and cliffs at Shore Acres State Park.

The trail leaves from next to the bathrooms and climbs up to bluffs above the ocean amid a forest of impressive coastal Sitka spruce. Soon you will pass a number of side trails to the right with excellent views of coves and sea stacks. The trail meets the access road again, but first turn right and follow the short trail down to Norton Gulch, a beautiful cove. When you return to the main trail where it follows the road. The trail then parallels the road for a few hundred yards, offering occasional views north to Cape Arago's lighthouse. Locate a wide trail departing right from the access road and follow it. This narrow lane was the former driveway of the Simpson mansion, on whose old estate you will be hiking. A short distance down this trail, turn right at an unmarked junction near a huge, multilimbed Sitka spruce. This is the beginning of the loop.

The trail wraps around the cliffs and coves here, at one point passing directly above colorful sea cliffs and rock formations on an unfenced section of trail directly above the ocean. What a spectacular spot! At a T-junction in the woods at about 2 miles from the trailhead, turn right into a dense thicket. The trail winds down and out of a gully using staircases to arrive at a viewpoint of the ocean. Soon you will arrive at the edge of Shore Acres State Park, where dogs and other animals are forbidden. At 2.4 miles you will arrive at the observation building, with views north to the honeycombed formations you just passed. Keep right at a sign for Simpson Beach, saving the botanical gardens for later. Louis J. Simpson built a house here for his wife Cassie in 1908, but the house burned down in 1921, not long after his wife's death. The trail passes a gated side entrance to the botanical gardens and winds downhill to diminutive Simpson Beach, set between colorful headlands. This is the first great destination here. From the beach, the Oregon Coast Trail continues south towards Cape Arago's windy headland. After the beach, you should return to the gate at the edge of the botanical gardens. Some hikers may want to skip this side trip, but I would strongly recommend taking the time to visit Shore Acre's gardens. Give yourself at least 15 – 20 minutes for the visit.

When you've finished visiting the gardens, make your way back to the trail. You can return to the trail through the garden's side gate, or you can follow the garden access road beyond the parking lot until you near the entrance booth. Here, locate the wide trail heading into the woods on your left. Follow this path, the old driveway of the Simpson estate, north. Along the way you'll pass through the old gates of the estate. After 0.3 mile, come to the junction with the trail near the multilimbed spruce, now on your left. Continue on the old road. From here, follow your way back on the trail to Sunset Bay and your car. Then go shoot some hoops!

13. Golden and Silver Falls

Distance: 3.6 miles out and back
Elevation Gain: 800 feet
Trailhead Elevation: 298 feet
Trail High Point: 731 feet
Season: all year
Best: March – June
Pass: none needed
On the traditional lands of: the Hanis Coos, Lower Umpqua, and Siuslaw peoples

Directions from Coos Bay:

- From the south end of Coos Bay, fork left onto OR 241 at a sign for the Coos River and Allegany.
- Drive this highway for 13.7 winding, lovely miles to the small community of Allegany.
- At a sign for Golden and Silver Falls, continue straight. The sign says it is 10 miles to Golden and Silver Falls. Continue following signs for Golden and Silver Falls. The road soon narrows.
- The road changes to gravel at 18.4 miles (or 4.7 miles from Allegany), just before mile marker 19. Keep left at a sign for the park.
- You will finally arrive at the trailhead at road's end, 23.3 miles from US 101 (and 9.6 miles from Allegany).
- There is a bathroom and several picnic tables here. No pass is required.
- **Drivetime from Coos Bay:** 40 minutes

Hike: One of Oregon's least heralded state parks contains two of the most spectacular waterfalls in the Coast Range. There are separate trails to both falls as well as a trail that climbs from Silver Falls to a precarious perch opposite the top of Golden Falls. For the best experience, come here in the spring when the falls are flowing at their best, and hike all three trails in this small park. You won't regret it!

Begin by hiking to Golden Falls first. From the parking lot, locate the trail leading across a bridge. Once across the bridge, keep right to hike to Golden Falls (left leads to Silver Falls and the top of Golden Falls). The trail follows Glenn Creek for 0.4 mile to the base of Golden Falls,

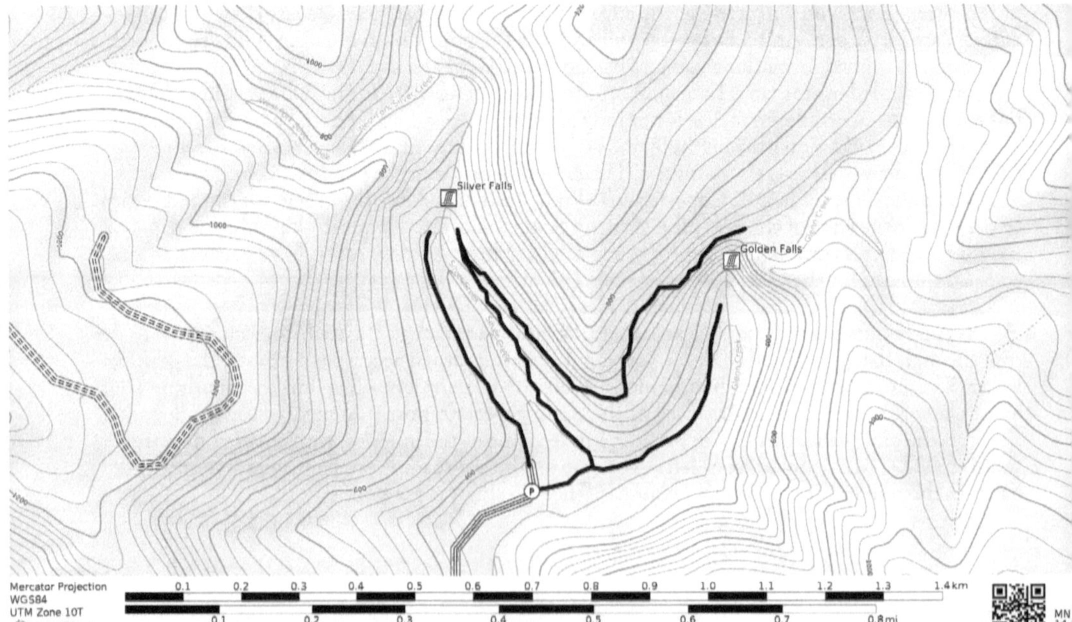

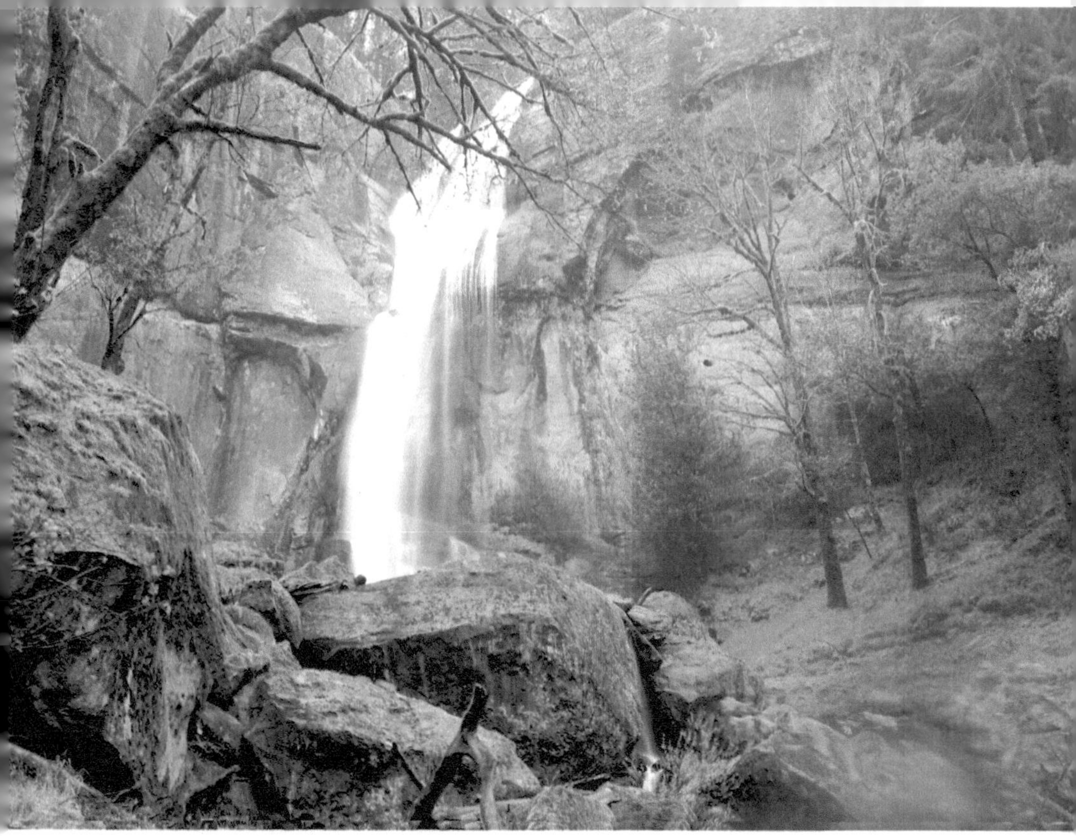

Golden Falls in early Spring.

which at 254 feet tall is one of the tallest waterfalls in the coast range. In winter and spring, the falls thunders over the huge red and black cliffs here, while the falls is more subdued in the summer and fall. It is not easy to access the base of the falls when they are running high.

When you are finished visiting Golden Falls, return to the trail junction near the bridge and turn right. You'll hike uphill under huge Douglas firs, which add to the moody atmosphere here on rainy days. As the trail begins to open up, keep a close eye on your hands and on your pets, as poison oak lines the side of the trail at times. You will reach a point directly below Silver Falls at about a mile into the hike. As you're almost at the base of the falls, the view isn't exactly the best; that being said, this is a fantastic spot to commune closely with this 259-foot-tall beauty of a waterfall. If you're up for more adventure, you can hike to the top of Golden Falls from here.

Hike back from Silver Falls a short distance to a trail junction. Hikers with small children should avoid the side trip to the top of Golden Falls as the trail passes huge cliffs without any sort of guardrail or protection. If you're up for the adventure, turn left and hike uphill on a wide trail, the remains of an old road. Soon you will begin to follow cliffs until the top of Golden Falls appears before you. Continue on this trail but remember to watch your step as the trail passes a 300-foot-high cliff to your right. The trail more or less ends just beyond the top of the falls, so you'll have to turn around here. As with the lower trail, keep an eye out for poison oak up here as well. Return the way you came back to the trailhead.

Before you go, there's one more trail worth exploring here. At the far end of the trailhead, locate a trail that leads up the left bank of Silver Creek and follow it for 0.3 mile to a vantage of Silver Falls. This view is better than the view on the other side of the creek, and you'll be able to see the graceful side of this falls as it tumbles 259 feet down an overhanging cliff. What a view! When you're done here, make your way back to the trailhead.

14. Coquille River Falls and Hanging Rock

	Coquille River Falls	Hanging Rock
Distance:	1.4 miles out and back	1.8 miles out and back
Elevation Gain:	500 feet	400 feet
Trailhead Elevation:	1,684 feet	3,678 feet
Trail High Point:	1,684 feet	3,937 feet
Seasons:	all year	May - November
Best:	all year	June - October
Pass:	none needed	none needed
On the traditional lands of:	the Tolowa Dee-ni', Takelma, and Cow Creek Umpqua peoples	the Tolowa Dee-ni', Takelma, and Cow Creek Umpqua peoples

Directions from Coos Bay:

- From Coos Bay, drive OR 42 southeast for 22.6 miles to a turnoff for Powers.
- Follow the ramp and exit south onto OR 542.
- Drive south for 18 miles to the small town of Powers.
- From Powers, continue south through town and turn right onto S. 4th Avenue. This road becomes the Rogue River-Coquille Road.
- Drive this road south of Powers 16.3 miles to a junction with FR 3348 on the left.
- Turn left and drive 1.5 very curvy miles to the signed Coquille River Falls trailhead at a pulloff on the left side of the road.
- **Drivetime from Coos Bay:** 90 minutes

Hike: Coquille River Falls might be the greatest waterfall in Oregon's Coast Range. Tumbling 115 feet in two tiers, its roar fills the canyon and ancient forests in all directions. Were it closer to a major city, this would be a very popular hike on par with some of the Columbia River Gorge's famous attractions. Instead, you might have it to yourself, as I did when I visited on a rainy October day. Despite the short length of this hike, the falls is worth the long drive from wherever you start the day. If you're looking for more hiking, plan on a driving east into the Coastal mountains to visit Hanging Rock's iconic viewpoint of the Rogue River.

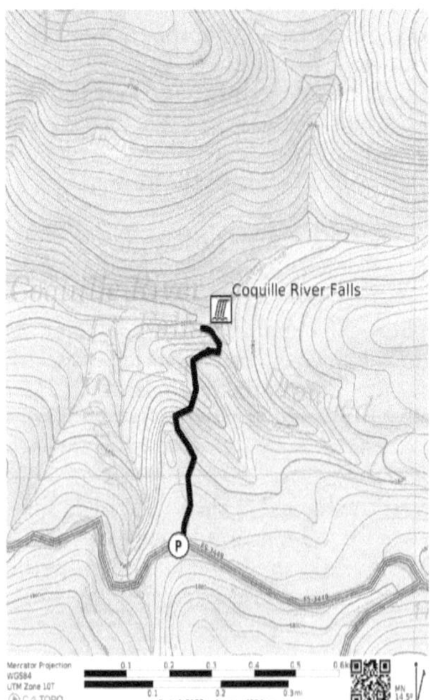

The trail begins with a quick descent below the road into a dark grove of huge, ancient trees. You'll continue a switchbacking descent towards the Coquille River until you reach a trail junction near the falls. When you near the falls, ignore a trail that says "Upper Falls" and instead follow the trail as it scoots around a narrow promontory above the river. In summer, Coquille River Falls is graceful, splitting into side-by-side tiers as it flows over its lower tier. For the rest of the year, the raging waterfall spills over the cliffs at an ear-splitting volume. Be careful on the trails around the falls, as they are slippery for most of the year. When you're done taking in the falls, return

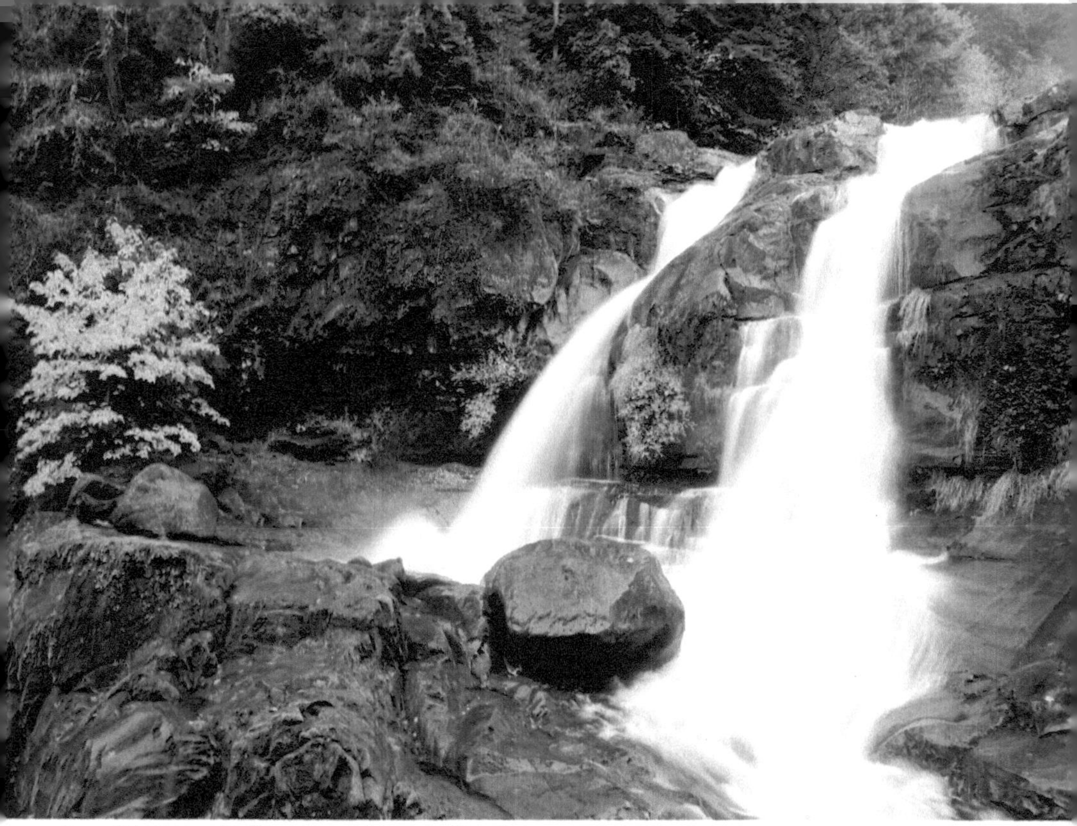

Coquille River Falls on a cold, rainy October morning.

the way you came, remembering to save some energy for the climb back uphill.

If you're planning on hiking to Hanging Rock's legendary viewpoint, drive 0.4 mile east to a junction with FR 5520. Ignore this junction and continue following paved FR 3348 for 7.3 more miles along the Coquille River. At 7.7 miles from Coquille River Falls, turn right onto FR 5520 at a junction opposite Buck Creek Campground. Turn right onto FR 5520 and drive 5.7 miles of good gravel road to a junction with FR 5520-140 on the left. Fork to the left here and drive 1 mile of narrow, bumpy gravel to the trailhead pullout on the right.

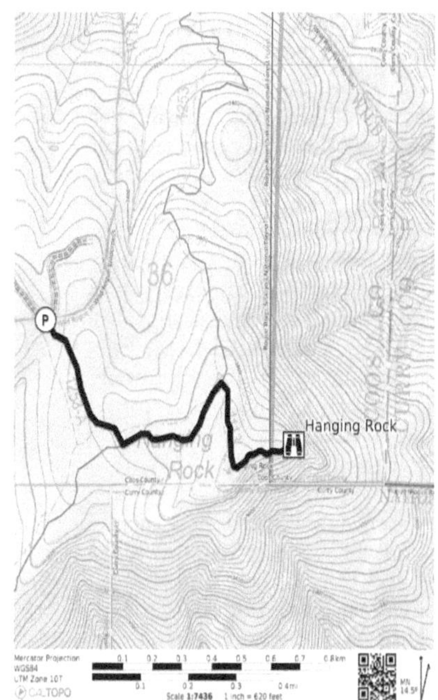

From the trailhead, follow the trail through deep woods. Rhododendrons hang tall above the trail, adding splashes of pink in June. Pass a trail junction at 0.3 mile, at which you continue straight. You'll continue climbing through the woods gradually to a junction with the Hanging Rock Trail at 0.6 mile. Turn right on the Hanging Rock Trail and climb through increasingly open woods. The trail drops a bit as you approach Hanging Rock. Follow the trail to the rock, which you reach at 0.9 mile. The true form of Hanging Rock does not reveal itself until you are almost on top of it. The rock is aptly named, as you'll have astounding views down some 3,600 feet to the Rogue River. Trails lead to better views of the rock from the side, but watch your step! Whenever you're ready, return the way you came.

15. Iron Mountain Botanical Area

Distance: 1.8 miles out and back
Elevation Gain: 500 feet
Trailhead Elevation: 3,497 feet
Trail High Point: 4,009 feet
Season: May – November
Best: June – July
Pass: none needed
On the traditional lands of: the Tolowa Dee-ni', Tututni, and Cow Creek Umpqua peoples

Directions from Gold Beach:

- From Gold Beach, drive Jerry's Flat Road east for 30.7 miles of paved road to a junction near the small community of Agness.
- Continue straight on a gravel road towards Agness Pass, following signs for Powers.
- Drive 11 miles of winding gravel road to Agness Pass. If you're ever in doubt, continue following signs for Powers.
- At Agness Pass, turn left onto gravel FR 5325, the Elk River Road.
- Following this winding, narrow road for 3.9 miles to a fork. Keep left.
- Continue 2.1 miles to the signed trailhead on the right side of the road, 6 miles from Agness Pass. There is room for 4 – 5 cars to park on the left side of the road, but you'll be surprised to see anyone at the trailhead.
- **Drivetime:** 90 minutes

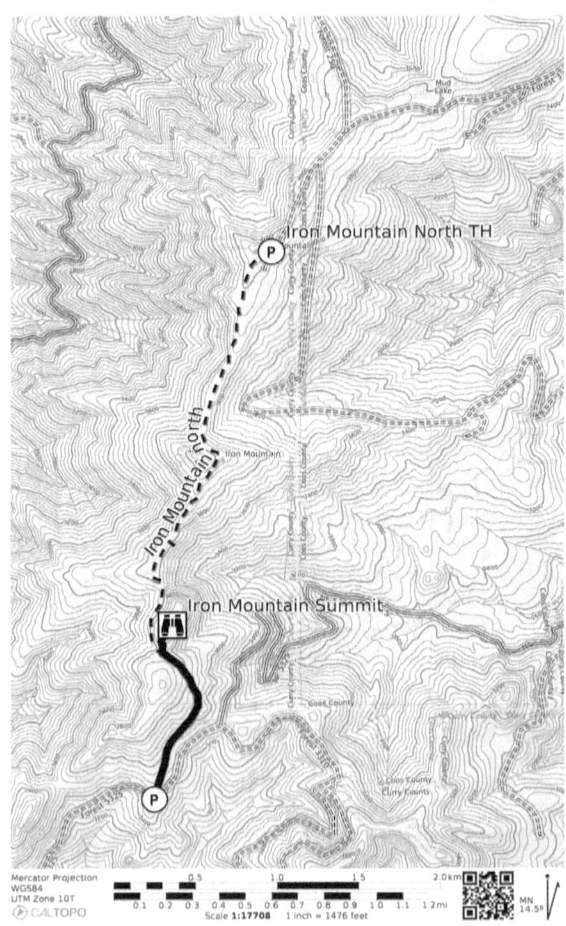

Hike: Not to be confused with Iron Mountain in the Old Cascades (Hike 57), this Iron Mountain seems lost in the rugged mountains of the southern Oregon coast range. It's a long drive from anywhere, whether it be Gold Beach, Port Orford, or Powers. This anonymity has helped keep this beautiful corner of southwest Oregon shrouded in secrecy, and yet there is so much to see! The Rogue River-Siskiyou National Forest has set aside this Iron Mountain as an area of botanical interest, and plant lovers should find much to see on this short hike. Hikers will love the great views on the summit of Iron Mountain. There is something for everyone here, even if it takes a long time to drive to the trailhead.

From the trailhead, follow the trail uphill through a fascinating forest of Port Orford cedar and Jeffrey pine. Masses of rhododendrons bloom here in June. If you're visiting in June (as I did), you will also note the proliferation of golden yellow

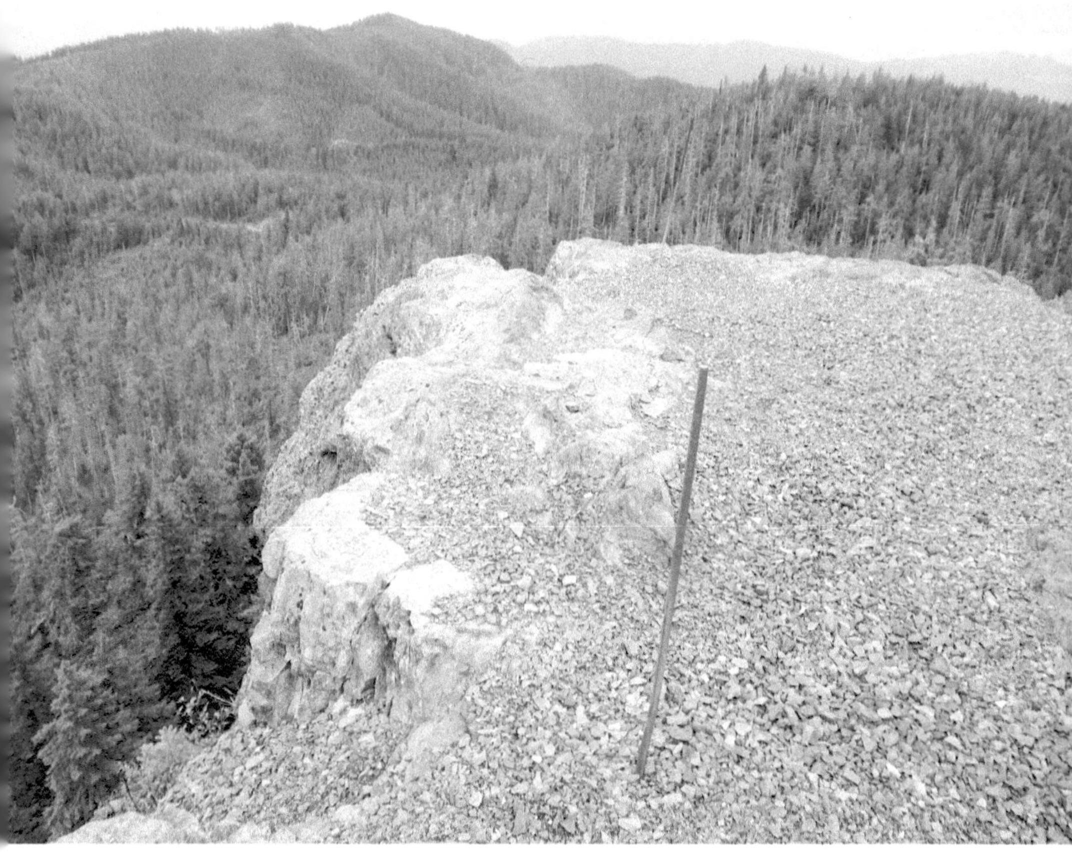

Remains of a long-gone lookout building on the rocky summit of Iron Mountain.

Siskiyou irises along the trail. The soil here is a reddish color, true to the name of the mountain. As you hike uphill along this old road that is now a trail, you will also note the fascinating mixture of flowers, plants, and trees that call this area home; indeed, this area is located at the confluence of plants commonly found both in the Pacific Northwest and Northern California. The Forest Service has noted that more than 300 different species of plants grow in this small area, some of which are quite rare.

After 0.7 mile of gradual hiking uphill, you will reach a trail junction with the spur trail to Iron Mountain's summit. Turn right here and hike this steep trail uphill another 0.2 mile to the summit of Iron Mountain at just over 4,000 feet above sea level. On clear days you can see waves break on the Pacific Ocean to the west, but your attention might also be drawn to the many crumpled ridges and mountains of this part of the Coast Range. A lookout stood here during the first half of the 20th Century. The summit teeters on the edge of a huge cliff on the mountain's east face, so be careful where you step and sit.

The recommended hike returns to the trailhead the way you came but if you're interested in a longer hike, you can continue following the old road north towards the northern trailhead of Iron Mountain. The trail stays mostly in the forest, but this is a pretty area and it's fun to explore if you have the time.

If you're driving a high-clearance vehicle and don't mind driving back a different way, you can follow FR 5325 for 11.7 miles of rocky gravel and another 18.6 miles of pavement to road's end at US 101. Signs help guide you back to the highway. Along the way you'll pass fens of Darlingtonia on the side of the road, several campgrounds, and many excellent views of the gorgeous Elk River. I spent a memorable evening driving through this canyon, blasting heavy metal and wondering what was around the next turn. I can't wait to go back.

16. Blacklock Point

Distance: 9.4 miles out and back
Elevation Gain: 400 feet
Trailhead Elevation: 16 feet
Trail High Point: 180 feet
Season: all year
Best: all year
Pass: $5 day use fee
On the traditional lands of: the Tututni and Siletz peoples

Directions from Port Orford:

- Drive north from Port Orford on US 101 for approximately 10 miles to a junction with Floras Lake Loop Road. Turn left here.
- Drive 0.8 mile and turn left on Floras Lake Road.
- Drive 1.4 miles and turn right at a sign for Boice Cope Park.
- Drive 0.2 mile to the Day Use area, where you should park.
- As of 2022, the day use fee is $5, which is payable at the parking lot.
- **Drivetime from Port Orford:** 20 minutes

Hike: The lonely stretch of coastline between Coos Bay and Port Orford is fun for exploring, but the labyrinth of trails, roads, and beaches can be confusing even for veteran hikers. This fun day trip to the rugged cliffs of Blacklock Point combines the best of this gorgeous area, but be sure to pay attention to tide tables, trail junctions, and your own intuition. More than most hikes in this book, you will need to be aware of where you are at any given point to experience this hike at its best.

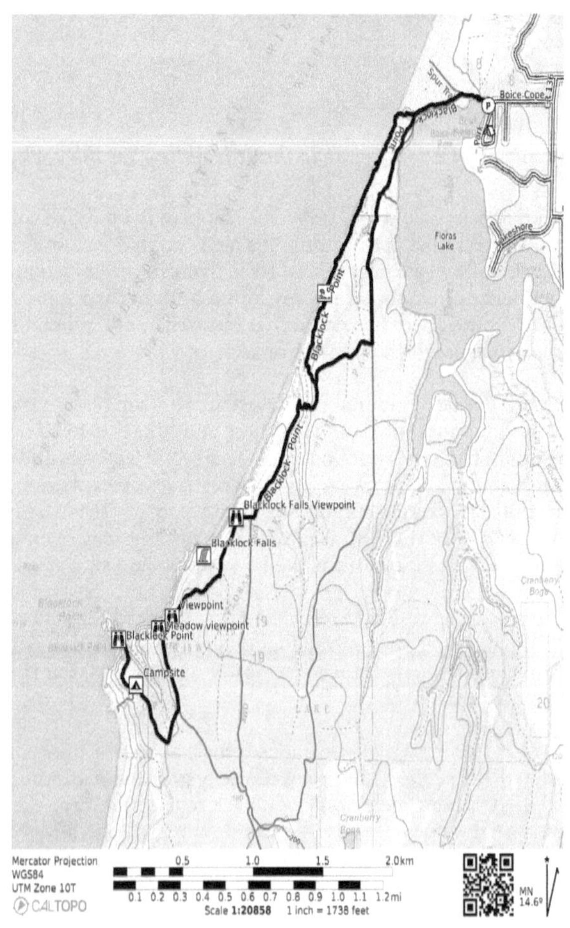

From the day use parking area, follow the trail out to Floras Lake. Continue along the north side of the lake until you reach a small sand dune. Cross the dune and head downhill to the beach. This is one of the more scenic beaches along this stretch of the Oregon Coast, but it is best experienced at low tide or close to it; at high tide, the beach disappears altogether. Be sure to check the tide tables before you do this part of the hike (you can avoid it, as you will see later). As you hike along the beach, the sandstone cliffs above the beach grow taller and taller, revealing small coves and weathered layers of rock that rise directly out of the sand. After 1.2 miles along the beach (and 1.7

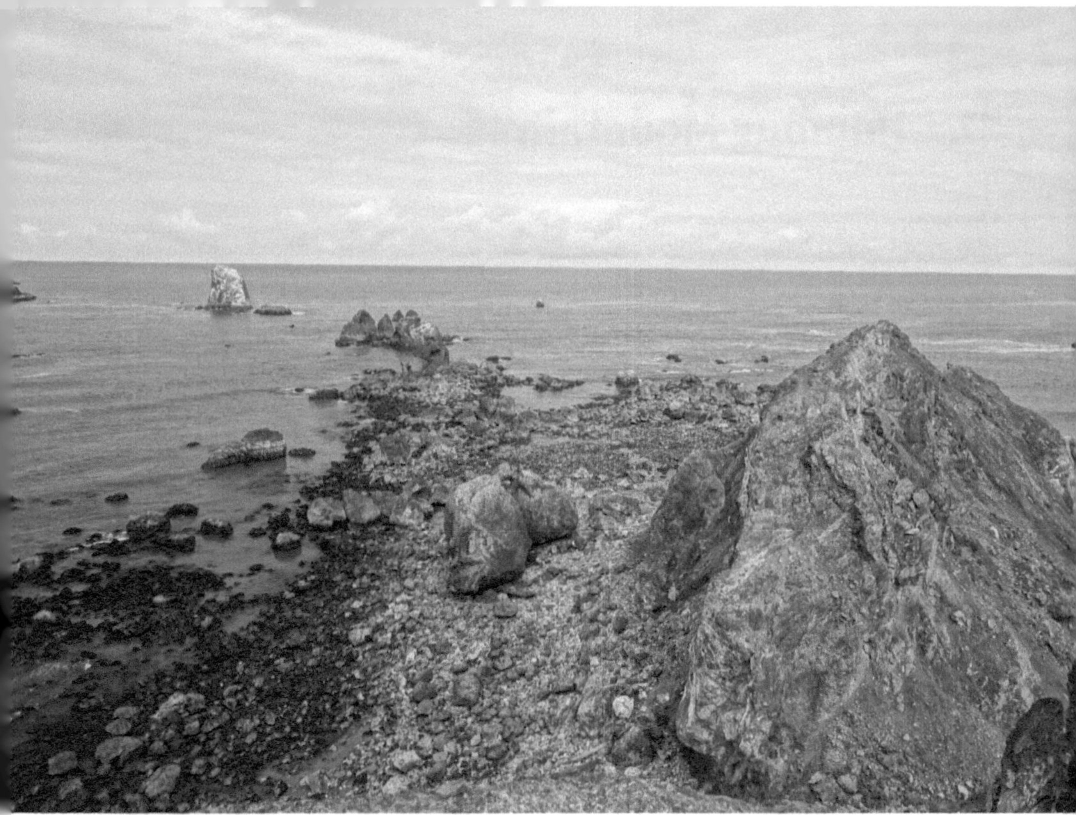

Blacklock Point

miles of hiking overall), you'll reach a small creek flowing into the ocean. Do not cross this creek; instead, locate a very brushy trail heading uphill to your left. The way soon becomes clear, and within 0.2 mile, you'll reach a junction with the Oregon Coast Trail (OCT). Turn right here.

The OCT drops into the basin holding the same creek mentioned above. The trail crosses the creek at a muddy ford; look downstream to your right for a bridge leading over the creek. The trail then climbs onto the cliffs above the sea as it tunnels through dense forest, and from this point on, it is easy to follow and well-signed. You will follow signs leading you to Blacklock Point. Side trails to the right lead to a view of a natural rock arch on the beach, a tall waterfall tumbling down the cliffs of Blacklock Point, and an attractive meadow full of June wildflowers just above the northern end of Blacklock Point. At about 4 miles from the trailhead, reach a junction in the woods above Blacklock Point; turn right and continue following trails down to Blacklock Point. Just above the point is a campsite if you're looking to backpack in this area. At 4.7 miles from the trailhead, the rugged cliffs of the point reveal themselves below you! A trail leads up to the highest part of the point but watch your step! Of all the places I visited along the coast working on this book, this was one of my favorites.

On your return trip, you have a lot of options. Without a good map however, you should probably just return the way you came. Skip the beach on the way back (unless you were not able to visit it earlier) and continue following signs towards Floras Lake. When you reach the lake, follow the left shoreline until you reach the trail connecting the day use area and the beach. Turn right to return to the day use area.

17. Humbug Mountain

Distance: 5.8 miles out and back
Elevation Gain: 1,700 feet
Trailhead Elevation: 39 feet
Trail High Point: 1,755 feet
Season: all year
Best: all year
Pass: none needed
On the traditional lands of: the Tolowa Dee-ni', Tututni, and Siletz peoples

Directions from Port Orford:

- Drive south from Port Orford on US 101 for approximately 6 miles until you reach the trailhead on the right side of the road.
- If you're driving north on US 101 from Gold Beach, drive approximately 21 miles north until you reach the trailhead on the left side of the road, just past the Humbug State Park campground entrance.
- **Drivetime from Port Orford:** 10 minutes

Hike: The tallest peak on the Oregon Coast, Humbug Mountain seems to rise directly from the Pacific Ocean itself. Driving south on US 101 along the coast south of Port Orford, the mountain appears larger than life, a wilderness unto itself. And yet, the hike to the summit of this peak is surprisingly gentle, with many switchbacks and few steep stretches. Most hikers will love this hike, but for the most extraordinary experience, plan on visiting during a sunny afternoon or evening to see the sun illuminating the coastline south of the summit in various shades and shadows.

From the signboard at the trailhead, the trail crosses a creek and begins climbing steadily through deep woods. Markers every quarter mile help you keep track of your progress. These

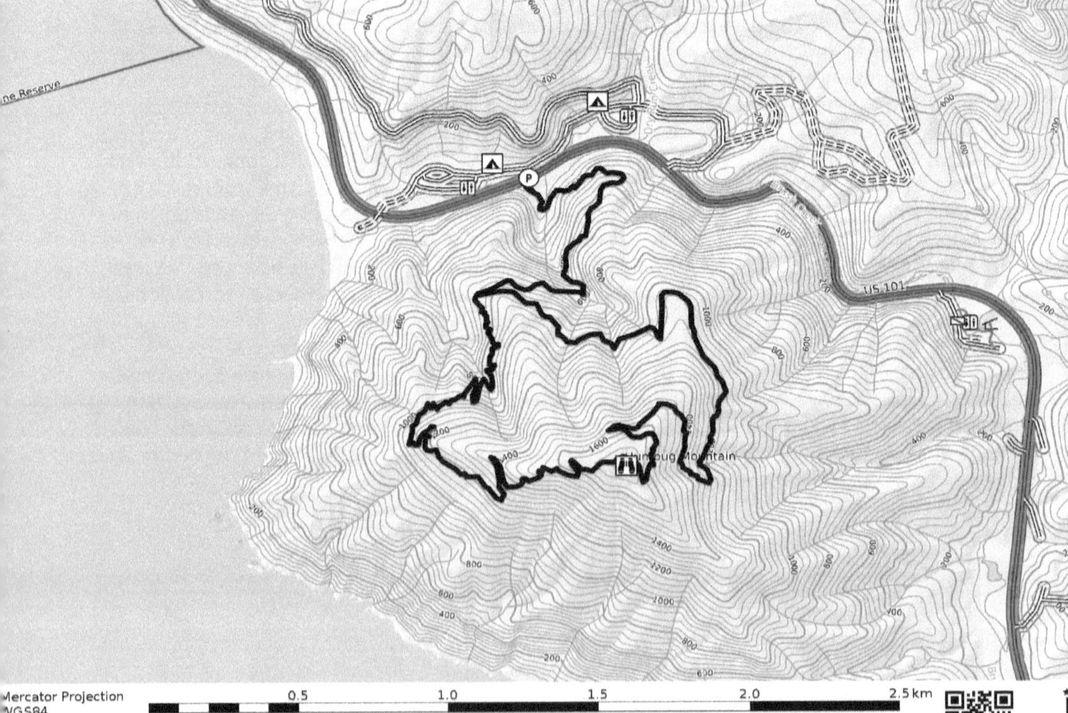

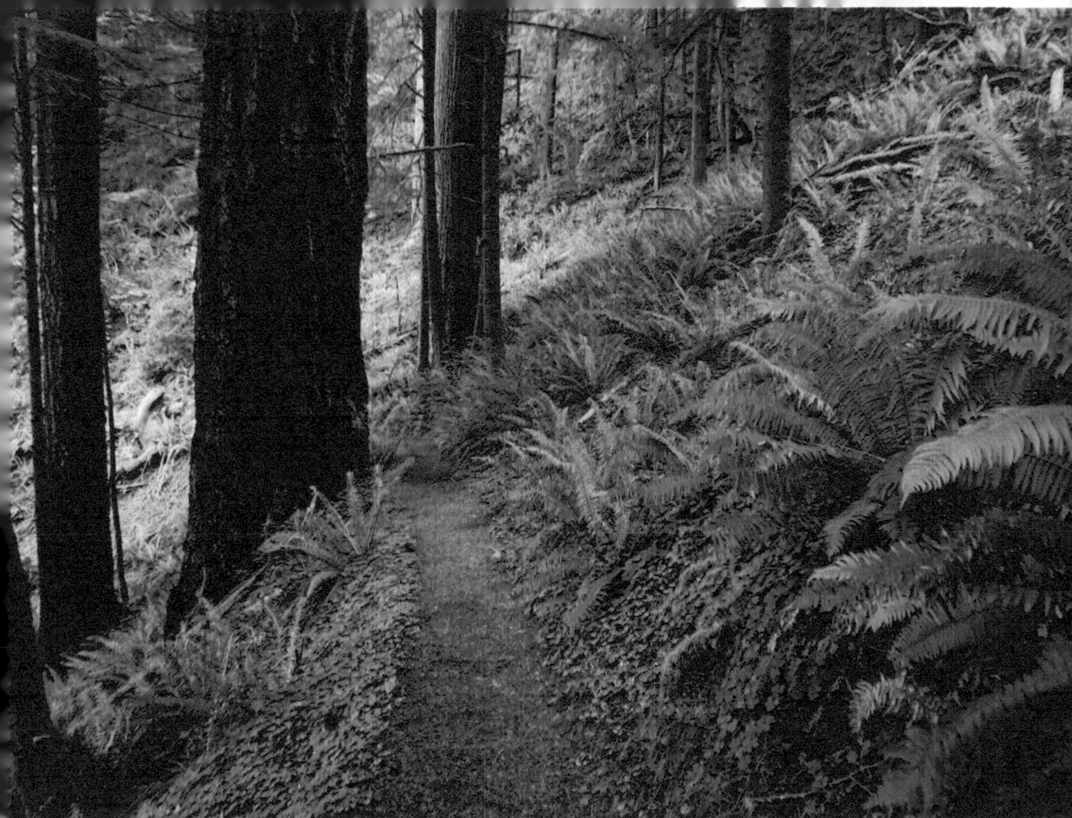

woods are beautiful, with lots of tall trees and spring flowers. Despite being on the coast, the ocean remains out of sight and the sounds of traffic on US 101 overwhelms the sound of waves beating against Humbug Mountain's cliffs. At 1.1 miles from the trailhead, you will reach a fork in the trail at the start of the loop. Both trails reach the summit so it's your choice how you want to get there. For a steeper but shorter ascent, fork to the right on the West Trail.

This end of the loop climbs through more grand forest, offering occasional looks north across the coastline to Port Orford and Cape Blanco. Keen eyes will note the light emanating from the Cape Blanco Lighthouse on cloudy days. This trail was reconstructed in 1993 after being obliterated during the legendary 1962 Columbus Day Storm. After 1.5 miles, the trail reaches a junction with the short spur trail to the summit of Humbug Mountain. Turn right and continue 0.1 mile uphill to the summit of Humbug Mountain at 2.7 miles from the trailhead. Here at last there is a view south towards Gold Beach, and what a view it is! A trio of benches invite a long rest to take in the scenery.

When you're ready to continue the hike, return the 0.1 mile back to the junction and commence hiking downhill on the longer, more gradual East Trail. You'll descend from the summit into a cool, mossy woods. In June, pink rhododendrons and white irises add color to the scene. The forest on this side of Humbug Mountain is considerably more open, with more tanoak and larger coniferous trees adding contrast. The trail winds gently around the southeastern slopes of the mountain, eventually reaching a reunion with the singular Humbug Mountain Trail after 2 miles. Here you will need to turn right and descend 1.1 miles to the trailhead, unless of course you want to turn around and do it again. Who could blame you?

Where to stay: There is plenty of camping at Humbug Mountain State Park near the trailhead, providing perhaps the shortest drive to a trailhead you will ever experience. Beware the campground's marauding blue jays however, as they will take every possible opportunity to abscond with any item of food that is not bolted down and well-concealed. Don't say I didn't warn you!

18. Boardman State Park

Distance: 7 miles out and back
Elevation Gain: 1,400 feet
Trailhead Elevation: 187 feet
Trail High Point: 314 feet
Season: all year
Best: all year
Pass: none needed
On the traditional lands of: the Tolowa Dee-ni', Tututni, and Siletz peoples

Directions from Gold Beach and Brookings:

- Drive south on US 101 from Gold Beach for 16 miles to the Arch Rock Picnic Area on the right side of the road. If you're driving here from Brookings, drive north on US 101 for approximately 12 miles to the Arch Rock Picnic Area on the left side of the road.
- **Drivetime from Gold Beach and Brookings:** 20 minutes

Hike: The rugged stretch of coastline between Gold Beach and Brookings is home to the most spectacular coastal scenery in the state. Here the Pacific Ocean has sculpted natural bridges, offshore sea stacks, pocket beaches, and some of the tallest sea cliffs in the state. Highway 101 follows the cliffs here, offering many different short hikes all along the Samuel Boardman State Scenic Corridor, named after the first superintendent of Oregon's state park system. You can do as the tourists do here: get out of your car, visit a few of the most scenic spots not far from any number of parking areas, and continue driving south or north along the highway. But you are a hiker: you should park at Arch Rock and experience the best of what this area has to offer on foot. The constant ups and downs along this stretch of the Oregon Coast Trail (henceforth referred to as the OCT) can be tiring, but you will absolutely love the experience.

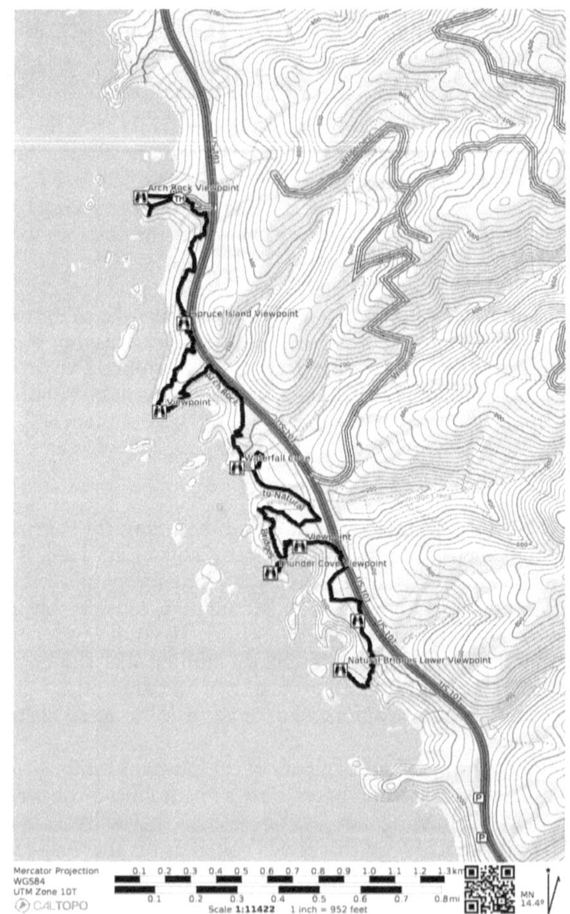

Begin at the Arch Rock Picnic Area. Before you start the hike in earnest, follow the paved trail down to a viewpoint of Arch Rock. When you've finished taking in the view, return to the parking area and follow the access road almost all the way back to US 101. Locate the Oregon Coast Trail on the right, heading into the woods. The OCT follows every headland and cove, for better or worse; expect to spend a lot of this hike rapidly gaining and then losing elevation. Occasionally the contours of this landscape will push you back to the highway, so

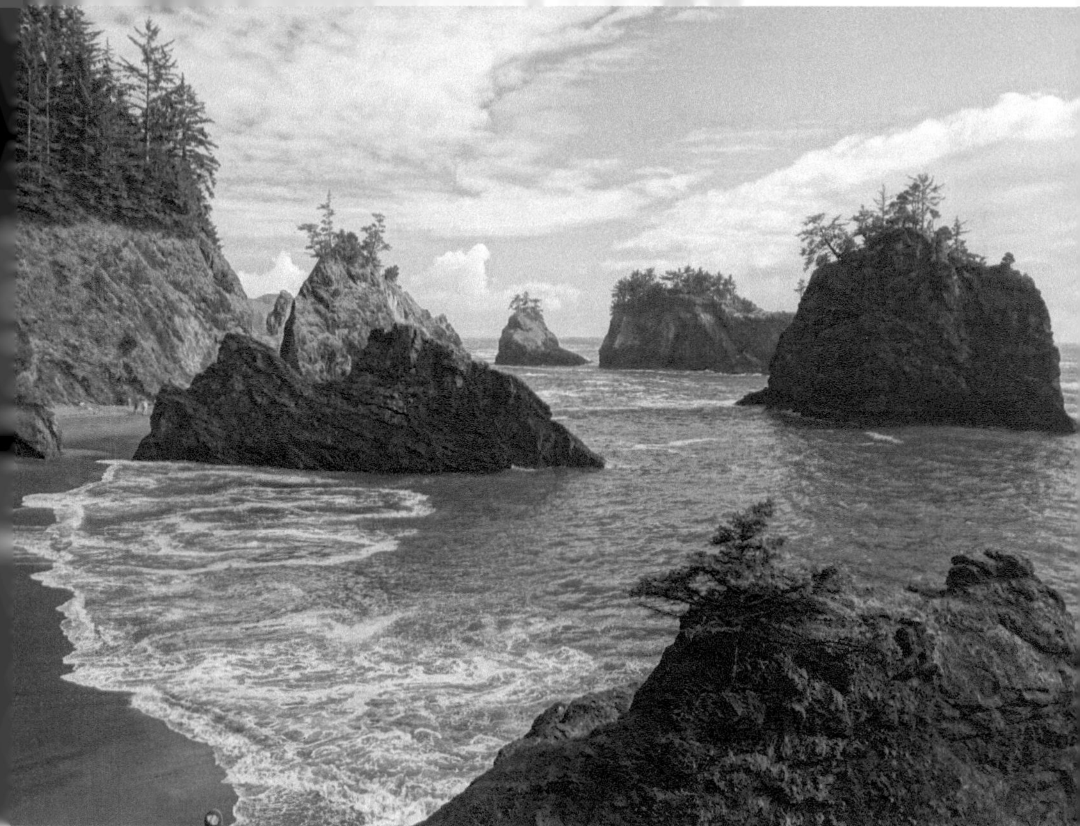

Secret coves abound in Boardman State Park.

pay attention to locating the trail during these short stretches along the highway guardrail (it's not that bad). After 1.5 miles, the trail descends to an absolutely spectacular spot: here, a waterfall on Miller Creek tumbles directly onto a narrow beach backed by sea stacks. You might be tempted to just call it a day here, and I would not blame you in the slightest.

If you're continuing the hike, you'll be sharing the trail with many fellow admirers. From here, the trail passes a junction with an optional loop down to Thunder Cove, then climbs steeply to Thunder Cove's parking area at 2.8 miles. Follow the trail along the highway until you locate the OCT and continue following it to the Natural Bridges parking area at 3.1 miles. The natural bridges below are fantastically beautiful, but also fantastically popular on social media. Expect to see lots of people here. The viewpoint down to the natural bridges is nice, but for the best experience, continue following the OCT south until you reach an obvious junction with a wide trail heading steeply downhill to the right. Turn here and follow this steep, muddy trail until you reach a wide flat above the ocean. Below you are the sea stacks and natural arches you came to see. This flat has plenty of excellent picnic spots, perfect for sitting down and watching the ocean continue to sculpt this most beautiful coastline. A rough trail continues past here onto the top of one of the natural bridges; some daring souls creep out onto the bridge to have their photo taken or just for the thrill of it. I'll leave the decision up to you, but do not be surprised if this trail is closed one day in the future to protect this fragile spot.

Return the way you came, remembering to note the spots where you need to follow the highway and then dip back into the forest. A car shuttle is a fun and obvious way to traverse this stretch of coastline, but not everyone has the ability to set that up.

If you're staying in the area or still have more energy, there are other trails in the Boardman Corridor further to the south. Perhaps my favorite of these leads a half-mile to Cape Ferrelo's windswept cliffs and then south to Lone Ranch Beach. Whatever you do in this area, it is certain to be a lot of fun.

19. Windy Valley

Distance: 4.0 miles out and back
Elevation Gain: 800 feet
Trailhead Elevation: 3,166 feet
Trail High Point: 3,254 feet
Season: May – November
Best: June – July
Pass: none needed
On the traditional lands of: the Tolowa Dee-ni', Tututni, and Siletz peoples

Directions from Brookings:

- From Brookings, follow the North Bank Road along the Chetco River for 8 miles to the Redwood Nature Trail parking lot on the left side of the road.
- Continue another 7.7 miles of narrow paved road to a T-junction just after a bridge.
- Turn left here onto FR 1376 and drive 9.7 miles of narrow gravel road to a fork with FR 360.
- Keep left and continue 0.3 mile to a fork. Keep right here.
- Continue another 2.8 miles to a T-junction with FR 1407. Turn right here to stay on FR 1376.
- Drive another 0.1 mile to the Snow Camp Trailhead on the left side of the road.
- There is a short spur road to the trailhead here with room for a few cars to park. If the lot is full, there are spots to park along FR 1376. The parking lot also has an old wooden pit toilet, but no other amenities.
- **Drivetime from Brookings:** 80 minutes

Irises line the trail to Windy Valley in June and July.

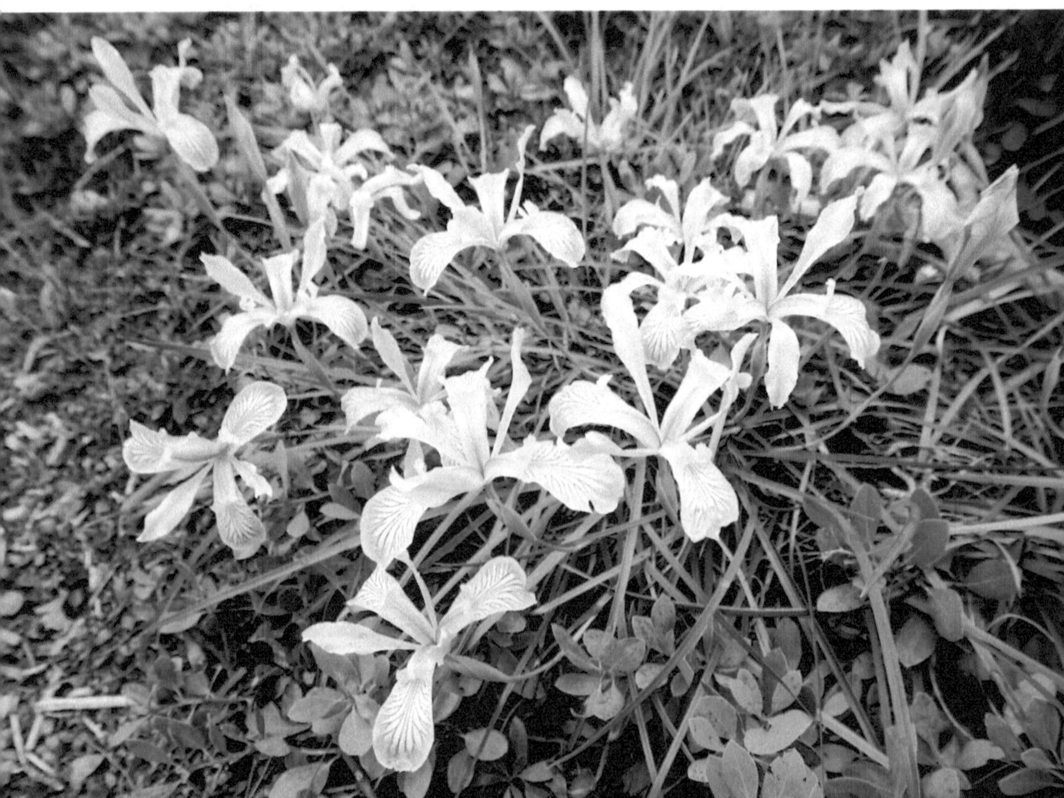

Hike: This lovely hike from the Snow Camp Trailhead down to secluded Windy Valley might just be the best wildflower hike in the state of Oregon. Come here in June and July and you will be absolutely mesmerized as you hike. Botanists and wildflower enthusiasts will find this hike slow going indeed as they struggle to gain any forward momentum – I found myself stopping every five minutes to photograph flowers. There are so many species of flowers and plants here, some of them quite rare, that attempting to list them would be impossible. This is not hyperbole – this hike is that good.

Begin at the Snow Camp Trailhead. The trail traverses an open hillside full of snags left behind by several previous fires (most notably, the massive 2002 Biscuit fire, the largest in Oregon history at that time), and the flower show begins almost immediately. There are more species of flowers than I could possibly list here, but most notable are the millions of irises that line the trail in some years. The view stretches west to the Pacific Ocean. After 0.4 mile, the trail drops to a creek crossing. Western azaleas grow profusely down in this draw, and there are several fens of insectivorous Darlingtonia plants just off the trail beyond the creek crossing. From here, you'll climb up to a saddle besides a rocky knob just off the trail; it is possible, but not easy, to scramble to the top of this knob. Stay on the trail and follow it as it traverses a steep slope gradually downhill into Windy Valley. The flower show here in June is intoxicating; in addition to the ubiquitous irises and azaleas as well as common flowers like paintbrush and penstemon, look for rare California lady slipper orchids in boggy spots just off the trail. This white and yellow orchid grows only in southwestern Oregon and northwestern California, and this is one of only a few trails you can see it in Oregon.

As you descend into Windy Valley, you'll trade open slopes for an impressive forest of knobcone pine and Port Orford cedar, the latter of which is quite rare and only grows near the southern Oregon coast. As with the slopes above, the valley has been repeatedly touched by the numerous fires that have burned through this corner of Oregon, but the fires were mostly on the ground here and the canopy feels as alive as ever. At 1.6 miles, the trail drops to an unsigned junction with the Snow Camp Trail, marked only by a post. To hike into the heart of Windy Valley, keep right and follow the trail as it passes by meadows and a few magnificently huge trees. You'll reach trail's end at a creek crossing in the heart of Windy Valley at 2 miles. To access the huge meadow in the center of the valley, you'll have to ford Windy Creek or find a log to cross the creek (there are several, if you look). There are several nice campsites around the edge of the meadow, should you wish to backpack into here. A bench dedicated to Gladys Mann, a longtime 4H leader in Curry County, sits at the edge of the meadow, offering hikers a place to sit and take in this special place.

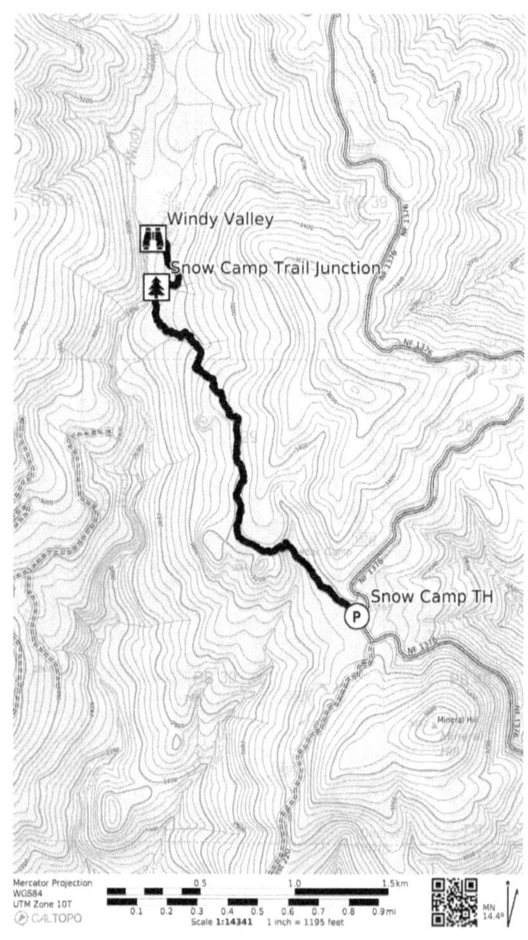

Whenever you can bear it, return the way you came.

20. Oregon Redwoods

Distance: 1.2 mile loop
Elevation Gain: 400 feet
Trailhead Elevation: 71 feet
Trail High Point: 370 feet
Season: all year
Best: all year
Pass: none needed
On the traditional lands of: the Chit-dee-ni (Chetco), Tolowa Dee-ni', and Siletz peoples

Directions:

- From Brookings, turn onto North Bank Chetco River Road, following signs for Alfred Loeb State Park.
- Drive 7.6 miles to Alfred Loeb State Park.
- Continue a little over a half-mile to a small parking area on the left side of the road signed for the Redwood Nature Trail. This is the trailhead.

Note: This is not to be confused with the Oregon Redwoods Trail, which is located further south, close to the California border. If you are searching for this hike on the internet, search for the Redwood Nature Trail.

Hike: Redwood trees are the tallest on the planet, and they only grow along a narrow strip of coastline from northern California to the extreme southwest corner of Oregon. The northernmost grove in the world is located in Alfred Loeb State Park, northeast of Brookings. Here, just 8 miles north of the California border, lies a magnificent grove of *Sequoia sempervirens*, the nicest to be found in the state of Oregon. While the trees here cannot compare to those found further south in California, this is as absolutely the nicest such grove in our state. Make this a mandatory stop if you're down in the Brookings area.

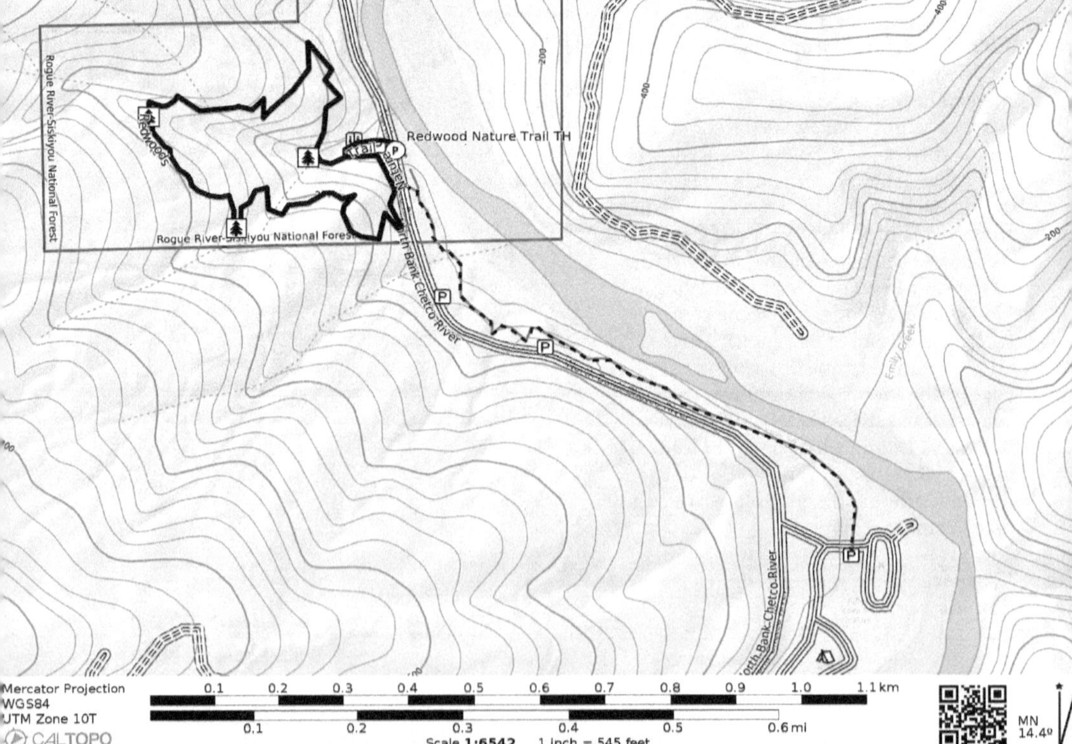

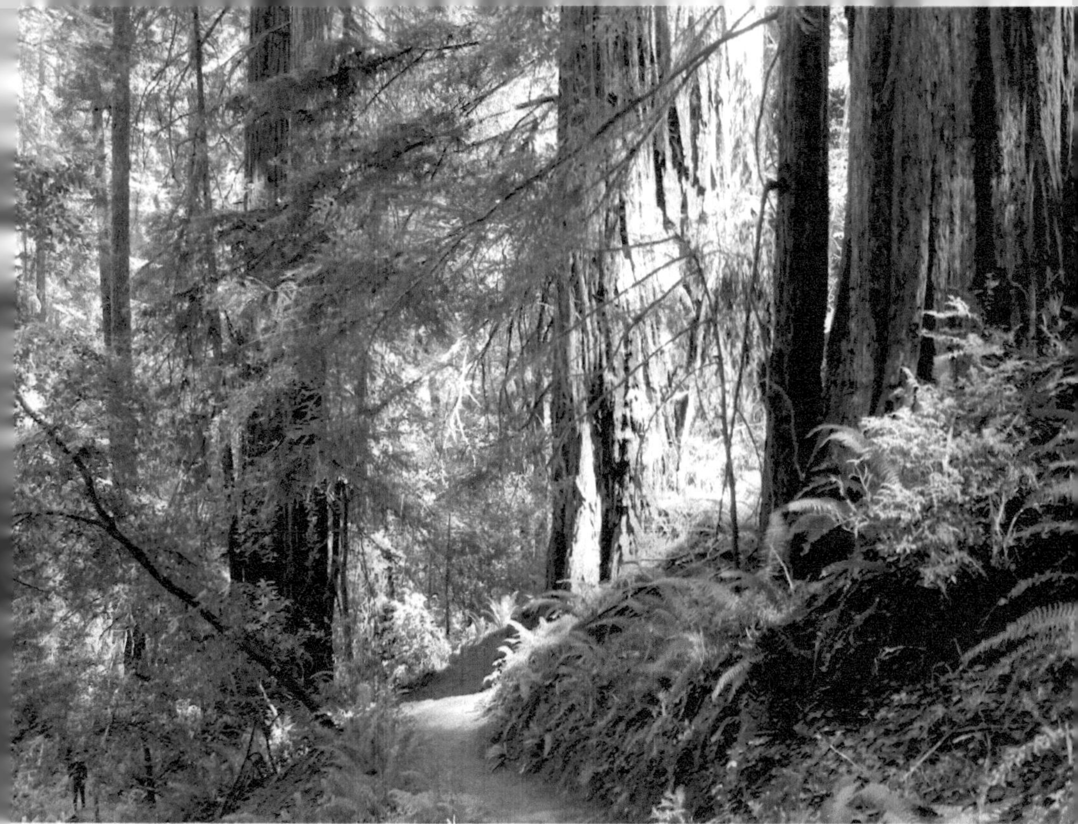

Redwoods along the Redwood Nature Trail east of Brookings.

The trail begins at a small parking lot just off the North Bank Chetco River Road. Follow the wide trail and immediately come to a junction, just below an impressive redwood and next to a bridge across the creek that runs through the redwood grove. Turn left here to begin the loop. The trail follows the road briefly before switchbacking uphill into an impressive redwood grove. Though not as awe-inspiring as the redwoods found south of the border, there are some massive trees in here, and you'll enjoy taking the time to crane your neck up to the heavens in awe of these giants. These are, after all, Oregon redwoods. You'll wind along a creek, pass under many tall trees, then switchback downhill to cross the creek again. When you cross the bridge, you'll reach the junction at the end of the loop. Turn left to return to the trailhead.

Other hiking options:
There are sadly very few good hiking options along the Chetco River. A trail beginning in Alfred Loeb State Park follows the river for 0.7 mile to the trailhead described above for the Redwood Nature Trail. You can extend your hike by starting at this lower trailhead but even then, this is still less than 3 miles round-trip.

Hikers looking for more hiking along the Chetco or in the mountains east of here should consider hiking to Windy Valley (Hike 19) or waiting for the trails on the western side of the Kalmiopsis Wilderness to be cleared. One such trail, the Tincup Trail, follows the Chetco River into its narrow canyon, eventually reaching remote Tincup Gorge. The trail is scheduled for maintenance sometime in the next year or two but was sadly not passable when I visited in the summer of 2022.

For more information on the trails in the Brookings area and Chetco valley, follow the Siskiyou Mountain Club here: **https://siskiyoumountainclub.org**.

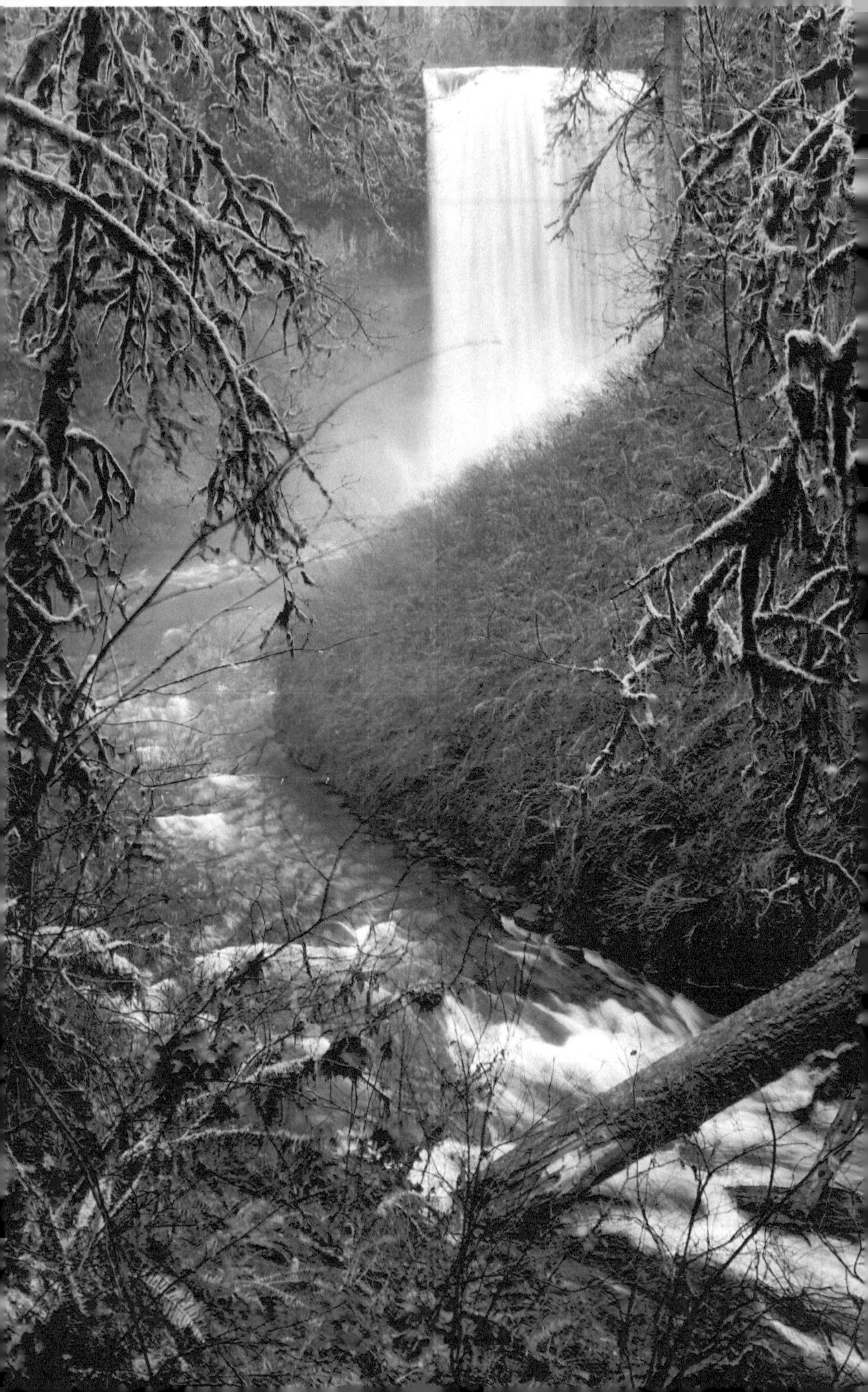

Portland and the Willamette Valley

		Distance	EV Gain	Page
21.	Lower Macleay Park to Pittock Mansion	5.2 miles	900 ft	62
22.	Powell Butte	4.6 miles	600 ft	64
23.	Eagle-Fern Park	1.7 miles	400 ft	66
24.	Silver Falls State Park	7.9 miles	1,000 ft	68
25.	McDowell Creek Falls	1.7 miles	300 ft	70
26.	Mount Pisgah	5.4 miles	1,100 ft	72

The Willamette Valley contains a surprising wealth of hiking options, all of which are open year-round. Here you'll find far-reaching views of the Cascade volcanoes, pocket groves of ancient forest, waterfalls in the foothills, and fields of spring wildflowers. Approximately 70 percent of Oregon's population lives in the Willamette Valley, and you should expect to encounter crowds on most of these hikes. The hikes featured here are among the most well-known of these, and with good reason. Were it anywhere else, Silver Falls State Park would likely be a national park, while Pittock Mansion's view of Mount Hood is among the most iconic in the state of Oregon. Further south, Mount Pisgah marks the southern end of the Willamette Valley, and is a popular destination for Eugene-area hikers.

The most attractive part of these hikes is that they are open year-round. I grew up in Salem, and we went to Silver Falls State Park often in the winter, a tradition I carry on to this day. In many ways, these hikes are best in winter and spring, when the waterfalls flow at their strongest and your chances of seeing wildlife are at their best. These are also wonderful places to explore during the occasional Valley snowstorm in the winter. Whenever you visit, you'll be sure to find something you love.

Photo on left: Middle North Falls in Silver Falls State Park (Hike 24)

21. Lower Macleay Park to Pittock Mansion

Distance: 5.2 mile semi-loop
Elevation Gain: 900 feet
Trailhead elevation: 101 feet
Trail high point: 955 feet
Season: all year
Best: April – May, October
Pass: None needed
On the traditional lands of: the Atfalati and Stl'pulmsh (Cowlitz) peoples

Directions from Portland:

- In Portland, drive up into northwest Portland to the corner of NW 25th & NW Thurman Street.
- Turn left on NW Thurman Street and drive two blocks to NW 27th Street. Turn right, drive one block to Upshur Street and turn left.
- The trailhead, Lower Macleay Park, is at the end of Upshur Street. There is a small parking lot there but you'll likely need to find parking in the neighborhood.
- Better yet, you can take either the #15 or the #77 bus to within a few blocks of the park. Consult http://www.trimet.org for more information.
- **Travel time in Portland:** less than 30 minutes from anywhere in town

Hike: One of Oregon's finest hikes is located just minutes from downtown Portland. If this seems difficult to believe, consider this: the hike from Lower Macleay Park up to Pittock Mansion follows a scenic canyon to an abandoned structure affectionately known as "the Witches Castle" and climbs gradually up to Pittock Mansion, where views worthy of a postcard stretch

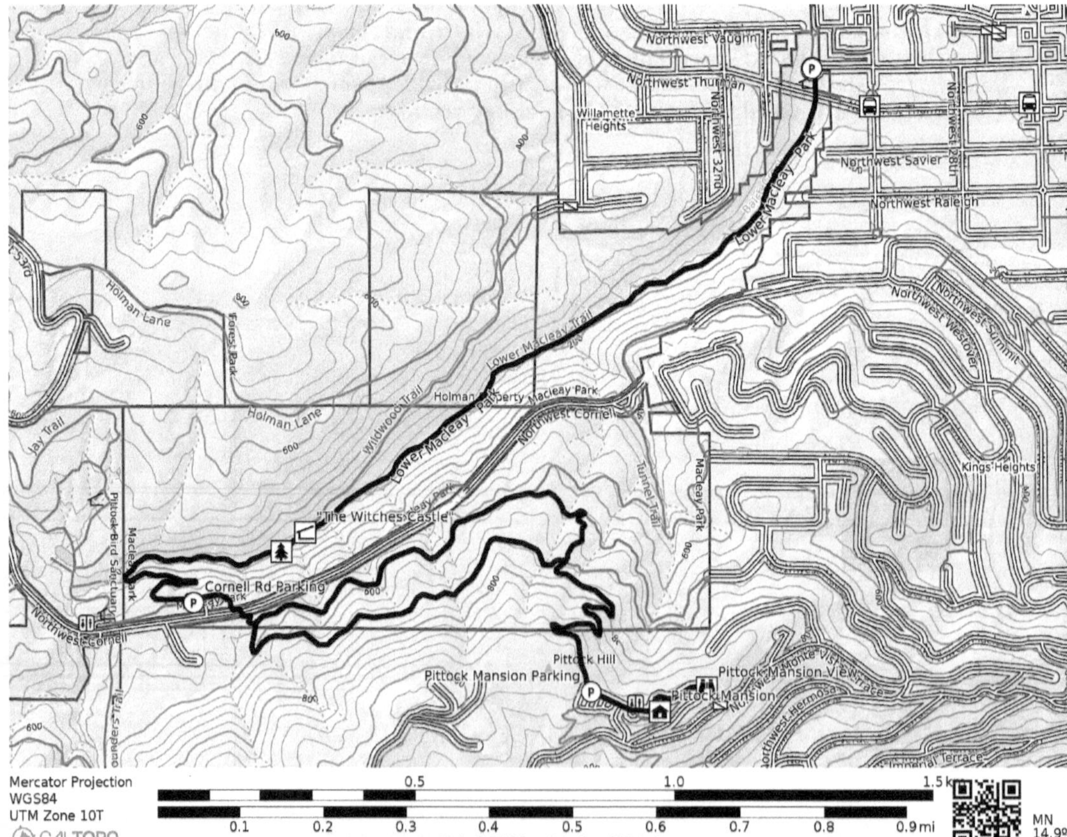

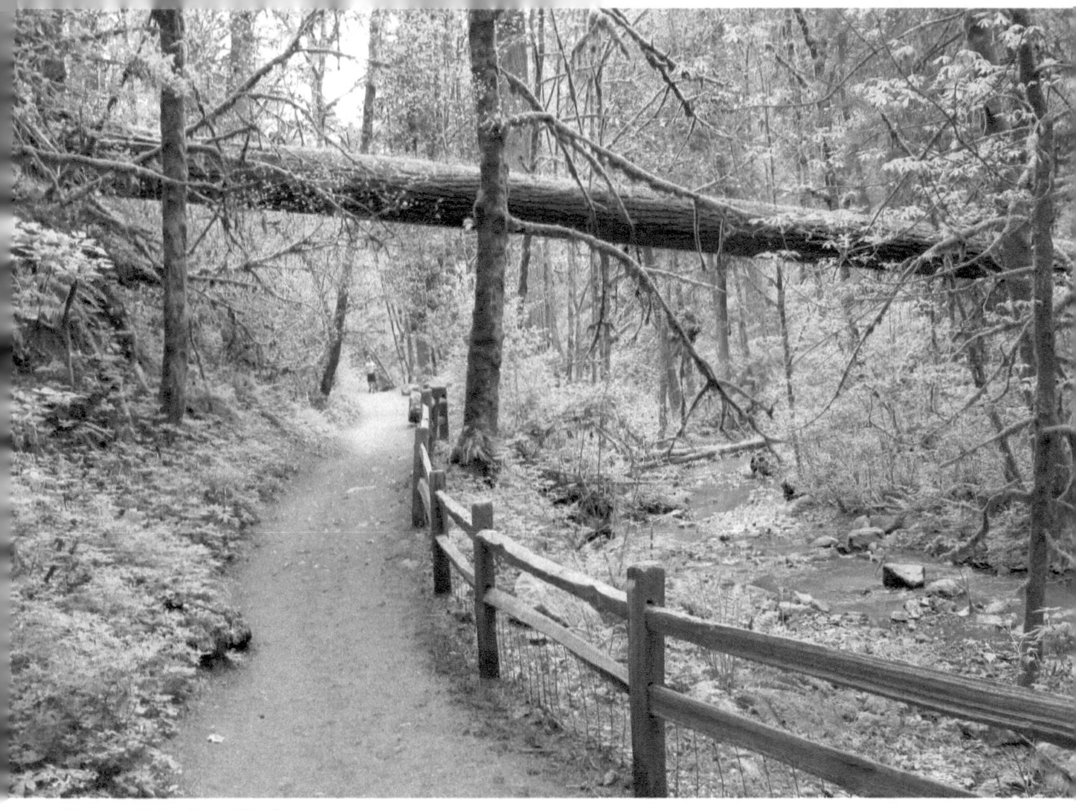

Lower Macleay Park in spring.

across the city of Portland to the Cascades. This is one of my favorites.

The hike begins at Lower Macleay Park's trailhead. Locate the wide trail and pass under the tall Thurman Street Bridge. The trail enters Balch Creek's canyon and proceeds to follow the creek at a close distance. You will cross the creek on a new bridge just above a small waterfall, a location that feels far more remote than it actually is. Enter increasingly dense and impressive forest; at just under a mile the trail passes by Portland's tallest tree, a giant that is over 300 years old. Another minute's walk leads hikers to a junction with the Wildwood Trail at a stone building (a former bathroom) known as the "Witches Castle". This is one of the most popular spots on a very popular hike, so expect to share the castle with many admirers.

Continue straight past the castle. From here, the trail continues up Balch Creek, crossing it not far beyond. You will then climb a pair of switchbacks to a trailhead along NW Cornell Road. Cross the road and continue on the Wildwood Trail. The trail climbs the forested bank above Cornell Road and enters deeper forest on the slopes below Pittock Mansion. You will pass several trail junctions on your way uphill; at each of these, you need to stay on the Wildwood Trail to reach Pittock Mansion. At 2.5 miles from the trailhead, the trail at last crests the hill and arrives at Pittock Mansion's large parking lot. Turn left here and follow the parking lot to the mansion. If you've got some extra time and you aren't too muddy, you can tour the mansion as part of your hike. Henry Pittock, an early employee of *The Oregonian* who eventually became the editor of the newspaper, had this mansion built in 1914. Even if you decide to skip the tour, you will no doubt enjoy the grounds around the mansion. Roses line the paths along the mansion, and a visit in June or July is the best time to enjoy these blooms. Past the grounds, the view stretches out to Mount Hood, towering over the tall buildings of downtown Portland. Also visible on the horizon from north to south are other Cascade peaks from Mount Rainier to Mount Jefferson. Return the way you came; along the way, you can make a short loop using the Upper Macleay Trail, which loops back to Cornell Road. From there, follow the Wildwood and Lower Macleay Trails backs to the trailhead.

22. Powell Butte

Distance: 4.6 mile loop
Elevation Gain: 600 feet
Trailhead elevation: 223 feet
Trail high Point: 629 feet
Season: all year
Best: all year
Pass: none needed
On the traditional lands of: The Confederated Tribes of the Grand Ronde people

Directions:

- From downtown Portland drive southeast on Powell Blvd, also known as US 26.
- Continue on Powell Blvd. for about 5 miles past Interstate 205 to a junction with SE 162nd Drive. Turn right here and drive uphill into the Powell Butte parking complex.
- If you're using public transit, take the #9 Bus to the corner of SE Powell Blvd. and SE 162nd Avenue (stop ID 13957). Walk back to the junction with SE 162nd Avenue, turn left here and walk uphill on SE 162nd Avenue into Powell Butte Nature Park.
- **Drivetime from Portland:** 20 minutes

Hike: Like many other hills in the Portland metro area, Powell Butte in outer southeast Portland is an extinct volcano. This diminutive hill that rises over Gresham and east Portland is part of the Boring Lava Field, a lava flow that also includes Mount Tabor, Mount Talbert, Rocky Butte, Mount Scott, and Larch Mountain among many others. Almost every one of these extinct volcanoes features a great view of the metro area, but few offer as much variety as Powell Butte. Not only will you find great views of the metro area and five Cascade volcanoes, but you can also visit the huge meadows on the summit of Powell Butte, hike through scenic forest on the mountain's flanks, and can see both wildflowers and wildlife seldom seen in the city. I might be biased though; I live within walking distance of Powell Butte, and I hike the trails here several times a year. There is so much to see here that you might enjoy coming to Powell Butte again and again to experience its charms throughout the year.

Visiting Powell Butte is a "Choose Your Adventure" kind of hike. There are many trails here, and maps on signposts throughout the park help you navigate the park should you decide to veer

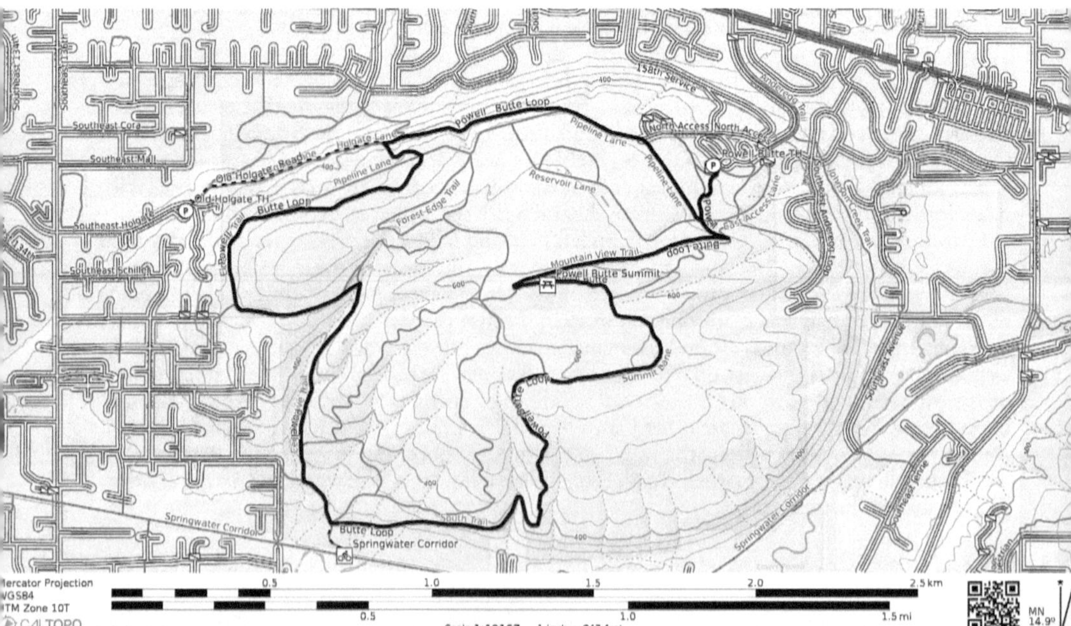

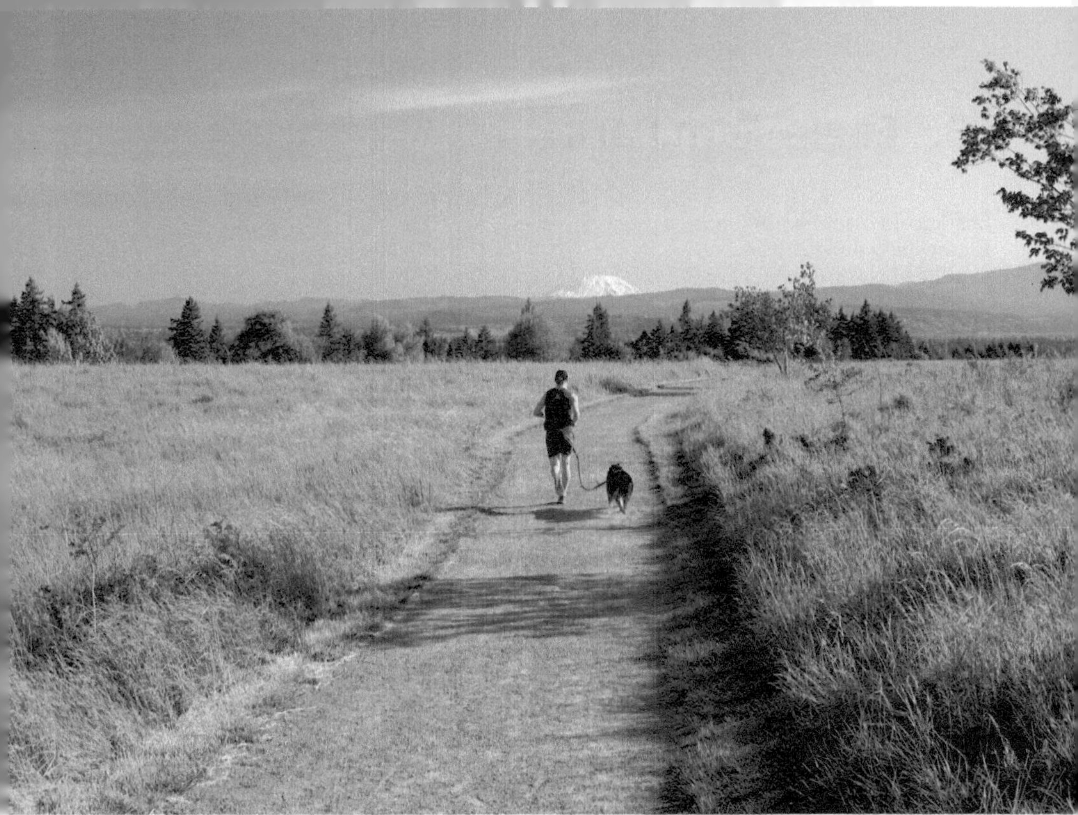

A runner and his dog running towards Mt. St. Helens at Powell Butte.

from the itinerary described below. To hike my favorite loop, begin at the trailhead and follow the paved Mountain View Trail uphill towards Powell Butte's summit. You'll pass several side trails on the way up, but you'll want to stay on the paved trail as it winds its way to the summit. Reach the summit of Powell Butte at 0.6 mile. A mountain finder at the summit helps you identify the many summits visible from Mount Rainier to Mount Jefferson, with the view of Mount Hood particularly impressive here. Beyond the summit, continue straight on what is now Summit Lane and follow this trail through the wildflower meadows around the east side of the summit. If you come here early in the day you'll likely spot deer in the meadow, but a midday visit will allow you the opportunity to birdwatch to your heart's desire. You'll reach a junction with the South Trail at 1 mile. If you're short on time, you can keep straight and follow this trail back to the trailhead, but for the longer loop through the woods, turn left on the South Trail.

The South Trail begins in the summit meadow but soon drops into cool forest on the south side of Powell Butte. After a mile of hiking through the woods, you'll reach a junction near the Springwater Corridor, the long-distance biking trail that passes through southeast Portland en route to nearby Boring. Turn right onto the Cedar Grove Trail and follow it for 0.5 mile to a junction with the Elderberry Trail. Turn left onto this trail and follow it clockwise around the northwest corner of Powell Butte. At every trail junction you are offered the possibility of returning to the top of the butte, but we're following the longest loop. Turn left on the Elderberry Trail and follow it around the west side of Powell Butte until it begins climbing again. You'll pass Pipeline Road (following this trail will take you immediately back to the trailhead parking lot) and continue on the Elderberry Trail until you meet Pipeline Trail a second time. Cross the trail and head downhill to complete the Elderberry Trail. At the bottom of a set of steps, meet Old Holgate Lane. Turn right and follow this lovely forest lane until you meet the Pipeline Road a third time. Turn left and follow this road back to the Mountain View Trail. Turn left here and follow this trail back to the parking lot.

23. Eagle-Fern Park

Distance: 1.7 mile loop
Elevation Gain: 400 feet
Trailhead elevation: 525 feet
Trail high point: 818 feet
Other seasons: all year
Pass: Pay $8 at the park entrance booth
On the traditional lands of: the Clackamas and Molalla peoples

Directions:

- Starting at Interstate 205, exit 13, drive 14.3 miles towards Estacada on OR 224.
- Approximately 1 mile past the junction with OR 211, turn left at a sign for Eagle Fern Park onto Wildcat Mountain Dr.
- Keep straight at a junction in just 0.2 mile. Continue another 1.8 miles to a junction with SE Eagle-Fern Road.
- Turn right and drive 2.3 miles to Eagle-Fern Park on your right.
- Turn right into the park and pay the $8 park access fee as soon as you park.
- **Drivetime from Portland:** 50 minutes

Hike: Having traveled all over the United States, I can honestly say that Oregon has some of the nation's best parks. Take for example Eagle-Fern Park, located near Estacada, about 40 minutes southeast of Portland. Here you'll find a scenic wooden bridge over a rushing creek that deserves to be called a river, and a easy loop trail that leads you through one of the finest groves of ancient forest in the Willamette Valley. For more ancient forest and river views, you can follow a longer loop up and down the slopes above Eagle Creek. Eagle-Fern Park can be quite crowded in the summer, so plan a visit here in the offseason when you only feel like being outside for a couple hours. It's worth it.

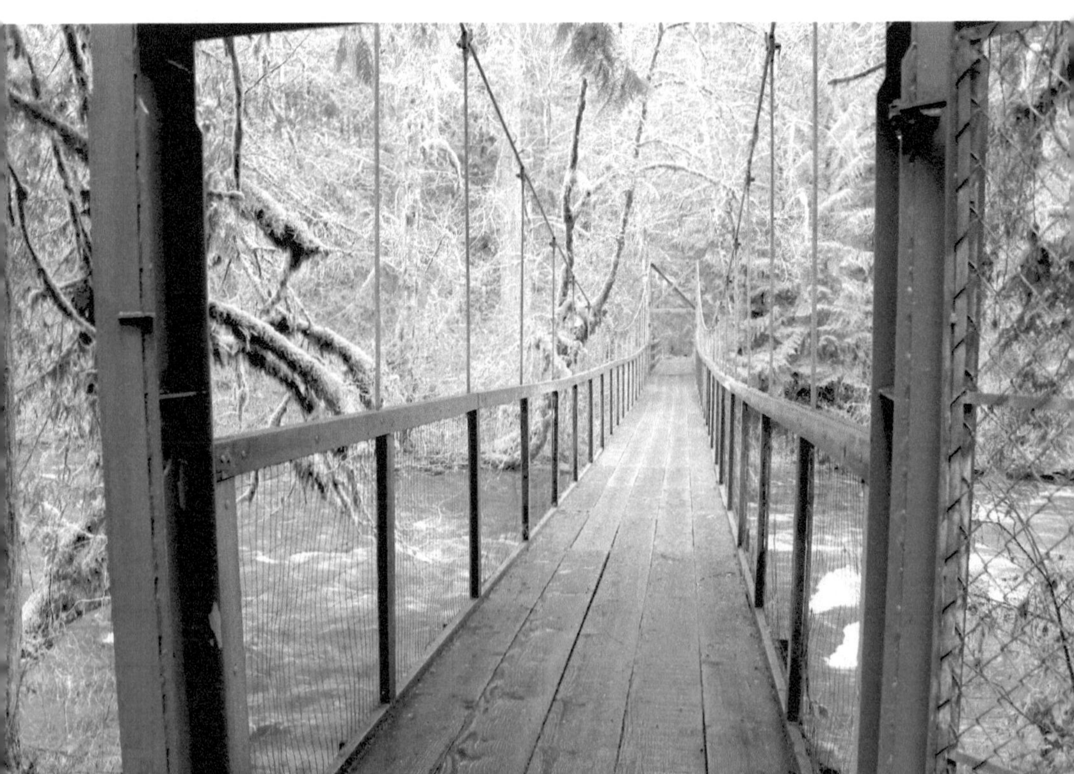

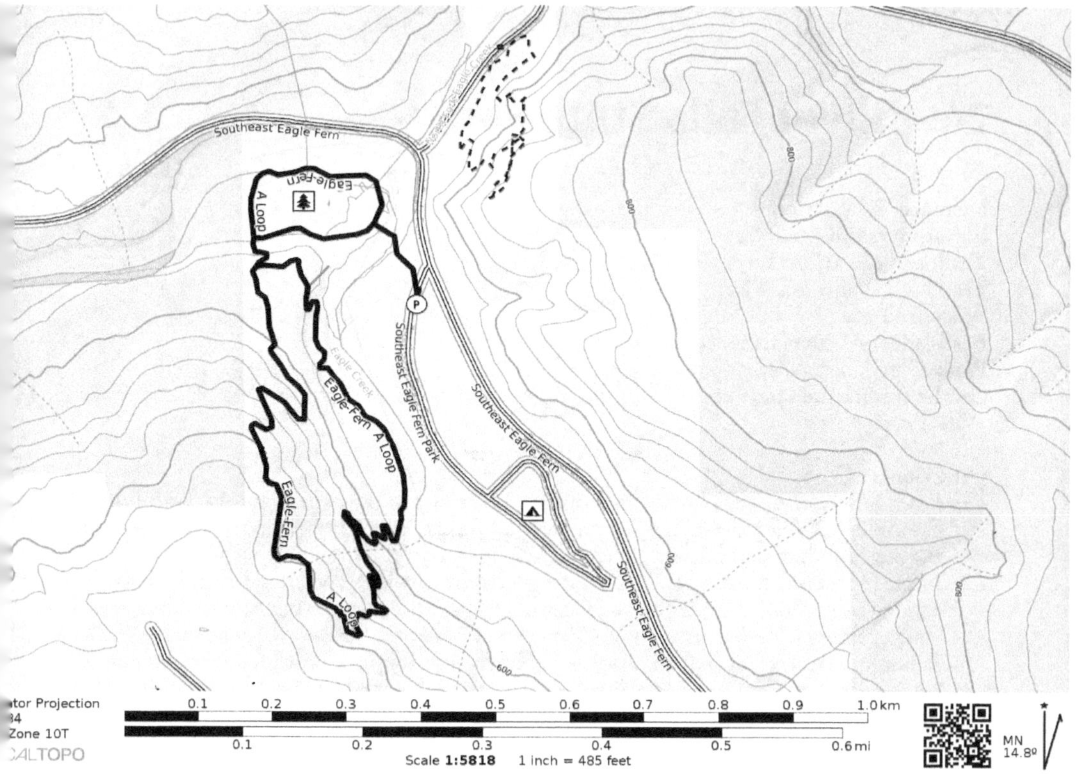

From the parking lot, locate the signboard that leads you to the wooden bridge over Eagle Creek. This scenic bridge is a wonderful place to stop and watch the rushing waters of the creek pass underneath you! On the far side of the bridge, you will reach a junction at the start of the loop. Turn right here to begin the loop. Signboards mark this all-access trail through the impressive forest here. A pamphlet is also available, with marked stops for even more information. After meandering your way through this gorgeous spot, reach a junction with the upper loop at 0.4 mile from the trailhead. Turn right here.

You will climb gradually above the forest floor here on a wide but occasionally muddy trail. Before long the trail switchbacks uphill along huge ancient Douglas firs and cedars to the trail's high point of just over 800 feet. On the rare sunny days in winter, the slopes here will often still be draped in fog, with sunbeams piercing the fog in a most scenic manner. This is when I love to visit Eagle-Fern Park. As you work your way across the forest at the upper end of the canyon, you will have the occasional view down through the trees and ferns to Eagle Creek; the name of the park is quite fitting.

At 1.2 miles into your loop, the trail begins to abruptly descend towards Eagle Creek. Every time I visit I wish this hike were longer, but the trail up here follows the general contours of the park boundary; this is as good as it's going to get in this small park. Follow the trail downhill until you reach the banks of Eagle Creek. From here the trail bends its way around sword ferns and the occasional boulder to a reunion with the all-access trail on which you started. Turn right and follow the trail a short distance to the wooden bridge over Eagle Creek and the conclusion of this loop.

Continuing your hike:
If you're still looking for a little exercise and a little more time in the woods, you can follow Loop D through the woods on the other side of Eagle-Fern Park. Return to the junction with southeast Kitzmiller Road and turn right. You'll find the trailhead for Loop D less than 0.2 mile from the junction. The trail network in Eagle-Fern Park is still under construction, so perhaps there will be more trails here in the future.

24. Silver Falls State Park

Distance: 7.9 mile loop
Elevation Gain: 1,000 feet
Trailhead elevation: 1,479 feet
Trail high Point: 1,574 feet
Season: all year
Best: January – June, October – December
Pass: $5 park entrance fee (pay at the parking lot)
On the traditional lands of: The Molalla, Grande Ronde, Siletz, Cayuse, Umatilla, and Walla Walla Peoples

Directions:

- From Silverton, drive OR 214 southeast for 13.4 miles to the parking lot at North Falls.
- Continue 2.3 miles to a turnoff on the right for South Falls. Turn right and drive through the huge series of parking lots to South Falls Lodge, the trailhead for this hike.
- Note: Directions to Silver Falls depend a great deal on where you are starting. If you're coming from the Portland area, you'll drive through Silverton on your way to Silver Falls. If you're coming from Salem and points south, you can avoid Silverton by following OR 22 to Sublimity. Turn left at Exit 13, drive to Sublimity and continue north for 2.5 miles until you reach a junction with OR 214. Turn right here and follow the highway for approximately 10 miles to the turnoff for South Falls on the left.
- **Drivetime from Silverton:** 20 minutes

Note: Dogs are not allowed in the Silver Falls canyon.

Hike: Silver Falls State Park is a place every Oregonian should visit at least once. Where else in Oregon can you easily visit ten waterfalls, four of which you can walk behind? As I've said before, Silver Falls would be a national park were it almost anywhere else. As it is, it is one of Oregon's most visited state parks, and you should expect crowds whenever you visit. This is truly one of Oregon's most extraordinary places, and I make it a point to visit at least once a year. My favorite time to visit Silver Falls is on rainy days in the winter when the falls are raging and the crowds at their least, but the park is beautiful in any season. There's never a bad time to visit Silver Falls State Park.

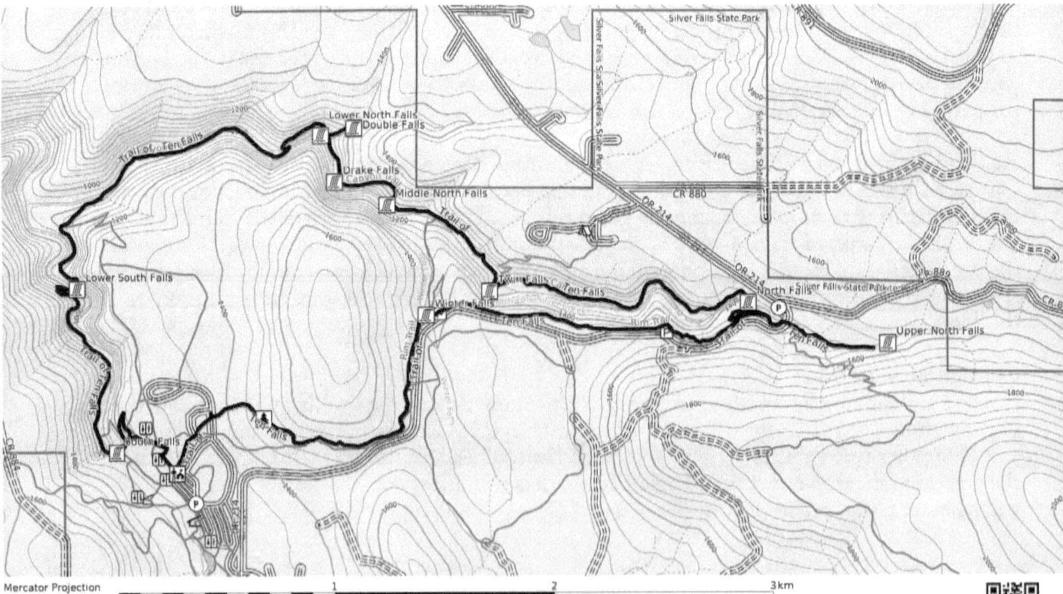

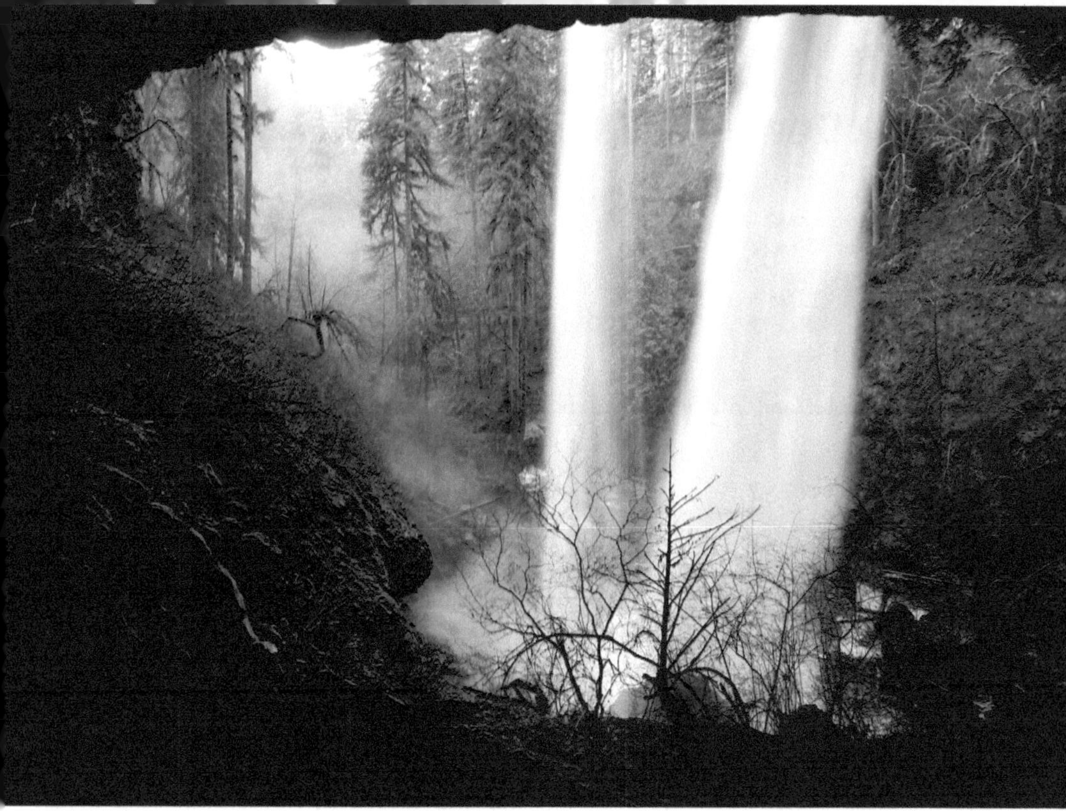

Hiking behind North Falls in the winter is a magical experience.

From the South Falls Lodge, follow the paved trail towards South Falls. You'll reach a junction near the viewpoint at the top of South Falls. Either way will take you to the bottom of South Falls but for the best experience, you should turn left on the trail that passes behind South Falls. This is the most famous and arguably the most impressive waterfall in the park, and you'll have to share either trail you take with lots of admirers. Beyond South Falls, the trail follows the rushing South Fork of Silver Creek to the top of Lower South Falls. The trail descends a series of switchbacks and stairs to the falls, then passes behind it so close you can almost touch the water. From here, you'll follow the Canyon Trail to a junction with the Maple Trail at 1.4 miles. Keep straight on the Canyon Loop Trail and follow it to a bridge over the North Fork of Silver Creek at 2.3 miles. Not far past the bridge, you'll reach Lower North Falls, one of the park's most scenic. The falls is especially beautiful in the fall when it is framed by yellow and orange fall foliage. From here the trail climbs a short distance to a junction with the short side trail to Double Falls. Follow this trail to the base of the falls, the tallest in the park. In the winter, this 184-foot double plunge is an impressive sight, but it dries up in the summer.

Beyond Double Falls, the trail passes Drake Falls and soon reaches views of impressive Middle North Falls. This falls is one of the most impressive in the park, as the North Fork falls 106 feet in a wide curtain. A short side trail leads you behind the falls to a viewpoint on the opposite side of the creek for an even better view. Beyond Middle North Falls, you'll meet a junction with the Winter Falls Trail. Keep straight here and follow the North Fork as it passes small but scenic Twin Falls. At 4.5 miles, North Falls comes into view. Though shorter than South Falls, this waterfall is even more dramatic and powerful, and the trail leads you far behind the falls, allowing hikers many different views of this fascinating place. Follow the trail uphill from North Falls to a junction with the Rim Trail at 5 miles. You'll need to turn right to complete the loop but before you do, be sure to turn left and follow the paved trail upstream for 0.3 mile to Upper North Falls. When you're done visiting this falls, follow the trail back to the North Falls parking area and continue on the Rim Trail through the woods for 2.3 miles to the South Falls Lodge, where you can warm up by the fire after the hike.

25. McDowell Falls Park

Distance: 1.7 mile loop
Elevation Gain: 300 feet
Trailhead elevation: 816 feet
Trail high point: 1,099 feet
Season: all year
Best: January – May
Pass: none needed
On the traditional lands of: the Santiam and Kalapuya peoples

Directions:

- From Albany, drive east 12 miles on US 20 into the town of Lebanon.
- Turn left onto E Grant St and drive almost a mile to a bridge over the South Santiam River.
- Cross the river and turn right on Berlin Road.
- Drive this road for 10.5 miles to a junction with McDowell Creek Road.
- Turn left and drive 3.4 miles to the first lot in the park, complete with an old wooden sign for Royal Terrace Falls.
- **Drivetime from Albany:** 45 minutes

Hike: Silver Falls gets all the fame in the Willamette Valley but there are other waterfalls to find here. McDowell Falls Park in rural Linn County contains a quartet of gorgeous cascades that are well worth the drive into the country between Lebanon and Sweet Home. This hike is wonderful in any season but never more so than in the spring, when the waterfalls are at their fullest and the forest in the canyon at its greenest. In the summer and fall the waterfalls here run very low, diminishing their scenic beauty considerably. If you're visiting on a sunny weekend day, this is when the park is most crowded so make sure you get here early to secure a parking spot.

Leave the parking lot and soon cross McDowell Creek not far above Lower McDowell Falls

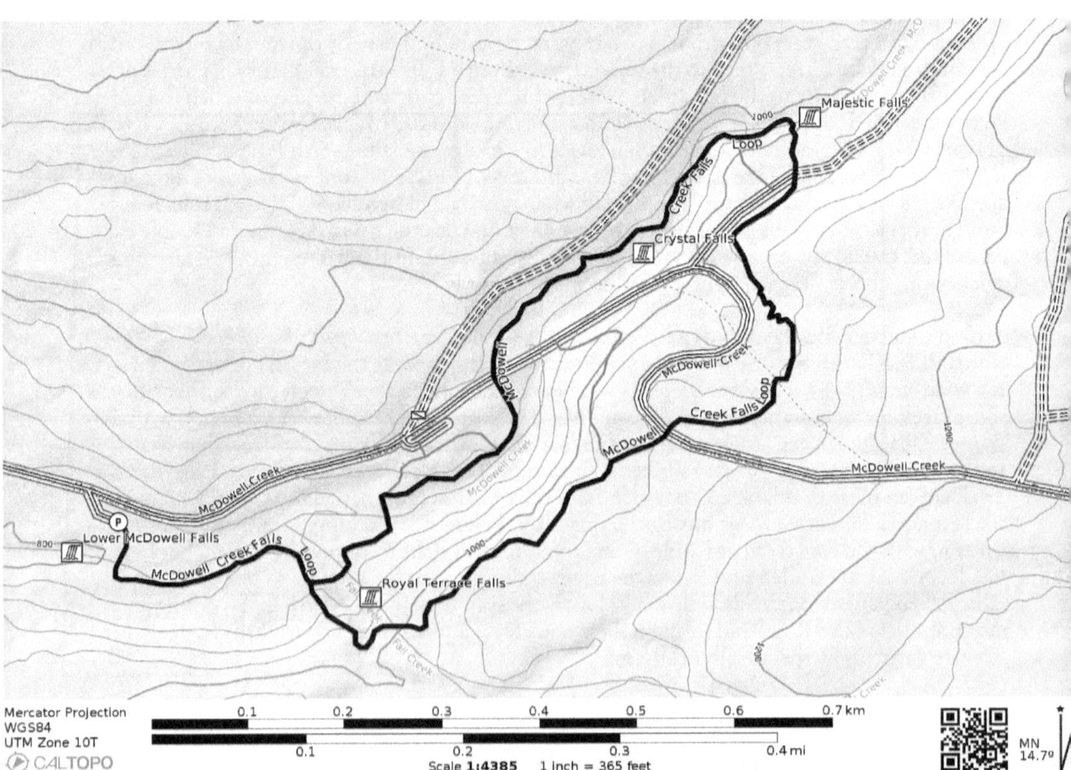

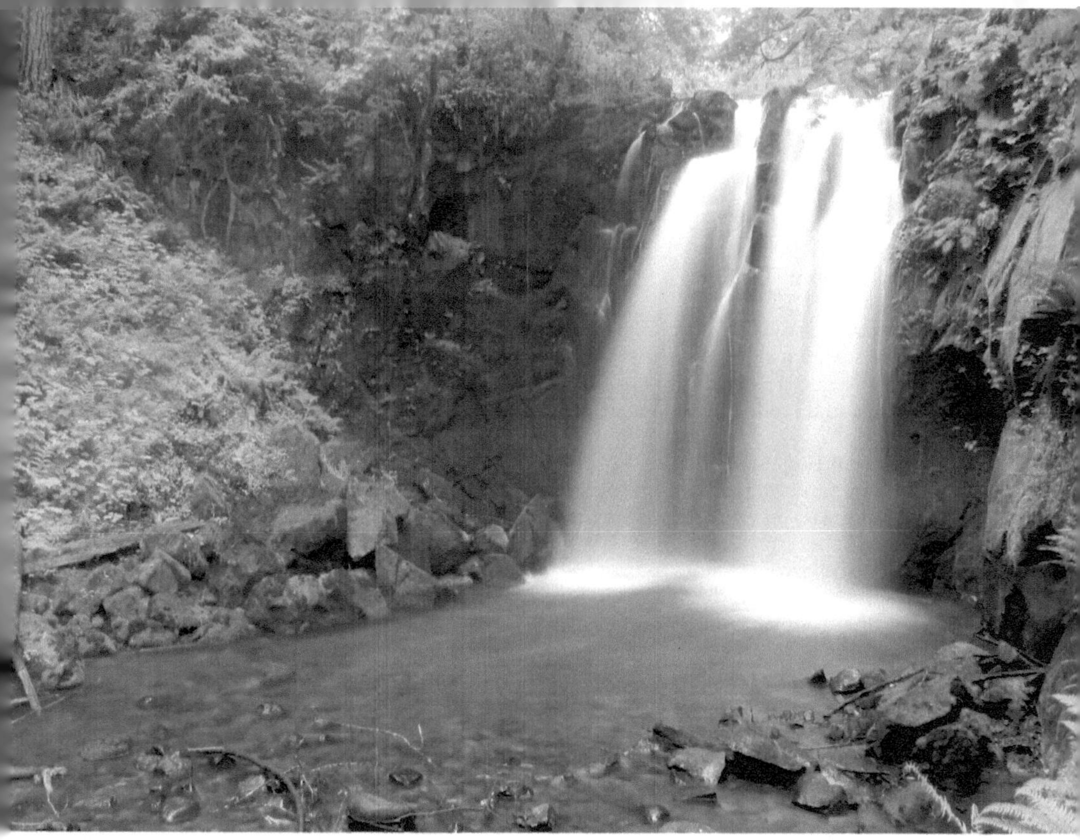

Majestic Falls on a rainy day in June.

(which, unfortunately, is quite difficult to see). Continue straight until you reach a trail junction at a set of stairs. For the recommended loop, turn right here (although you might want to see Royal Terrace Falls, which is just a few hundred feet up the trail at a bridge). To begin your loop, climb up the stone stairs to the top of Royal Terrace Falls. When you reach the top of the falls, you may notice a recent clearcut just a few hundred yards away, a sad testament to the small size of McDowell County Park and the preponderance of logging in the private land holdings in the Cascades north of Sweet Home. Cross a bridge and climb a bit more until you reach a road crossing. Cross the road and follow a trail that descends through second-growth forest to Majestic Falls' parking lot.

Look for a trail that leaves the parking lot here and descends a set of stairs to a viewing deck at the top of Majestic Falls, then descend an impressive and elaborate set of stairs to a viewing deck face-to-face with the falls. Although the falls is only 39 feet tall, it lives up to its name and is exceptionally photogenic. From here, head downstream on a trail paralleling McDowell Creek. You'll pass above Crystal Falls, where a rough trail leads down to the base of the falls. The trail soon crosses the park road before returning you to Royal Terrace Falls. This magnificent tiered falls is the star of the park, and is best saved for last. Here Fall Creek veils off the cliffs above in two steps for a total of 119 feet. A close look at the falls reveals holes in the rock created by erosion, where the water disappears into the rock only to reappear a bit further down. From the falls, cross the bridge over Fall Creek and walk the 0.2 mile back to your car. Lower McDowell Falls is located off-trail below the the trailhead; you'll need to look for user trails to find this beautiful but small falls.

26. Mount Pisgah

Distance: 5.4 miles
Elevation Gain: 1,100 feet
Trailhead elevation: 528 feet
Trail high point: 1,529 feet
Season: all year
Best: March – May
Pass: $5 day use fee per vehicle
On the traditional lands of: the Winefelly, Yoncalla, Chelamela, and Kalapuya peoples

Directions from Eugene:

- From Eugene, drive south on I-5 to exit 188, signed for OR 58.
- Drive southeast on OR 58 for 4.3 miles to a junction on the left with South Ridgeway Road.
- Turn left and drive 1.7 miles to the trailhead on the left at a sharp curve. If you search for the destination online, this is the Mt. Pisgah Southeast Parking lot.
- **Drivetime from Eugene:** 20 minutes

Hike: Mount Pisgah was the place where Moses first saw the holy land, as reported in the book of Deuteronomy. Though the name of that peak is in actuality Mount Nebo, the name Pisgah (meaning summit) has been applied to many places across the world. Oregon's Mount Pisgah features views of a less noteworthy place, towards the fertile farmlands at the southern end of the Willamette Valley. This outstanding loop through the eastern side of Mount Pisgah Arboretum passes fantastic displays of spring wildflowers and excellent views not only of the Eugene area but also of the Cascade Crest. Whether or not you think the Eugene area is Oregon's holy land, you'll almost certainly enjoy this hike a great deal.

From the parking lot, follow wide Trail #6 underneath powerlines for 0.4 mile to a junction at

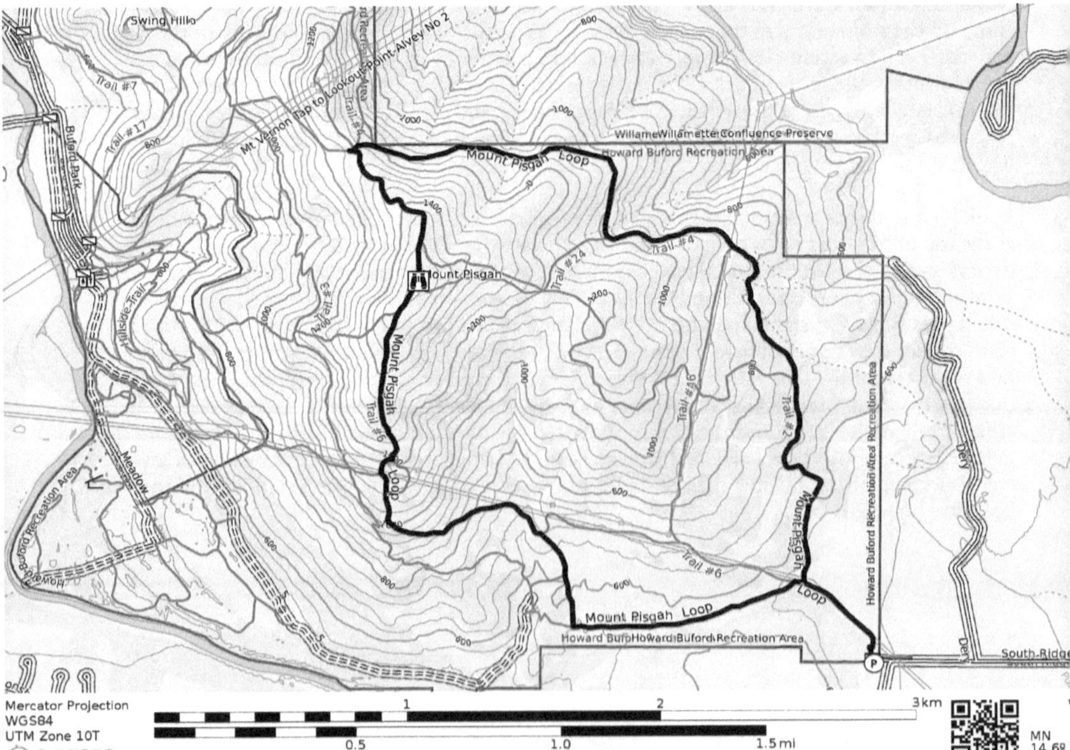

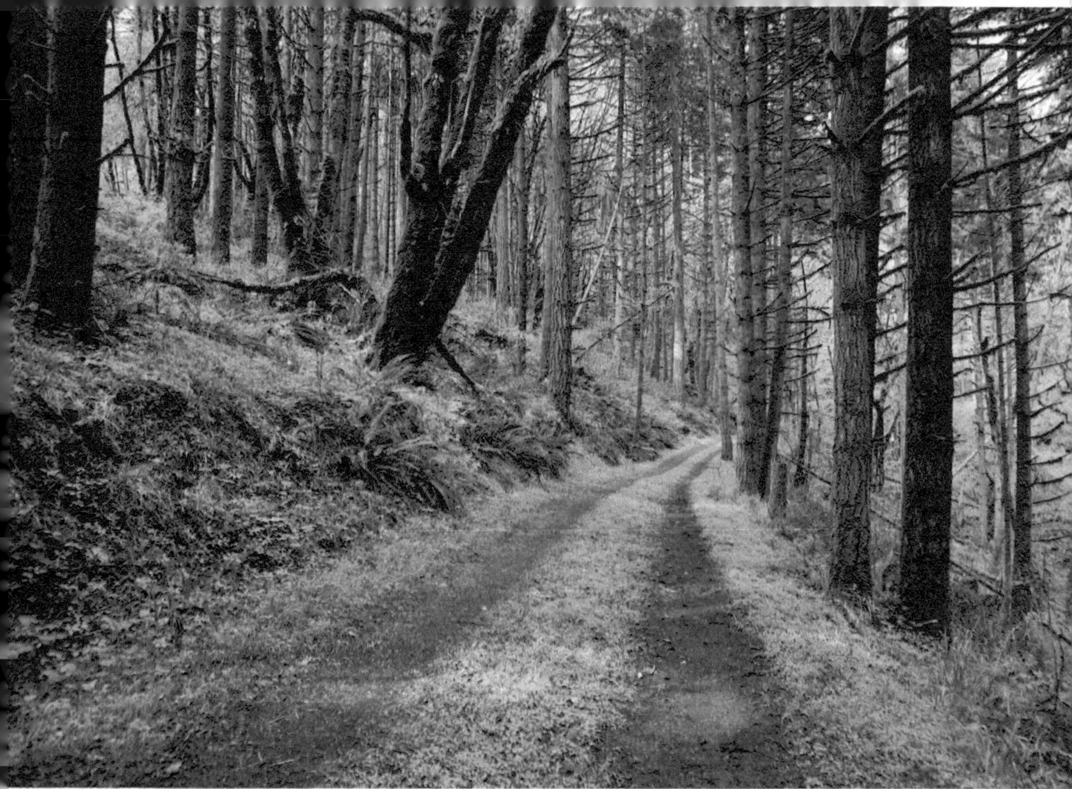

Forest lanes in Mount Pisgah Arboretum.

the base of Mount Pisgah. Fork to the right on Trail #4. There are many trails in the arboretum, offering many different loops; whether you stick to my directions or you want to opt for a shorter or longer hike using one of the many connecting trails, be sure to keep an eye on the map to help you navigate this area. Trail #4 begins by passing through open forest with several meadowed openings. In April look for purple irises, blue and purple camas, lots of white fawn lilies, and many more in both the meadows and in the forest along these trails. Soon Trail #4 trades the oak woods and meadows of the lower part of the trail for deeper forest higher on the slopes of Mount Pisgah, but the grade is never steep. The forest along this trail is exceptionally scenic in spring, when everything is bright green and full of life. At 2.6 miles, the trail reaches a fork with Trail #14E on the left, marked by a post. Fork to the left onto Trail #14E; the sign states that you are only 0.5 mile from the summit.

You will follow Trail #14E uphill and turn onto Trail #1, will lead you steeply uphill to the summit of Mount Pisgah at 3.1 miles. By the time you near the summit, you will almost certainly encounter plenty of other folks hiking the trails here. Most hikers approach this trail network from the west as it is closer to Eugene and the hike to the summit is shorter; I wouldn't blame you for choosing this option, but the hike described here is much nicer. The summit offers lots of room to spread out. On clear days the views of the Cascades are excellent, but even on cloudy days you'll be able to see much of the Eugene-Springfield area.

When you're ready to continue your loop, follow Trail #6 downhill from the summit and into the huge meadows on the south side of Mount Pisgah. As with everywhere else on this hike, you'll pass junctions with several other trails; stay on Trail #6 to complete the loop. The displays of camas in the meadows are particularly impressive in the spring and help compensate for the necessity of hiking under or near powerlines for much of the way back. Keep your dogs close for this stretch of trail (and really for the entire hike), as poison oak grows profusely in the meadows and oak woodlands here. You'll meet Trail #4 at the completion of your loop at 5 miles. Turn right onto what is actually Trail #2 and follow it back 0.4 mile to the trailhead.

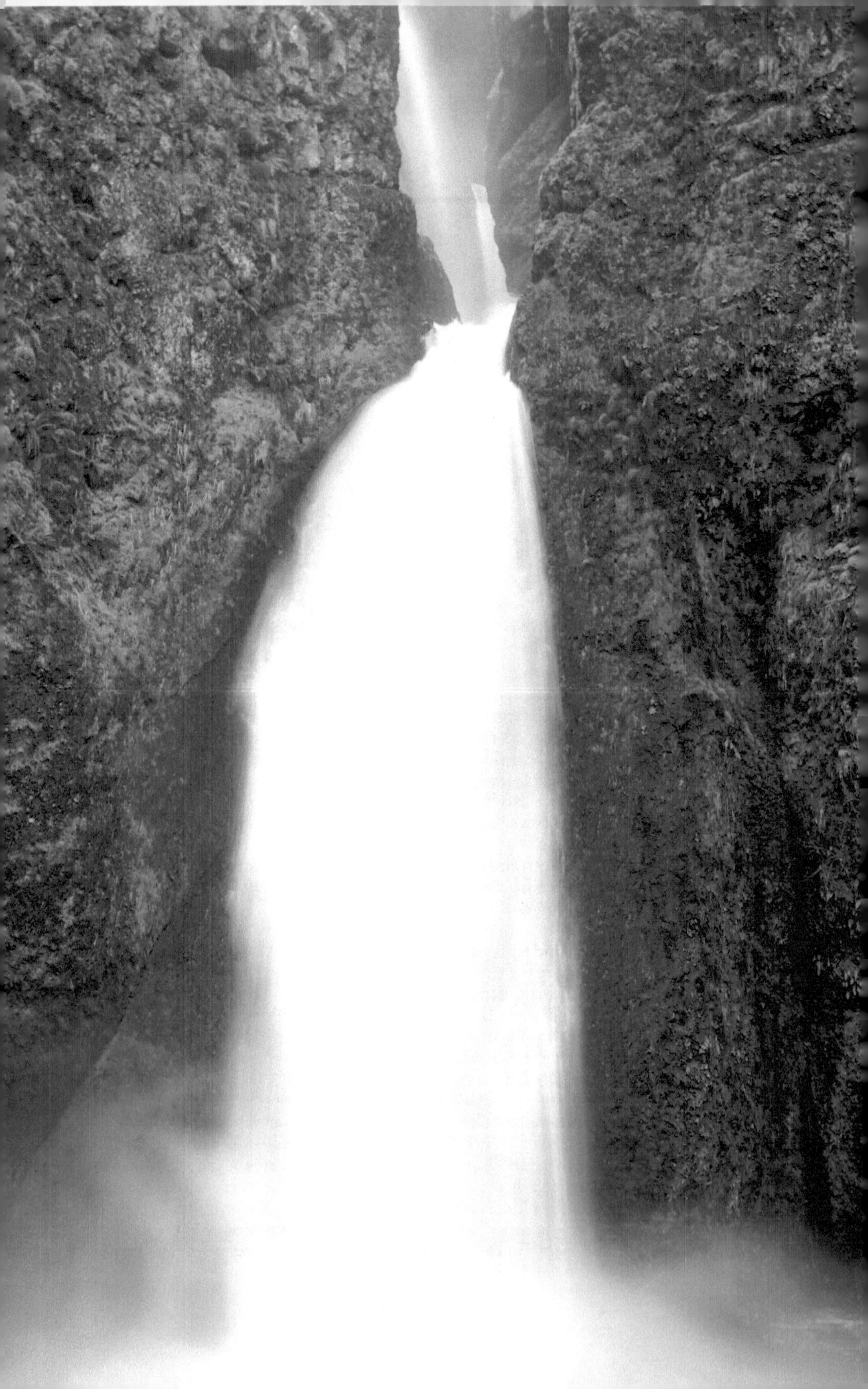

Columbia River Gorge

		Distance	EV Gain	Page
27.	Angels Rest	4.4 miles	1,500 ft	76
28.	Multnomah-Wahkeena Loop	5.4 miles	1,500 ft	78
29.	Wahclella Falls	2 miles	300 ft	80
30.	Eagle Creek	13 miles	1,300 ft	82
31	Chinidere Mountain	4.8 miles	1,300 ft	84
32.	Mitchell Point	2.4 miles	1,200 ft	86
33.	Mosier Twin Tunnels	8.4 miles	600 ft	88
34.	Tom McCall Preserve	5.6 miles	1,500 ft	90
35.	Deschutes River Trail	7.6 miles	200 ft	92

The Columbia River Gorge is home for many hikers in the Portland area. When I first moved to the Portland area many years ago, I found myself hiking primarily in the Gorge. Over the next several years I hiked almost every trail in the Gorge, and to this day the Gorge is my go-to destination when I cannot think of somewhere else to go. Presented here are nine of my favorite hikes in the Gorge; here you'll find waterfalls, far-reaching views, spring and summer wildflowers, and many reminders of Oregon's past and present. As you head east through the Gorge, the climate becomes much drier, becoming almost desert-like by the time you reach the Deschutes River.

Although most people visit the Gorge during the warmer months, the best time to explore the Gorge is between October and May. During fall and winter, the waterfalls run at their fullest, and the eastern Gorge is a fantastic place to escape the rainy doldrums of western Oregon in search of sunshine and blue skies. Spring brings frequent showers and sunbreaks to the Gorge, and wildflowers line every one of these trails. Summer in the Gorge can be very hot, especially east of Hood River. Rattlesnakes are frequently seen in the eastern Gorge in the spring and summer, particularly on hot days. Whenever you visit, you'll be sure to find something to love on these hikes.

Photo on left: Wahclella Falls (Hike 29)

27. Angels Rest

Distance: 4.4 miles out and back
Elevation Gain: 1,500 feet
Trailhead Elevation: 121 feet
Trail High Point: 1,617 feet
Seasons: all year
Best: January - June, October - December
Pass: none needed
On the traditional lands of: the Cascades and Stl'pulmsh (Cowlitz) peoples

Directions:

- From Portland, drive east on Interstate 84 to exit 28, signed for Bridal Veil.
- Continue onto E Bridal Veil Road for 0.3 mile to a junction with the Historic Columbia River Highway.
- At the junction, turn right into the Angels Rest Trailhead.
- **Drivetime from Portland:** 30 minutes

Hike: Angels Rest is a rite of passage for Portland hikers. It's hard to imagine a more beautiful hike located closer to a major city than this one, and as a result the hike is routinely one of the most crowded hikes in the entire state of Oregon. A moderate trail leads to one of the best views of the Columbia River Gorge, and for many Portland hikers, this is their favorite hike – and for some hikers, it's the only hike they know. Speaking as a Portlander, if you're looking to blame anybody for the crowds here, take your complaints elsewhere and be happy that we have such a beautiful hike so close to home. You can still find solitude at Angels Rest if you visit in the winter, on rainy days, or if you come early in the day. During the summer this hike get so crowded you should probably just plan on going elsewhere.

From the Angels Rest Trailhead, follow the wide and well-signed Angels Rest Trail uphill. The

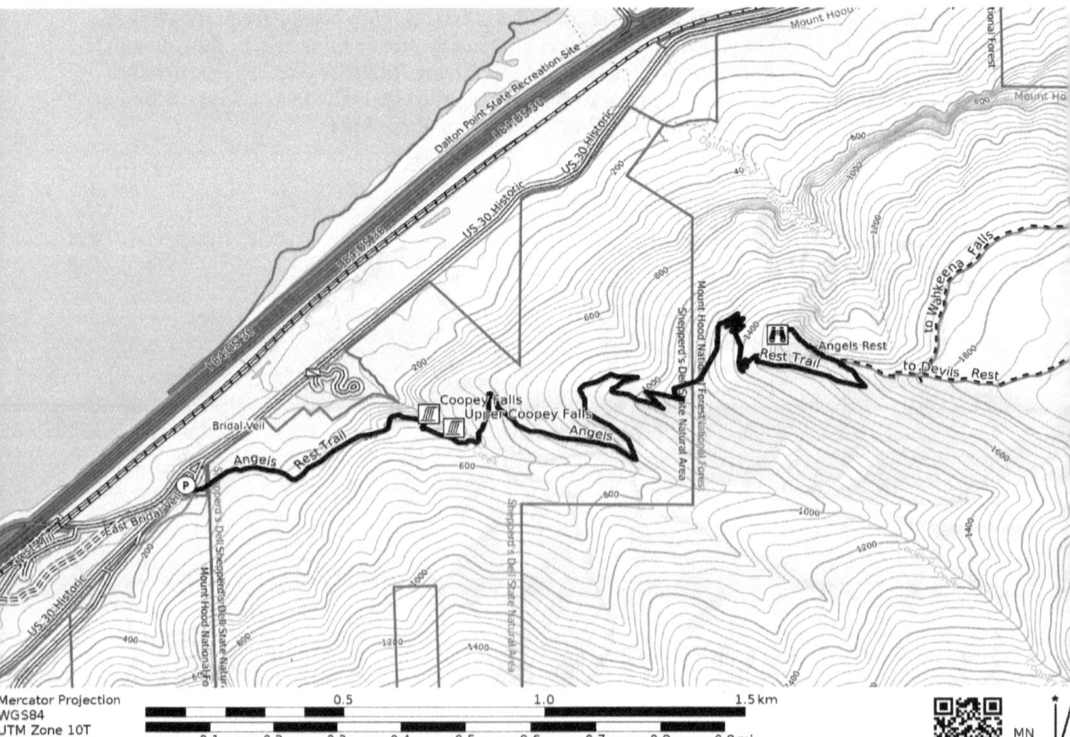

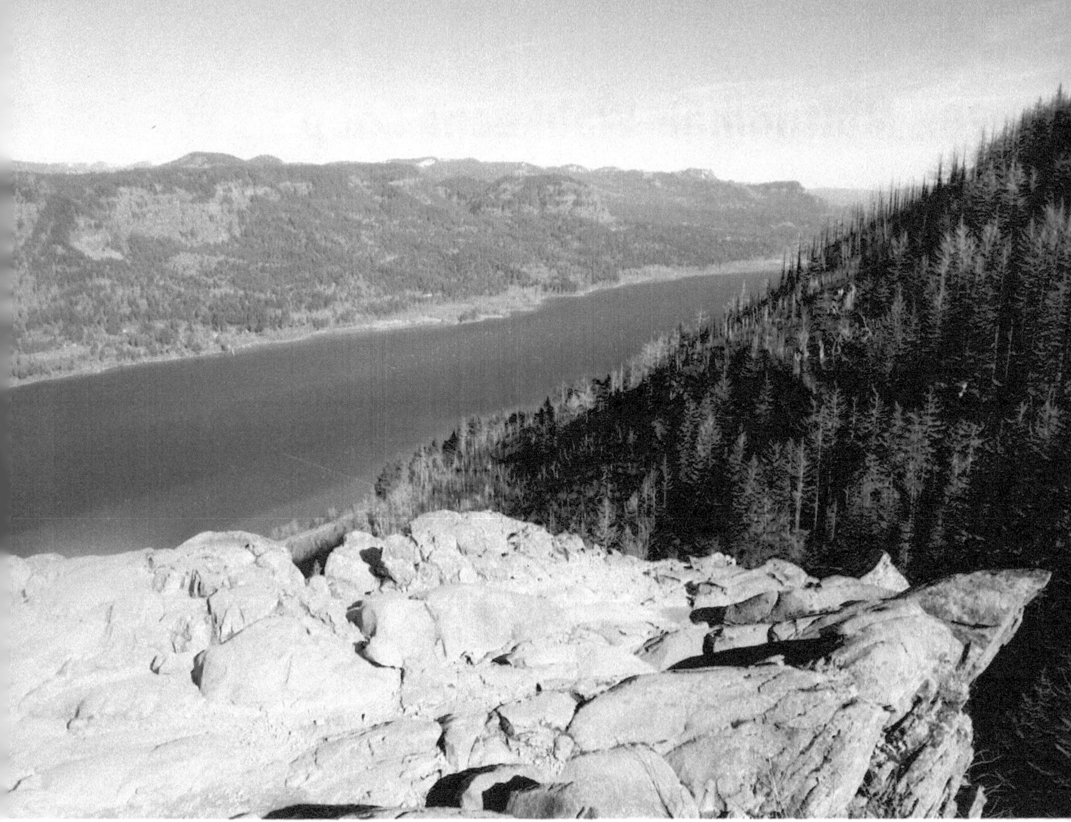

Looking east from the cliffs of Angels Rest.

trail climbs at a steady but mostly gradual grade through a scenic forest that offers views out to the Columbia River and down to Coopey Falls, a large waterfall on the grounds of a Catholic convent at the base of the cliffs here. The flower show in the forest here is impressive in spring; in addition to the ever-present trillium, the harbinger of spring, look for lots of blue and purple larkspur, brown chocolate lily, and many other flowers commonly seen in forests west of the Cascades. As you ascend, you will also begin hiking through forest that burned during the 2017 Eagle Creek Fire. This fire burned quickly through the western Gorge in the days following Labor Day in 2017, cutting a swath of nearly thirty miles through the Gorge. The damage along the Angels Rest Trail is not bad compared to some other places further east.

Wildfires are not all bad; the fire opened up views along the trail that were not here before, and in many ways, I like this trail more than I did before the fire. After a series of switchbacks, the trail passes a rockslide near the base of Angels Rest's cliffs at 1.8 miles; you're getting close now. Continue uphill another 0.3 mile to junction with a side trail on the left. Almost everyone turns left here, so you can't miss the junction (if you do, the trail immediately begins to climb towards Devils Rest; unless this is your plan, turn around and look for the trail ahead of you as you descend). Follow this short side trail up a rocky slope with huge views up and down the western Gorge. You may need to use your hands in a few places, but the last few hundred yards are easy otherwise. You should keep an eye out for poison oak on this side trail, as it grows in a few spots near the trail. Reach the end of Angels Rest at 2.3 miles, where there is ample room to spread out even on crowded days. The view up here is extraordinary, particularly to the west toward the Portland metro area. Sunsets up here are glorious as the lights come on all over the Portland metro area. This is a wonderful way to spend an evening but be prepared to hike out in the dark. When you're ready, return the way you came.

28. Multnomah-Wahkeena Loop

Distance: 5.4 mile loop
Elevation Gain: 1,500 feet
Trailhead elevation: 50 feet
Trail high point: 1,546 feet
Seasons: all year
Best: February – May, October – November
Pass: none needed
On the traditional lands of: the Cascades and Stl'pulmsh (Cowlitz) peoples

Directions:

- Drive east from Portland on Interstate 84 to Multnomah Falls, exit 31. Beware that this is a left-lane exit. Park anywhere in the huge lot.
- **Drivetime from Portland:** 30 minutes

Hike: Multnomah Falls is Oregon's most famous waterfall and also its best. An estimated 2 million people visit the falls every year, and it is hard to find a time when the parking lot at the falls isn't full. Most of the tourists who visit Multnomah Falls are unaware of the half-dozen other waterfalls in the area, and few take the time to do the Multnomah-Wahkeena Loop, one of Oregon's best, most iconic hikes. You will encounter plenty of people on the trails along this hike, but not as many as you might expect. This is one of my favorite places to hike in the winter, as the falls are powerful, the forest lush, and the crowds at their smallest. During the summer this hike get so crowded that ODOT employs flaggers to help people find parking spots. During the summer months you should probably just plan on going elsewhere.

As this is a loop, you can do this hike in either direction; I like to save Multnomah Falls for the grand finale of my hike, so I can get a coffee at the lodge and take one last look at the falls. From

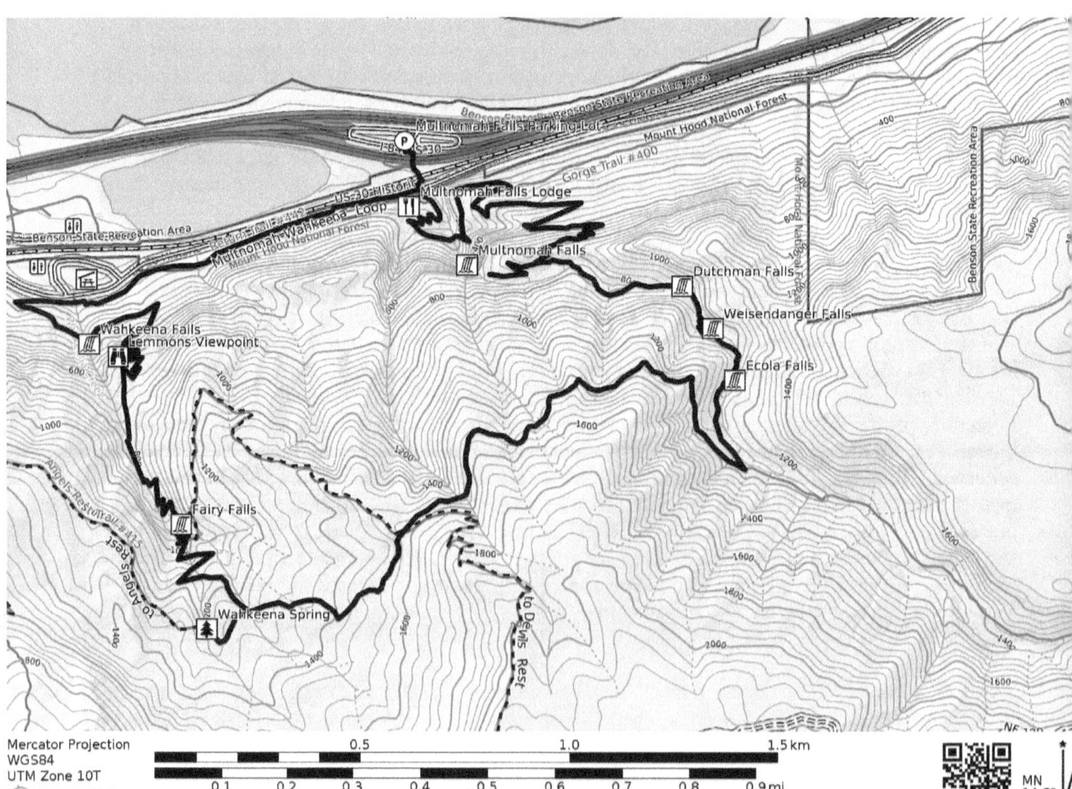

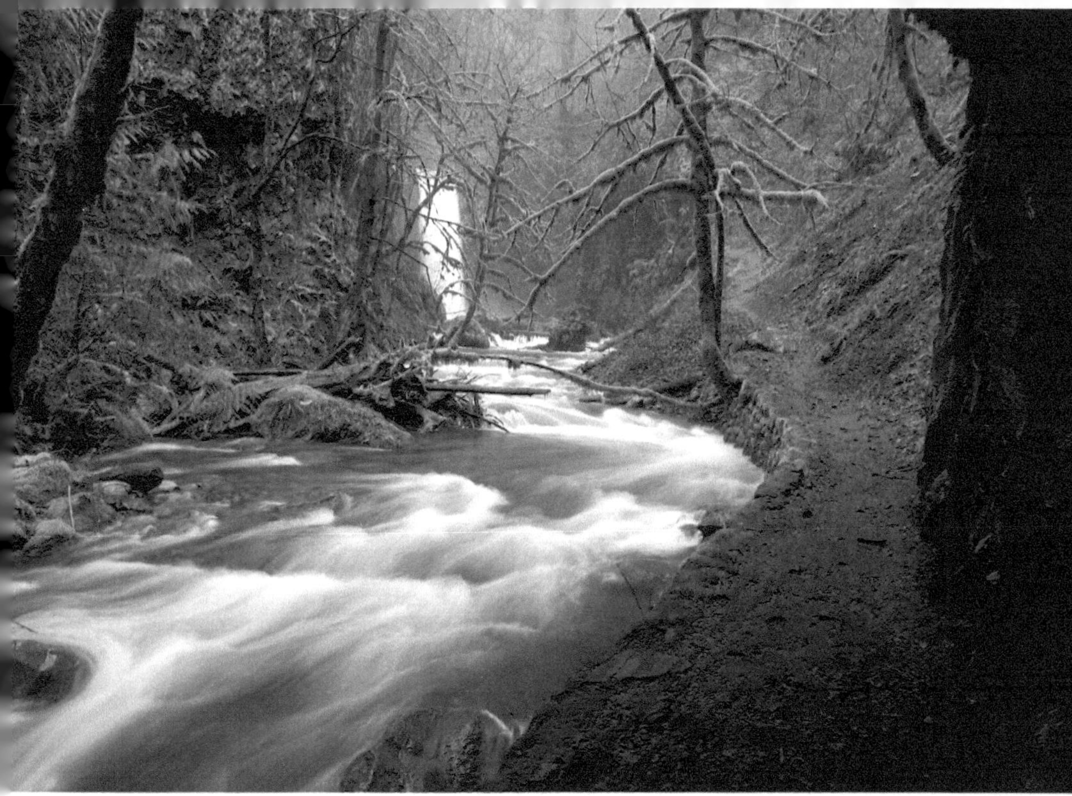

Weisendanger Falls on Multnomah Creek.

the parking lot, follow the paved path under the freeway to the Multnomah Falls Lodge. Once you reach the lodge, follow the historic highway west until you locate the trail to Wahkeena Falls. Take this trail and follow it for 0.5 mile until you reach the Wahkeena Falls Trailhead. From here, turn onto the Wahkeena Falls Trail and follow it uphill for 0.2 mile to the base of Wahkeena Falls. Wahkeena is a Yakama word meaning "most beautiful", and when you see the falls, it's obvious why it has this name. When you're ready to continue, follow the paved trail uphill as it switchbacks a half-mile to the top of Wahkeena Falls. When the trail reaches the basalt shelf at the top of the falls, turn right for the short side trail to Lemmon's Viewpoint for a quick breather. Beyond the viewpoint, the trail follows Wahkeena Creek through its exceptionally beautiful slot canyon for a half-mile to the base of diminutive Fairy Falls at 1.9 miles. Continue uphill another 0.1 mile to a junction on the left with the Vista Point Trail. Both trails go to the same place, but I like the Wahkeena Trail a little more. Continue uphill on the Wahkeena Trail another 0.4 mile to a junction with the Angels Rest Trail (another approach to Angels Rest; see Hike 27). You'll turn left here to continue following the Wahkeena Trail, but if you're looking for a nice place for a rest, consider stopping at Wahkeena Spring. For Wahkeena Spring, turn right and follow the Angels Rest Trail 0.1 mile to the source of Wahkeena Creek, a huge spring that gushes out of the hillside directly below the trail. This is a perfect spot for a lunch break!

Return to the Wahkeena Junction and continue heading east (straight). You'll reunite with the Vista Point Trail at 2.7 miles near the trail's high point. The trail switchbacks down through burned forest to Multnomah Creek's canyon, meeting the Larch Mountain Trail at 3.5 miles. From here it's a succession of highlights. You'll pass Weisendanger Falls and many gorgeous cascades in the creek on the way to the top of Multnomah Falls. The trail reaches a junction with the side trail to the top of Multnomah Falls at 4.2 miles. Take the time to go check out the the eye-popping view of the top of the falls, then pass hundreds of tourists as you hike the paved trail downhill 1 mile to the base of Multnomah Falls.

29. Wahclella Falls

Distance: 2 miles out and back
Elevation Gain: 300 feet
Trailhead elevation: 55 feet
Trail high point: 276 feet
Seasons: all year
Best: November – May
Pass: NW Forest Pass
On the traditional lands of: the Cascades and Stl'pulmsh (Cowlitz) peoples

Directions:

- From Portland, drive east on Interstate 84 to Exit 40, signed for Bonneville Dam. Exit the freeway here and turn right immediately.
- Upon turning right, you will almost immediately reach another junction. Left is the Tooth Rock parking lot while straight leads you directly to the Wahclella Falls lot. Continue straight to the Wahclella Falls lot. If it is full, go back and park at Tooth Rock.
- **Note:** Leave nothing of value in your car here, as break-ins have sometimes occurred at this trailhead in the past.
- **Drivetime from Portland:** 45 minutes

Hike: Whenever I'm looking for a short but spectacular hike, my first thought is to hike to Wahclella Falls. This 127 foot falls is among the most beautiful and impressive in the entire Columbia River Gorge, and the hike to the falls is an absolute delight. There is never a bad time to hike this trail, but my favorite time of year to visit Wahclella Falls is in early spring, when the falls are roaring and the mosses and trees along the trail seem almost electric green in the early spring sunshine. There is much to love here, and you'll find yourself returning to this hike again and again over the years.

Sun pierces the fog above Wahclella Falls.

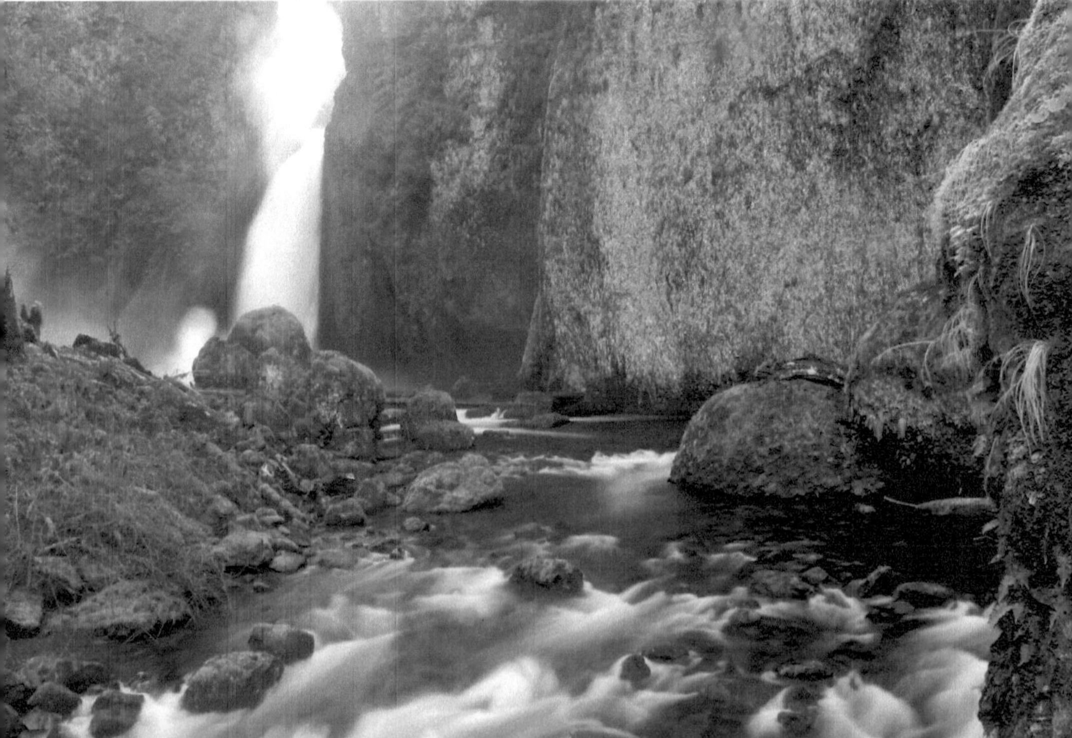

From the trailhead, you'll pass a small dam used by the Bonneville Fish Hatchery and very soon arrive at a bridge beside raucous Munra Falls, which tumbles across a steep basalt slope just an arm's length from the trail. You'll follow beautiful Tanner Creek into a deep canyon that burned during the 2017 Eagle Creek Fire. The fire began in the Eagle Creek canyon only a few miles to the east during Labor Day weekend in September 2017 and touched everywhere in this part of the Gorge. The damage along the trail is noticeable but the area is recovering nicely. Trail crews did an excellent job reconstructing and reopening this trail in the aftermath of the fire, a feat that is particularly impressive given the uneasy geology in this canyon. At 0.8 mile, you'll reach a fork in the trail, the start of a short loop to Wahclella Falls. Fork to the right here to follow the most scenic route.

The trail switchbacks downhill to a bridge over rushing Tanner Creek and enters the huge rocky amphitheater that holds Wahclella Falls. You'll notice a number of truly huge boulders in Tanner Creek and along the trail here; a 1973 landslide dropped these boulders into the canyon, temporarily damming Tanner Creek (see the map) and permanently changing the look of this canyon. Fifty years later, the boulders remain a fixture of this canyon. Wahclella Falls soon comes into view at the head of the canyon but you'll need to follow the trail across a bridge to the base of the falls before its true stature becomes apparent. Wahclella Falls pours out of an extremely narrow gorge, and the upper tier of the falls is only visible from the face-to-face vantage at the unofficial picnic area above the base of the falls. The falls is in fact the last in a series of waterfalls along Tanner Creek, but all the waterfalls upstream are incredibly difficult to see, let alone access. You'll have plenty of competition for the best photo spots here, but you should take your time and bask in the beauty of Wahclella Falls for as long as you deem necessary.

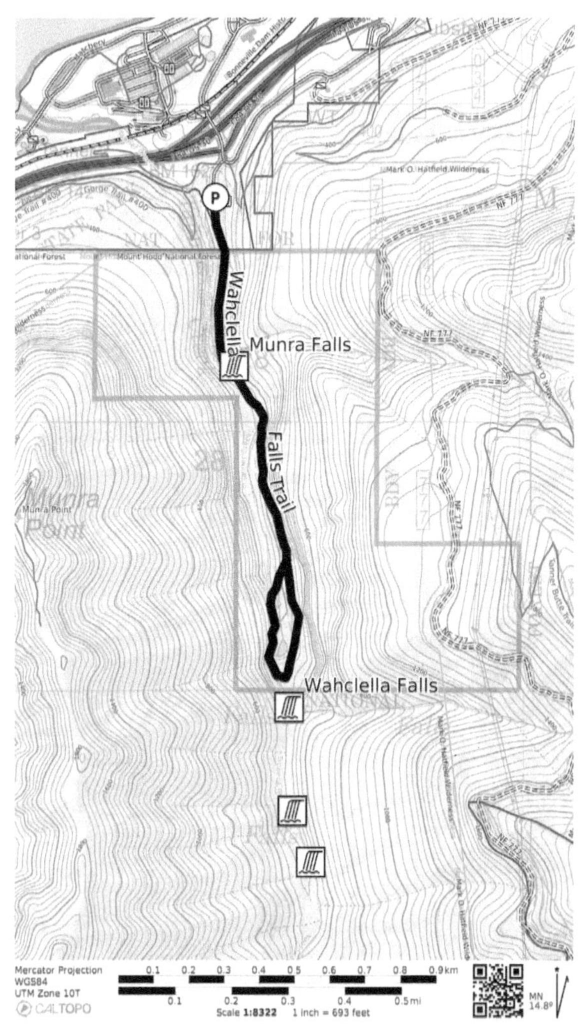

When you're ready to continue the hike, follow the trail uphill from Wahclella Falls to complete the loop. After 0.4 mile, you'll reach the fork at the beginning and end of the loop. Continue downhill along Tanner Creek to return to the trailhead, taking in the excellent views across the Columbia River to Table Mountain on the Washington side of the river.

If you're looking for another hike after this one, consider driving three miles west on I-84 to Exit 37, signed for Warrendale. From here, turn left to cross over the freeway, then turn left again onto Frontage Road for 0.7 mile to the Elowah Falls Trailhead. The trail to Elowah Falls and Upper McCord Falls begins here. Both of these waterfalls are spectacular and well worth the time it takes to visit them, but the trails are frequently closed due to slides and washouts.

30. Eagle Creek

Distance: 13 miles out and back
Elevation Gain: 1,300 feet
Trailhead elevation: 60 feet
Trail high point: 1,357 feet
Seasons: all year (avoid winter ice and snow)
Best: March - May, October - November
Pass: NW Forest Pass
On the traditional lands of: the Cascades and Stl'pulmsh (Cowlitz) peoples

Directions:

- Drive Interstate 84 east of Portland to Eagle Creek Exit 41.
- Almost immediately after exiting the freeway, there is a parking lot on the left next to a fish hatchery. Continue another half-mile to the trailhead at road's end. This lot fills very early on most days. If the lot is full, drive back towards I-84 a half-mile to the lot at the fish hatchery. Leave nothing of value in your car here, as break-ins have sometimes occurred at this trailhead in the past.
- **Drivetime from Portland:** 45 minutes

Hike: One of the most popular hikes in Oregon is also one of the best. Follow a spectacular trail above a narrow gorge featuring waterfall after waterfall, each one better than the last. Good things come at a cost though; this is one of the most popular hikes in the state of Oregon, so expect a lot of traffic on the trail. Furthermore, the Eagle Creek Fire began here in September 2017, and burned much of this canyon. Punch Bowl Falls is no longer easily accessible, and slides are common in the winter. On the flip side, the fire opened up views of a few waterfalls that were previously difficult to see from the trail. The damage is not all that bad for the most part - this is still one of Oregon's most extraordinary hikes.

The Eagle Creek Trail mostly stays along cliffs for much of its scenic journey.

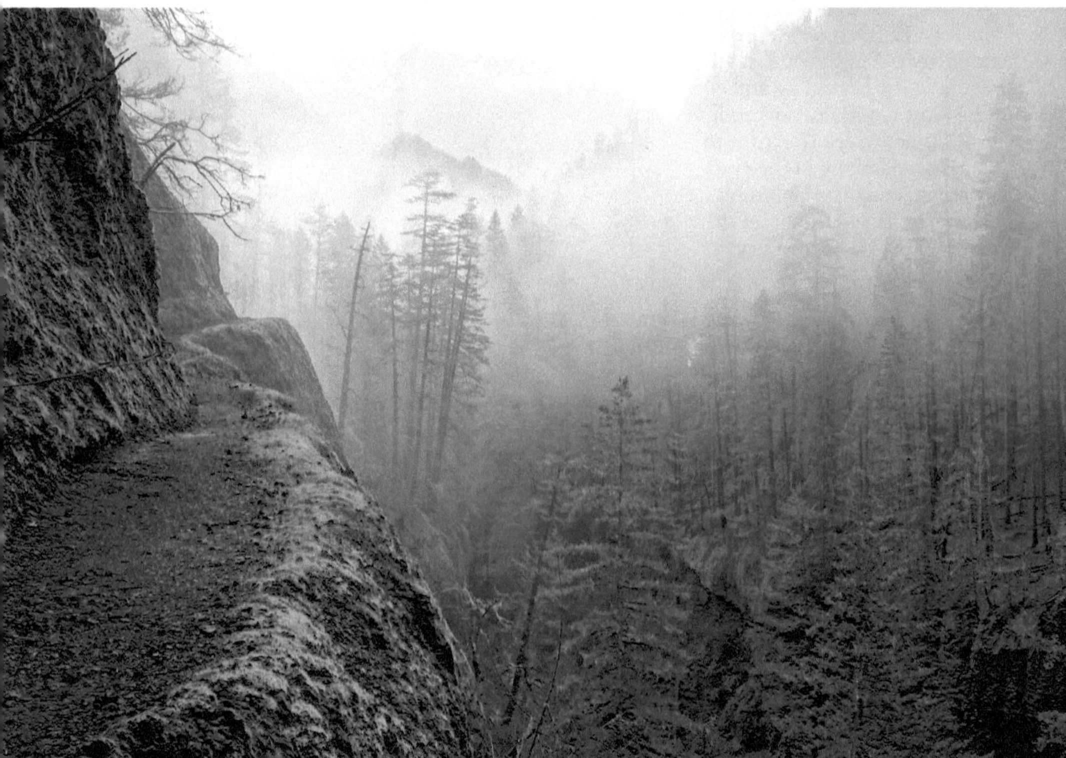

Begin on the wide trail as it parallels wide Eagle Creek. In the winter, this part of the trail can be very icy – and indeed, if it looks too icy here, turn around and go hike somewhere else. The Eagle Creek Trail is not a place you want to be when it's too icy to hike safely. Begin slowly climbing, as the trail ascends to a narrow ledge above the canyon of Eagle Creek. In some places, the trail was blasted out of the ledge – thankfully, chains are in place to help out those uncomfortable with heights. At 0.6 miles, look across the canyon to Wauna Falls, a 150-foot tiered waterfall – this is your first taste of the many waterfalls here. The trail then passes obstructed views of Metlako and Sorenson Falls ahead, cascading side by side. From here, the trail continues another 0.9 mile to a junction with the spur trail down to Punch Bowl Falls. Ignore this side trail and continue on the Eagle Creek Trail. From here, the trail returns to the ledge above the creek, and in a little more than a mile later, traverses a cliff edge opposite Loowit Falls. Those afraid of heights may struggle with this stretch of the trail. At 3.3 miles, reach the aptly-named High Bridge, where the trail crosses Eagle Creek high above a narrow gorge. This is an incredible spot and well worth it for those looking for a moderate hike. There were once many campsites just beyond here, but they burned in the 2017 fire and are no longer a safe place to camp.

For a more difficult hike, continue upstream as the canyon opens up somewhat. You will pass a view of Skoonichuck Falls before crossing the creek again on a bridge at 4.5 miles. Just a short while later, pass Wy'East Camp and its namesake falls, Wy'East Falls. From here, pass a junction with the abandoned Eagle-Benson Trail and enter the Hatfield Wilderness. At a little under 6 miles from the trailhead, you'll pass by Grand Union Falls and enter the Potholes, a series of boulders along the trail that are somewhat hollowed out by water, and reach Tunnel Falls at 6.2 miles. At 165 feet tall, this gorgeous waterfall is an impressive sight indeed. Even more impressive is the tunnel that was blasted out of the rock behind the falls, allowing safe passage upstream. You'll feel the falls shake the rock, but you'll be safe in this passage behind the falls.

Don't turn around yet! The trail continues around a bend as it clings to the side of the cliff above Eagle Creek, and becomes downright frightening (or awesome, depending on your perspective) as it passes above 130-foot Twister Falls. The stretch of trail from Tunnel to Twister Falls is one of the most extraordinary in the Pacific Northwest, and by this point the crowds have thinned out, allowing you to enjoy it in relative peace. If you have a bit more energy, you can continue another 0.2 mile to Sevenmile Falls, the final waterfall on Eagle Creek and by far the quietest. If you're hiking past here, you can follow signs to Wahtum Lake (Hike 31), some 6 miles to the south.

When you are finally ready to turn around, return the way you came.

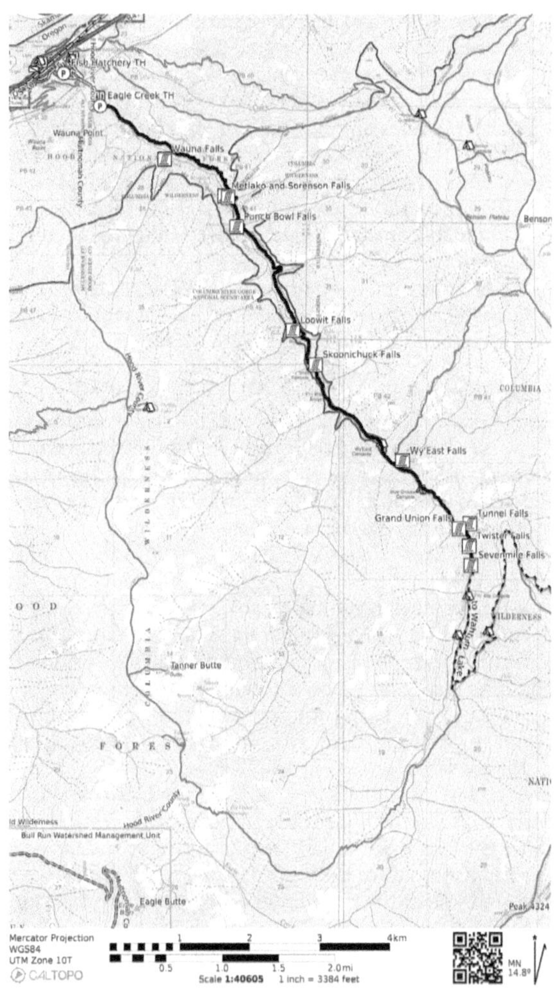

31. Chinidere Mountain

Distance: 4.8 mile loop
Elevation Gain: 1,300 feet
Trailhead elevation: 3,944 feet
Trail high Point: 4,674 feet
Season: June – October
Best: June – October
Pass: NW Forest Pass
On the traditional lands of: the Cascades, Stl'pulmsh (Cowlitz) and Warm Springs peoples

Directions:

- From the west end of Hood River, leave Interstate 84 at Exit 62.
- Just after you exit the freeway, turn right onto Mount Adams Avenue opposite a gas station. This road becomes Country Club Road.
- Drive 3.2 miles to a T-junction with Barrett Drive. Turn left.
- In just 0.2 mile, keep straight at a stop sign. Continue 1 more mile to a junction with OR 281. Turn right.
- Drive 2 miles to a junction on your right, immediately after passing the Apple Valley Country Store, signed "Dee Parkdale Next Right". Turn right here (do not continue straight uphill).
- Drive 2.2 miles on this highway, passing Tucker Park along the way, to another junction on your right, signed for Lost Lake. Veer right here.
- Drive 4 miles on this road to a junction with Lost Lake Road. Turn right.
- Cross the West Fork of the Hood River and reach a junction with Rainy Lake Road in just 0.3 mile. Keep left to continue towards Lost Lake.
- Continue 5 miles to a junction on your right signed for Wahtum Lake. Veer right here.
- Drive this one lane paved road 4.3 miles to a junction with FR 13. Keep straight here to continue on FR 1310.
- Continue on this one-lane paved road another 5.9 miles to the trailhead at Wahtum Lake's small campground. NW Forest Pass is required here.
- **Drivetime from Hood River:** 1 hour

Hike: Wahtum Lake is where the Columbia River Gorge meets the Cascades. Long a destination of many Gorge backpacks, the lake also makes an excellent base camp to explore the area's many scenic high points. Of these high points, you would be hard-pressed to find a better destination than Chinidere Mountain. From this high vantage, you will be able to see from Mount Rainier to Mount Jefferson, with Mount Hood the star attraction some fifteen miles to the southeast. In summer flowers blanket the rocky summit, offering gorgeous scenery even on days when clouds block the views.

From the trailhead, you have two choices for descending to lake level: you can either hike directly downhill on the steep wooden stairs of the Wahtum Express Trail, or you can turn right on the Wahtum Horse Trail and follow it gradually downhill to 0.4 mile to the lake. Choose this latter option to start, and proceed downhill to the lake, where you will meet the Pacific Crest Trail at a junction. From here, turn right and hike along the lakeshore on the PCT. Before long the trail begins to gradually climb away from the lake, heading north towards the Benson Plateau, the Columbia River, and eventually, Canada. Before we leave the lake, pause for a moment to consider how remarkable it truly is. Wahtum Lake has a maximum depth of 184 feet, making it the deepest lake in the Mount Hood National Forest. This depth is noticeable from the ridgelines above the lake, from which the lake appears the deepest shade of indigo. Wahtum Lake narrowly escaped the wrath of the Eagle Creek Fire, and the ancient timber found along the edges of the lake are some of the most impressive forest in this part of the Cascades.

The PCT climbs above the lake to a junction with the Herman Creek Trail at 2 miles from the trailhead. In June and July, look for showy beargrass blooms along this section of the trail. Continue north on the PCT another 0.2 mile or so to a junction with the Chinidere Mountain Trail on your right. Before you climb to the summit, you should probably continue straight on the PCT another tenth of a mile as it passes under hanging wildflower meadows below the rocky slopes of Chinidere Mountain. The meadows are just a taste of the best yet to come. Return to the Chinidere Mountain junction and turn left (uphill). This spur trail climbs a half-mile through the woods to the summit, where you will have views across the entire region. Wildflowers blanket every green nook and cranny of the rocky summit, while off-trail rock formations beckon the fearless explorer. Directly below you is the grey-green mosaic of Eagle Creek's famed canyon; keen eyes can even pick out the confluence of the East and West Forks of Eagle Creek in the canyon below. This is one of the finest picnic spots in this corner of the Gorge.

When you're ready to return, hike back downhill to the PCT. Turn left and almost immediately begin looking for the potentially unsigned junction with the Chinidere Cutoff Trail on your right. If you can't find the trail there's no shame in returning the way you came. If you find the trail, follow it steeply downhill to the west end of Wahtum Lake. Along the way you'll notice a pipe running along the trail; this was the former water line that pumped spring water into a campground along the lake that is now abandoned. At 0.7 mile from the PCT, cross Eagle Creek on downed logs at the lake's outlet. You will then immediately reach a junction with the Eagle Creek Trail. Continue straight another fifty yards or so to another junction with the PCT, which runs along the lakeshore. Turn left and hike 0.2 mile along the lake to a junction with the Wahtum Express Trail. If the thought of climbing a few hundred stairs seems daunting, locate the horse trail and follow it back uphill to the trailhead. Otherwise, turn right on the Express and scurry up the stairs to the parking lot and your vehicle. This last part of the hike is invigorating, and you will probably feel better for saving it for last!

Note that you can also backpack here from Eagle Creek (Hike 30). The trek south on Eagle Creek to Wahtum Lake is a classic Gorge backpacking trip, and hikers often return via either the Pacific Crest Trail or the Herman Creek Trails. Consult a map of the area for more information.

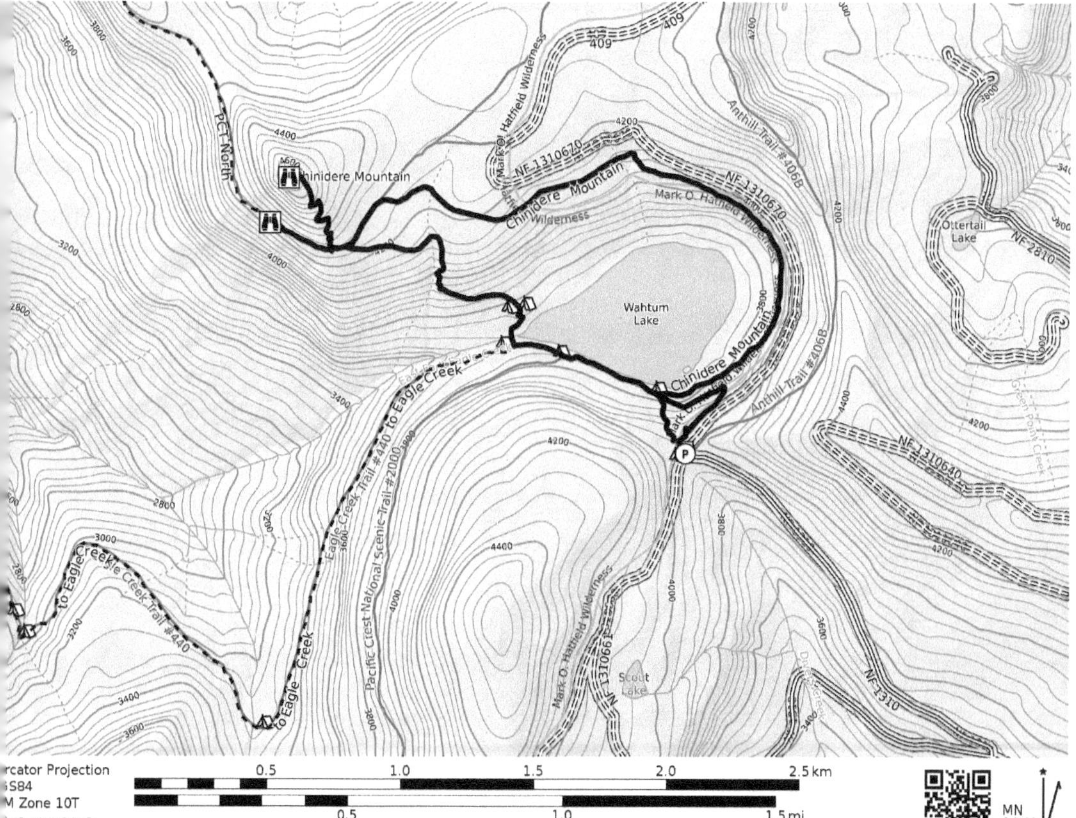

32. Mitchell Point

Distance: 2.4 miles out and back
Elevation Gain: 1,200 feet
Trailhead elevation: 100 feet
Trail high point: 1,200 feet
Season: all year
Best: March - April
Pass: None needed
On the traditional lands of: the Warm Springs, Grand Ronde, Wasco and Wishram peoples

Directions:

- From Portland, drive east on Interstate 84 to Exit 58, where you will see a sign for the Mitchell Point Overlook.
- Exit the freeway here and drive into the parking lot below Mitchell Point. This is the trail-head.
- **Note:** The Mitchell Point Trailhead can only be reached from eastbound Interstate 84. If you are coming from Hood River, drive to the Viento Exit 56; turn around here and head east to Exit 58.
- **One more important note;** The Mitchell Point Exit will be closed through at least the end of 2023 while ODOT rebuilds the Historic Columbia River Highway through this area. Check ODOT's website for more information. There is no access to this trail while this project is ongoing.
- **Drivetimes:** 1 hour from Portland, 10 minutes from Hood River

Hike: Mitchell Point gives you a lot of bang for your buck. In less than an hour you can climb a solitary trail to a superb viewpoint of the Columbia River Gorge. In April the upper reaches of the trail are covered in wildflowers, among them balsamroot and the lovely pink calypso orchid.

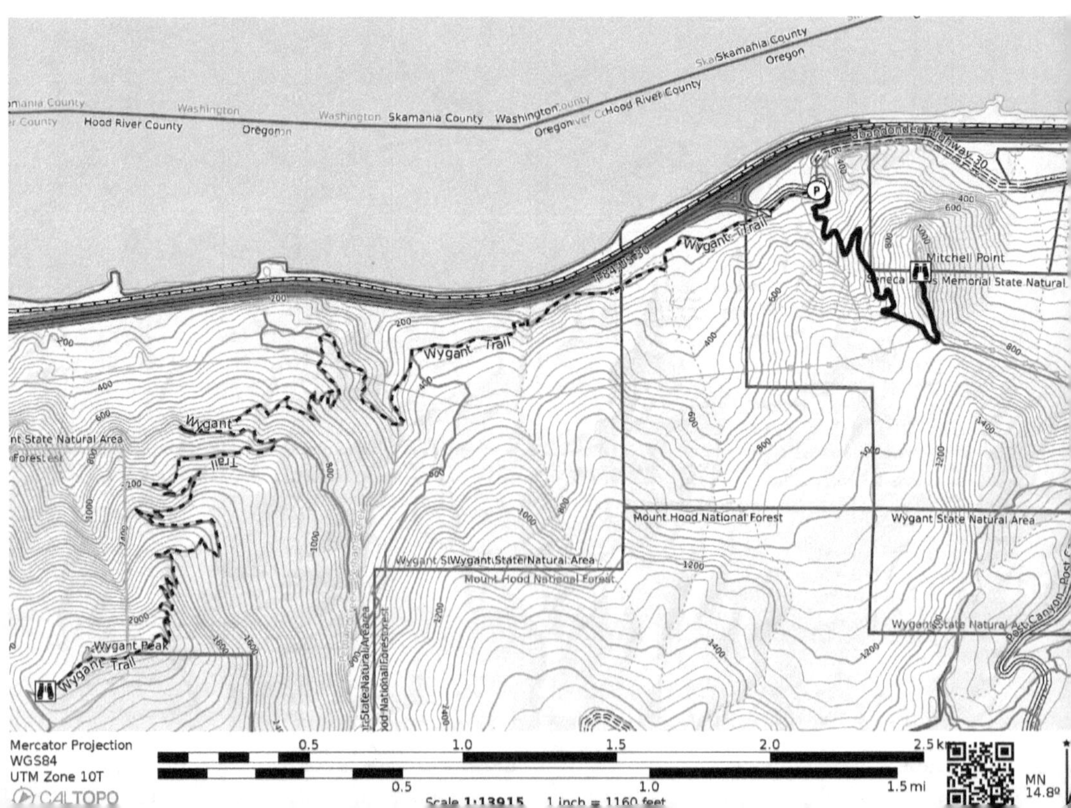

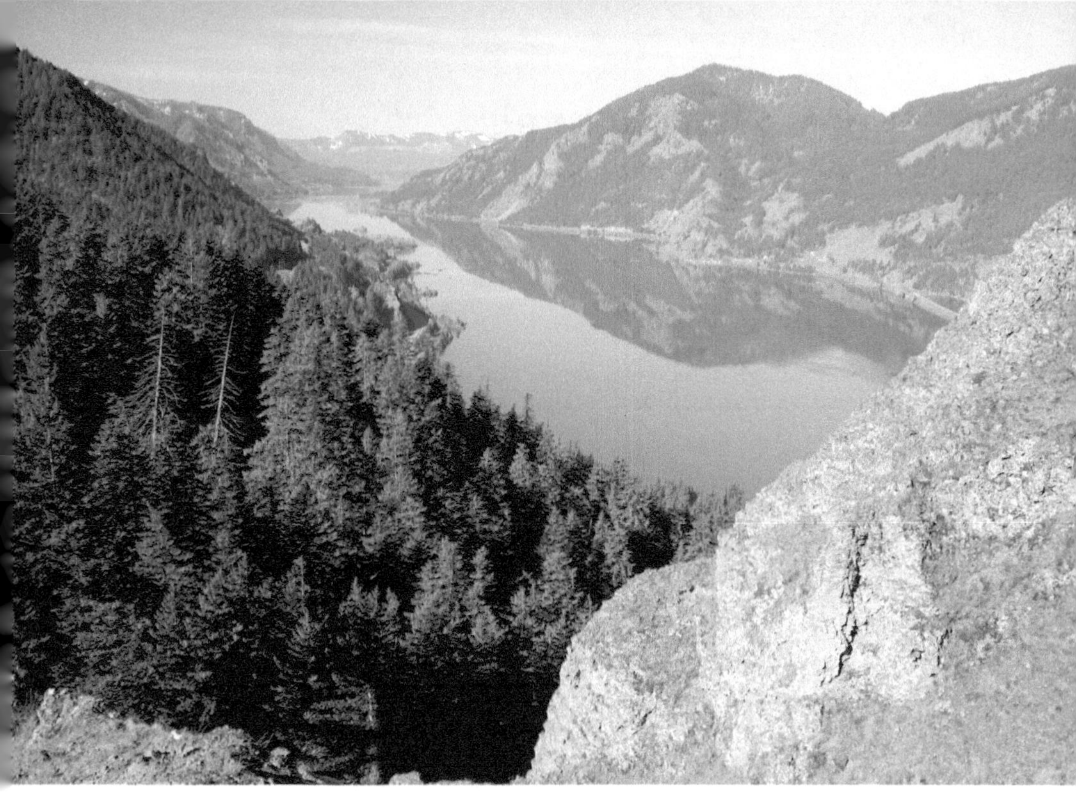

Looking west from the cliffs of Mitchell Point towards Dog Mountain.

You can easily do this trip in two hours and have time to do another hike afterwards; alternately, this makes a great sunset hike if you come after work. The view cannot be beat! Keep an eye out for poison oak along the trail as it can be profuse in some spots.

From the south end of the parking lot, look for a trail heading south towards the cliffs. The trail climbs gently through lovely forest following a small creek before climbing away, becoming steeper and steeper as it works its way up Mitchell Point. Eventually the trail reaches a talus slope framed dramatically by white oak and great views of the west end of the Gorge. After cresting above the talus, the trail winds through some nice older forest. In April the forest floor here is carpeted with the lovely pink calypso orchid. Freshly-risen orchids give off an incredible perfume that only lasts for a day or two – you may need to get down on your hands and knees and sniff a great number of flowers until you find one that is scenting – you won't regret it! One mile from the trailhead, reach a set of powerlines at an open saddle.

Look to your left up at the green ridgeline of Mitchell Point and follow the steep trail up through meadows 0.3 mile to the top of the ridge. In March and April look for grass widows, desert parsley, larkspur, balsamroot and other Gorge wildflowers. When the ridge narrows into an exposed summit with a 180-degree panorama of the Columbia River Gorge, stop and take in the views; you might just want to stay awhile. Return the way you came.

Hikers desiring more time on the trail can check out the recently restored route to Wygant Peak. Though less scenic and much longer than the short trail to Mitchell Point, this is a fun hike that takes you to a less-visited spot in the Gorge. From the Mitchell Point Trailhead, follow the Wygant Trail as it parallels the freeway for a mile. The trail then crosses Perham Creek and proceeds to steadily climb the slopes of Wygant Peak for more than three miles. Significant trail work has pushed back the thickets of poison oak that once grew along the trail but you should be on the lookout for it for much of the way up. At 4.4 miles, you'll reach the viewless summit of Wygant Peak. For a better view, follow the trail below the summit another 0.2 mile until you reach a hanging meadow with a nice view west to the Gorge. Not many people visit this spot, and it's a lovely place. Return the way you came.

33. Mosier Twin Tunnels

Distance: 8.4 miles out and back
Elevation Gain: 600 feet
Trailhead elevation: 348 feet
Trail high Point: 527 feet
Season: all year
Best: November – May
Pass: Oregon State Parks Pass (electronic fee box available at the trailhead)
On the traditional lands of: the Warm Springs, Grand Ronde, Wasco and Wishram peoples

Directions:

- From Portland, drive east on Interstate 84 to Hood River.
- At Exit 64, leave the freeway, following signs for Government Camp.
- At the bottom of the exit ramp, turn right and drive a short way uphill to a four way stop.
- Turn left here and drive 1.2 miles to road's end at Mark Hatfield State Park. Park in the lot here.
- **Drivetimes:** 5 minutes from Hood River, 65 minutes from Portland

Hike: The Historic Columbia River Highway once traversed the entire Columbia River Gorge from The Dalles to the outskirts of Portland. When Interstate 84 was completed in the 1960s, the historic highway was abandoned, and left to nature. Over time, many segments of the highway have been recovered and converted into bike paths and hiking trails. This beautiful segment from Hood River to Mosier might be the best of these, featuring fantastic views across the Columbia River Gorge and a series of tunnels that offer a unique destination that is attractive in any season – especially in the dead of winter. Although the entire hike is on a paved road, there is much to love about this charming relic of a bygone day.

From the trailhead, follow the road as it climbs gently above the bluffs above the Columbia River. Interstate 84 is audible for much of this hike, but the highway noise rarely intrudes. Each end of this trail is quite popular, but the wide road ensures you'll have enough space to enjoy this hike without feeling like it's too crowded. As you hike along, consider the juxtaposition of the busy freeway below you, and the quaintness of the restored highway on which you are hiking. Keep this in mind as you follow this road around its many twists and turns. You will pass a side trail at

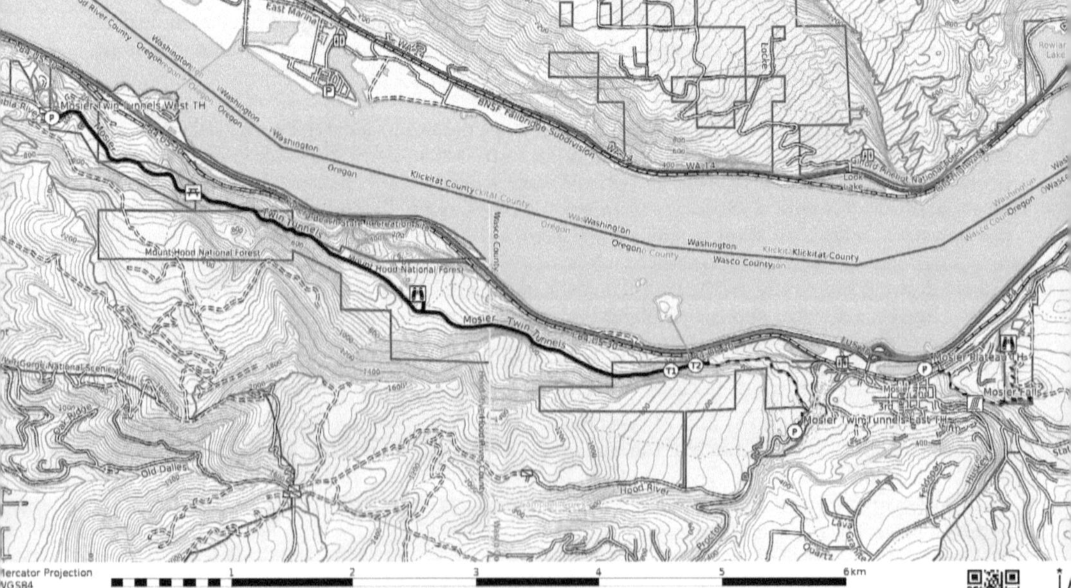

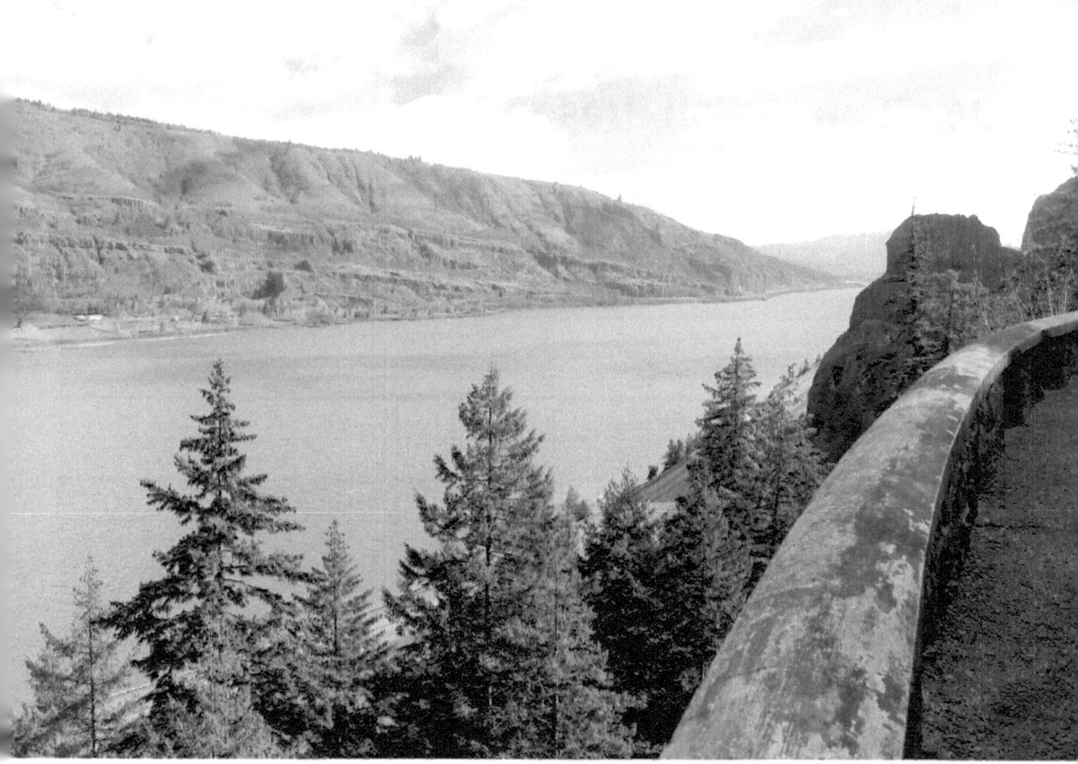

Looking east from the Historic Highway to the Washington side of the Gorge.

just under 2 miles. The trail that takes off here ends at a fence before it goes anywhere interesting, but it's worth a look just the same.

After about 2.5 miles from the trailhead, the road passes a wide spot with a spectacular view across the Columbia River. The mountain on the other side is Burdoin Mountain, rising above Bingen on the Washington side of the river. From here, continue another mile or so to the Mosier Twin Tunnels. The first of these is rather utilitarian, as it was built to catch falling rock from the cliffs above. The second tunnel is far more interesting. Restored to its original glory in the 1990s, this short but captivating tunnel passes two wonderful viewpoints out to the Gorge through open, rocky windows in the tunnel walls. These viewpoints are excellent stopping points on rainy days. Once out of the tunnel, you will quickly reach a picnic area and viewpoint out to the eastern Gorge at just over 4 miles from the western trailhead. Notice also how it seems like you've reached the eastern Gorge – around you are grassy slopes and ponderosa pines. Balsamroot blooms here in April, adding color to the scene. The road continues another mile to the road's eastern terminus at the edge of Mosier, but this stretch of trail is much less interesting than what you've already seen. Unless you're a completist or just want a couple more miles of hiking, it's best to stop here. Return the way you came.

Other hiking options;

The Mosier area is full of fantastic hiking options if you're looking for something else to do after you finish this hike. You could drive east 10 minutes to the Tom McCall Preserve (see Hike 34) and hike the trails there. Another fantastic option is the Mosier Plateau Trail, a delightful path in Mosier that has much to love. To find this latter trail, drive Interstate 84 east 5 miles to Mosier (Exit 69). Leave the freeway and follow old US 30 through the small town of Mosier. Plan on parking at a small lot on the left side of the road just before a bridge over Mosier Creek. The trail begins just across the bridge and climbs up the slopes above Mosier Creek, passing a historic cemetary and Mosier Falls along the way. You'll hike through gorgeous hanging meadows of spring wildflowers to the top of Mosier Plateau at 1.3 miles from the trailhead. The view here stretches west across the Gorge to the slopes of Burdoin Mountain on the Washington side.

34. Tom McCall Preserve

	Rowena Crest	Tom McCall Point
Distance:	2 miles out and back	3.6 miles out and back
Elevation Gain:	450 feet (on the return)	1,017 feet
Trailhead Elevation:	703 feet	703 feet
Trail High Point:	703 feet	1,720 feet
Seasons:	all year (avoid summer heat)	March 1 – October 31
Best:	March - May	March - May
Pass:	None needed	None needed
On the traditional lands of:	the Warm Springs, Grand Ronde, Wasco and Wishram peoples	the Warm Springs, Grand Ronde, Wasco and Wishram peoples

Directions:

- From Hood River, drive east on Interstate 84 east to Mosier.
- At Exit 69, signed for Mosier, leave the freeway and turn right to follow old US 30 through the small community of Mosier.
- Drive through Mosier and continue 6 more miles to the Rowena Crest parking area on the right side of the road. You'll need to park somewhere along the short road to the Rowena Crest viewpoint; come early on most days to ensure you find a parking spot.
- The Rowena Crest Trail departs from the north side of the road, while the Tom McCall Point Trail departs from the south side of the road.
- **Drivetimes:** 15 minutes from Hood River, 1 hour and 15 minutes from Portland

An old fenceline marks a scenic viewpoint on Rowena Crest.

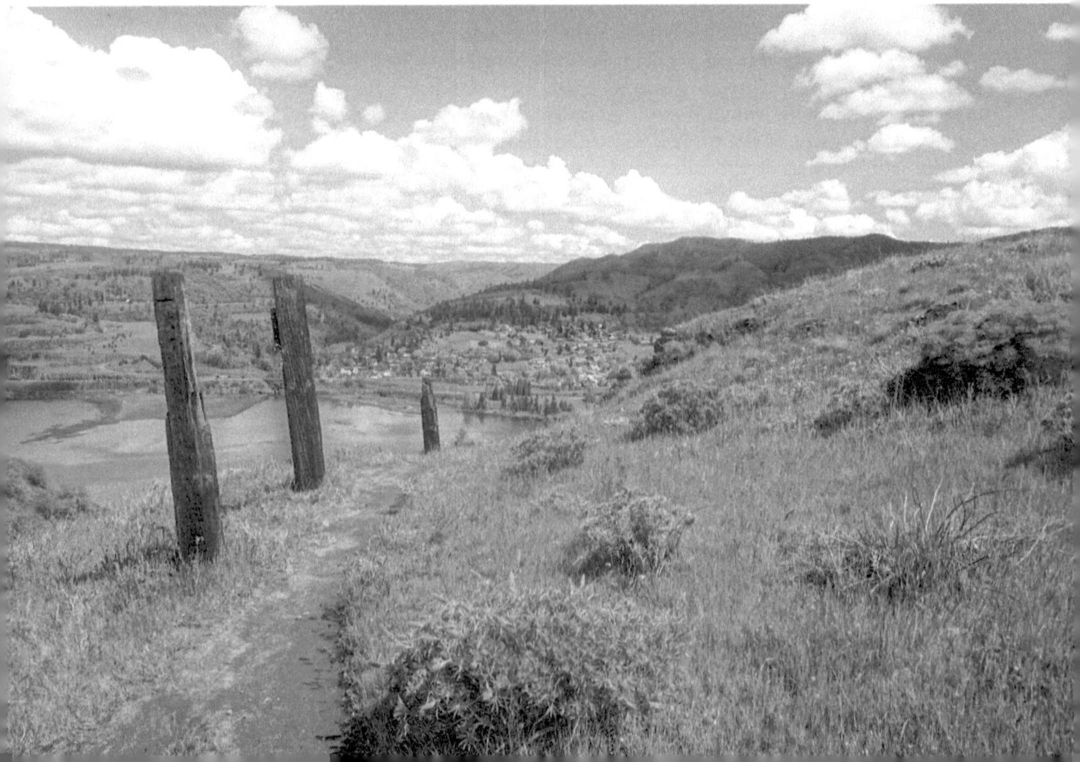

Hike: Tom McCall was perhaps the most beloved governor in Oregon's history. Governor from 1967 to 1975 and a Republican for his entire political career, McCall nevertheless believed in preserving Oregon's environment, and his advocacy helped win some of the most important environmental victories in Oregon's history, among them passage of the Bottle Bill, the cleanup of the Willamette River, and the Beach Bill to renew Governor Oswald West's declaration that all Oregon beaches must be public land. His relentless environmental activism is the reason there are so many public spaces named after Tom McCall. The prettiest of these places is the Tom McCall Preserve between Mosier and The Dalles. Here you'll find fantastic displays of spring wildflowers and extraordinary views of the Columbia River Gorge as well as Mount Adams and Mount Hood. There are two great hikes here, one easy and one a bit less easy; for the best experience, take the time to do both.

Before you start the hike, it is important to note that the Nature Conservancy owns this property, and that you should follow any and all rules in place on each trail. The first and most important rule is that **dogs are prohibited here,** as they are at all Nature Conservancy properties. Also important to know is that the Tom McCall Point Trail is closed between November and February to help prevent erosion along the trail surface during the wet winter months; the Rowena Crest Trail is open all year. Last but not least, but sure to watch out for poison oak and ticks, both of which are commonly found in the eastern Gorge in the warmer months; rattlesnakes are also occasionally seen in the preserve on hot days.

The order in which you hike each trail is not important, but you might want to warm up by hiking the easy Rowena Crest Trail downhill from the trailhead. This wide trail passes through spectacular wildflower displays from March through June, among them yellow balsamroot and blue and purple lupine. The trail ambles downhill from Rowena Crest, passing a pond and several fantastic viewpoints of the eastern Gorge. Watch your step here, as poison oak grows along the trail in a few spots. The trail ends at a rocky viewpoint at 1 mile, after which you'll need to turn around and return the way you came to the trailhead.

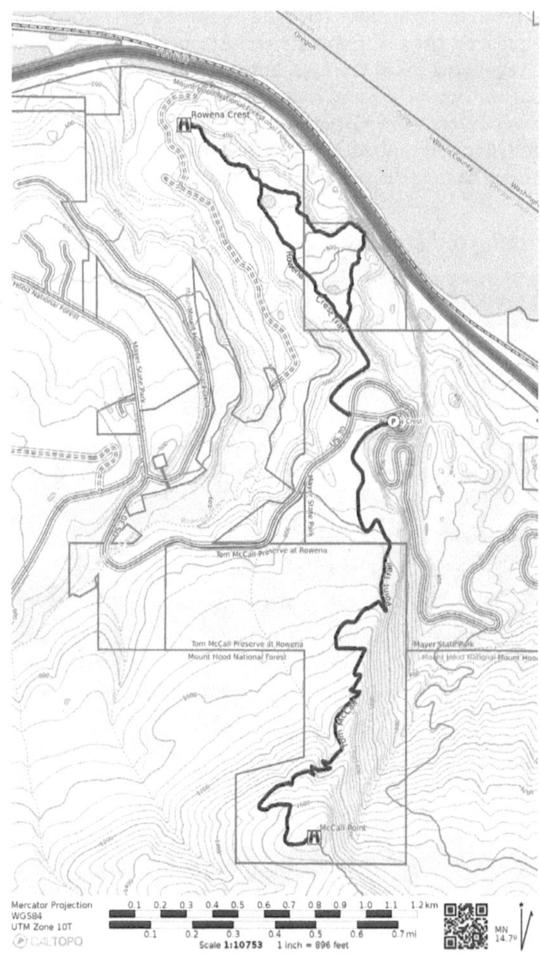

For Tom McCall Point, locate the trail heading due south from the Rowena Crest Viewpoint and follow across a meadow full of spring wildflowers and views east to Mount Hood. The trail enters the woods and climbs 1.8 miles to the open summit of Tom McCall Point. The spring wildflower displays are even more impressive up here than down at Rowena Crest, and the view is truly magnificent, spreading east and west along the Gorge, north to Mount Adams and south to Mount Hood. Tom McCall may have never visited this spot, but he certainly would have loved it. Return the way you came.

35. Deschutes River Trail

Distance: 9 miles out and back (with partial loop)
Elevation Gain: 200 feet
Trailhead elevation: 217 feet
Trail high point: 331 feet
Season: January - May, October - December
Best: January - April
Pass: none ($5 fee if parked overnight)
On the traditional lands of: the Tenino, Wasco, Wishram, and Warm Springs peoples

Directions:

- From The Dalles, drive east 13 miles on Interstate 84 to Exit 97. Following signs for the Deschutes Recreation Area, leave the freeway at Exit 97 and arrive at a junction.
- Turn left and drive 3 miles to Deschutes State Park.
- Cross the river and turn right into the campground.
- Drive through the campground and park at the south end of the B campground loop, near the camp host and bathrooms. The trail is straight ahead at the end of a grassy field.
- **Drivetime from The Dalles:** 15 minutes

Hike: The Deschutes River flows some 250 miles from its source at Little Lava Lake to the river mouth on the Columbia River, just upstream of the submerged wonders of Celilo Falls. Most Oregonians know the Deschutes River as it flows peacefully through Central Oregon, from LaPine State Park and through Sunriver into Bend. North of Redmond, however, the Deschutes River enters a deep desert canyon that is known primarily for its glorious river rafting. A series of dislocated railbeds, long since converted to trails, follow the river's east bank, offering excellent hiking during the colder months of the year. This beautiful hike along the Deschutes follows the

Hiking the Deschutes River Trail is a delight on a sunny day in the winter.

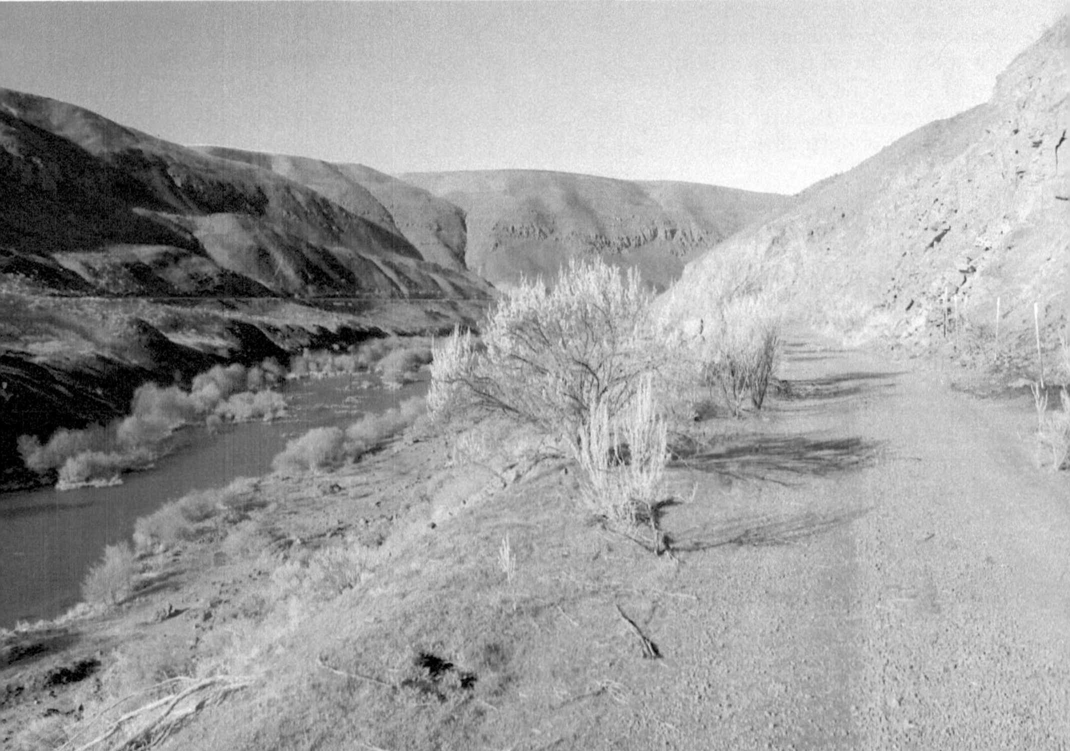

lowest reaches of the river, from just above the mouth to deep inside the river's inner canyon. Come here between November and May for the best hiking; in summer, the canyon is insufferably hot and the rattlesnakes numerous.

Begin on the grassy flat at the far end of the campground. Walk to the end of the flat, where you'll be faced with a trail junction. It does not matter much which way you do this hike, but I say you should turn left here. Follow this short trail uphill past another trail junction to trail's end at the gravel road that follows the river upstream. Turn right here. From here, how far you go is up to you. If you're looking for a different view of the Deschutes Canyon, hike upriver on the old road 1 mile to the Ferry Springs Trail on your left. Follow this scenic but windy, exposed trail up and over the slopes above the river for 1.7 miles, gaining and then losing 500 feet along the way. You'll reach a reunion with the road at 3 miles into your hike. If you'd rather just stay on the road, continue 0.9 mile to a saddle where the Ferry Springs Trail rejoins the Deschutes River Trail. From this junction, continue following upstream, well above the rushing Deschutes River. At 3.3 miles (or 4.2 miles if you hiked the Ferry Springs Trail), you'll reach a junction. To the right is a campsite along the river, complete with a vault toilet. Truth be told, this was a much prettier spot before the 2018 Substation Fire ripped through the canyon, burning much of the vegetation. For a moderate hike, continue straight on the main road another half-mile to a series of fantastical basalt rock formations. The most interesting is a small cave well above the trail, 4 miles from the trailhead (or 4.9 miles if you hiked the Ferry Springs Trail).

If you're turning around here, hike back to the junction and follow its access road down to the camp area. Locate a user trail following the river and follow it just over 3 miles back to the trailhead. Along the way you'll pass a tricky spot where large boulders have fallen on the riverbank, necessitating stopping here and there to negotiate the various trails through these spots. This is a lot of fun, but some hikers may find this stretch of trail frustrating. When you arrive at the trailhead at the end of your loop, you will have hiked approximately 8 miles, or 9 miles if you chose to add on the loop to Ferry Springs.

If you're interested in a longer hike, continue upriver from the basalt formations for as long as you wish. There are no big highlights (a much-loved boxcar at nearly 6 miles upriver burned in the 2018 fire, alas), but the scenery is uniformly beautiful. This is a fantastic place to spend a few days exploring, deep in the Deschutes canyon among the sagebrush and stars. For more information on hiking further into the inner canyon, see the entry for Macks Canyon in Hike 88.

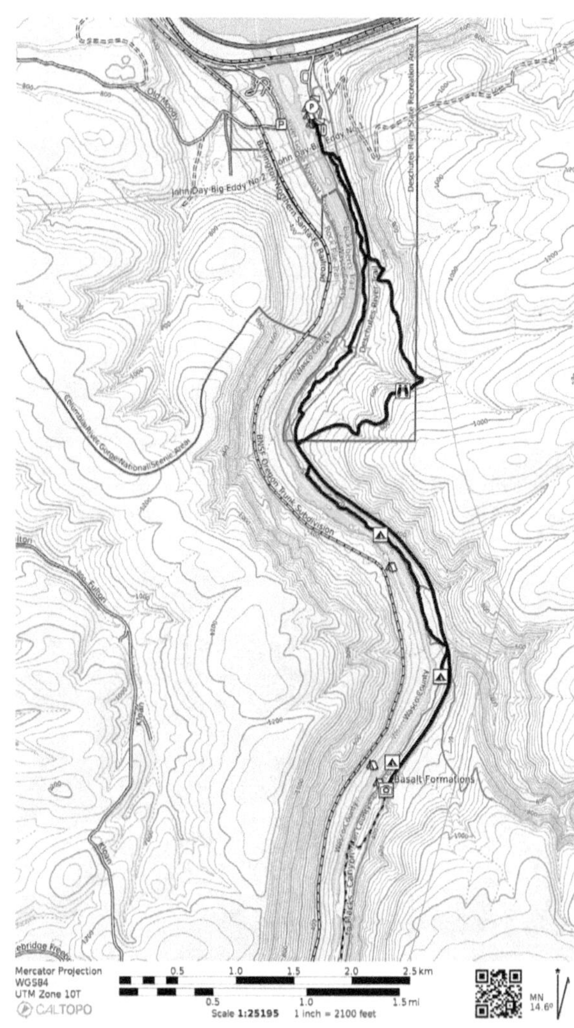

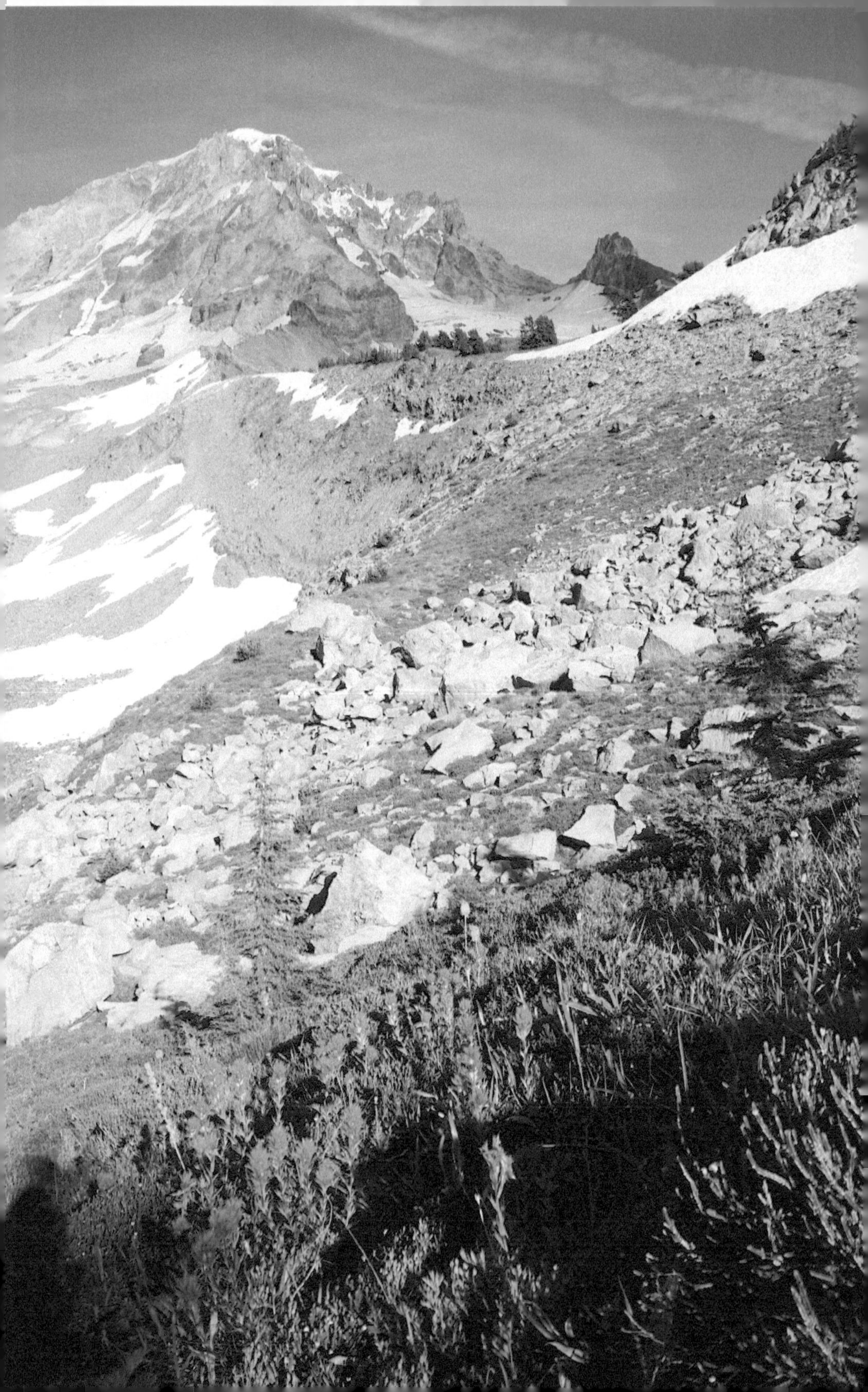

Northern Oregon Cascades

		Distance	EV Gain	Page
36.	Lost Lake	3.8 mi	100 ft	96
37.	Paradise Park	12.6 mi	2,800 ft	98
38.	Ramona Falls and Yocum Ridge	7.8 mi	1,100 ft	100
39.	Bald Mountain and McNeil Point	11 mi	2,700 ft	102
40.	Elk Cove	9 mi	1,900 ft	104
41.	Gnarl Ridge	10.8 mi	2,300 ft	106
42.	Lookout Mountain	3 mi	600 ft	108
43.	Fifteenmile Creek	11.2 mi	2,100 ft	110
44.	School Canyon	7.6 mi	1,700 ft	112
45.	Boulder Lake Loop	10.3 mi	1,700 ft	114
46.	Salmon River Trail	9.2 mi	400 ft	116
47.	Serene Lake Loop	12.3 mi	2,700 ft	118
48.	Bagby Hot Springs	3.2 mi	300 ft	120
49.	Battle Ax	5.6 mi	1,800 ft	122
50.	Olallie Lake	6.7 mi	100 ft	124

Ranging from the Columbia River Gorge to the Olallie Plateau, the Northern Oregon Cascades are where the residents of Portland and the northern Willamette Valley go to play. You'll find some of Oregon's most extraordinary scenery here, from lacy waterfalls to alpine meadows to peaceful moutain lakes. Mount Hood is the center of this area, and every single hike featured in this section is located in the Mount Hood National Forest. With so many amazing destinations to discover, I had some trouble narrowing down this list to fifteen hikes. Presented here is the best of the best, my favorite hikes in the Northern Oregon Cascades.

Forest fires have affected this area greatly in recent years, and many of my favorite places in this area burned during the Riverside and Beachie Creek Fires in 2020. The Clackamas River canyon and the Bull of the Woods Wilderness areas were particular altered by the fires, and many of the trails in these areas are either still closed or in rough shape. To the south, the Lionshead Fire in 2020 burned much of the Olallie Lake Plateau, and many of the trails in this area have yet to be reopened as of 2023. Several of the hikes in this section have been touched by fires, most notably Elk Cove (Hike 40) and Olallie Lake (Hike 50). As our climate continues to warm with every passing year, fires have become an unfortunately frequent occurance; let's hope that none touch this area for a long time to come.

Photo on left: Yocum Ridge (Hike 38) on the northwest side of Mount Hood.

36. Lost Lake

Distance: 3.8 mile loop
Elevation Gain: 100 feet
Trailhead elevation: 3,163 feet
Trail high Point: 3,195 feet
Season: May - November
Best: May - November
Pass: $11 day use fee (May - October)
On the traditional lands of: The Cowlitz, Cayuse, Walla Walla, and Umatilla Peoples

Directions:

- Beginning in Hood River, leave Interstate 84 at Exit 62.
- Just after you exit the freeway, turn right onto Mount Adams Avenue opposite a gas station. This road becomes Country Club Road.
- Drive 3.2 miles to a T-junction with Barrett Drive. Turn left.
- In just 0.2 mile, keep straight at a stop sign. Continue 1 more mile to a junction with OR 281. Turn right.
- Drive 2 miles to a junction on your right, immediately after passing the Apple Valley Country Store, signed "Dee Parkdale Next Right". Turn right here (do not continue straight uphill).
- Drive 2.2 miles on this highway, passing Tucker Park along the way, to another junction on your right, signed for Lost Lake. Veer right here.
- Drive 4 miles on this road to a junction with Lost Lake Road. Turn right.
- Cross the West Fork of the Hood River and reach a junction with Rainy Lake Road in just 0.3 mile. Keep left to continue towards Lost Lake.

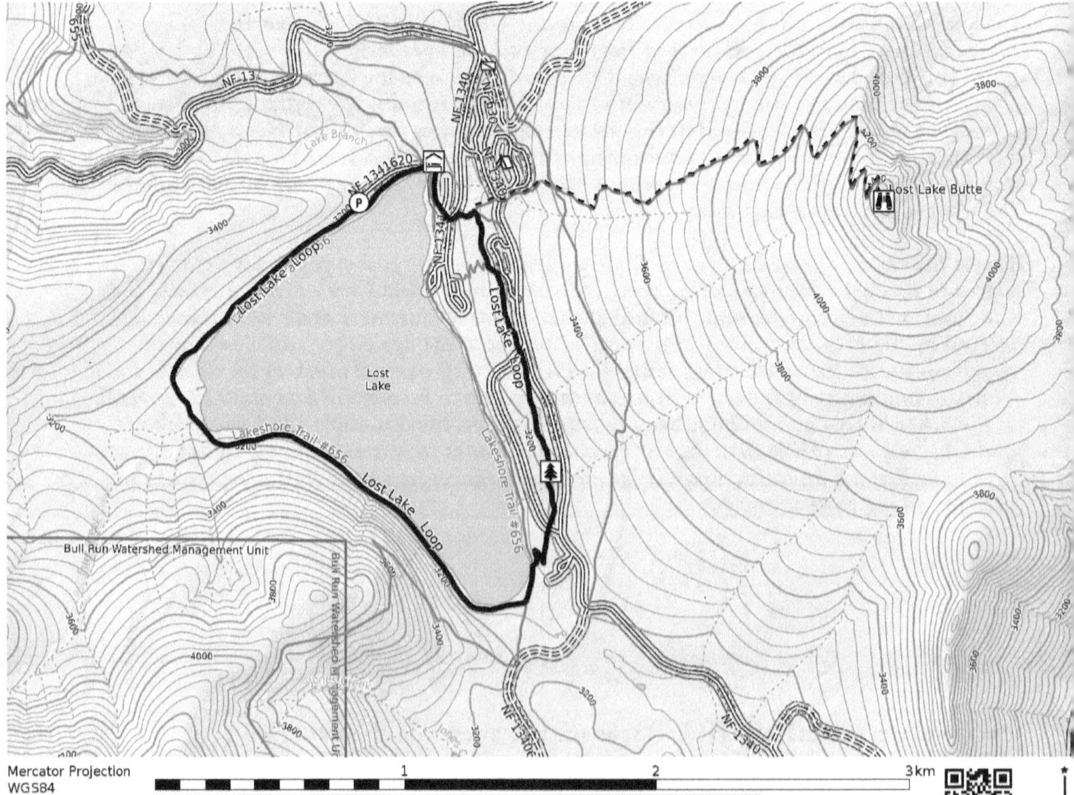

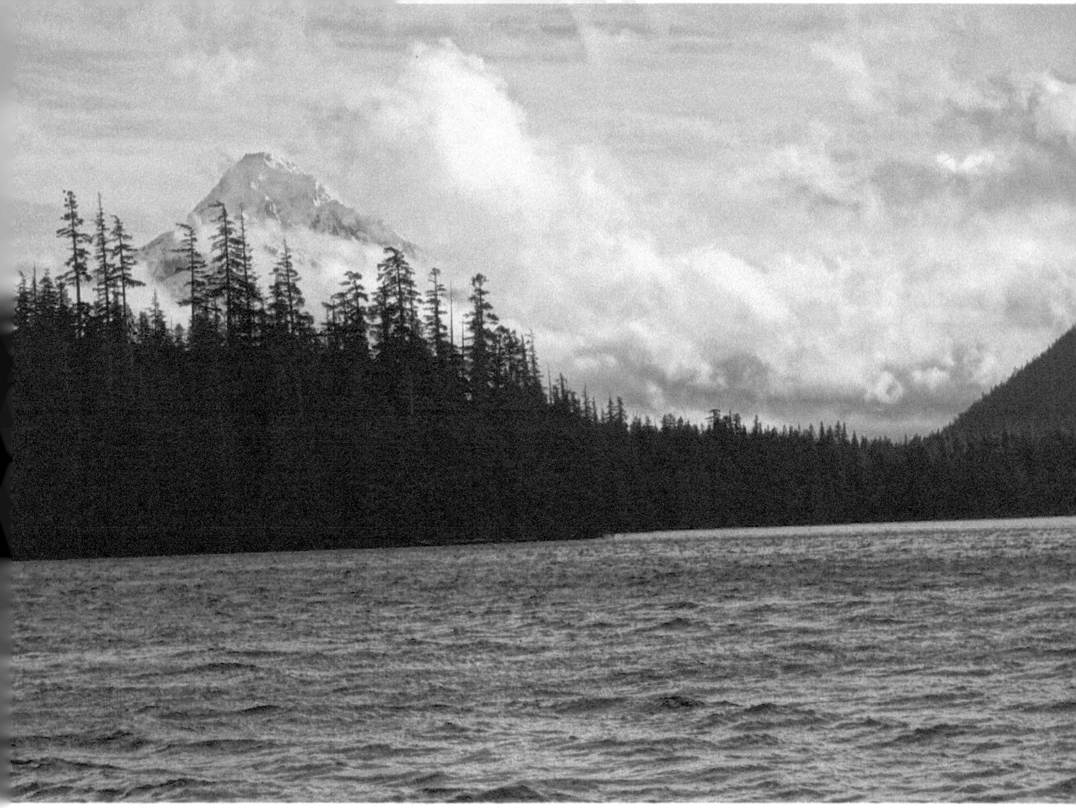

Lost Lake's iconic view of Mount Hood on a cloudy fall day.

- Drive 13.3 miles on this paved road to Lost Lake's entrance booth.
- Pay the $11 fee and drive through the resort complex to the picnic area at the lakeshore, 0.4 mile from the booth. This is the trailhead.
- **Drivetime from Hood River:** 55 minutes

Hike: Lost Lake has one of Oregon's most iconic views. The view of Mount Hood here is so good that it was featured on a quarter in 2010 – so millions of people all over the country know this view. And yet, obtaining such scenery requires little effort. Once you're at the lake however, there is a lot more to do than just take in the view. A trail circles the lake, offering an easy hike that is sure to please the whole family.

Start at the day use area on the lakeshore. Locate the trail around the lake, which follows the lakeshore as you might expect. You can hike around the lake in either direction, but consider hiking in a counterclockwise direction. The trail follows the lakeshore, passing the iconic view of Mount Hood you see in the photo above. Boardwalks help you navigate the occasional swampy spots along the trail. Eventually you'll lose the view of Mount Hood but the lake is so beautiful and the forest so lush and impressive that you'll enjoy almost every moment of this hike. At 1.8 miles, you'll reach a junction with the Huckleberry Mountain Trail, which leads uphill to the Pacific Crest Trail in 2.2 miles. Stay on the lakeshore trail for a short distance to a junction with the Old Growth Trail on the right. Either trail will take you back to the trailhead, but the Old Growth Trail passes through some of the most impressive ancient forest in this part of the Oregon Cascades. Follow the Old Growth Trail as it passes under some gargantuan Western red cedars. You'll have several opportunities to drop back down to the lakeshore, as there is a proliferation of trails along this side of Lost Lake. At 3.8 miles, you'll reach the picnic area again at the completion of the loop. Adventurous hikers can hike up to the summit of Lost Lake Butte for its equally fantastic view of Mount Hood. To locate the Lost Lake Butte Trail, look for a signed junction leaving from the campground not far from the lodge. The trail climbs 1,200 feet in 1.9 miles to the summit of Lost Lake Butte, a former lookout site.

37. Paradise Park

Distance: 12.6 miles out and back
Elevation Gain: 2,800 feet
Trailhead elevation: 5,874 feet
Trail high Point: 6,092 feet
Season: July – October
Best: mid-July – August
Pass: NW Forest Pass
On the traditional lands of: The Cascades, Cayuse, Walla Walla, and Umatilla Peoples

Directions:

- From Portland, drive US 26 east for approximately 50 miles to a junction with the Timberline Lodge Road at the eastern end of Government Camp.
- Turn left at a sign for Timberline Lodge and drive 5.5 miles uphill to the large parking lot at Timberline Lodge, the trailhead.
- **Drivetime from Portland:** 1 hour and 20 minutes

Hike: The name Paradise Park is a lofty title indeed, but when you visit these beautiful alpine meadows on the southwest side of Mount Hood, it's easy to see why it was so named. Hiking to paradise is easier said than done, however, and you may wish to spend a night or two on this side of the mountain. This is one of the most extraordinary hikes on Oregon's tallest mountain, without question. Hiking to Paradise Park also gives you the opportunity to visit another iconic destination, Timberline Lodge. The lodge was built by the Civilian Conservation Corps in the 1930s and has served as Oregon's most famous hotel ever since; it is worth taking the time after your hike to go explore the lodge, to get a beer in one of the bars, or to just sit on the patio and

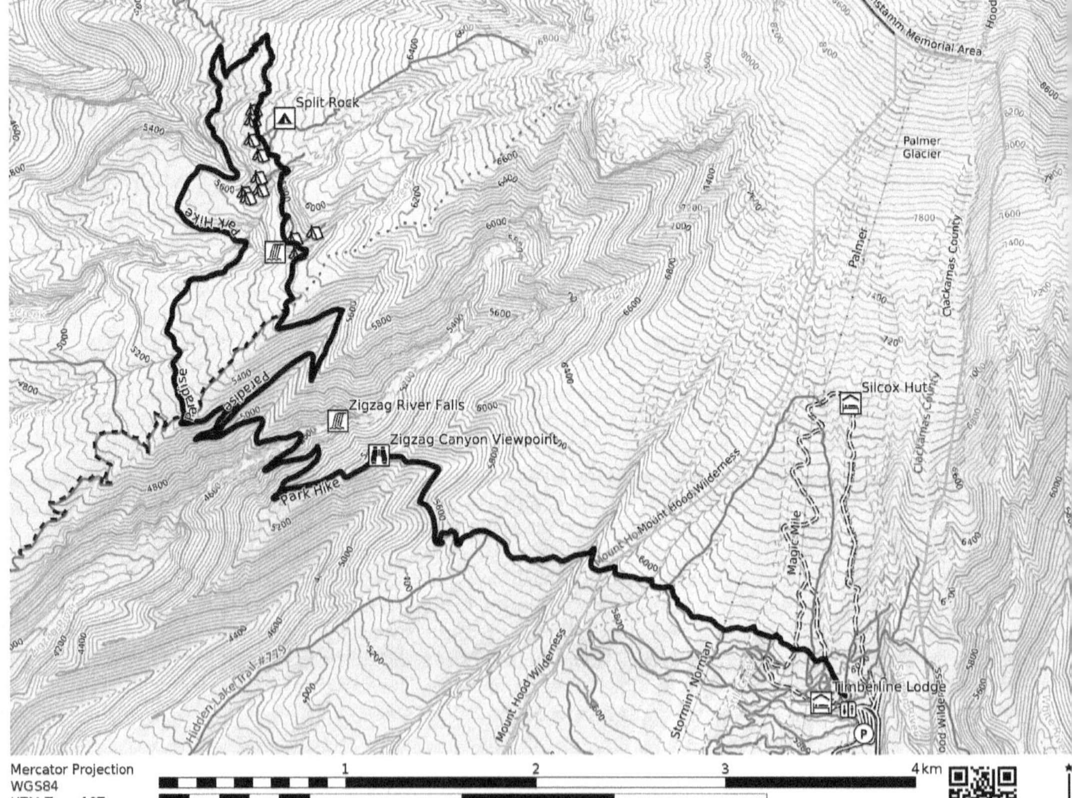

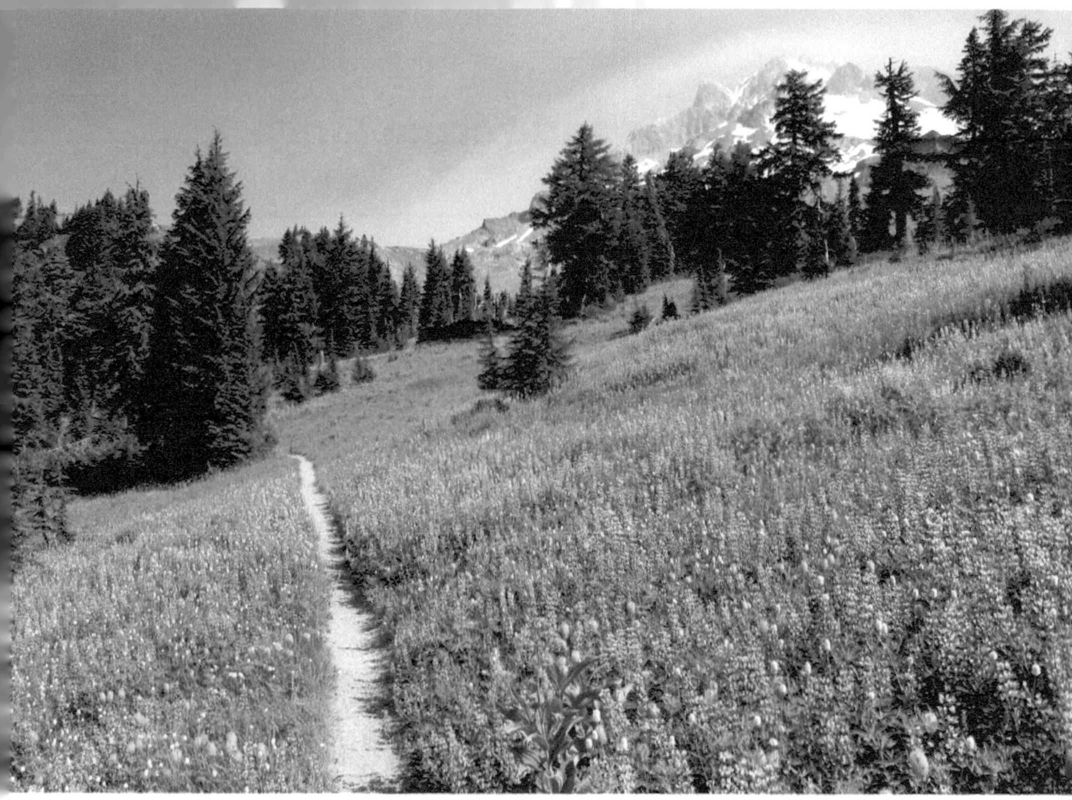

Lupine lines the trail through Paradise Park, with Mount Hood towering overhead.

marvel at the views of Mount Hood and Mount Jefferson. Plan on a full day up here, or even a full weekend.

The hike begins at Timberline Lodge. Follow the service road uphill for a brief distance until you intersect the Pacific Crest Trail (PCT). You'll follow the PCT for much of your hike. Turn left and follow the PCT as it passes under ski lifts and intersects with many different trails to and from the lodge (see the map). At every junction for the first several miles, stay on the PCT. You'll have numerous fantastic views up the slopes of Mount Hood for the entire hike, as well as far-reaching views to Mount Jefferson and even the Three Sisters on very clear days. During late July and into August, lupine grows profusely along each side of the trail, adding a fragrant bonus to an already beautiful hike. After 2.5 miles of gradual downhill, the PCT reaches an outstanding viewpoint at the head of Zigzag Canyon, where the Zigzag River pours out of the rapidly dwindling Zigzag Glacier high on the slopes of Mount Hood. Follow the PCT downhill to a ford of the Zigzag River. On hot days this crossing can be tough, but most of the time it can be done with dry feet. From here, follow the PCT uphill to a junction with the Paradise Park Loop Trail at 3.9 miles. Turn right here.

The Paradise Park Loop Trail follows a forested side canyon into the huge meadows that gave Paradise Park its name. In some years, the display of beargrass along the slopes here is a truly astonishing sight, as this lily is the dominant plant in the meadows on this side of the mountain. You'll reach a junction with the Paradise Park Trail at 5 miles (this trail is a cromulent approach to the park, but mostly stays in the forest for miles and miles and is thus much less exciting). If you're feeling tired you can follow this trail downhill for a half-mile to the PCT to complete the loop, but the best is yet to come. You'll follow the Paradise Park Loop Trail through huge wildflower meadows and fantastic campsites to Split Rock at 5.8 miles. This is the best place to stop and take it all in. From here, follow the loop trail downhill another 0.6 mile to the PCT, and turn left. You'll follow the PCT for the rest of your hike back. You'll pass under waterfalls below the Paradise Park meadows, then follow the PCT down into and back out of Zigzag Canyon. From there, hike 2.5 miles of gradual uphill back to Timberline Lodge.

38. Ramona Falls and Yocum Ridge

	Ramona Falls	Yocum Ridge
Distance:	7.8 mile semi-loop	17.4 miles out and back
Elevation Gain:	1,100 feet	3,700 feet
Trailhead Elevation:	2,468 feet	2,468 feet
Trail High Point:	3,494 feet	6,150 feet
Season:	May - November	July - September
Best:	May - October	August
Pass:	NW Forest Pass	NW Forest Pass
On the traditional lands of:	The Cascades, Cayuse, Walla Walla, and Umatilla Peoples	The Cascades, Cayuse, Walla Walla, and Umatilla Peoples

Directions:

- From Portland drive east on US 26 to Zigzag and Rhododendron.
- Just after a stop light with a sign for East Lolo Pass Road (FR 18), turn left on Lolo Pass Road and follow the Sandy River north.
- Stay on Lolo Pass Road for 4 paved miles.
- Immediately after a large sign for Mount Hood National Forest, turn right at a junction with FR 1825 that is labeled "campgrounds trailheads".
- Drive 0.6 mile of paved road to a junction with FR 1825 at a bridge.
- Turn right to stay on FR 1825. Continue on FR 1825 another 1.3 miles, staying left at every junction, until you reach a junction with FR 100.
- Turn left and drive 0.5 mile of rough pavement to the large Ramona Falls parking lot.
- Drivetime from Portland: 1 hour and 15 minutes

Hike: Tucked away at the foot of Mount Hood, Ramona Falls is one of Oregon's most recognizable waterfalls. With such fame comes crowds and notoriety; the falls is so famous that a Portland indie rock band named itself Ramona Falls. You should expect crowds any time you

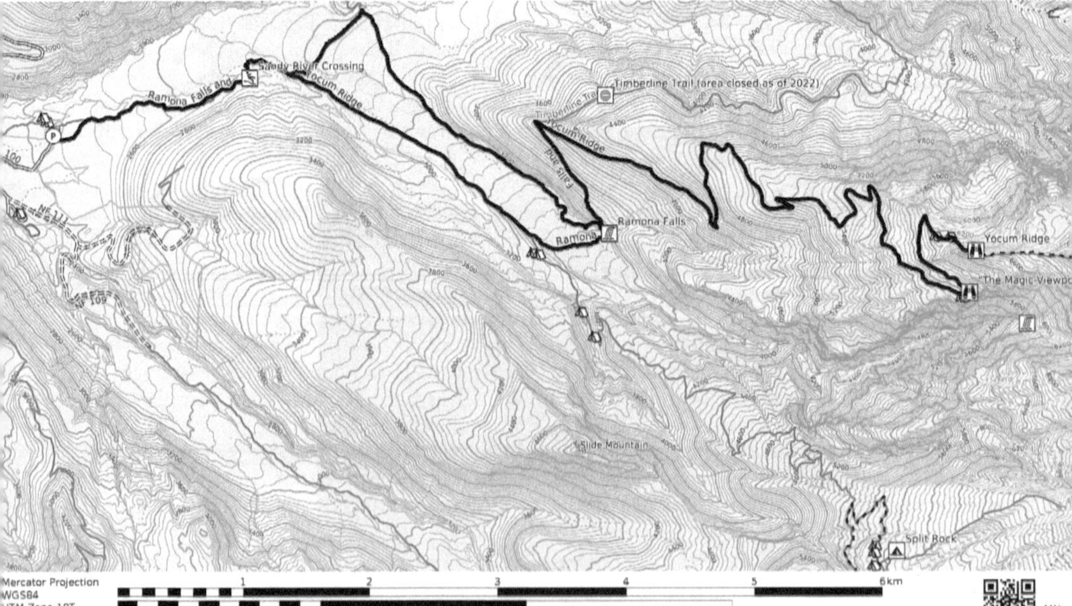

visit the falls, and yet you can still find solitude here by visiting here on weekdays, and in the offseason. No matter when you hike the falls, the way there is a delight and the falls is a scenic marvel, a rare place that never gets old. With a lot more time and energy, and when the weather is just right, you can hike many more miles to the fabled meadows and views on Yocum Ridge. Most hikers will be content to stop at Ramona Falls, however.

The trail departs from a signboard on the right side of the enormous parking area. You will follow the Sandy River for a little over a mile until the trail reaches a bridgeless crossing of the torrent. Here, Mount Hood comes into view, towering over the river's sandy canyon. Once upon a time there was a bridge across the river here (and before that, a trailhead near here that made this a shorter hike), but the river's crumbly banks, changing whims, and raging current have made a bridge here a practical impossibility. Cross the river on downed logs or rocks as best you can. If the crossing is unnerving, or if it's been raining a lot recently, there's no shame in turning around here. Once across the river, locate the trail as it crosses the Sandy's flood plain, and continue on the north bank another quarter mile to a junction with the Pacific Crest Trail. The most direct access to the falls is straight ahead on the PCT, but this is also the less interesting approach. Instead turn left here and hike a half-mile northwest to a junction with the Ramona Falls Trail on your right. Turn right here, and soon you will be following the charming banks of Ramona Creek. Here the creek meanders through a luxurious carpet of moss, tumbling over decaying logs and miniature waterfalls in a most photogenic manner. The ramparts of the lowest end of Yocum Ridge tower over the trail. Eventually the trail leaves Ramona Creek, but then you're almost at the falls. At about 3.5 miles, you will arrive at lacy Ramona Falls and a junction with the Timberline Trail. There's lots of room to spread out here, and you'll need it; this is routinely one of the busiest places on Mount Hood.

When you're ready to move on, you are faced with choices. If you're up for the challenge of Yocum Ridge, turn left at the falls and climb 0.7 mile to a junction with the Yocum Ridge Trail. From there it's 4 miles of gradual uphill, most of it uneventful, until the trail breaks out into glorious meadows with a stupendous view of Mount Hood. At 7.6 miles from the Ramona Falls Trailhead, you will arrive at one of Oregon's greatest viewpoints. Here the Sandy River flows directly out of the Reid Glacier high on the northwest face of Mount Hood, tumbling over waterfall after waterfall, in a rugged gorge below you. This is an awe-inspiring place, and this is where you should turn around if you're day hiking. Hikers with even more energy can follow the Yocum Ridge Trail further uphill for 0.8 mile to the top of the ridge, where the trail becomes rough and the terrain even rougher. If you're backpacking, there are campsites tucked into every nook and cranny of this dramatic spot. Sunsets up here are glorious, and you can watch the lights come on over the Portland metro area. When you decide to return, you'll have to hike nearly 5 miles downhill just to make it back to Ramona Falls – so if you're only here for the day, don't linger too long.

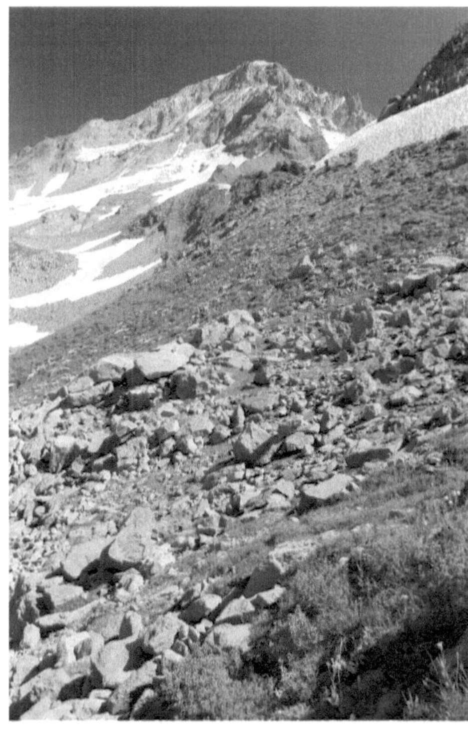

If the thought of Yocum Ridge is too daunting, then simply turn right at Ramona Falls and follow the Timberline Trail to a junction with the Pacific Crest Trail. Here you'll turn right and hike through open woods to the conclusion of your loop. Turn left here, cross the Sandy again, and hike a little over a mile to the trailhead.

39. Bald Mountain and McNeil Point

	Bald Mountain	McNeil Point
Distance:	1.8 miles out and back	11 miles out and back
Elevation Gain:	664 feet	2,700 feet
Trailhead Elevation:	3,921 feet	3,921 feet
Trail High Point:	4,585 feet	6,181 feet
Season:	June – October	July – October
Best:	June – July	July – October
Pass:	NW Forest Pass	NW Forest Pass
On the traditional lands of:	The Cascades, Cayuse, Walla Walla, and Umatilla Peoples	The Cascades, Cayuse, Walla Walla, and Umatilla Peoples

Directions:

- From Portland, drive east on US 26 for approximately 40 miles to the junction of US 26 and Lolo Pass Road on your left.
- Turn left and drive Lolo Pass Road 4.2 miles to a junction on your right with FR 1825.
- Turn right and drive 0.6 mile to a junction at a bridge. Keep straight (do not cross the bridge) on what is now FR 1828.
- Follow this paved road for 5.5 miles of rough pavement to a junction with FR 118 on your right. Turn right here.
- Drive 1.6 gravel miles to the overcrowded Top Spur Trailhead. Parking is limited despite the trailhead's popularity; come early if you want a good parking spot.
- **Drivetime from Portland:** 1 hour and 20 minutes

Hike: Of the many places named Bald Mountain in Oregon, this Bald Mountain on the northwest side of Mount Hood must certainly be the most beautiful. From afar this Bald Mountain looks like a diminutive bump on the ridge, but from the mountain's open slopes Mount Hood fills the sky above in one of northwest Oregon's most extraordinary views. If you're looking for an adventure fit for a longer day or a full weekend, you can follow the Timberline Trail towards

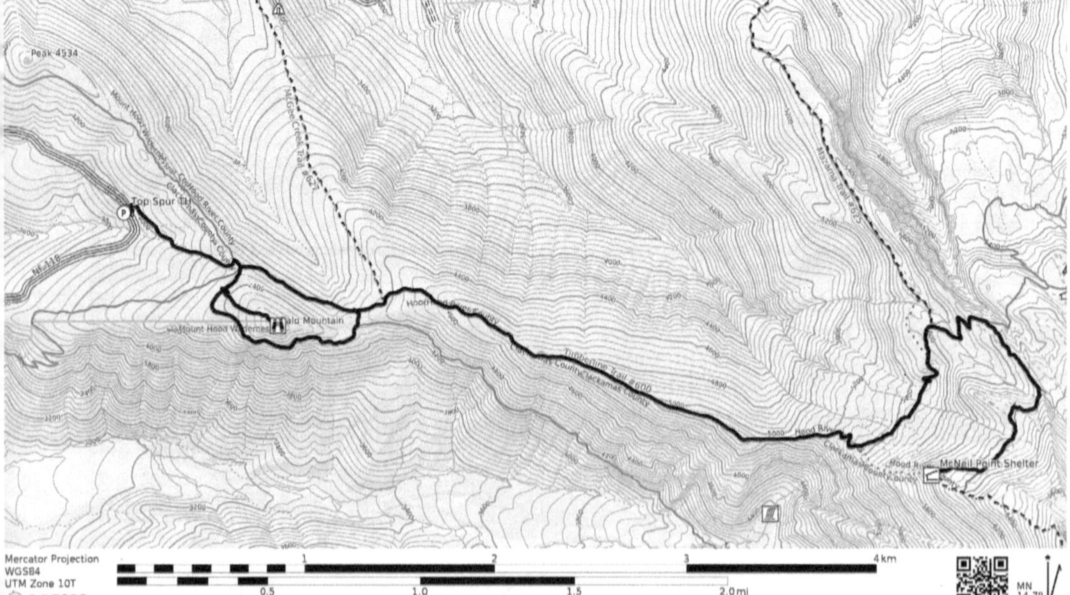

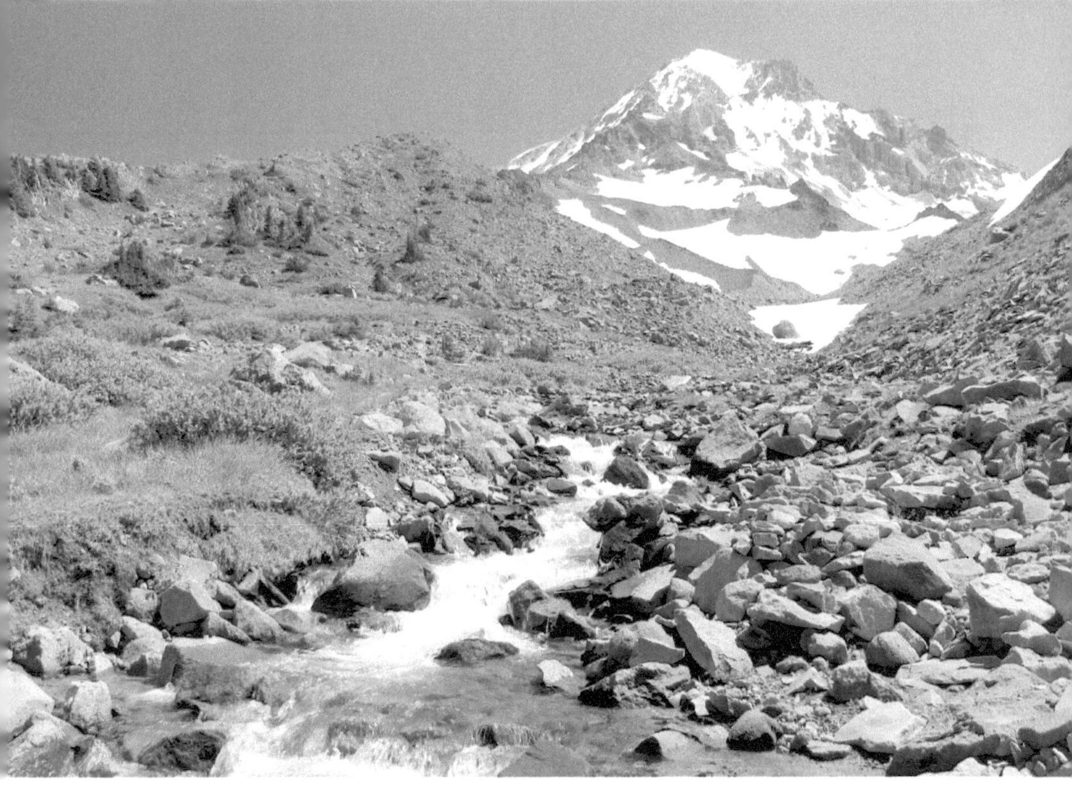

McGee Creek flows out of the Ladd Glacier just below McNeil Point on Mount Hood.

McNeil Point's stone shelter, another iconic spot on this side of Mount Hood. Just make sure you get to the trailhead early in day – the Top Spur Trailhead is among the most popular on this side of the mountain, and there isn't much room to park anywhere else.

From the trailhead, follow the Top Spur Trail gradually uphill through deep forest for 0.5 mile to a junction with the Pacific Crest Trail. Delicate white avalanche lilies grow in abundance along the trail in late June and early July. when you reach the PCT, turn right and just 300 feet later, arrive at a confusing junction with the Timberline Trail. Continue straight on the Timberline Trail and follow it for 400 feet to an unsigned but obvious junction on the left. Turn left and follow this spur trail steeply uphill for 0.3 mile to the summit of Bald Mountain. All that remains of the lookout tower that once stood here are the concrete foundations. While the summit is forested, continue another 100 feet on the trail to a magnificent view of Mount Hood at the edge of Bald Mountain's steep cliffs. The Timberline Trail is only a few hundred feet below you but the steep slopes make a shortcut impossible. When you're ready, return to the Timberline Trail. If you're ready to be done, turn right and return the way you came. For McNeil Point, turn left.

Beyond the Bald Mountain junction, the trail emerges from the woods at a splendid view of Mount Hood along the hanging meadows below Bald Mountain's summit. Continue along the hillside to a junction with a connector trail on your left at 1.3 miles from the trailhead (not counting the side trip to Bald Mountain's summit). Turn left and hike a short distance over a ridge to another junction with the Timberline Trail, where you turn right. You'll continue uphill along this forested ridge, passing a junction with the McGee Creek Trail at 1.6 miles and hiking into forest decimated by the 2020 windstorm that fueled the Labor Day fires further south in the state. Follow the Timberline Trail past a couple of ponds to a junction with the Mazama Trail at 4.2 miles. Continue another 0.3 mile to a junction with the McNeil Point Trail on your right. This spur trail follows McGee Creek uphill and then bends back to the south through meadows of heather and wildflowers. You'll reach McNeil Point's stone shelter at 5.5 miles, where the view of Mount Hood is astounding. You can continue uphill along the rocky ridge above McNeil Point, but whenever you're ready, return the way you came.

40. Elk Cove

Distance: 9 miles out and back
Elevation Gain: 1,900 feet
Trailhead elevation: 4,501 feet
Trail high Point: 5,835 feet
Season: July – October
Best: July – October
Pass: none needed
On the traditional lands of: The Warm Springs, Cayuse, Walla Walla, and Umatilla Peoples

Directions from Hood River:

- Beginning in Hood River, leave Interstate 84 at Exit 62.
- Just after you exit the freeway, turn right onto Mount Adams Avenue opposite a gas station. This road becomes Country Club Road.
- Drive 3.2 miles to a T-junction with Barrett Drive. Turn left.
- In just 0.2 mile, keep straight at a stop sign. Continue 1 more mile to a junction with OR 281. Turn right.
- Drive 2 miles to a junction on your right, immediately after passing the Apple Valley Country Store, signed "Dee Parkdale Next Right". Turn right here (do not continue straight uphill).
- Drive 2.2 miles on this highway, passing Tucker Park along the way, to another junction on your right, signed for Lost Lake. Veer right here.
- Drive 4 miles on this road to a junction with Lost Lake Road. Turn right.
- Cross the West Fork of the Hood River and reach a junction with Rainy Lake Road in just 0.3 mile. Keep left to continue towards Lost Lake.
- Drive 8 miles to a fork in the road. Right leads to Lost Lake, but you want to turn left onto the Lolo Pass Road.

Mount Hood and Barrett Spur loom over Wy'east Basin near Elk Cove.

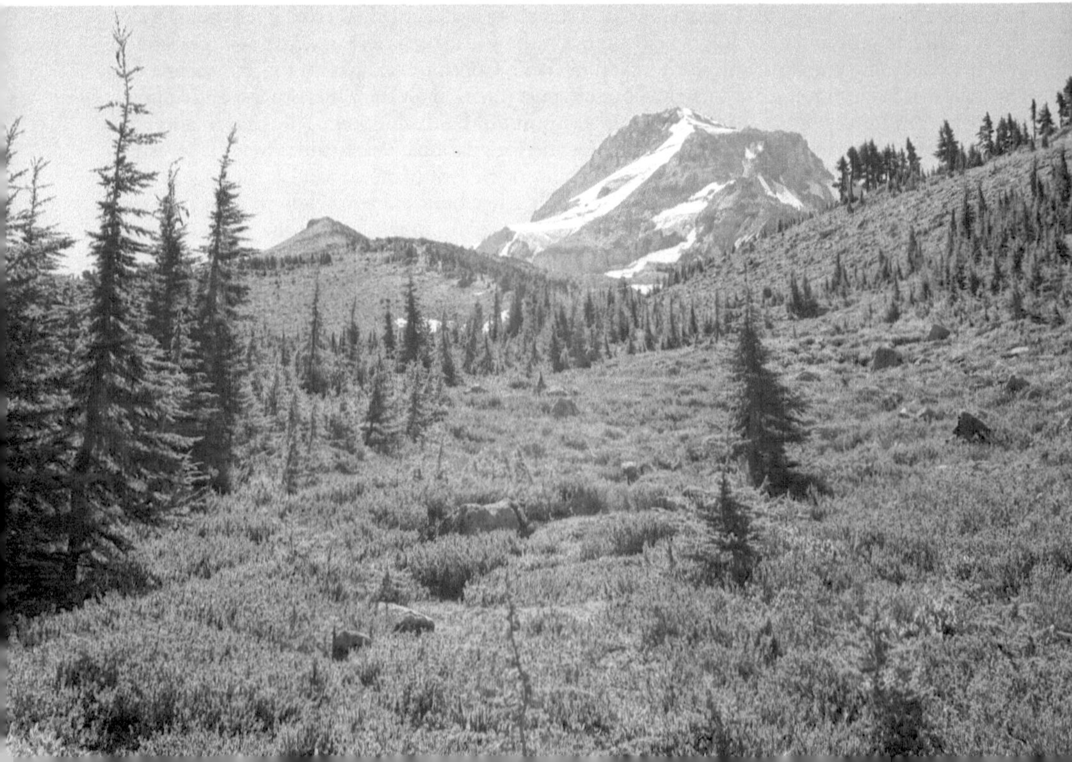

- Drive the Lolo Pass Road for 3 miles to a junction with FR 16. Turn left onto FR 16.
- Follow FR 16 for 5.4 miles to a very sharp turn right at a junction with FR 1650.
- Turn a sharp right onto FR 1650 and drive 2.9 miles of rocky gravel road to a fork.
- Keep left and drive 0.9 mile to road's end at the Vista Ridge TH. Parking is limited and you may need to park several hundred yards before the trailhead on busy summer weekends.
- **Drivetime from Hood River:** 1 hour

Hike: Some places just make you happy. There's something to be said for arriving at a place that gives you joy for no other reason other than it's beautiful and it's there. Elk Cove is one of these places. There are more spectacular spots on Mount Hood along the Timberline Trail and yet, hikers routinely cite Elk Cove as one of their favorite places on the mountain. Everything here seems in balance – the mountain towers over Elk Cove's wildflower meadows, while craggy Barrett Spur seems to keep watch over the area like a bodyguard. The Dollar Lake Fire in 2011 narrowly avoided Elk Cove, and everything here looks as it has always looked for as long as people have been visiting this place. While the constant crowds can occasionally bum me out elsewhere on the mountain, I never tire of visiting Elk Cove.

Beginning at the Vista Ridge Trailhead, you'll follow the wide and dusty Vista Ridge Trail for 0.4 mile to a junction at the edge of the Mount Hood Wilderness. Left follows the Old Vista Ridge Trail to a spectacular viewpoint at Owl Point, but for Elk Cove you'll need to turn right. The Vista Ridge Trail soon enters forest that is recovering from the Dollar Lake Fire. Huckleberries line the trail, offering countless tasty treats in August and September. You'll follow the Vista Ridge Trail uphill through the burn to a junction with the Eden Park Trail at 2.6 miles. Turning right here leads to Eden Park and eventually Cairn Basin, you should keep straight to continue toward Elk Cove. You'll leave the burn behind and reach a junction with the Timberline Trail at 2.9 mile. Turn left here.

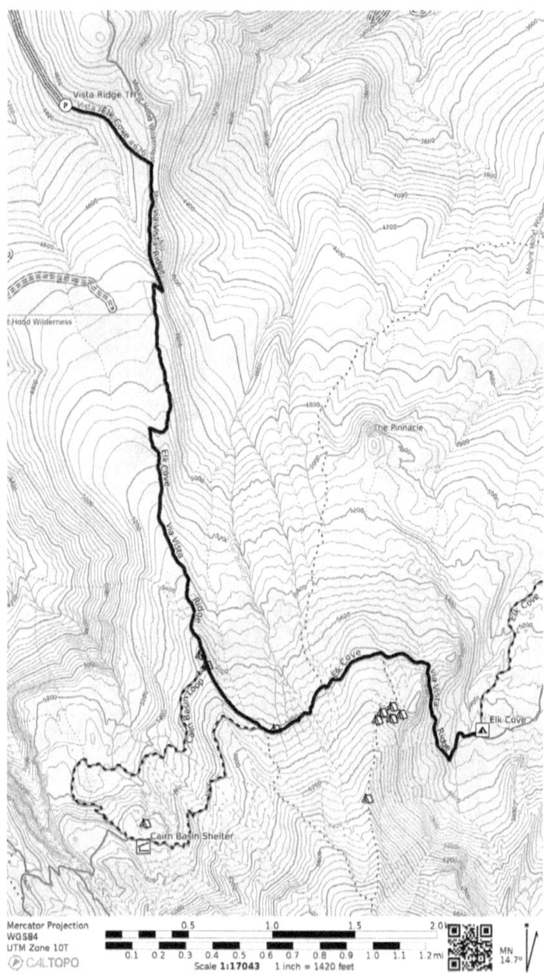

Once you reach the Timberline Trail, the scenery is gorgeous. You'll dip in and out of gullies lined with summer wildflowers and even patches of snow for much of the summer. You'll pass a junction with the seldom-traveled Pinnacle Ridge Trail at 3.3 miles and continue following the Timberline Trail gradually uphill to a ridge end at 3.8 miles. The trail then follows the rocky slopes of Barrett Spur downhill to Elk Cove at 4.4 miles. Here you can explore to your hearts content! You'll need to continue another 0.1 mile to a junction with the Elk Cove Trail at 4.5 miles to find the camping area here. This trail is another way to hike to Elk Cove, but it is longer, steeper, and more exposed. Whenever you're ready, return the way you came.

41. Gnarl Ridge

Distance: 10.8 miles out and back, with loop
Elevation Gain: 2,300 feet
Trailhead elevation: 4,452 feet
Trail high point: 6,550 feet
Season: July - October
Best: July - October
Pass: NW Forest Pass
On the traditional lands of: The Warm Springs, Cayuse, Walla Walla, and Umatilla Peoples

Directions:

- From Portland, drive US 26 to Government Camp and then continue to the junction with OR 35.
- Turn right onto OR 35 and drive north on this highway around Mount Hood for 7.7 miles to a signed junction for the Elk Meadows TH, on your left.
- Turn left and drive 0.3 mile to the trailhead.
- If you are coming from Hood River, drive south on OR 35 for 31 miles to a turnoff on your right for the Elk Meadows Trailhead. Turn right here and drive 0.3 mile to the trailhead on the right side of the road.
- **Drivetimes:** 80 minutes from Portland, 40 minutes from Hood River.

Hike: In an area with no shortage of extraordinary views of Mount Hood, the view from Gnarl Ridge might just be the best. Here the east face of the mountain spreads out before you, from the sharp summit pinnacle and down across the massive Newton Glacier. This is no walk in the park, however; to get there, you'll have to deal with at least one potentially difficult creek crossing and climb up and up onto the mountain's flanks. Despite these difficulties, you'll want to do this hike again and again. I have!

The Timberline Trail and Mount Hood along Gnarl Ridge.

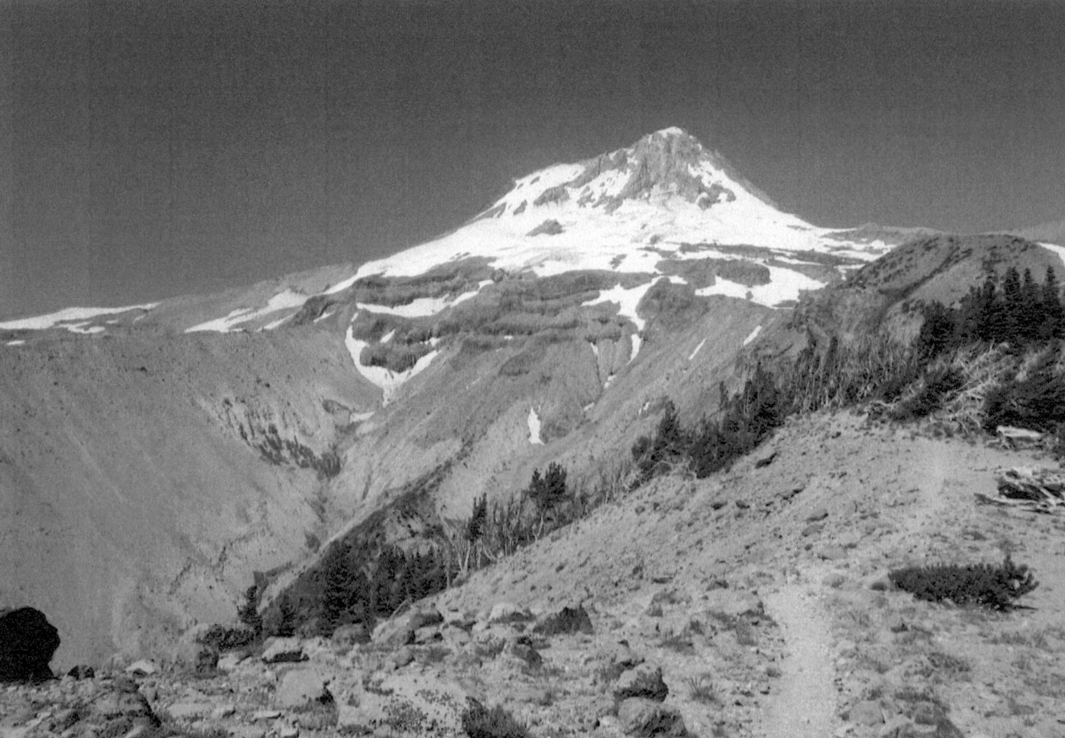

The trail begins at the Elk Meadows Trailhead. Follow this trail northeast through a dusty forest whose understory seems to consist entirely of huckleberries. In August and September, your progress will be slowed as you graze on this most delicious of mountain fruits. Along the way, you will pass several trail junctions; stay on the Elk Meadows Trail. You will cross Clark Creek on a wooden bridge at 0.8 mile; continue another 0.4 mile to a bridgeless, somewhat irritating crossing of Newton Creek at 1.2 miles. There is usually a log over the creek, but don't count on this; you might need to ford the creek. Once across, locate the Elk Meadows Trail heading into the woods away from the creek.

From here, the trail climbs about 650 feet in 0.9 mile via a series of switchbacks. Not long after the trail levels out, reach a four-way trail junction at 2.1 miles from the trailhead. Right leads up to Elk Mountain, while straight leads into Elk Meadows, a popular backpacking destination with a rustic shelter and a fantastic view of Mount Hood. You can visit the meadows too, but doing so adds 1.5 miles to your hike; instead, you should turn left here on the Gnarl Ridge Trail. The Gnarl Ridge Trail climbs gently for 1.1 miles to a junction with the Timberline Trail at 3.2 miles. Turning left here will take you down to a tough crossing of Newton Creek; save this for the return hike, or don't do it at all. To continue hiking up Gnarl Ridge, continue straight on what is now the Timberline Trail. You will climb through the woods another 1.8 miles, passing increasingly spectacular wildflower meadows on the north side of Lamberson Butte. At 5 miles, the trail rounds a corner and breaks out of the woods, and here before you is the view of Mount Hood for which you worked so hard. The mountain fills the sky, and lupine lines the trail at your feet. Gnarled trees guard the ridgetop, offering a million and one photo compositions.

You can continue along the Timberline Trail as far as you like but the view does not get better than this. So return to the junction with the Gnarl Ridge Trail, 1.8 miles back down the trail. If you're up for a short loop to spice things up, turn right here and follow the Timberline Trail for 0.8 mile to a crossing of Newton Creek. This is known as one of the most difficult creek crossings on the Timberline Trail, so be careful and choose your route well. Some years there is a log across the creek, so you may get lucky. Once across the creek, switchback uphill past a campsite to a junction with the Newton Creek Trail at 7.8 miles. The Timberline Trail continues into Heather Canyon (a worthy destination in its own right), but you should turn left here. Follow the Newton Creek Trail downhill for 1.9 miles until you reach the Elk Meadows Trail, then turn right and hike 1.1 miles to the trailhead.

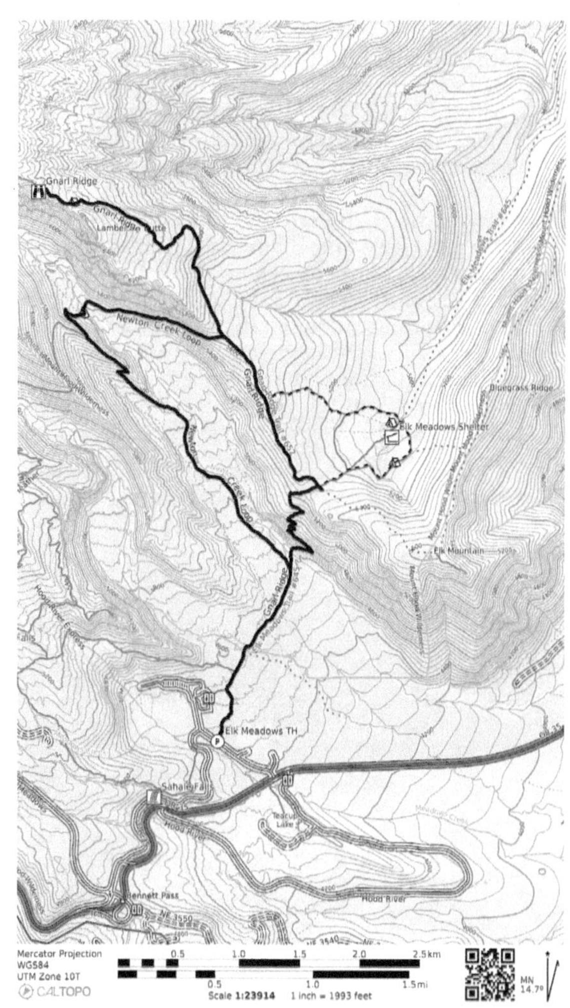

42. Lookout Mountain

	High Prairie Loop	Lookout Mtn via OR 35
Distance:	3 mile loop	11.2 mile semi-loop
Elevation Gain:	600 feet	3,000 feet
Trailhead Elevation:	5.954 feet	3,551 feet
Trail High Point:	6.529 feet	6.529 feet
Season:	July - October	July - October
Best:	July - October	July - October
Pass:	NW Forest Pass	none needed
On the traditional lands of:	the Grand Ronde, Siletz, and Warm Springs peoples	the Grand Ronde, Siletz, and Warm Springs peoples

Directions to the Gumjuwac Trailhead :

- From Portland, drive US 26 east to a junction with OR 35 just east of Mount Hood.
- Turn right onto OR 35 and drive north for 10.7 miles to the Gumjuwac Trailhead on the right side of the road, just after the highway crosses the East Fork of the Hood River. There is parking on the left side of the road. If you're coming from Hood River, drive south on OR 35 for 27.8 miles to the trailhead.
- **Drivetimes:** 80 minutes from Portland, 35 minutes from Hood River.

Directions to the High Prairie Trailhead:

- If you're opting for the shorter hike which starts at High Prairie, continue another 0.8 mile north on OR 35 to a junction with FR 44 (Dufur Mill Road), just after Little John Sno-Park. This junction is 27 miles south of Hood River.
- Turn right and continue on FR 44 for exactly 3.8 miles to a poorly-marked junction with FR 4410. Turn right here. Drive this washboarded and dusty gravel road uphill 4.5 miles to its end at a junction with the Bennett Pass Road.
- Turn left and drive 100 yards to the trailhead on the left side of the road.
- **Drivetimes:** 110 minutes from Portland, 65 minutes from Hood River.

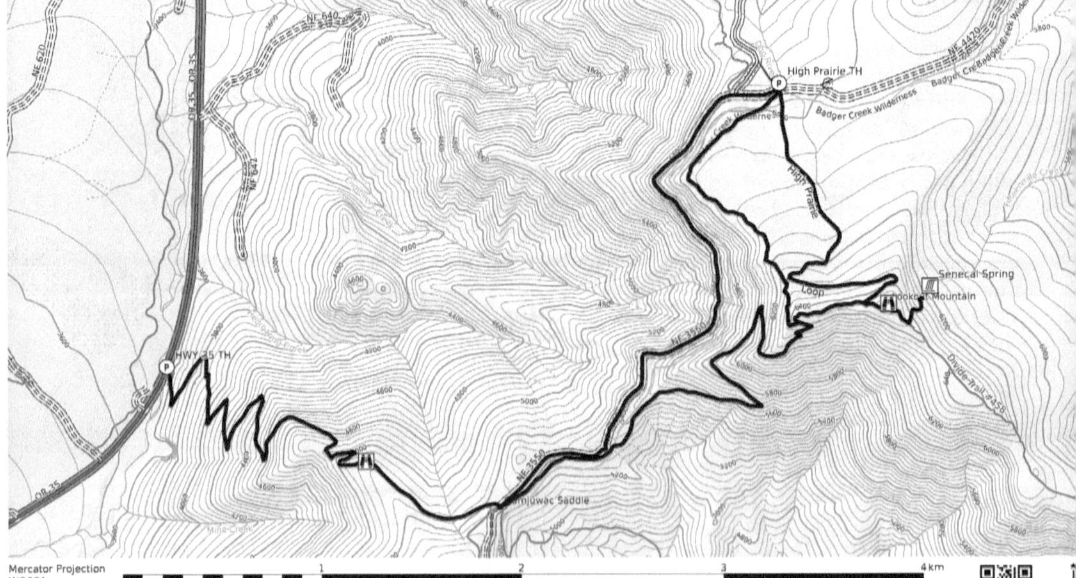

Hike: Located just east of Mount Hood, the Badger Creek Wilderness seems to be mostly forgotten by Oregon hikers. Lookout Mountain is the exception to this rule, due to its extraordinary front-row view of Mount Hood's eastern face. There are several different routes to the summit; presented here is a short loop that everyone can enjoy and a long approach with easy road access. For the best experience, come here often and explore to your heart's desire!

For the short loop, start at the High Prairie Trailhead. Immediately after leaving the trailhead, you'll arrive at a trail junction and the start of your loop. You'll hike gradually up the northern slopes of Lookout Mountain, passing a spectacular view west to Mount Hood at a rock pinnacle along the way. At 1 mile from the trailhead, reach a junction with the Divide Trail. Turn left here and continue 0.2 miles along a scenic ridge to a junction with the old road that forms the rest of your loop. Continue another 0.2 mile to the summit of Lookout Mountain, where the view is truly extraordinary! In addition to the view of Mount Hood, you'll be able to look north to Mounts Adams, Rainier, and Saint Helens, and south all the way to the Three Sisters. Behind you to the east stretches the brown hills and canyons of Central Oregon. Hikers sometimes camp on the summit to watch the sun set and then rise over the Cascades. If you're backpacking, Senecal Spring is just downhill from the summit on the Divide Trail; continue 500 feet east on the Divide Trail, and look for a small trail heading downhill to the left. At the bottom of this side trail is Senecal Spring, the source of Fifteenmile Creek (Hike 43). Even if you've opted for the longer hike described below, this is a neat spot to stop! When you can at last pull yourself away from the summit, you could very easily just return the way you came. To make a loop, however, return to the junction 0.2 west of the summit described above, and turn right on this old road to descend 1.4 gradual miles through the woods to return to the High Prairie Trailhead.

If you're up for a longer hike, consider starting at the Gumjuwac Trailhead along Oregon 35. The Gumjuwac Trail climbs 1,700 feet in 2.6 miles to Gumjuwac Saddle, where the trail meets the Bennett Pass Road. An old wooden sign explains the origins of the name Gumjuwac: "Years ago a French-Canadian sheep herder whose name was Jack and who always wore gum shoes camped here". You could drive here, of course, but this road is notoriously rocky, narrow, and occasionally frightening. What is an awful drive can make for a fun walk; instead of continuing on the mostly viewless Divide Trail, turn left to follow the Bennett Pass Road. The road passes some fantastic summer wildflowers and several excellent views west to Mount Hood. You will likely meet a few brave souls driving the road; feel free to admire and pity them at the same time. After 2 miles, the road turns a corner and meets FR 4410 near the High Prairie Trailhead. Keep right and almost immediately reach the trailhead. From here, follow the directions above to the summit of Lookout Mountain.

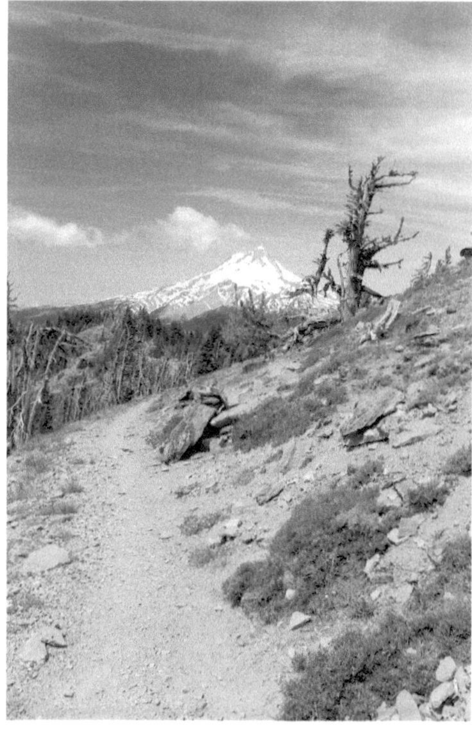

On the way down, follow the Divide Trail back towards High Prairie for 0.4 mile until you reach a junction. The High Prairie Trail continues north towards the trailhead you already passed; instead, turn left to continue hiking downhill on the Divide Trail towards Gumjuwac Saddle. Blowdown can be a problem on this trail, but your efforts are compensated with excellent displays of summer wildflowers. Follow this trail for 2 miles downhill to Gumjuwac Saddle. From there, locate the Gumjuwac Trail and turn right. You'll hike downhill for 2.6 miles to the trailhead along OR 35.

43. Fifteenmile Creek

Distance: 11.2 mile loop
Elevation Gain: 2,000 feet
Trailhead elevation: 4,627 feet
Trail high point: 4,627 feet
Season: June - October
Best: June - July
Pass: none needed
On the traditional lands of: the Wasco, Wishram, and Warm Springs peoples

Directions:

- From Portland drive US 26 east to a junction with OR 35 on the side of Mt. Hood
- Turn onto OR 35 and continue for 13.5 miles to a junction with FR 44 (Dufur Mill Rd.) between mileposts 70 and 71. If you're coming from Hood River, this junction is on the left, 27 miles south on OR 35.
- Turn right and continue on FR 44 for 5.2 miles.
- At a junction, turn right and continue on FR 44 for 3.1 miles.
- Turn right on unsigned but paved FR 4420 and continue for 2.2 miles to a junction.
- Drive straight, now on paved FR 2730 for 2.1 miles to the small but charming Fifteenmile Campground. The trail departs from a sign on the left side of the campground, near the outhouse. The campground is a nice base camp for adventures in the area.
- **Drivetimes:** 110 minutes from Portland, 65 minutes from Hood River.

Hike: Hiking is about the experience as much as it is the destination. Not every hike has to lead to a stunning viewpoint or a crashing waterfall; sometimes a scenic meadow, or a stand of tall trees, or a rock pinnacle can be just as awe-inspiring. This long loop down into and then back out of Fifteenmile Creek's canyon east of Mount Hood does not have any views of the great volcano, but it does have so much else: secret meadows, impressive ponderosa pines, mysterious and intriguing rock hoodoos, and enough variety to keep you wondering what's around the next turn. This is one of my absolute favorite hikes anywhere, especially in June and July when the flower show along the hike is one of the best in the Mount Hood National Forest. Rather than a lack of views, the major detriment of this hike is that you start at the top; thus, you need to hike downhill, then return uphill. Consider it a fair tradeoff for this hike's many virtues.

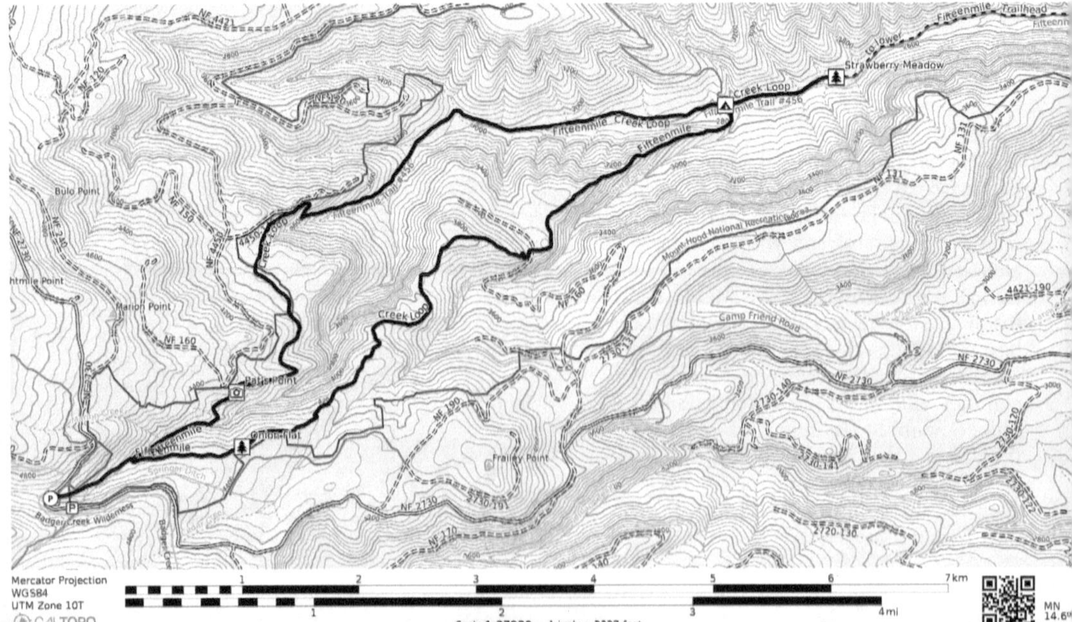

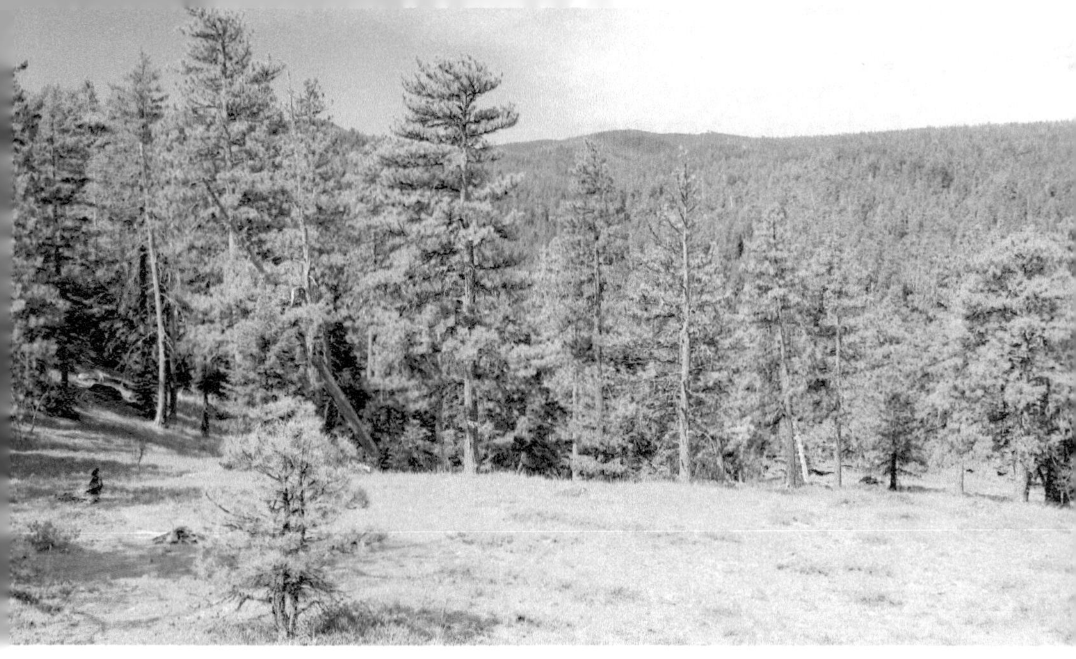

The Fifteenmile Creek Trail, with Lookout Mountain (Hike 42) on the horizon.

The trail begins by the outhouse and continues slightly downhill through open woods. At a half-mile from the trailhead, you arrive at a junction with the Cedar Creek Trail at the start of the loop. Turn right here and quickly drop down to a bridge over rushing Fifteenmile Creek. The Cedar Creek Trail never approaches Cedar Creek, instead opting to climb back to the rim of Fifteenmile Creek's canyon. You'll have glimpses across the canyon here; see if you can spot the trail on the other side! The trail passes through Onion Flat's stand of ancient ponderosa pines and continues a gradual descent among scenic rock hoodoos and early summer wildflowers. In June and July, look out for balsamroot, lupine, paintbrush, Oregon sunshine, and even the small pink blooms of bitterroot. At 3.5 miles from the trailhead, you will cross an old road, now long decommissioned. From here, the trail begins to drop more steeply as it follows a narrow ridge between Cedar and Fifteenmile Creeks. At 5 miles, the trail levels out suddenly in dark forest and crosses Fifteenmile Creek on a bridge. Just across the bridge is a four-way trail junction. To continue your loop you'll need to turn left on the Fifteenmile Creek Trail; the unsigned but scenic Underhill Trail heads uphill here, straight ahead; but for the time being, turn right on the Fifteenmile Trail. Just 0.3 mile downstream is lovely Strawberry Meadow, flanked by massive ponderosa pines. Plan on a long stop here to take in the scene. The trail continues beyond here but does not get any more interesting. If you are continuing, it's 3 miles downstream to the remote and almost inaccessible lower Fifteenmile Trailhead, in the hot and dry hills west of Dufur.

When you're ready to continue your loop, return to the four-way junction and continue straight on the Fifteenmile Trail. This trail is primarily used and maintained by local mountain bikers, so expect to step out of the way for our friends on two wheels. This stretch of the trail starts out gradual as you follow the creek, passing a few massive cottonwood trees on the way. After 1.5 miles, the trail begins to climb more significantly as you leave Fifteenmile Creek. You'll pass more rock formations, flowers, and ponderosa pines on the way up, as well as a rarely-traveled gravel road. At 3.2 miles from the four-way junction, the trail meets an old road. Turn left here to continue, and soon you'll be back on the open slopes of the canyon wall. Reach Pat's Point at 3.9 miles from the four-way junction, and at 9.5 miles into your hike. Sedums grow profusely here year-round, with flowers in June and July. As with earlier in the hike, see if you can spot the Cedar Creek Trail on the slopes across the canyon. From Pat's Point, continue 1.1 miles into the woods to the junction with the Cedar Creek Trail, where you'll keep straight. From here, it's 0.5 mile back to the Fifteenmile Creek Trailhead.

44. School Canyon

Distance: 7.6 miles out and back
Elevation Gain: 1,700 feet
Trailhead elevation: 2,687 feet
Trail high point: 4,043 feet
Season: April – November
Best: May – June
Pass: none needed
On the traditional lands of: the Tenino, Warm Springs, and Siletz peoples

Directions:

- From The Dalles, drive US 197 south 27 miles to a junction with Shadybrook Road, just north of Tygh Valley.
- Turn right on Shadybrook Road and drive 1.1 miles to a junction with Fairgrounds Road. Turn left here.
- After just 0.7 mile, turn right on the Badger Creek Road and drive this gravel road 6.6 miles to a junction with Ball Point Road, FR27.
- From the junction of Badger Creek Road and Ball Point Road, turn right onto Ball Point Road (FR 27).
- Drive 2.1 paved miles to the School Canyon Trailhead on your left.
- **Drivetime from The Dalles:** 1 hour

Hike: The pine oak grassland for which the Badger Creek Wilderness south of The Dalles is known is unique to this part of Oregon. The mountains here are a fascinating mix of the lush Cascade crest and the high desert found east of the Cascades. In addition to the ubiquitous pines and oaks in the mountains here, you'll also observe lots of spring and summer wildflowers and even the occasional juniper tree, here at the western edge of its habitat. The trails here are delightfully uncrowded, and it's possible to hike trails in the area and not see another person for hours or even days at a time. Perhaps the best trail on the east side of the Badger is this scenic

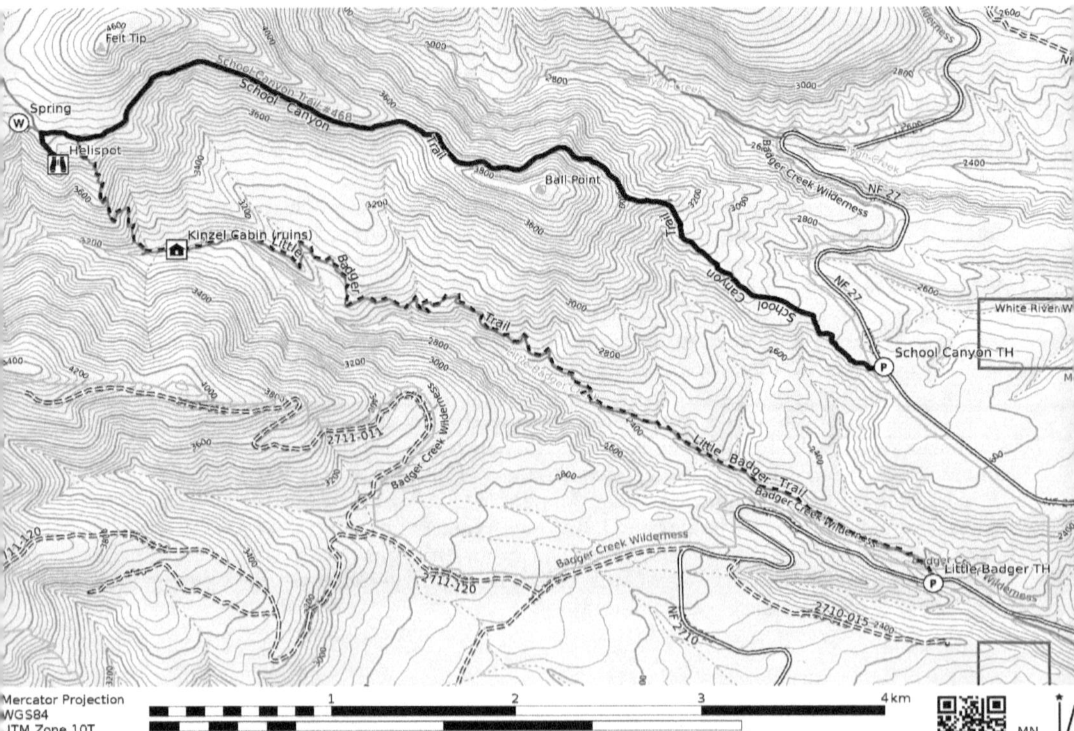

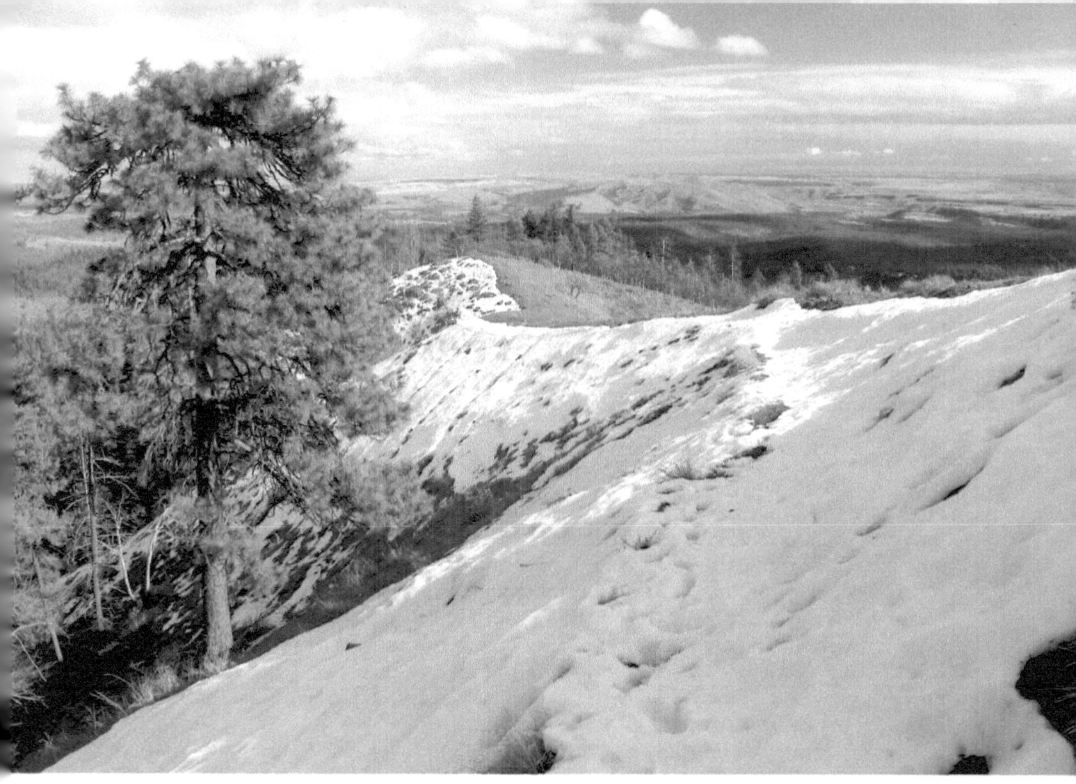

The School Canyon Trail on a cold but dry February day.

trail around the slopes of Ball Point to the fluted rock pinnacles and wildflower gardens of School Canyon. Adventurous hikers can make a loop out of this adventure by returning via the lovely Little Badger Creek Trail.

The School Canyon Trail begins at a roadside pullout along FR 27. You'll follow the trail through open woods characteristic of the pine oak grasslands in the area. Fragrant and colorful lupine dominates the understory in May. You'll have occasional views through the trees to rounded Ball Point ahead of you. The trail leaves the oak woods and ascends a scenic open hillside full of spring wildflowers and excellent views to a saddle below the upper slopes of Ball Point. The forest here burned in a 2007 fire but is recovering nicely. You'll have views south to Mount Jefferson and even the Three Sisters far to the south. Beyond the saddle, the trail follows the backside of Ball Point. This trail only receives maintenance every few years so you may need to climb over a few trees. The School Canyon soon leaves the slopes of Ball Point, passing into a deep forest of impressive ponderosa pine. At 3.6 miles, the trail reaches a junction with the Little Badger Trail on the left. Continue another 0.1 mile to an unsigned junction on the left. Turn left and follow this short trail out to a helispot (a spot where helicopters can land during forest fires) amid fluted rock pinnacles and clumps of spring wildflowers. This is the recommended stopping point for this hike. If you're backpacking, there is a spring another few hundred feet to the west. Unless you're planning a longer hike, return the way you came.

If you're looking for a longer hike, consider hiking down Little Badger Creek. This trail drops steeply down the open slopes below the helispot for 0.7 mile to the remains of Kinzel Cabin, then follows the scenic open slopes above Little Badger Creek for a couple miles, only to return to creek level in a scenic grove of tall ponderosa pines. The Little Badger Trail is just as scenic as the School Canyon Trail, but at 4.5 miles one way with a lot more elevation gain, it makes for a longer day. Connecting the two trails requires a 1 mile bushwhack or a short car shuttle. To locate the Little Badger Trailhead, drive back FR 27 to its junction with the Badger Creek Road. Turn right and drive down the Badger Creek Road for 1.5 miles to the trailhead in a pullout beside Little Badger Creek.

45. Boulder Lake

Distance: 10.3 miles (includes all trails)
Elevation Gain: 1,700 feet
Trailhead elevation: 4,369 feet
Trail high point: 5,596 feet
Season: June – October
Best: July – October
Pass: none needed
On the traditional lands of: Grande Ronde, Siletz, and Warm Springs peoples

Directions:

- From Portland, drive east on US 26 for 49 miles to a junction with OR 35. Exit US 26 and drive north on OR 35.
- Drive OR 35 around the southeast side of Mount Hood for 4.7 miles to a poorly marked junction on the right with FR 48 in a parking lot, just after OR 35 crosses the White River. If you're coming from Hood River, this junction is on the left just before the highway crosses the White River, approximately 34 miles south of Hood River.
- Turn onto FR 48 and drive down FR 48 for exactly 6.9 miles to a poorly-marked turnoff on FR 4890 on your left.
- Drive this paved road for 3.7 miles to a junction and continue straight, now on FR 4881 for 2.5 paved but brushy miles.
- Reach a junction with FR 4880 and turn left for 4 narrow, washboarded gravel miles to the well-marked trailhead on your left.
- **Drivetimes:** 2 hours and 10 minutes from Portland, 1 hour and 20 minutes from Hood River

Hike: Lakes are rare in the rugged country east of Mount Hood, and sparkling blue Boulder Lake is without a doubt the most beautiful of the few lakes in the area. A quick and easy trail climbs to the lake, where you'll find a campground set amid the rocky cliffs and tall trees that line the lake. It's a long drive to the trailhead from wherever you started, so consider making a longer loop that takes in the best of what this area has to offer. This hike is fantastic in any time but never more so than in September and October, when you'll find the vine maple, larches,

Boulder Lake is located deep in the eastern slopes of the Cascades.

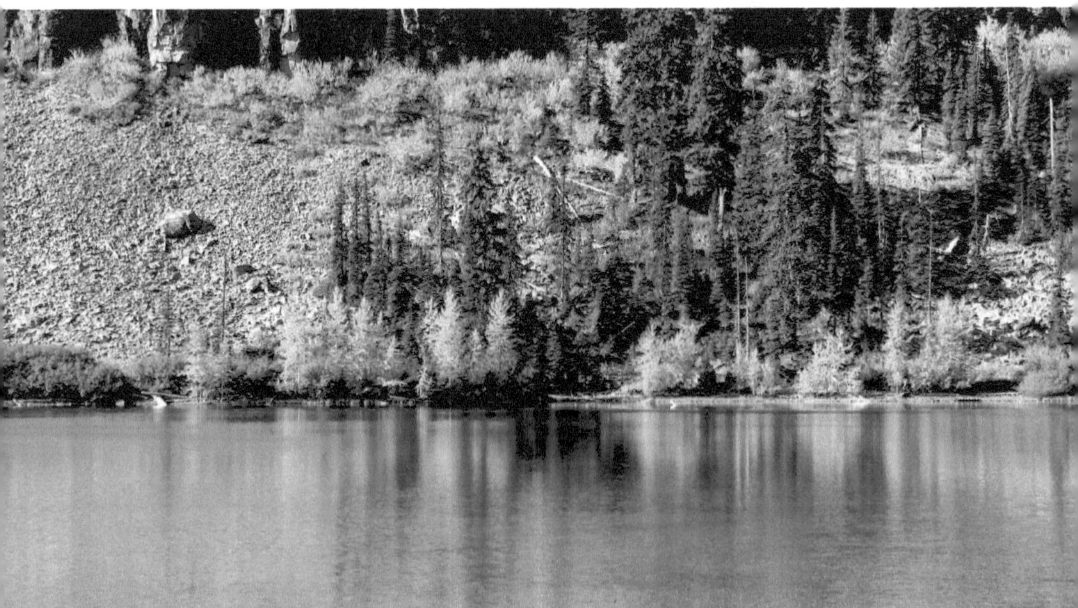

cottonwoods, and aspens on this hike in varied and glorious shades of fall color. Whenever you visit, you're sure to find something to love here.

From the trailhead, follow the wide Boulder Lake Trail uphill to small Spinning Lake on the left side of the trail. Just a short distance beyond Spinning Lake, you'll reach deep blue Boulder Lake at 0.3 mile from the trailhead. As it's only a ten-minute walk from the trailhead, the lake is a popular backpacking destination. Your loop begins here. Before you continue your hike, you may want to take the time to walk the loop trail around this gorgeous lake. You'll pass a number of larch trees, a deciduous conifer whose needles change color in the fall. A large colony of pikas lives in the rockslide above the lake, and you'll no doubt hear the ***meep!*** of these adorable rock rabbits. Back at the head of the lake, you'll begin the larger loop above and beyond Boulder Lake. Turn left (south) and hike 0.6 mile to Little Boulder Lake. From here, follow the trail until it dead ends at a gravel road. You'll follow this road uphill for 1 mile to a junction with the Forest Creek Trail at a saddle. Turn right and follow this trail through deep forest along the cliffs above the basin that holds both Boulder Lakes. Along the way you'll pass a few nice viewpoints down to the lakes and out to the mountains and forested canyons east of here, but for the most part you'll just stay deep in the woods for this stretch of the hike. After passing over Echo Point, the Forest Creek Trail reaches huge Bonney Meadows at 5.1 miles (including the loop around Boulder Lake). Turn right on the Hidden Meadows Trail and follow it around the edge of this vast, scenic prairie. After 0.3 mile you'll reach a junction with the Boulder Lake Trail on the far end of Bonney Meadows. If you're ready to be done with the hike, you'll turn right here to hike back down 1.8 miles to Boulder Lake. If you're interested in visiting Bonney Butte, the area's best viewpoint, you'll want to turn left.

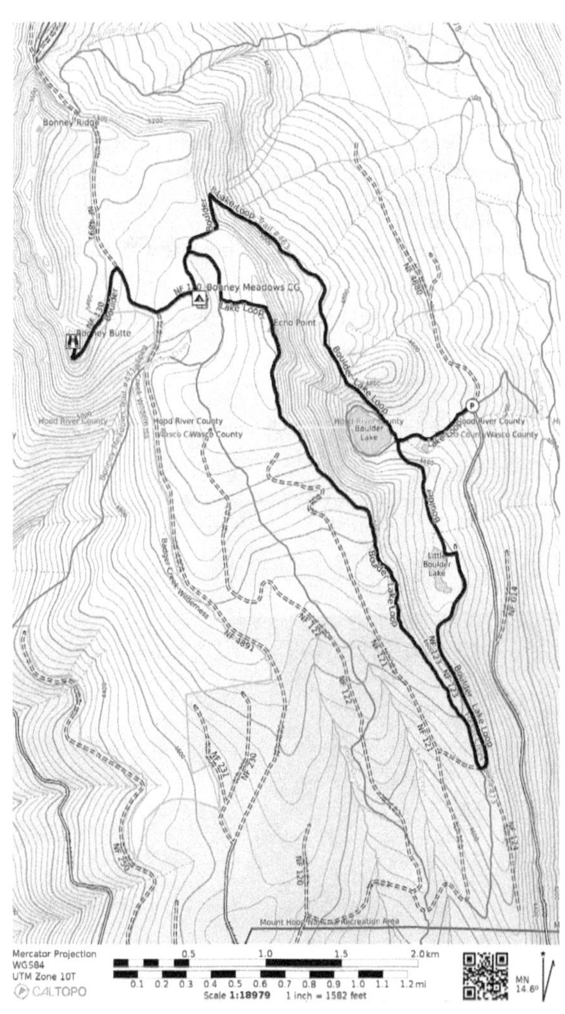

To hike up to Bonney Butte, follow the Boulder Lake Trail for 0.2 mile to Bonney Meadows Campground and turn right to follow the campground access road out to FR 4891, the extremely rough road that traverses this area. Turn right on FR 4891 and walk this road for 0.3 mile to a junction with FR 130 on the left. Follow this road uphill for 0.5 mile to the summit of Bonney Butte. The view of Mount Hood here is spectacular! Every fall a group called Hawkwatch gathers here to track migrating hawks; if you visit during this time, you may even get to see a hawk up close.

When you're ready to return, hike back to Bonney Meadows Campground and locate the Boulder Lake Trail. Follow it downhill through an impressive forest of ancient Douglas firs for 2 miles to Boulder Lake. When you reach the trail junction at the far end of the lake, turn left and walk downhill 0.3 mile to the trailhead.

46. Salmon River Trail

	Old Salmon River Trail	to Rolling Riffle Camp
Distance:	5.2 miles out and back	9.2 miles out and back
Elevation Gain:	300 feet	400 feet
Trailhead Elevation:	1,524 feet	1,524 feet
Trail High Point:	1,599 feet	1,739 feet
Season:	all year	all year
Best:	all year	all year
Pass:	none needed	none needed
On the traditional lands of:	The Cascades and Molalla peoples	The Cascades and Molalla peoples

Directions::

- From Portland southeast on US 26 for 35 miles to the small community of Welches.
- Approximately 1 mile past the stoplight and shopping center in Welches, turn right at the Subway in Zigzag onto E Salmon River Road.
- Drive 2.7 miles south passing several homes along the way to the Old Salmon River Trailhead on your right just after the road enters the Mount Hood National Forest.
- There are several trailheads along this stretch of road, but the one you want is the first one you will see on the right.
  Note: Leave nothing of value in your car as break-ins have occurred here in the past.
- **Drivetime from Portland:** 1 hour and 10 minutes

Ancient Western red cedars line the Old Salmon River Trail south of Welches.

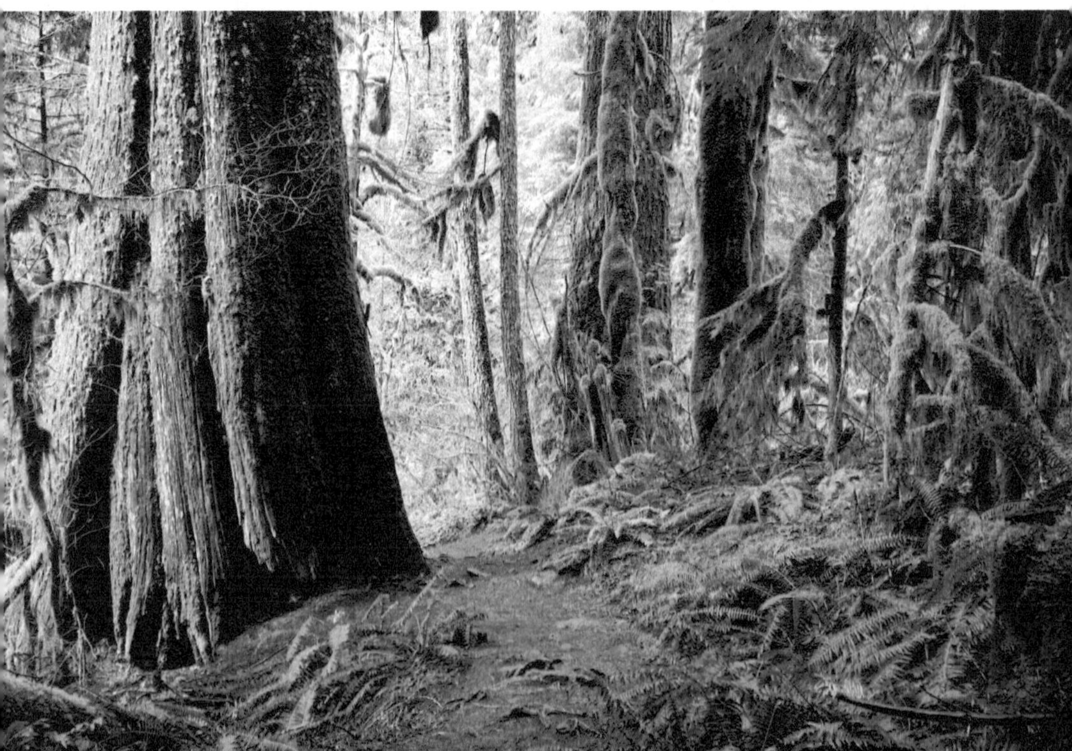

Hike: Less than ten percent of Oregon's extraordinary ancient forest remain, and most of these old-growth groves are located deep in the wilderness far from our major cities. Very little ancient forest is located near any of Oregon's major cities for the simple reason that, if a forest was easy to access, it was probably logged sometime long before anyone had the idea to protect the area. The Salmon River Trail south of Welches is a wonderful exception to this rule. You'll start your hike only a stone's throw from houses before entering a glorious green world of tall trees, lush mosses and ferns, and rushing water. This hike is especially wonderful in the winter when so much of the surrounding terrain is buried under several feet of snow.

This first section of trail is known as the Old Salmon River Trail. From the trailhead, follow the trail downhill into a lush forest dominated by huge sword ferns. You're just across the national forest boundary here, and houses are visible through the trees downstream. After just a few minutes on the trail, you'll hike between two massive Western red cedar trees near the Salmon River. The trail follows the river for the entirety of this hike, sometimes dipping deep into the forest but mostly staying near the river. Along the way, you'll need to cross a few seasonal creeks; getting across is easy much of the year but it can be difficult to keep your feet dry in the winter. At 1.4 miles, the trail seems to end at the Salmon River Road at a narrow spot along the river. Follow the road for 500 feet and locate the continuation of the trail on your right. The next mile follows the river closely, passing by Green Canyon Campground and more impressive ancient forest. At 2.6 miles, you'll reach the end of the Old Salmon River Trail at a crossing of the Salmon River Road just before the bridge over the river. If you're looking for an easy hike, turn around here.

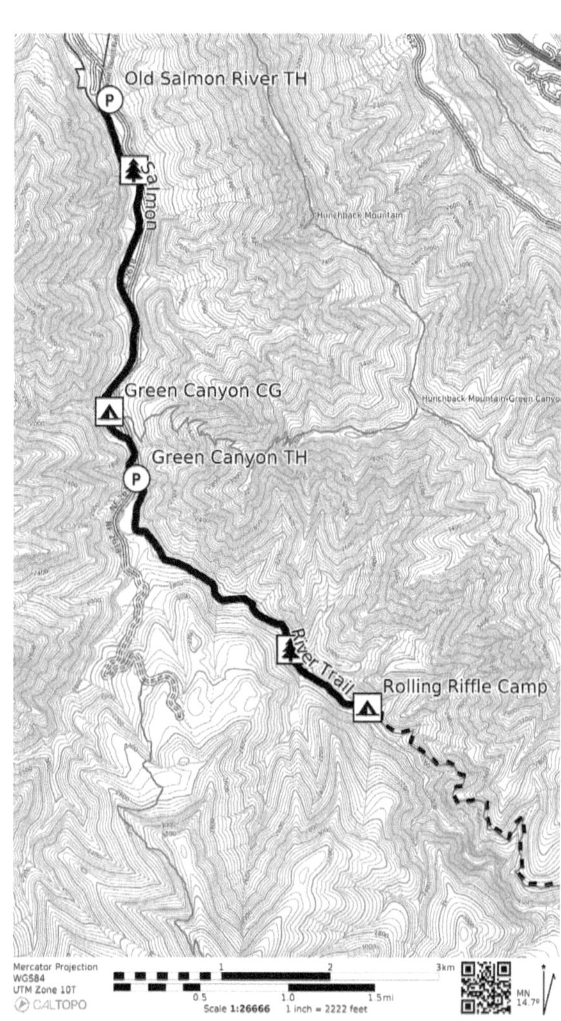

For the longer hike to Rolling Riffle Camp, cross the road and locate the Salmon River Trail on the other side. The trail follows the Salmon River closely before leveling out into an impressive grove of ancient forest that seems far more remote than it is. The trail through the forest here is glorious, as the sun filters through the tree canopy on sunny days, illuminating everything in a thousand shades of green and brown. You'll follow the Salmon River Trail to spacious Rolling Riffle Camp, which you reach at 4.6 miles from the Old Salmon River Trailhead. If you're backpacking, you should find a site here. Unless you're feeling especially energetic, you should turn around here. Beyond this point the trail climbs for the next 2 miles above a narrow gorge in the river. Some folks come up here looking for views of the string of waterfalls in the Salmon River canyon, but safely viewing any of these falls is almost impossible. Beyond the viewpoint the trail continues several more miles to a remote upper trailhead. From wherever you decide to turn around, return the way you came.

47. Serene Lake Loop

Distance: 12.3 mile loop
Elevation Gain: 2,700 feet
Trailhead elevation: 4,080 feet
Trail high point: 4,988 feet
Season: June – November
Best: August – September
Pass: none needed
On the traditional lands of: The Molalla People

Directions:

- From Portland, drive south on OR 224 to Estacada. Continue driving on OR 224 along the Clackamas River another 25 miles to Ripplebrook. This former ranger station is now a store. There is a pit toilet to the left of the store that is open to the public.
- A short distance after Ripplebrook, OR 224 becomes FR 46 at a junction with FR 57.
- Following a sign for Timothy Lake, turn left on FR 57. Drive this paved road 6.9 miles to a junction with FR 58 on your left.
- Turn left and drive FR 58 for 3.4 miles of one-lane paved road to a junction with FR 5810 signed for Hideaway Lake.
- Turn left and follow FR 5810 for 5.3 miles of good gravel road to a junction on the left with Hideaway Lake Campground.
- Continue straight on FR 5810 another 0.3 mile to the Shellrock Lake TH on your right.
- **Drivetime from Portland:** 2 hours

Hike: Located about halfway between Mount Hood and Mount Jefferson, the Roaring River Wilderness is a land of deep forest, rugged canyons, inviting backcountry lakes, huge wildflower meadows, and scenic viewpoints with views to the High Cascades on the horizon. With many miles of uncrowded trails and many fantastic campsites, backpackers will love this area. The best hike in Roaring River country takes you on a loop tour to Serene Lake, maybe the best mountain

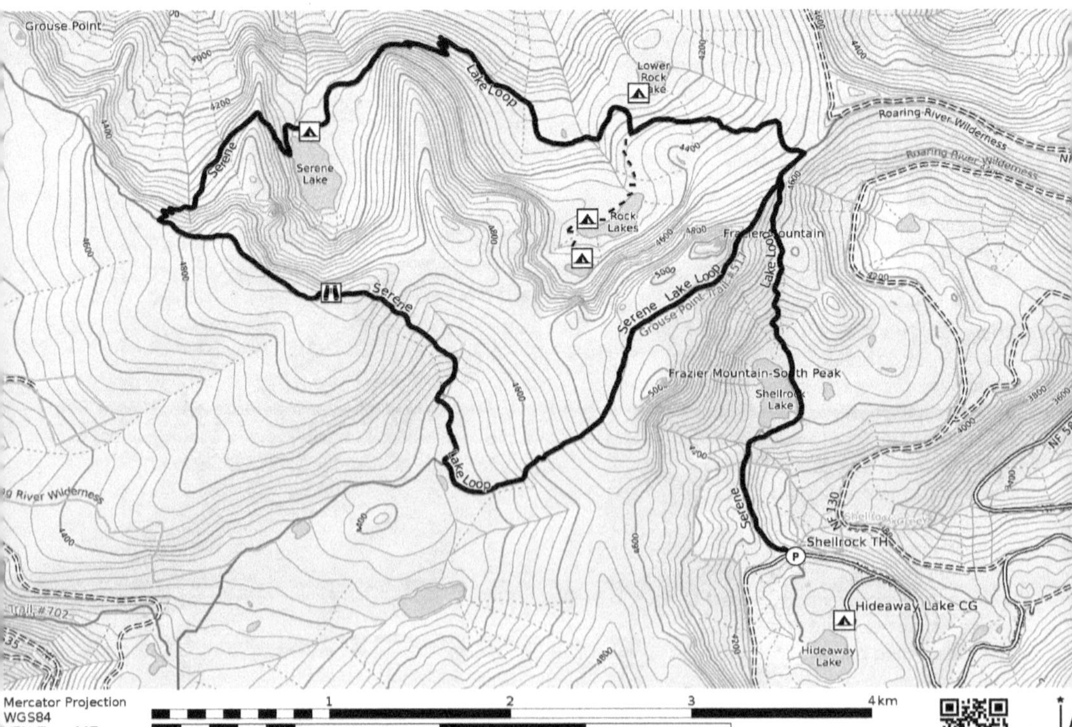

lake in the area. You'll also visit secluded Cache Meadow, pass a number of fantastic viewpoints, and hike through mile after mile of deep, dark mountain forest. The best time to visit this area is in August and September, when the nights are warm, the mosquitoes are long gone and the huckleberries are ripe.

From the Shellrock Lake Lake TH, follow the trail uphill through the woods before descending a bit to reach Shellrock Lake at 0.6 mile. The trail curves around this scenic lake, passing several excellent campsites. Beyond Shellrock Lake, the trail climbs steadily through scenic forest to a junction with the Grouse Point Trail at 1.8 miles. This is the start of the loop. As with most loops, it doesn't really matter which way you turn, but the loop is easier to navigate if you turn right. You'll drop 0.2 mile to the Frazier Turnaround Trailhead. You can shorten this hike by 4 miles round-trip if you drive to this spot, but the road is horrendous and receives little if any maintenance. To continue the loop, turn left on the Serene Lake Trail and hike downhill through the woods. At 0.8 mile from Frazier Turnaround, you will pass two junctions – one on the left leads to Middle and Upper Rock Lakes in 0.8 mile, while the next trail on the right leads to Lower Rock Lake in just 0.1 mile. If you're backpacking, all three lakes have nice campsites. From these junctions, the Serene Lake Trail continues west towards its namesake. You'll lose some elevation as the trail passes along rocky slopes high above the upper reaches of the Roaring River. At 5 miles from the trailhead, you will at last reach Serene Lake. The trail follows the lakeshore to a camping area on the lake's western end. There are a number of fantastic campsites here, one of which even has a picnic table. Expect company though, as this is the most popular backpacking destination in this area. The Riverside Fire in 2020 narrowly missed this area, and it should go without saying that campfires are an extremely poor idea here. If you're backpacking, bring a camping stove and enough clothing to stay warm.

Many hikers will be tempted to make Serene Lake their destination, but if you're planning on doing the full loop, follow the Serene Lake Trail uphill for 1 mile to a T-junction with the Grouse Point Trail. Turn left and hike uphill towards the crest of the ridge above Serene Lake. When the trail reaches a junction on the left, turn here and follow this spur trail 100 yards to a fantastic view overlooking blue and green Serene Lake and north to Mount Hood and the trio of Washington volcanoes. If you're looking for the best place on this hike to spread out for lunch, this is it. Return to the Grouse Point Trail and follow it steeply downhill to Cache Meadow at 7.6 mile. Expect voracious mosquitoes here in June and July, but otherwise this is a peaceful and quiet place. The trail through the meadows is confusing. At the far end of the meadow, reach a pair of confusing junctions: first, turn left just before you reach a pond. You will soon reach a four-way junction at the site of the old Cache Meadow shelter. There will be a sign for the Cripple Creek Trail. Keep left to stay on the Grouse Point Trail. The trail then leaves the meadow, passes a trail sign that reads only "517" (the trail's number) and then begins climbing furiously one final time on its way out of Cache Meadow's basin. At a little over 9 miles, finally crest the ridge holding Frazier Mountain and reach a junction on the remains of an old road. Turn right and begin working your way downhill. The trail passes through huckleberry bushes full of ripe fruit in late summer as well as a few nice views south to Mount Jefferson. Finally, at 10.5 miles, you'll reach a reunion with the Shellrock Lake Trail on your right. Turn right and hike 1.8 miles back to the trailhead.

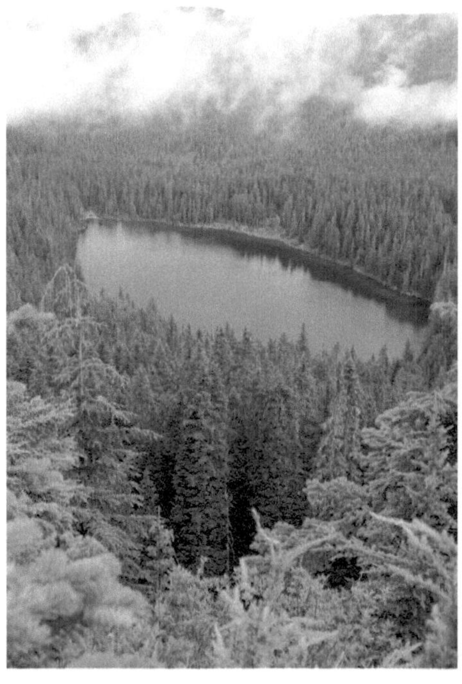

48. Bagby Hot Springs

Distance: 3.2 miles out and back
Elevation Gain: 300 feet
Trailhead elevation: 2,093 feet
Trail high point: 2,269 feet
Season: March – November
Best: April – October
Pass: NW Forest Pass + Special Soaking Pass
On the traditional lands of: the Molalla people

Directions:

- From Portland, drive south on OR 224 to Estacada. Continue driving on OR 224 along the Clackamas River another 25 miles to Ripplebrook. This former ranger station is now a store. There is a pit toilet to the left of the store that is open to the public.
- A short distance after Ripplebrook, OR 224 becomes FR 46 at a junction with FR 57. Continue straight (right) on FR 46. Drive 4.2 miles on FR 46 to a junction with FR 63, where you turn right, following signs for Bagby Hot Springs.
- Drive this 2-lane paved road for 3.5 miles to a junction with FR 70, signed for Bagby Hot Springs.
- Turn right on FR 70 and drive 6.8 miles to the well-signed trailhead on your left.
- **Note 1:** Leave nothing of value at this trailhead. Break-ins have been a problem in the past at Bagby Hot Springs. The parking lot is monitored but vigilance is a good idea.
- **Note 2:** A special $5 pass is required to use the hot springs. You can purchase the pass at the trailhead or at the Ripplebrook store.
- **Drivetime from Portland:** 1 hour and 30 minutes

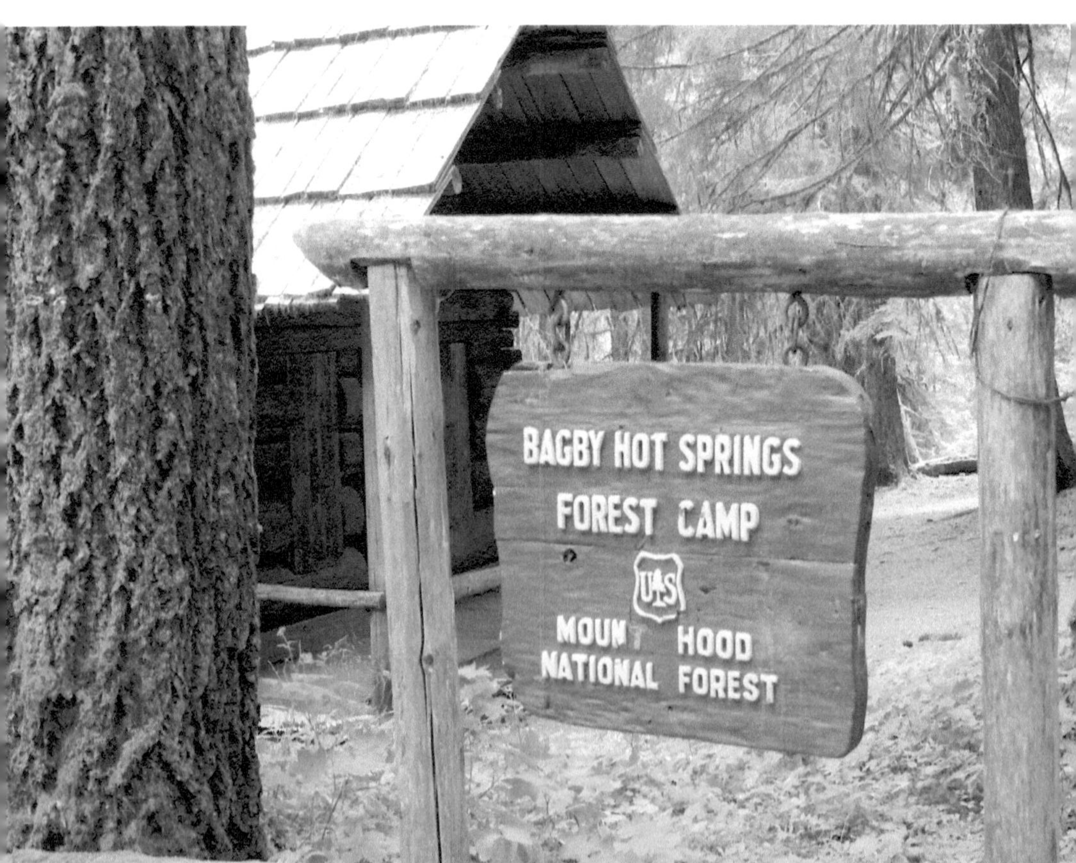

Hike: Once upon a time, Bagby Hot Springs were among the most famous backcountry destinations in Oregon. Hot springs lovers from all over the state and region would congregate on the busy trail to the springs, and it was not uncommon to wait for as much as two hours to soak in the delightfully rustic tubs at the springs. Legend has it that prospector Robert Bagby discovered the site in the 1880s, but in truth area tribes had soaked here for hundreds of years before Bagby set foot in the area. The popularity of the springs in recent times led to the springs being managed by concessionaires. An Oregon couple bought the rights to manage the site in 2021 and have invested a considerable amount of time and money into restoring the aging buildings at the springs. Bagby Hot Springs is expected to fully reopen sometime in 2023.

From the trailhead, locate the wide trail and follow it to a bridge over the Hot Springs fork of the Collawash River. You will soon enter a magnificent forest of ancient Douglas firs, some as many as eight feet thick. Take the time to appreciate the ancient forest along this trail; this valley was among the only places spared during the ravages of recent fires. Nearby Opal Creek suffered almost total devastation during the Beachie Fire in 2020 and few places have burned worse or more frequently than the surrounding Bull of the Woods Wilderness in recent times. The forest along the Bagby Trail remains blissfully cool and majestic, and a lush carpet of moss lines the trail almost the entire way to Bagby Hot Springs. The trail is almost level, allowing you to hike as slow or as fast as you like. At 1.5 miles from the trailhead, the Bagby Trail crosses another bridge and arrives at the hot springs.

Bagby Hot Springs feels like an outpost deep in the wilderness. A Forest Service guard station, now closed to the public, is located near the numerous bathhouses and soaking pools at the hot springs. If you're planning to soak, you may need to wait your turn. Heated water emerges from the ground here at temperatures between 120° – 138°, and you will need to fill up buckets with cold water to help regulate the water temperature in the pools to your liking. Public nudity and consumption of alcohol or other controlled substances is prohibited. Do not enter the guard station or any other locked buildings. Even though this is a relatively short and easy hike, you will likely spend all day in the woods here.

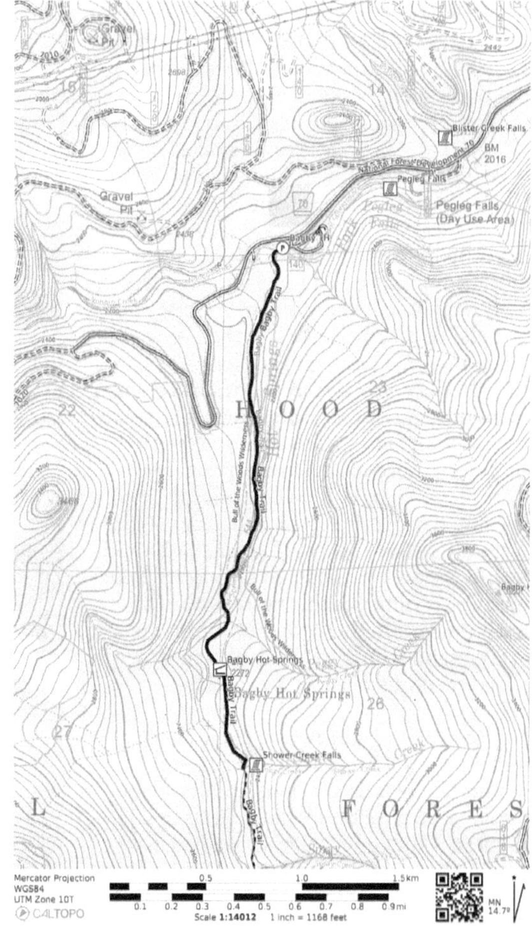

If you're still interested in a longer hike, the Bagby Trail continues south beyond the hot springs and enters the Bull of the Woods Wilderness. Many hikers venture 0.2 mile beyond the hot springs to trickling Shower Creek Falls, where you can cool off after a hot soak. Beyond Shower Creek Falls the trail passes through stupendous ancient forest before reaching the boundary of the 2020 fires. You'll eventually reach the southern end of the Bagby Trail just west of Elk Lake's Campground (Hike 49) some 10 miles south of Bagby Hot Springs. Expect rough trail conditions and many downed trees if you're heading further up the trail.

49. Battle Ax

Distance: 5.6 mile loop
Elevation Gain: 1,800 feet
Trailhead elevation: 3,808 feet
Trail high Point: 5,550 feet
Season: July – October
Best: July – October
Pass: none needed
On the traditional lands of: the Molalla people

Directions:

- From Salem, drive OR 22 for 49 miles to Detroit.
- Immediately after crossing the Breitenbush River, turn left at a sign for Breitenbush and Elk Lake on FR 46.
- Drive 4.5 miles to a poorly-signed junction with FR 4696.
- Turn left here and drive this paved road 0.8 mile to a junction with FR 4697.
- Turn left again, pass a sign stating that this road is not maintained for passenger cars and begin climbing. The first two miles of this road are good gravel but soon the road becomes rough and rocky. After 4.5 miles, turn left at a junction marked only by a green post to continue on FR 4697.
- Drive 1.4 rough, rocky miles to a bridge at the east end of Elk Lake.
- Continue another 0.6 mile of terrible road to a sign for Elk Lake's campground. There are several wide spots here where you can park. You can usually park a little further up the road, but it soon deteriorates to the point of becoming impassible.
- Be very aware of your car's ability to handle FR 4697 – a vehicle with low clearance and good tires can handle these roads if you drive very, very slowly; I've even seen a Prius here. Vehicles with higher clearance will manage just fine.
- **Drivetime from Salem:** 75 - 90 minutes

Hike: Battle Ax is in the middle of nowhere but is firmly in the middle of some of Oregon's finest mountain scenery. Located at the southwest end of the rugged Bull of the Woods Wilderness, the mountain has long been at the center of a vast network of trails stretching across this end of the Cascades. It's a chore to drive to the trailhead, but once you're there the flowers, tall trees, and stupendous views that have brought visitors here are still there. The slopes of Battle Ax miraculously escaped the ravages of the Beachie Fire in 2020, which burned almost everything to the west of here, including Mount Beachie nearby. With so much changed in this corner of the mountains, I am grateful that Battle Ax is almost exactly as it was when I first visited way back in 1994.

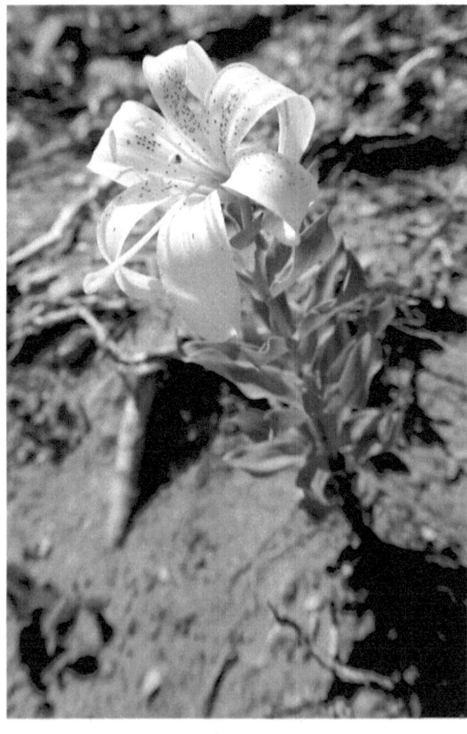

Begin by parking somewhere along the road near the turnoff for Elk Lake's car campground. There is no developed trailhead for Battle Ax because there's nowhere to build a trailhead – the rocky, steep slopes here have kept further development at bay ever since the road into Elk Lake was built. Walk the road some 0.3 mile to a junction with the Bagby

Trail. This is the same Bagby Trail that departs from the Bagby Hot Springs Trail (see Hike 48, but this end is far more rugged and solitary). Save this trail for the other side of your loop and continue walking up the rocky road. Before long you'll reach the point of no return for vehicles, and from here the road becomes so rugged and rocky that it's actually a chore to walk. Views open up to the craggy slopes of Mount Beachie, and southeast to Mount Jefferson. After 1 mile, you'll reach Beachie Saddle and the eastern edge of the Beachie Fire, which began a few miles from here on the steep slopes of Mount Beachie. Turn right here to begin your climb up Battle Ax. The way up is occasionally steep but rewards you with views down to Elk Lake and out to Mount Jefferson. In July a wide array of wildflowers covers the open slopes of Battle Ax. Look for yellow Oregon sunshine, red paintbrush, purple penstemon, the showy pink and white Cascade Lily, and many more. After 1.6 miles of uphill, you will arrive at the rocky summit of Battle Ax, marked by the remains of a long-lost lookout tower. The views up here are truly panoramic. To the north you'll see Mount Saint Helens, Mount Rainier, Mount Adams, and Mount Hood. To the southeast is Mount Jefferson, and further south, Three-Fingered Jack, Mount Washington, and the Three Sisters. Directly below you is deep blue Elk Lake. The lake is close enough that you'll even be able to hear people at the campground below.

Many hikers will opt to turn around and return the same way, but if you've got more energy, you can continue on a fun loop. Locate the trail beyond the remains of the lookout tower and continue along the narrow crest of Battle Ax's summit ridge. Eventually you'll switchback steeply downhill to a junction with the Bagby Trail. Turn right here and follow this brushy trail across a series of talus slopes and through ancient forest to a viewpoint of Elk Lake and Mount Jefferson. From here, the Bagby Trail continues downhill to its southern terminus at the Elk Lake Road. Turn left here and hike 0.3 mile to the trailhead at the campground road junction.

If you wish to spend the night, note that the Elk Lake Campground fills early on weekends, has no running water, and is a popular party spot. It's still a great place to spend a weekend, though.

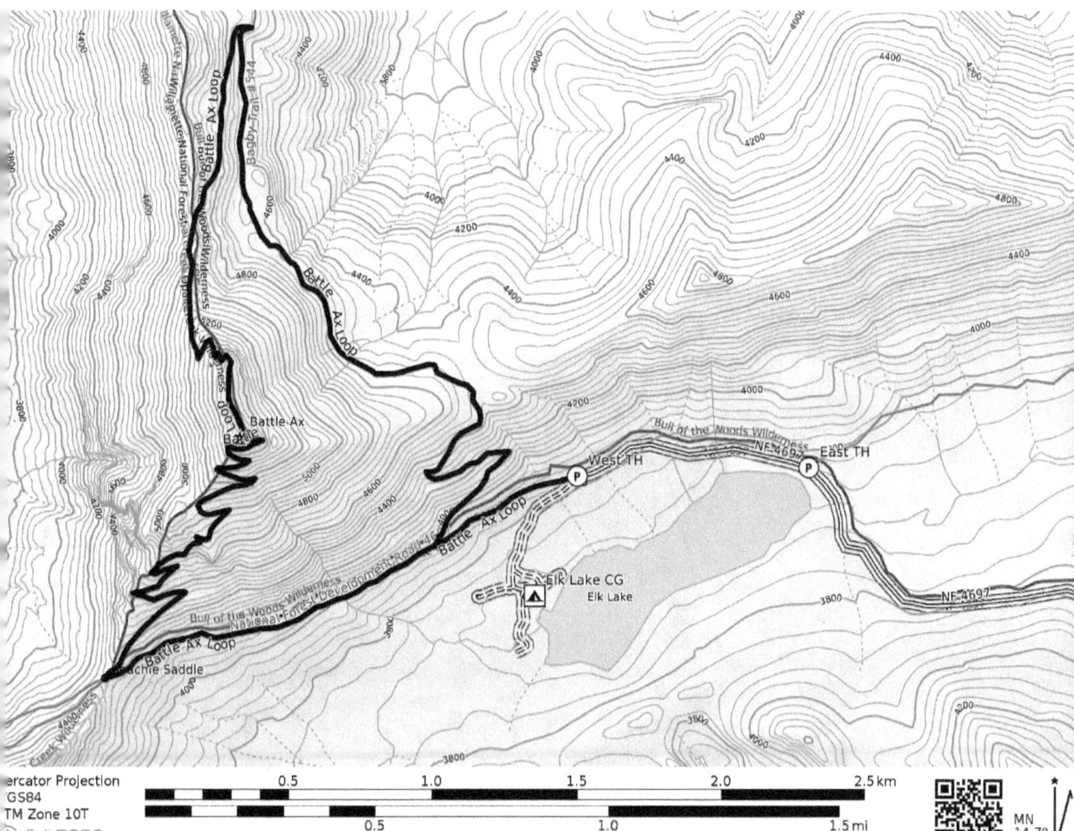

50. Olallie Lake

Distance: 6.7 mile loop
Elevation Gain: 100 feet
Trailhead elevation: 4,971 feet
Trail high Point: 4,994 feet
Season: June – October
Best: August – October
Pass: none needed
On the traditional lands of: The Warm Springs, Molalla, and Tenino peoples

Directions:

- From Portland, drive south on OR 224 to Estacada. Continue driving on OR 224 along the Clackamas River another 25 miles to Ripplebrook. This former ranger station is now a store. There is a pit toilet to the left of the store that is open to the public.
- A short distance after Ripplebrook, OR 224 becomes FR 46 at a junction with FR 57. Continue straight (right) on FR 46.
- Drive another 22.3 miles on FR 46 to a junction on the left with the Olallie Lake Road (FR 4690) – you will notice that "Olallie" is painted on the road here. with an arrow to mark the direction.
- Turn left here onto FR 4690 and drive 6.1 miles of narrow pavement and another 1.9 miles of rocky gravel to a junction with the Skyline Road, FR 4220.
- Turn right here and drive 5.1 miles of rutted gravel road to the Olallie Lake Resort.
- Drive past the resort entrance and 100 feet later, turn right into the signed parking area for the Pacific Crest Trail.
- **Drivetime from Portland:** 2 hours and 30 minutes

Olallie Lake in June 2022, the day before the resort opened for the season.

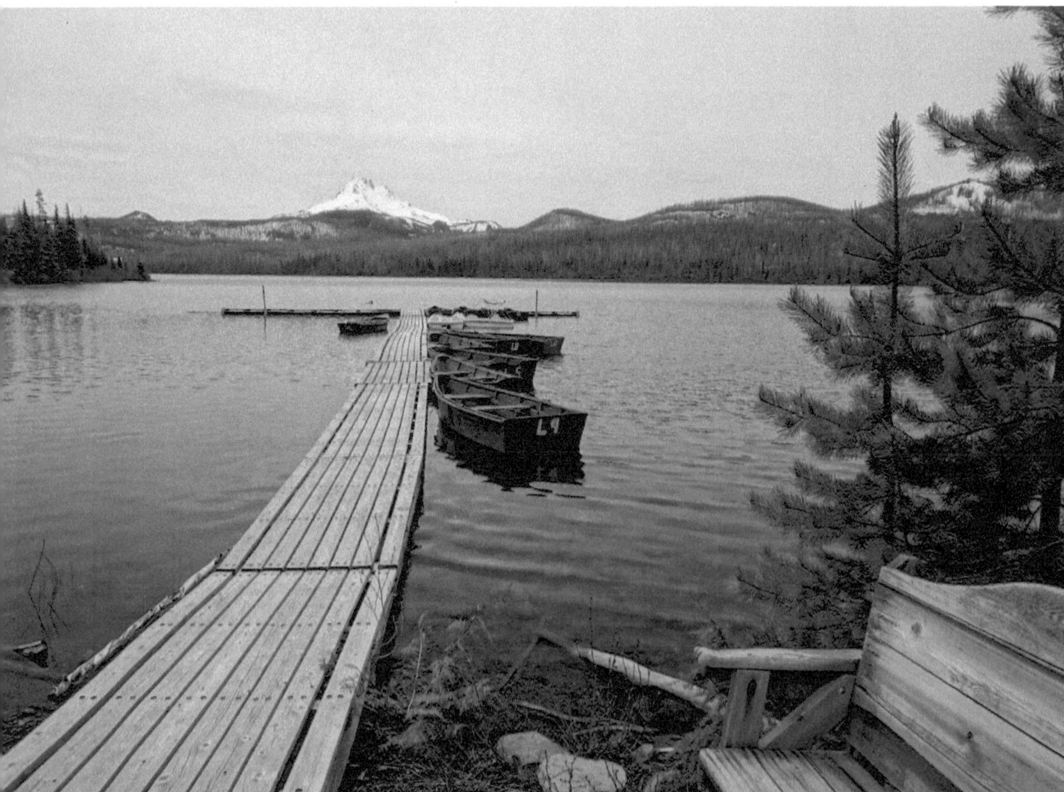

Hike: Located at the crest of the Cascades, Olallie Lake and its glorious view of Mount Jefferson has been an iconic Oregon destination for millennia. Olallie means "berry" in the Chinook jargon used by area tribes, and when hiking around the lake, you'll see why. The entire lakeshore is ringed with huckleberries, and huckleberry bushes are the dominant plant in the understory all throughout this part of the Cascades. The Warm Springs, Tenino, Molalla and other area tribes gathered in this area at the end of every summer to harvest berries. Unfortunately, the Olallie area has burned repeatedly in recent years, most notably in the Lionshead Fire in 2020. The Olallie Lake Resort was miraculously spared the ravages of the fire, and Olallie Lake remains one of the most beautiful places in this part of the Cascades. The loop trail around Olallie Lake and its equally beautiful neighbor Monon Lake is still worth the effort. Unfortunately, the trails along both lakes suffered significant damage in the 2020 fires and may still be closed when you read this. Check online at my website or at the Olallie Lake Resort page (https://www.olallielakeresort.com) for more information.

To begin the loop along Olallie Lake, follow the lakeshore east from the resort towards Paul Dennis Campground. You'll note that swimming is banned in Olallie Lake, as it is the drinking water source for the resort; you'll also need to keep your dogs out of the lake too along the lakeshore. The lakeshore trail eventually pushes you into Paul Dennis Campground. At the far end of the campground, look for the Olallie Lake Trail between sites 14 and 16. The trail follows the lake, passing fantastic views of Mount Jefferson. Along the way you'll enter the Warm Springs Reservation, at which point you will need to stay on the trail. At 0.9 mile, the trail reaches an unmarked junction with a trail heading to lakes deeper into the Reservation; keep right here and continue following the lakeshore. The trail curves around the southeastern side of the lake, leaves the Reservation, and reaches a junction at a cairn at 1.4 miles. Turn left here and hike past a pair of small lakes to a junction above Monon Lake at 1.5 miles. Turn left here.

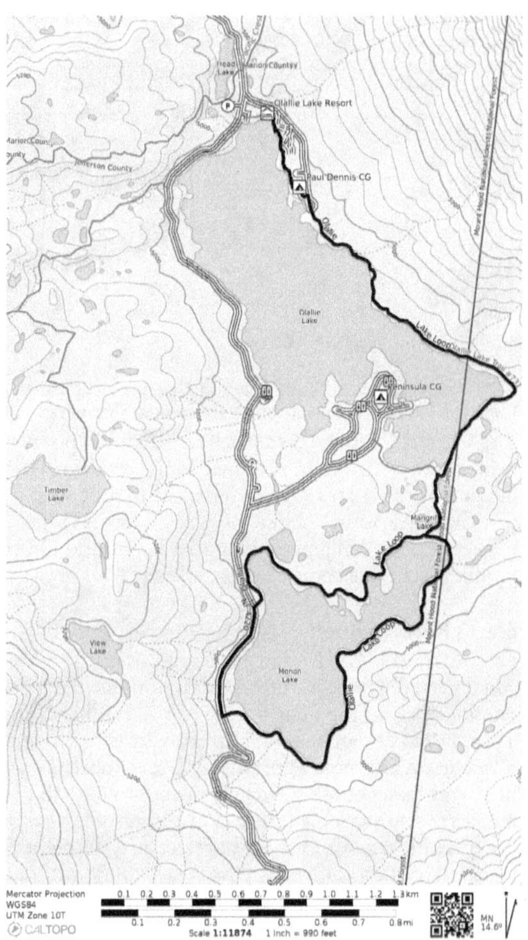

Monon Lake is just as beautiful as its neighbor to the north. Though the view of Mount Jefferson is not as impressive as the view found at Olallie Lake, the lake is deep and features many peninsulas, coves, and isolated campsites. Swimming is allowed in Monon Lake as well, should you wish to jump in. In addition to the ubiquitous fire damage, one thing you may not appreciate at both lakes is the tremendous and voracious population of mosquitoes early in the summer; you'll find yourself hiking as fast as you can around the lakes until at least mid-August. At 3.1 miles, the Monon Lake Trail dead ends at the Skyline Road. Turn right here and follow the Skyline Road north 0.3 mile until you locate the Monon Lake Trail on the north side of the lake. Turn right here and follow the north shore of Monon Lake for 0.9 mile to the connector trail, where you turn left. When you arrive at Olallie Lake, turn right and follow the lakeshore trail back to the resort.

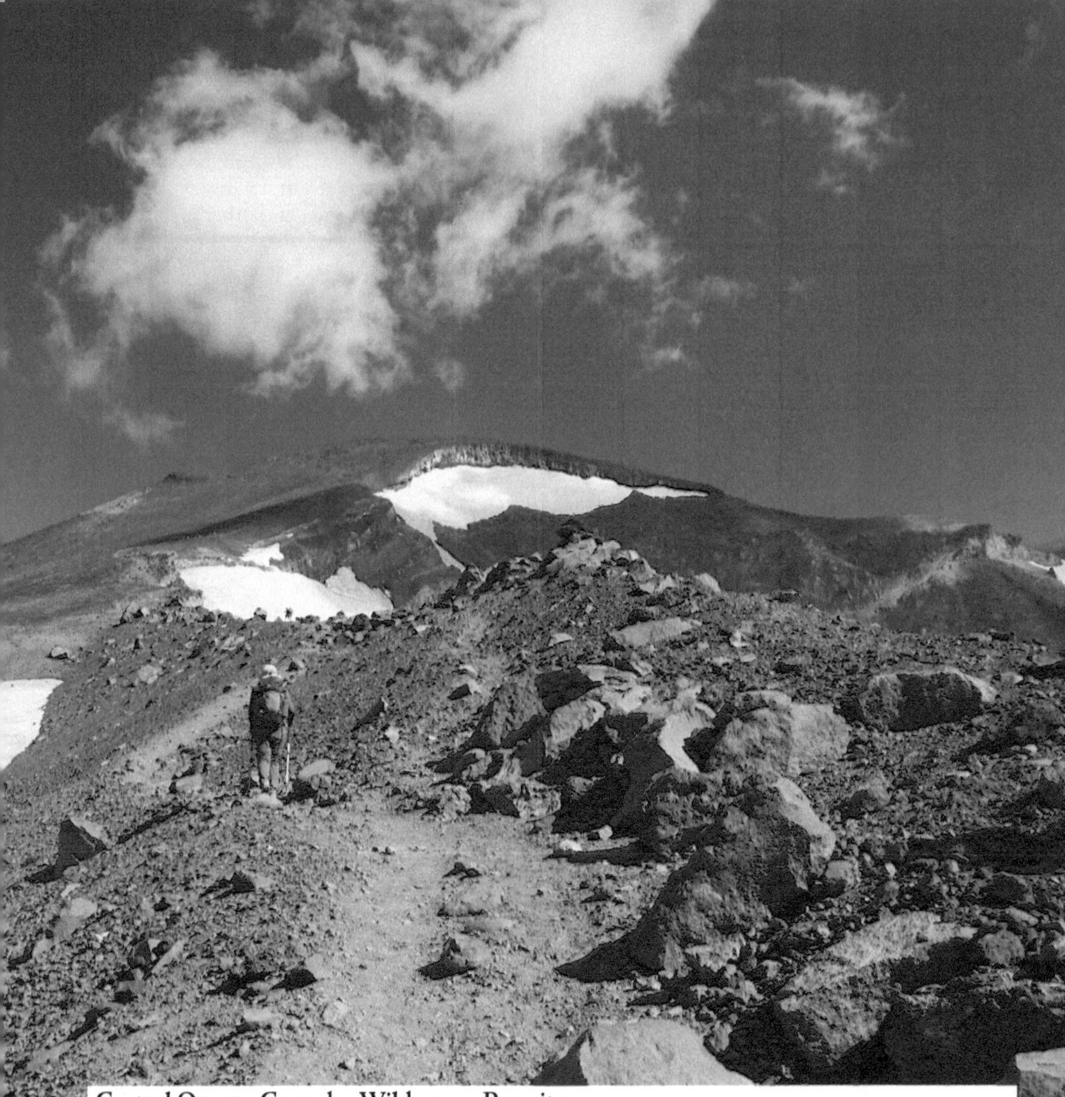

Central Oregon Cascades Wilderness Permits:

The Central Oregon Cascades have surged in popularity in recent years, and some places were being loved to death. In response to the resulting environmental problems caused by extremely heavy usage in places such as Jefferson Park (Hikes 51 and 52), Marion Lake (Hike 53), Canyon Creek Meadows (Hike 59), Green Lakes (Hike 70), and the South Sister Summit Trail (Hike 71), the Willamette National Forest and Deschutes National Forest have implemented a permit system for some of these hikes.

Here's how it works:

For any trails in the Mount Jefferson, Mount Washington, and Three Sisters Wilderness areas, you'll need to check in the hike descriptions here to see if they need a permit. Some hikes will require a permit for a day hike, while all trailheads in these three wilderness areas will require a permit to backpack. To obtain the permit, go to www.recreation.gov and search for Central Cascades Wilderness Permit, Day Use; choose the trailhead at which you plan to begin your hike, and then choose the day you want to hike this trail. Permits go on sale in the winter, but many are also available ten days in advance of the day you want to hike. If you're planning a backpacking trip, you'll need to select an Overnight permit instead for the trailhead at which you plan to start your hike. Don't leave home without your permit as backcountry rangers patrol these three wilderness areas and will warn or even cite you for not having the required permit.

Central Oregon Cascades

		Distance	EV Gain	Page
51.	Park Ridge	6.8 mi	1,400 ft	128
52.	Jefferson Park via South Breitenbush	13.6 mi	3,600 ft	130
53.	Marion Lake	6.2 mi	1,200 ft	132
54.	Coffin Mountain and Bachelor Mtn	6.8 mi	2,247 ft	134
55.	House Rock	1.2 mi	100 ft	136
56.	Middle Santiam Wilderness	13.6 mi	2,500 ft	138
57.	Iron Mountain Loop	6.8 mi	1,900 ft	140
58.	West Browder Ridge	11.4 mi	2,000 ft	142
59.	Canyon Creek Meadows	7.9 mi	1,600 ft	144
60.	Black Butte	4.2 mi	1,553 ft	146
61.	Metolius River	5.3 mi	300 ft	148
62.	Clear Lake and the McKenzie River	6.3 mi	500 ft	150
63.	Proxy Falls and Linton Lake	2.2 mi	200 ft	152
64.	Benson Lake	3.6 mi	402 ft	154
65.	Matthieu Lakes	6 mi	900 ft	156
66.	Demaris and Camp Lakes	15.4 mi	1,800 ft	158
67.	Tam McArthur Rim	5.6 mi	1,200 ft	160
68.	Tumalo Falls Loop	7.8 mi	1,400 ft	162
69.	Sparks Lake	2.7 mi	100 ft	164
70.	Green Lakes	9.6 mi	1,200 ft	166
71.	South Sister Summit	12.4 mi	4,909 ft	168
72.	Shale Ridge Trail	6 mi	400 ft	170
73.	Bohemia Mountain	1.6 mi	613 ft	172
74.	Salt Creek and Diamond Creek Falls	4.4 mi	1,000 ft	174
75.	Diamond View Lake	10.8 mi	1,008 ft	176

The Central Oregon Cascades are the state's playground, and no region deserves more entries than this one. From Mount Jefferson to the Three Sisters to Diamond Peak, this is the heart of Oregon's Cascade range. Here you will find majestic glacier-clad mountains, awe-inspiring ancient forests, stupendous waterfalls, and mile after mile of gorgeous trails. Of all the sections in this book, this one had the most hikes cut from the final list - I could have made an entire book of extraordinary hikes just in the Central Oregon Cascades. Every hiker will find lots to love in this area. The only downside is that many of these hikes are crowded, and some require a limited-entry permit to hike.

Photo on left: The final steep climb to the summit of South Sister (Hike 71)

51. Park Ridge

Distance: 6.8 miles out and back
Elevation Gain: 1,400 feet
Trailhead elevation: 5,506 feet
Trail high point: 6,886 feet
Season: July – October
Best: July – October
Pass: NW Forest Pass + limited entry permit
Permit required: day use or overnight (if backpacking)
On the traditional lands of: the Molalla and Tenino peoples

Directions from Salem:

- From Salem, drive OR 22 east approximately 49 miles to Detroit.
- Turn left at a sign for Breitenbush, Elk Lake and Olallie Lake onto FR 46.
- Drive 16.6 miles on FR 46 to a pass where you enter the Mount Hood National Forest.
- Turn right here on the Skyline Road (FR 4220) and drive 1 mile of gravel road to a large gate. Continue past the gate, where the road abruptly worsens into a rocky, narrow and severely rutted track that will severely test the patience of any passenger car driver. Drive another 5.8 excruciatingly slow miles to the signed trailhead on your right, at a large parking lot made of bright red cinders.
- Most passenger vehicles can make it if driven extremely carefully but you'll be a lot happier in a higher clearance vehicle.
- If you're driving from Portland, drive southeast on OR 224 to Estacada, then continue 25 miles to Ripplebrook, where OR 224 becomes FR 46. Continue 28.9 miles to Breitenbush Pass, where you turn left on the Skyline Road (FR 4220). Follow this awful road 6.8 miles to the trailhead just before Breitenbush Lake.
- **Drivetimes:** 2 hours and 30 minutes from both Salem and Portland

Mount Jefferson from Park Ridge, only three weeks before the 2020 fires.

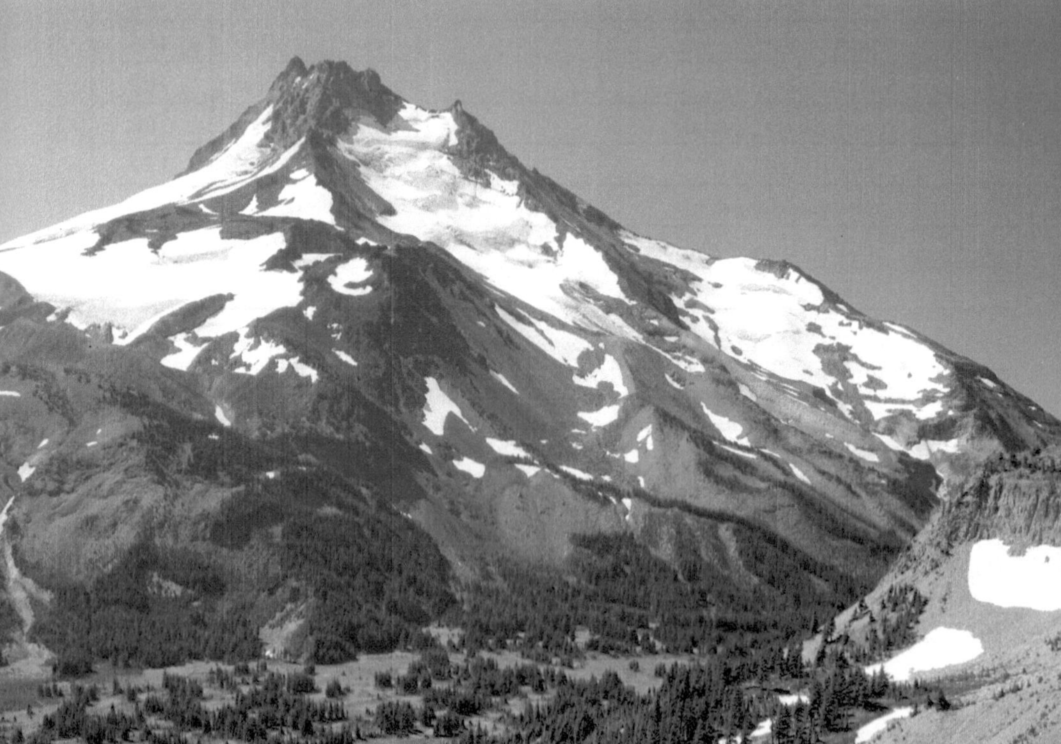

Hike: Park Ridge and Jefferson Park might be the most beautiful place in Oregon. Mount Jefferson towers over the rugged ridges and sublime meadows of Jefferson Park, and all the mountains of Oregon seem to line up on the horizon to the north and south. Flowers line the trail in the summer, and the ubiquitous huckleberry bushes turn various shades of orange and red in the fall, offering yet more color to an already beautiful scene. Getting there is a chore, but once you're there, you won't want to leave. All of this beauty comes at a price however, even beyond scoring a permit to hike the trail. The road to the trailhead is the worst in this book; we once got our 1997 Nissan Sentra to the trailhead, but not without considerable nailbiting and some choice swear words. This area burned in the 2020 Lionshead Fire, leaving behind scars on the surrounding ridge and mountains, and closing the trail for two years. It will be open by the time you read this. Before you go, don't forget to secure your day use or overnight permit; see the introduction to the Central Oregon Cascades on page 126 for more information.

From the trailhead, follow the Pacific Crest Trail south into the high country surrounding Breitenbush Lake. The Lionshead Fire mostly spared large stretches of this section of the PCT, but expect fire damage for much of the hike. The trail follows a rocky ridge with views west to Pyramid Butte, which burned badly in a 2010 fire and again during the 2020 fires; the old trail heading over to the basin below the butte (see the map) is in rough shape and should be ignored until it is restored. Stay on the PCT as it continues climbing gradually through meadows and high-elevation forest. The top half of Mount Jefferson peeks out above the rocky crest of Park Ridge on occasion, but you'll have to wait for the best views. At approximately 2.5 miles from the trailhead, you'll leave the forest behind and enter an alien landscape of rockslides, snowfields, and scattered ponds. The trail meanders through the tundra on the northern slopes of Park Ridge, occasionally getting lost in the snow. Expect large snow patches up here well into August. At 3.4 miles, the PCT reaches the summit of Park Ridge, where one of Oregon's greatest views awaits you. Mount Jefferson fills the sky above the meadows and lakes of Jefferson Park, only three miles to the south. I've been here several times when the mountain was lost in the fog and I still found this spot beautiful; on a clear day, it is very, very difficult to leave Park Ridge. Return the way you came.

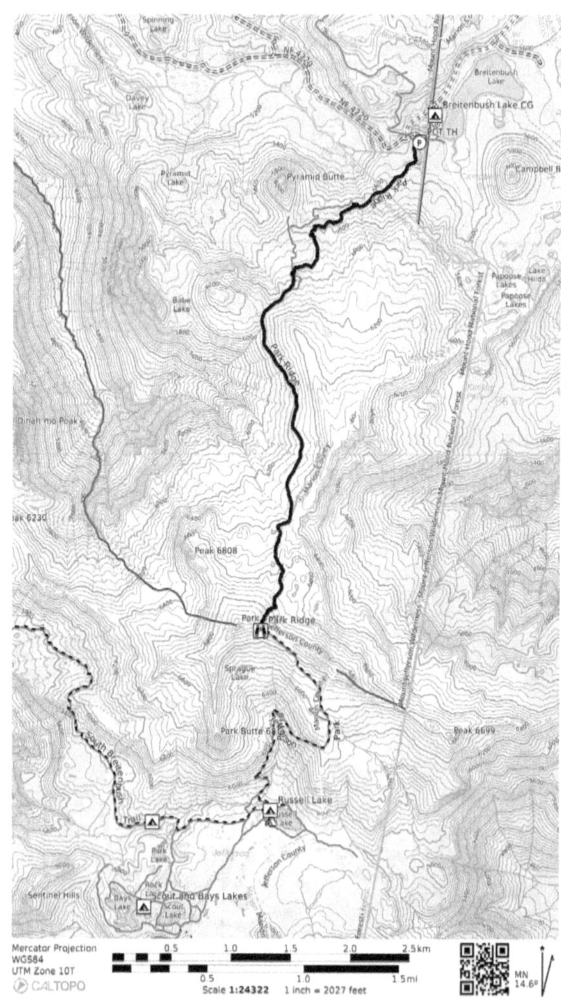

Energetic hikers can follow the PCT south for two of the most beautiful miles of trail in Oregon to Russell Lake at the northern end of Jefferson Park. I strongly encourage this if you have the energy, but you'll have to hike uphill out of Jefferson Park on the way back. For an alternative route into Jefferson Park, see the South Breitenbush approach in Hike 52.

52. Jefferson Park via South Breitenbush

Distance: 13.6 miles out and back
Elevation Gain: 3,600 feet
Trailhead elevation: 3,058 feet
Trail high point: 5,974 feet
Season: July – October
Best: July – October
Pass: NW Forest Pass + limited entry permit
Permit required: day use or overnight (if backpacking)
On the traditional lands of: the Molalla and Tenino peoples

Directions from Salem:

- From Salem, drive OR 22 east for approximately 49 miles to Detroit.
- Turn left at a sign for Breitenbush, Elk Lake and Olallie Lake onto FR 46.
- Drive 11.6 miles to a junction with FR 4685 on your right. Turn right.
- This road begins as pavement, crosses the North Fork Breitenbush River on a one-lane bridge, and immediately transitions to gravel.
- Drive 4.6 miles to a large parking lot on your right, located in a large open flat with lots of room to park.
- **Drivetime:** 1 hour and 30 minutes

Hike: Jefferson Park is one of the most beautiful and extraordinary places in the state of Oregon. Hikers from across the state flock to the area in droves during the summer to take in the incredible views of Mount Jefferson, the fields of summer wildflowers, and some of the most swimmable lakes in Oregon. This beauty comes with a price; to hike into Jefferson Park, you'll need to hike at least 11 miles through terrain that has repeatedly burned in recent years. There are several ways to hike into the park, but the approach via the South Breitenbush Trail has always been my favorite. The way is long, rough, and rocky, but this trail allows you to experience everything this area has to offer. As with the other trails into Jefferson Park, the South Breitenbush Trail has been closed since the 2020 fires but is expected to be reopened during the summer of 2023. Before you go, don't forget to secure your day use or overnight permit; see the introduction to the Central Oregon Cascades on page 126 for more information.

Backpackers in Jefferson Park on a gorgeous summer weekend.

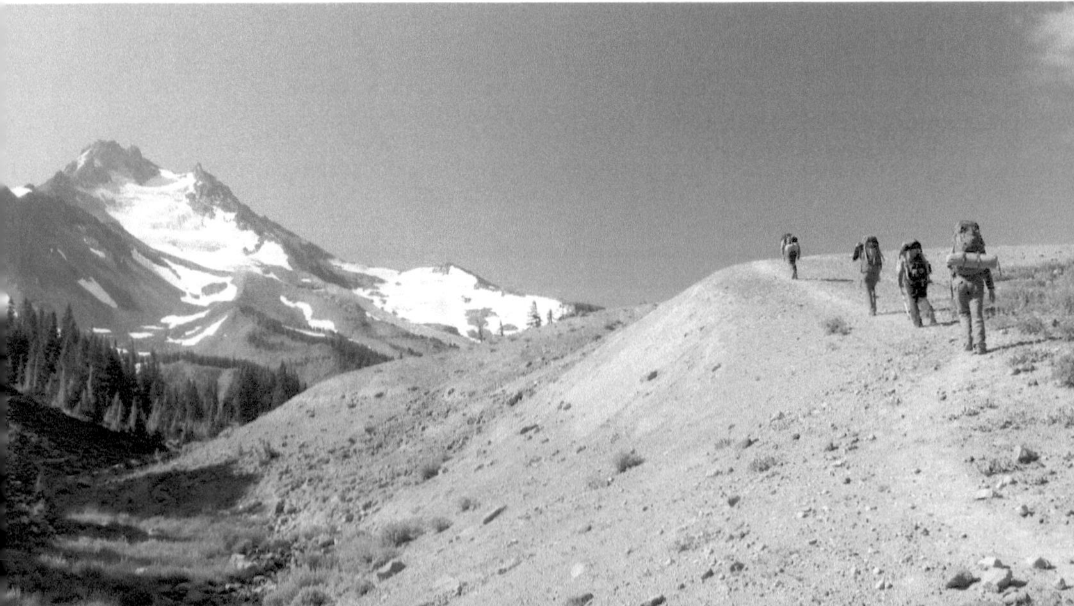

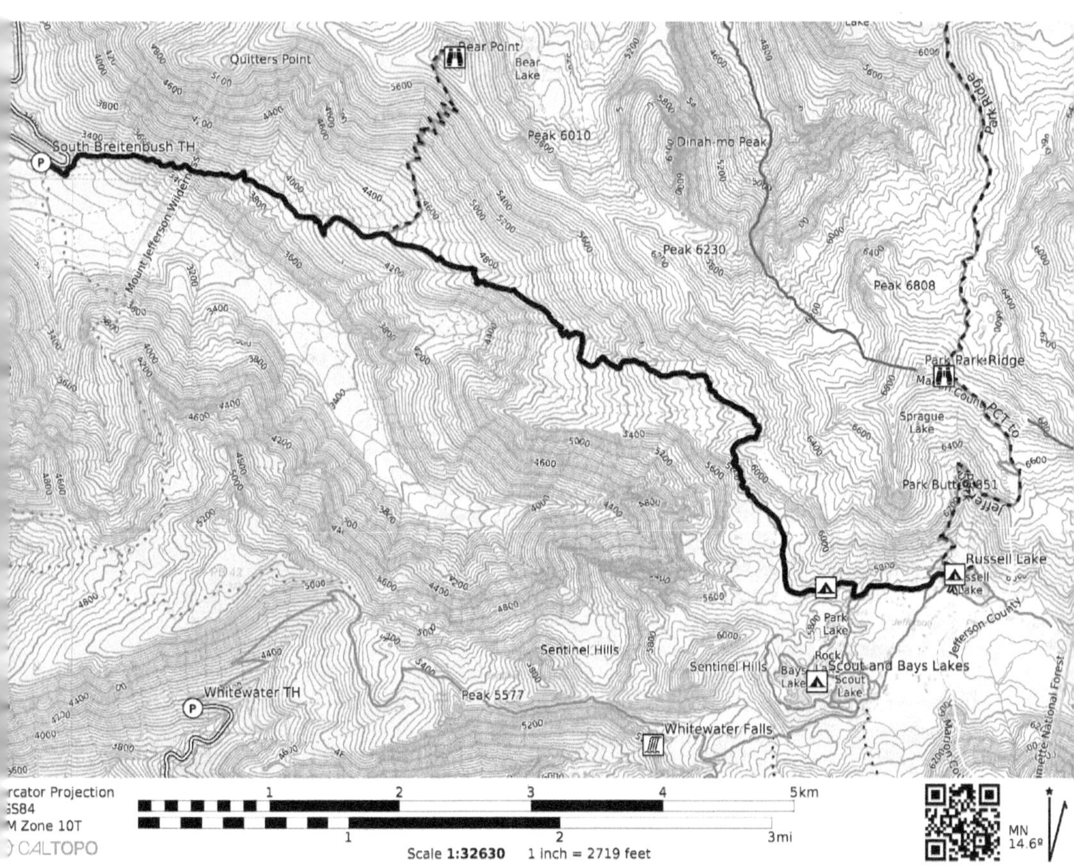

From the trailhead, follow the South Breitenbush Trail through a mossy bottomland as it follows the hairpin curve of FR 4685. Before long, you'll begin a long uphill traverse along the steep slopes above the South Breitenbush River. The trail passes through patches of forest that burned during the Lionshead Fire in 2020, but the South Breitenbush canyon is believed to have burned at a far lower severity than the damage found along neighboring ridges to the south and east. At 2.1 miles, you'll reach a junction with the Bear Point Trail on the left. This trail climbs up steep, open slopes 1.7 miles to an incredible view of Mount Jefferson, but it is not known when this trail will be reopened. From the junction, ignore the Bear Point Trail for now and continue straight on the South Breitenbush Trail.

As the trail climbs, the tread becomes rocky and tedious. You'll have the occasional view ahead to Mount Jefferson, but for the most part you'll remain in a forest regrowing from a previous fire in the 1960s. As you hike, consider that this trail is the historic approach to Jefferson Park; rangers once traveled along this path, which is in fact a single trail from Breitenbush Hot Springs to Jefferson Park. At 3.5 miles, the trail at last begins to level out and enters a lovely stretch of alpine woods and meadows. You'll pass a scenic tarn next to the trail and have excellent views up to Park Ridge above the trail. At 4.5 miles, the South Breitenbush Trail curves around the end of Park Ridge and begins to drop into Jefferson Park. A few short switchbacks through a rockslide lead you into the park, and soon you'll join the South Breitenbush River once more. The river is a small alpine stream here, with banks lined with a kaleidoscope of summer wildflowers. The trail follows the river for over a mile to a junction with the Pacific Crest Trail at 6.2 miles. Turning right here will lead you to Scout and Bays Lakes a mile to the south, but the easier destination is Russell Lake, some 200 yards to the east. Turn left on the PCT, then follow signs to Russell Lake, where you'll find amazing views of the mountain and fantastic wildflower meadows. Jefferson Park is very difficult to leave. so plan on backpacking here at least once. Campsites abound, but make sure to camp only in designated sites. The sunsets are amazing, and sometimes even life-changing. Return the way you came.

53. Marion Lake

Distance: 6.2 miles out and back
Elevation Gain: 1,200 feet
Trailhead elevation: 3,328 feet
Trail high point: 4,148 feet
Season: May – October
Best: May – October
Pass: NW Forest Pass + limited entry permit
Permit required: day use or overnight (if backpacking)
On the traditional lands of: the Molalla and Tenino peoples

Directions from Salem:

- From Salem, drive OR 22 east for approximately 49 miles to Detroit.
- Continue on OR 22 another 16.2 miles to a junction with Marion Road (FR 2255), just opposite the Marion Forks Restaurant.
- Turn left here and drive this one-lane paved road for 0.8 mile to the end of pavement.
- Continue another 3.7 miles of gravel road to road's end at the Marion Lake Trailhead.
- **Drivetime from Salem:** 1 hour and 30 minutes

Hike: Marion Lake has long been one of the most popular destinations in the Central Oregon Cascades and it's easy to see why. You'll find an enormous and wildly scenic backcountry lake, excellent campsites, gorgeous views of the surrounding mountains, and one of Oregon's best waterfalls on what is a relatively easy hike. Even more impressive is the display of vine maple around the lakeshore in the fall, when it seems like the entire lakeshore is on fire with millions of orange and red leaves. Before you go, don't forget to secure your day use or overnight permit; see the introduction to the Central Oregon Cascades on page 126 for more information.

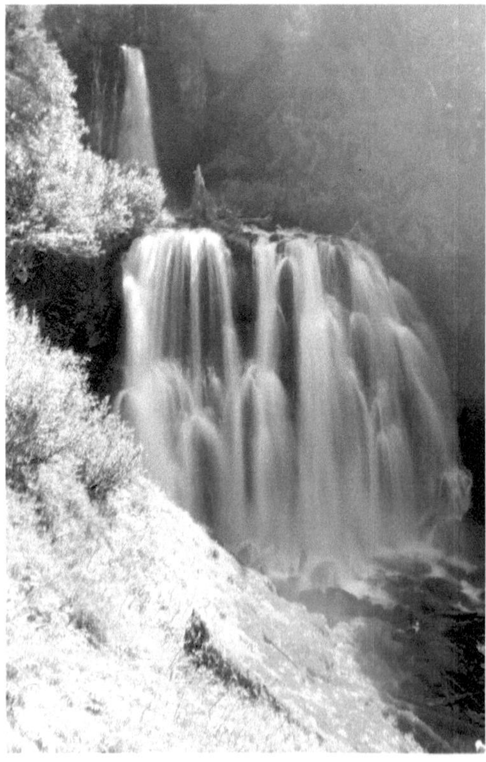

From the trailhead, follow the wide trail to Marion Lake through deep, mossy forest beside trickling Moon Creek. At about a mile from the trailhead, the trail crosses a pair of springs and begins a gradual ascent through deep woods. You'll reach scenic Lake Ann at 1.4 miles. Note how the lake's outlet disappears into the rocks below the trail, the source of the sound of running water you hear as you approach the lake. Beyond Lake Ann, the trail climbs another 0.4 mile to a fork, the beginning of the loop around the western shore of Marion Lake. Both trails take you to the lake, but this loop is best done counterclockwise, so fork to the right here. After just 0.2 mile from this junction, you'll see an unsigned but obvious trail branching off to the right. This out and back path leads you 0.2 mile to Marion Falls, one of Oregon's truly great waterfalls. Adventurous hikers will love this fun detour to the 150-foot twin falls (whose lower tier is known as Gatch Falls), but hikers uncomfortable with brushy trails, steep and slippery slopes, and considerable exposure should skip this detour. Beyond the Marion Falls side trip, you'll continue another 0.6 mile to a trail junction at the southwestern corner of huge Marion Lake. At 360 acres in size, the lake is the largest lake in Oregon that is located entirely in a wilderness area. The lake also has a maximum depth of 180 feet, making it by far the deepest lake in the Mount Jefferson Wilderness.

To continue the loop around the lakeshore you'll need to turn left at the junction. Before you continue the loop, however, you should consider another fun side trip to a view of Mount Jefferson. Turn right at the junction and follow the Blue Lake Trail for 0.1 mile until the trail begins to climb across a rockslide. Leave the trail here, following social trails back towards Marion Lake. Once you leave the rockslide, you'll see a handful of campsites just above lake level. Walk down to the lakeshore, where at last Mount Jefferson comes into view across the lake in all its glory. This is one of the best views of the mountain in the entire wilderness and few people know to look for it. If yu're planning an overnight stay, the campsites here are quite nice. When you're ready to leave the mountain behind, return the way you came to the bridge over Marion Creek and the junction just beyond where you left the loop.

You'll follow the Blue Lake Trail around the lake's western shore. Here the views across this vast lake are mostly filtered through the trees but are still impressive. Walking around Marion Lake, you would never expect that this was once the social and cultural hub of the Mount Jefferson area. Naturalist A.G. Prill had a cabin along the lake's north shore, and a Forest Service guard station once stood near the junction of the Marion Lake and Blue Lake Trails. Fishing enthusiasts kept boats here year-round to allow them access to the deeper parts of the lake. When Marion Lake became part of the Mount Jefferson Wilderness in 1968, the Forest Service removed both cabins as they were deemed incompatible with the wilderness designation. After following the lakeshore for 0.9 mile, you'll reach a junction with the Marion Lake Trail near the site of the old Forest Service guard station. Turn left here for the conclusion of the loop, but before you do, consider detouring to the lakeshore for an excellent view of Three-Fingered Jack across the lake. The forest on the eastern side of the lake burned during the B+B Fire in 2003 but is recovering nicely. From here, return to the Marion Lake Trail and hike 2.2 miles back to the trailhead.

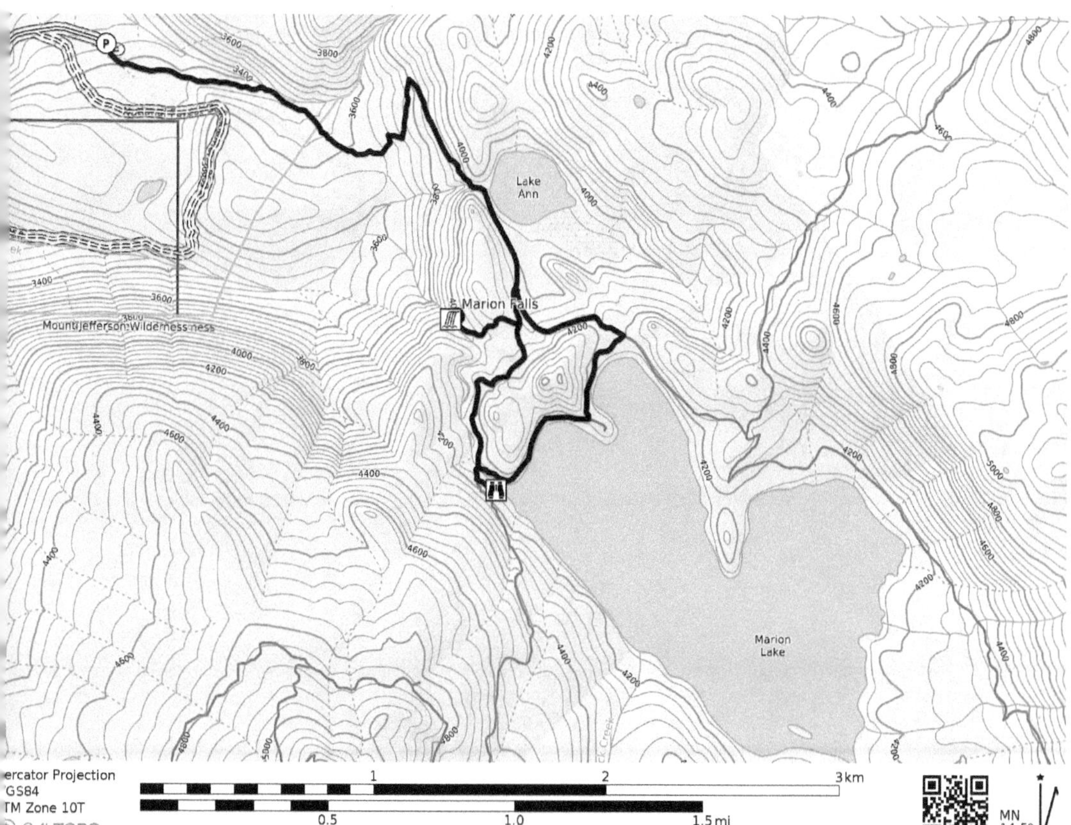

54. Coffin and Bachelor Mountains

	Coffin Mountain	Bachelor Mountain
Distance:	3 miles out and back	3.8 miles out and back
Elevation Gain:	1,047 feet	1,200 feet
Trailhead Elevation:	4,735 feet	4,831 feet
Trail High Point:	5,782 feet	5,941 feet
Season:	June – October	June – October
Best:	June – July	June – July
Pass:	none needed	none needed
Permit:	none needed	none needed
On the traditional lands of:	the Molalla people	the Molalla people

Directions from Salem:

- From Salem, drive OR 22 east approximately 49 miles to Detroit.
- Continue past Detroit on OR 22 for 19 miles to a junction with the Straight Creek Road (FR 11) on your right.
- Turn right and drive this winding but paved road for 1.4 miles to a junction with FR 1168. Ignore this junction and continue on paved FR 11.
- Continue 2.6 miles to another junction with FR 1168, veering sharply off to the right.

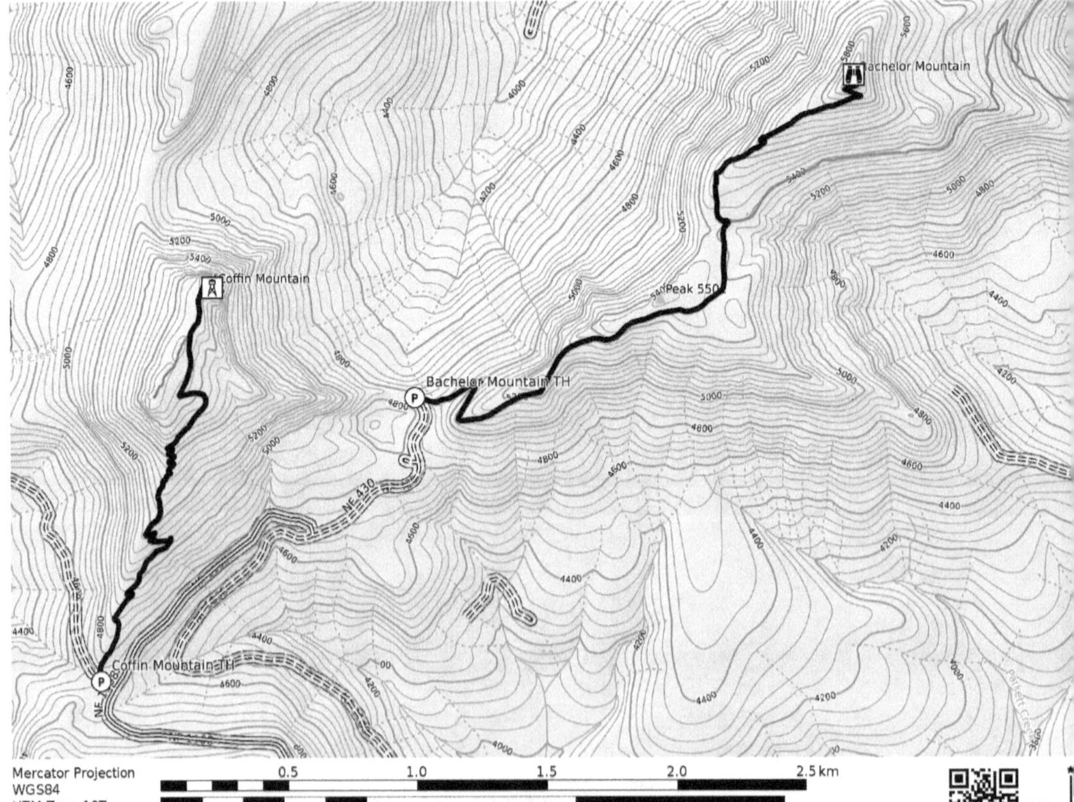

- Turn right and drive this gravel road 1.4 miles to a fork with FR 368.
- Keep left on FR 1168 and continue another 2.4 winding miles to a junction with FR 450.
- Turn left and drive 50 yards to the signed trailhead.
- For Bachelor Mountain, continue another 0.7 mile on FR 1168 to a junction with FR 1168-430, angling away to the left.
- Turn left here and drive 0.5 mile of narrow, rocky gravel to road's end at the Bachelor Mountain trailhead on your right. Above the trailhead is an exceptional view of Coffin Mountain to your left.
- **Drivetime:** 1 hour and 45 minutes from Salem

Hike: A member of the lily family, beargrass is a tall white flower that grows on mountain slopes all over the West. Pinning down the growth cycle of this flower is difficult, and predicting a good beargrass year is nearly impossible. In 2019, Coffin Mountain south of Detroit experienced a brief period of intense popularity during an especially impressive beargrass bloom. There is so much more to this hike than just beargrass; the flower displays here are fantastic all throughout the summer, and the views of the surrounding mountains and Cascade peaks are hard to beat. For a similar experience with less beargrass but better flower variety and equally impressive views, you can hike to the summit of nearby Bachelor Mountain.

From the Coffin Mountain Trailhead, follow the trail steeply up the open slopes of Coffin Mountain. When seen from most vantages, the mountain takes on a flat-topped perspective that makes it look impossible to climb. The trail to the summit is shockingly well-graded in fact, and you'll be no doubt helped along by the spectacular flower displays and views to be found here. In addition to beargrass, look for masses of red paintbrush, purple larkspur, yellow arnica, white irises, orange tiger lilies, and so many more. The trail reaches the summit at 1.5 miles, where you'll find spectacular views up and down the Cascade Range from Mount Rainier to Diamond Peak. A closer look also reveals a thin sliver of Detroit Lake in the valley to the north. The view is so great and the summit so exposed that the lookout that stands here sits on the ground, rather than on a tower as so many do. The lookout on the summit is staffed during the summer and you should leave the staffer be unless they come out to speak to you. Return the way you came.

If you're planning on hiking to the summit of Bachelor Mountain, you'll need to return to the trailhead and drive east 1.2 miles to the Bachelor Mountain Trailhead. From the trailhead, you'll hike uphill through an impressive forest of Douglas fir and mountain hemlock before emerging on the open slopes of Bachelor Mountain. The flower display is even more impressive here than at Coffin Mountain, with fewer beargrass blooms but with more scarlet gilia, Cascade lilies, and xeric flowers than you'll find on Bachelor Mountain's neighbor to the west. At 1.3 miles, you'll reach a junction with the Bruno Meadows Trail. Fork to the left and follow this trail 0.6 mile to the summit, where you'll find the remains of a lookout that was dismantled in the 1960s. The view is even better here than at Coffin Mountain, and you'll have a unique, front-row vantage of the damage caused by the 2020 wildfires. The view is just as good here, and the view of Mount Jefferson is particularly amazing. Return the way you came.

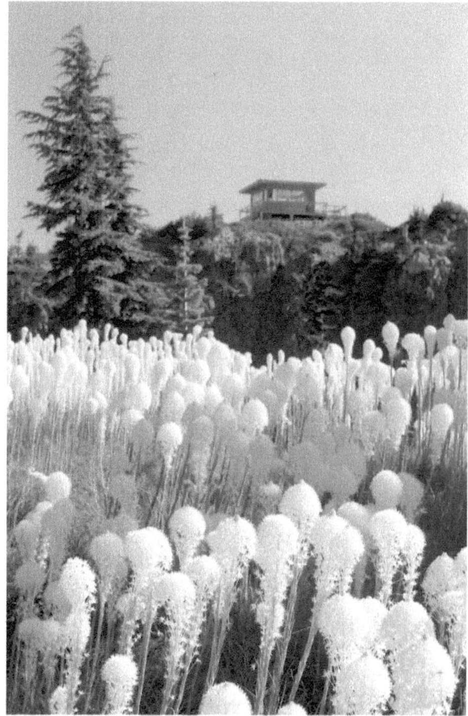

55. House Rock

Distance: 1.2 mile loop
Elevation Gain: 100 feet
Trailhead elevation: 1,606 feet
Trail high point: 1,716 feet
Season: all year
Best: all year
Pass: none needed
Permit: none needed
On the traditional lands of: the Molalla people

Directions:

- From Sweet Home, drive 26 miles on US 20 up the South Santiam River to a junction with Latiwi Creek Road (US 2044), signed for House Rock Campground.
- Turn right here and drive 200 yards downhill to a junction.
- Turn right and drive downhill 0.3 mile to a parking area on your right, just before a bridge. The trail leaves from the signboard at this lot.
- **Drivetime from Sweet Home:** 35 minutes

Hike: In a state full of wonderful campgrounds, House Rock is one of my favorites. Here the South Santiam River flows through a rocky, narrow canyon full of ancient and massive Douglas firs. The campsites here are tucked away next to the river or under the tall trees, offering a peaceful and gorgeous spot to spend a night, a weekend, or an entire week. The easy and fully gorgeous House Rock Loop begins at the campground, allowing campers and hikers alike the opportunity to take in the best of what this area has to offer. The only downside of this hike is

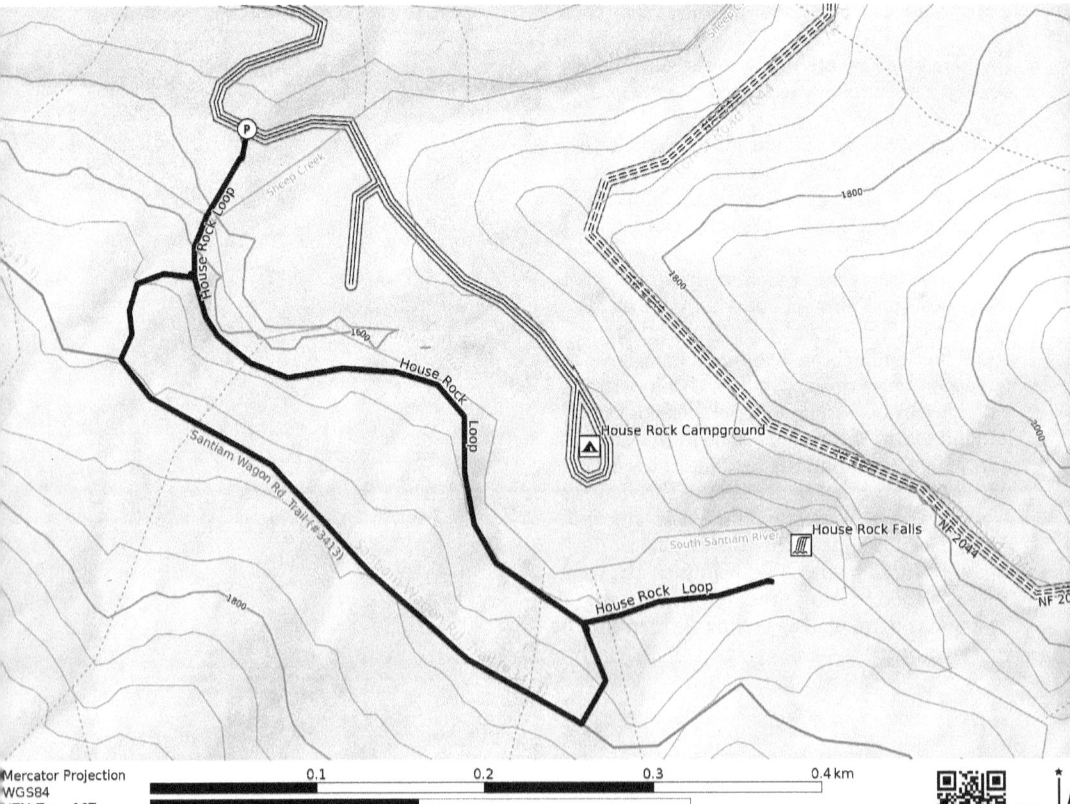

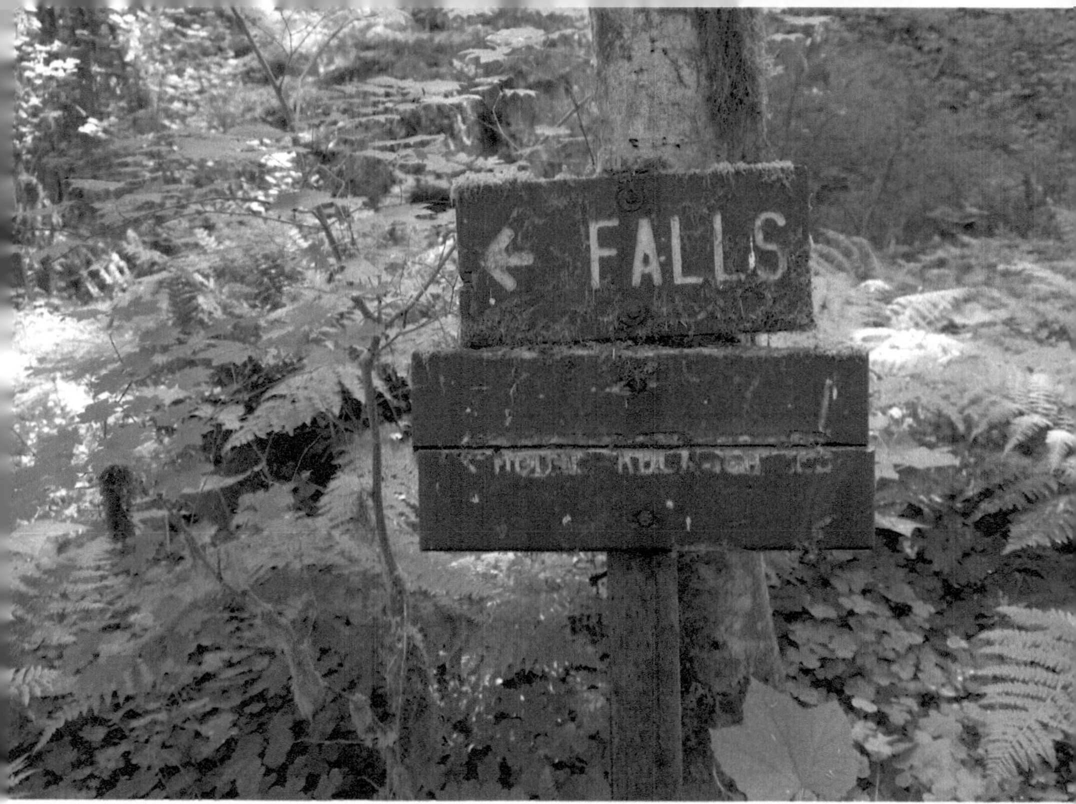

The old wooden sign on the Santiam Wagon Road.

that it isn't longer; this is one of the best short hikes in Oregon.

From the trailhead at the beginning of the campground loop, follow the signed trail to a bridge over the South Santiam River. Once across the bridge, follow the trail upriver to a trail junction. Turn left here to begin the loop. After just a few moments, the trail passes under the House Rock, the namesake of the campground where you started. Pioneer families took refuge under the rock during storms while traveling the Santiam Wagon Road, which you'll visit in a little bit. The trail continues beyond the boulder to a junction with a spur trail on the left. Right takes you to the wagon road, but first you should turn left to go visit House Rock Falls. Follow this trail downhill to an obstructed view of the falls, a 20-foot chute in a narrow crevice on the South Santiam River. The rocks above the falls are fun to explore but getting an unobstructed view of the falls is almost impossible. When you're ready to continue, return to the last junction and turn left. You'll switchback uphill through impressive old-growth forest to a junction with the Santiam Wagon Road, where you turn right to continue on the loop.

The Santiam Wagon Road was constructed in the 1860s and served as the primary route through the Central Cascades for the next several decades. The construction of US 20 during the 1920s led to the abandonment of the old wagon road. Today it serves as an excellent hiking trail, particularly during the winter months when the higher Cascades are under snow. Follow the old wagon road downhill under more impressively tall trees for 0.3 mile to another junction, which may be unsigned. Turn right and follow this trail downhill to the beginning of the loop trail near the bridge over the South Santiam River. Turn left here to cross the river and return to the trailhead.

If you're looking for a longer hike you can follow the Santiam Wagon Road east or west from the House Rock area through lovely forest. The scenery does not improve, however, and this is best saved for those rainy days when you just want to go for a walk in the woods.

56. Middle Santiam Wilderness

Distance: 13.6 miles out and back
Elevation Gain: 2,500 feet
Trailhead Elevation: 2,405 feet
Trail High Point: 2,734 feet
Season: June – October
Best: June – October
Pass: none needed
Permit: none needed
On the traditional lands of: the Molalla people

Directions from Sweet Home:

- Drive 19 miles east of the Quartzville Road Bridge at the east end of Sweet Home to a junction on the left with Soda Fork Road (FR 2041). Turn left onto Soda Fork Road next to an old garage, and reset your odometer here.
- Drive 0.8 mile and keep left to stay on FR 2041. You will drive this gravel road into the heart of many old and recent logging operations. The road is gravel and mostly good, with a few rough spots.
- At 7.6 miles, you will arrive at a six-way junction at a pass. Keep straight on the main road (FR 2041) to continue.
- At 8.2 miles, keep left to stay on FR 2041.
- At 9.6 miles, keep left.
- At 11.9 miles, reach a three-way fork with Spur Road. Take the middle road, FR 646.
- Follow this narrow dirt road for 0.6 mile to its end at the Shedd Camp Trailhead. There is room for about 10 cars.
- **Drivetime from Sweet Home:** 1 hour and 20 minutes

Hike: While Oregon is home to many wild places, few feel as wild as the Middle Santiam Wilderness. Designated in 1984 to protect one of Oregon's largest and most impressive remaining stands of old-growth forest, hiking into the Middle Santiam feels like a trip back in time to the days before most of our ancient forest was logged. Hikers looking for an easy hike can hike downhill to Shedd Camp Shelter, just above a gorgeous waterfall and one of Oregon's finest swimming holes. But you drove all this way, so you should plan on the longer hike to Donaca Lake. Better yet, plan this hike as a backpacking trip to spend one night or many deep in the heart of this wild, wild place.

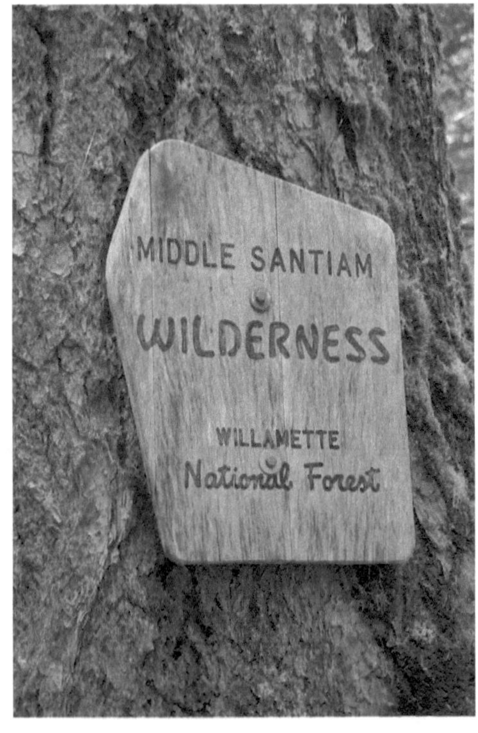

From the signboard at the trailhead that is signed for the Chimney Peak Trail, follow the trail downhill into deep forest. After a fast 0.6 mile, you'll arrive at Shedd Camp Shelter. Set amid huge trees, the shelter is a delightful place to spend a few hours (or a few nights). User paths lead to viewpoints of Shelter Falls and its amazing swimming hole. Continue another 0.1 mile from the shelter to a crossing of the Middle Santiam River just above the falls. You can usually cross with dry feet but you may need to ford the river early in the season when the river is swollen with snowmelt. Once across the river, you'll pick up the Chimney Peak Trail and follow it to a junction with the South Pyramid Trail at 1.1 miles. Keep left to stay on the Chimney Peak Trail. The trail passes through a grove of truly magnificent old-growth Douglas firs and hemlocks as it follows the steep canyon slopes of Pyramid Creek. At 3.2 miles, the trail reaches a bridgeless crossing of wide Pyramid Creek. Just before the creek crossing, look to your right for a fantastic campsite by the creek – a worthy goal for hikers looking for an easy hike or an easy backpacking trip. If you're continuing, you'll have to get your feet wet to cross Pyramid Creek.

Once across the creek, the trail climbs a short distance to a crossing of FR 2041 – the very road you followed most of the way to the trailhead. Before the Middle Santiam Wilderness was officially designated a wilderness area in 1984, the Forest Service had attempted to extend FR 2041 deep into this rugged area. The road washed out repeatedly, and since becoming wilderness, has taken on the appearance of a trail. Mountain bikers use the old road to access other trails outside the wilderness, so you may encounter a group or two here. Cross the road and at last enter the Middle Santiam Wilderness. The trail continues deeper into ancient forest, where the only sounds are those of the forest: the wind, the birds, the occasional stream. The Chimney Peak Trail is quite brushy through here but is still easy to follow; if you visit on a wet day, expect to get soaked as you hike through the brush. After awhile hiking through the deep forest here, the Chimney Peak Trail reaches a junction with the Gordan Peak Trail on the right at 5.4 miles. Keep straight to continue following the Chimney Peak Trail.

You're in the home stretch now. The Chimney Peak Trail continues even deeper into ancient forest another mile to Donaca Lake at 6.6 miles from the trailhead. An oasis deep in the heart of the Middle Santiam Wilderness, this scenic lake has several good campsites. Huge trees line the lake, offering shade on sunny days and protection on rainy days. Several inlets on the north side of the lake provide excellent drinking water. This is a wonderful place to spend the night, far away from all the trappings of modern living. When you're ready, return the way you came.

Extending your hike:
The Chimney Peak Trail continues several miles to the west, eventually reaching its namesake. This is an adventure best suited for a longer backpacking trip. There are many other worthy adventures in this wild place but you will need to plan ahead. The trails are faint, steep, and brushy, and water can be scarce. Everything here is a true adventure, for better and for worse.

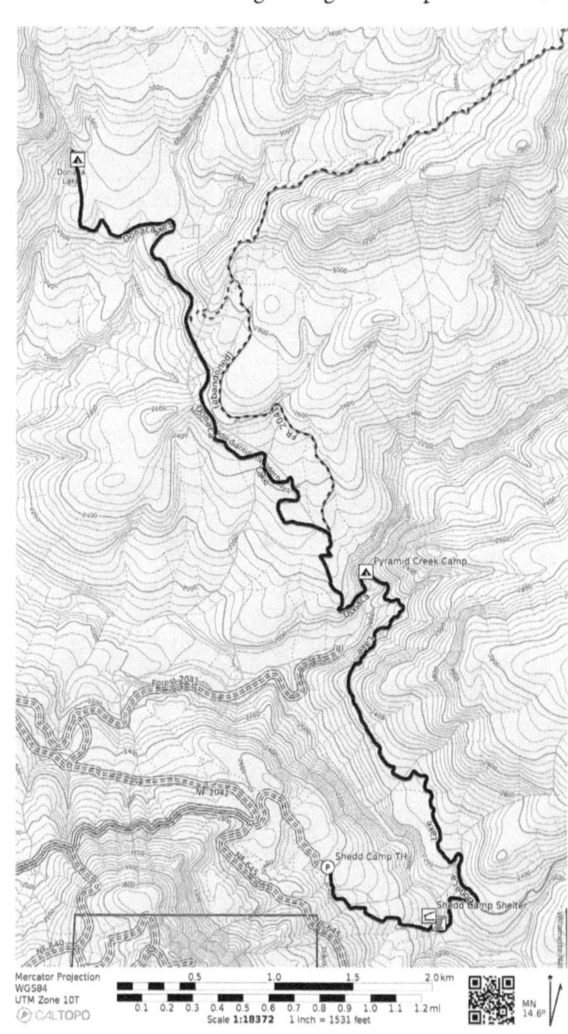

57. Iron Mountain Loop

Distance: 6.8 mile loop
Elevation Gain: 1,900 feet
Trailhead elevation: 4,225 feet
Trail high point: 5,439 feet
Season: June – October
Best: June – July
Pass: NW Forest Pass
Permit: none needed
On the traditional lands of: the Molalla people

Directions:

- From Sweet Home drive east on US 20 for 35 miles to Tombstone Pass.
- Turn right into a large lot with a bathroom.
- If you are coming from the east, the trailhead is 11.1 miles west of the split with OR 22.
- **Drivetime from Sweet Home:** 45 minutes

Hike: The mountains west of the Cascade crest between the Santiam and McKenzie River valleys are known as the Old Cascades. These mountains are considerably older than the volcanoes that dominate the horizon to the east, and the volcanic soil and rocky peaks in this area are home to some of Oregon's most extraordinary wildflower meadows. This classic loop passes along the base of Cone Peak on its way to the summit of Iron Mountain in the heart of the Old Cascades, passing numerous stupendous wildflower meadows along the way. Unlike many other hikes in this region, expect crowds here during wildflower season in June and July as this is one of the most beloved hikes in the central Oregon Cascades.

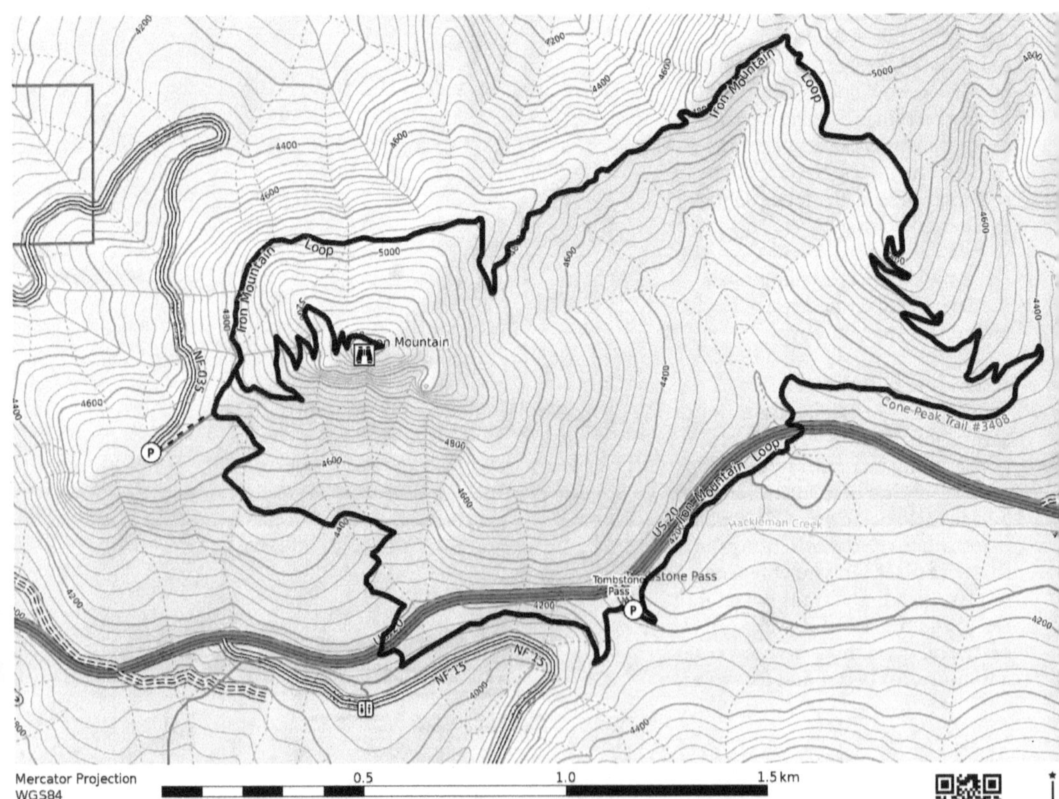

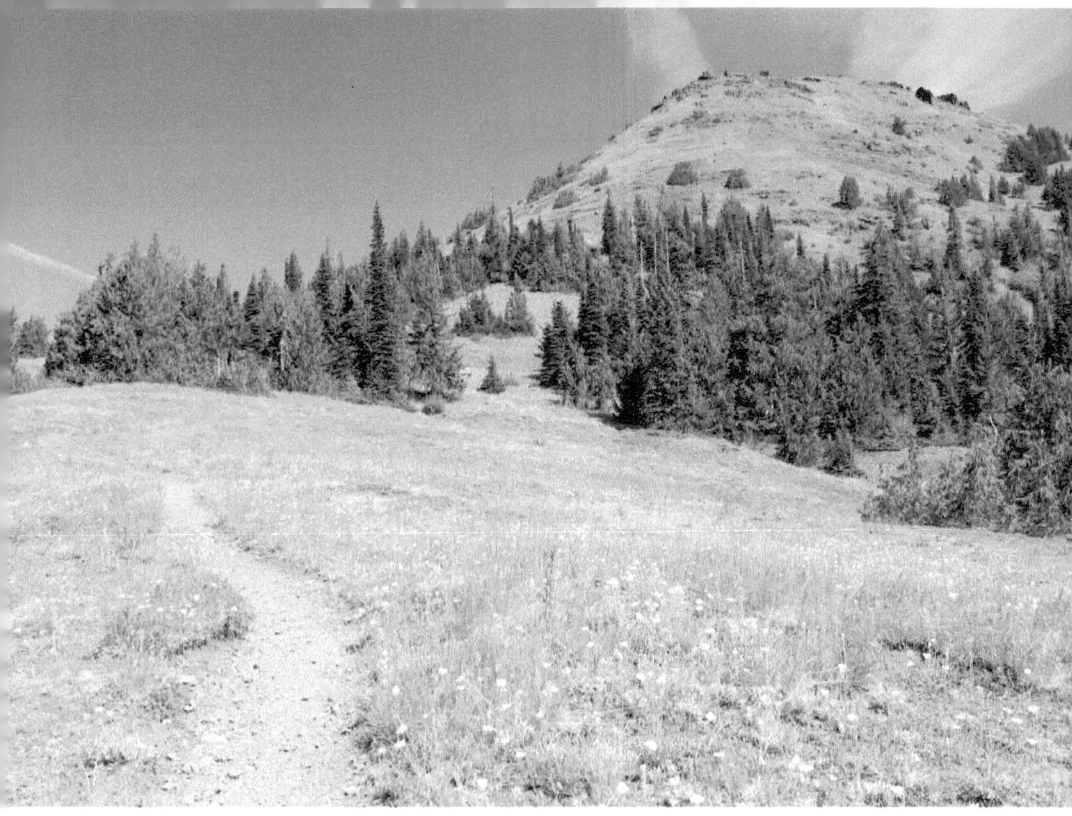

The wildflower meadows at the base of Cone Peak are fun to explore.

From the trailhead at Tombstone Pass, locate the Tombstone Nature Trail and hike downhill slightly through the forest paralleling US 20. At about a half-mile from the trailhead, you will cross US 20. Look both ways and carefully cross the highway. From here, you'll pick up the Cone Peak Trail and climb gradually up through the forest until you reach Cone Peak's meadows at a little over 2 miles. In flower season, the next mile of trail is among the finest in the Cascades: acres of wildflowers carpet the meadows, while Iron Mountain with its distinctive rock pinnacle looms across the valley to the west. Look for countless blue and purple larkspur, red paintbrush, and yellow Oregon Sunshine, a small daisy-like flower. You may want to bring a wildflower guidebook or have an app on your phone to help you identify the many and varied flower species found in the meadows here.

Beyond Cone Peak's meadows, the trail dips into the forest a bit as it traverses around Iron Mountain's forested north face. Snow can linger on these slopes late into June and early July, as this side of Iron Mountain does not see much sunshine. At 3.9 miles, meet the Iron Mountain Spur Trail on your left. Turn left and switchback uphill 0.7 mile to the summit, where you will find a fenced observation deck and benches. The view is extraordinary, stretching from Mount Adams to Diamond Peak. A lookout tower stood on the summit here until 2008, when it was dismantled and replaced by the observation deck on which you now stand. The summit can feel a bit crowded on sunny summer days but you should resist the temptation to wander off trail here; the cliffs are huge, and even the lookout tower once blew off the summit in a winter storm.

When you're ready to finish the hike, hike back to the Iron Mountain Trail and turn left. You will quickly reach a junction with the Iron Mountain Trail on your right; this trail arrives from a trailhead only a few hundred yards to the right, offering a shorter approach to this area if you need one. To complete this loop, continue downhill until you reach a crossing of US 20. Look both ways and carefully make your way across the highway. From here, the trail descends into the forest below the highway. You'll need to regain a bit of elevation over the next 0.6 mile on the way back to Tombstone Pass to complete the loop.

58. West Browder Ridge

Distance: 11.4 miles out and back
Elevation Gain: 2,000 feet
Trailhead elevation: 4,015 feet
Trail high Point: 5,729 feet
Season: June – October
Best: July
Pass: none needed
Permit: none needed
On the traditional lands of: the Molalla people

Directions:

- From the junction of US 20 and Quartzville Road east of Sweet Home, drive approximately 30 miles on US 20 up the South Santiam River to a junction with FR 15. If you are coming from the east, this junction is on your left 11.7 miles after the OR 22 / US 20 split.
- Turn right here onto FR 15 and drive 2.5 paved miles to the trailhead, a small parking lot with a "P" sign on the right. The trailhead is located at the junction of FR 15 and FR 080.
- The trail departs from the left side of the road at a signboard.
- **Drivetime from Sweet Home:** 55 minutes

Hike: The Old Cascades are where wildflower lovers go on vacation. Here you will find the finest displays of July wildflowers anywhere, with more variety than you could possibly imagine. But there's so much more to see here beyond blooms – many of the trails climb through impressive groves of ancient forest meadows, and on towards spectacular viewpoints east towards the volcanoes of the high Cascades. Perhaps the best hike in the Old Cascades is this long and varied trek along the western end of Browder Ridge. Along the way you'll pass tall trees and endless meadows in full bloom with July wildflowers, and views south to the Three Sisters. Patience and energy will take you to the summit of Browder Ridge, where you'll have views northeast to Mount Jefferson and across the rugged heart of the Old Cascades. Pack a hearty lunch, enough water, a camera, and your wildflower identification guide and you are assured of a wonderful time.

The hike begins at a signboard just across FR 15. You'll climb above the road and hike into a

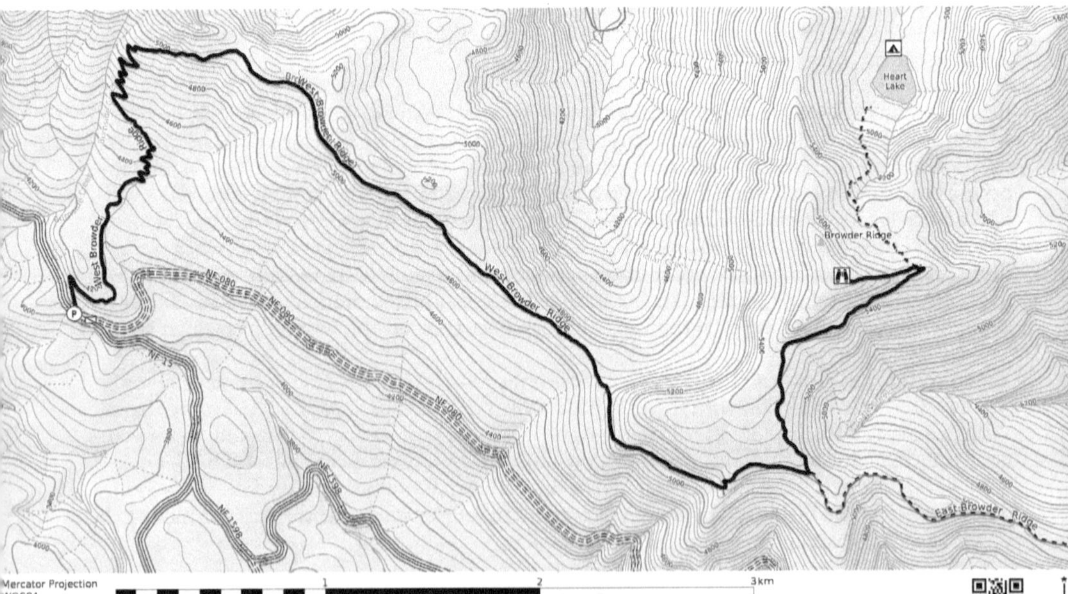

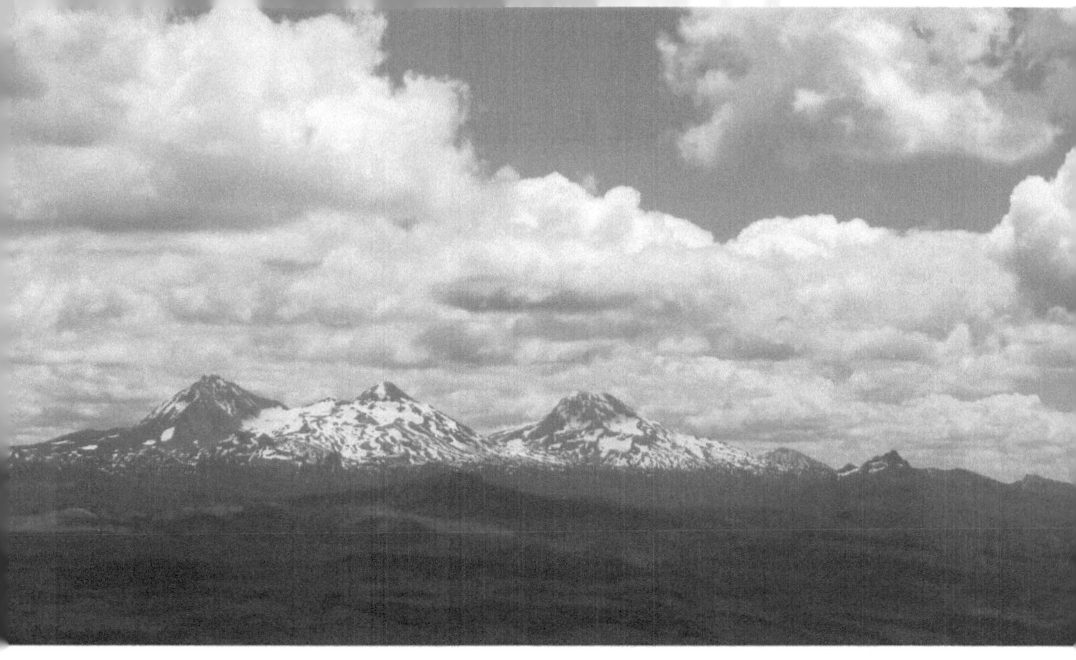

West Browder Ridge features fantastic views of the Three Sisters.

cool wood, where the climbing relents. At a little under a mile from the trailhead, reach the base of Browder Ridge's west face at the foot of an enormous meadow of bracken fern. At first glance, you may be wonder if you must climb straight up this madness; but in fact, the trail climbs gently along the edge of the meadow, offering your first glimpses southeast to the Three Sisters. Orange tiger lilies line the trail through the fern meadow in July. Once you've reached the top of the meadow, the trail settles down and you'll soon reach the first of what seems like an endless succession of meadows. Each one is a kaleidoscope of color – note the red paintbrush, the blue and purple lupine, the pink owl's clover, the yellow monkeyflower, the white mariposa lilies, and so much more. The trail passes through impressive ancient forest, emerging anew in yet more meadows. The views keep coming and coming as you hike along the crest of Browder Ridge.

At around 3 miles from the trailhead, the trail passes through a brief section of trail where the forest burned in a spot fire some ten years ago. Here you are sure to spot orange tiger lilies in season. From here, you will begin climbing on tread that is occasionally plagued with blow-down. The West Browder Trail meets the more popular Gate Creek Trail in deep woods at 4.7 miles. Turn left here and begin a gentle ascent towards the summit of Browder Ridge. Soon the trail emerges below Browder Ridge's summit cliffs. Continue the climb through meadows until you reach a saddle at 5.5 miles from the trailhead. Veer to the left to follow a rougher trail that scrambles up to the summit of Browder Ridge's rocky crest. At times this trail seems sketchy but keep the faith – simply pushing forward will eventually take you to the rounded summit of Browder Ridge. Take the time to seek out different views – there are many to be had, north-east to Mount Jefferson, southeast to the Three Sisters, and across the wide scope of the Old Cascades.

When you're ready to turn around, return the way you came to the saddle below the summit of Browder Ridge. A trail departs here and heads steeply downhill (and I mean steep – it loses 700 feet in 0.7 mile) to beautiful Heart Lake. Backpackers will be tempted by Heart Lake, but know that there are few sites along the marshy lakeshore, and the trail down is murder on your knees. My wife described this trail the one time we hiked it as "not for the faint of heart", and I agree with her. Most hikers will be content to return the way they came along Browder Ridge's meadows. Along the way, you'll get to experience the meadows, the ancient forest, and the views again – and no, it just does not get old.

59. Canyon Creek Meadows

Distance: 7.9 mile semi-loop
Elevation Gain: 1,600 feet
Trailhead elevation: 5,146 feet
Trail high point: 6.547 feet
Season: July – October
Best: July – October
Pass: NW Forest Pass + limited entry permit
Permit required: day use or overnight (if backpacking)
On the traditional lands of: the Warm Springs, Tenino, and Molalla peoples

Directions from Sisters:

- Drive US 20 for 12 miles northwest to a turnoff on your right for FR 12, signed for "Mt. Jefferson Wilderness Trailheads".
- Turn right on FR 12 and drive 1.1 miles to a fork in the road. Keep right for another 3.3 miles to a sign for Jack Lake. Turn left and drive 0.6 mile of narrow pavement to a bridge over Jack Creek by Jack Creek Campground.
- Keep straight 0.7 mile of pavement to a junction on the right signed for Cabot Lake TH.
- Keep straight, now on FR 1234, another 0.7 mile of washboarded gravel to a junction with FR 1235, Bear Valley Road, on your right.
- Keep left and drive 5.1 miles of wide but extremely bumpy, washboarded gravel road to Jack Lake and the huge trailhead for Canyon Creek Meadows.
- **Drivetime from Sisters:** 45 minutes

Hike: Canyon Creek Meadows is one of the most spectacular places in the Oregon Cascades.

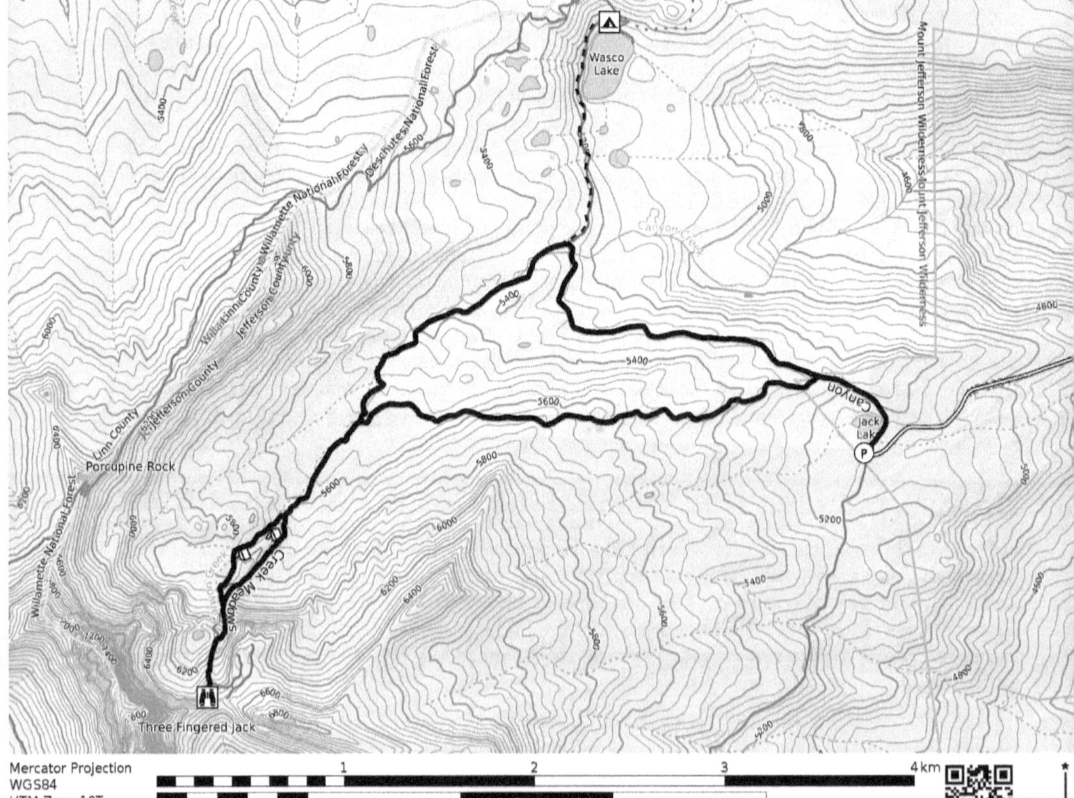

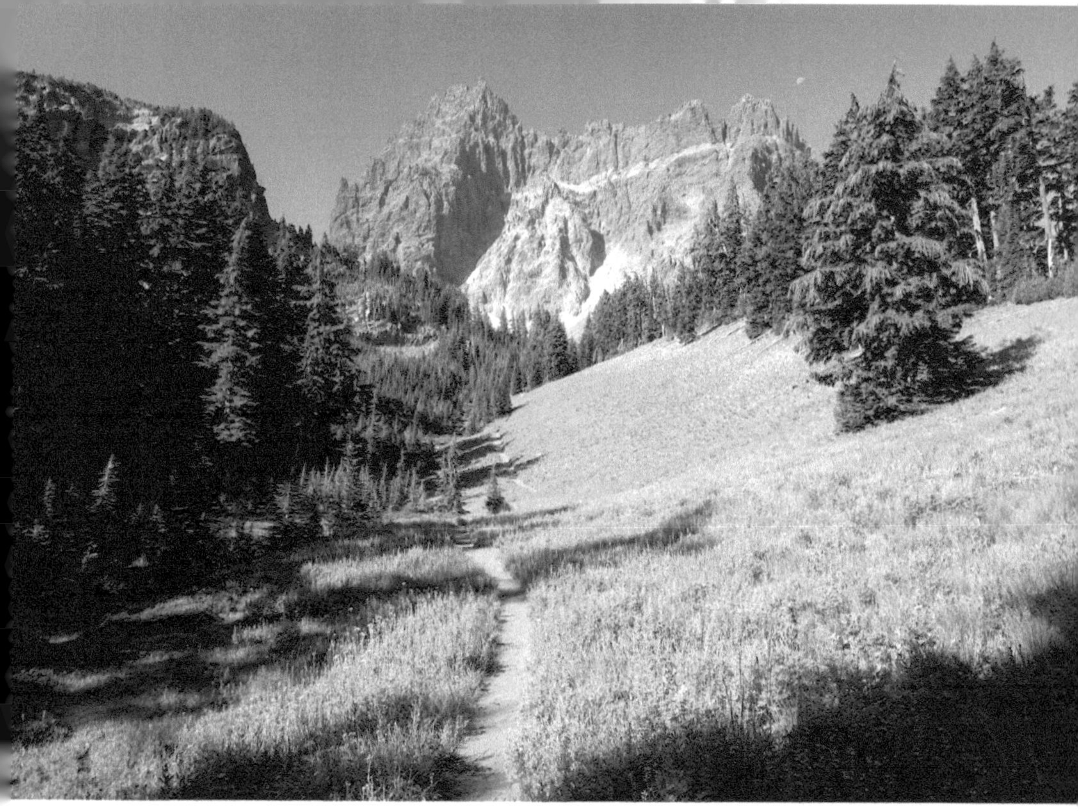

Three-Fingered Jack towers over Canyon Creek Meadows.

The massive, heavily eroded wall of Three-Fingered Jack towers over fields of wildflowers, while cascading Canyon Creek is at turns glassy and roaring, providing myriad photo opportunities. This is a magical place! Before you go, don't forget to secure your day use or overnight permit; see the introduction to the Central Oregon Cascades on page 126 for more information.

From the trailhead, follow the Old Summit Trail for 0.4 mile to a fork in the trail. Turn left here. As you hike along, you'll be in the scar left by the 2003 B+B Fire, one of the largest and most destructive in Oregon's history. This fire began at Booth Lake, not far south of here, before eventually burning more than 90,000 acres, most of it in the Mount Jefferson Wilderness. Today, the land is recovering nicely, and many young conifers now line the trail. You'll leave the fire scar behind at 1.6 miles as the trail passes into deep woods in the basin that holds Canyon Creek Meadows. At a junction at 2.2 miles, turn left on the Glacier View Trail and hike into Canyon Creek Meadows. This unofficial trail is obvious all the way into the meadows, which you reach at 2.6 miles. Three-Fingered Jack is your constant companion; follow the trail into the slopes of this sharp, craggy colossus as it climbs above the huge wildflower meadows below. Look for the notch in the sandy glacial moraine above you and climb steeply on the unofficial trail to a spectacular view of a glacial tarn at the base of Three-Fingered Jack's precipitous slopes at 3.3 miles. The glacier that once filled this moraine has retreated and is now considered deceased. The trail continues steeply uphill to a wide shoulder on the east face of Three-Fingered Jack at 3.8 miles. Mountain goats, reintroduced into the Mount Jefferson Wilderness in 2010, are frequently sighted on the slopes along the moraine. Look north to a fantastic view of Mount Jefferson, looming over the sweep of its namesake wilderness.

To complete the loop, return to the junction you passed at 2.2 miles and continue north on the Canyon Creek Trail along the creek for 2.5 miles to a junction with the Old Summit Trail at 6.3 miles. Peaceful and serene Wasco Lake is only 0.7 mile to the north, offering the possibility of a pleasant detour or a cool swim on a hot day. If you're ready to finish the hike, however, turn right and follow the Old Summit Trail 1.6 miles back to the Jack Lake Trailhead.

60. Black Butte

Distance: 4.2 miles out and back
Elevation Gain: 1,553 feet
Trailhead elevation: 4,887 feet
Trail high point: 6,440 feet
Season: May – October
Best: June – July
Pass: NW Forest Pass
Permit: none needed
On the traditional lands of: the Warm Springs and Tenino peoples

Directions from Sisters:

- From Sisters, drive US 20 for 8 miles northwest to a turnoff on your right for FR 11, also known as Green Ridge Road.
- Turn right and drive this paved road for 3.8 miles to a junction with FR 1110, signed for the Black Butte Trailhead.
- Turn left here and drive 4 miles of washboarded and dusty gravel to a junction with FR 700. Fork to the right to stay on FR 1110.
- From here, the road is rocky and rough in a few spots but remains passable. Drive slowly for 1.1 miles on FR 1110 to the trailhead.
- **Drivetime from Sisters:** 30 minutes

Hike: Everywhere you go in Central Oregon. Black Butte's dark, conical form is on the horizon. This extinct volcano is located just east of the Cascade Crest, towering over the ranches and vacation homes in Black Butte Ranch and along the Metolius River. One would assume that the

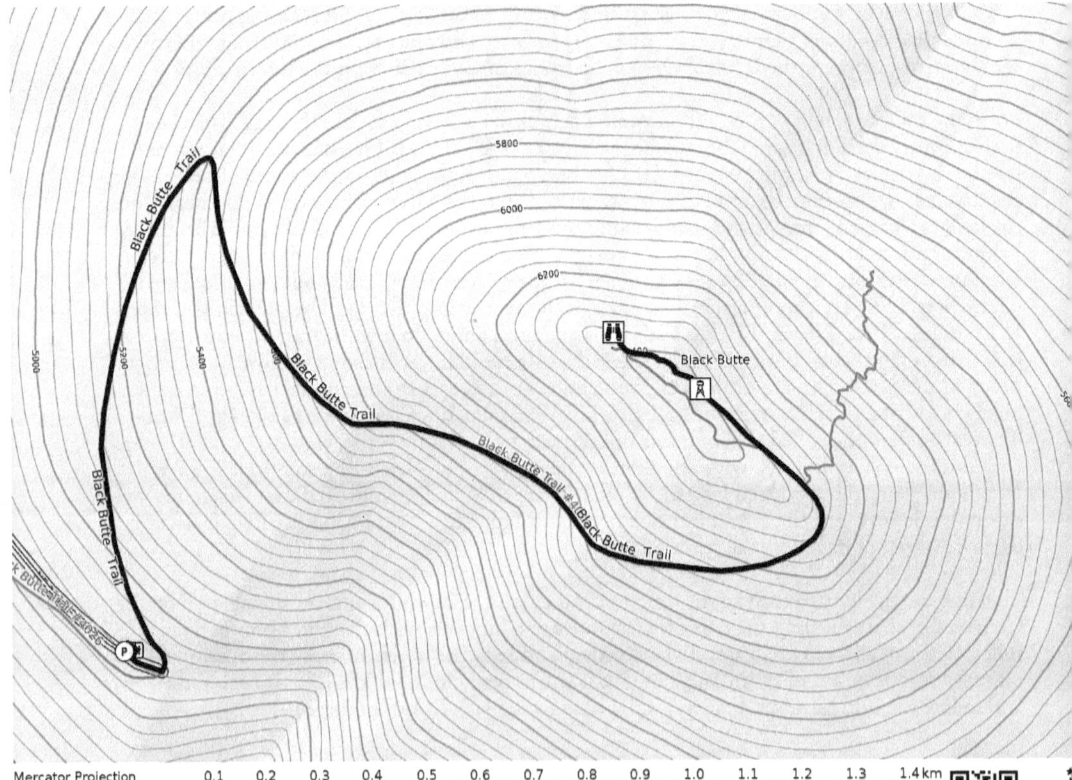

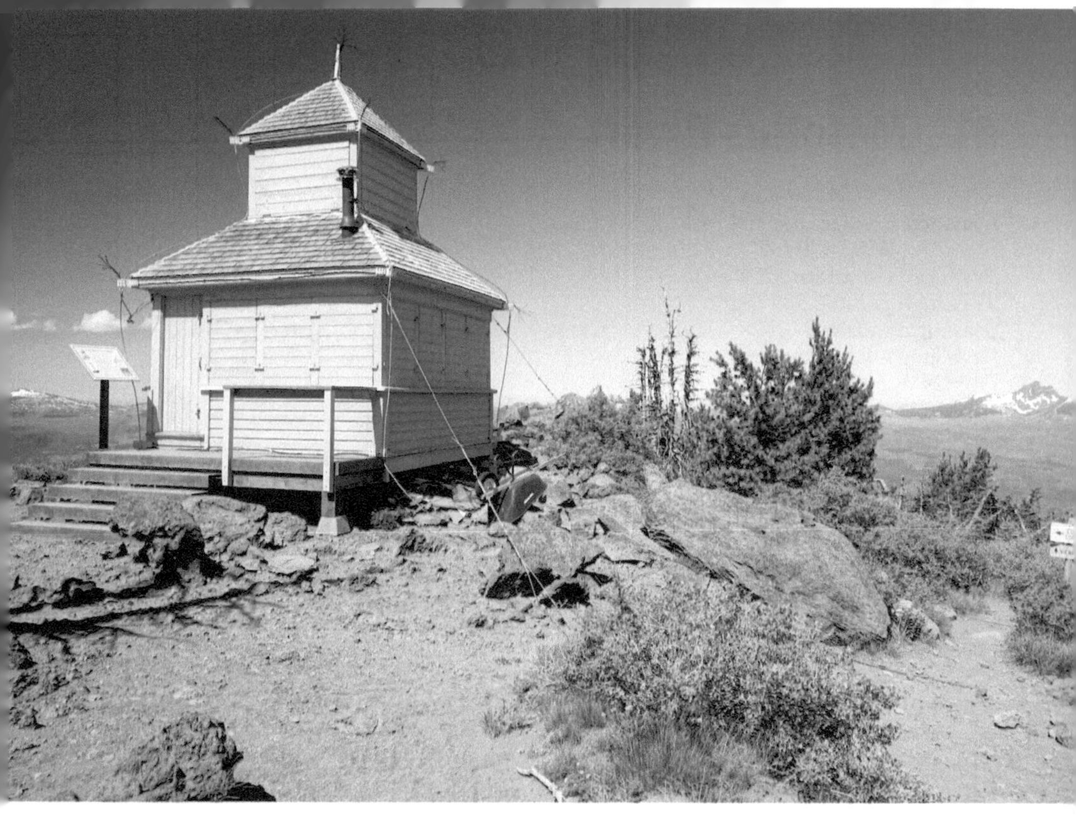

The cupola lookout on the summit, with Three-Fingered Jack in the background.

view from the summit of Black Butte would be excellent, and you would be correct. The hike to the summit is about more than just great views, however; you'll also hike under huge ponderosa pines, pass spectacular displays of wildflowers in June and July, and visit a historic lookout building that has been restored in recent years. This hike has something for everyone. Pack sunscreen for this hike, as much of it is exposed to the sun.

From the trailhead, follow the Black Butte Trailhead uphill. The forest here is predominantly ponderosa pine, and these are some truly impressive specimens. The trail leaves the forest at about a mile and enters a sunny hillside with lots of early summer flowers. Look for yellow balsamroot, red paintbrush, columbine, and scarlet gilia, false Solomonseal, blue and purple larkspur, and so many more. Fragrant snowbrush (better known as ceanothus) lines the trail, discouraging any attempts to cut switchbacks. As soon as you leave the forest, you will be able to see the lookout on the summit, but you should resist the call of summit fever. Sunny days on this stretch of trail feel particularly hot, and you'll want to stop frequently to take in the flowers and views visible around every corner.

The Black Butte Trail reaches the summit at 2 miles from the trailhead, at an elevation of 6,440 feet. The 62-foot lookout tower that stands atop the summit was built in 1995 and is staffed every summer. The lookout tower is off-limits to visitors. Follow the trail across the summit to a white cupola-style building on the western edge of the summit. This building, once a lookout, was built in 1923 and has been restored in recent years. This lookout is also closed to visitors, but a trail behind the building leads to a platform with one of the best views in Central Oregon. Look north to Mount Jefferson, with Mount Hood on the northern horizon. Look east to Three-Fingered Jack, and south to Mount Washington and the Three Sisters, all seemingly within arm's length. The meadows below you to the south are Black Butte Ranch. To the north, the Metolius River (Hike 61) flows north from the springs at the base of Black Butte, stretching out like a snake towards its rugged inner canyon. Cartophiles will love this viewpoint, as it almost feels like a map of Central Oregon is spread out below you. Whenever you are ready to turn around, return the way you came.

61. Metolius River

Distance: 5.3 miles out and back
Elevation Gain: 300 feet
Trailhead elevation: 2,870 feet
Trail high point: 2,884 feet
Season: all year
Best: June – July, October
Pass: NW Forest Pass
Permit: none needed
On the traditional lands of: the Warm Springs and Tenino peoples

Directions:

- From Sisters, drive northwest on US 20 for 9 miles to a junction on the right with FR 14, signed for the Metolius River.
- Turn right and drive north on FR 14 for 2.6 miles to a split in the road. FR 14 for 2.6 miles to a split in the road. While left takes you to the town of Camp Sherman, you need to keep right here, following the pointer for area campgrounds.
- From this point, drive north another 7.7 miles to the signed turnoff on your left for Wizard Falls Fish Hatchery.
- Turn left here and drive downhill to a large parking lot on the eastern bank of the Metolius River, just before a bridge over the river. The trail is located across the bridge in the Fish Hatchery. Do not park at the Fish Hatchery unless you're planning on visiting the hatchery.
- **Drivetime from Sisters:** 30 minutes

Hike: With flower-spangled islands, gushing springs and huge ponderosa pines towering above, the Metolius River is pure magic. Equally magical is the ease of the hikes along the river, making this area a great destination for families and inexperienced hikers. For the best experience, try coming in June and July when the river's scenic islands overflow with a wide array of flowers, or in October when the vine maple along the river and the larch trees overhead turn a dozen shades

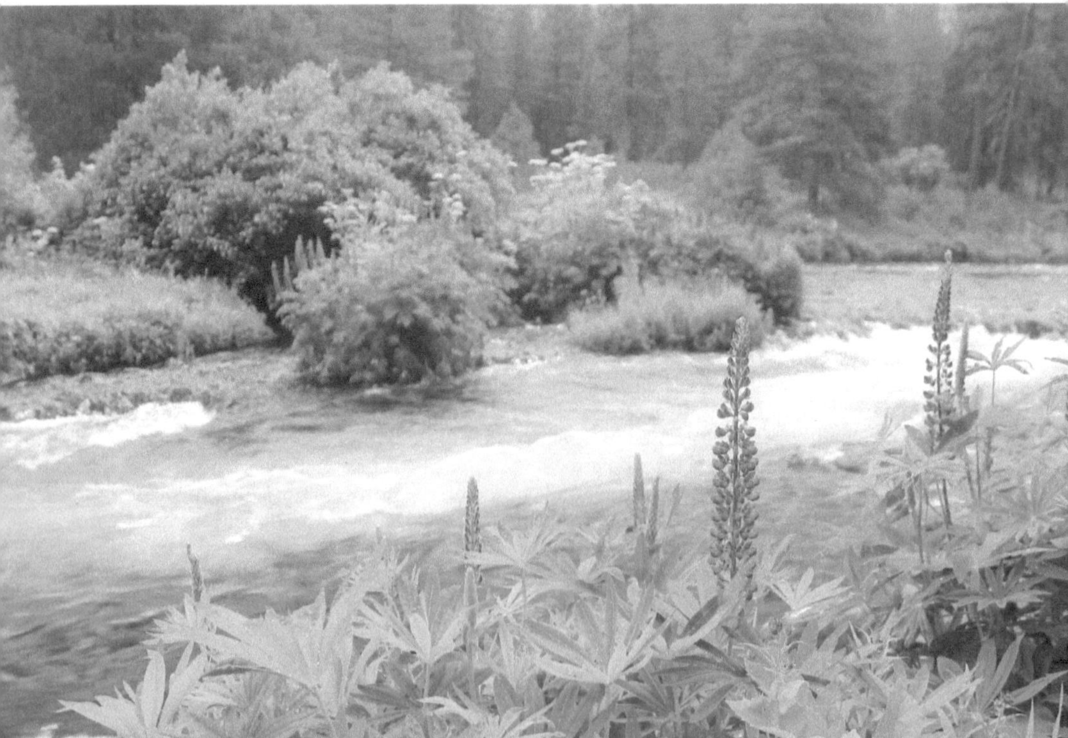

of gold and orange. No matter when you visit, this river will entrance you every time you see it; William L. Sullivan, the dean of Oregon guidebook authors, calls the Metolius "the most magical of all Oregon rivers", and I could not agree more.

From the trailhead, follow the West Metolius River Trail south from the trailhead. The trail mostly stays a hundred feet or more from the riverside, but a number of fishing paths offer access to the river. The river is a surreal shade of electric blue, and flowers line the riverbanks for much of the summer. One notable feature of the Metolius is the numerous islands in the river, which feature bushes of summer wildflowers as well as valuable bird habitat. Although this hike is quite easy, you'll find yourself stopping regularly to watch the river pass by. At 2.5 miles, the trail reaches a viewpoint of a series of gushing springs across the river which flow directly into the Metolius. This is a very popular spot, as many hikers visit the springs from the Canyon Creek Trailhead just 0.3 mile away (the road to this trailhead is gravel and parking is limited, which is why I have you start at Wizard Falls instead). A car shuttle is easy to establish if you want to hike the trail one-way, but you'll love this trail even more hiking back towards Wizard Falls. Return the way you came, stopping hundreds of times along the way to take in the river and its many, many charms.

Other Adventure Options:

There are a dozen campgrounds along the Metolius River and nearly all of them are fantastic places to spend a few nights. Most of these campgrounds require reservations in advance on www.recreation.gov but most do not fill except on the busiest of summer weekends. You may get lucky if you pull in here on summer weekdays, or early and late in the season on weekends. Dispersed camping is also possible throughout the canyon.

If you're planning on hiking some more, you can follow the West Metolius River Trail north from Wizard Falls for 3 lovely miles to Bridge 99, also known as Lower Bridge. If you're planning on a loop, cross the river here and pick up the East Metolius Trail, which you can follow 3.2 miles back to Wizard Falls. The West Metolius Trail continues north of Lower Bridge another 1.5 miles to its end at Candle Creek Campground, just before the boundary with the Warm Springs Reservation.

Backpackers will enjoy following the old road along the river's eastern bank deep into the dark and mysterious Horn of the Metolius, the river's lower canyon. From Lower Bridge, follow the river north on an unofficial trail for 1.5 miles, then pick up the road and follow it as far as you like. You'll find great campsites, an old farmstead, a number of summer cabins, and many great views of the magical Metolius.

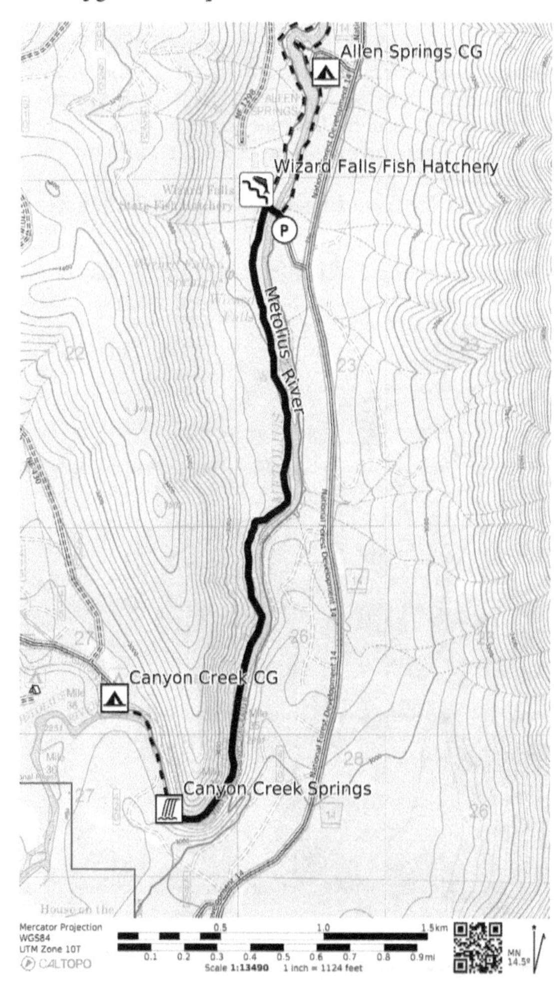

62. Clear Lake

	Sahalie and Koosah Falls	Clear Lake Loop
Distance:	1 mile out and back	5.3 mile loop
Elevation Gain:	200 feet	300 feet
Trailhead Elevation:	2,876 feet	3,036 feet
Trail High Point:	2,876 feet	3,081 feet
Season:	all year (be careful in winter)	all year (be careful in winter)
Best:	all year	all year
Pass:	none needed	none needed
Permit:	none needed	none needed
On the traditional lands of:	the Molalla people	the Molalla people

Directions from Eugene:

- Drive east on OR 126 for approximately 70 miles to a turnoff on the right for Clear Lake. If you're coming from Salem, Sweet Home, or Sisters, you'll need to drive south on OR 126 from the junction with US 20 for 3.7 miles to the turnoff on your left for Clear Lake.
- Drive downhill for 0.4 mile to the day use parking lot at the Clear Lake Resort.
- For Sahalie Falls, continue 1.9 miles south on OR 126 to the signed trailhead for Sahalie Falls on the right.
- **Drivetime from Eugene:** 1 hour and 20 minutes

Stunning Sahalie Falls on the McKenzie River.

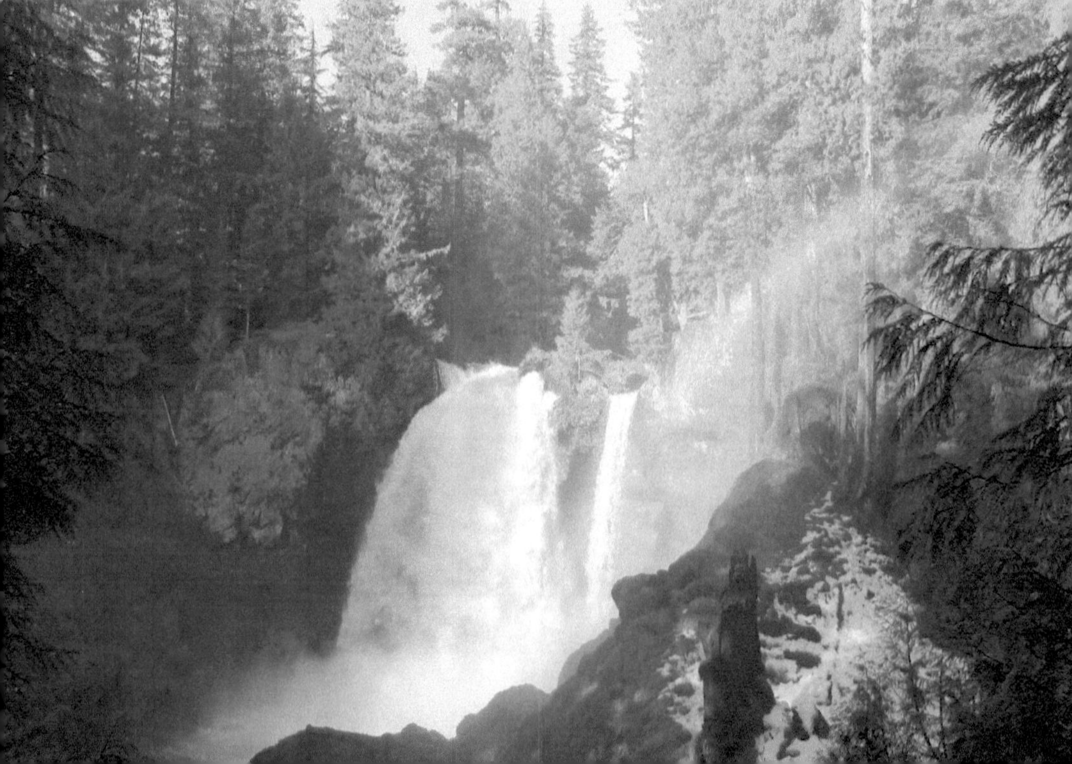

Hike: Clear Lake is one of Oregon's most extraordinary lakes. This intensely blue and clear lake was created by lava flows from nearby Sand Mountain that dammed the McKenzie River approximately 3,000 years ago, creating a very cold, very deep lake that drowned the forests along the banks of the river. The drowned trees are still visible in the lake, adding even more intrigue to an already fascinating place. This easy loop around the lake crosses the McKenzie River at its source, weaves through a rugged lava flow, and passes excellent views of Mount Washington and the Three Sisters across the lake. Located just a few minutes drive to the south, you can also visit two extraordinary waterfalls on the McKenzie River, another iconic place in an area full of them. With so much to do here, you might want to consider spending the weekend at the Clear Lake Resort, or at least getting a camping spot nearby.

As the parking lots at Sahalie and Koosah Falls are small and fill quickly, you should probably start your day here. From the small lot at Sahalie Falls, a trail leads 100 yards to a fenced viewpoint of Sahalie Falls, one of Oregon's most beautiful waterfalls. Here the McKenzie River plunges 73 feet into an incredibly mossy pool where rainbows are common on sunny days. If you're up for more hiking, continue downstream along the gorgeous McKenzie River a half-mile to a fenced overlook of Koosah Falls, a 74-foot curtain in a spectacularly rocky canyon. Several viewpoints along the trail offer excellent views of the falls. A longer loop that follows the west bank of the McKenzie River is possible but it's probably best to just return the way you came.

To hike around Clear Lake, you'll need to start at the day use lot by the resort. Follow the Clear Lake Loop trail south from the parking lot. Soon you'll pass excellent views across lake to Mount Washington's spire, located just a few miles to the east. At 1.2 miles, you'll cross a bridge over the McKenzie River just a few feet below its source. Once across the bridge, you'll reach a junction with the McKenzie River Trail. Continue straight here.The south shore of Clear Lake is exceptionally beautiful. As soon as the sun hits the lake's waters in the morning, you'll notice that the shallow parts of the lake are a luminous shade of turquoise, while the deeper parts of the lake are profoundly blue. The vine maple that grows along the lakeshore turns yellow, orange, and red in the fall, adding contrast to an already beautiful scene. The trail winds through the lava flow that dammed the lake, passing Coldwater Cove's campground and views directly across the lake to the resort. At a little under 4 miles, you'll reach the turquoise waters of Great Spring, which is tucked away in an isolated corner of the lake among enormous Douglas fir trees. From here, you'll follow the trail around the lakeshore another 1.3 miles to the completion of the loop at the Clear Lake Resort.

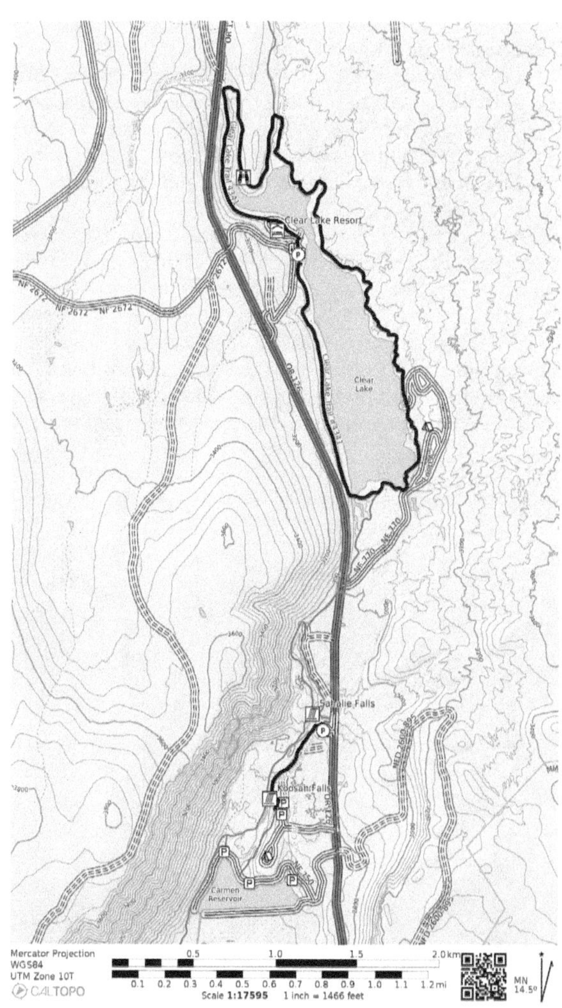

63. Proxy and Linton Falls

	Proxy Falls Loop	Linton Falls
Distance:	2.2 mile loop	5.8 miles out and back
Elevation Gain:	200 feet	800 feet
Trailhead Elevation:	3,117 feet	3,564 feet
Trail High Point:	3,230 feet	4,000 feet
Season:	May – November	May – November
Best:	May – November	May – November
Pass:	NW Forest Pass	NW Forest Pass + permit
Permit:	none needed	for overnight stays only
On the traditional lands of:	the Molalla people	the Molalla people

Directions from Eugene:

- From Eugene, drive east on OR 126 for approximately 55 miles to a junction on the right with OR 242, about 4 miles past McKenzie Bridge.
- Turn right onto OR 242 and drive 8.6 miles to the Proxy Falls Trailhead. For Linton Lake, continue 1.6 more miles to the Linton Lake Trailhead.
- **Drivetime from Eugene:** 1 hour and 20 minutes

Hike: Proxy Falls is one of Oregon's most famous waterfalls, and it is certainly one of its most photogenic. Proxy Creek drops 226 feet in a pair of cascades over one of the mossiest slopes you'll ever see. Just to the east, Upper Proxy Falls beckons hikers to investigate its quiet pool. The easy loop to both falls has long been one of Oregon's most popular easy hikes, and one of its best. Hikers with more time and energy should drive east to the Linton Lake Trailhead, where a longer but still easy hike leads to scenic Linton Lake. Adventurous hikers can follow a rough, steep unofficial trail up to stunning views of two spectacular waterfalls on Linton Creek above the lake. Whatever you do in this area, it is certain to be fun!

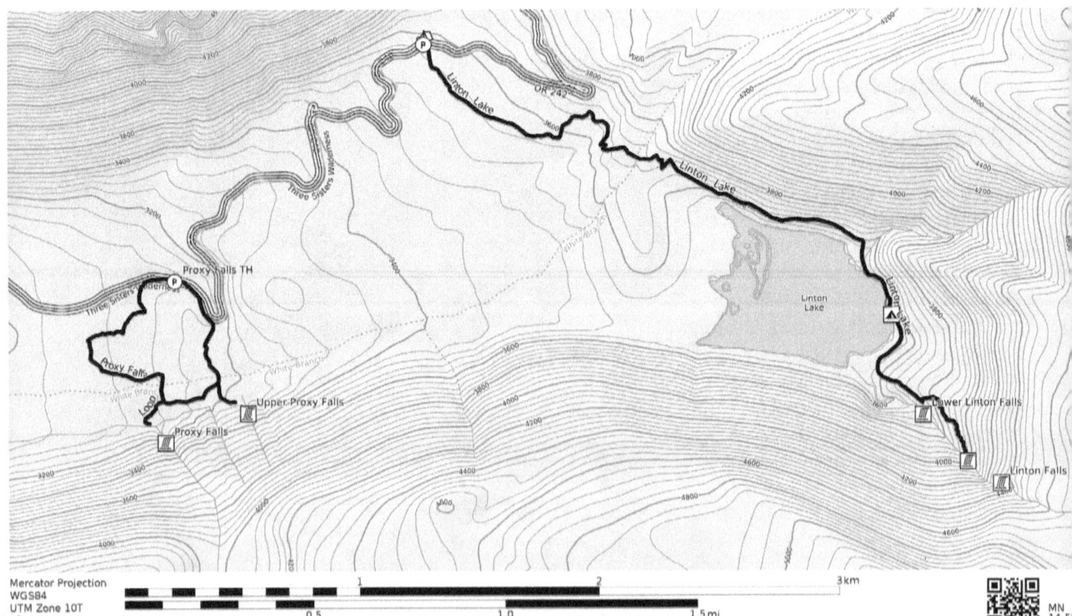

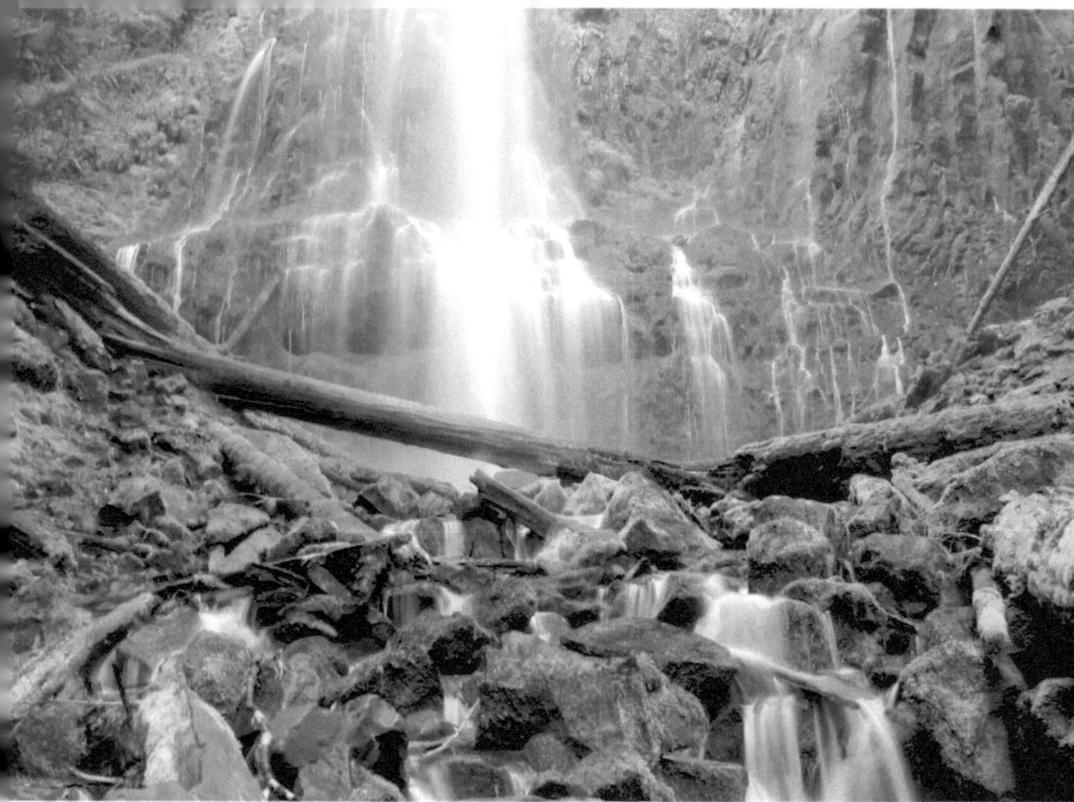

Proxy Falls is one of Oregon's most spectacular waterfalls.

For Proxy Falls, locate the trail on the south side of OR 242 and follow it to the right until it climbs above the highway. You'll follow this easy trail through the lava flows that dominate this area for 0.8 mile to a junction in the woods near Proxy Falls. Turn right and continue 0.1 mile to a view of the falls from a rocky shelf above Proxy Creek. The view here is excellent, but most people continue on an unofficial trail that leads to the base of the falls in another 0.2 mile. The best views of Proxy Falls are found down here but watch your step; hikers with limited mobility should avoid this steep and slippery path into the canyon. When you're done here, return to the last trail junction and turn right. You'll follow the loop trail another 0.2 mile to a junction on the right with the short trail to Upper Proxy Falls. Turn right and follow this trail 0.1 mile to the deep pool at the base of tumbling Upper Proxy Falls. This 129-foot falls seems to emerge from the moss above, tumbling into a deep and mysterious pool. The creek disappears into the lava here; it will reemerge several miles to the west. When you're ready, return the 0.1 mile to the last junction and turn right to hike 0.4 back to the trailhead.

For Linton Lake and Falls, follow the Linton Lake Trail through the forest for 1.2 miles to the edge of Linton Lake. Vine maple turns yellow, orange and red in October, brightening these dark woods considerably. Follow the trail above the lakeshore another 0.6 mile until it seems to disappear along the steep lakeshore. If you want to continue the hike, you'll have to pick your way over some downed trees and keep your eyes peeled for the trail, now unofficial and rough in spots due to damage from the 2017 Separation Fire. A few nice campsites along the lakeshore invite overnight stays (don't forget to get your permit first!), At the lake's southeast end, the trail launches steeply uphill, following roaring Linton Creek. Fifteen minutes of climbing will take you to a precarious overlook of raging Lower Linton Falls. Watch your step here, as getting a good view of the falls requires walking to the edge of a steep slope above the creek. Another ten minutes of climbing will take you to trail's end at the base of huge, multi-tiered Linton Falls. With a height of nearly 500 feet, the falls is among the tallest in Oregon and is certainly one of the most impressive. It's a tough climb to these two waterfalls, but you'll certainly be glad you did. Whenever you're ready, return the way you came.

64. Benson Lake

Distance: 3.6 miles out and back
Elevation Gain: 402 feet
Trailhead elevation: 4,843 feet
Trail high point: 5,245 feet
Season: July – October
Best: July – October
Pass: NW Forest Pass + limited entry permit
Permit required: day use or overnight (if backpacking)
On the traditional lands of: the Molalla people

Directions:

- If you're coming here from Eugene, drive OR 126 east for approximately 56 miles to the intersection with OR 242 not far beyond McKenzie Bridge.
- Drive OR 242 for 15.8 winding, slow miles to the signed turnoff for Scott Lake on the left. If you're coming from Sisters, OR 242 for 20.4 miles to the turnoff for Scott Lake on the right.
- Turn onto the Scott Lake Road and drive this bumpy gravel track for 0.9 mile to the trailhead on the left, just before the road reaches the north side of Scott Lake.
- **Drivetimes:** 90 minutes from Eugene, 40 minutes from Sisters

Hike: Scott Lake and Benson Lake are two of the most beloved lakes in Central Oregon for good reason; here, you can spend days exploring the shores of each lake, camping, fishing, and swimming in turquoise water against a backdrop of the Three Sisters. This popularity comes with a price; if you're planning on camping or backpacking here, expect stiff competition.

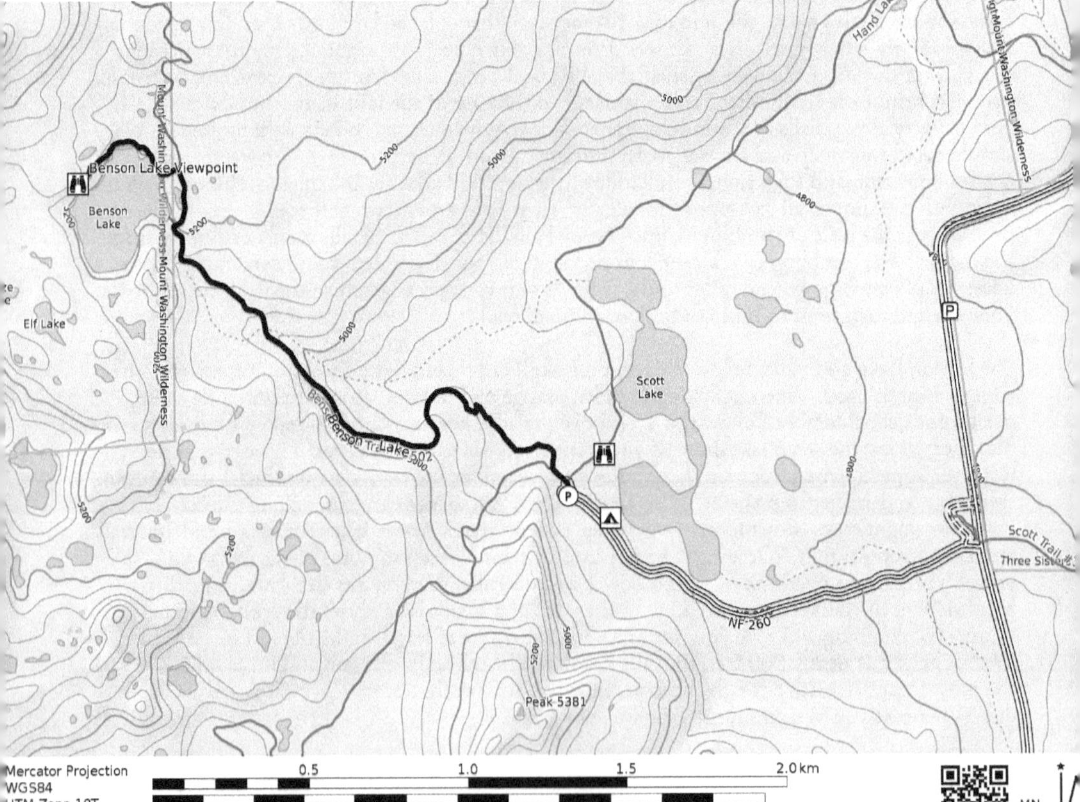

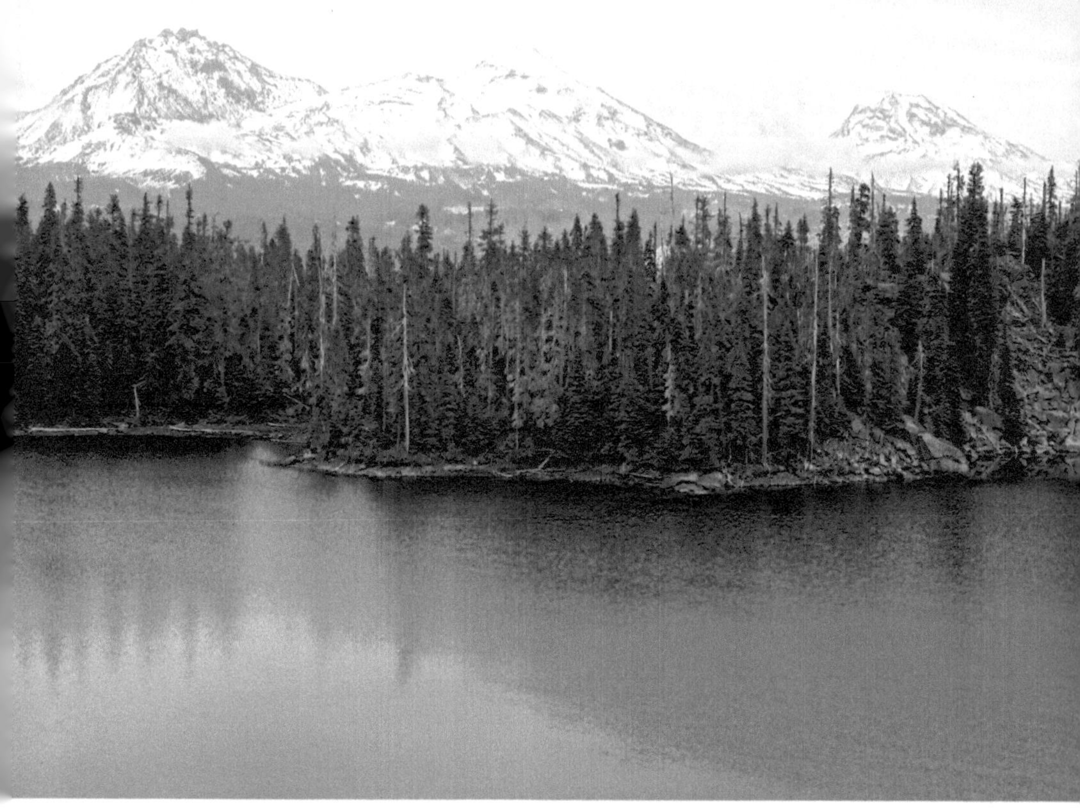

The Three Sisters and Benson Lake on a cold October day.

Despite the popularity, the hike from Scott Lake to Benson Lake is both easy and beautiful, and once there, you can hike up to one of Oregon's most extraordinary views: the Three Sisters looming over Benson Lake's deep blue waters. Before you go, don't forget to secure your day use or overnight permit; see the introduction to the Central Oregon Cascades on page 126 for more information.

From the trailhead, follow the Benson Lake Trail gradually uphill through the woods. In the fall, the red leaves of the ubiquitous huckleberry bushes that line the trail add color to an already beautiful scene. The trail reaches the edge of Benson Lake at 1.4 miles. Even with the permit system now in place, expect to meet lots of hikers here. A social trail follows the south side of the lake, but for the best view, continue following the main trail around the east side of the lake until you reach its north shore. Look for a trail junction here with a sign that says "User trail - not maintained". Turn left here and follow this trail to a campsite. Beyond the campsite, follow the trail along the north shore of Benson Lake until you see bluffs above you. Follow the trail up the bluffs, or simply scramble up them if you lose the trail. The Three Sisters soon come into view above the lake, and at 1.6 miles, you'll reach a rocky outcrop with a view of all Three Sisters, with the deep blue waters of Benson Lake below you. This viewpoint is a sacred spot to local tribes, who have been visiting this viewpoint for millennia. Please disturb nothing up here and pay this spot the respect it deserves.

If you're planning on a longer hike, the Benson Lake Trail continues north to Tenas Lakes and Scott Mountain. Both of these are worthy destinations meriting further exploration. You can also hike east from Scott Lake to Hand Lake, another lovely place. If you're hoping to camp, the primitive Scott Lake Campground has excellent campsites that fill on summer weekends. Beyond the location, the prime attraction here is the spectacular view of the Three Sisters rising above Scott Lake from the lake's north end. Even if you aren't camping, you might want to hang around at Scott Lake until sunset, as the Three Sisters turn pink in the evening light. Sunsets here are worth the wait and are not to be missed!

65. Matthieu Lakes

Distance: 6 mile semi-loop
Elevation Gain: 900 feet
Trailhead elevation: 5,277 feet
Trail High Point: 6,044 feet
Season: July – October
Best: July – October
Pass: NW Forest Pass + limited entry permit
Permit required: day use or overnight (if backpacking)
On the traditional lands of: the Tenino people

Directions:

- From Sisters, drive OR 242 for 14.4 winding, curving miles to a junction on your left signed for the Lava Lake Trailhead. If you're coming from the west, this junction is on your right just 0.5 mile beyond McKenzie Pass.
- Turn left here and drive 0.4 miles of rocky dirt road to a sign for the Pacific Crest Trail. Turn right and drive just 0.1 mile to the trailhead. Watch out for ruts and sharp rocks on both gravel roads.
- **Drivetime from Sisters:** 30 minutes

Hike: The Three Sisters Wilderness is a veritable outdoor playground with something for everyone. Backpackers will love the long-distance trails circling the wilderness, climbers love scaling the peaks here, and hikers enjoy hikes of all levels of difficulty. Many of the best hikes in the wilderness are quite difficult, but this lovely loop to Matthieu Lakes is a joyous exception. Here you'll hike the Pacific Crest Trail south to a pair of lakes set at the foot of North Sister, with views stretching far across the wilderness. The hike is easy enough for most hikers, with enough

North Sister towers over windy South Matthieu Lake.

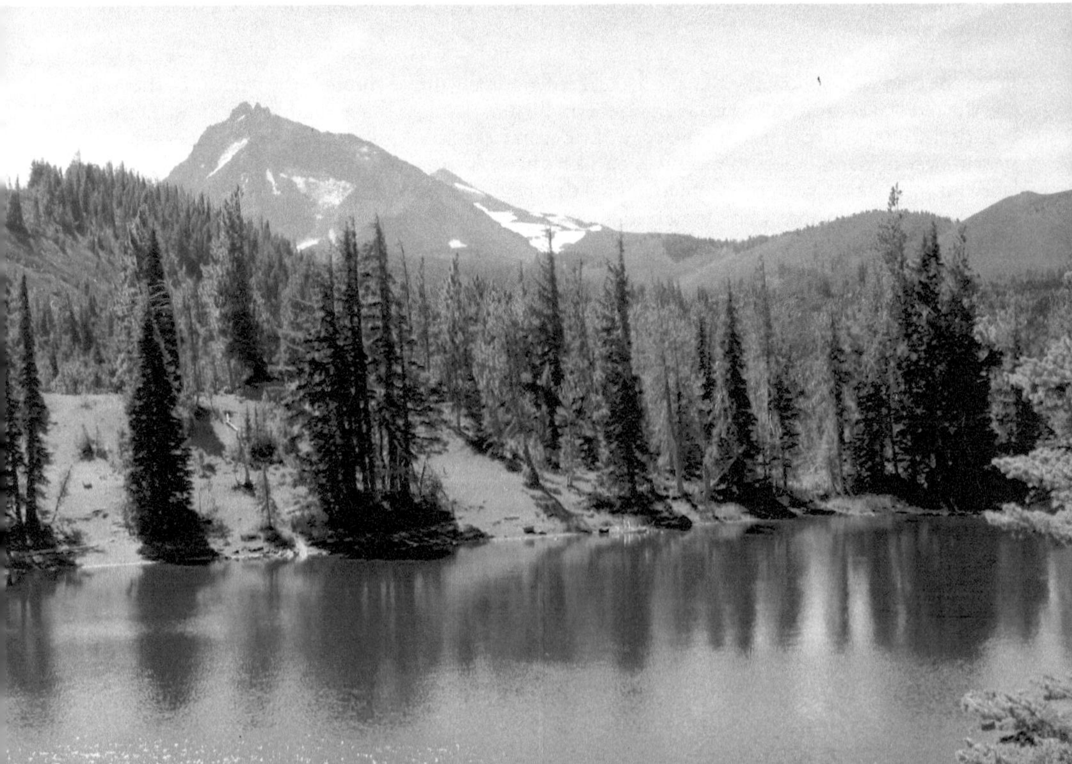

reward to keep you moving along the trail even when you're tired. Before you go, don't forget to secure your day use or overnight permit; see the introduction to the Central Oregon Cascades on page 126 for more information.

Begin at the Lava Lake Trailhead. Follow a level trail through the woods a quarter mile to a junction with the Pacific Crest Trail. Turn left here and ramble through the woods a half mile to a junction with the trail to North Matthieu Lake, a segment of the old Oregon Skyline Trail. Either way is fine, but for now keep left to stay on the PCT. Along the way you'll be hiking through forest that burned during the Milli Fire in 2017; much of the way is now in burned forest, but at least this fire opened up better views of the surrounding terrain. The PCT then begins a gradual climb through the woods. At one point, you can look back towards Mount Washington and Mount Jefferson, further north on the rolling Cascade crest. The climbing then intensifies a bit, and views open up to the south towards North Sister. At 3 miles, reach a reunion with the North Matthieu Lake Trail. Continue straight and almost immediately reach South Matthieu Lake. Set in a bowl at the dusty crest of the Cascades, the lake is a spectacularly exposed spot with jaw-dropping views south to North Sister's rugged crown. The lake is a popular backpacking destination, so if you've planned an overnight stay make sure you have your wilderness permit handy, and make sure you only camp in designated sites.

Once you're ready to move on to North Matthieu Lake, return to the trail junction mentioned above and turn left. You will descend lightly to North Matthieu Lake, tucked away in the woods near a lava flow. Hike around the scenic lake, a worthy companion to its exposed sibling to the south. If you're backpacking, again remember to set up camp only in designated sites. Beyond the lake the trail follows the lava flow through the woods to a reunion with the Pacific Crest Trail. Turn left and continue a half mile to the aforementioned Lava Camp Trail junction. Turn right here and hike a quarter mile to the trailhead.

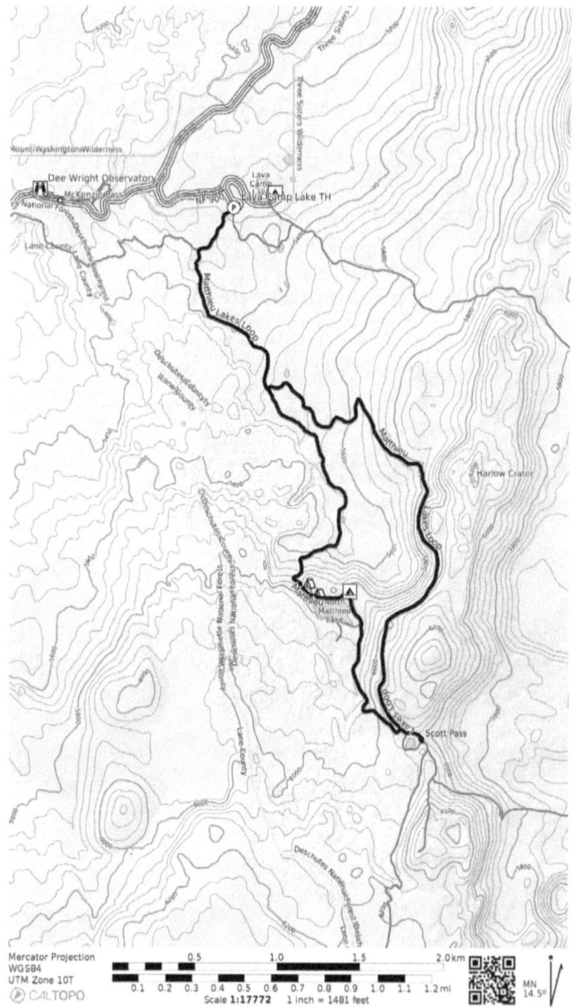

Before you leave the area, make sure you stop at the Dee Wright Observatory at McKenzie Pass, just a half-mile west of the Lava Camp Lake turnoff. At the observatory you'll find incredible views of the vast lava flows that stretch across the landscape here. You can follow paved trails for a little under a mile through this surreal landscape that is more reminiscent of Mordor than Central Oregon. The stone house at the summit of the observatory features fantastic views of North and Middle Sisters across the lava fields, as well as fantastic views of the mountains to the north.

66. Demaris and Camp Lakes

	Demaris Lake	Camp Lake
Distance:	11.6 miles out and back	15.4 miles out and back
Elevation Gain:	1,200 feet	1,800 feet
Trailhead Elevation:	5,307 feet	5,307 feet
Trail High Point:	6,245 feet	7,022 feet
Season:	July - October	July - October
Best:	July - October	July - October
Pass:	NW Forest Pass + limited entry for overnight stays	NW Forest Pass + limited entry for overnight stays
Permit:	limited entry for overnight stays	limited entry for overnight stays
On the traditional lands of:	the Molalla people	the Molalla people

Directions:

- From Sisters, drive west on OR 242 for 1.3 miles to a turnoff on the left with the Pole Creek Road (FR 15).
- Turn left and drive 10.5 miles of mostly good gravel road to the trailhead at road's end. Along the way, be sure to follow signs for the Pole Creek Trailhead; if you're not sure, keeping right at almost every junction will get you there.
- **Drivetime from Sisters:** 30 minutes

Camp Lake offers stunning views of South Sister and very cold swimming.

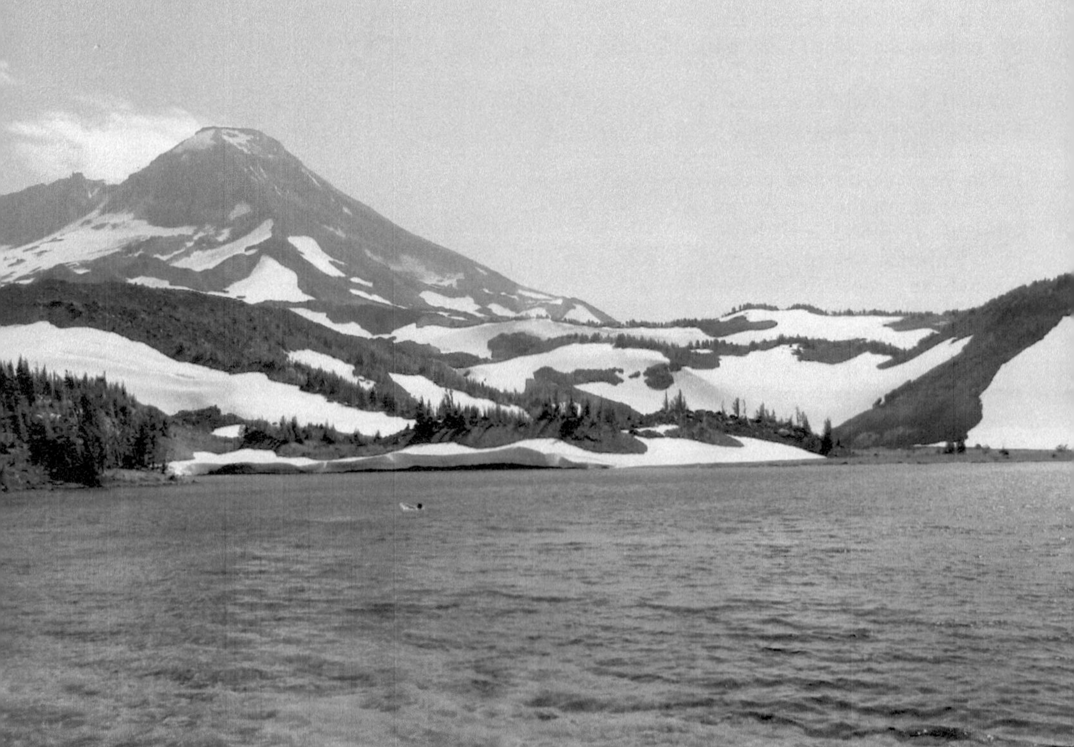

Hike: There's no easy way into the heart of the Three Sisters Wilderness, but the long trek to Camp Lake is easier than most. Sure, this hike is 15 miles out and back, but it's never steep and the views more than make up for the effort. If you're looking for an easier day and a neat place to spend the night, you can skip Camp Lake and stroll down to Demaris Lake, where you'll find similarly excellent views and a better shot at privacy. Just be sure to skip this hike on hot days, as the first few miles pass through exposed, dusty terrain that burned in a 2012 fire. If you're backpacking, don't forget to get your overnight permit to spend the night; see the introduction to the Central Oregon Cascades on page 126 for more information.

From the trailhead, locate the Pole Creek Trail. The 2012 Pole Creek Fire started not far from here, burning through most of the large ponderosa pines that grew here. A few of the trees survived, and the fire has opened up spectacular views of all Three Sisters, particularly North Sister. The trail climbs for 1.4 miles to a junction with the Green Lakes Trail. Continue straight here onto the Green Lakes Trail and hike gradually downhill another 0.7 mile to a crossing of Soap Creek. Cross the creek and immediately reach a junction with the Camp Lake Trail, where you turn right. The Camp Lake Trail climbs gradually for 1.5 miles to the edge of the burn, and continues another 1.2 miles to a crossing of the roaring North Fork Whychus Creek, which flows out of the glaciers on Middle Sister. There are usually logs on which you can cross the creek but some caution is nevertheless prudent. Just across the creek, you'll reach a junction with the spur trail to Demaris Lake. For the shorter hike, turn left here.

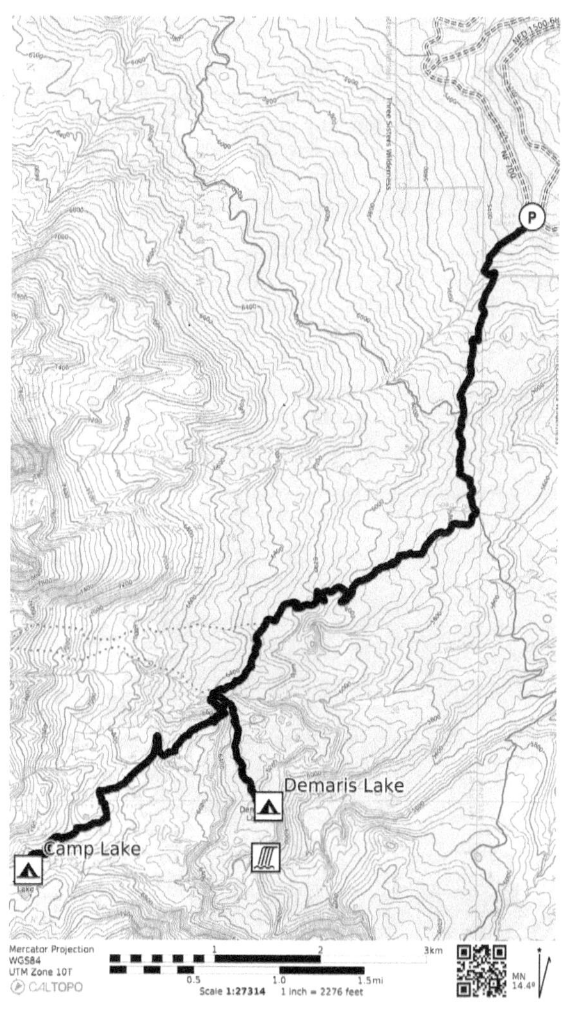

The Demaris Lake Trail descends gradually through the woods for 0.7 mile to the lake. Upon first glance the lake does not seem all that exciting, with only views of the top of South Sister; further exploration around Demaris Lake reveals fantastic views and excellent campsites on the lake's east side. A short user trail leads to a stunning viewpoint of South Sister and the canyonlands of Whychus Creek at a cliff edge. You could spend days exploring this area.

If you're continuing towards Camp Lake, you should instead keep right at the junction just after the crossing of the North Fork of Whychus Creek. The Camp Lake Trail climbs gradually for 2.8 miles of gorgeous, rolling terrain to Camp Lake at 7.6 miles from the trailhead. The view of South Sister towering over Camp Lake is among the most iconic in the Oregon Cascades. Whether you're here for the day or the weekend, you'll want to take the time here to soak in the incredible mountain views in this spectacular corner of the Three Sisters Wilderness.

If you're backpacking, there are sites all over the lake. Plan on very cold, windy nights and hope to be surprised.

67. Tam McArthur Rim

	From the Rim to the Prow	From the rim to Broken Top
Distance:	5.6 miles out and back	12.8 miles out and back
Elevation Gain:	1,200 feet	2,500 feet
Trailhead Elevation:	6.527 feet	6,527 feet
Trail High Point:	7,733 feet	8,360 feet
Season:	July - October	July - October
Best:	July - October	July - October
Pass:	NW Forest Pass + limited entry	NW Forest Pass + limited entry
Permit:	day use or overnight	day use or overnight
On the traditional lands of:	the Confederated Tribes of the Warm Springs	the Confederated Tribes of the Warm Springs

Directions:

- From Sisters, drive Elm Street south, where it becomes Three Creek Road (FR 16).
- Continue up this road for 14 miles of pavement and 1.5 miles of occasionally rough gravel road to a junction on your right for Driftwood Campground.
- Turn right here and drive 100 bumpy feet to the trailhead parking lot on your right. The trail is across the main road on your left.
- **Drivetime from Sisters:** 30 minutes

Hike: From Tam McArthur Rim the view seems to stretch on towards forever – but your eyes will be locked on Broken Top's craggy summit directly ahead. This is one of Oregon's best hikes, and with a lot of patience and energy, it can be truly unforgettable. Just make sure to pack sunscreen, enough water, and a windbreaker; the hike tops out at an elevation of over 8,000 feet, or higher than most of the mountains in the Oregon Cascades. With that in mind, you won't regret a single step of this hike. Before you go, don't forget to secure your day use or overnight permit; see the introduction to the Central Oregon Cascades on page 126 for more information.

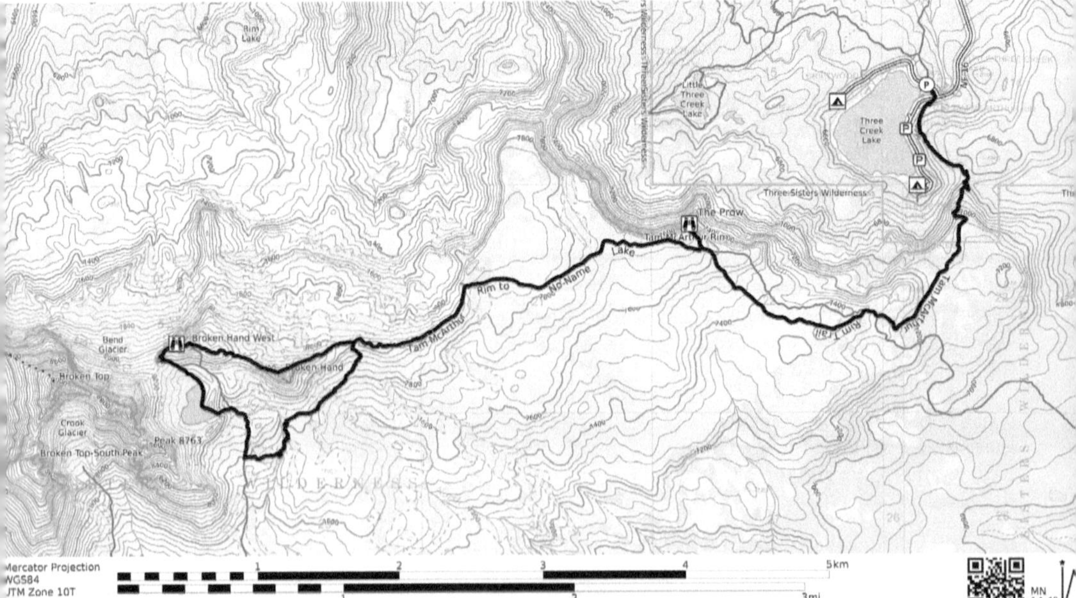

Begin by climbing up above Three Creek Lake on a wide and well-maintained trail. Along the way you'll have a few looks down to the lake, and out to the Three Sisters. At a little over a mile from the trailhead, the trail crests the lip of the rim and continues climbing gently towards the more open, higher part of the rim to the west. Before long you will find yourself at a junction with a horse trail that arrives from the south. Continue straight, passing a possibly unmarked junction with a trail that follows the edge of the rim more closely. However you decide to go, you will reach the official end of the Tam McArthur Rim Trail at 2.8 miles from the trailhead at a viewpoint known as The Prow. For less able hikers, this is an ideal turnaround spot. Here you will be standing at 7,700 feet above sea level, and more than 1,000 feet above both Three Creek and Little Three Creek Lake. Hikers with a fear of heights will want to stand well back of the rim edge, but there's plenty of room to spread out here just the same. The view seems to stretch into infinity, with the Three Sisters looming across the fire-scarred canyons of Park and Whychus Creeks below. On very clear days you can see all the way to Mount Hood, and even Mount Adams in Washington.

If you've got more energy and are up for a more serious adventure, return to the main trail and soon pass a "Trail Not Maintained" sign (don't fret, it's in great shape). The eye-popping views of Broken Top and the Three Sisters get better with every step west. The unofficial trail continues gently uphill across a rolling ridgetop of red cinders for 2 more miles. The way is generally obvious and the trail wide and well-tread, but there are occasional spots that may necessitate a bit of route-finding. At 4.8 miles from the trailhead, you will climb to a saddle below Broken Hand's cliffs. The views here are even better than they were at trail's end, save for one thing: Broken Hand blocks most of the view west towards Broken Top. Hikers not skilled in the art of following faint, unofficial trails should declare victory here. On the other side of Broken Hand lies fabled No Name Lake, an aquamarine glacial tarn at the base of Broken Top's summit glaciers. But getting there requires some ingenuity and persistence, if not dogged determination.

If you're up for the challenge, you've got options. You can follow a faint trail to the left that descends into a scenic basin on the south side of Broken Hand. Should you lose this trail, you cannot possibly get lost as long as you follow the base of Broken Hand. From here, you can pick up user trails and continue until you hit the maintained trail to No Name Lake, not far from the lake. If you'd rather take the high route, you'll have to follow the rough, exposed trail along the north side of Broken Hand. Neither of these trails are all that obvious, but they will all take you to No Name Lake in about a mile. The advantage of the high trail across Broken Hand is the views ahead to the lake. The high trail eventually drops to a narrow, exposed ridge perched between No Name Lake and the Bend Glacier on Broken Top's north face. The views here are mind-blowing. From there, drop down to No Name Lake and fight the crowds for your pictures, and pat yourself on the back for getting to this special place the hard way. Most people hike to No Name Lake via the Broken Top Trailhead, a 6-mile round-trip hike that begins at the Broken Top Trailhead. This would be a great choice were it not for the absolutely horrendous access road. Most people you meet here won't believe that you hiked here from Tam McArthur Rim, and you should feel free to tell them whatever horror story you'd like about the route. You've earned it. Camping is possible but banned within a quarter-mile of No-Name Lake. From wherever you ended up, return the way you came.

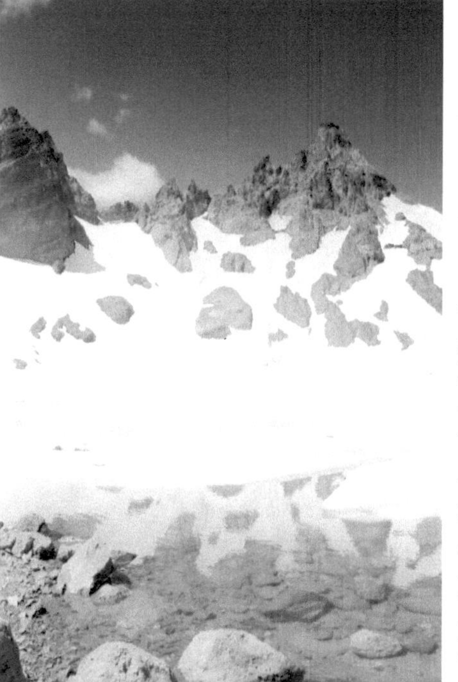

68. Tumalo Falls Loop

Distance: 7.8 mile loop
Elevation Gain: 1,400 feet
Trailhead elevation: 4,977 feet
Trail high point: 6,089 feet
Season: June – October
Best: June – October
Pass: NW Forest Pass
Permit: none needed
On the traditional lands of: the Confederated Tribes of the Warm Springs

Directions from Bend:

- From Bend, follow NW Galveston Avenue west through town until it becomes Skyliners Road. At a traffic circle with NW Mount Washington Avenue, drive around the traffic circle and continue onto Skyliners Road.
- Drive west on Skyliners Road for 8.8 miles to a bridge over Tumalo Creek, where the road becomes gravel.
- Continue on the gravel road for 2.6 miles to the Tumalo Falls parking lot at road's end.
- **Drivetime from Bend:** 25 minutes

Hike: Tumalo Falls is Central Oregon's answer to Silver Falls State Park. Here you'll find a dozen waterfalls and a scenic canyon that calls out to be explored. Just as at Silver Falls, the most impressive waterfall is the one at the trailhead, but the others are not to be missed. Hikers looking for a full day's adventure can follow trails to the head of Tumalo Creek's impressive canyon, only to return on quiet trails along Bridge Creek. Best of all – unlike many Central Oregon trailheads, no permits are required here, just enough time and energy to complete this loop.

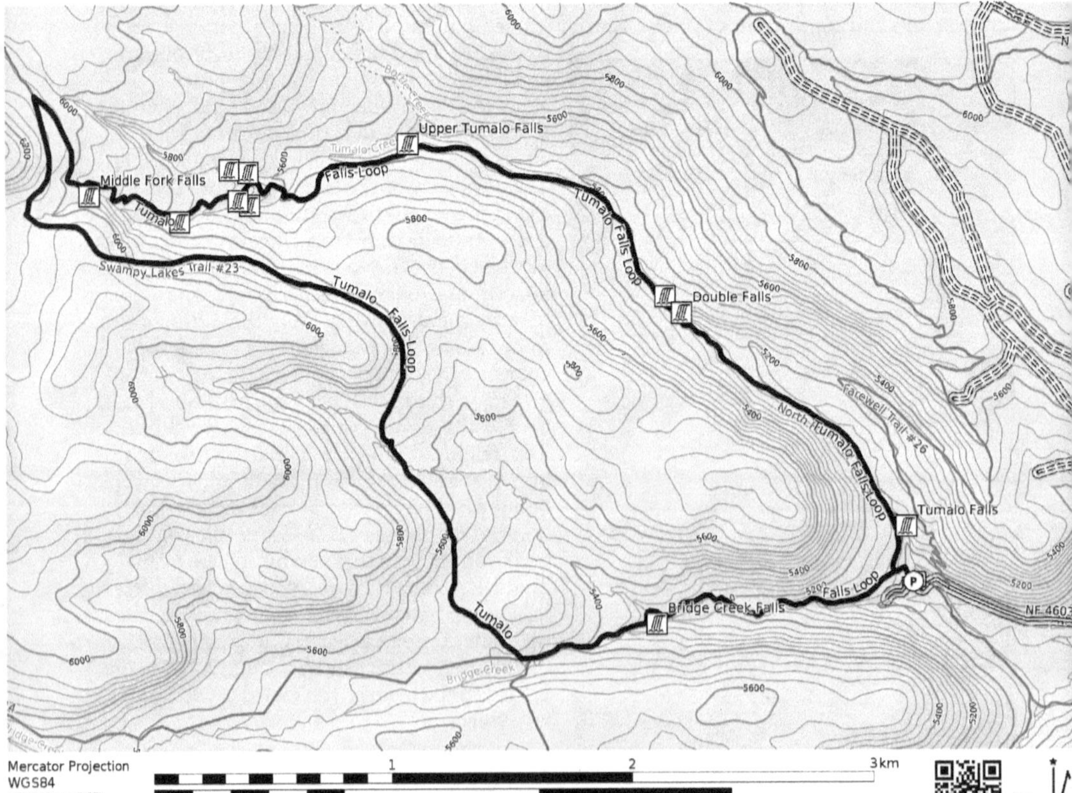

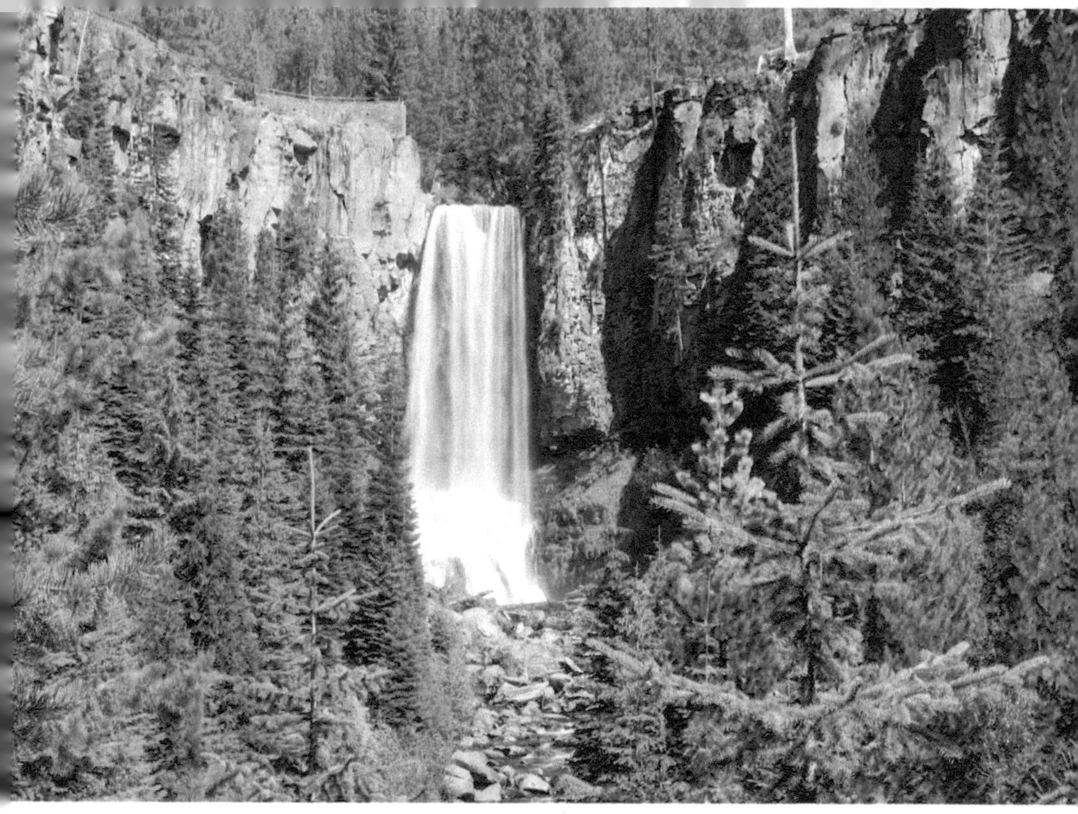

Tumalo Falls is a popular destination for Central Oregon hikers.

One important note: dogs are only allowed along the Tumalo Creek section of this loop, so you'll have to make this hike an out and back.

From the pit toilet at the trailhead, follow the trail to a fenced viewpoint of Tumalo Falls. This is the best view you'll have of this 89-foot curtain, and it's a great one. You may have to wait your turn to take photos of the falls, as this viewpoint is quite popular. When you're ready to continue, follow the trail uphill along the canyon wall above Tumalo Creek. You'll pass another fenced overlook of the top of the falls at 0.3 mile. The trail above the falls is delightful, with views of the tumbling creek and its many small waterfalls and small cascades. At 1.2 miles, a short side trail to the right leads to an exposed overlook of Double Falls in the creek below. Watch children and pets closely here, as there are no fences to prevent a fall. Just a short distance upstream is another waterfall. Continue hiking upstream another mile to another signed spur trail, this one to Upper Falls. The view from this short spur trail isn't all that good, but an unofficial and very steep trail leads downhill to the base of the falls. Beyond this "upper" falls, the trail continues uphill, descends briefly to cross the Middle Fork of Tumalo Creek on a log bridge, then continues gaining elevation in deep forest above the creek. At 3.5 miles, a short side trail to the left leads you to beautiful Middle Fork Tumalo Falls. This 53-foot falls is one of the scenic highlights of this loop and is well worth an extended stop to bask in its beauty.

If you're planning on hiking the full loop, continue on the North Fork Trail another 0.3 mile to a junction with the Spring Creek Trail on the left. Turn left here at a post, signed for Bridge Creek. This trail climbs briefly and then descends to a crossing of the Middle Fork. The creek is placid here and logs allow hikers to cross with dry feet for most of the year. The Spring Creek Trail then proceeds to gradually descend along the canyon walls above first the Middle Fork, then Spring Creek. Along the way you'll pass into Bend's watershed, where all pets are prohibited. The trail reaches a four-way junction with the Bridge Creek Trail at 6.4 miles. Turn left. You're in the home stretch now! The Bridge Creek Trail follows its namesake downhill, passing scenic Bridge Creek Falls along the way. Follow this trail 1.4 miles to the trailhead.

69. Sparks Lake

Distance: 2.7 mile loop
Elevation Gain: 100 feet
Trailhead elevation: 5,446 feet
Trail high point: 5,492 feet
Season: June – October
Best: August – October (after the mosquitoes!)
Pass: NW Forest Pass
Permit: none needed
On the traditional lands of: the Warm Springs, Klamath, and Molalla peoples

Directions:

- From Bend, drive Century Drive west until it becomes the Cascade Lakes Highway.
- From the last traffic circle in Bend, continue approximately 24 miles to a signed turnoff for Sparks Lake on the left.
- Turn left, then turn left again almost immediately (right leads to the Soda Creek Campground) onto the lake's gravel access road.
- Drive 1.6 miles of bumpy, potholed gravel to the Ray Atkeson Trailhead at road's end. A NW Forest Pass is required.
- **Drivetime from Bend:** 45 minutes

Hike: Sparks Lake features stunning reflections of both South Sister and Broken Top, but many who visit choose to only walk out to the viewpoint. There is much more to do and see here! If you've got some extra time, you can follow an easy loop through the lava flow that dammed the lake. This fun hike passes another great viewpoint and weaves through a small slot canyon that

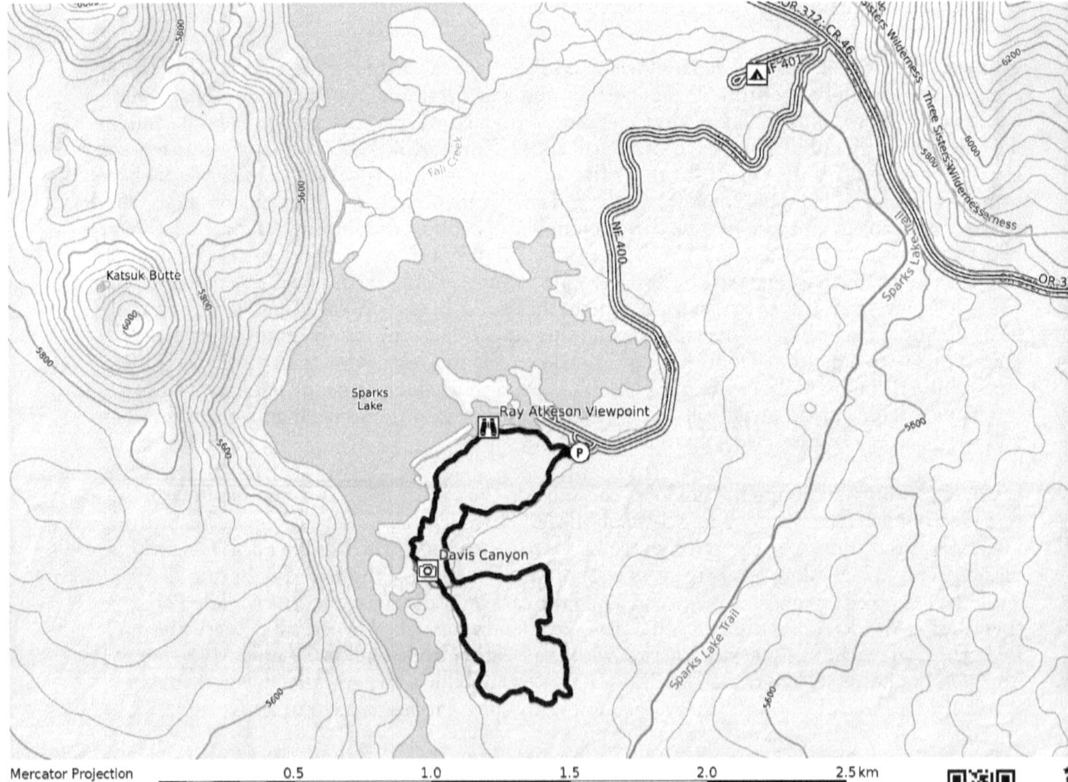

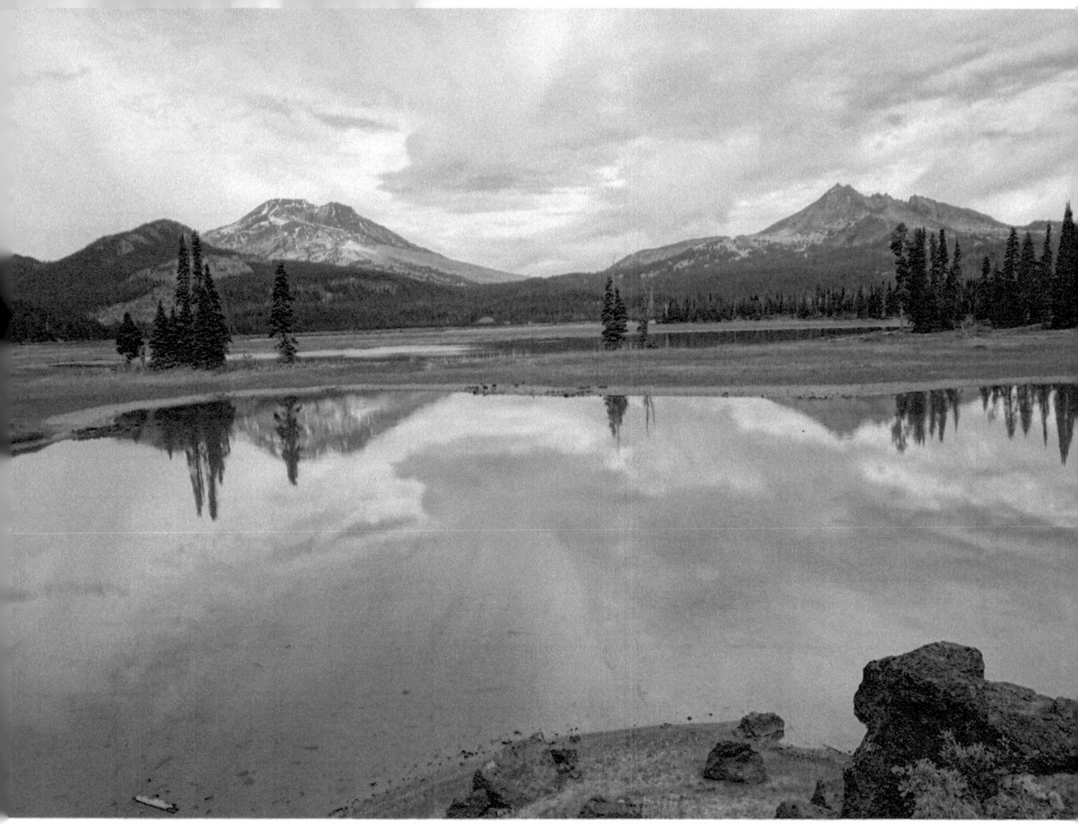

South Sister and Broken Top rise over Sparks Lake on a cloudy day in October.

children will love. The lake was a favorite of Oregon's photographer laureate Ray Atkeson, for whom the trailhead and paved trail are named. It is likely that it will be a favorite of yours, too.

From the trailhead, follow the paved trail towards Sparks Lake. After just 0.1 mile, you will reach a junction. The lakeshore turns right here, but save this for the end of the hike and instead continue straight. The trail passes over and through fissures in the lava rock that formed gaps and slot canyons. At 0.6 mile from the trailhead, you'll reach a junction with a short cut trail to your right; you can cut the distance of this loop in half, something to keep in mind if you're short on time or are hiking with children. Instead, keep left here for the longer loop. The trail soon begins climbing gradually through the forest and reaches a nice viewpoint of South Sister and Broken Top at 1.1 miles. From here, you will descend to a view of a huge rock amphitheater that my friend calls "The Pit of Doom". The trail then proceeds to follow this rocky valley for a few hundred yards. The volcanic rock formations on this hike are endlessly fascinating!

At 1.8 miles, you'll reach a junction with the short cut trail described above. Turn right here and almost immediately you'll reach a signed junction on your left for the Davis Canyon Loop. Don't miss this fantastic spot! The short trail takes you through a narrow slot canyon in the lava reminiscent of Crack In The Ground (Hike 96). In some spots, the crack is only a few feet wide. After a few hundred yards, you'll emerge back on the main trail at the shore of Sparks Lake. Follow the shore of this shallow lake. Soon South Sister comes into view across the rugged lakeshore, offering several breathtaking views. After a few tenths of a mile more, you'll rejoin the hiking trail near the trailhead. Turn left here to return to the trailhead…or turn right to do it all again!

70. Green Lakes

	Green Lakes via Fall Creek	Green Lakes Loop
Distance:	9.6 miles out and back	13.6 mile loop
Elevation Gain:	1,200 feet	1,800 feet
Trailhead Elevation:	5,443 feet	5,443 feet
Trail High Point:	6,583 feet	6,802 feet
Season:	July - October	July - October
Best:	July - October	July - October
Pass:	NW Forest Pass + limited entry	NW Forest Pass + limited entry
Permit:	day use or overnight	day use or overnight
On the traditional lands of:	the Warm Springs and Molalla peoples	the Warm Springs and Molalla peoples

Directions:

- From Bend, drive Century Drive west until it becomes the Cascade Lakes Highway.
- From the last traffic circle in Bend, continue approximately 25 miles to a signed turnoff for the Green Lakes Trailhead on the right.
- Turn right and drive into the large trailhead, where there is ample room to park.
- **Drivetime from Bend:** 30 minutes

Hike: If you asked most Central Oregon hikers about their favorite hike, Green Lakes would

South Sister rises over the largest of the Green Lakes

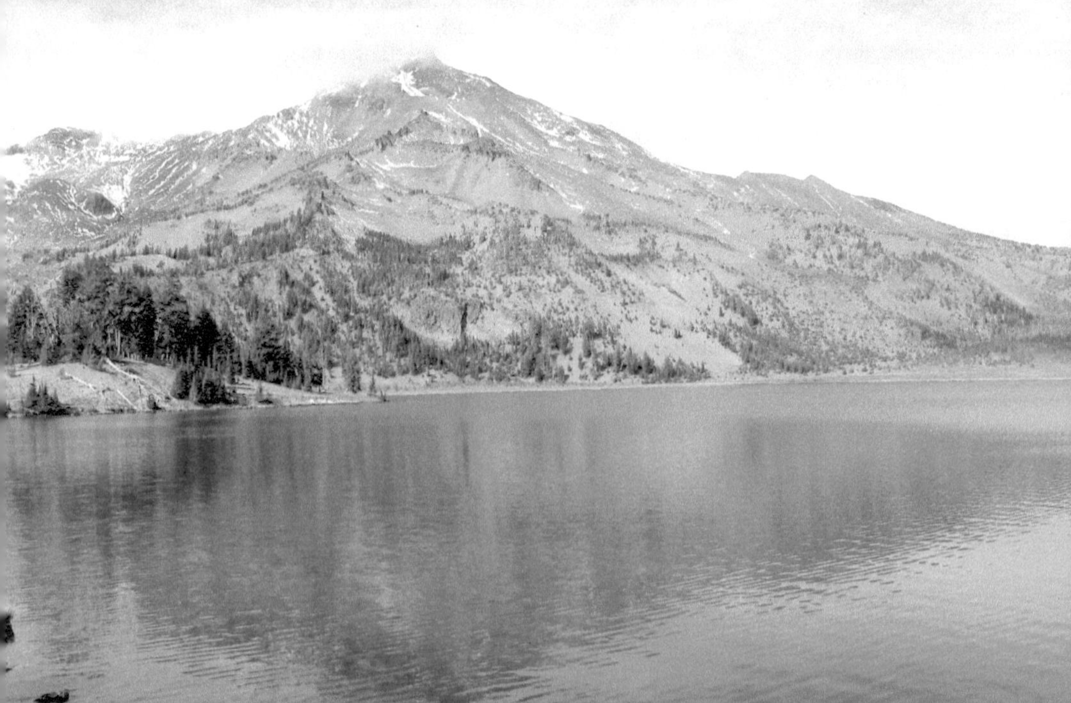

win this unofficial survey in a landslide. This seems to be everyone's favorite hike, and it's easy to see why. You follow Fall Creek gradually uphill, passing waterfalls, spectacular displays of wildflowers, and lava fields to a trio of turquoise lakes set directly between South Sister and Broken Top. Combine this scenic beauty with easy access from Bend and the Green Lakes Trail was among the most crowded in Oregon before the implementation of a permit system in 2021. Hikers looking for a longer hike can make a loop under the slopes of Broken Top along tumbling Soda Creek en route to Green Lakes. Before you go, don't forget to secure your day use or overnight permit; see the introduction to the Central Oregon Cascades on page 126 for more information.

For the out and back hike along Fall Creek, locate the Green Lakes Trail at the trailhead and follow it to a bridge across glassy Fall Creek, The creek is your companion all the way to Green Lakes. The creek is aptly-named; you'll pass several cascades and waterfalls in the first two miles of the hike. At 2.2 miles, the trail reaches a junction with the Moraine Lake Trail, which takes you west to Moraine Lake and the South Sister Climber's Trail (Hike 72). Continue along the Fall Creek Trail, following signs for Green Lakes. At 3.3 miles, the trail begins to follow a huge lava flow on the west side of the creek, remnants of a long-ago South Sister eruption. This lava flow dammed Fall Creek, creating the Green Lakes. The trail climbs above the creek for a short distance before reaching a wide plain at 4.4 miles from the trailhead. South Sister towers over this valley, and two of the three Green Lakes can be seen. Continue straight another 0.4 mile to a peninsula with excellent views of both South Sister and Broken Top towering over the turquoise waters of the largest Green Lake. The traul continues north another few hundred yards to the third of the Green Lakes, by far the greenest of the trio. There are campsites all over this basin, but be sure to camp only in designated sites away from the fragile lakeshores of all three lakes. Return the way you came from here; if you're planning on the loop, start on the Soda Creek Trail first.

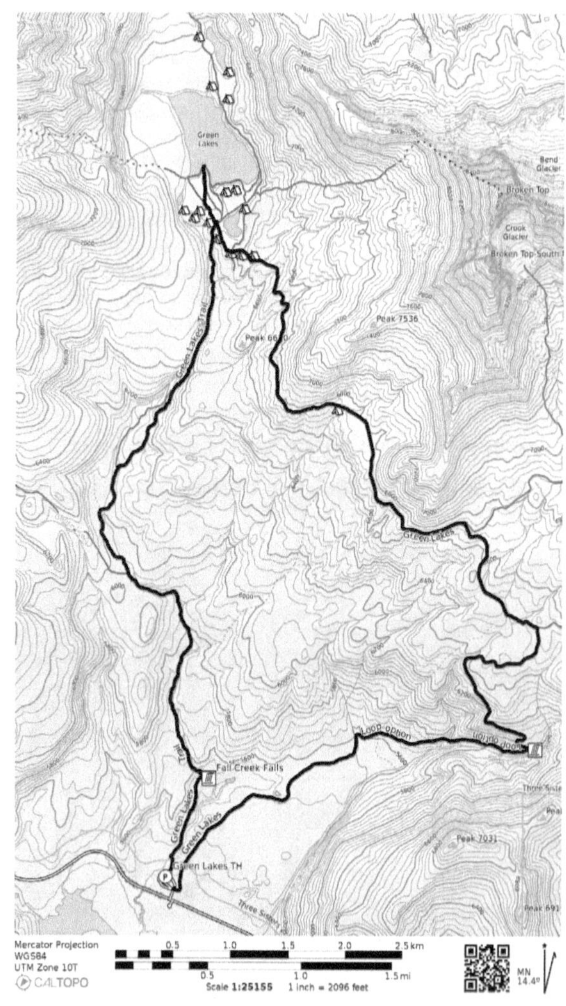

For the longer loop, locate the Soda Creek Trail on the far-right side of the trailhead. Follow this trail gradually uphill for 4.3 miles. Most of the way is in the forest but views gradually open up to the ruddy slopes of Broken Top as you ascend. The trail reaches a junction with the Todd Lake Trail at 4.3 miles. Turn left here and hike 0.9 mile of gradual uphill to a junction with the Broken Top Trail at 5.2 miles. Turn left here and follow this gorgeous trail west for another 3 miles to a junction with the Fall Creek Trail beside the first of the Green Lakes. Follow the directions above to the largest of the Green Lakes and then back to the trailhead.

71. South Sister Summit

Distance: 12.4 miles out and back
Elevation Gain: 4,909 feet
Trailhead elevation: 5,449 feet
Trail high Point: 10,358 feet
Season: July – September
Best: August
Pass: NW Forest Pass + Limited Entry Permit
Permit required: day use or overnight (if backpacking)
On the traditional lands of: the Warm Springs and Molalla peoples

Directions:

- From Bend, drive Century Drive west until it becomes the Cascade Lakes Highway.
- From the last traffic circle in Bend, continue 26 miles to the Devils Lake Trailhead. Just after the road curves to the south, turn left into the trailhead.
- Continue straight until you reach the trailhead at the end of the loop.
- **Drivetime from Bend:** 35 minutes

Hike: The best things in life do not come easily. Oregon is full of tall mountains and extraordinary viewpoints, and yet few can compare to the summit of South Sister. It takes a herculean effort to hike to the summit, but thousands of hikers make the trek every year. You can too, but get in shape first! This is one of Oregon's most extraordinary, and extraordinarily difficult hikes. I recommend packing at least four liters of water and prepare for almost any weather; if thunderstorms or snow are in the forecast, skip this hike and go somewhere else! Before you go, don't forget to secure your day use or overnight permit; see the introduction to the Central Oregon Cascades on page 126 for more information.

From the trailhead, you will follow the wide trail for 0.2 mile to a crossing of the Cascade Lakes Highway. Carefully scurry across this busy road, then locate the South Sister Climbers Trail on the far side. The trail begins to climb steeply through deep forest, gaining 1,250 feet in this first stretch of the hike. At 2 miles, you will reach a four-way junction at the lip of a wide, dusty plateau. South Sister towers above this scenic spot, and the route of your hike is before you.

Looking north from the summit of South Sister.

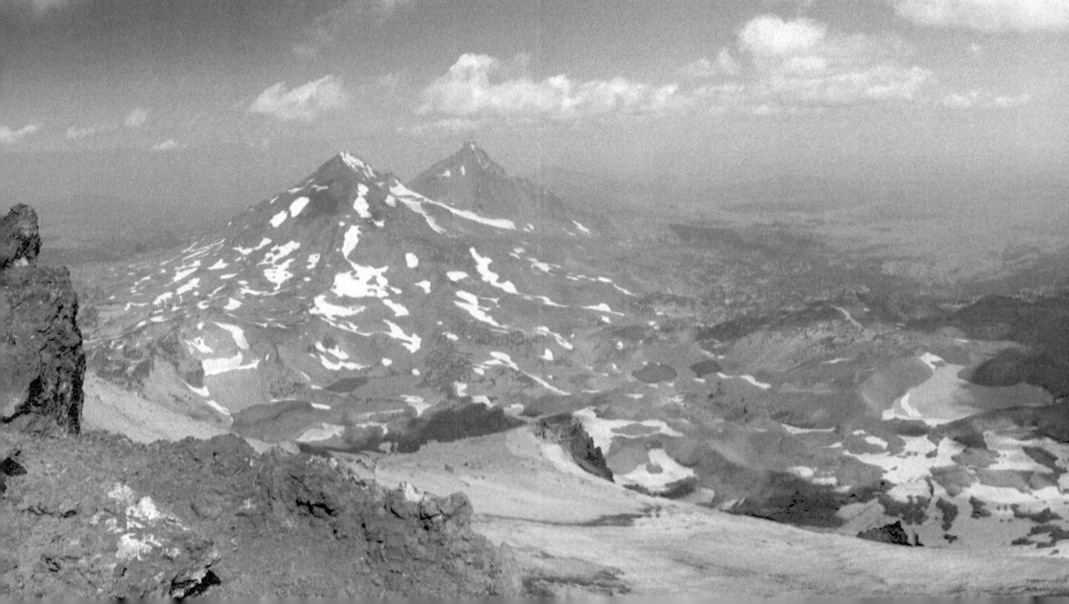

Turning right at this junction will take you down to Moraine Lake in a little under a mile; the lake makes for a scenic place to spend the night before summit day, but staying there requires a separate overnight permit (see the instructions above, and search for overnight permits instead). Assuming you're just doing this hike in a day, continue straight another 1.2 miles to the far end of this wide plateau. Once you pass the route of the now-decommissioned Canyon Trail down to Moraine Lake, the trail begins to climb in earnest.

From here, you will climb 1,900 feet over the next 1.6 miles. Somehow, it feels steeper than that! When I first hiked this trail in 1994, we met a gentleman coming down from the summit who referred to this stretch as "Hell 1", and that the final steep summit push was "Hell 2"; all this time later, that description still feels fitting. After huffing and puffing your way up the rocky, sandy, dusty slopes to the base of the moraine below the Lewis Glacier, a most amazing view is attained: below you is a turquoise glacial tarn at the base of the Lewis Glacier, and above you are the steep red cinder upper slopes of South Sister's summit. From the moraine, you will climb another 1,400 feet in 1 mile of rocky red cinders until you at last reach the lip of the summit crater at 5.8 miles. Many hikers reach this spot and declare victory, and it's hard to blame them; you've already climbed almost a vertical mile!

To reach the true summit of South Sister, follow the trail along the right side of the summit crater another 0.4 mile and another 150 feet of uphill until you reach the true summit at 6.2 miles from the trailhead. Spread out before you are Middle and North Sisters, with the Chambers Lakes (Hike 66) dotting the basin between South and Middle Sister. Even Broken Top looks small from this vantage point. The view stretche for more than a hundred miles in every direction on clear days. This is a view fit for such a difficult trek, and you will feel a sense of accomplishment worthy of the adventure. Some hardy folks even camp on the summit to watch the sun rise over Central Oregon. Expect an extremely cold and windy night if this is your plan.

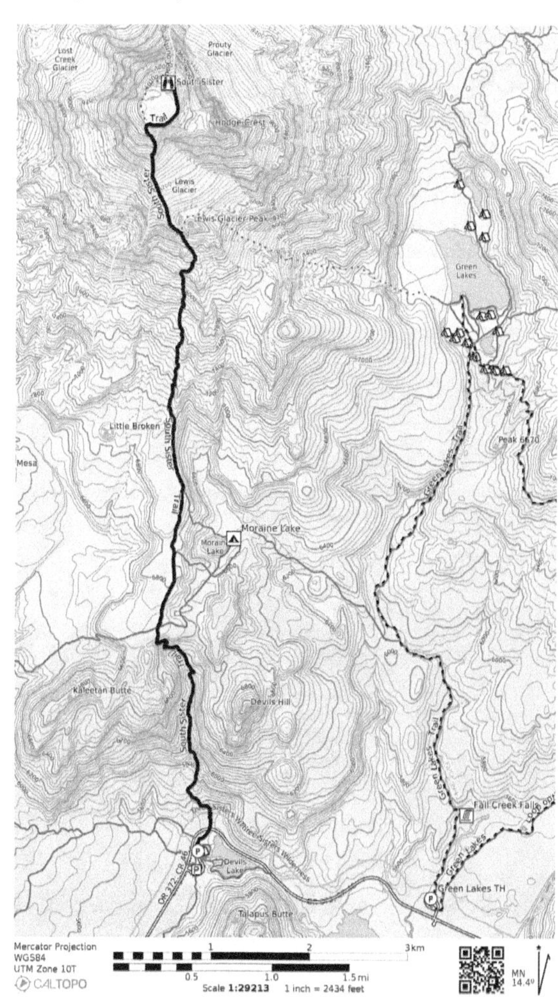

Return the way you came, and rejoice! You just climbed Oregon's third-tallest peak – it calls for a celebration!

Note: You can also summit South Sister from Green Lakes (Hike 70) but this approach is longer and and more demanding. If you'd like to make a weekend of it, you can start at the Green Lakes Trailhead, hike to Green Lakes, and see if you can find the rough climber's trail to South Sister. If that doesn't work, backtrack to the Moraine Lake junction and follow the trail until it intersects with the South Sister Trail, at which point you'll follow the directions above.

72. Shale Ridge Trail

Distance: 6 miles out and back
Elevation Gain: 400 feet
Trailhead elevation: 2,923 feet
Trail high Point: 3,095 feet
Season: May – November
Best: May – November
Pass: none needed
Permit: none needed
On the traditional lands of: the Yoncalla and Kalapuya peoples

Directions:

- From Eugene, drive south on OR 58 for approximately 38 miles.
- Just before you reach Oakridge, turn left onto Westfir Road. Drive 0.5 mile to a junction just after you cross the Willamette River, then turn left to continue on Westfir Road.
- Drive 2.7 miles to the small town of Westfir, where Westfir Road becomes FS 19, also known as the Aufderheide Drive.
- Drive 29 miles on this winding road as it follows the serpentine North Fork Middle Fork Willamette River.
- At a sharp curve in the road, turn right into the Shale Ridge Trailhead. There is room for 4 – 5 cars. No pass is required.
- **Drivetime from Eugene:** 2 hours.

Hike: Sometimes Oregon's wildest places are surprisingly easy to reach. This stroll into the deep, dark canyon of the North Fork Middle Fork Willamette River is as relaxing as it is intriguing. You'll hike through a green tunnel to a magnificent grove of ancient forest at the head of this canyon's valley, where the North Fork Middle Fork Willamette River roars out of the Waldo

Hiking through Cedar Bog.

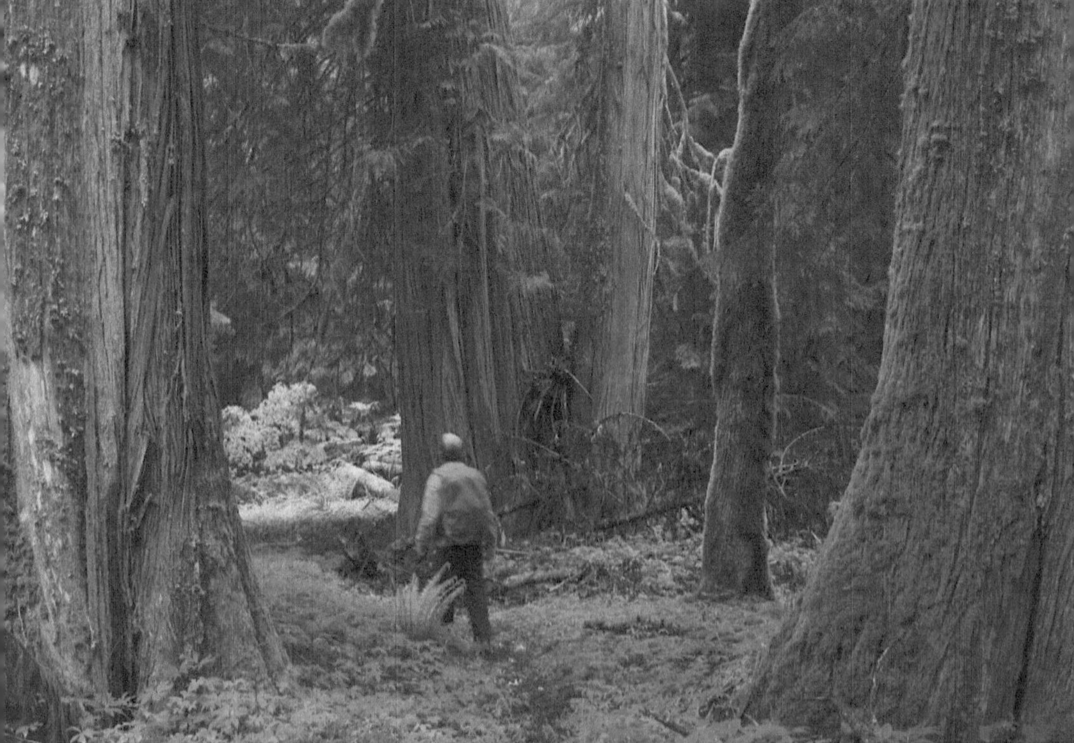

Lake Wilderness. Plan on a full day to make the most of this extraordinary place. This trail was closed for most of the summer and fall of 2022 due to the Cedar Creek Fire near Waldo Lake, just south of here. This fire prevented me from visiting Waldo Lake, which burned significantly during this fire. The Cedar Creek Fire did not burn any of this hike, but if you're planning an expedition deeper into this rugged wilderness, you may encounter fire damage. Check the Middle Fork Ranger District online for more information.

From the trailhead, locate the Shale Ridge Trail heading straight, and ignore the North Fork Trail which heads right to follow the river downstream. The Shale Ridge Trail soon enters the Waldo Lake Wilderness, and from here on out, it's just you and the trees. The river is often heard but rarely seen here, as it is located on the far end of the swamp to your right. The trail passes through some fantastic groves of ancient Douglas fir, and the understory here is indescribably mossy and verdant. Everything seems green. Although this is the Shale Ridge Trail, it should really be the North Fork Middle Fork Willamette River Trail; while the river is rarely seen, its presence is always felt.

At 1.8 miles, the trail reaches Skookum Creek's many channels. Pick your way across the creek on rocks and logs and continue deeper into the wilderness. The trail continues another mile through increasingly impressive forest to a flat known as Cedar Bog. The North Fork Middle Fork Willamette River emerges from a deep, dark canyon into this swamp, through which the river has carved many channels. The route through here can be complicated; follow orange flagging across downed logs to keep going. At the center of the bog, you'll pass some truly astounding cedars, believed to be hundreds of years old. When the trail reaches the center of the bog beside the main channel of the North Fork Middle Fork, this is your destination.

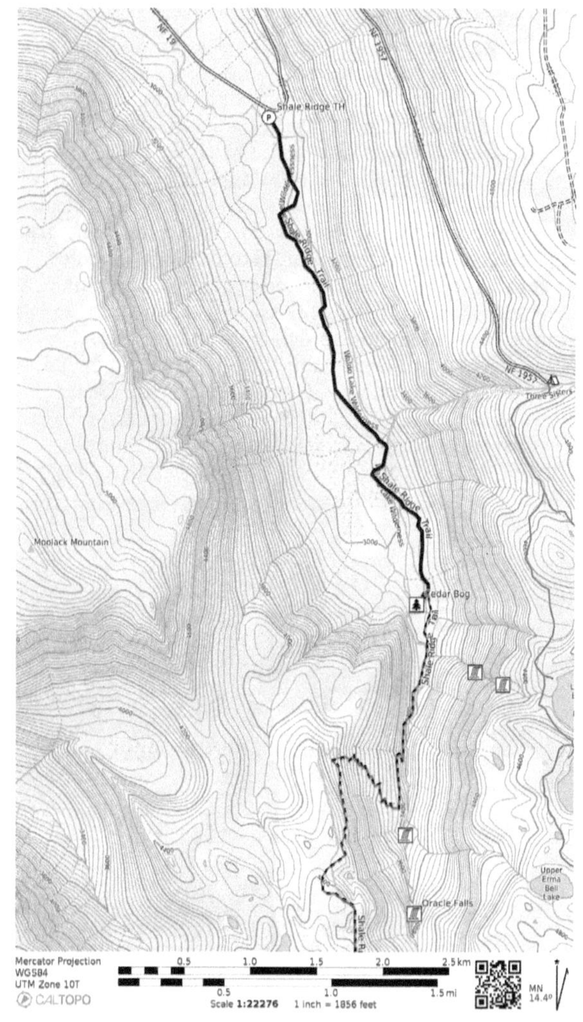

The Shale Ridge Trail does in fact continue upriver towards Shale Ridge but becomes extremely rough and faint immediately after you cross the river. This section of trail has not been maintained for many years and is difficult to follow. Deeper in the North Fork Middle Fork canyon is Oracle Falls, one of Oregon's most extraordinary waterfalls. Reaching Oracle is extraordinarily difficult and requires significant experience in off-trail travel through brush, downed logs, and perilously steep slopes, as well as a level of patience bordering on extreme. These days, many of the folks attempting to hike beyond deeper into the North Fork canyon are in search of this magical place. Most do not make it. Try this at your own risk. Return the way you came.

73. Bohemia Mountain

Distance: 1.6 miles out and back
Elevation Gain: 613 feet
Trailhead elevation: 5,381 feet
Trail high Point: 5,994 feet
Season: June – October
Best: June – October
Pass: none needed
Permit: none needed
On the traditional lands of: the Cow Creek Umpqua, Kalapuya, and Yoncalla peoples

Directions:

- From Eugene, drive south on Interstate 5 approximately 20 miles to Cottage Grove. Leave I-5 at Exit 174, signed for Cottage Grove and Dorena.
- Turn left and drive along Row River Road, which passes through Dorena and eventually begins to follow Brice Creek. At 15 miles from the freeway, you'll pass a sign for the Bohemia Mines. Ignore this junction, as it follows extremely rough Sharps Creek Road. Continue driving along Brice Creek.
- You will continue another 3.5 miles of paved road to an intersection with a road signed for Brice Creek and Bohemia Saddle.
- Keep right and 8 miles to a junction with Champion Creek Road (FR 2473) at the East Brice Creek Trailhead. The Champion Creek Road has a sign that reads "Bohemia Saddle", and this road does indeed also reach Bohemia Mountain; you should ignore this road, as it is incredibly rough. You should instead keep left to continue following Brice Creek.
- Drive 3.8 more miles along Brice Creek to a junction with FR 2212 on your right.
- Following signs for Fairview Mountain and Bohemia Saddle, turn right here and drive this good gravel road for 6.3 miles to Noonday Saddle.
- From Noonday Saddle, keep straight and continue 1.9 miles of worsening gravel road to Champion Saddle. If you're sick of sitting in the car, you can park here and walk the rest of the way, making for a much longer 5 mile hike.
- Otherwise, continue on the narrow dirt road for 1.1 miles to the trailhead at Bohemia Saddle. Along the way, you'll pass both Musick Guard Station (a rentable cabin) as well as the road into Bohemia City. Save this exploration for after your hike.
- **Drivetime from Eugene:** 1 hour and 20 minutes

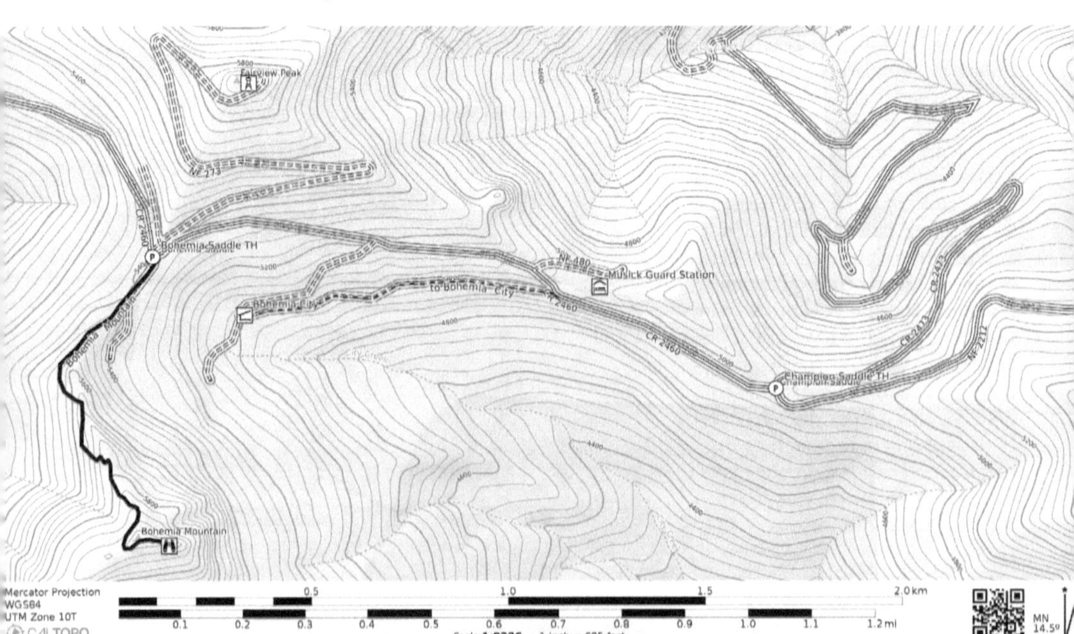

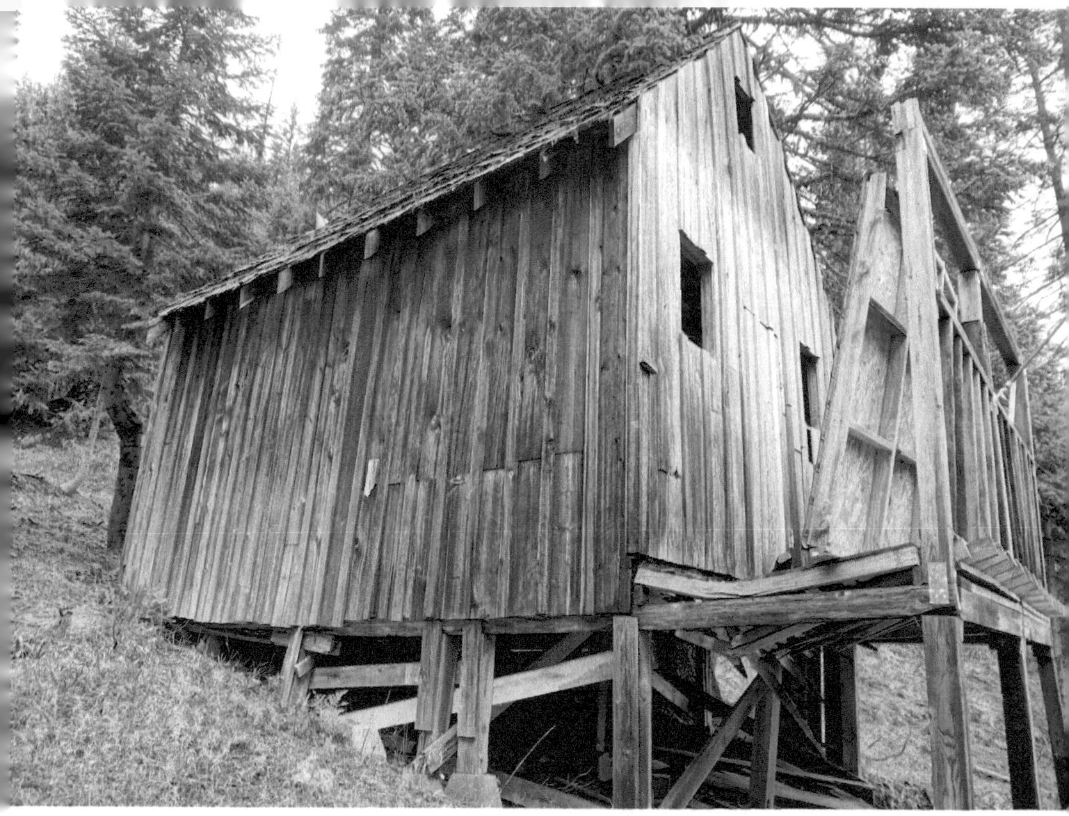

The remains of the old post office below Bohemia Mountain.

Hike: Like so many other places in the remote corners of Oregon, the trails and roads at Bohemia Mountain southeast of Cottage Grove were built for mining. Ivan Lorky, better known as James "Bohemia" Johnson, found gold on the slopes of the mountain along with George Ramsey in 1863, and proceeded to form a company to mine the gold and other minerals, deep in the heart of the Cascade foothills. A town grew in the footsteps of the mines, only to be abandoned after less than a decade. When James Musick came to the area to mine in the 1880s, Bohemia City was resurrected and eventually grew to a size of thirty houses, among them a post office, hotel, store, and saloon. The second incarnation of the town was abandoned once more by the late 1920s, but the names of these two men remain all over the scenic country around Bohemia Mountain. In addition to a beautiful hike to a panoramic viewpoint, you can also explore the remains of Bohemia City at the foot of the mountain. This is a short hike, but there's so much to do here you'll want to spend a full day exploring.

Begin your hike at Bohemia Saddle. If you walked here from Champion Saddle, stay on the main road and ignore the side roads leading to Bohemia City on the left (save this for later) and the Musick Guard Station (which can be reserved on www.recreation.gov) and walk 1.1 miles to Bohemia Saddle. From the saddle, follow the Bohemia Mountain Trail uphill to the left. On the way up you'll pass countless summer wildflowers, among them impressive displays of Cascade lilies. The steep trail reaches the summit at 0.8 mile. The views up here are truly amazing, and you'll see Cascade summits from Mount Hood to Mount Thielsen. It is said that Mount Shasta is visible on extremely clear days. Look below you to the remains of Bohemia City. When you're ready to return, hike back down to Bohemia Saddle.

If you'd like to visit the remains of Bohemia City, follow the road halfway back to Champion Saddle and look for a road forking sharply downhill to the right, immediately after you pass Musick Guard Station. This road is rough and it's better to walk. You'll reach Bohemia City after 0.6 mile. All that's left is the old post office, which is constantly in the process of being restored. Ignore the temptation to explore further, as the road to the mine is on private property and mining still occurs on occasion in this area.

74. Salt Creek and Diamond Creek Falls

Distance: 4.4 miles (all trails)
Elevation Gain: 1,000 feet (all trails)
Trailhead elevation: 4,092 feet
Trail high Point: 4,330 feet
Season: May – November
Best: June – October
Pass: NW Forest Pass
Permit: none needed
On the traditional lands of: the Kalapuya people

Directions:

- From Eugene, drive southeast on OR 58 for approximately 57 miles to a turnoff on the right signed for Salt Creek Falls Observation Point. If you're coming from the east, this turnoff is 29 miles west of the OR 58 / 97 split north of Chemult.
- Turn right here and drive 0.1 mile to a fork in the road. Keep right here and drive 0.5 mile to the large parking area at the brink of Salt Creek Falls.
- **Drivetime from Eugene:** 1 hour and 15 minutes

Hike: Salt Creek Falls is one of Oregon's most extraordinary waterfalls, and it takes almost no effort to see it. Driving east on OR 58, you will catch glimpses of this glorious falls, and all it takes is a short drive and walk off the highway to see it up close. Don't make this a simple pit stop, however; there is much to see here, from fantastic views of Salt Creek's rugged canyon to another waterfall that is just as spectacular as Salt Creek Falls. This is one Oregon's premier easy hikes, and you should make the time for it even if you're just passing through the area.

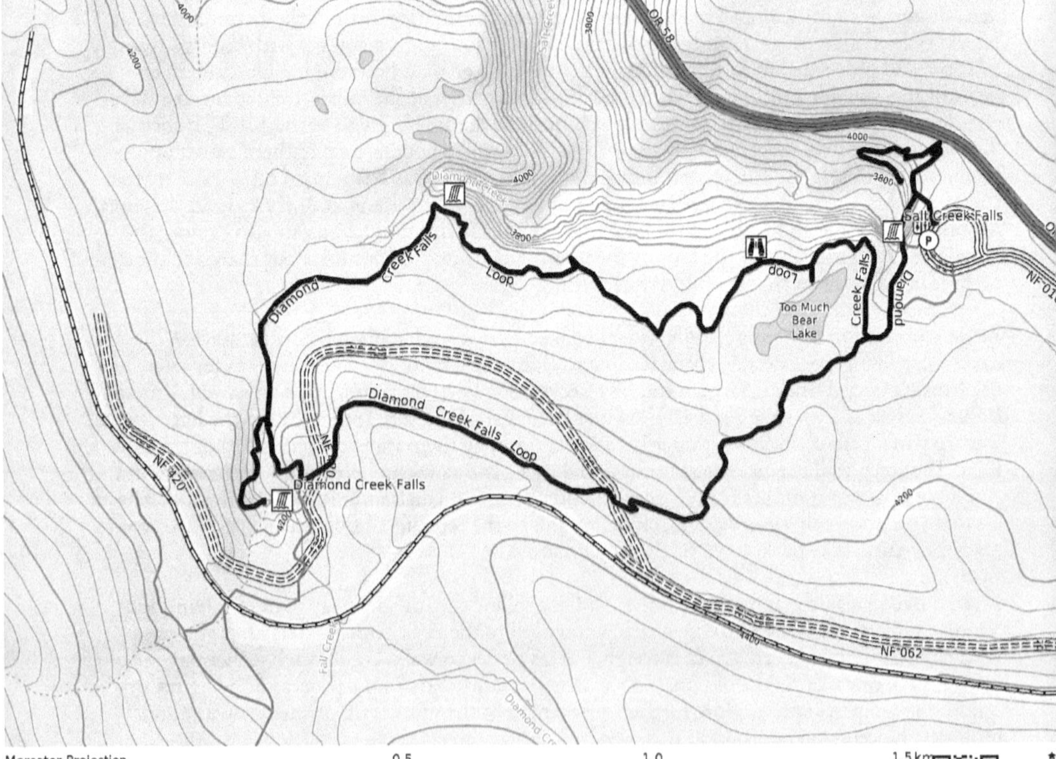

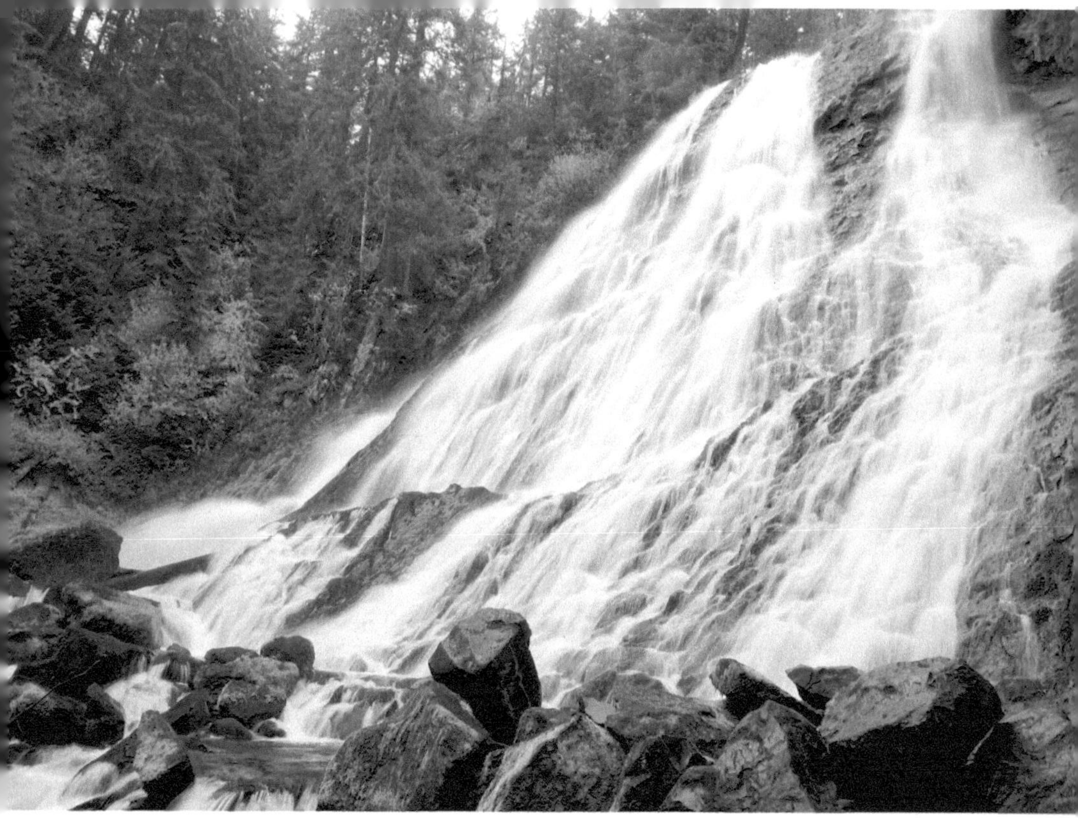

Diamond Creek Falls

From the trailhead walk past the observation kiosk to go check out the view of Salt Creek Falls. Once you reach a fenced viewpoint of the falls, you have the option of following down the trail down to the base of the falls either now, later, or not at all. You might not feel like checking out the view of the base of the falls later, so I recommend visiting this spot first. Follow the wide trail downhill for 0.4 mile to its end at a head-on view of this most impressive waterfall. When you're done, return to the top of the falls and turn right to follow the paved trail along the rim of the creek.

You'll soon cross a bridge and reach the beginning of the loop. Turn right to hike this loop counterclockwise. The trail follows the top of Salt Creek's canyon, reaching a side trail to the delightfully-named Too Much Bear Lake at just over a half-mile from the trailhead. Take a moment to ponder the curious origins of this small lake's name, then return to the trail. Turn left again and continue following the trail along the rim of the canyon. You'll pass a pair of viewpoints; the first is a view of Salt Creek's canyon, and the second is an obstructed view of Lower Diamond Creek Falls, mostly out of sight in the canyon below. At a little over 2 miles, reach a junction on the right with a trail signed for "Lower Diamond Falls". This is the side trail for what is actually upper Diamond Falls, more commonly known as Diamond Creek Falls. Turn right and follow this steep and somewhat sketchy side trail to a bridge across the creek. Continue past the bridge a short distance to spectacular Diamond Creek Falls. Here Diamond Creek tumbles 120 feet down and across a basalt cliff reminiscent of Ramona Falls near Mount Hood. In a state full of gorgeous waterfalls, Diamond Creek Falls is one of the best.

When you're ready to continue your hike, return to the main trail and turn right. You will climb to a viewpoint overlooking Diamond Creek Falls, then reach an unsigned junction with the Vivian Lake Trail near the top of the falls. Turn left here to continue the loop. The loop follows this trail over a hill and across two decommissioned roads. Eventually you'll reach the junction near the Salt Creek bridge at the close of the loop. Once across the bridge, turn left to skirt above Salt Creek Falls again, and then turn right to the trailhead.

75. Diamond View Lake

Distance: 10.8 miles out and back
Elevation Gain: 1,008 feet
Trailhead elevation: 4,830 feet
Trail high Point: 5,838 feet
Season: July – October
Best: August – October
Pass: none needed
Permit: none needed
On the traditional lands of: the Klamath and Molalla peoples

Directions:

- From Eugene, drive southeast on OR 58 for 69 miles to Willamette Pass.
- Continue east beyond Willamette Pass a 0.5 mile to a turnoff on the right for the West Odell Lake access road. If you're coming from the east, this turnoff is on the left, 23.6 miles from the OR 58 / 97 split north of Chemult.
- Turn right and drive 2 miles to the Shelter Cove Resort. Turn right here at a sign for the Trapper Creek Trail.
- Drive this small gravel road 100 yards to a small trailhead parking area before the road reaches train tracks.
- **Drivetime from Eugene:** 1 hour and 20 minutes

Hike: Diamond Peak is one of Oregon's most beautiful and least-known major peaks. Instead of a single summit, Diamond Peak spreads its broad shoulders wide across the horizon south of the Three Sisters, offering multiple summit peaks atop a reddish-orange cone of cinders. Most Oregon hikers see Diamond Peak from a distance, note the mountain's wide profile, and keep driving or hiking somewhere else. The best views of this impressive peak are found on its eastern

Diamond View Lake offers stunning reflections of Diamond Peak.

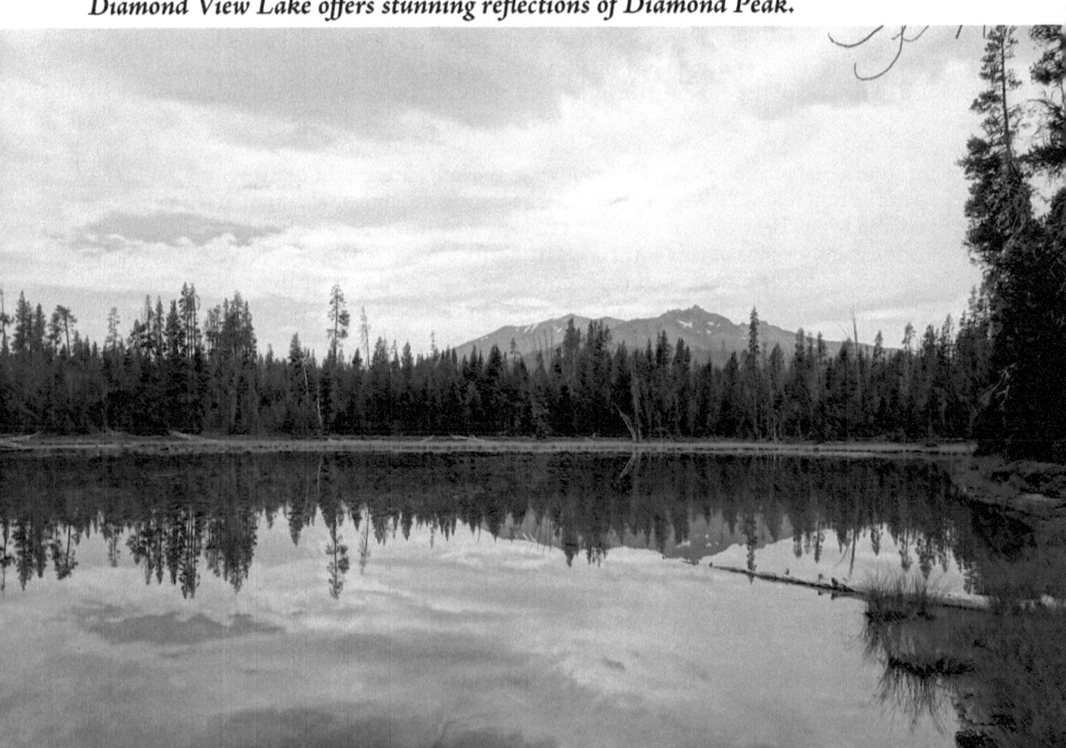

slopes, and this delightful and surprisingly easy hike to Diamond View Lake may just be the best in the entire wilderness. You'll absolutely love it!

Begin the hike by crossing the train tracks. Once across the tracks, follow a hiker sign and arrow to the start of the Trapper Creek Trail. In just a moment you will reach a signboard. Fill out your free permit and then set out on the Trapper Creek Trail. After just 0.2 mile, you'll reach a junction with the Whitefish Creek Trail. Right leads to the Pacific Crest Trail, but you want to go straight. The next two miles are an absolute delight! You will follow Trapper Creek, often closely at times. This glassy, crystal-clear stream puts on a show for two miles, tumbling over mossy ledges and bending gracefully through rocky gorges. At a little over 2 miles, the trail reaches a ledge overlooking the splashing creek. This is an excellent rest stop, as the trail leaves the creek from here to climb to the lake. Up to this point, the Trapper Creek Trail has been gradual. Surprisingly, it is even more gradual from here to the lake. At times it hardly even seems like you're gaining elevation!

The forest begins to thin out as you approach the lake. The yellowish rock you see strewn all over the ground here is pumice, a remnant of Mount Mazama's eruption some 7,700 years ago, which created Crater Lake. After hiking through the woods for a spell, you'll know you're getting close before you even reach the lake. Clouds of mosquitoes, ever the bane of the Diamond Peak Wilderness, swarm you as soon as you reach the basin holding the lake for much of June and July. It is for this reason that it's better to wait to do this hike until mid-August at the earliest. The trail reaches Diamond View Lake at a little over 5 miles from the trailhead. Follow the trail around the lakeshore of the shallow lake for a few hundred yards until Diamond Peak comes into view across the lake. On clear days, the reflection of the peak in the lake's shallow, glassy waters is absolutely stunning. Campsites abound if you're backpacking but make sure you camp away from the lake's fragile shores. Campfires are prohibited, in addition to being a terrible idea in this fragile environment. Return the way you came.

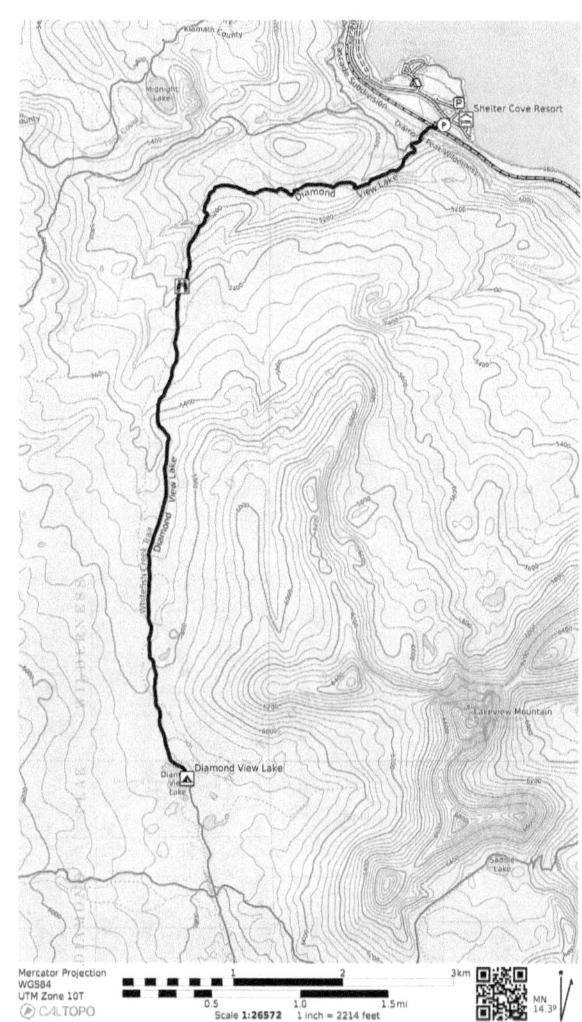

If you're looking for a longer hike, you've come to the right place. The trail continues past Diamond View Lake, eventually reaching Crescent Lake. Along the way you'll pass a junction with the Crater Butte Trail, which you can follow east to Stag Lake or west to the slopes of Diamond Peak. Make sure to consult a good map if you plan on exploring this area further. The Diamond Peak Wilderness is quite fun to explore, but bring a good map to make the most of your time in this special place.

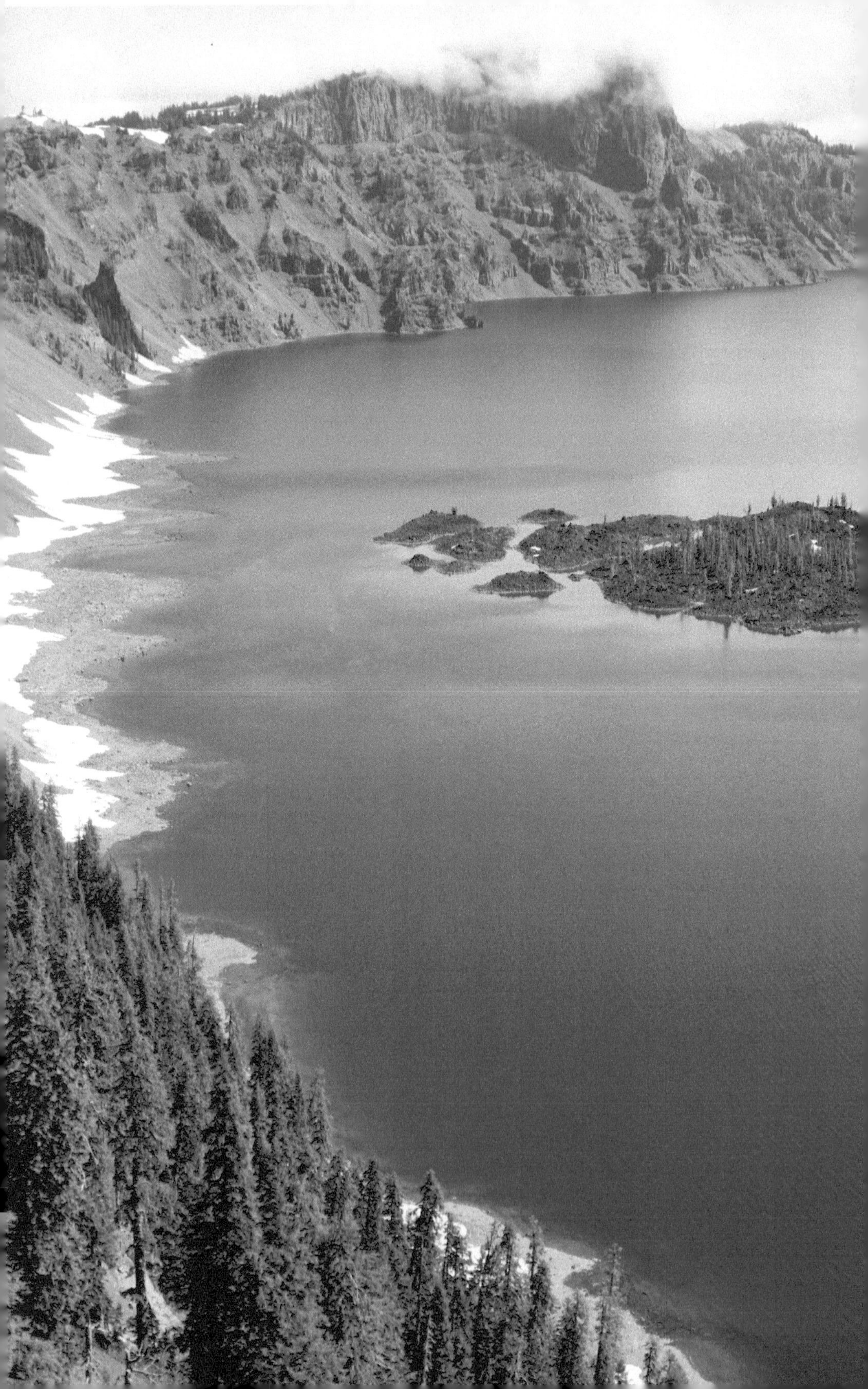

Southern Oregon and Southern Cascades

		Distance	EV Gain	Page
76.	King Mountain Rock Garden	1 mi	200 ft	180
77.	Lemolo Falls	4.6 mi	500 ft	182
78.	Mount Thielsen Meadows	11.8 mi	1,600 ft	184
79.	Crater Lake	6.2 mi	1,400 ft	186
80.	Mount Bolivar	2.8 mi	1,163 ft	190
81.	Rogue River Trail	7 mi	1,000 ft	192
82.	Illinois River Trail	11 mi	3,000 ft	194
83.	Kerby Peak	7.2 mi	2,700 ft	196
84.	Sucker Creek Gap & Swan Mountain	11.4 mi	2,200 ft	198
85.	Siskiyou Peak	5.6 mi	900 ft	200
86.	Lower and Upper Table Rock	8.4 mi	1,530 ft	202
87.	Hobart Bluff	2.6 mi	400 ft	204

Southern Oregon isn't just a place; it's also a feeling. The climate is warmer and drier than in many other parts of Oregon, the days are longer, and the flora and fauna unique and fascinating. You'll find much to love here, from intriguing wildflower meadows to deep, remote canyons, and from thunderous waterfalls to the incomparable Crater Lake. Much of what you'll find down here is unique to southern Oregon (and far northern California). As this part of Oregon feels distinctly different, it should not be surprising that a movement to carve out a new state - the state of Jefferson - has been active down here for decades.

I would have preferred to offer more hikes in this section but a constant parade of fires and poor weather kept me out of Southern Oregon more than I would have liked. Few places in Oregon have felt the ravages of climate change more than the state of Jefferson, and many places in this part of Oregon have burned in the recent past. The Kalmiopsis Wilderness (Hike 82, but also mentioned in Hike 20) has seen two of Oregon's largest fires (The Biscuit Fire in 2002 and the Chetco Bar Fire in 2017), and many trails in the Kalmiopsis remained closed or impassible to this day. To the east, the North Umpqua River was the site of the massive Archie Fire in 2020 that blackened more than 130,000 acres in the area along and around the North Umpqua River. Many of the places I would have loved to visit were closed or impassible; I look forward to seeing them reopen as the years go by.

Nevertheless, presented here are twelve of my absolute favorite hikes. Some of these hikes are well-known to many southern Oregon hikers, but others are seldom visited. There is something for everyone here, and you should find many reasons to return to these hikes again and again.

Photo on left: The incomparable Crater Lake (Hike 79).

76. King Mountain Rock Garden

Distance: 1 mile out and back
Elevation Gain: 200 feet
Trailhead elevation: 4,921 feet
Trail high point: 5,029 feet
Season: June – November
Best: June – July
Pass: none needed
On the traditional lands of: the Tolowa Dee-Ni', Modoc, Takelma, and Cow Creek Umpqua peoples

Directions:

- Drive Interstate 5 north of Grants Pass to Exit 76, signed for Wolf Creek. Leave the freeway here and turn right onto Coyote Creek Road. If you're coming from Roseburg, drive south on I-5 for approximately 44 miles to Exit 76 and follow signs for Old State Hwy 99. Just past Wolf Creek, turn left onto Bridge Avenue, then continue onto Coyote Creek Road.
- Drive 5.4 miles on this road to the end of pavement. Continue 0.7 mile of gravel road to a fork, where you keep left.
- Continue on this road, now known as BLM 33-5-21, for 2 miles to a 4-way junction. Keep straight on 33-5-21.
- Drive 1.2 miles to where the road curves sharply uphill, becoming BLM 33-5-26.
- Follow this steep road uphill for 2 miles to a small brown "Trail" sign on the left. Turn left into the small parking area that serves as the trailhead. The last mile of this road is rocky and rough but should be passable for most passenger cars.
- **Drivetimes:** 50 minutes from Grants Pass, 1 hour and 15 minutes from Roseburg

Hike: Driving Interstate 5 is a boring but inescapable part of traveling in Oregon. Even the prettier stretches of the highway offer little relief from the tedium of passing trucks, speeding Californians, and long distances between towns. This short hike to King Mountain Rock Garden offers an antidote to the boredom. This excellent leg-stretcher is just 12 miles from the freeway but feels surprisingly remote. This small preserve features rare flowers, stupendous views, and stately trees. Just as attractive is the nearby ghost town of Golden, perhaps the best-preserved ghost town in the state of Oregon.

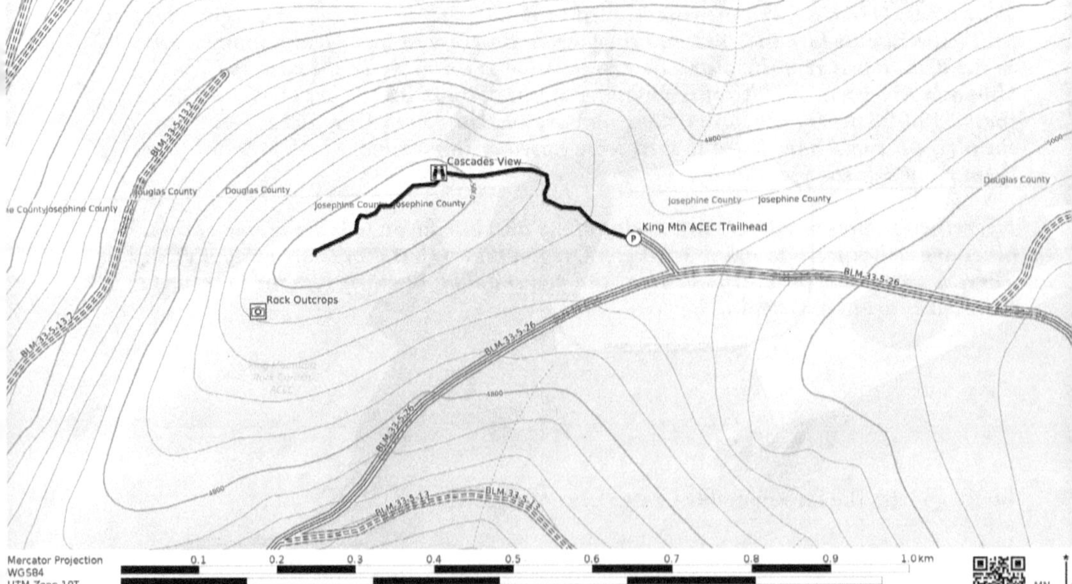

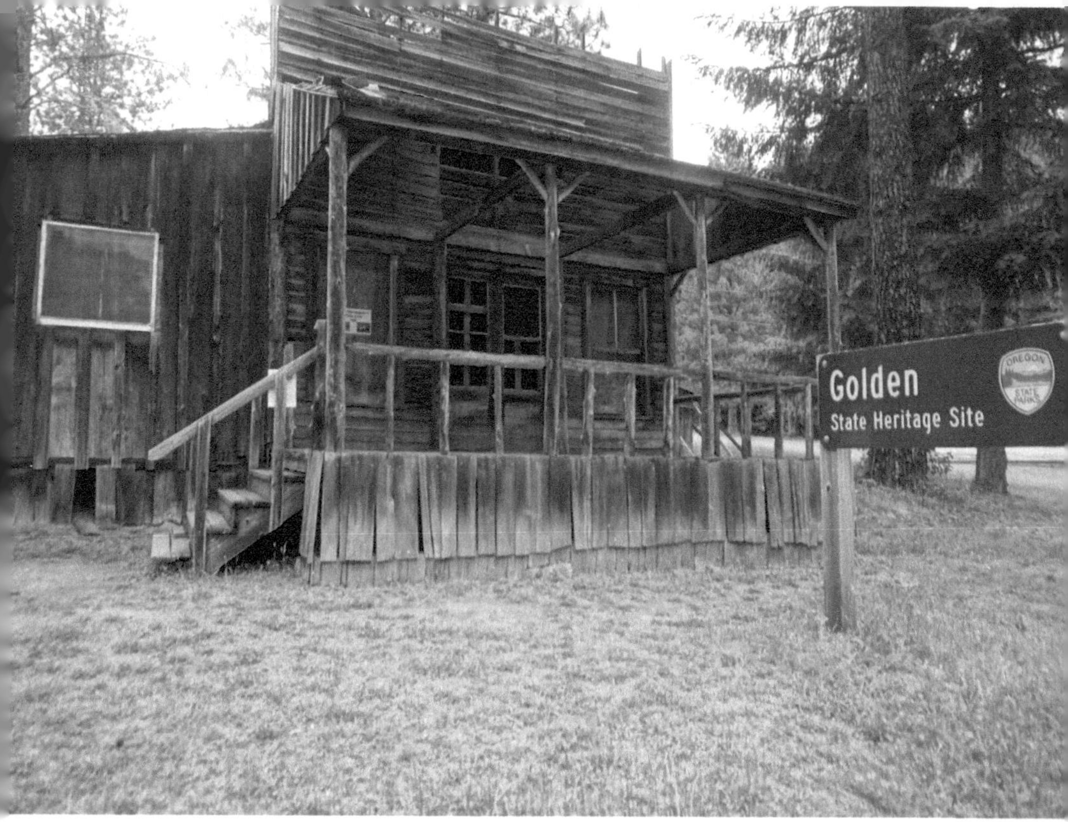

The ghost town of Golden is a fun place to explore after the hike.

Beginning at the King Mountain Trailhead, follow the trail, an obvious jeep road, uphill between stately ponderosa pines. In just a few minutes, you'll near the rocky summit of King Mountain. Your attention might be on the flowers at your feet; in season, look for stonecrop and paintbrush, as well as two very rare flowers endemic to King Mountain: the small, brown and yellow Siskiyou Missionbell and the fuzzy white and purple Umpqua phacelia. The BLM established the 90-acre King Mountain Area of Critical Environment Concern to protect these two flowers, both of which are rarely found in Oregon. After only ten minutes of walking, you'll reach the rocky western summit of King Mountain. The views here are massive, stretching east to the Cascades. The trail then drops to the equally rocky west summit, where you'll have excellent views down to the Rogue Valley and the I-5 corridor. The meadows here are fun to explore but try your best not to trample the plants and flowers that make this place special. When you're ready, return to the trailhead the way you came. The meadows and ponderosa pine groves at the trailhead are similarly fun to explore, and you could easy spend another hour or two exploring the King Mountain area.

Before you get back on the freeway, be sure to stop at the Golden State Heritage Site, which you passed on the drive to King Mountain. This unheralded state park is the site of the town of Golden, which was built during a 1890s mining boom. Four buildings remain in the town: a church, a former residence, a shed, and a building that once housed the town's post office and store. The town became known for being dry, as well; unlike many mining communities, there was never a saloon in Golden. When the gold boom ended, the town's population dwindled, and Golden was fully abandoned by the middle of the 20th Century. Lovers of history will find this place fascinating, and when you add the ghost town to your fun little hike on King Mountain, you'll be glad you left the freeway for a bit.

Note: The Golden State Heritage Site is closed as of December 2022 but is expected to reopen sometime in 2023.

77. Lemolo Falls

	Lemolo Falls North	Lemolo Falls South
Distance:	4.6 miles out and back	2.2 miles out and back
Elevation Gain:	500 feet (on the return)	700 feet (on the return)
Trailhead Elevation:	4,085 feet	4,193 feet
Trail High Point:	4,085 feet	4,193 feet
Season:	May – November	May – November
Best:	May – November	May – November
Pass:	none needed	none needed
On the traditional lands of:	the Cow Creek Umpqua and Modoc peoples	the Cow Creek Umpqua and Modoc peoples

Directions:

- From Roseburg, drive east on OR 138 for 73 miles to a turnoff on the left signed for Lemolo Lake. If you're coming from Crater Lake, this junction is 5.9 miles west of Diamond Lake.
- Turn left onto FR 2610 and drive 4.9 miles to a junction just across the dam that forms Lemolo Lake. Turn left here.
- The Lemolo Falls Trailhead is 0.6 mile beyond the dam. Turn left across a narrow bridge that spans a canal, and cross the bridge. Park wherever you can as space is limited, and make sure you leave yourself space to turn around.
- **Drivetime from Roseburg:** 1 hour and 30 minutes

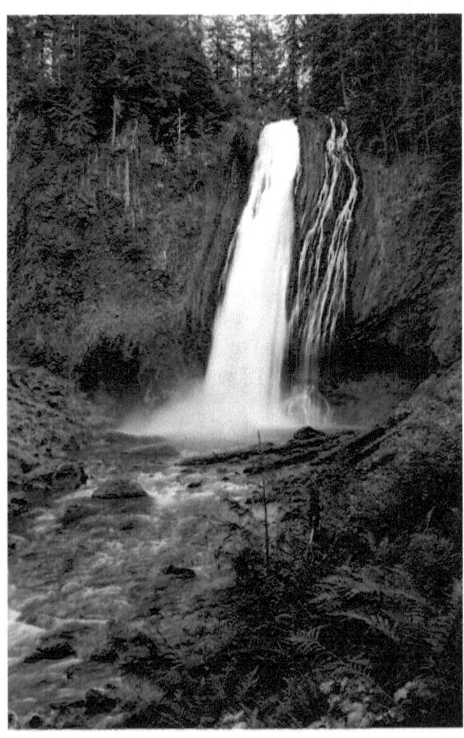

Hike: Lemolo translates to "wild" or "untamed" in the local Chinook jargon, and this is quite a fitting name for spectacular Lemolo Falls. The North Umpqua River plummets 165 feet across a mossy basalt slope, and the rumble of the falls fills the canyon for nearly a mile in every direction. On any list of Oregon's best waterfalls, Lemolo Falls belongs near the top. There are two trails to this extraordinary place, and unfortunately, each comes with its advantages and disadvantages. The North Umpqua River Trail leads you along a gorgeous stretch of the river leading to the falls, but only has one good view of Lemolo Falls. On the other side of the North Umpqua River, an old trail drops to the base of the falls, offering breathtaking views and many photographic possibilities; unfortunately, the road access to this trail is worse, the trail is shorter and steeper, and does not contain any of the river views that make the North Umpqua Trail so lovely. For the best experience, hike both trails!

For the North Umpqua Trail, you'll leave the trailhead and hike downhill through dark woods along the spectacular North Umpqua River. You'll pass fantastic displays of summer wildflowers, among them iris, columbine and rhododendron, while the river rumbles over basalt ledges and boulders to your left. A number of side trails lead to stellar viewpoints of the river. At just over 2 miles, the trail reaches the lip of Lemolo Falls. A proliferation of trails lead to the top of the falls, but you should ignore these dangerous detours and stay on the North Umpqua Trail. Just a short distance downhill, look for a steep side trail angling downhill to the left. Follow this trail very carefully down to a rocky promontory with a spectacular side view of the falls. This is the only viewpoint of Lemolo Falls from the north side of the river, but it's a great one. The trail continues downhill another mile to a bridge over the North Umpqua River but there are no views of the falls here, nor is it possible to connect this trail to the other trail that reaches the base of Lemolo Falls. Unless you're planning a larger car shuttle on the North Umpqua River to somewhere downstream, return the way you came.

To hike to the base of Lemolo Falls from its south side, return to the trailhead and drive back across Lemolo Lake's dam. Drive 0.5 mile south to a junction on the right with FR 3401, Thorn Prairie Road. If you skipped the North Umpqua Trail hike described above, this junction will be on your left 4.2 miles north of OR 138. Follow FR 3401 for 0.4 mile and turn right onto FR 800. Drive this road for 1.6 miles to a junction on the right with a sign that reads "Lemolo Falls Road No. 840". Turn right here and drive this narrow, bumpy, high-centered road for 0.2 mile to the trailhead at road's end. Park at any number of spots along the road. The southern trail to Lemolo Falls is a far less interesting hike than the northern approach described above but wastes no time directing you to the base of the falls. Follow the trail as it switchbacks downhill to river level at 0.7 mile. Soon massive Lemolo Falls comes into view in front of you at the far end of the canyon. The views are jaw-dropping, breathtaking, and utterly unforgettable. The spray down here near the base of the falls can be intense, so you might want to bring a raincoat on a cooler day even if it's dry everywhere else.

When you're ready, return the way you came.

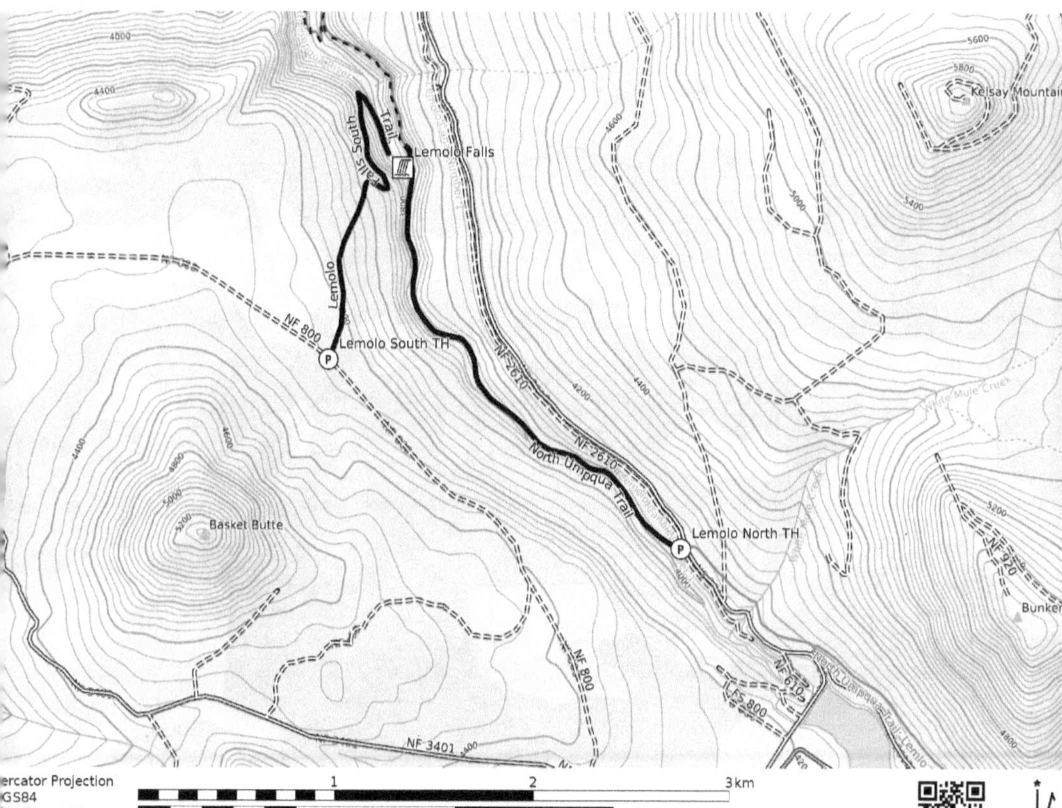

78. Mount Thielsen Meadows

Distance: 11.8 miles out and back
Elevation Gain: 1,600 feet
Trailhead elevation: 5,323 feet
Trail high point: 6,933 feet
Season: July – October
Best: July – October
Pass: NW Forest Pass
On the traditional lands of: the Cow Creek Umpqua and Klamath peoples

Directions:

- From Roseburg, drive OR 138 east for approximately 78 miles to Diamond Lake's north entrance. If you're coming from Bend, drive south on US 97 for 74 miles to a junction on the right with OR 138, signed for Crater Lake. Turn right and drive OR 138 for 22.8 miles to the north turnoff for Diamond Lake.
- Turn left and drive 0.3 mile downhill to the Howlock Mountain Trailhead on the left. Turn into the trailhead and drive around to the day-use trailhead next to the trail and away from the horse corrals.
- **Drivetimes:** 90 minutes from Roseburg, 100 minutes from Bend

Hike: Located near both Crater Lake and Diamond Lake, Mount Thielsen is one of Oregon's most photographed mountains. The mountain's sharp summit pinnacle has earned it the nickname of "Oregon's lightning rod", and its summit is a cherished ascent for climbers without any fear of heights (don't bother otherwise!). Despite this notoriety, few people take the time to hike on the mountain's slopes. This fantastic hike climbs gradually through a recently burned forest

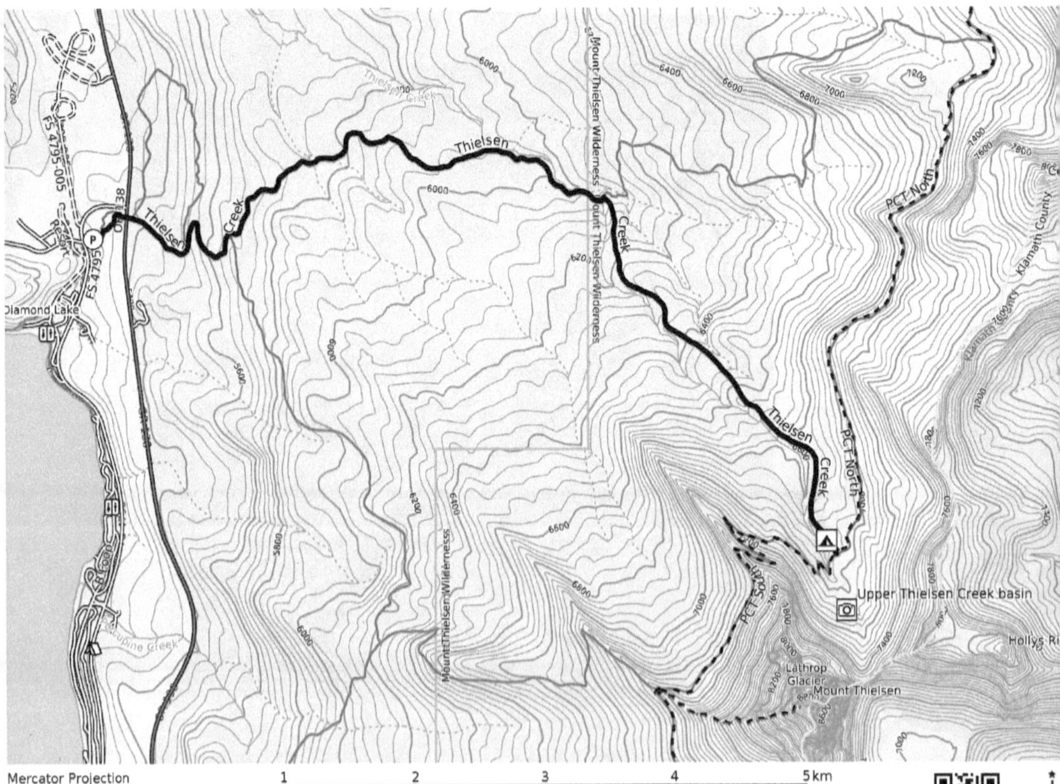

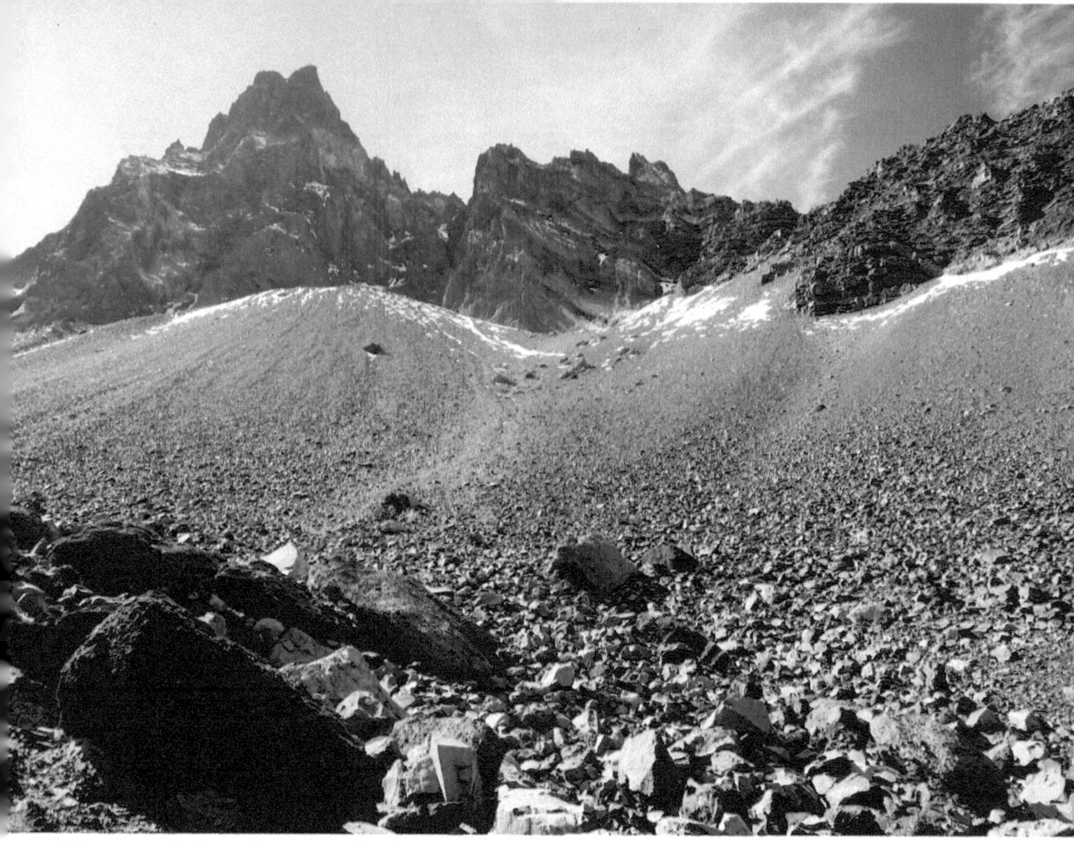

The rugged face of Mount Thielsen rises over the headwaters of Thielsen Creek.

to gorgeous meadows below the sharp northern face of Mount Thielsen. If you're backpacking, you'll love exploring this area even more.

From the trailhead, turn left and follow the trail as it passes under OR 138 via a large tunnel. Stay on this trail and ignore all junctions (there are a great number of equestrian trails here that lead all over the place). At 1 mile, ignore the Spruce Ridge Trail to keep left on the Howlock Mountain Trail, following signs for Thielsen Creek. From here, you'll enter a forest that burned in the 2020 Thielsen fire and continue climbing gradually through burned forest. Just after crossing Thielsen Creek at 3.5 miles you'll reach a junction with the Thielsen Creek Trail. Turn sharply to the right here. You'll climb steadily for 2.2 miles, passing increasingly fantastic views of Mount Thielsen along the way. At 5.8 miles from the trailhead, you'll at last meet the Pacific Crest Trail. Turn right here and hike south 0.1 mile on the PCT to a crossing of Thielsen Creek. Mount Thielsen towers over this idyllic glen, in perhaps the most impressive view of the mountain that is reachable by trail. There are several excellent campsites here tucked away in the trees.

It is great fun to wander around the upper reaches of Thielsen Creek at the very foot of the mountain. A rough trail continues upstream along the creek, revealing even more exceptional views of the steep north face of Mount Thielsen. The Lathrop Glacier, for many years the southernmost glacier in Oregon, once resided in a narrow crack above the small moraine at the foot of the mountain but has disappeared in recent years after a long series of hot summers. You can likewise hike further north or south on the PCT to your heart's desire, but the meadows here make for the best destination. If you're one of those brave souls planning on climbing the mountain, you can follow the PCT south for 2.4 miles until you intersect the Mount Thielsen Trail. Turn left here and follow the trail up the mountain, turning around when you reach your limit. The last 80 feet to the summit is a free climb that is incredibly exposed.

Return the way you came, remembering to turn left on the Thielsen Creek Trail, and again on the Howlock Trail to the trailhead.

79. Crater Lake

	The Watchman	Garfield Peak
Distance:	2 miles out and back	4.2 miles out and back
Elevation Gain:	400 feet	1,000 feet
Trailhead Elevation:	7,592 feet	7,124 feet
Trail High Point:	7,993 feet	8,049 feet
Season:	July - October	July - October
Best:	July - October	July - October
Pass:	$30 park entrance fee or America the Beautiful Pass	$30 park entrance fee or America the Beautiful Pass
On the traditional lands of:	the Klamath and Molalla peoples	the Klamath and Molalla peoples

Directions from Roseburg:

- From Roseburg, drive OR 138 east for 85 miles to a junction with OR 230 at the north end of Crater Lake National Park.
- Turn right here and enter the national park. Pay the $30 entrance fee and continue 11 miles to the Watchman Trailhead on the left. For Garfield Peak, continue 4 more miles to Rim Village and park in one of the many lots here.
- **Drivetime:** 2 hours

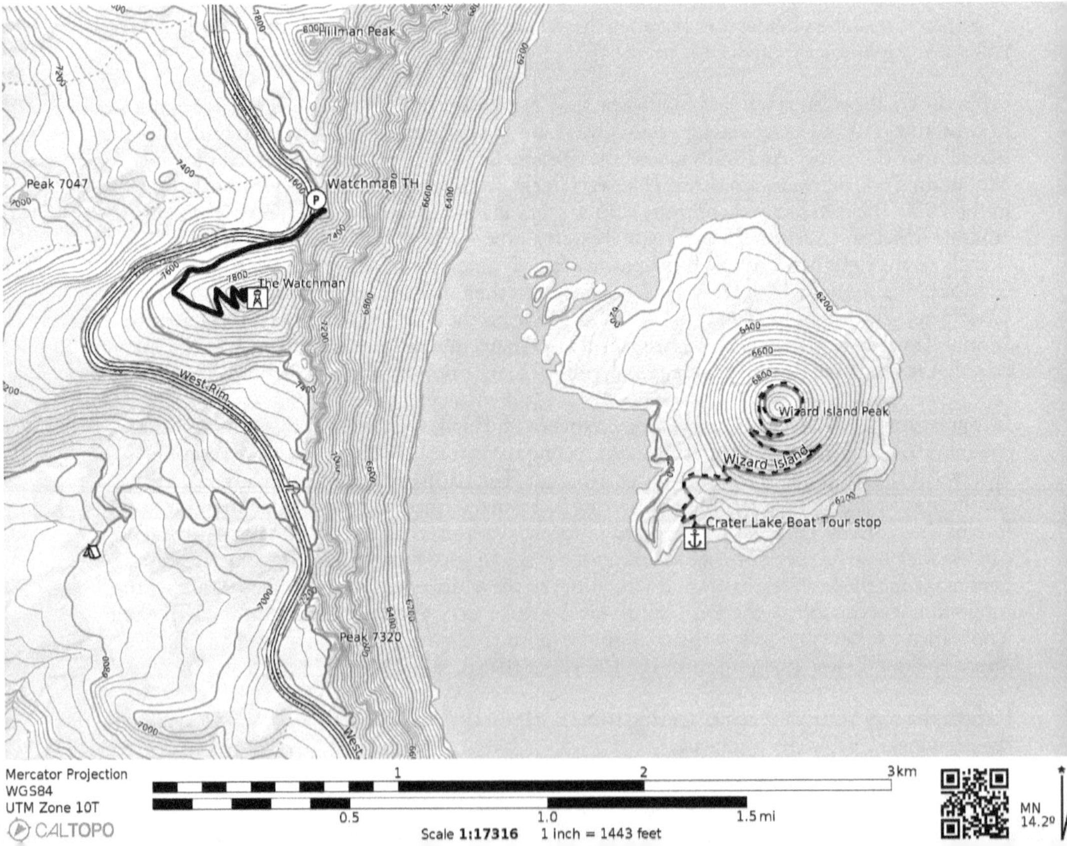

Hillman Peak
Peak 7047
Watchman TH
The Watchman
West Rim
Wizard Island Peak
Wizard Island
Crater Lake Boat Tour stop
Peak 7320

Mercator Projection
WGS84
UTM Zone 10T
CALTOPO

1 2 3km
0.5 1.0 1.5 mi
Scale 1:17316 1 inch = 1443 feet

MN
14.2°

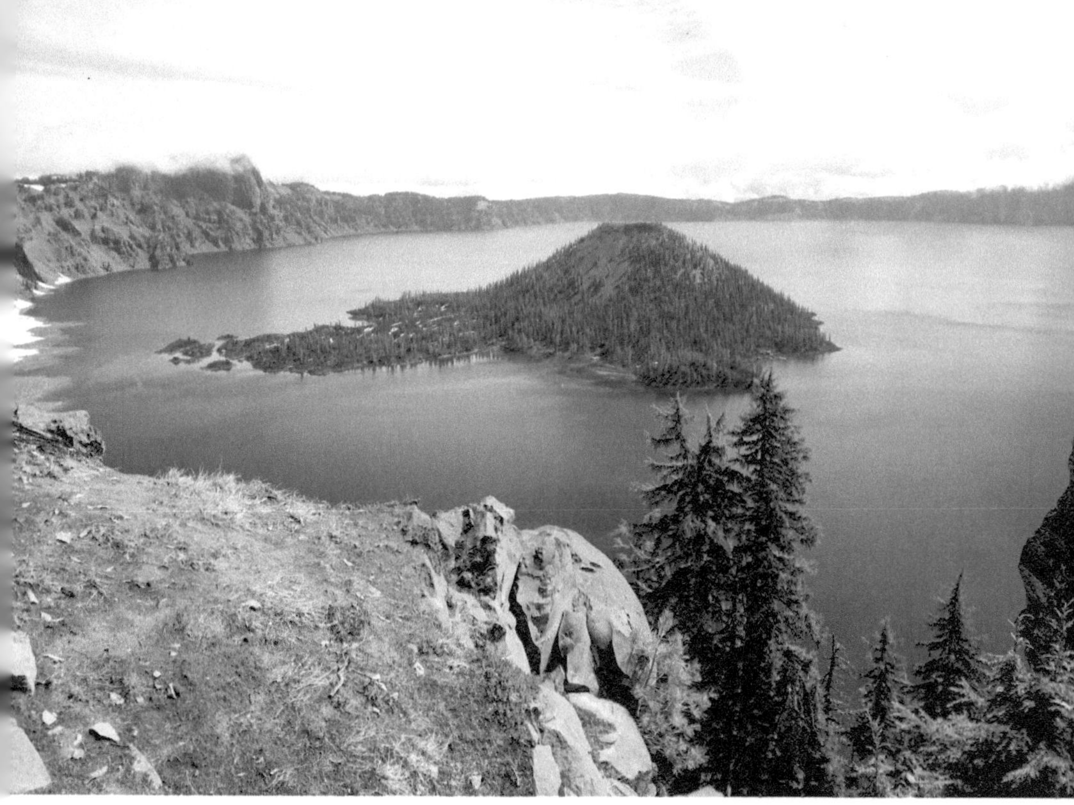

Crater Lake and Wizard Island from the slopes of The Watchman.

Directions from Medford:
- From Medford, drive northeast on OR 62 for 56 miles to a junction with OR 230. Fork to the right here to stay on OR 62.
- Continue on OR 62 another 16 miles to a junction with Munson Valley Road at the south end of the national park.
- Turn left here, pay the $30 park entrance fee, and continue 6.7 miles to Rim Village; park in one of the many lots here for Garfield Peak. For the Watchman, continue 4 more miles to the Watchman Trailhead on the right side of the road.
- **Drivetime:** 2 hours

Directions from Bend:
- Drive south on US 97 for 74 miles to a junction on the right with OR 138, signed for Crater Lake.
- Turn right and drive OR 138 for 14.7 miles to a junction with OR 230 on your left.
- Turn left here and enter the national park. Pay the $30 entrance fee and continue 11 miles to the Watchman Trailhead on the left. For Garfield Peak, continue 4 more miles to Rim Village and park in one of the many lots here.
- **Drivetime:** 2 hours

Note: Dogs are banned on all trails in Crater Lake National Park.

Hikes: There is nothing like the first time you see Crater Lake. It doesn't seem possible that such a place should exist. The deep blue lake in the middle of a collapsed volcano entrances everyone who sees it, and once you're there, you simply cannot look away. This is Oregon's only national park, and it would be hard to argue that there is a more extraordinary place in all of Oregon. There are lots of trails here, but the two best lead to exceptional viewpoints of the lake atop the Watchman and Garfield Peak. There are many other trails in the park worth your time, and the trails to Wizard Island and Mount Scott are also described here.

For the Watchman, leave the trailhead and set out uphill on a wide trail. There are excellent views down to Crater Lake and Wizard Island at the trailhead, but even better views await. In early summer, you may encounter deep snow patches at the trailhead and on these high slopes, so exercise caution. At such a high elevation it is easy to lose your breath, so take your time with this one. Follow a trail signed for The Watchman south for 0.5 mile to a junction and turn left. Another 0.5 mile of climbing leads you to the summit of the Watchman at nearly 8,000 feet above sea level. A fire lookout sits on the summit that is staffed during the summer. The staffer has one of Oregon's most extraordinary views at their feet: the entirety of Crater Lake, with Wizard Island almost directly below. The views of the Cascade peaks to the north and south are equally impressive, here at the top of the world. You'll have plenty of competition for the best spots here, but you won't mind spending a lot of time on the summit. Take at least a few minutes to soak up the view but save some energy - an even better viewpoint awaits a few miles south at Garfield Peak.

For Garfield Peak, drive down to the Crater Lake Lodge on the south side of the rim. Once you're at the parking lot, follow the rim edge east from the Rim Village lot. Even from the parking lot you'll have spectacular views across the wide sweep of Crater Lake, but don't turn around – it only gets better! Soon you'll trade pavement for a wide gravel trail. Even after dozens of fabulous views across the lake, your attention will still be pulled down to its deep azure waters. As with the trail to the summit of The Watchman, take your time on this hike, as the thinner air at this high altitude will force you to stop and catch your breath more often than you would at lower elevations. After 2 miles and nearly 1,000 feet of elevation gain, you'll puff up to the wide summit of Garfield Peak. You'll have views to the north across Crater Lake to Mount Thielsen and Mount Bailey above Diamond Peak, while the view stretches south all the way to Mount Shasta in northern California. Here it becomes more apparent that you are standing on what was once a great volcano. This peak, known as Mount Mazama, erupted 7,700 years ago, spreading ash all over western North America. The eruption obliterated the mountain's summit, causing it to collapse into a huge hole known as a caldera. Over time the caldera filled with rain,

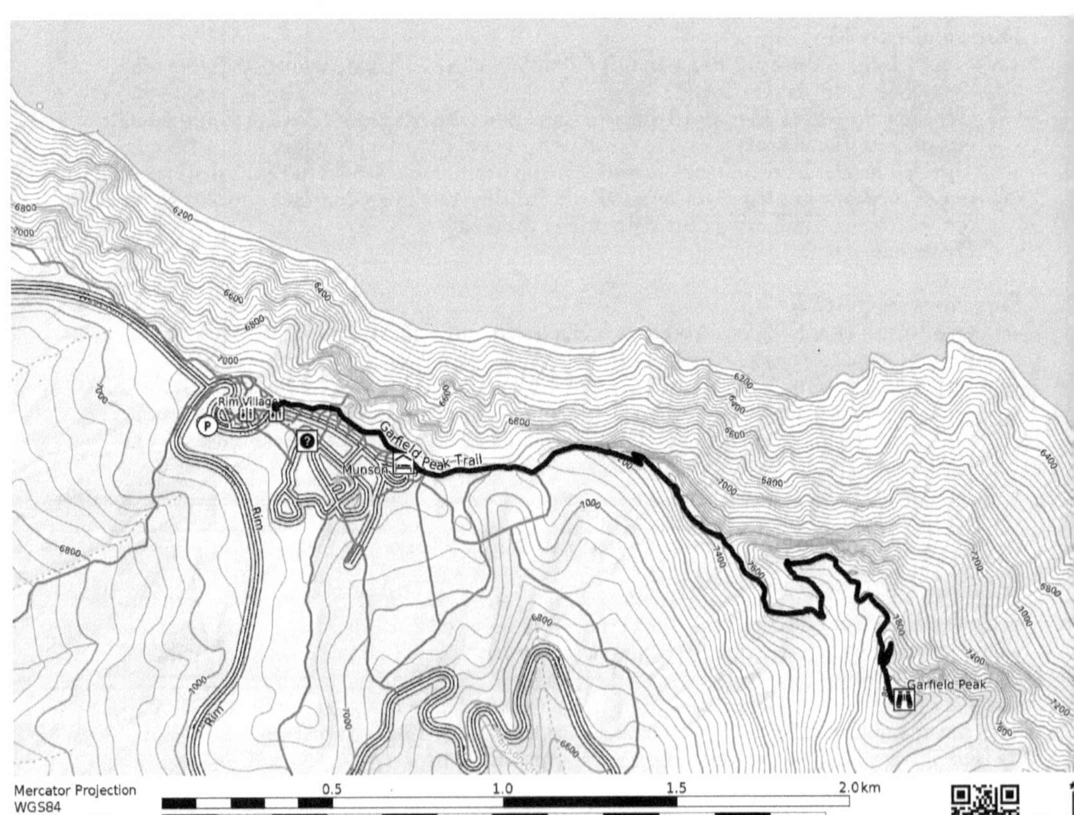

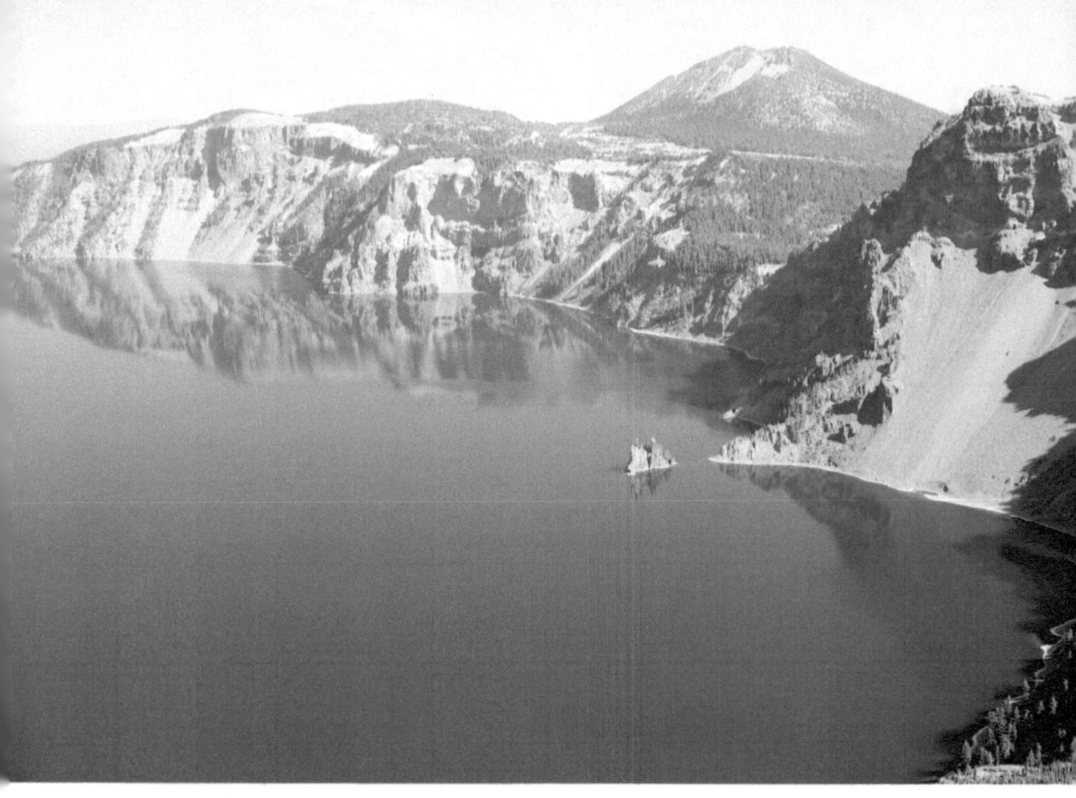

Mount Scott and Phantom Ship as seen from the summit of Garfield Peak.

becoming Crater Lake. Where you are standing on the summit is more than 4,000 feet below the elevation of Mount Mazama's former summit. Phantom Ship is the rocky island visible in the lake below the summit; this formation is part of a former cone that was inside Mount Mazama when it erupted, and Phantom Ship is in fact the oldest exposed rock in Crater Lake. You could easily spend hours looking across the lake and reading about the unique series of geologic events that created this most extraordinary place. Whenever you're ready, return the way you came.

Other Hiking Options:
While only two trails are described above, there are many others in Crater Lake worth hiking. Two of the best lead down to the shore of Crater Lake for a boat tour to Wizard Island, where you can hike to the summit of the island, and to Mount Scott, where a 5 mile round-trip hike will take you to one of the highest peaks in the Oregon Cascades.

For Wizard Island, you'll need to purchase a ticket for the Wizard Island boat tour. The tour was not offered from 2020 – 2022 due to the COVID-19 pandemic, and thus was not surveyed for this book. If tours are being offered again, they generally cost $55 per person. It is a good idea to purchase the tickets in advance. You'll need to hike over a mile downhill to Cleetwood Cove for the boat tour, and then hike 2.2 miles uphill to the summit of Wizard Island – a cinder cone that grew in the aftermath of Mount Mazama's collapse. The island is, in fact, a volcano inside of a volcano. There are few places like this in the entire world, making this perhaps the most unique hike in Oregon.

For Mount Scott, follow a trail from the East Rim Drive for 2.5 miles to the summit at 8,929 feet, the highest in the park and the tenth highest in the Oregon Cascades. This is said to be the only place where you can see the entirety of Crater Lake. A lookout sits on the summit, and just as at The Watchman, the staffer has one of the most extraordinary views in Oregon. Return the way you came from the summit.

80. Mount Bolivar

Distance: 2.8 miles out and back
Elevation Gain: 1,163 feet
Trailhead elevation: 3,156 feet
Trail high point: 4,319 feet
Season: May – October
Best: May – October
Pass: none needed
On the traditional lands of: the Tolowa Dee-Ni' and Cow Creek Umpqua peoples

Directions from Roseburg:

- From Roseburg, drive south on Interstate 5 for 16 miles to Exit 103, for Riddle.
- Exit the freeway and turn right on the Riddle Bypass Road. After 5.3 miles, the Riddle Bypass Road becomes the Cow Creek Road. Continue 19.3 miles to a junction on the right with West Fork Road (or approximately 25 miles from I-5).
- Turn right on the West Fork Road and drive 10 miles to a fork in the road with Walker Prairie Road.
- Turn left (uphill) on Walker Prairie Road, also known as BLM 32-9-35. Drive 4.5 miles, always staying on the paved road. You will arrive at a 6-way junction at Anaktuvak Saddle.
- Fork to the left onto BLM Road 32-9-3, following a sign for the Oregon Coast.
- Drive 3.3 miles to the trailhead on the left in a small turnout with room for 2 - 3 cars.
- **Drivetime from Roseburg:** 2 hours (90 minutes from Powers if coming from the west).

Hike: Mount Bolivar is truly in the middle of nowhere. Described by some as one of the highest points in the Oregon Coast Range, this impressive peak seems to belong to no place in specific.

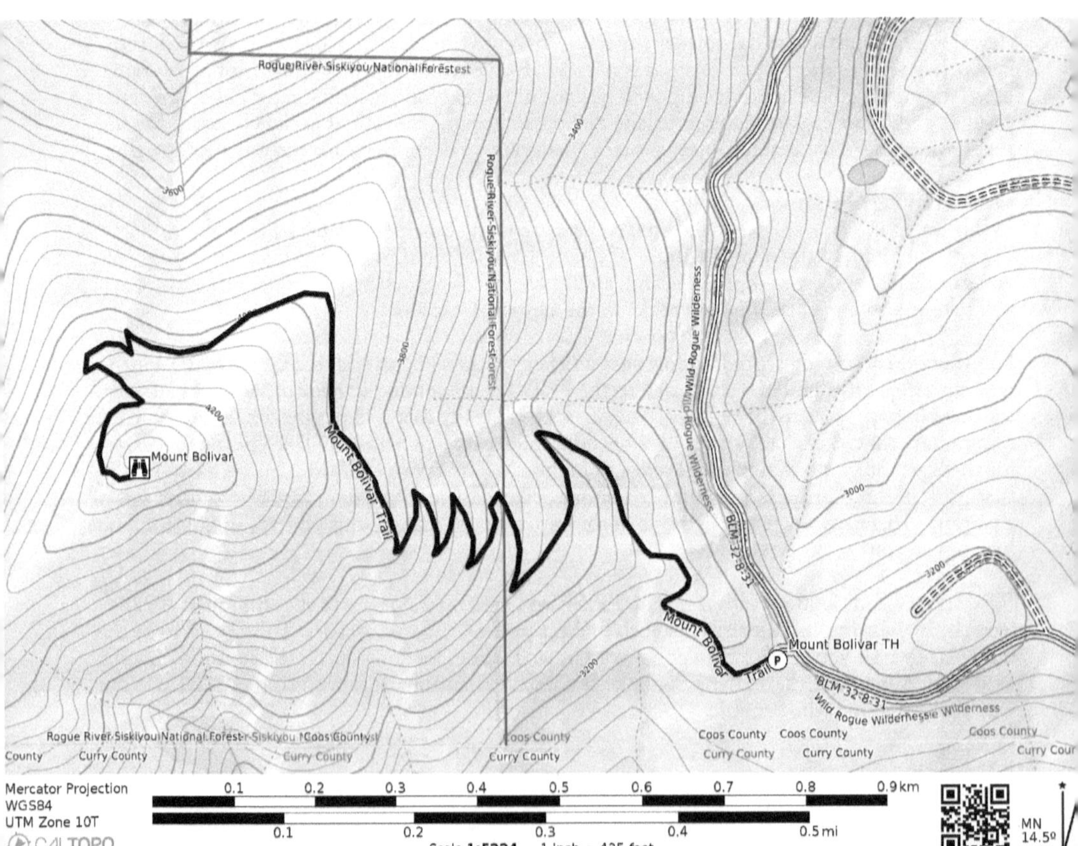

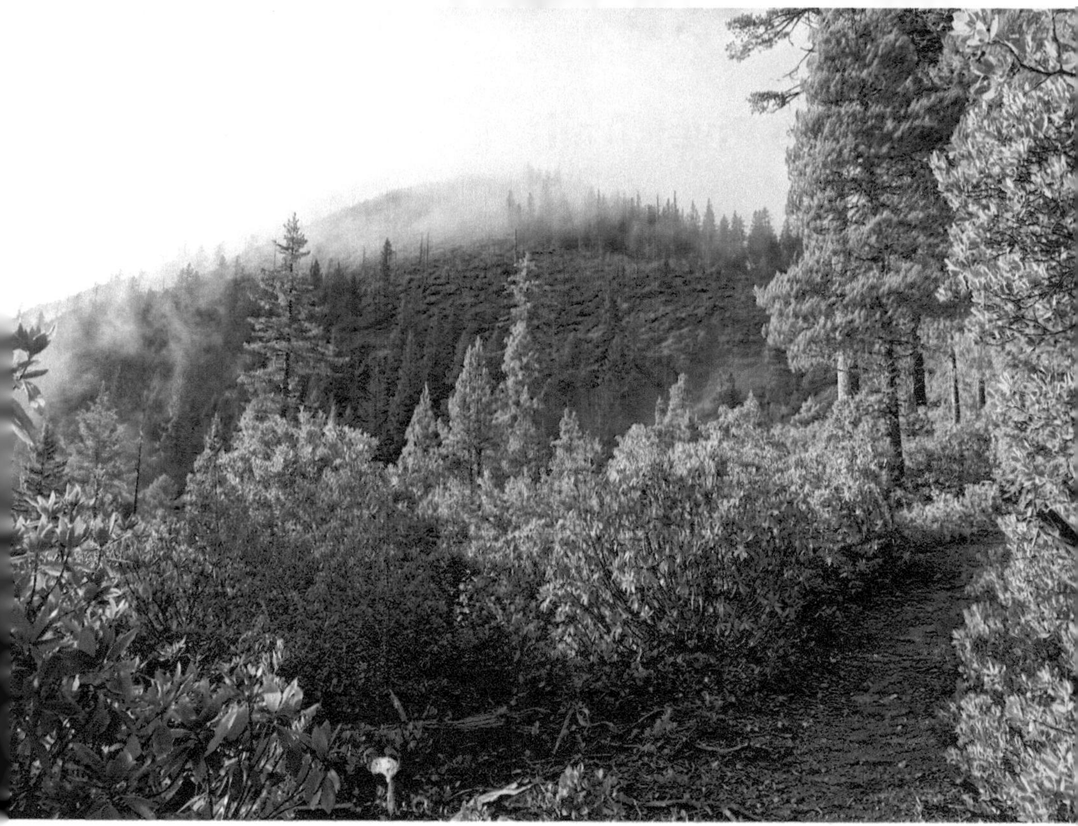

The foggy slopes of Mount Bolivar after a late fall rain shower.

You might feel this way too when you attempt to find the trailhead, which requires significantly more patience than most places in this book. Regardless of when you visit and how long it takes you to get there, this is an extraordinary hike that is well worth the effort. A well-graded trail climbs to the summit of this rocky peak, where you'll find stupendous views that are said to stretch from Mount Hood to Mount Shasta on clear days.

From the trailhead, the Mount Bolivar Trail switchbacks uphill among scattered manzanita bushes that flourish here in the wake of a 2005 fire. Being at the crossroads of the coastal and warmer interior ecosystems, you will see a surprising amount of biodiversity here. Among the trees are scattered madrones, yews, ponderosa pines, and many more. After 0.8 mile, the trail rounds a corner and passes into a cool coastal rainforest, with huge Douglas firs and twisted yews. The trail then switchbacks steeply up the rocky slopes, passing impressive wildflowers in the summer. Reach the summit of Mount Bolivar at 1.4 miles from the trailhead, where the views stretch far into the distance. Even on cloudy days you'll be able to spot the Rogue River canyon to the south. Scattered about the summit are cables and bits of broken glass that remain from the last lookout that stood here, which was dismantled sometime in the late 50s. Also located on the summit is a plaque dedicated to the state of Oregon from the people of Venezuela. The mountain was named by Simon Bolivar Cathcart, a Coos County surveyor who decided to name the mountain after Simon Bolivar, the Venezuelan military and political leader after whom Cathcart had been named. You can hike thousands of miles across the state of Oregon and still be surprised when you find such a monument – an extraordinary place indeed! When you're ready, return the way you came.

Note: As you might expect based on the sign, you can also drive here from the Oregon Coast. To locate the trail from this direction, drive to the intersection of FR 33 and FR 3348 south of Powers that is described in the directions for Coquille River Falls (Hike 14). Turn onto FR 3348 and continue 19 miles east, following signs for Glendale. Along the way you'll pass a turn-off for Hanging Rock, which you can also do from this direction. I did all three of these hikes in one very long day!

81. Rogue River Trail

Distance: 7 miles out and back
Elevation Gain: 1,000 feet
Trailhead elevation: 699 feet
Trail high point: 783 feet
Season: all year
Best: March – June, October – November
Pass: NW Forest Pass
On the traditional lands of: the Tolowa Dee-Ni' and Cow Creek Umpqua peoples

Directions:

- From Grants Pass, drive north on Interstate 5 to Exit 61, signed for Merlin.
- Exit the freeway and turn left towards Merlin.
- Drive towards Merlin and what becomes Galice-Merlin Road.
- At 10.7 miles from I-5, you'll pass Indian Mary Park. Continue on what is now Galice Road another 4.4 miles to a fork in the road at a sign for Agness (a small town on the other side of the Rogue Divide closer to Gold Beach). Stay straight and continue following the Rogue River.
- Continue following Galice Road for 7.5 miles to a turnoff for the Grave Creek Boat Ramp and trailhead, just after the road crosses the Rogue River at the Grave Creek Bridge.
- **Drivetime from Grants Pass:** 45 minutes

Hike: Emerging fully grown from the slopes of Mount Mazama (Crater Lake) and flowing all the way to the Pacific Ocean, the Rogue River is one of Oregon's most iconic and spectacular rivers. The lower stretch of the Rogue River west of Grants Pass and east of the Pacific is a natural wonder, a deep canyon marked by rugged cliffs, tall trees, and the serpentine path of the Rogue. Backpacking and rafting are the best way to visit this canyon, but day hikers can sample the best of what this area has to offer on this fun hike to the Whiskey Creek Cabin.

Begin by follow the trail uphill above the trailhead, which marks the beginning of a 40-mile route along the Rogue as well as the put-in point for rafters in the lower canyon. The trail passes above Grave Creek Rapids just a short distance downriver of the trailhead. You will also note the presence of poison oak – so much poison oak – as it grows **profusely** along the trail. While

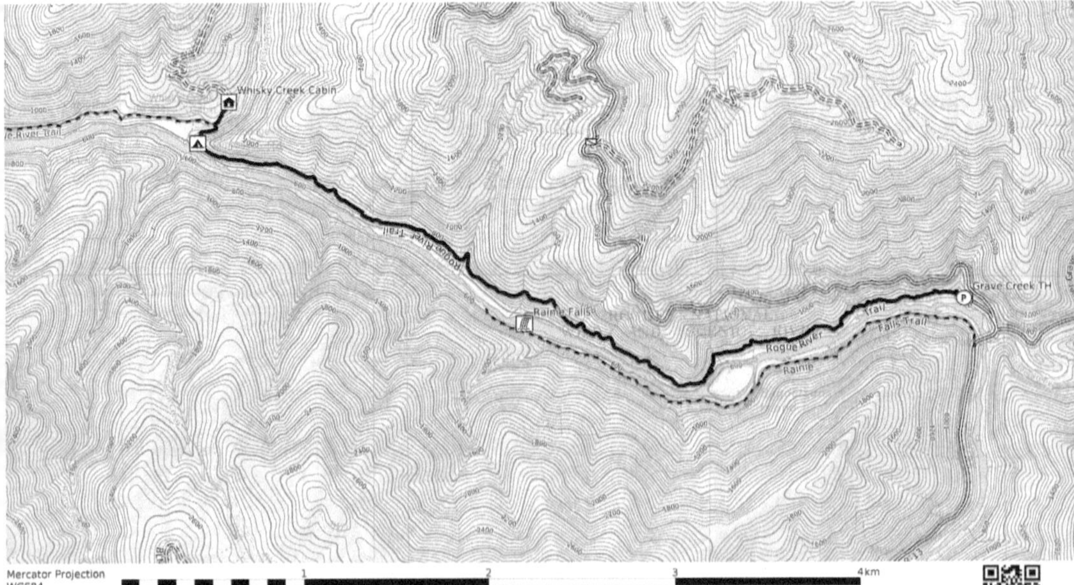

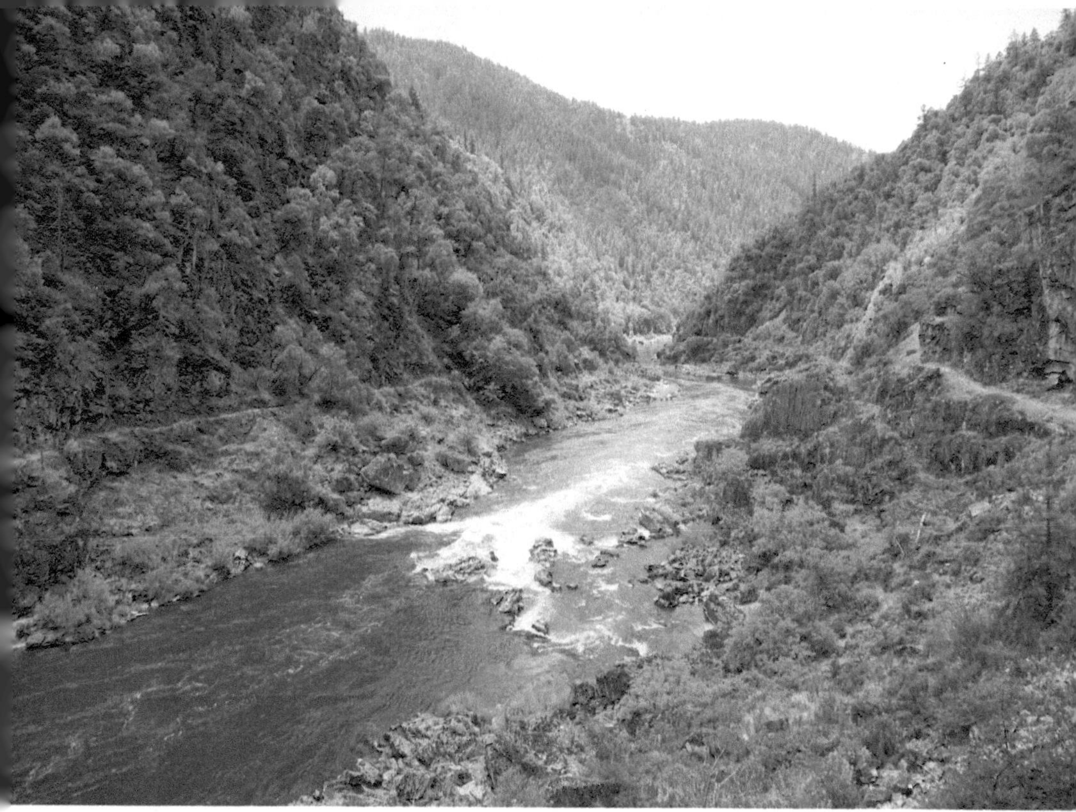

The Rogue River Trail passes high above the river in a spectacular canyon.

staying on the trail is a good idea wherever you hike, it is especially important here. Hikers who are sensitive to poison oak should avoid this hike, unfortunately. At 1.2 miles, the trail passes above a spot marking the highest floodwaters ever recorded in the canyon; take a moment and try to imagine the Rogue River flowing this high above its banks. You'll continue to follow the bluffs above the river to a view down to Rainie Falls, a cataract in the river. The view of the falls from the trail is not all that great; if you're looking for an easier hike with a better view of the falls, consider the trail on the opposite side of the river, which ends at Rainie Falls.

After the trail passes Rainie Falls, you'll enter a more wooded stretch of trail that can be quite muggy on warm days. The trail passes over China Gulch and under some impressive madrone trees before emerging once more on the cliffs above the Rogue River. At a little over 3 miles from the trailhead, the Rogue River Trail rounds a bend and arrives at Whiskey Creek Camp. Here, at last, you can walk down to the river! Before you settle into lunch, follow the Rogue River Trail up Whiskey Creek to a bridge over the scenic creek. Once across the bridge, turn right on a side trail and hike a few minutes to Whiskey Creek Cabin, the oldest cabin in the Rogue canyon and the site of mining operations for nearly one hundred years. The cabin was built in the late 1800s and inhabited until 1973. It is in great shape now and is on the National Register of Historic Places. Then return to Whiskey Camp's grassy flat by the river. You can continue downriver from here, but for this hike, return the way you came.

Backpackers can of course continue many miles down the river, passing many more spectacular views and several cabins. You may want to establish a car shuttle to hike the trail one-way, and you should expect to encounter the black bears who roam this canyon in search of an easy meal. One particularly fun backpacking trip is the Wild Rogue Loop, a 29-mile trek that connects a lower segment of the Rogue River Trail with Hanging Rock (Hike 14). Whatever you do in this area, it is certain to be fun.

82. Illinois River Trail

Distance: 11 miles out and back
Elevation Gain: 3,000 feet
Trailhead elevation: 874 feet
Trail high point: 1,666 feet
Season: all year
Best: March – May, October – November
Pass: none needed
On the traditional lands of: the Tolowa Dee-Ni' and Cow Creek Umpqua peoples

Directions:

- From Grants Pass, drive southwest on US 199 for approximately 20 miles to the town of Selma.
- At the flashing light in the middle of Selma, turn right onto the Illinois River Road.
- Follow this road for 6.7 miles of mostly paved road to a fork with FR 4105 on the right. While turning right will also take you to the trailhead, it's more direct to continue straight on what is now FR 4103.
- Continue on FR 4103 for 11 miles on a that starts out good but slowly deteriorates to a junction on the right with FR 4105-152.
- Continue straight on what is now a bumpy, muddy, potholed road another 0.6 mile to the trailhead at road's end, at Briggs Creek Trailhead and Campground.
- Passenger cars can make it to the trailhead if driven with extreme caution, but you may wish to have a vehicle with considerably higher clearance. The Illinois River Road has a reputation for being awful, and until the last few miles, it is not. There are places to park on the side of the road in the last mile before the trailhead if you don't feel like subjecting your vehicle to any more punishment.
- **Drivetime from Grants Pass:** 1 hour and 30 minutes

Hike: The Illinois River flows through the heart of the state of Illinois, eventually emptying into the Mississippi River just north of St. Louis. It is muddy, wide, and mostly not very attractive. Oregon's Illinois River, however, is an absolute stunner. The emerald river roars through a deep, rugged gorge, eventually flowing into the Rogue River not far from Gold Beach. The settlers from Illinois who named the river obviously never saw this inner canyon, as it is truly one of Oregon's most extraordinary places. You can enjoy the best of this canyon, but you'll need to get in shape first, as the constant ups and downs and exposure test even the most experienced hikers. The spectacular views, rare and colorful flowers, and the red and brown rock in the canyon should be enough to spur you on and keep you hiking long after you start feeling the fatigue set in. Beware though: poison oak also grows profusely in the canyon, rattlesnakes are frequently seen on hot days, and due to steep drop-offs along much of the trail, this hike is not recommended for hikers with a fear of heights. Last but not least, this trail gets very hot in the summer and is best avoided between July and September.

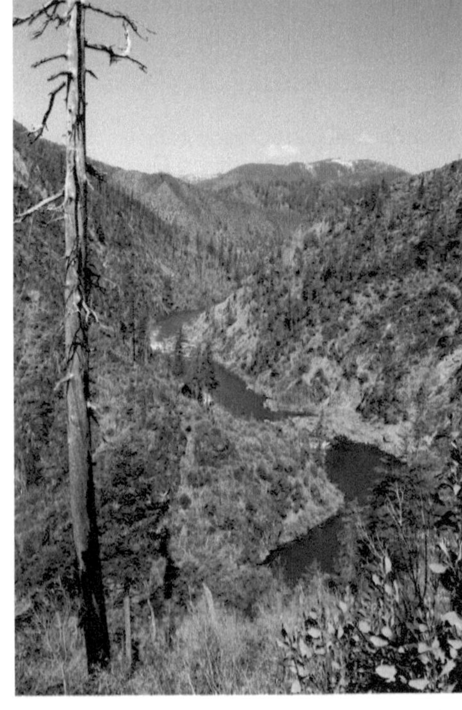

From the trailhead, cross the bridge over Briggs Creek and begin hiking uphill as the trail climbs up a bench above the creek. You should be thankful for the bridges along the trail, as almost all the side creeks that you cross would be impassible without them. You will round a bend and continue climbing towards a rocky shelf above the river. The spring flower show starts almost immediately; look for copious displays of iris, phlox, paintbrush, mariposa lilies, and so many more. Before long you'll be several hundred feet above the river, where you have continuous and exceptional views of the serpentine Illinois River, flowing through this deep gorge. The river is a beautiful shade of emerald green, and offers a lovely contrast to the reds and browns of the canyon, and the white snags of trees that burned in the Biscuit Fire in 2002. At 2.5 miles from the trailhead, the trail rounds a bend to cross York Creek. Before you cross the creek, look on the right side of the trail for a large patch of small, pink flowers that grow in April and May. These blooms are the rare *Kalmiopsis leachiana*, the namesake of the Kalmiopsis Wilderness where you are hiking. This flower, a small shrub with numerous pink blooms, is endemic to the Kalmiopsis and grows nowhere else in the world but in this wilderness. If you're feeling tired or running short on time, the York Creek bridge is a good spot to turn around. Before you go any further, you should wander a few feet up York Creek to find a small patch of *Darlingtonia californica*, an insectivorous plant sometimes found in this part of Oregon.

If you're continuing, the trail climbs and then descends to a crossing of Clear Creek at 3.9 miles. The unsigned Shorty Noble Way Trail departs here on the left. You'll stay on the Illinois River Trail and continue uphill for another 0.8 mile to a junction with the Pine Flat Way Trail at a saddle. The trail is unmarked but departs from the left side of the saddle, heading downhill. Follow this trail steeply downhill for 0.8 mile, losing almost 1,000 feet along the way down. You'll end up in Pine Flats' cool woods, just a stone's throw from the Illinois River. If you're backpacking, there are numerous excellent campsites here. A number of user trails lead to the banks of the river, where it is wonderful to sit, deep in the heart of one of Oregon's great wilderness areas.

Return the way you came.

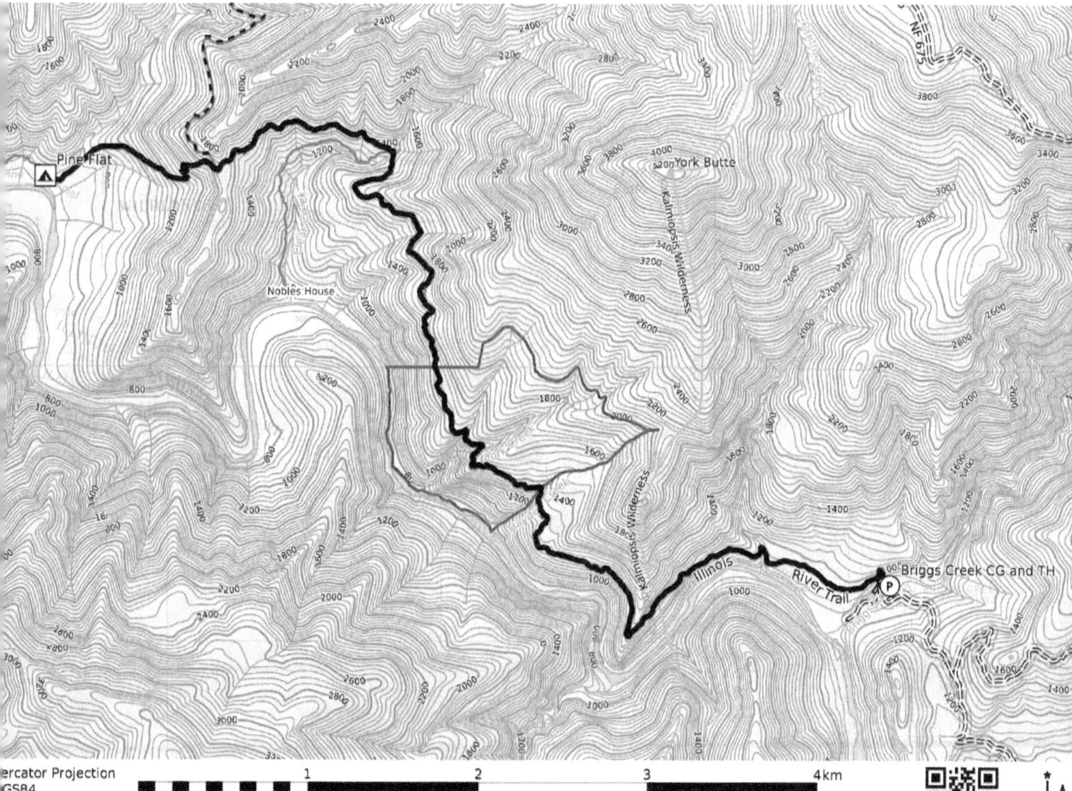

83. Kerby Peak

Distance: 7.2 miles out and back
Elevation Gain: 2,700 feet
Trailhead elevation: 2,931 feet
Trail high point: 5,548 feet
Season: May – November
Best: June – July
Pass: none needed
On the traditional lands of: the Tolowa Dee-Ni', Takelma, Modoc, and Cow Creek Umpqua peoples

Directions:

- Drive to the town of Selma, on US 199 some 20 miles southwest of Grants Pass.
- From the flashing light in the middle of Selma, turn left on Deer Creek Road.
- Drive on Deer Creek Road for 8.5 miles to a junction with White Creek Road. There will be a sign for the Kerby Peak Trail.
- Turn right onto White Creek Road and drive 0.4 mile of paved road to a junction.
- Turn left onto E White Creek Road and drive 2.6 miles of winding, steep, rocky gravel to the trailhead on the left.
- **Drivetime from Selma:** 25 minutes (50 minutes from Grants Pass)

Hike: Southwest Oregon is the most botanically diverse region of Oregon, and hikers in this area enjoy discovering exotic and beautiful flowers around every bend in the spring and summer. Few hikes are better for this than Kerby Peak, in the mountains between the valleys of the Applegate and Illinois Rivers. Botanical diversity is more than just flowers; you'll also get to hike among madrones, Brewer's spruces, and other trees not commonly found elsewhere in Oregon.

Siskiyou Lewisia grows along the rocky slopes of Kerby Peak.

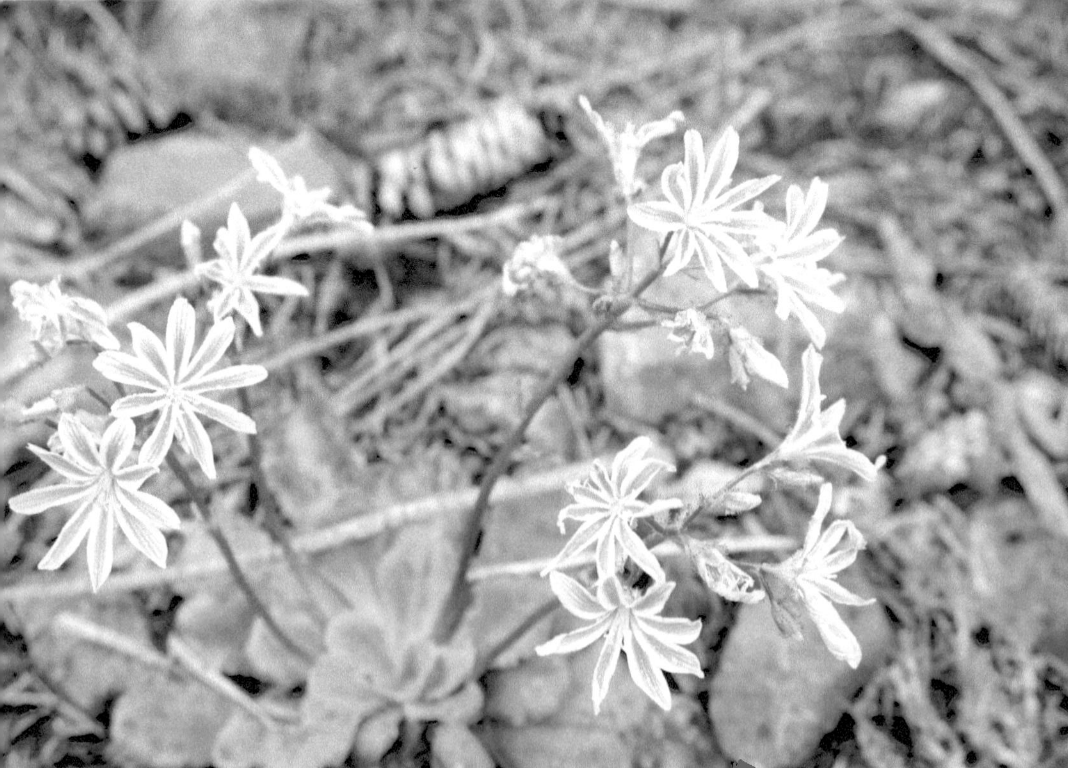

Perhaps best of all, you can also expect spectacular views from the summit of Kerby Peak. Just remember to get in shape first, as this is no walk in the park!

From the trailhead, look for what appears to be an old road. Look for a brown hiker symbol post that marks the start of the Kerby Peak Trail. You will immediately begin hiking uphill on a wide trail through open forest. Red and orange madrones line the trail here. Keep an eye on the ground for groundcone, a purple parasitic flowering plant that resembles a pinecone. This odd and lovely flower is frequently seen along the lower part of the trail. The forest becomes more montane as you ascend, eventually giving way to the Douglas firs more commonly seen elsewhere in Oregon. Beargrass and iris bloom here in June, and you may even spot the bright red blooms of snow plant, a saprophytic flower that is seldom seen Oregon.

The trail climbs steeply across a rocky ridge end and reaches a pass at 1.8 miles near Point 4463. From this point on, you'll traverse around the eastern face of Kerby Peak, passing under rocky slopes where scarlet gilia, paintbrush, and beargrass grow profusely. You may even spot another rare flower endemic to this region, the cream, orange, and pink blooms of Siskiyou Lewisia (*Lewisia cotyledon*). On the slopes below the summit you will also note a strange tree with drooping limbs; this is the rare and fascinating Brewer's spruce. You won't see this tree almost anywhere else in Oregon, and in fact it is among the rarest trees in the entire Pacific Northwest.

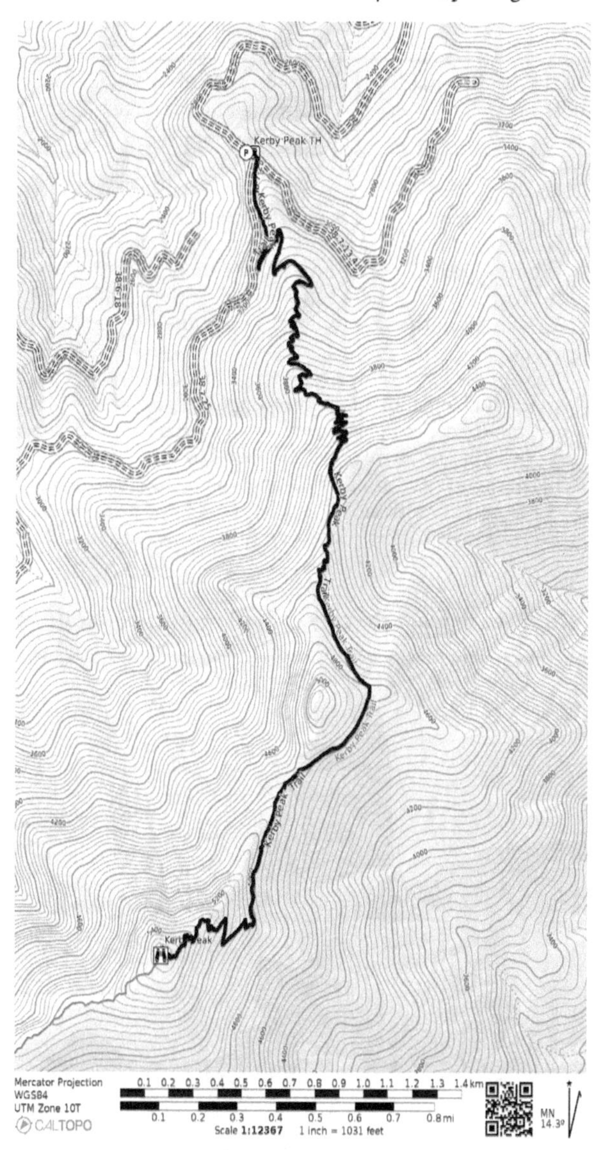

The trail climbs furiously from here, reaching the summit of Kerby Peak at 3.6 miles. On a clear day the view stretches from Mount McLoughlin in the east to Preston Peak and the high peaks of the Siskiyous in California. The lookout that once stood here was demolished in 1966, but you will still note a few remnants of the lookout on the summit. The summit is a wonderful place to spend an hour or two taking in the views, but it is also quite exposed and windy on rainy days, so make sure you pack a raincoat or at least a windbreaker.

Return the way you came.

84. Sucker Creek Gap and Swan Mountain

	Sucker Creek Shelter	Swan Mountain
Distance:	7.6 miles out and back	11.4 miles out and back
Elevation Gain:	1,200 feet	2,200 feet
Trailhead Elevation:	4,281 feet	4,281 feet
Trail High Point:	5,203 feet	6,272 feet
Season:	June - October	June - October
Best:	June - October	June - October
Pass:	none needed	none needed
On the traditional lands of:	the Tolowa Dee-Ni', Modoc, Takelma, and Cow Creek Umpqua peoples	the Tolowa Dee-Ni', Modoc, Takelma, and Cow Creek Umpqua peoples

Directions:

- From Medford or Grants Pass, drive to the community of Applegate. Applegate is 19 miles south of Grants Pass on OR 238 and 20 miles west of Medford via Jacksonville on OR 238.
- From Applegate, turn onto Thompson Creek Road and drive south towards the California border. Drive 9.2 miles south to where the road changes to one lane of pavement.
- Continue another 2.4 miles to a junction at the end of pavement, a total of 11.6 miles from Applegate.
- Fork to the left to stay on Thompson Creek Road, ignoring the two roads that branch off to the right. Continue on Thompson Creek Road for 2.6 miles to a junction on the right with FR 1030, marked by a sign that says "One lane road with turnouts".
- Turn right and drive gravel FR 1030 for 10.8 miles to road's end at the Steve Fork Trailhead. If you reach a junction and you are unsure of which way to go, follow signs for the Steve Fork Trailhead.
- **Drivetimes:** 1 hour and 40 minutes from both Grants Pass and Medford

Looking south from the summit of Swan Mountain into California.

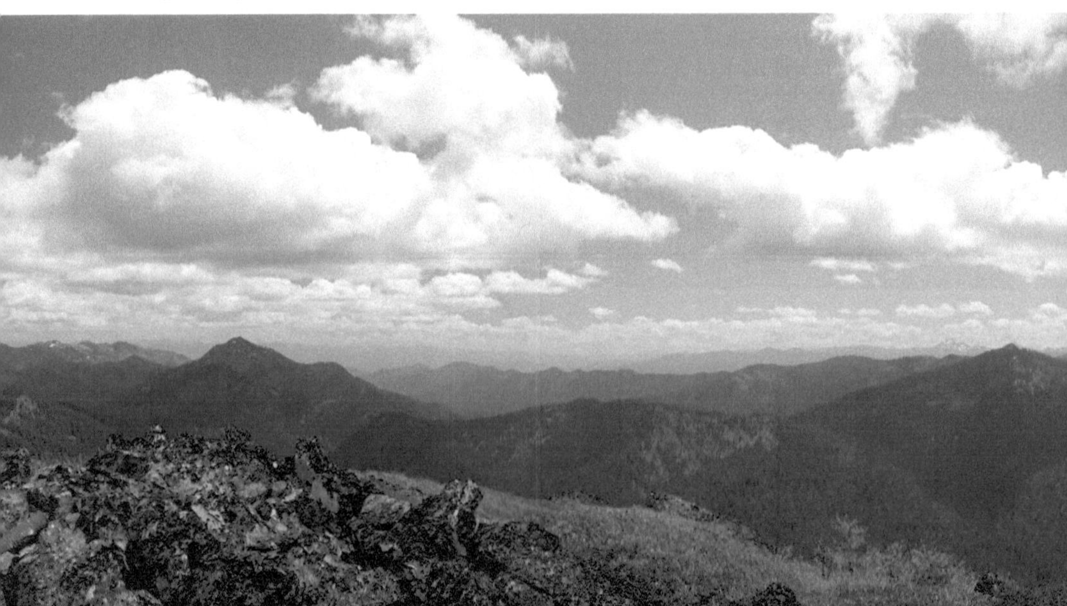

Hike: Located in the remote Red Buttes Wilderness less than a mile north of the California border, Sucker Creek Gap is a magical place. Here you'll find enormous trees, a quiet lily pad lake, a historic shelter, and tremendous views. You'll even get to hike into and back out of California, a novelty that is possible on this hike due to the nature of the rugged topography of this area. There is much to love here, and you'll be planning your return to this area before you even get back to your car.

From the Steve Fork Trailhead, follow the trail south into the Red Buttes Wilderness. After just 0.3 mile, you'll cross into California. There are no signs marking the state line. At 1 mile, you'll reach a trail junction. Turn right here at a sign for Sucker Creek Gap. You'll soon begin climbing through open woods of incense cedar, Jeffrey pine, and Douglas fir. At 2.4 miles, the trail passes a few huge Jeffrey pines and crosses back into Oregon. Continue another 0.8 mile to a trail junction at a cairn. The way to Sucker Creek Gap turns right, but you should turn left. You'll follow a brushy trail for 0.2 mile to a cirque lake that was formed by a small Ice Age glacier. There is an excellent campsite here, should you wish to backpack. When you're ready to continue the hike, return to the main trail and turn left. You'll continue 0.4 mile to a four-way junction with the Boundary Trail at Sucker Creek Gap. To find Sucker Creek's shelter, turn left on the Boundary Trail and follow it for 0.1 mile until you see an obvious user trail heading downhill on the right. Turn right and follow this steep trail down 0.1 mile to a meadow surrounded by enormous incense cedars, some of the largest you'll ever see. The shelter is at the end of the trail, at the western edge of the meadow. This is a gorgeous place, and it is difficult to leave. To continue the hike, return to Sucker Creek Gap. If you're ready to hike back, turn right at the four-way junction to hike back to the Steve Fork Trailhead. If you're planning on hiking to the summit of Swan Mountain, turn left on the Boundary Trail at a sign for Oregon Caves.

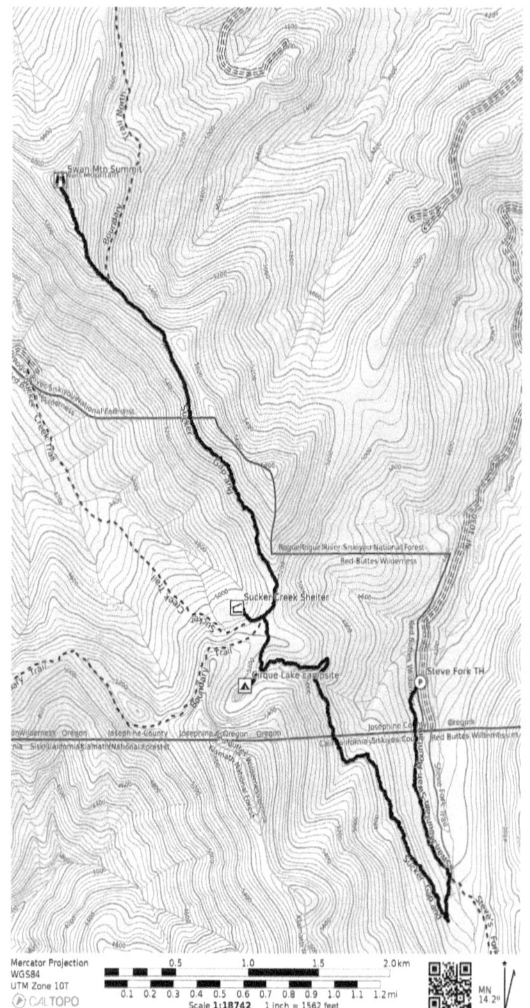

The Boundary Trail climbs gradually through a dark forest. Blowdown can be an issue here if trail crews have not been through recently. After a mile or so, you'll leave the forest and continue climbing along an open slope. Just as the Boundary turns and begins to descend the eastern slope of Swan Mountain at 5.6 miles (all side trips included), look for a faint trail heading left up the open slopes of Swan Mountain. Follow this occasionally faint trail uphill 0.6 mile to the summit of Swan Mountain, elevation 6,272 feet. The views from the summit are stupendous, stretching east to the summits of the Cascades and south, from the twin summits of Red Buttes and far into California. A cool breeze keeps you company while you take in the panoramic views. Whenever you're ready, return the way you came.

85. Siskiyou Peak

Distance: 5.6 miles out and back
Elevation Gain: 900 feet
Trailhead elevation: 6,600 feet
Trail high point: 7,141 feet
Season: June – October
Best: July – October
Pass: none needed
On the traditional lands of: the Shasta, Takelma, and Modoc peoples

Directions:

- From Ashland, drive south on Interstate 5 for about 8 miles to Exit 6, signed for Mount Ashland. Exit the freeway and turn right onto the Mount Ashland Road.
- Drive 0.6 mile and turn right at a sign for Mt. Ashland Ski Area.
- Drive up Mount Ashland Road for 8.8 miles to the ski area.
- Continue beyond the ski area 0.2 mile, where the road turns to gravel. Continue another 2 miles of bumpy, rocky gravel to the Grouse Gap Trailhead on the right side of the road. There is room for 2 or 3 cars. There is an absolutely fantastic view of Mount Shasta on the southern horizon at the trailhead.
- **Drivetime from Ashland:** 45 minutes

Hike: At the crossroads of Oregon and California, the Pacific Crest Trail passes over the alpine meadows at the crest of the Siskiyou Mountains. This beautiful and fascinating stretch of trail takes you across the slopes of Mount Ashland to the summit of Siskiyou Peak, where the view stretches from Mount McLoughlin to Mount Shasta, well into California. Along the way you'll pass gorgeous meadow after gorgeous meadow and a number of huge Shasta red firs, more typically associated with California. While this hike might seem like a slice of northern California, it is an extraordinary Oregon hike. This is an especially great hike on hot days, as you can usually find cooler air this far up in the mountains.

At the Grouse Gap Trailhead, locate the Pacific Crest Trail just below the road. You'll set about hiking very gradually through meadows with fantastic views southeast to Mount Shasta. The meadows along the trail here are an intriguing mix of the Cascades, the Great Basin, and the

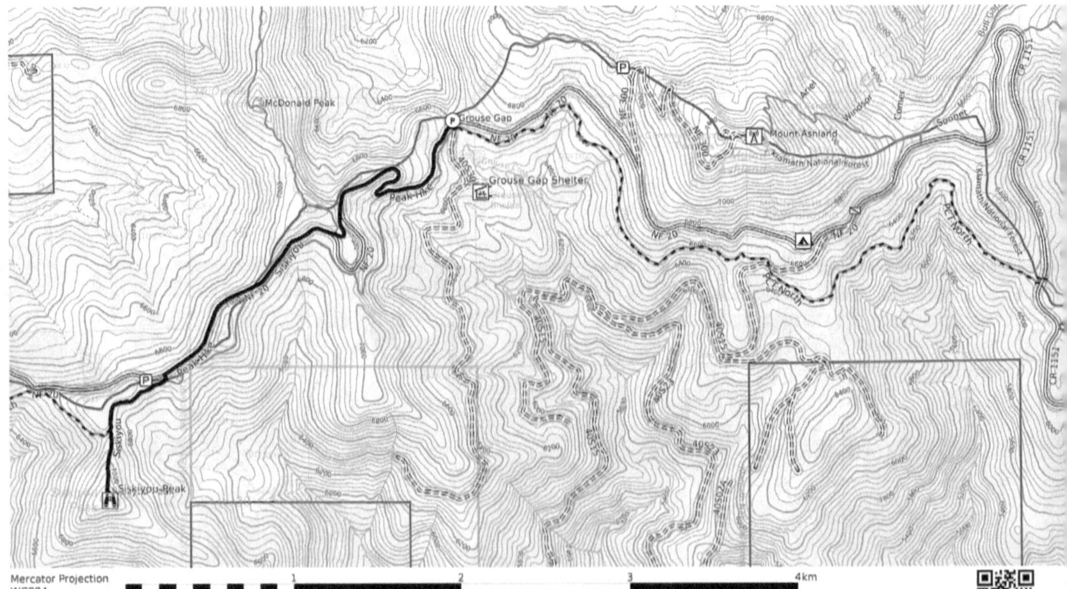

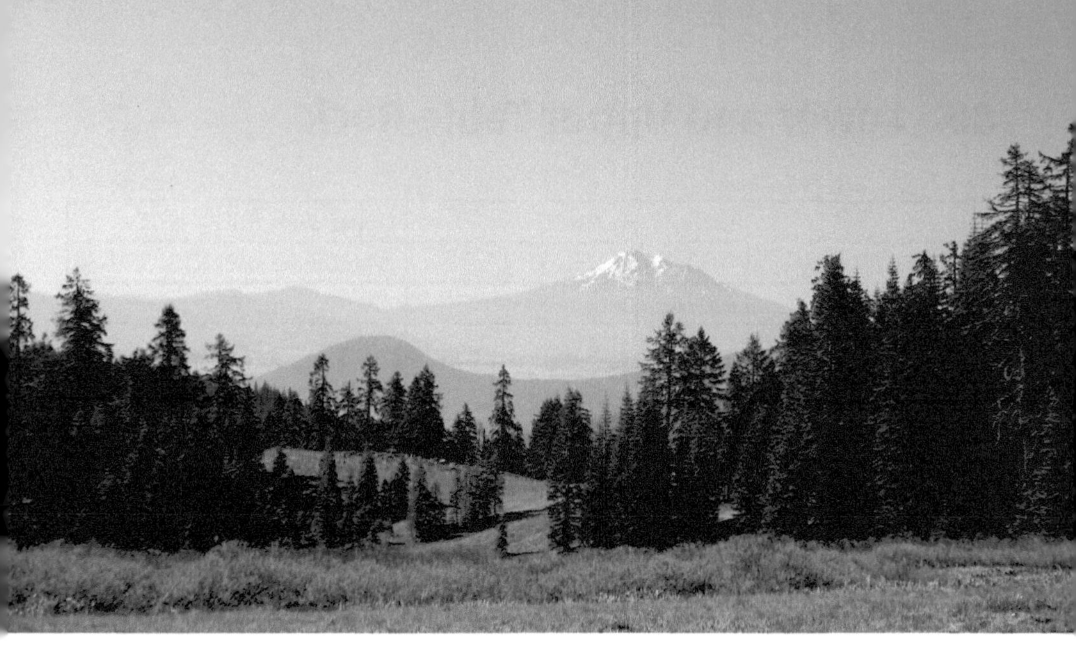

Mount Shasta dominates the southern horizon at Grouse Gap.

Siskiyous, with several varieties of plants found only on these slopes. Especially interesting is the prolieration of sagebrush lining the trail, which is usually found in desert environments as opposed to the slopes of a peak nearly 7,000 feet in elevation. Larkspur lines the trail in late June and into July, while chocolate lilies and several species of paintbrush grow in more open areas along the trail. Huge Shasta red fir tower over the trail in forested areas, offering shade on even the warmest days. Also be on the lookout for snow patches in the forested stretches of trail that last well into July.

The trail climbs around a rocky gap and begins to parallel FR 20, the road you drove to the trailhead. The road becomes quite rough beyond the Grouse Gap Trailhead, so you shouldn't encounter much traffic here to interrupt your hiking splendor. Mount Shasta comes into view again and the slopes become increasingly dry as you near Siskiyou Peak. Views open north to the summit of Mount Ashland, topped by a huge radar that resembles a rising moon. At 2.5 miles from the trailhead, look for an unmarked spur trail on the left, just before the PCT begins to descend the southern slopes of Siskiyou Peak. Turn left and climb this unofficial trail 0.3 mile and 200 feet of elevation to the summit of Siskiyou Peak, at elevation 7,141 feet. The view here is exceptional, especially south into California. Look for snowy Mount Shasta on the southeast horizon, while the Marble Mountains and Trinity Alps rise to the south above the valleys containing the towns of Weed and Mount Shasta. Back in Oregon, Mount McLoughlin rises above Mount Ashland's white dome, while aptly-named Big Red Mountain dominates the western horizon. It's fun to wander around the slopes of Siskiyou Peak in search of new views and shady spots to sit on hot days.

Return the way you came. South of the spur to Siskiyou Peak, the Pacific Crest Trail begins its long descent into California. If you want to extend your hike, continue north on the PCT beyond the Grouse Gap Trailhead for more meadows and views. The trail continues 3.3 miles to an obscure trailhead along the Mount Ashland Road. If you continue south on the PCT beyond the junction to Siskiyou Peak, you'll reach Siskiyou Gap in 3.8 miles and the California border in a little over 14 miles.

Before you leave the area, be sure to drive down to the Grouse Gap Shelter just below the trailhead. Here you'll find a huge three-sided shelter with a picnic table and circular fire pit, complete with a chimney. The shelter seems to be used more in the winter than in the summer, and it's possible that you'll have it to yourself even in the middle of the day.

86. Lower and Upper Table Rock

	Lower Table Rock	Upper Table Rock
Distance:	5 miles out and back	3.4 miles out and back
Elevation Gain:	800 feet	730 feet
Trailhead Elevation:	1,243 feet	1,311 feet
Trail High Point:	2,021 feet	2,040 feet
Season:	all year	all year
Best:	March – June	March – June
Pass:	none needed	none needed
On the traditional lands of:	the Takelma, Shasta, Modoc, and Cow Creek Umpqua peoples	the Shasta, Takelma, Modoc, and Cow Creek Umpqua peoples

Directions from Medford:

- From Medford, drive north on Interstate 5 to Central Point Exit 33.
- Leave the freeway and turn right onto Biddle Road.
- Drive 1 mile and then turn right onto Table Rock Road.
- Drive this road 5.1 miles to a junction with Modoc Road, signed for Upper Table Rock. If you're hiking Upper Table Rock first, turn right and drive Modoc Road 1.5 miles to the trailhead. For Lower Table Rock, continue on Table Rock Road 2.5 miles to a junction with Wheeler Road.
- Turn left on Wheeler Road and drive 0.8 mile to the trailhead.
- **Drivetime from Medford:** 20 minutes

Note: Dogs are prohibited on both Table Rock trails.

Hike: Relics of a volcanic eruption millions of years ago, the twin plateaus of Lower and Upper Table Rock tower over the farms and houses north of Medford. The plateaus have been a popular gathering place for millennia, as the Takelma people hunted and gathered at the base of

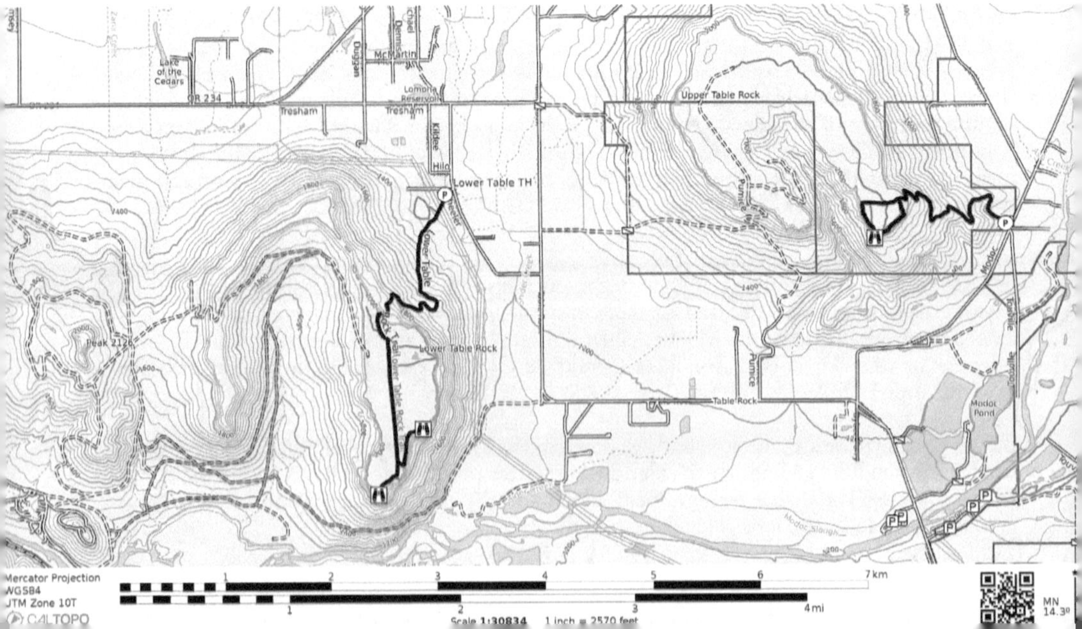

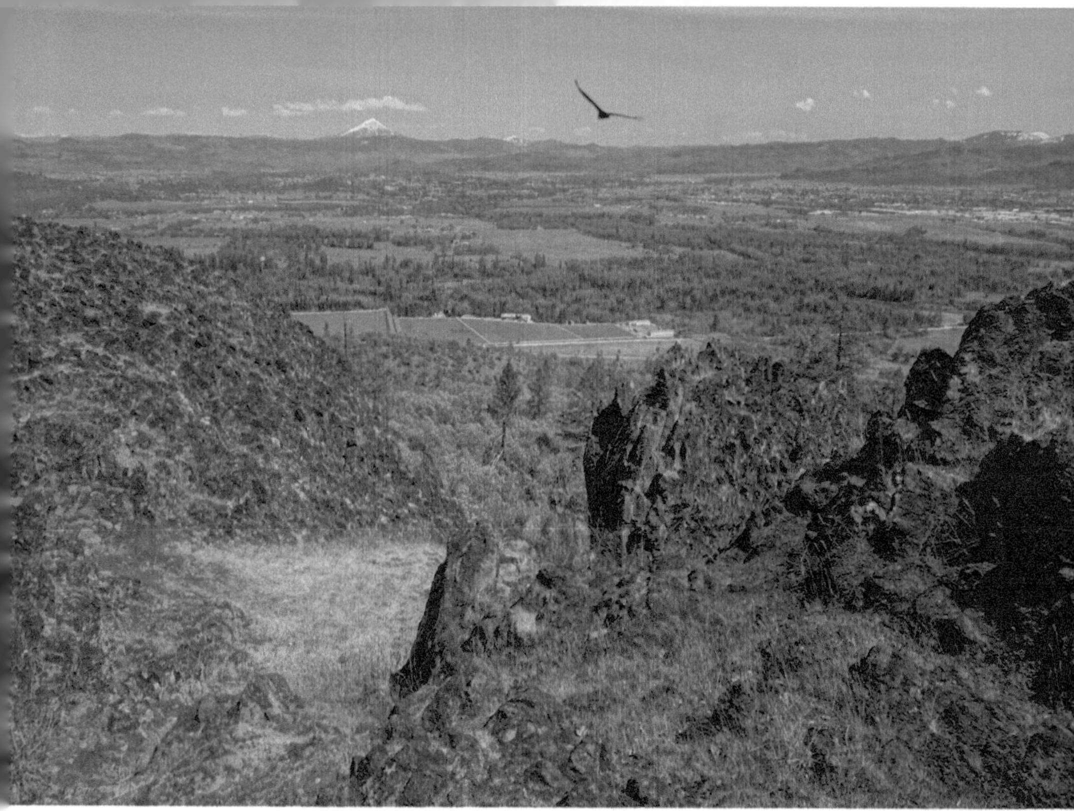

A hawk takes flight from Upper Table Rock, with Mount McLoughlin in the background.

the rocks and used the rocks as a sanctuary. Today, Lower and Upper Table Rocks provide a fun and easy hiking escape all year round for hikers in southern Oregon. The best time to visit is in spring, when the hillsides are covered in flowers and the summits of both rocks retain water that provides vital habitat for a number of rare plant species. Just make sure to avoid this area on hot days, as you'll bake in the summer sun before you even make it to the summit of both plateaus.

Begin at Lower Table Rock. From the trailhead, follow the wide trail through an attractive oak wood. The trail climbs gradually at first, then steeply as it ascends Lower Table Rock. Look for masses of spring flowers from March to June – so many, in fact, that it would be impossible to list them all here. Signboards provide details about the flowers along the trail, as well as the geologic and human history of this area. After 1.5 miles, the trail crests the summit of Lower Table Rock. Follow the trail across the huge summit plateau, passing seasonal ponds known as vernal pools. The trail follows an old airstrip across the summit plateau of Lower Table Rock for a mile to the edge of the plateau, where views open up to the Rogue River valley. The Rogue River itself is right below you, flowing from the Cascades across the heart of southern Oregon. Hawks and eagles are frequently sighted flying on the thermals just off the edge of the cliffs. Mount McLoughlin looms snowy and solitary across the valley. The rocks on the summit plateau's edge offer a nice place to sit and take in the view. When you're ready, return the way you came.

For Upper Table Rock, you'll want to drive to the Upper Table Trailhead a few miles to the east. Follow this gradual trail uphill through the woods, passing spectacular flower displays that cover the hillside from March to June. Stay on the trail, as poison oak lines the trail all the way to the summit. The trail emerges from the woods at 1.3 miles on Upper Table Rock's huge summit plateau. The trail forks here. Turn left and follow a wide trail 0.2 mile to the southeast edge of Upper Table Rock, where the view is spectacular. In addition to the Rogue Valley and Mount McLoughlin, you'll also have views south to Medford, Ashland, and the snowy peaks of the Red Buttes Wilderness on the southern horizon. Whenever you're ready, return the way you came.

87. Hobart Bluff

Distance: 2.6 miles out and back
Elevation Gain: 400 feet
Trailhead elevation: 5,317 feet
Trail high point: 5,494 feet
Season: June – October
Best: June – July
Pass: none needed
On the traditional lands of: the Shasta and Modoc peoples

Directions:

- From Ashland, leave Interstate 5 at Exit 14, signed for Ashland, Klamath Falls, and OR 66.
- Turn left onto OR 66 and drive 14.8 miles to a junction with Soda Mountain Road on the right at a sign for Cascade-Siskiyou National Monument. Soda Mountain Road is also called BLM 39-3c-32.3.
- Drive 3.7 miles of bumpy, potholed gravel road to the trailhead at a pass under powerlines. The Pacific Crest Trail crosses the road here. There is an outhouse and room for about a dozen cars.
- The trail to Hobart Bluff leaves from the north side of the road at a sign.
- **Drivetime from Ashland:** 40 minutes

Hike: The Cascade-Siskiyou National Monument southeast of Ashland sits at the confluence of the Cascade, Siskiyou, and Klamath Mountains. Here you'll find sagebrush and balsamroot mixing with oaks and junipers, and grassy, flower-spangled slopes mixing with dense forests and rocky slopes. While such scenery is commonly found all over southern Oregon, it reaches its

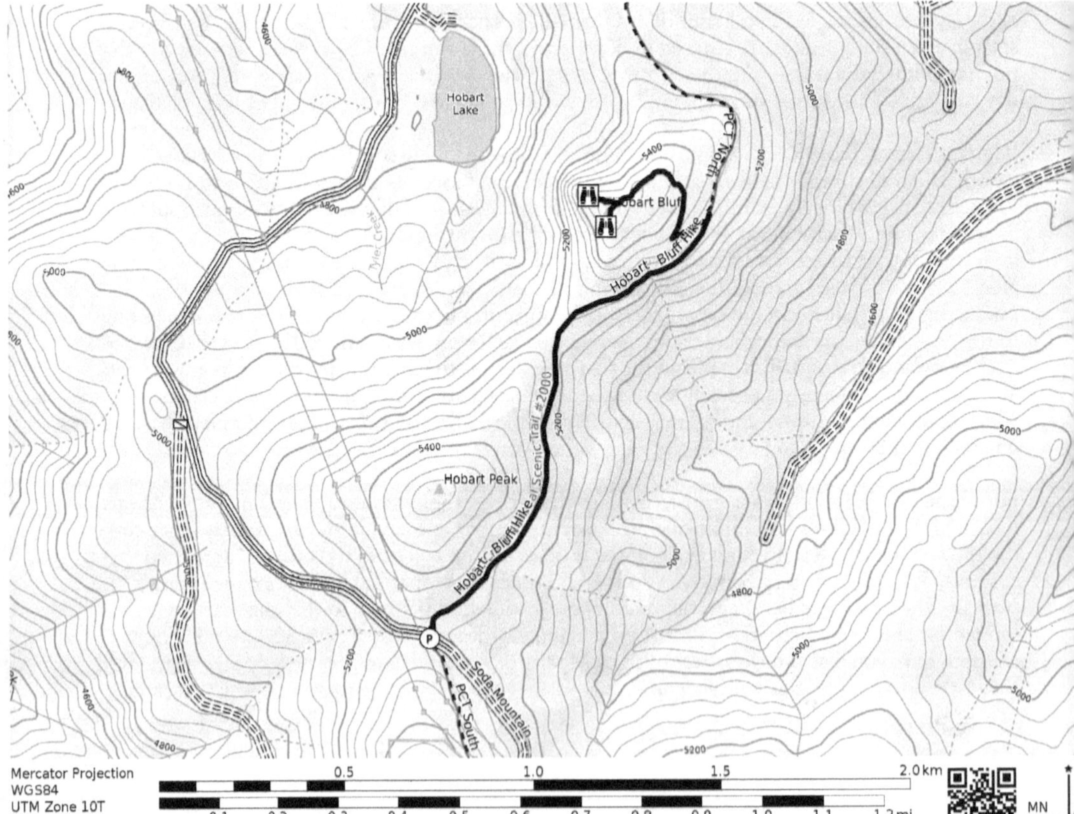

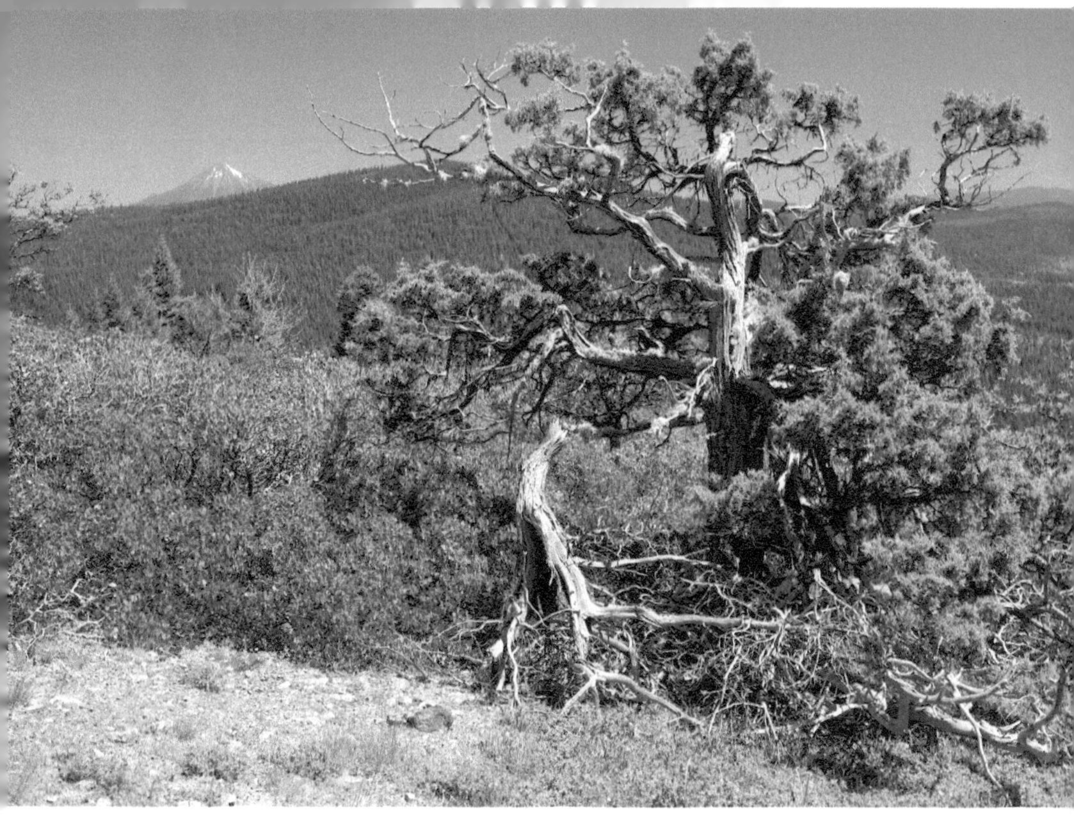

Mount McLoughlin rises above the junipers and oaks at Hobart Bluff.

zenith in the monument. This short hike to the summit of Hobart Bluff encompasses much of the best traits of this beautiful area, offering fantastic flower displays and extraordinary views north and south to the high peaks of the southern Cascades. This short hike has something for everyone.

Begin by following the Pacific Crest Trail (PCT) north from the grassy trailhead. You will soon enter a forest of Douglas fir and incense cedar. In June and July, the forest floor comes alive with flowers and butterflies. Look for larkspur, flax, columbine, and irises growing among scrub oak and wild cucumber. Keen eyes can spot the yellow and brown blooms of Brown's peony, usually found in dry environments such as this. The PCT descends slightly, then regains elevation gradually as you traverse along the southeast slopes of Hobart Bluff. At about 0.5 mile, you will pass an unmarked junction. Stay on the PCT and climb slightly to a signed junction with the spur trail to Hobart Bluff at 0.8 mile. Turn left here.

The summit trail climbs along the grassy slopes of Hobart Bluff, passing oaks and junipers, here at the western edge of their range. Balsamroot blooms profusely here in May and June of most years. As you climb, views open up northwest to Mount McLoughlin and south to huge and snowy Mount Shasta. The trail reaches the summit of Hobart Bluff at 1.3 miles. The summit plateau resembles a huge castle. You'll find several viewpoints east to mountains, west to Mount Ashland, and northwest to Ashland. Keen eyes can pick out cars driving on OR 66, the highway you drove to get here. In a region with many great views, this is one of the best.

Return the way you came. Hikers looking for a longer hike can follow the PCT north from the Hobart Bluff junction but it does not get more interesting and there are no views to speak of; you might want to follow the PCT south instead from the trailhead towards Soda Mountain, where you'll find a staffed lookout tower with similarly excellent views. Consult a map of the Cascade-Siskiyou National Monument for more information.

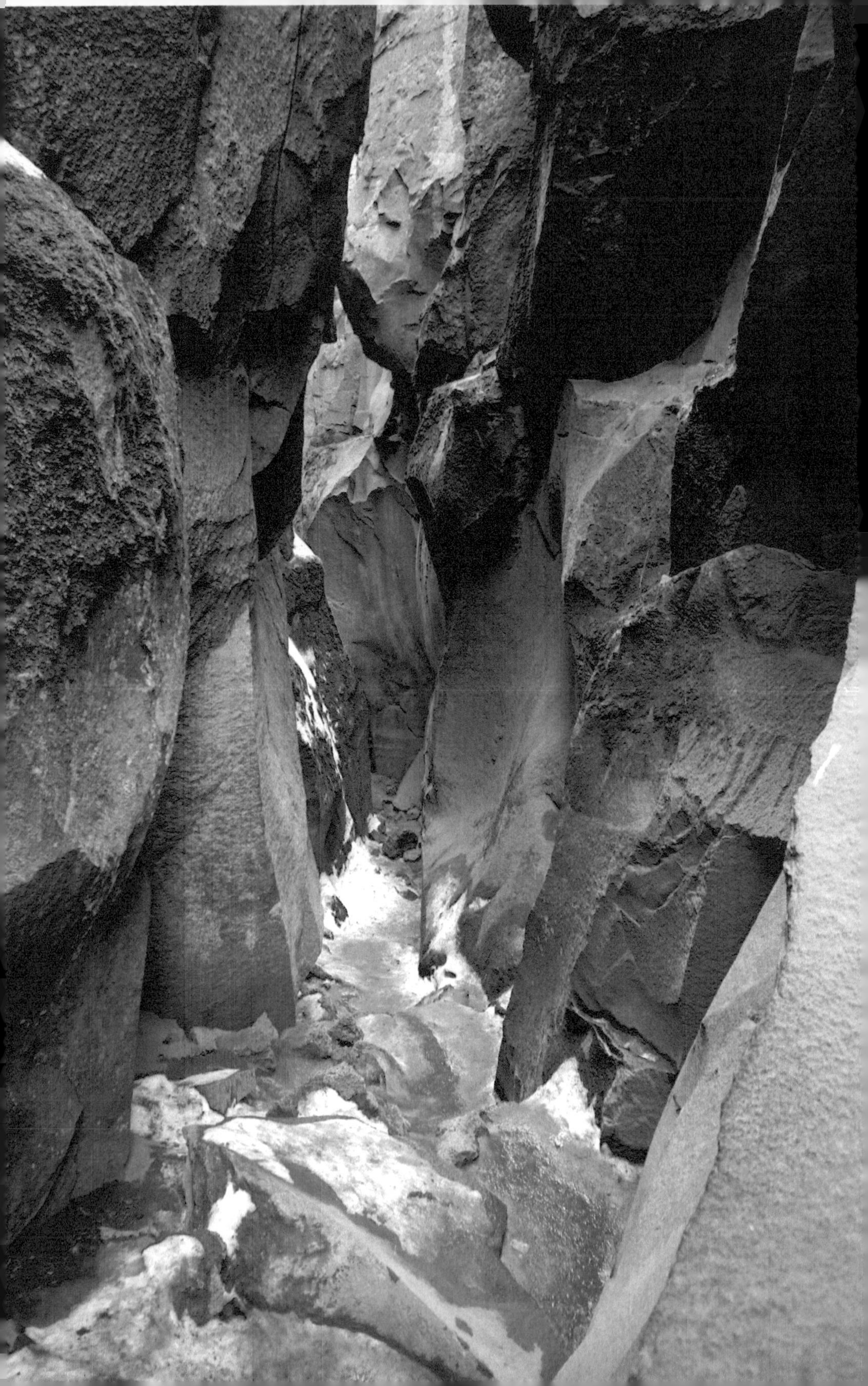

Central Oregon High Desert

The Central Oregon High Desert is the largest section in this book geographically. There are many definitions of what constitutes Central Oregon, but for the purposes of this book, this section covers the middle third of the state - that is, everything from the Deschutes River east to the Blue Mountains, and everything west of John Day and Lakeview further south. This vast area is larger than many US states, and multiple hiking guidebooks could be written about the area. I visit Central Oregon frequently in winter and spring, when the constant rain at home in Portland prompts me to head east in search of sunshine and adventure. Many of these hikes are old favorites of mine, and I am very happy to share them with you here.

For Central Oregon residents, these places are home. This is where you go hiking in the winter and spring when you don't feel like dealing with the snow and the crowds in the mountains. For the rest of us, the best time to visit the Central Oregon high desert is from October to May. Fall and winter bring cold weather but frequent sunshine, and spring brings a parade of wildflowers to what is typically an arid region. Most of these hikes are uncomfortably hot in the summer, and rattlesnakes are frequently seen in the Deschutes and Crooked River canyons in the summer. The exceptions to this rule are Newberry Crater, a huge collapsed volcano southeast of Bend, and Hager Mountain, another volcano in the so-called Oregon Outback. Both of these peaks top 7,000 feet and feature weather more typical of the Cascades than the rest of the High Desert. Wherever you go here, it is certain to be an adventure!

Photo on left: Crack In The Ground (Hike 96)

88. Macks Canyon

Distance: 9.4 miles out and back
Elevation Gain: 700 feet
Trailhead elevation: 473 feet
Trail high point: 543 feet
Season: January - May, October - December (avoid summer heat)
Best: October - May
Pass: none needed
On the traditional lands of: the Confederated tribes of the Warm Springs, and the Tenino people

Directions:

- From The Dalles, drive south on US 197 for 28 miles to Tygh Valley.
- Just before the highway reaches Tygh Valley, turn left onto OR 216 at a four-way intersection.
- Drive 8.4 miles to a bridge over the Deschutes River at Sherars Bridge. Cross the river and just a short distance later, turn left onto the Deschutes River access road.
- Drive 17 miles of generally excellent gravel road to Macks Canyon at road's end.
- **Drivetime from The Dalles:** 1 hour and 20 minutes

Hike: The Deschutes River flows some 250 miles from its source in central Oregon to the Columbia River. Along the way the river passes through some of the most impressive canyon country in Oregon. Several hikes in these canyonlands are described in this book, and all of them are beautiful in their own way. The trek from Macks Canyon north towards the river's mouth on the Columbia River is perhaps my favorite of these hikes. Here you will hike along the remains of a failed rail line, in and out of rugged side canyons under cliffs and vivid displays of columnar basalt. While not all that far from civilization, this corner of the Deschutes Canyon feels like one of the most remote corners of the state. Just make sure you avoid this hike in the summer, when highs in the canyon routinely reach the triple digits.

From the Macks Canyon Trailhead, locate what looks like a jeep road on the north end of the campground. This is the trail. Follow this wide path to a vantage point above a gully. Here the

The Deschutes River Trail at Macks Canyon.

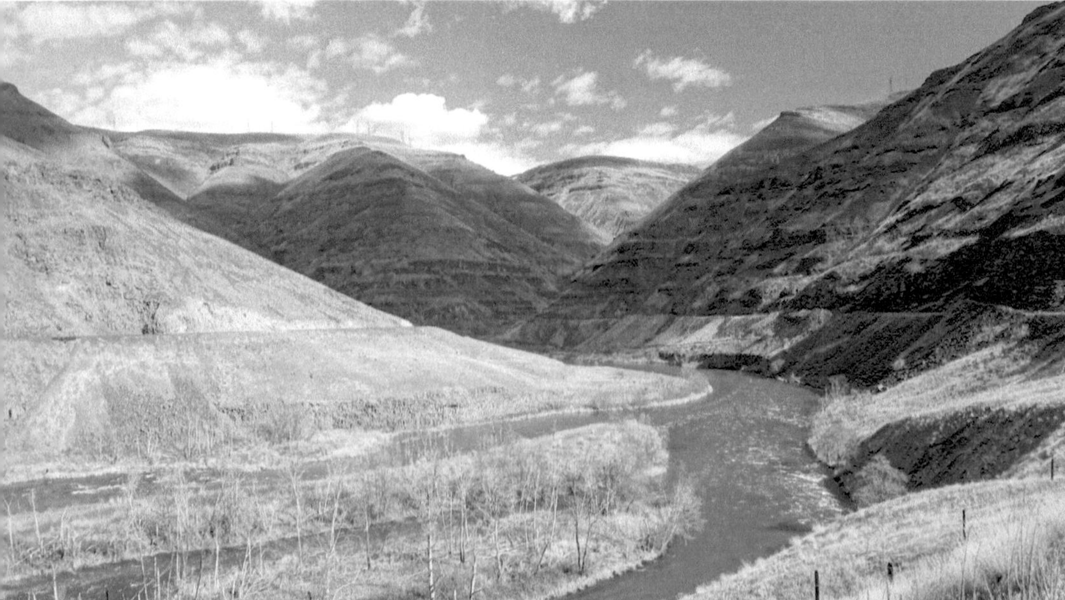

trestle that once held the rail line has collapsed into the canyon. Look for a well-defined user trail that scrambles into and back out of this gully. From here, you'll continue hiking downstream along the remains of the rail line, passing two more major gullies in similar fashion. As you hike along, take the time to ponder the origin of this trail. In the early 20th Century, this canyon was the site of one of the last of the so-called railroad wars in the United States. The Des Chutes Railroad Company and the Oregon Trunk Railroad Company each built rail lines along the banks of the Deschutes River from its mouth to Bend, each attempting to control the flow of timber and natural resources along the river. Each railway was built with hand tools and a considerable amount of effort, occasionally resorting even to sabotage. In the end, the Oregon Trunk Railroad on the western bank of the river won the war, and trains continue to use the railway to this day. The remains of the Des Chutes Railway are what make up this trail, as well as the Deschutes River Trail (Hike 35) and the road to the Criterion Ranch Trailhead (Hike 91). Today you will hike over weathered rail ties and see relics from the period when this line was still an active railroad. As you hike, you will be awed and amazed by the fantastic displays of columnar basalt in the canyon. Some of the finest displays of these vertical rock columns in Oregon are found along this trail, stopping hikers in their tracks to snap photos by the dozen. You should also keep your eyes on the slopes above, as a herd of bighorn sheep inhabit this canyon, along with many different species of birds. Less awesome is the barbwire fence found along the trail in spots; although the entire hike is on public land, the fences have not been removed. Also keep an eye out for ticks and rattlesnakes in the canyon during the warmer months.

At 4 miles, the trail follows a huge bend in the Deschutes River and becomes rough and faint. Follow the old railway another 0.7 mile to a knoll above both trail and river, perhaps the best stopping place along this hike. Here at the bottom of a 2,000 foot deep canyon, it is easy to feel small. If you're willing to scramble in and out of another gully, you'll find the end of the road that leaves from the Deschutes River State Recreation Area, some 19 miles downstream. If you're able to establish a car shuttle, the possibilities are enticing. For more information about this end of the Deschutes River Trail, see Hike 35. In the absence of a car shuttle, return the way you came.

Where to camp:
If you drove all this way to hike Macks Canyon, why not stay the night at one of the small but lovely campgrounds found on this stretch of the Deschutes River? The skies get very dark at night, offering fantastic stargazing. Just make sure to bring your own water and expect windy conditions in any season.

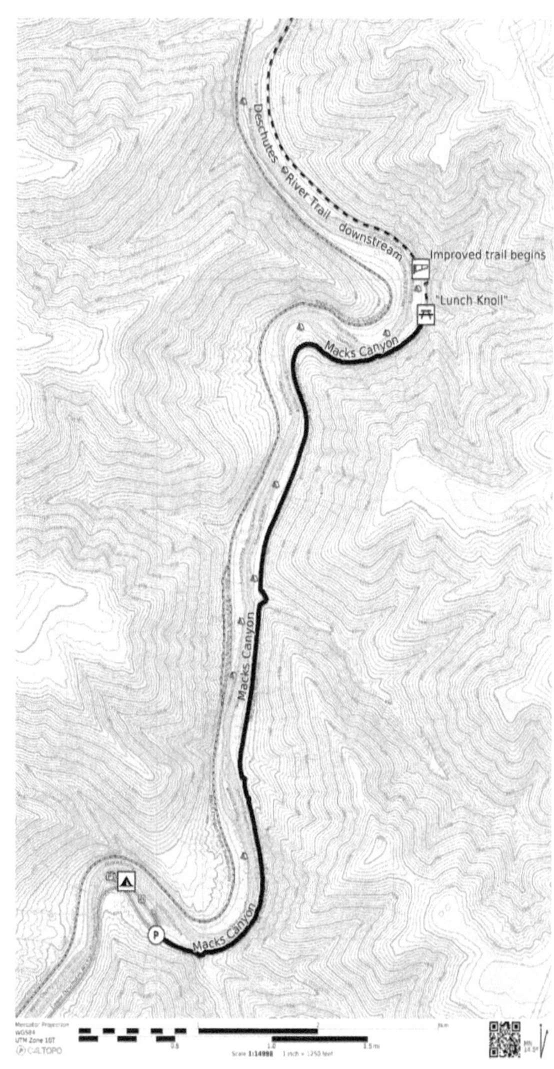

89. Cottonwood Canyon

	Gooseneck Viewpoint	Pinnacles Trail
Distance:	2.2 miles out and back	10 miles out and back
Elevation Gain:	900 feet	100 feet
Trailhead Elevation:	579 feet	579 feet
Trail High Point:	1,453 feet	590 feet
Season:	all year (avoid summer heat)	all year (avoid summer heat)
Best:	March - May	March - May, October
Pass:	none needed	none needed
On the traditional lands of:	the Confederated tribes of the Warm Springs, and the Tenino people	the Confederated tribes of the Warm Springs, and the Tenino people

Directions from The Dalles:

- From The Dalles, drive Interstate 84 east for 20 miles to Biggs Junction.
- At Exit 104, leave the freeway and turn onto US 97 heading south towards Wasco.
- Drive south on US 97 for 8.5 miles to an exit for OR 206. Take the exit for OR 206 and turn left at the top of the exit ramp onto OR 206, in the direction of Wasco.
- After almost 1 mile, arrive in Wasco. Follow signs for OR 206 through this small town.
- Drive 14.8 miles beyond Wasco on OR 206 to the bottom of the John Day River's canyon.
- Turn right at the sign for Cottonwood Canyon State Park, loop under the highway and drive to a large day-use lot on the north side of the highway. Do not drive into the campground.
- **Drivetime from The Dalles:** 45 minutes

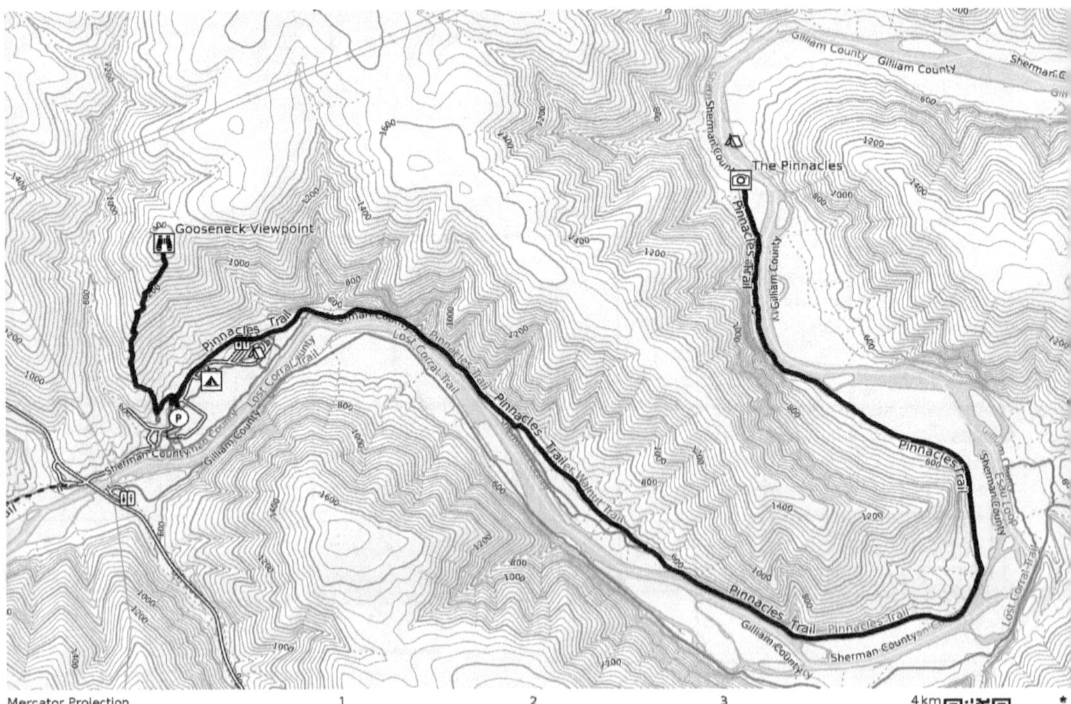

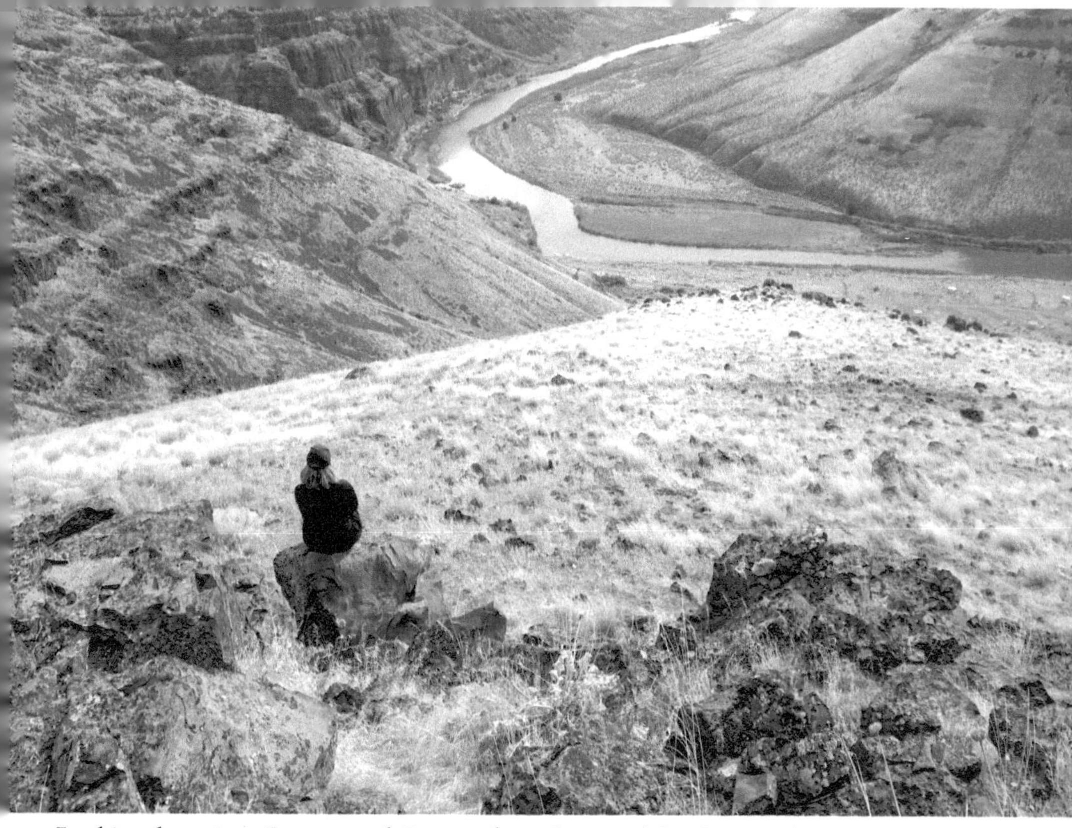

Looking down into Cottonwood Canyon from the top of the Gooseneck.

Hike: Cottonwood Canyon State Park along the lower John Day River opened in 2013 and quickly established itself as a favorite destination of Oregon high desert lovers. Although it's more than a two-hour drive from my home in Portland, I love coming out here in the winter and spring to get away from the incessant rain of the Willamette Valley. There is much to love here, and with a wide variety of trails, many adventures await hikers willing to make the drive from wherever they live. The two best of these adventures take you up a social trail to the top of Gooseneck Ridge for a spectacular view down into the John Day River canyon, and along the John Day for an easy day of mellow hiking.

For the short but invigorating hike up to the top of Gooseneck Ridge, make your way to the Sage Steppe Trail, just above the campground access road. Follow it in the direction of the obvious arch on the hill above the day use parking lot. Take a right on the Sage Knob Trail towards the arch, and once you reach the arch, continue hiking uphill on an unofficial but obvious social trail. As you near the top of the ridge, the trail becomes faint in spots but views open up to the graceful curve of the John Day River downstream of the campground. Bighorn sheep are frequently seen on these slips. After a little over a mile of climbing, you'll crest the top of the ridge where the views are extraordinary! An off-trail traverse between the top of the ridge and the Pinnacles Trail is possible but is quite difficult, requiring steep scrambling up and down the ridge. From the viewpoint, it is best to just return the way you came to the day use area.

If you're up for the long but easy hike along the Pinnacles Trail, follow the trail downriver from the campground. You'll gain excellent views up to the slopes on each side of the John Day River as you hike along, and keen eyes may spot bighorn sheep on the canyon walls. Spring flowers add color to the scene. At 2.5 miles from the trailhead, you'll reach a gate, a closure intended to protect nesting golden eagles from February to September. If you're here during that time, you'll have to turn around here. If the gate is open, continue 2.2 more miles to trail's end at the base of the pinnacles along the John Day River. From wherever you turn around, return the way you came.

90. White River Falls

Distance: 1 mile out and back
Elevation Gain: 200 feet
Trailhead elevation: 1,040 feet
Trail high point: 1,040 feet
Season: all year (avoid winter storms and summer heat)
Best: March – May
Pass: none needed
On the traditional lands of:the Confederated tribes of the Warm Springs, and the Tenino people

Directions:

- From wherever you begin, make your way to the town of Tygh Valley. This small town is 29 miles south of The Dalles and 100 miles north of Bend via US 97 and 197.
- From just north of Tygh Valley, turn east on OR 216 at a sign for White River Falls and Sherars Bridge.
- Once on this road, drive east for 4 miles to the well-marked state park on the right.
- During winter months, you will have to park at a lot just off the highway, but from April through October you can drive through the gate and continue 0.2 mile to a parking lot with a bathroom.
- **Drivetimes:** 40 minutes from The Dalles, 1 hour and 50 minutes from Bend

Hike: The White River flows off the east side of Mount Hood and tumbles through a deep canyon that few other than river rafters ever see. Near its confluence with the Deschutes River, this canyon climaxes in a jaw-dropping, awe-inspiring waterfall that some have called the very best in the entire state. When I first visited White River Falls many years ago few hikers had ever heard of it, and in the years since it has become a popular destination portrayed in many photos, videos, and even on the state highway map. White River Falls is most definitely one of Oregon's most extraordinary waterfalls, and worthy of a stop or even a road trip from wherever you call

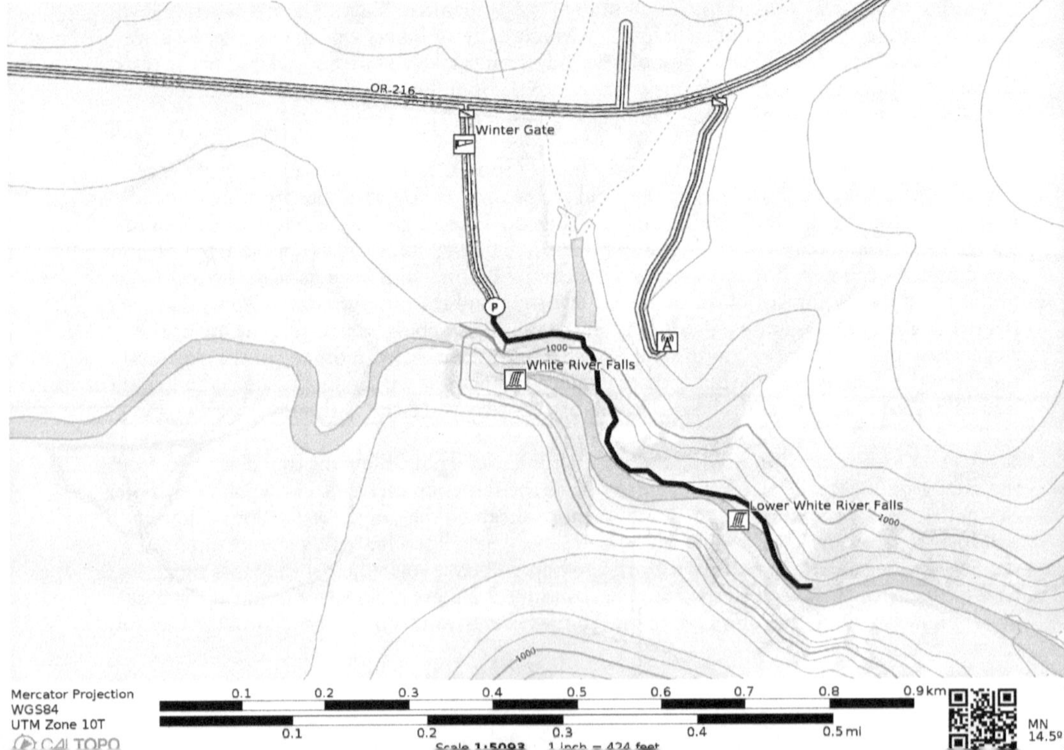

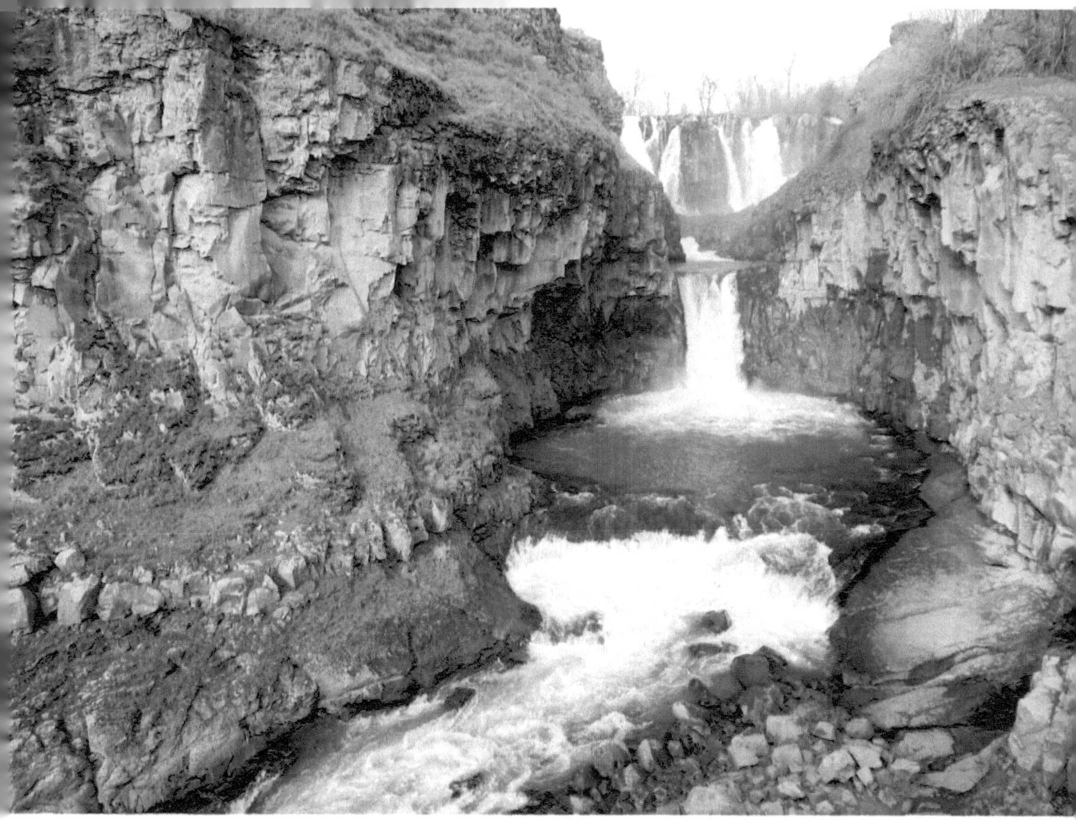

White River Falls is located only a few miles from Tygh Valley.

home. The only problem here is the brevity of the hike; you'll find yourself wishing the hike was much, much longer. Make a visit to the falls part of a longer trip to the Badger Creek Wilderness (Hike 44) or one of the other hikes in this area such as Macks Canyon (Hike 88) or Criterion Ranch (Hike 91).

From the parking lot, follow the sound of raging water to a fenced overlook of the falls. The view of the falls from this side is obstructed but breathtaking. Note the number of fences asking visitors to stay out of the water, advice you should heed. Locate the paved trail heading across a bridge and downhill. At a junction just beyond this bridge, turn right and proceed to hike downhill on a rough set of stairs. In April and May balsamroot lines this slope, adding color to the scene. Near the bottom of this set of stairs is a rocky promontory with a direct view of the falls, where at last both tiers have come into view. You may have to wait your turn here; this is the best view of White River Falls and you should expect competition from awestruck hikers and photographers. The falls is a two-tiered monster, dropping 110 feet first down a wide shelf, then a narrow plunge. The lower tier of the falls is named Celestial Falls.

Below this viewpoint, the stairs lead you to the bottom of the canyon. On your right here is the remains of a hydroelectric plant from the 1920s. Hikers were once able to explore the rusting machinery and rotting innards of this building but today everything is fenced off here. Please adhere to this closure, as the building is dangerous and is justifiably condemned. Hikers should instead continue downstream beyond the building, where the trail becomes brushy, passing through dense sagebrush and wild rose. Continuing downstream another 10 minutes will take you to the brink of Lower White River Falls. This cataract is far less impressive than its upstream sibling but compensates with fantastic columns of columnar basalt. There are numerous rocky outcrops to sit and gaze upon the river and falls here, in this oasis in the high desert. Even though you've only hiked a half-mile from the trailhead, you should stop here. Beyond this point the trail becomes rough and faint as you scramble over steep, muddy slopes in this rugged, narrow canyon. It's over 2 miles to the Deschutes River and there are no waterfalls downstream. You should instead return the way you came and continue your day on a different adventure.

91. Criterion Ranch

	Juniper Point	Stag Point
Distance:	4.6 miles out and back	11.6 miles out and back
Elevation Gain:	1,000 feet	2,500 feet
Trailhead Elevation:	955 feet	955 feet
Trail High Point:	1,851 feet	2,720 feet
Season:	all year (avoid summer heat)	all year (avoid summer heat)
Best:	March - May	March - May, October
Pass:	none needed	none needed
On the traditional lands of:	the Confederated tribes of the Warm Springs, and the Tenino people	the Confederated tribes of the Warm Springs, and the Tenino people

Directions:

- From wherever you begin, make your way to the town of Maupin. Maupin is 45 minutes south of The Dalles on US 197, 2 hours southeast of Portland via Government Camp (or The Dalles), and 1 hour and 45 minutes north of Bend via US 97 and 197.
- From downtown Maupin, cross the Deschutes River and turn right onto the Deschutes River Access Road. This junction will be on your left just before crossing the Deschutes if you're coming from the south.
- Once on this road, follow it for 3.6 miles of pavement and another 3.4 miles of good gravel to the trailhead at a locked gate. Along the way, you'll pass a number of small but welcoming campgrounds should you wish to spend the night.
- **Drivetimes:** 1 hour from The Dalles, 2 hours from Bend, 2.5 hours from Portland

Hike: The Criterion Tract of BLM land south of Maupin is very much a place where you can choose your own adventure. There are many satisfying adventures to be had here, but perhaps

The Deschutes River below the Criterion Tract.

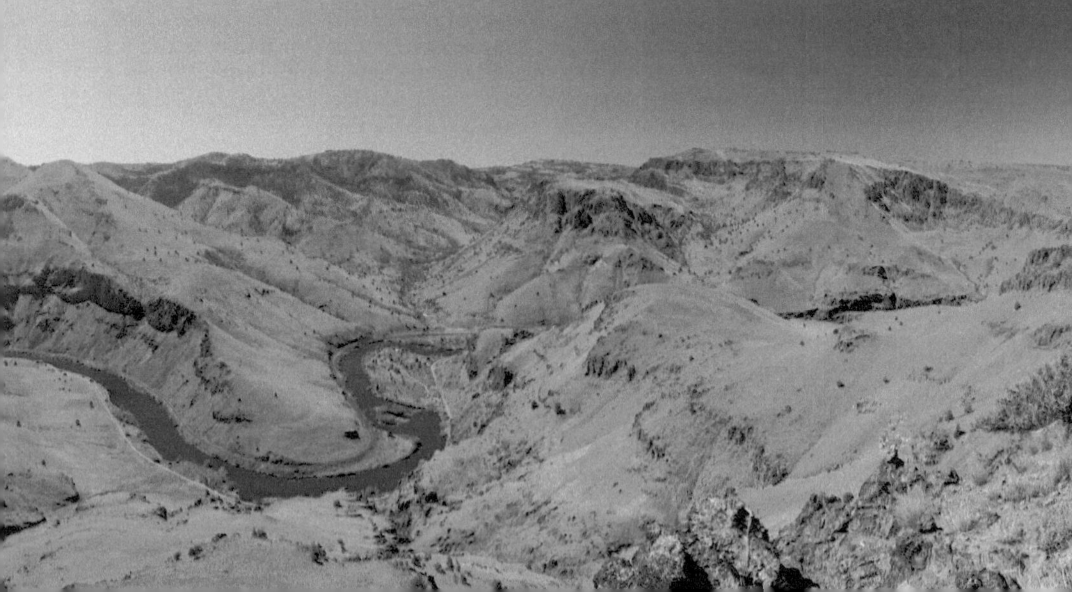

the best follows an old ranch road to a viewpoint looking out to Mount Hood and directly down to a scenic bend along the Deschutes River. Hikers comfortable with off-trail travel can continue several more miles to an even more extraordinary viewpoint of the Deschutes River and the hidden peaks of the Warm Springs Reservation. This is a beautiful hike in any season but never more so than in spring, when flowers bloom and the hillsides turn a striking shade of green. Avoid this area in the heat of summer and during cold periods in the winter. There is no shade on this hike, so avoid the area when conditions are unkind.

From the trailhead, ignore the road beyond the gate and instead follow the trail climbing through a gap behind the pit toilet. You will pass a gate and quickly climb onto a meadowed bench above the river. The trail passes through a cattle gate at a half-mile; make sure to close it behind you after you hike through. This entire hike is on public land, but the gates are designed to keep cattle out of certain sections of the area. From here, the trail climbs gradually beneath the rocky ramparts of the Deschutes canyon. Birds of all varieties patrol the skies overhead. As you ascend, look behind you for Mount Hood on the northwestern horizon, towering over the high plains west of Maupin and Tygh Valley. The trail then passes through another fence and continues climbing. At 2.3 miles, the trail passes by a pair of promontories on the right with views down to the river. At the second of these viewpoints, leave the trail and head down to this rocky vantage, where a single juniper stands sentinel above the Deschutes canyon. You will very quickly reach the cliff-edge below the juniper, where the views are eye-popping. The serpentine and deep blue Deschutes River is below you, while Mount Hood looms behind you on the horizon. In an area with many great viewpoints, this is one of the best.

Hikers uncomfortable with off-trail travel should turn around here. Beyond Juniper Point, the trail continues climbing another 1.3 miles to the top of the canyon at 3.6 miles. Keep an eye out for cows along the way, who roam this upper section of the Criterion Tract. When the trail tops out, you will see a fence in front of you; this fence marks the boundary of a section of private land. Leave the trail here and follow the fence steeply downhill to a spring, then uphill over a knoll. When you reach the top of the knoll, you will see Stag Point, your destination, in front of you. Although the way is steep at times, navigating this off-trail section is quite easy. You should meet another dirt road at about 5 miles from the trailhead. Follow the road until you near Stag Point, then set off cross-country to Stag Point itself, marked by a tall post. When you reach the point at 5.8 miles, the view from the slopes down to the river and out to Mount Hood are absolutely incredible! The open slopes along the canyon walls are immensely fun to explore, but eventually you'll have to return the way you came.

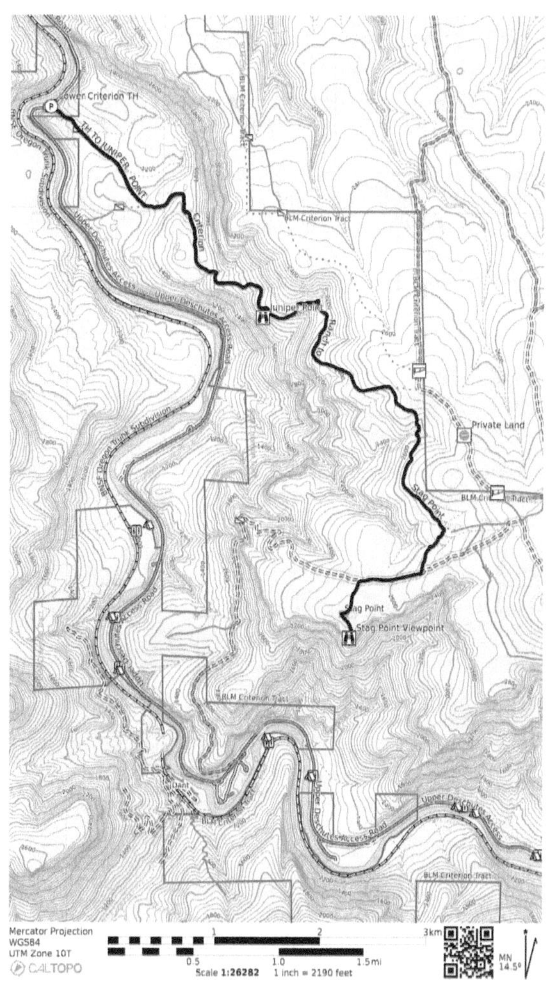

92. Otter Bench

Distance: 9.9 miles (all trails)
Elevation Gain: 1,500 feet
Trailhead elevation: 2,408 feet
Trail high point: 2,536 feet
Season: all year (avoid winter storms and summer heat)
Best: October – May
Pass: none needed
On the traditional lands of: the Confederated tribes of the Warm Springs, and the Tenino people

Directions:

- From Redmond, drive north on US 97 for 6 miles to Terrebonne.
- Just beyond Terrebonne, turn left onto Lower Bridge Road at a sign for Crooked River Ranch. If you're coming from Madras or points north, drive south for 20 miles to this intersection, just before US 97 enters Terrebonne.
- Turn left onto Lower Bridge Road (or right if coming from the north) and drive 2.1 miles to a junction with NW 43rd Avenue.
- Turn right and follow this road for 1.7 miles to a junction with NW Chinook Drive.
- Turn left on NW Chinook and drive 4.9 miles until you reach an intersection.
- Continue on SW Horny Hollow Road. Drive 1.7 miles to road's end at a gravel turnaround. This is the trailhead.
- **Drivetime from Terrebonne:** 20 minutes

Hike: Oregon's high desert is a delight to visit in winter and spring. Hikers who live west of the Cascades regularly visit Central Oregon in search of precious winter sunshine, and hikers who live in Central Oregon can leave the snow behind and take the time to explore the rugged can-

The Crooked River from Otter Bench.

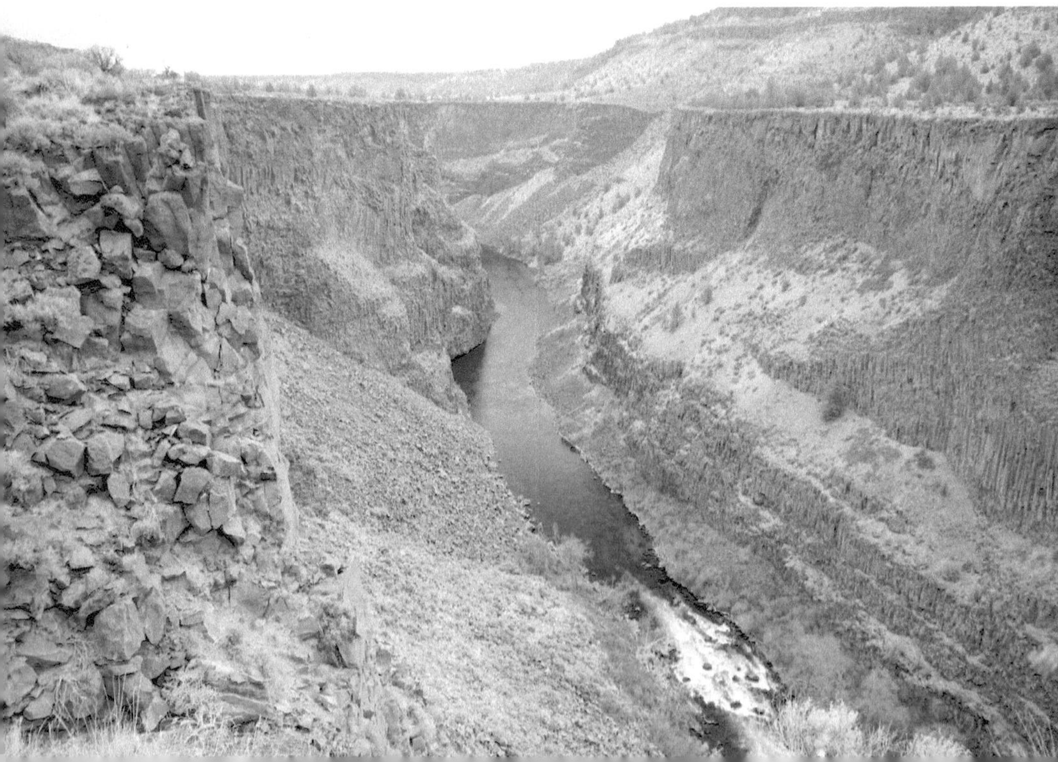

yons that cut through the region. This series of new trails along the canyon of the Crooked River is a winner. You'll explore the scenic benches above the Crooked River, and two spectacular trails offer steep entries into the river's inner canyon. These trails are a delight!

At the trailhead, you'll have your choice of adventures before you even begin. The Lone Pine Trail departs from the right side of the trailhead and drops 1 mile to the Crooked River. This section of trail is disconnected from the rest of the trail system at Otter Bench and should be hiked either first, last, or not at all. For the purposes of this description, we will save the Lone Pine Trail for the end of the hike. From the trailhead, locate the Horny Hollow Trail and Otter Bench Trails which branch off just beyond the trailhead. The Horny Hollow Trail is spectacular and follows the canyon wall closely. Unfortunately, this trail is closed from February 1 to August 31 to protect nesting eagles. If you're here in the fall and winter (before February 1), continue straight on the Horny Hollow Trail. Otherwise, fork to the left on the Otter Bench Trail. Follow this trail for 1.9 miles until you reach a reunion with the Horny Hollow Trail. The Pink Trail sets off to the right here; save this trail for later. Continue straight on what is now the Opal Canyon Trail. Keep left and follow this trail to spectacular views of the Crooked River Gorge. After 1.2 miles, the trail reaches its northern terminus with excellent views of the Crooked River just below where it enters Lake Billy Chinook. The trail then curves back to the south and continues 1.2 miles back to the fork in the trail. Continue south 0.4 mile to the junction with the Pink Trail.

Although you've already hiked 5 miles, the best is yet to come! For the most spectacular spot on this hike, turn left here and hike steeply downhill via a series of boulder stairs to a riverside rock garden along the Crooked River. Along the way you'll pass spectacular views of basalt formations above the Crooked River. Keep your eyes peeled for birds in this narrow, gorgeous canyon. Several rock benches offer a great place to stop for a break.

When you're ready to return, hike steeply back uphill to the junction with the Horny Hollow and Otter Bench Trails. If the Horny Hollow Trail is open, turn left and follow it; otherwise, hike the Otter Bench Trail for 1.9 miles back to the trailhead. If you've still got the energy, now is the time to tackle the Lone Pine Trail. Follow this path south from the trailhead first uphill, then downhill for 1 mile down to another lovely riverside vantage of the Crooked River. If you're only here for a couple hours, do this hike first and figure out the rest later. Regardless of when you visit, you'll love this chance to get up close and personal with the mighty Crooked River. Return the way you came. You'll have to hike uphill on the way out, so remember to save some energy for the return trip!

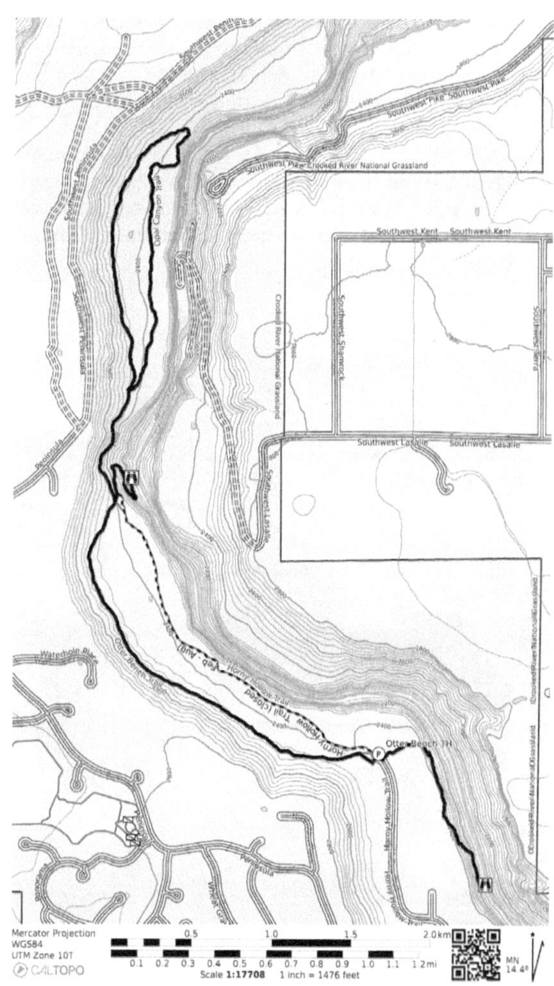

93. Scout Camp

Distance: 2.3 mile semi-loop
Elevation Gain: 800 feet
Trailhead elevation: 2,723 feet
Trail high Point: 2,723 feet
Season: all year (avoid summer heat)
Best: March – May, October
Pass: none needed
On the traditional lands of: the Confederated tribes of the Warm Springs, and the Tenino people

Directions:

- From Redmond, drive north on US 97 for 6 miles to Terrebonne.
- Just beyond Terrebonne, turn left onto Lower Bridge Road at a sign for Crooked River Ranch. If you're coming from Madras or points north, drive south for 20 miles on US 97 to this intersection on the right, just before US 97 enters Terrebonne.
- Turn left onto Lower Bridge Road (or right if coming from the north) and drive 2.1 miles to a junction with NW 43rd Avenue.
- Turn right here and drive 1.8 miles to a junction with NW Chinook Drive.
- Turn left and drive 2.4 miles to a junction with Mustang Road.
- Turn left and drive 0.2 mile to another junction. Turn right to stay on Mustang Road.
- Continue 0.9 mile to a junction with NW Shad Road.
- Turn right and drive 1.4 mile to a junction with SW Peninsula Drive.
- Turn right here and drive 3.2 miles to a junction on the left with SW Meadow Road.
- Drive 0.6 mile to a junction with SW Scout Camp Trail.
- Turn right and drive 0.3 mile to road's end at the Scout Camp Trailhead.
- **Drivetimes:** 20 minutes from Terrebonne, 40 minutes from Redmond, 60 minutes from Bend.

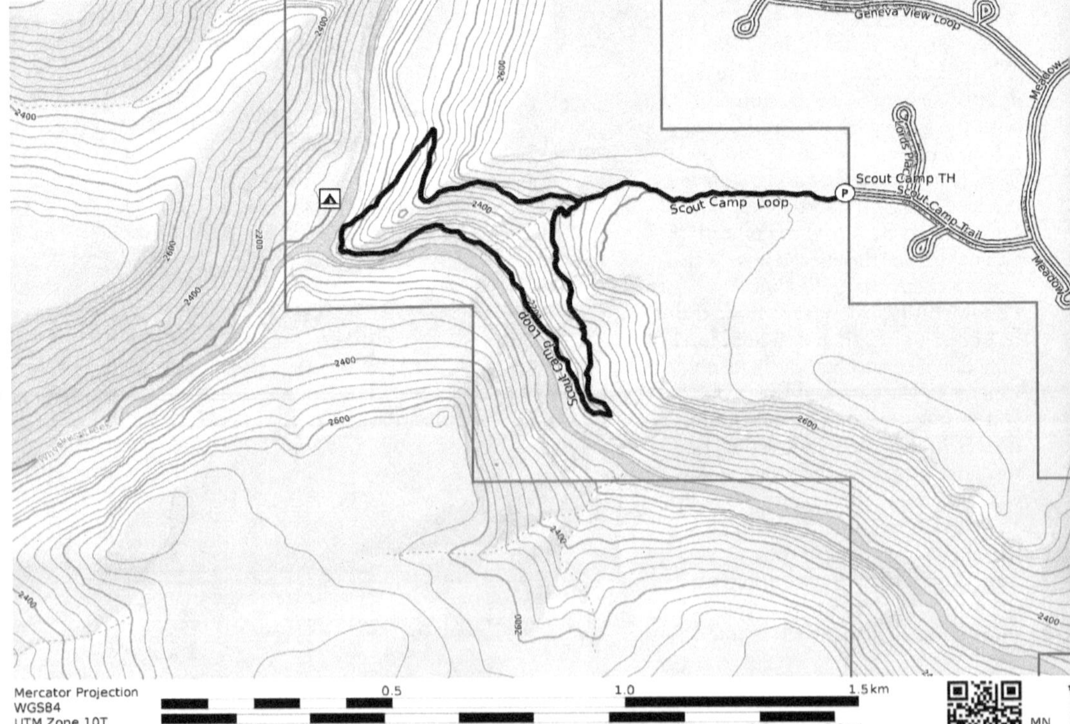

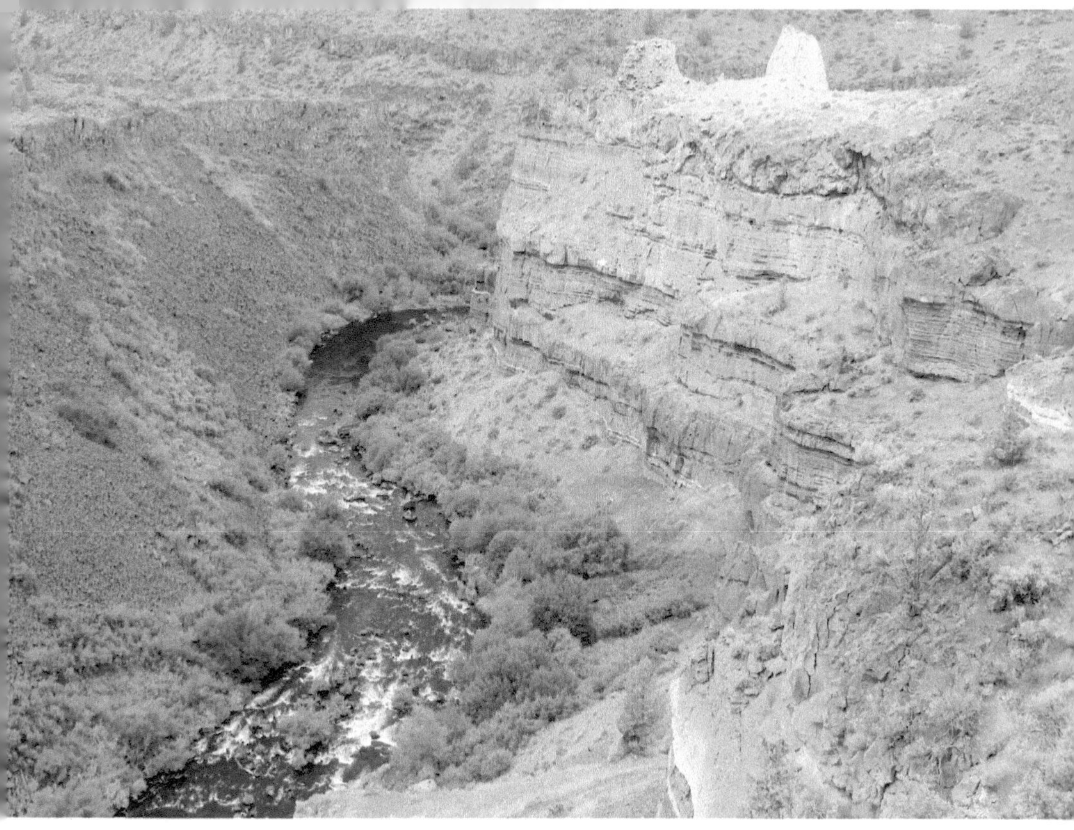

The Deschutes River flows below rainbow cliffs near Scout Camp.

Hike: Hidden at the edge of the labyrinth of roads in Crooked River Ranch is one of Oregon's most extraordinary hikes. Just minutes after leaving a subdivision, you'll enter a remote stretch of the Deschutes River Canyon and have spectacular views west to the high peaks of the Cascades. The trail then plunges into one of Oregon's most beautiful canyons, passing kaleidoscopic displays of spring wildflowers, before guiding you back to the top of the canyon. It's hard to believe that such intense beauty could be so close to civilization and yet, such is life in Central Oregon.

From the trailhead, follow the wide trail through spring wildflowers and open juniper woods for 0.4 mile to a fork in the trail at the beginning of the loop. Turn left here to hike the loop clockwise; doing so brings you the best views and allows you to avoid hikers at narrow spots in the trail. The trail begins switchbacking furiously into the narrow canyon, offering views to the mesmerizing rainbow cliffs above the Deschutes River. The flower display along the canyon walls here in spring is impressive; look for masses of yellow balsamroot, red paintbrush, blue and purple lupine, and so much more. The trail finally bottoms out at a bench above the river at 0.9 mile. You'll follow the rocky and rough trail above the river, passing under spectacular cliffs. At 1.4 miles, the trail appears to disappear at the base of a huge cliff. Scramble up the rocks here some fifteen feet to find the continuation of the trail on the other side. Across the river, Whychus Creek flows into the Deschutes. Continue hiking along the river another 100 yards or so until the trail at last begins to climb again. You may notice hikers and campers on the other side of the river; they've all hiked down to this spot from the Alder Flats Trailhead, which departs from near Sisters. Crossing the rampaging Deschutes River to join them is impossible, so you should wave your friendliest wave and then continue on your way. The trail then gains 470 feet over the next half-mile as it climbs steadily to the fork in the trail you passed earlier; some hikers may have issues with exposure on this section of trail, so slow down and take your time if needed. When you reach the fork, turn left and hike 0.4 mile to the trailhead.

94. Smith Rock

Distance: 4.2 mile loop
Elevation Gain: 900 feet
Trailhead elevation: 2,848 feet
Trail high Point: 3,293 feet
Season: all year
Best: March – May, October – November
Pass: $5 park entrance fee (pay at the parking lot)
On the traditional lands of: the Confederated tribes of the Warm Springs, and the Tenino people

Directions:

- From Redmond, drive north on US 97 for 6 miles to Terrebonne.
- At a signed junction in the middle of Terrebonne, turn right onto Smith Rock Way.
- From here, follow signs to Smith Rock State Park.
- **Drivetime from Redmond:** 15 minutes

Hike: Smith Rock is one of Oregon's most unique and captivating places. Located just two miles off bustling US 97 in Terrebonne, the orange cliffs and graceful rock formations at Smith Rock are reminiscent of Utah's famous national parks. Rock climbers come from all over Oregon and the rest of the world to scale the cliffs here, and you will almost certainly share some of the trails here with them. This extraordinary loop takes you around the base of Smith Rock's cliffs before taking you up and over the middle of the park, where you'll have some of the finest views in all Central Oregon. Just make sure to avoid this hike in July and August when the park regularly bakes in the summit heat.

The spectacular views of Smith Rock begin at the parking lot. From wherever you parked, locate the paved trail that heads downhill toward the Crooked River. There are two trails to the

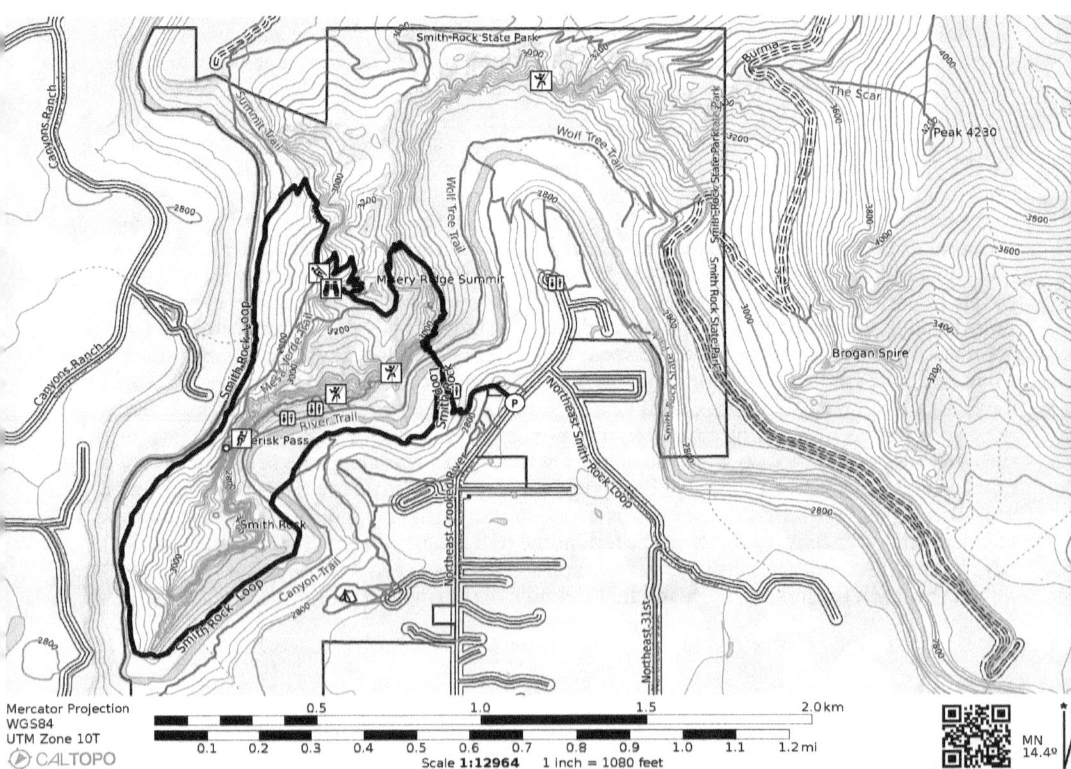

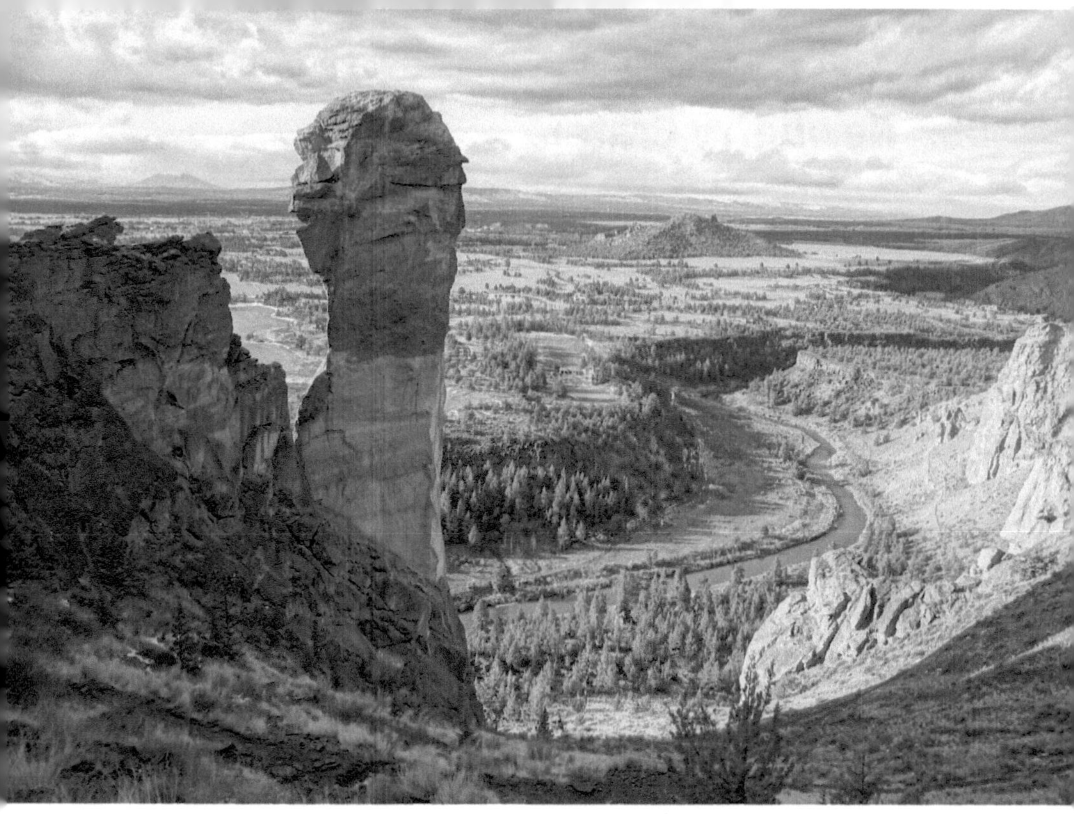

Monkey Face and the Crooked River from the west end of Misery Ridge.

river: one short and steep, the other longer and more gradual. Once you reach the bottom of the canyon, cross the bridge over the Crooked River and reach a junction at the beginning of the loop. As with most loops, the direction in which you do this hike does not matter, but I like to hike along the river first and save Misery Ridge for later. So turn left and hike along the river on a wide, dusty trail along the base of Smith Rock's cliffs. It is fun to venture off the River Trail on side paths that lead to climbing spots, but please give climbers their space and don't distract them. As the trail winds around the far side of Smith Rock, you'll leave the climbers behind, as most of the primary climbing routes are on the sunny eastern side of the rock. You'll also have views ahead to Monkey Face, a 350-foot tall rock pinnacle whose distinct visage is one of Oregon's most recognizable places. You'll reach a junction with the Mesa Verde Trail at 2.1 miles, a shortcut to Misery Ridge. If you're feeling tired, you can fork to the right here. Otherwise, continue hiking along the Crooked River another 0.5 mile to a junction at a huge boulder. Turn right here to continue the Misery Ridge Loop.

The trail climbs gradually at first but steepens after you reach a junction with the Mesa Verde Trail. Soon you'll be switchbacking steeply up the backside of Smith Rock. As you climb, wide-ranging views open up to a lineup of Cascade peaks from the Three Sisters to Mount Jefferson. The perfectly conical peak on the horizon is Black Butte. The trail passes along the base of Monkey Face, and with some luck, you'll be able to watch climbers attempting to scale the sheer cliffs of this pinnacle. After some fairly intense climbing, the trail reaches the top of Misery Ridge at 3.2 miles. A side trail leads to an intimate look across to Monkey Face. If it wasn't obvious before, this view should make it obvious how the rock got its name. Climbers like to rest in the monkey's mouth after making their way up the rock, and you are close enough to have a conversation with them without even raising your voice. Beyond Monkey Face, the trail crosses the narrow plateau of Misery Ridge's summit to a viewpoint at the eastern end of the ridge. From here, you'll follow the wide and popular trail downhill (many hikers choose to do the loop in this direction, so expect to pass a lot of people) until you reach the Crooked River again, just a few steps away from the beginning of the loop. Cross the bridge over the river and hike uphill to the trailhead.

95. Newberry Crater

Distance: 9.3 miles (all trails)
Elevation Gain: 700 feet
Trailhead elevation: 6,342 feet
Trail high Point: 6,593 feet
Season: July – October
Best: August - September
Pass: NW Forest Pass
On the traditional lands of: the Yahooskin people

Directions:

- From Bend, drive south for approximately 23 miles to a junction with the Newberry Crater Road on your left.
- Turn left and drive this paved road 11 miles to a fee booth, where you will need to show your NW Forest Pass or pay for a day pass.
- Continue 1 mile to a turnoff on your left for Paulina Falls (see below).
- Drive just under a mile further up the road to Paulina Lake. For the hike around the lake, park in the day-use lot.
- **Drivetime from Bend:** 45 minutes

Hike: Located well east of the Cascade Crest, Newberry Crater is the outcast among Cascade volcanoes. Here you will find two lakes inside the collapsed caldera of an ancient volcano, but you won't find the eye-popping, life-altering scenery that defines a visit to nearby Crater Lake. Instead, Newberry Crater charms with subtlety: with quiet mornings along a gentle lakeshore, with cold sunsets from the windswept summit of Paulina Peak, and with tumbling waterfalls in a wilderness canyon. While there is much to do in Newberry Crater, the hike around gorgeous Paulina Lake (pronounced Puh-Line-uh) is the cream of the crop. The loop is a scenic feast for the senses, with views across the azure waters to the rocky summit of Paulina Peak, a hidden

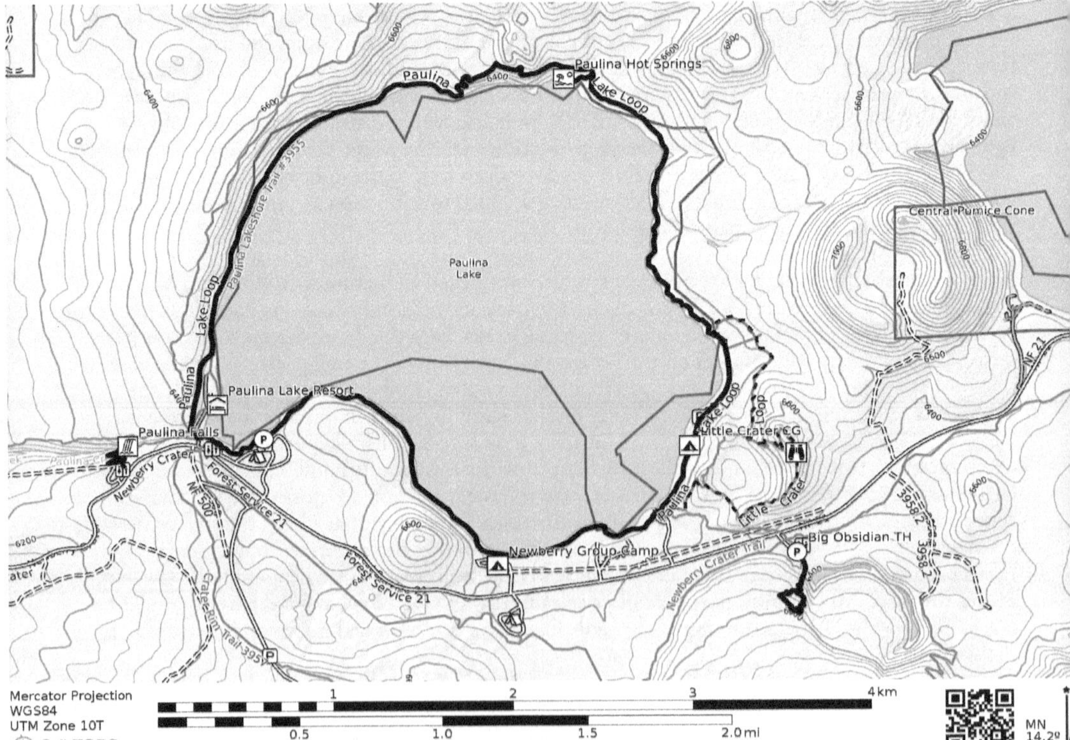

hot springs, and peeks west to some of the Cascade high peaks. Best of all, even if you do the full loop around the lake, you should still have enough energy to do three other worthwhile side trips while you're in the area.

From the day use area, follow the trail left to a bridge across Paulina Creek just below the lakeshore. Just across the bridge, you will reach a junction. Left leads you downstream along the creek, passing views of Paulina Falls and then along the tumbling creek to more waterfalls. Save this trip for a different day. Instead continue straight and reach another junction above some cabins. Fork to the left to avoid the cabins, and before long you'll be back hiking along the lakeshore, where the trail mostly stays. Occasionally you'll wander away from the lake for a bit, only to quickly return. Paulina Peak's rugged summit looms across the lake to the south. At 3 miles, reach a spur trail down to Paulina Hot Springs. The hot springs is proof that the area is still quite geothermally active, in case you'd forgotten that you're hiking around a lake inside a collapsed volcano. On this end of the lake, hot water bubbles up along the lakeshore, and you will find several shallow pools here right at water's edge. As with all hot springs, you are likely to encounter hot water enthusiasts. Your best chance of solitude is to visit after Labor Day, and plan on soaking in the morning. The pools are fairly unsatisfying but you may find one to your liking with some patience. Beyond the hot springs, the trail skirts the lava flow that separates Paulina Lake from East Lake. Keen eyes will notice obsidian in the lava rocks. At 4.2 miles from the trailhead, reach Little Crater Campground. At the day use area here, you can follow a trail up to the top of Little Crater for a view out to East Lake. Otherwise, just follow the paved road through the campground until you locate the resumption of the lakeshore trail. Follow the lakeshore, passing summer cabins and campgrounds, for 2.5 miles back to the trailhead at the day use area.

While you're still here, there are three other fantastic side-trips well worth your time. Begin by driving a half-mile downhill to the Paulina Falls parking lot. Here, one short trail leads to a view across the 80-foot double falls, while another drops 0.2 mile to a viewpoint at the base of the falls. After the falls, drive back to Paulina Lake, and locate the signed trailhead for Big Obsidian Flow. Here, you'll hike a fun 0.8-mile trail through a massive obsidian flow that tumbled down from Paulina Peak's crater just 1,300 years ago. At the top of this fun loop, you'll have a view back across Paulina Lake to Mount Bachelor and South Sister. Watch where you put your hands; the obsidian is so sharp that you may cut yourself, as I accidentally did here.

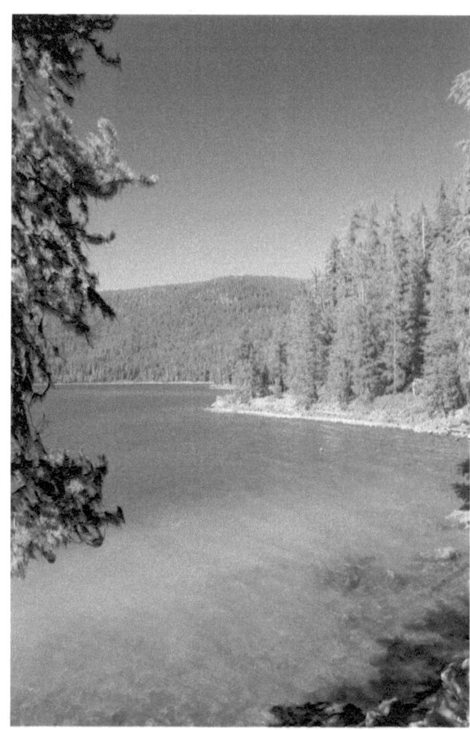

Before you leave the area, save time for a drive up to the summit of Paulina Peak, where you will find some of the most jaw-dropping views in the entire state of Oregon. From a junction near the trailhead day use area, turn uphill and drive 3.9 miles of washboard gravel to the summit of Paulina Peak, where you'll find a privy and a large parking area. The view up here stretches across the entire state of Oregon, from Mount Adams in Washington to Mount Shasta in California, and across Oregon's high desert for many miles to the east. The best photo lighting here is at sunrise and sunset but prepare for the icy winds that sweep across the mountain's 7,984 foot summit. Bring a thermos of coffee or hot cocoa and prepare to be amazed!

96. Fort Rock and Crack In The Ground

	Fort Rock	Crack in the Ground
Distance:	1.2 mile loop	3.6 miles out and back
Elevation Gain:	185 feet	112 feet
Trailhead Elevation:	4,354 feet	4,482 feet
Trail High Point:	4,536 feet	4,485 feet
Season:	all year	all year
Best:	March - May, October	March - May, October
Pass:	none needed	none needed
On the traditional lands of:	the Yahooskin people	the Yahooskin people

Directions from Bend:

- From Bend, drive south on US 97 for 31 miles to a junction with OR 31 just after LaPine.
- Turn left and drive 28.8 miles to a sign on the left for Fort Rock and Christmas Valley. You can see Fort Rock on the horizon.
- Turn left here and drive 6.2 miles to the town of Fort Rock.
- Turn left and drive 1 mile to a junction, signed for the state park. Turn left here.
- Drive 0.7 mile to the Fort Rock entrance on the right. Park in the trailhead lot.
- **Drivetime from Bend:** 70 minutes to Fort Rock

Hiking around Fort Rock.

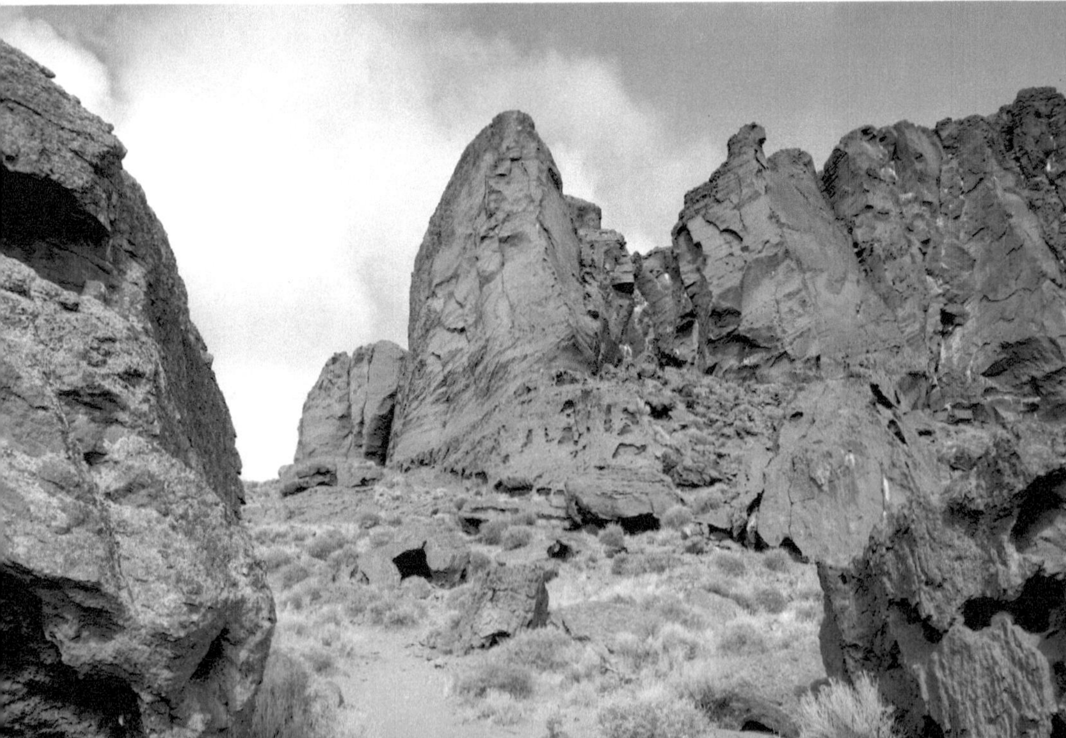

Note: As these are both short hikes in which it would be very difficult to get lost, no map is provided here. A good road map of this part of Oregon is very helpful, though.

Fort Rock Hike: Fort Rock is fascinating and beautiful, and pictures do not do it justice. Located far out in Oregon's outback, this huge horseshoe-shaped rock appears on the horizon like the Oregonian equivalent of Australia's famed Ayers Rock. Fort Rock has a history of human habitation going back thousands of years. Sandals found in a cave in this area date back nearly 10,000 years, and are some of the oldest ever found. This is an interesting thought to contemplate when you visit Fort Rock, as this place is now among the most remote in the state of Oregon. The outside edge of Fort Rock's rim is closed from February 1 to August 31 to protect nesting eagles.

The trail network leads you around the interior of the rim of Fort Rock, with side trails to viewpoints and outcrops. In general, you can go anywhere you please. The main loop here follows the interior for 1.2 miles. The exterior of Fort Rock can be explored on a rough loop between September 1 and January 31. This loop is quite fun but can only really be done in the fall, as this area can be quite cold and windy in the winter. When you're finished with Fort Rock, it's time to head east to Crack In The Ground.

Crack In The Ground directions:

- From Fort Rock, return to Fort Rock Village and turn left.
- Follow signs for 26 miles to the small town of Christmas Valley.
- At the far end of Christmas Valley, turn left at a sign for Crack In The Ground. This junction is 27.5 miles from the Fort Rock junction.
- Drive 7.1 miles to the unmarked trailhead on the left, complete with pit toilet.
- The trail departs from the opposite side of the road at a post and signboard.
- **Drivetime from Bend:** 130 minutes to Crack in the Ground.

Crack In The Ground Hike: A fissure in the ground far out in the Oregon Outback, Crack In The Ground is an intriguing location. Earthquakes and volcanic activity in this area formed the crack, and you'll enjoy hiking at the bottom of this narrow chasm. Unless you live in Christmas Valley it's a long drive for everyone, but anyone who loves exploring a unique piece of Oregon's geological past will love this hike.

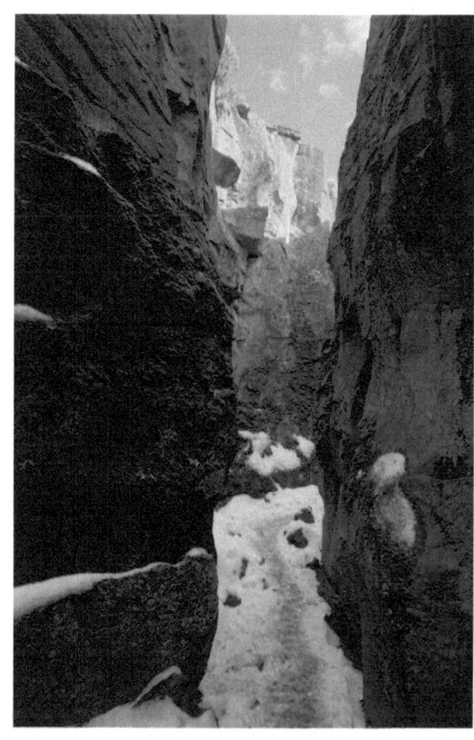

Begin by following the wide dirt trail to a picnic table at the entrance to the Crack. Before you go in, take a look at the other crack on the opposite side of the trail, a dangerous and deep chasm that should not be explored without climbing gear. Follow the obvious trail down into the Crack, which narrows to a few feet wide. Snow lingers here well into spring, and it feels downright cold here for much of the year. You will exit the Crack after only 0.3 mile. Many hikers will want to turn around here, but adventurous hikers can and should continue on a longer hike.

The Crack does continue for another 1.5 miles, with trails dipping down into the fissure and back out. Social trails follow the top of the Crack, offering loop possibilities. Both the trail and fissure end (at least the explorable part) end at 1.8 miles. Return the way you came, remembering to duck into the deepest, most popular part of the Crack one more time before you return to the trailhead.

97. Hager Mountain

Distance: 7.8 miles out and back
Elevation Gain: 2,000 feet
Trailhead elevation: 5,194 feet
Trail high Point: 7,187 feet
Season: all year (bring snowshoes in winter)
Best: May – June
Pass: none needed
On the traditional lands of: the Yahooskin and Klamath peoples

Directions:

- From LaPine, drive south for 2 miles to a turnoff on the left for OR 31.
- Drive southeast through Oregon's Outback for 46.4 miles.
- Just after the Silver Lake Ranger Station but before you enter the small town of Silver Lake, turn right onto East Bay Road. This road soon becomes FR 28.
- Drive 8.8 miles southeast on this road to a pullout on the left side of the road at a sign for the Hager Trail.
- The trail begins at a signboard.
- **Drivetime from LaPine:** 60 minutes

Hike: Located considerably east of the Cascades, Hager Mountain seems like it wandered off into the desert and stayed there. This hike resembles many hikes on the eastern slopes of the Cascades, but offers views from Mount Jefferson to Mount Shasta, and out into Oregon's high desert. A lookout tower at the summit can be rented during the winter and spring months, and arrows guide hikers to the summit even in the depths of winter. While this would be a beautiful winter adventure, the best time to do this hike is in May and June, when wildflowers grace the slopes of Hager Mountain and the skies are at their bluest.

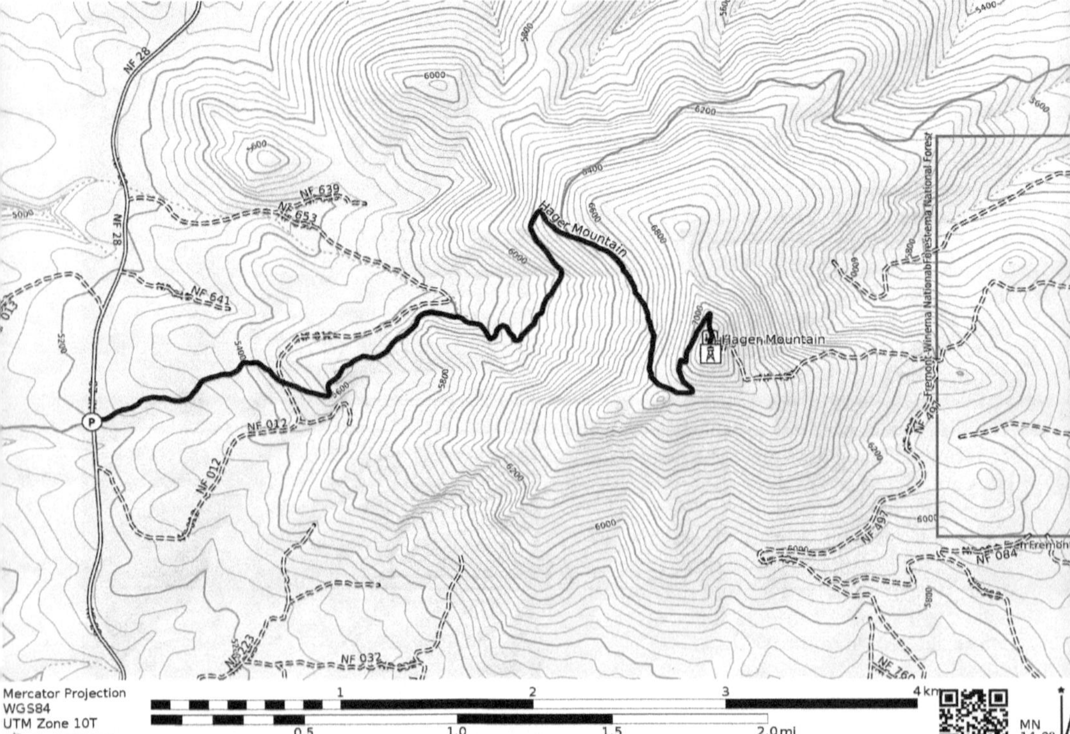

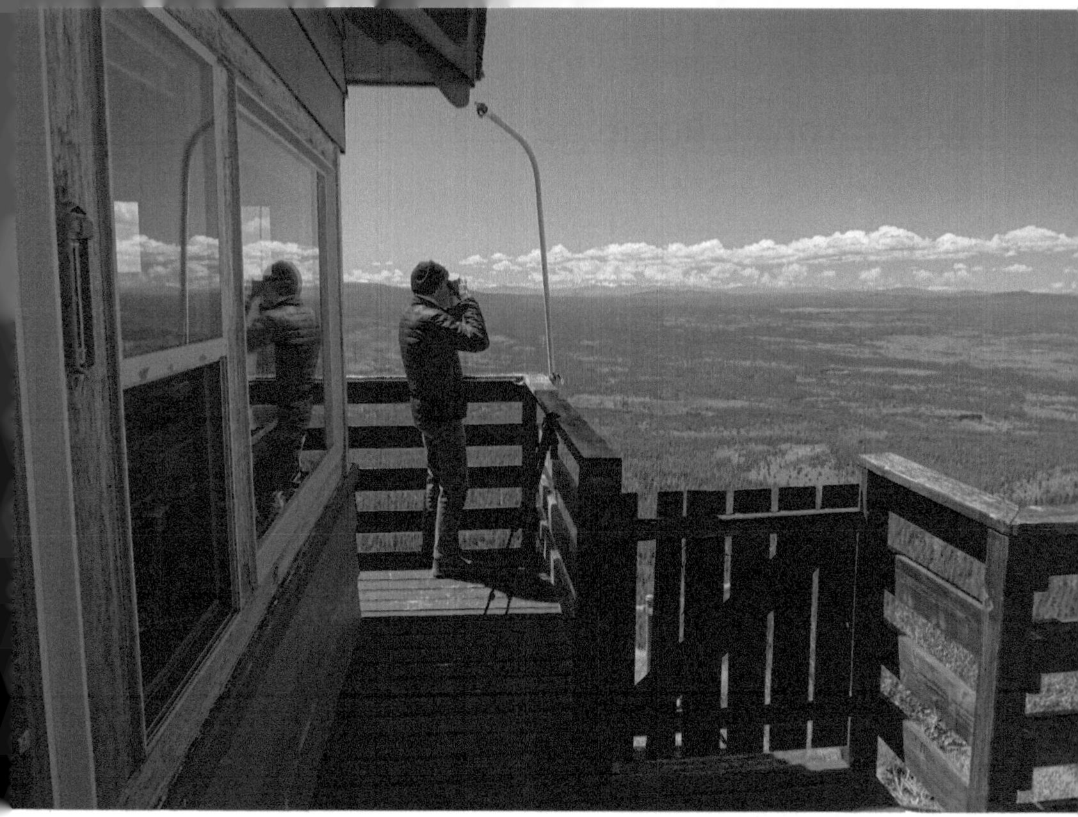

One could spend hours scanning the horizon at Hager Mountain Lookout.

Begin at the signboard and climb gradually through open Ponderosa pine forest with views ahead to the summit of Hager Mountain. Look for blue larkspur and lupine, red paintbrush, and many other spring flowers. After 0.7 mile the trail crosses a gravel road, offering a way to shorten the hike if so desired. You'll continue straight as the trail begins to climb more strenuously. Blue arrows on the trees above guide the way in winter and help keep hikers oriented. At 1.5 miles, you'll reach a junction with the Farm Well Trail on your left. Keep right and continue climbing through the deep woods.

The trail leaves the woods at 2.4 miles, where the trail switchbacks back to the south towards the summit of Hager Mountain. Pass a junction with the Fremont Trail at 2.7 miles and continue climbing steeply as the trail switchbacks around the slopes just below the summit. At 3.8 miles, the trail ends at a picnic table and dirt road just below the summit. Follow a trail uphill past the pit toilet to the lookout at the summit of Hager Mountain. The views are massive! Cascade peaks from Mount Jefferson to Mount Shasta line the western horizon. To the north, look for Newberry Crater's huge volcano (Hike 95), with Fort Rock (see Hike 96) sticking out of the ground like a rotten tooth. To the east, the view stretches far into the Oregon Outback's high desert. With such a view like this, it's no surprise that there's a lookout here. The lookout is staffed during the summer, and you should leave the staffer alone unless they come out to speak to you.

The lookout is available to reserve from November 15 to May 15. To make a reservation, visit www.recreation.gov six months before you want to stay, and make sure that you are on the website at 7AM sharp (Pacific Time) to reserve the lookout. As with all other reservable lookout towers, you should expect lots of competition. Weekdays are easier to reserve than weekends.

Unless you're spending the night or the week up here, return the way you came.

98. Chimney Rock

Distance: 2.8 miles out and back
Elevation Gain: 600 feet
Trailhead Elevation: 3,038 feet
Trail High Point: 3,604 feet
Season: all year except in winter storms
Best: May – June
Pass: none needed
On the traditional lands of: the Confederated tribes of the Warm Springs

Directions from Prineville:

- From downtown Prineville, turn right at the junction of US 26 / 126 onto Main Street, which is also OR 27.
- Drive 16.3 miles on this curvy, winding, and incredibly scenic highway following the Crooked River to the Chimney Rock Trailhead, on the left side of the road, just beyond Chimney Rock Campground.
- **Drivetime from Prineville:** 25 minutes

Hike: Following the Crooked River south from Prineville, the high desert scenery just gets better and better. The canyon walls rise and the air comes alive with the pungent aromas of juniper and sage. As you drive along, you'll pass several lovely campgrounds on your way to Chimney Rock, the scenic apex of the Crooked River canyon. Any time of year is a good time to visit but this area is never more beautiful than in May and June, when the canyon walls are green and covered in flowers and the weather mild.

Locate the Chimney Rock Trail departing from the left side of the small trailhead lot, opposite the signboard. You will switchback uphill and away from the road until the trail crosses a small gully. The trail then follows this gully uphill amid many gnarled, twisted juniper trees. At a

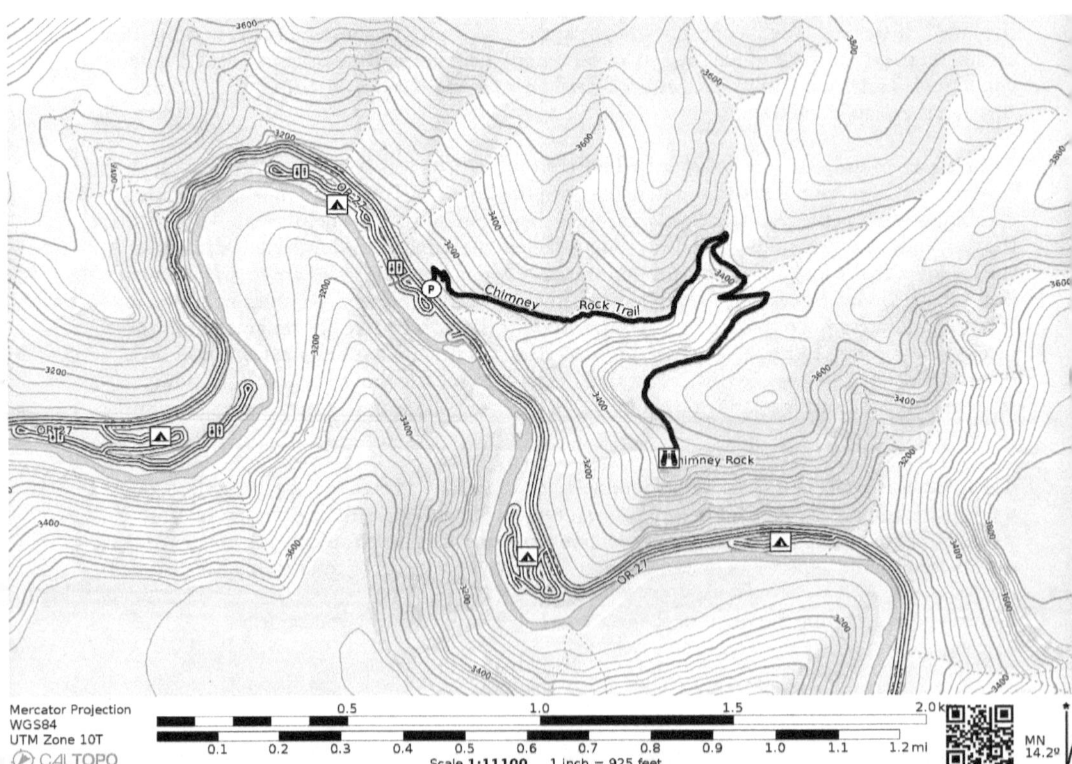

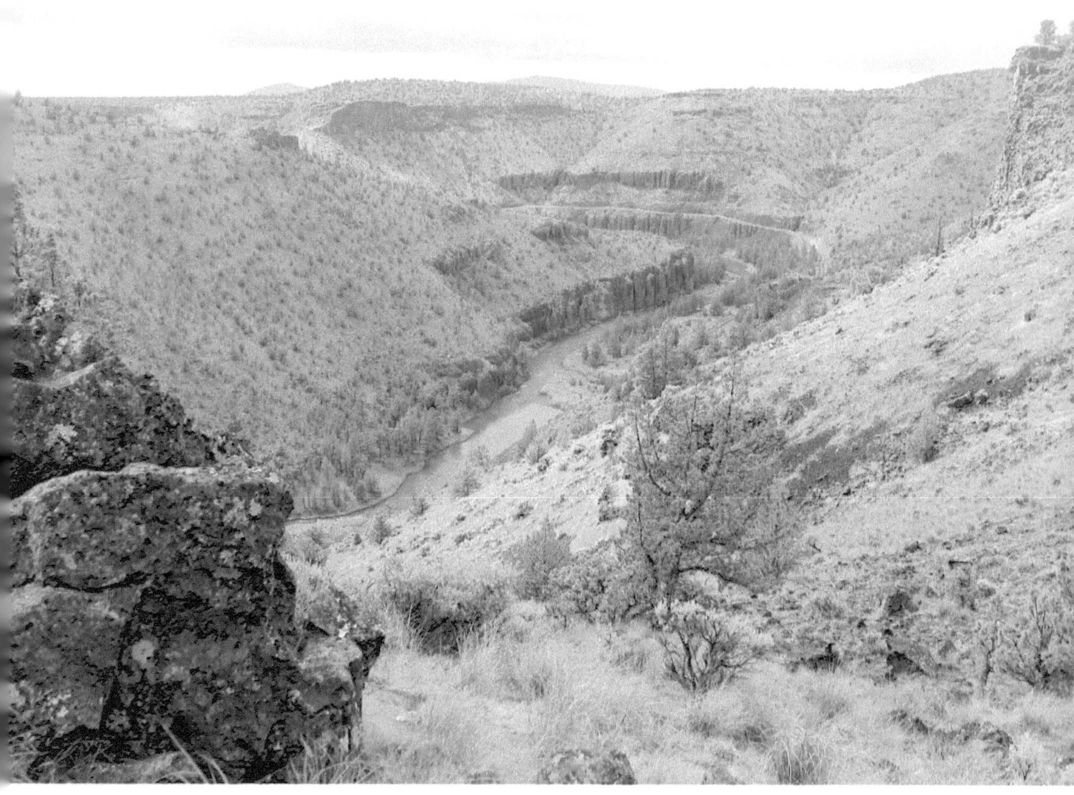

Looking down into the Crooked River Canyon from near Chimney Rock.

property boundary, the trail switchbacks uphill and soon crosses another gully just above a dry waterfall. The High Cascades begin to come into view here. First you will see Mount Bachelor, then Broken Top, then all Three Sisters, looming on the western horizon. A few more switchbacks lead you to the ridgetop, where the trail mellows out. From here, you'll hike across a rocky plateau with great views down to the Crooked River Canyon. White and pink bitterroot blooms line the trail in May and June. Native to the Oregon high desert, bitteroot (*Lewisia rediviva*) is an edible plant that tribes all over the west prized for its fleshy, even starchy texture. This may be the best place in Oregon to find this beautiful flower.

After ten minutes or so of hiking along this ridgetop, the trail rounds a corner and Chimney Rock comes into view at last. Follow the trail to the base of the rock at 1.4 miles from the traulhead, where a wooden bench invites a nice stop. The views down into the Crooked River canyon are excellent here, and it's fun to scramble around the base of this 30-foot rock. The trail ends here, alas, so you'll have to return the way you came.

While the Chimney Peak hike is less than 3 miles round-trip, you could easily spend a day exploring the beautiful canyon of the Crooked River. As you drive south from Prineville, you will pass a number of fantastic campgrounds with river access. All of these would make an excellent place to spend an evening or weekend, should you wish. The wonderful scenery continues as you drive south beyond the Chimney Rock Trailhead. You'll reach Bowman Dam at the head of Prineville Reservoir just 3.3 miles south of the trailhead. If you drove here from Prineville, you can return the way you came. If you drove here from Bend, you can continue south another 3.1 miles to a junction with Reservoir Road on the right. Turn right here and follow this road as it changes names several times, and passes through the small community of Willard, eventually reaching the outskirts of Bend some 28 miles from the junction on OR 27.

99. Steins Pillar

Distance: 4.2 miles out and back
Elevation Gain: 800 feet
Trailhead Elevation: 4,295 feet
Trail High Point: 4,572 feet
Season: all year except in winter storms
Best: May – June
Pass: none needed
On the traditional lands of: the Confederated tribes of the Warm Springs, and Nüümü (Northern Paiute) people

Directions from Prineville:

- From the junction of US 26 and Main Street, drive east on US 26 for 9.2 miles.
- Just after milepost 28 at the far end of the reservoir, turn left on Mill Creek Road.
- Drive 5 miles of 2-lane pavement on Mill Creek Road until the road enters the Ochoco National Forest and becomes gravel.
- Continue another 1.6 miles on Mill Creek Road to a junction with FR 500 at a sign for the Steins Pillar Trailhead.
- Turn right and drive 2 miles of narrow, rocky gravel road to the trailhead on the left side of the road.
- **Drivetime from Prineville:** 30 minutes

Hike: Hidden in the mountains north of Prineville is Steins Pillar, one of Oregon's most extraordinary rock pinnacles. This free-standing pillar is the remnant of an exposed volcanic plug from a larger volcano in the area, and to see it closely boggles the mind. This fun hike rambles over a forested ridgetop to the base of the pinnacle, where you can have a lot of fun exploring

Steins Pillar rises 350 feet above the surrounding terrain.

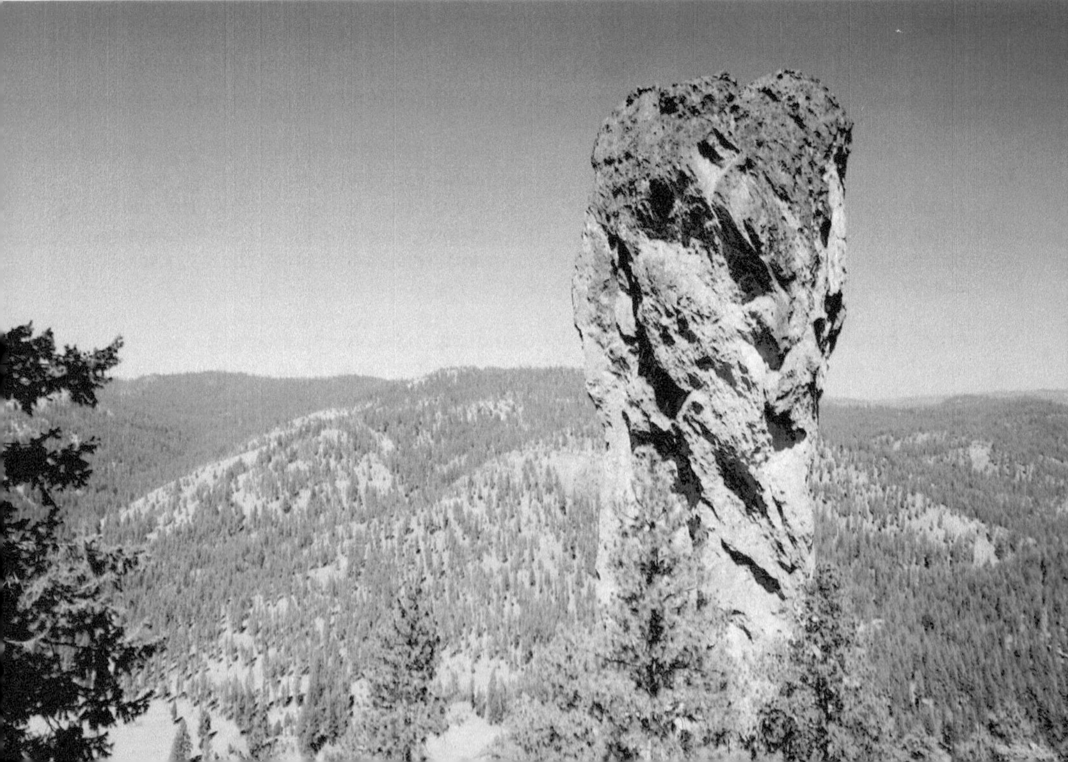

and climbing, if you are adequately equipped and so inclined. The pillar was named after Major Enoch Steen, who explored the area in the 1860s and after whom Steens Mountain is also named. It is for this reason that Steins Pillar is pronounced "steens" and not "steins", as the name would suggest.

Begin at the trailhead sign and signboard. You'll cross over a small spring and climb gradually amid junipers and ponderosa pines to a dusty ridgetop with views west to the Cascades. Along this stretch of trail you'll see lots of spring wildflowers, among them balsamroot, lupine, paintbrush, and many others. Cross a prairie and reach a junction with a short side trail that leads to your first view of Steins Pillar in the valley below. Take a moment to check out the view before returning to the main trail. The trail then descends for approximately a mile to the base of the pillar at just over 2 miles from the trailhead. Pictures do not do the pillar justice, as it rises above the surrounding forest in a most extraordinary way. You'll have lots of fun exploring the area around the trail, and a rocky overhang makes for a nice and shady place to stop for lunch on even the warmest days. Whenever you're ready to go, return the way you came.

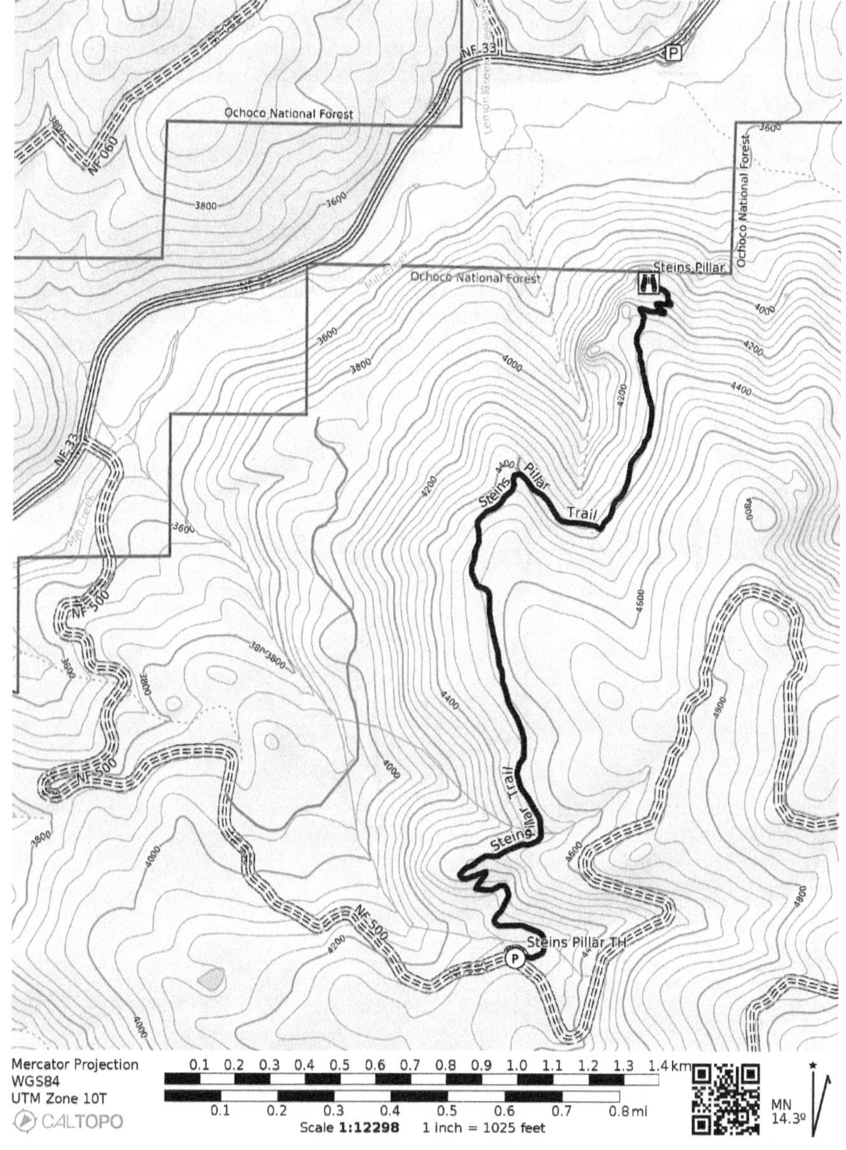

100. Sutton Mountain

Distance: 7.6 miles out and back
Elevation Gain: 1,700 feet
Trailhead Elevation: 3,071 feet
Trail High Point: 4,693 feet
Season: all year except in winter storms
Best: May – June
Pass: none needed
On the traditional lands of: the Confederated tribes of the Warm Springs, and the Tenino and Nüümü (Northern Paiute) peoples

Directions from Prineville:

- From Prineville, drive 47 miles east over the Ochoco crest to a junction with OR 207 just before you reach Mitchell.
- Turn left and drive 9.2 miles to a sudden and obscure junction with a dirt road on your left in the middle of a curve. This road is very easy to miss, so you'll have to pay attention. If you miss the turnoff and reach Girds Creek Road, turn around and drive 0.4 mile to the trailhead road on your right, right before milepost 15.
- Turn left here and drive to a wire fence. Open the fence, drive through it, and then close it behind you. Park in the grassy pasture by the road. This is the trailhead!
- **Drivetime from Prineville:** 60 minutes

Hike: Sutton Mountain rises above the Painted Hills and John Day River, marking the horizon for miles in every direction. Unsurprisingly, the views from the summit are excellent, stretching across this part of Oregon's high desert to the volcanoes of the Cascades. This hike to the dual summits of Sutton Mountain is immensely fun, passing lots of spring wildflowers and high desert scenery worthy of a postcard. Finding the trailhead can be an irritating experience (see the directions above), but as soon you hit the trail you'll be all smiles.

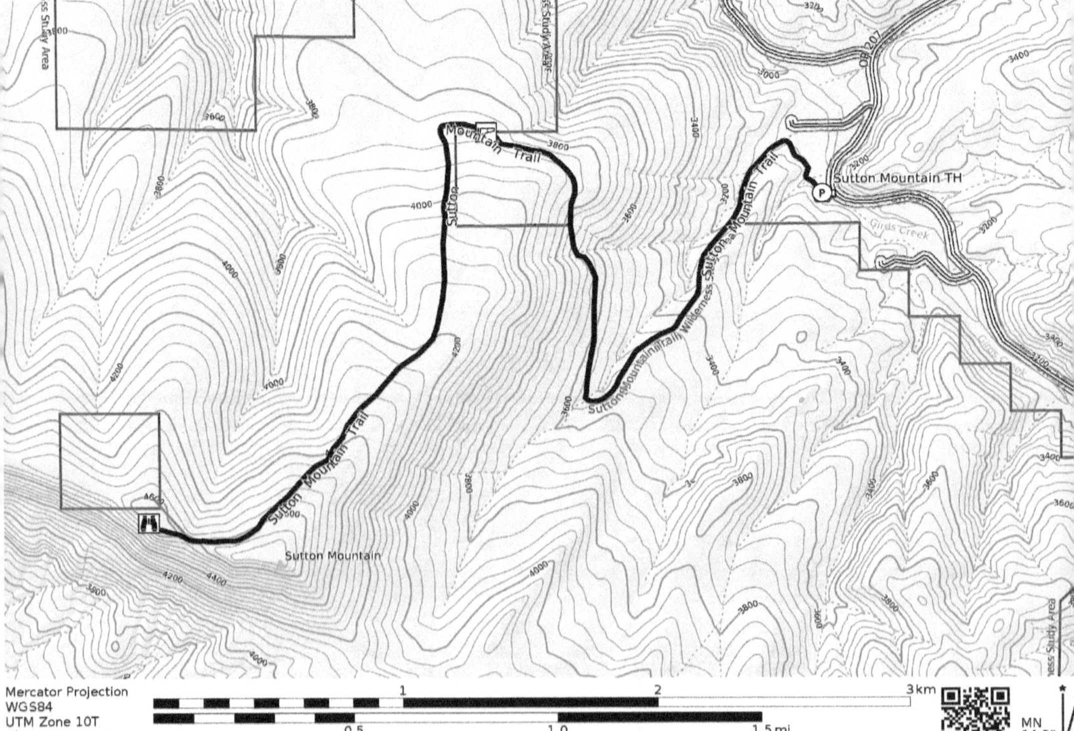

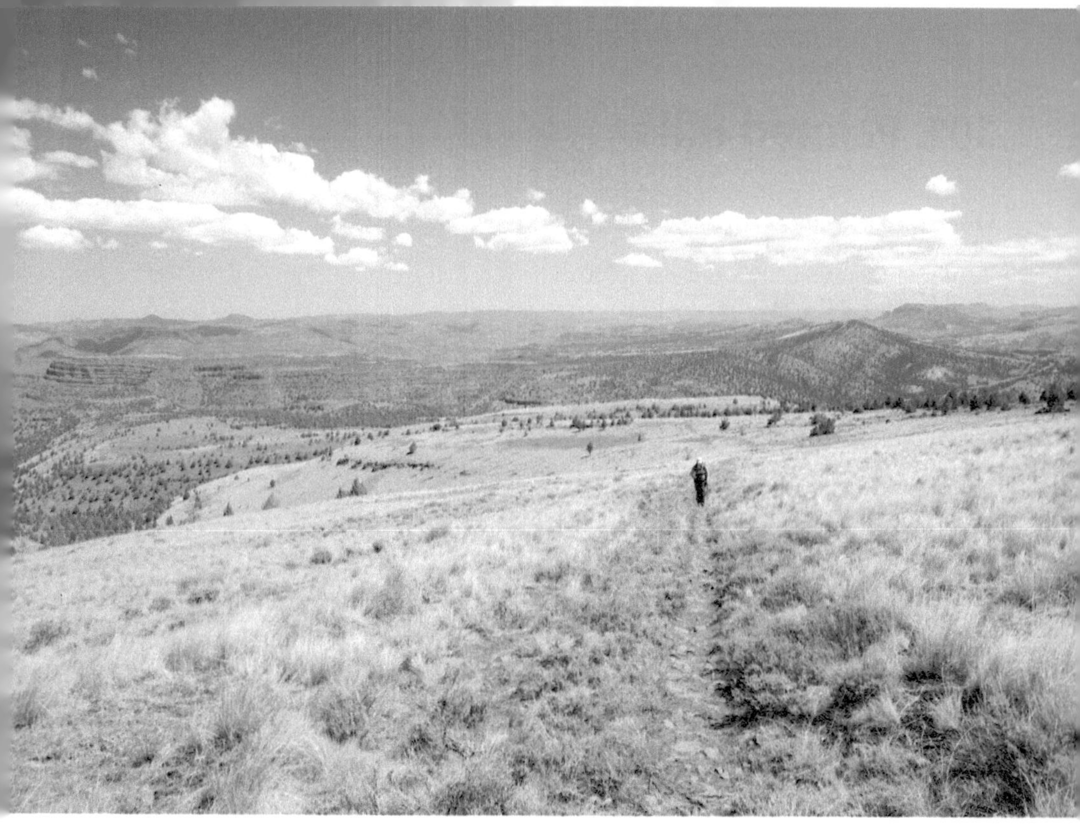

Climbing Sutton Mountain on a beautiful day

Once you've located the trailhead, the rest of the hike is easy to navigate. Follow the old road uphill from the trailhead amid junipers. You may encounter cattle on this hike, so be sure to keep your distance and be willing to detour around them if needed. After 1.4 miles or so, the road curves around a gully and begins to climb more. Look for lupine and yellow paintbrush here in the spring. Along the way, you'll pass into a small parcel of private property, so stay on the road as much as possible.

At 2 miles, you'll reach a ridge crest where views open up to the tip of Mount Hood and across the canyonlands to the north. Continue another half-mile of level road to a fenced gate. Open the gate and close it behind you, and then look for the road continuing steeply uphill to the left. You are now back on public land. Wild onions and purple larkspur grow profusely here in the spring. You may also encounter cattle here, unfortunately. The road climbs along the eastern end of Sutton Mountain to a saddle. The true summit is on the left at the mountain's eastern end, but the better views are found on the western summit. If you come here in April and May, you may also notice the small, vivid pink blooms of hedgehog cactus; blooming cactus are quite rare in Oregon, and this may be the best place to see them. Leave the road at the saddle and scramble a short distance to the western summit of Sutton Mountain. The view from the summit stretches across the Painted Hills and out to Mount Jefferson and Mount Hood on the western horizon. In addition to blooming cactus, you may also see bitterroot, paintbrush, and more wild onion blooming here in the spring. This is a fantastic spot!

If you have more time and energy you can complete the easy scramble to the true summit on the eastern end of Sutton Mountain, where you will find excellent views south and east to the summits of the Ochoco Mountains. The view is not as good as on the western summit, but it is worth the scramble off the trail. Regardless of where you decide to stop, return the way you came.

101. Painted Hills

Distance: 3 miles total (all trails)
Elevation Gain: 600 feet
Trailhead Elevation: approximately 2,000 feet
Trail High Point: 2,441 feet
Season: all year except in winter storms
Best: May – June
Pass: none needed
On the traditional lands of: the Confederated tribes of the Warm Springs, and the Tenino and Nüümü (Northern Paiute) peoples

Directions from Prineville:

- From Prineville, drive 42 miles east over the Ochoco crest to a turnoff on the left signed for the Painted Hills.
- Turn left and drive 5.4 miles to a junction with Bear Creek Road.
- Turn left here and drive 1 mile of gravel to the Painted Hills Overlook on the left. Although there is ample parking, the lot fills on spring and summer weekend days.
- Directions to the other destinations here are listed below.
- **Drivetime from Prineville:** 60 minutes

Hike: On any list of Oregon's most extraordinary and iconic places, the Painted Hills rank near the top. The red, orange, yellow, and black hues on the slopes here are the result of millennia of erosion combined with the mineral composition of the dust and rocks. This is an otherworldly place, and you'll have to contend with scores of tourists, photographers, and sightseers when you visit. Here's a pro tip: The colors are best in the late afternoon and after rains, especially after thunderstorms. Presented here are five short trails to help you make the most of your visit to this most special place.

Painted Overlook Trail: If you've only got time for one trail at the Painted Hills, make it this one. Most of the photos you've ever seen of the Painted Hills were taken here or along the road near this trailhead, and you'll be snapping photos by the dozen here as well. The Painted Overlook Trail departs from the trailhead and leads uphill to spectacular views down and into the Painted Hills. As with everywhere else in this extremely fragile area, stay on the trail and keep

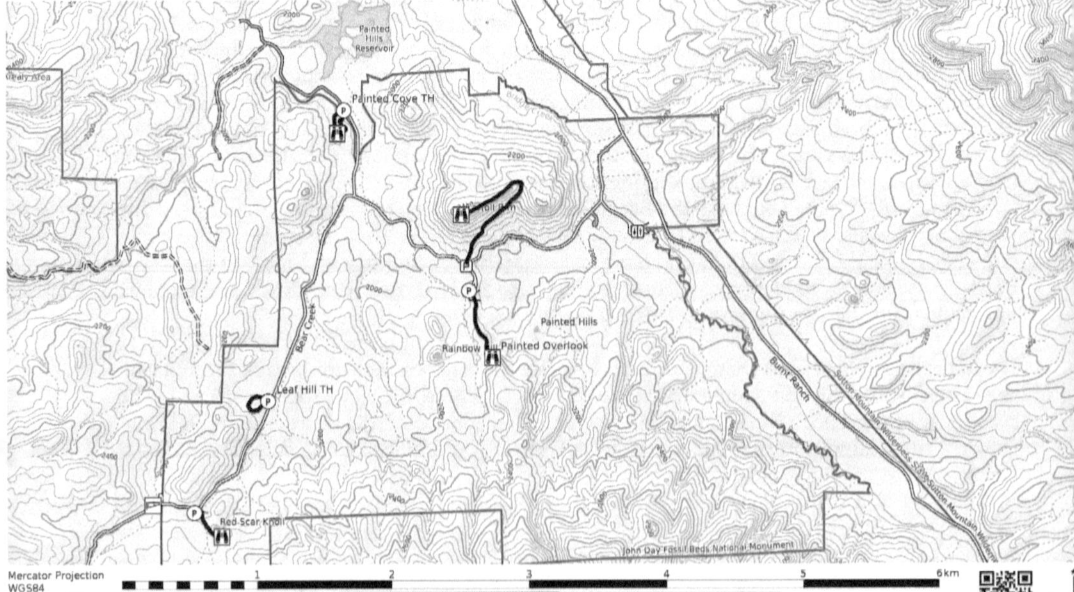

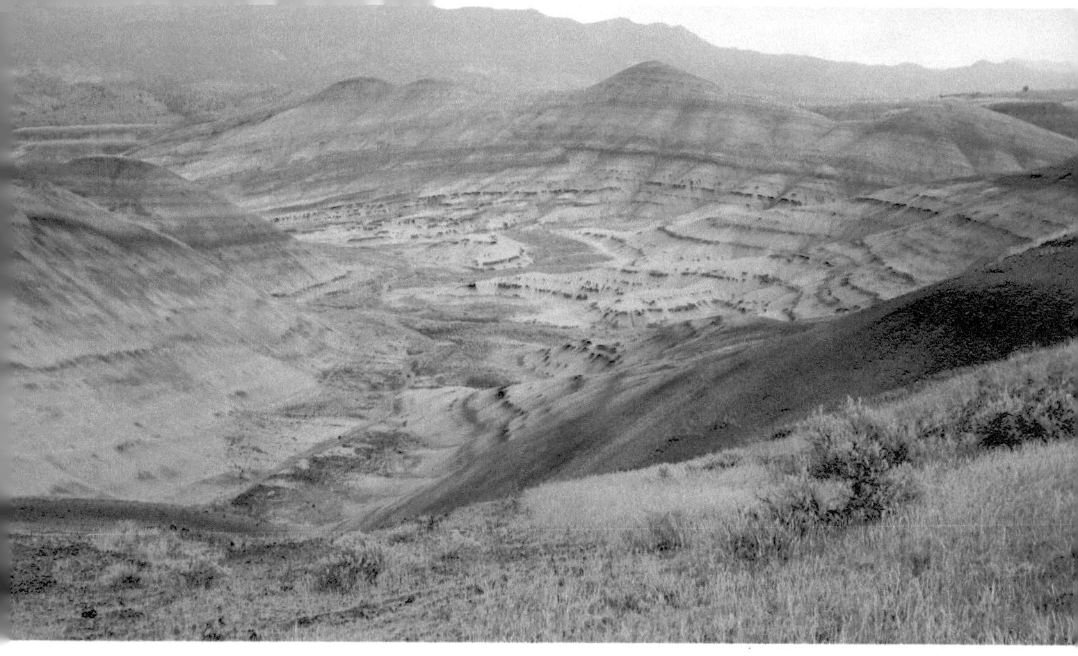

Looking down into the Painted Hills from the Overlook Trail.

your dogs on leash. The trail ends at a overlook at 0.3 mile. Return the way you came.

Carroll Rim: Located across the road from the Painted Overlook Trail, the Carroll Rim Trail leads uphill 0.8 mile to an overlook of the Painted Hills, gaining almost 400 feet along the way. At 1.6 miles out and back, this is the longest and most difficult trail in the Painted Hills area. It may be tempting to skip this trail in favor of some of the other, easier trails listed below, but trail gives you a wider view of the Painted Hills than any other.

Painted Cove: This short but beautiful trail curves around a hill that is a deep shade of red more reminiscent of Mars than of Oregon. Although this loop is only 0.3 mile in total, you'll probably take more photos here than anywhere else in the Painted Hills area. To find the Painted Cove Trail, drive beyond the Painted Hills Overlook 0.6 mile to a junction. Turn right here and drive 0.4 mile to a parking area signed only as "Nature Trail". In May and June, bitterroot grows all around the parking area at the trailhead.

Leaf Hill: You might wonder while you're visiting the Painted Hills area just where the fossils are; you are, after all, visiting the John Day Fossil Beds. While the other two units of the monument contain the most obvious and accessible fossil displays, the Leaf Hill Trail is a veritable goldmine for fossils. Over 2,000 different fossil specimens have been found here in this small area, believe it or not! Keep that in mind while you hike this short and not very scenic quarter-mile loop around Leaf Hill. To find the Leaf Hill Trail, drive back from the Painted Cove Trail 0.4 mile to the last road junction and turn right. Drive this excellent gravel road to Leaf Hill's small parking lot.

Red Scar Knoll: Last but definitely not least, the Red Scar Knoll Trail is like a small combination of the Painted Cove and Painted Overlook Trails, leading to several different perspectives of a red, orange, and pink hill known as Red Scar Knoll. From the trailhead, the trail crosses a bridge and forks. Left leads to a view of the knoll from below, while right leads up and around the knoll. Take the time to investigate both. The trail up and over the knoll dead ends at a view of the backside of the knoll at 0.25 mile, at a vantage where bitterroot blooms profusely in late spring. Although unsigned and tucked away at the far end of the Painted Hills area, this trail is absolutely worth your time! To locate the Red Scar Knoll Trail, drive to the Leaf Hill Trail and continue another 0.6 mile on Bear Creek Road to a turnaround on the left side of the road. The road is gated closed due to private property just beyond the trailhead, so you won't miss it – nor should you!

102. Blue Basin

Distance: 4.2 mile loop
Elevation Gain: 1,000 feet
Trailhead Elevation: 2,137 feet
Trail High Point: 2,904 feet
Season: all year except in winter storms
Best: March – June
Pass: none needed
On the traditional lands of: the Nüümü (Northern Paiute) people

Directions from Mitchell:

- Assuming that you are combining a visit to this area from the Painted Hills unit of the John Day Fossil Beds, the directions here are from Mitchell. If you're driving here from Prineville, drive US 26 east for 46 miles to Mitchell, then follow the directions below.
- From Mitchell, drive east on US 26 for 31 miles to a junction with OR 19 on the left, signed for Kimberly. If you're coming from John Day, drive 38 miles west on US 26 to this junction.
- Turn left on OR 19 and drive 5.1 miles to the Blue Basin turnoff on the left.
- Turn right and drive into the trailhead parking lot.
- **Drivetimes:** 45 minutes from Mitchell, 1 hour and 30 minutes from Prineville, 60 minutes from John Day.

Hike: In a region full of otherworldly places like Crack In The Ground, Newberry Crater, and the Painted Hills, there is perhaps no place more otherworldly than Blue Basin, between Mitchell and John Day. Here, you'll hike above heavily-eroded blue and green hills that are more evocative of some distant planet than anywhere you would typically associate with Oregon. Every Oregonian should visit Blue Basin at least once in a lifetime. The trail into Blue Basin is quite easy, and almost anyone can hike it. If you've got more energy, you can follow a fun loop up and over Blue Basin for excellent views of this most extraordinary place.

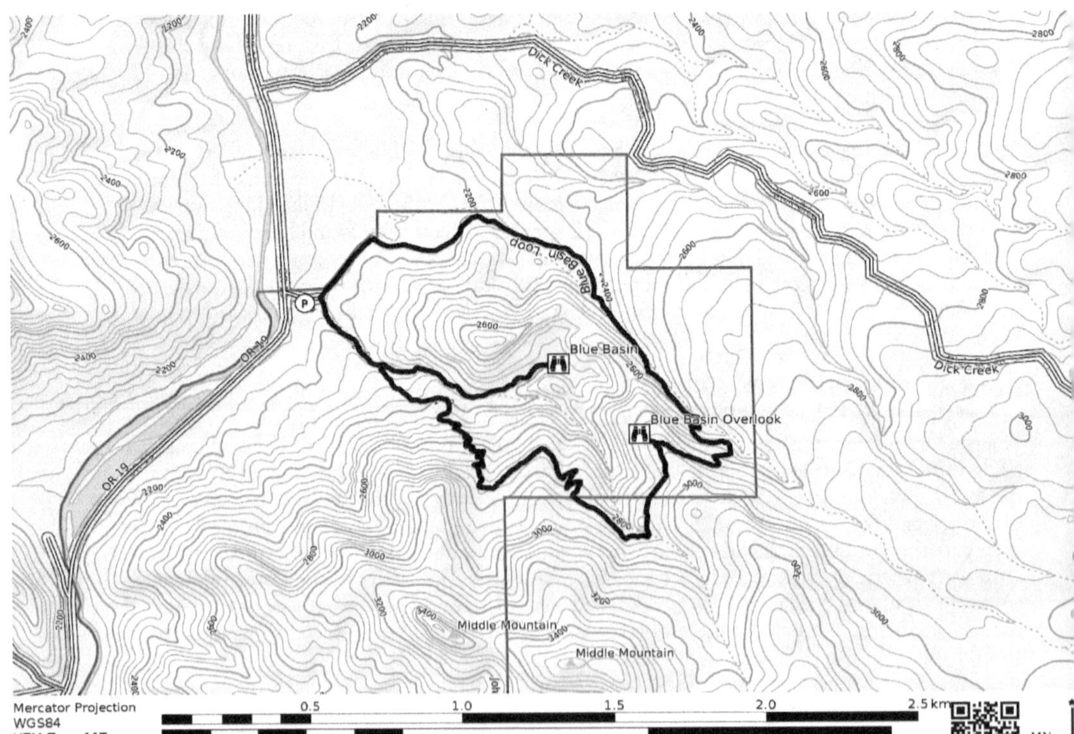

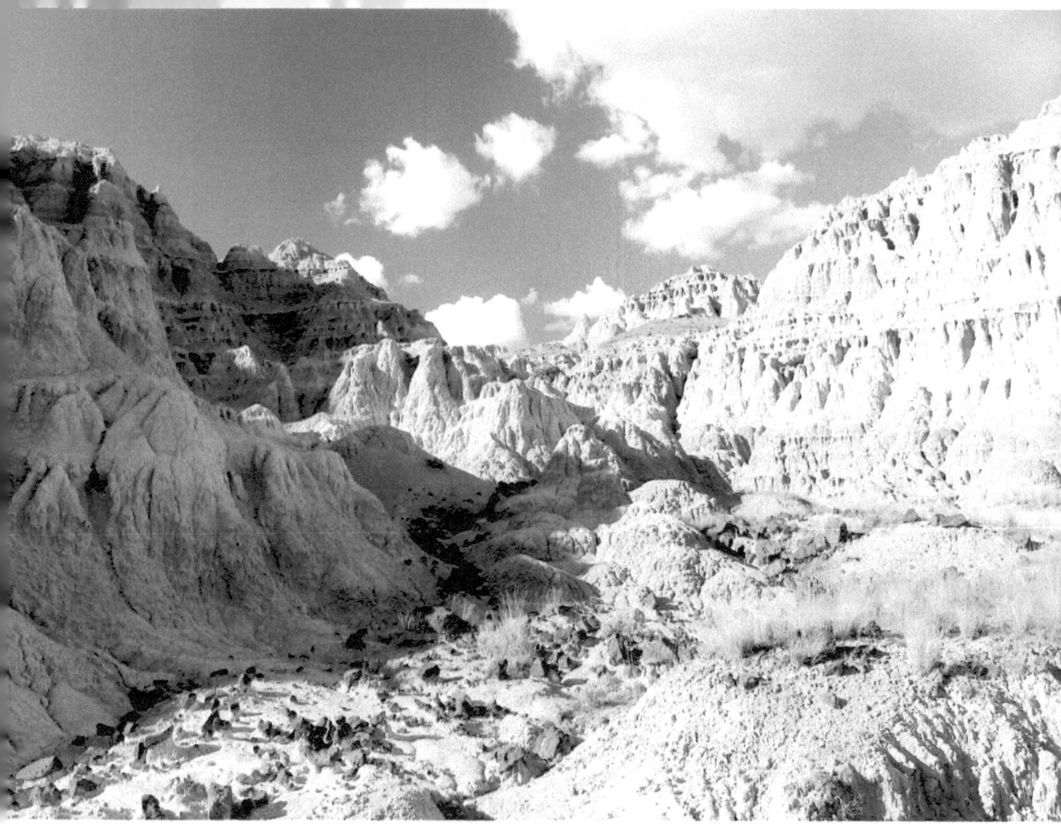

The surreal badlands of Blue Basin in the John Day Fossil Beds.

Starting at the trailhead you are faced with two choices: do you head into Blue Basin itself, or do you begin the loop on and over Blue Basin on the longer hike. For the purposes of this write up we'll head into Blue Basin first, saving the loop for later. From the trailhead, follow the Blue Basin Trail for 0.2 mile to a fork with the longer loop. Keep left and hike the trail into the basin. Along the way, you'll pass a number of fossils and take in every shade of blue and green imaginable. A visit on a rainy day is even more remarkable, as the creek here comes to life with pistachio-colored water, something that must be seen to be believed. Signs along the way explain how this came to be, a result of volcanic activity to the west. You'll pass a number of fossils encased in plexiglass (most are replicas) as well as a number of side trails that lead to different viewpoints of this fascinating place. The trail ends at 0.7 mile in huge, surreal basin of striated electric blue and green cliffs. As with everywhere here, it is imperative that you stay on the trail to help keep this place pristine.

When you're ready for the longer loop, return to the junction 0.2 mile from the trailhead and turn left. The loop trail climbs the slopes above Blue Basin, passing many spectacular views down into the basin. Along the way you'll also pass a number of wooden benches that offer winded hikers a place to stop and catch their breath. At 3 miles from the trailhead, you'll begin descending into Turtle Cove. From here, follow the trail back to the trailhead at 4.2 miles. There's nowhere else in Oregon quite like Blue Basin, and it is so extraordinary that you may be tempted to go hike it again.

If you're curious to know more about this area, be sure to stop at the Thomas Condon Visitor Center, located 3.4 miles south of the Blue Basin Trailhead and 2 miles north of the junction with US 26. Here you can see hundreds of fossil specimens, watch a 20 minute park orientation film, and learn as much as you could possibly want to know about all three units of the John Day Fossil Beds.

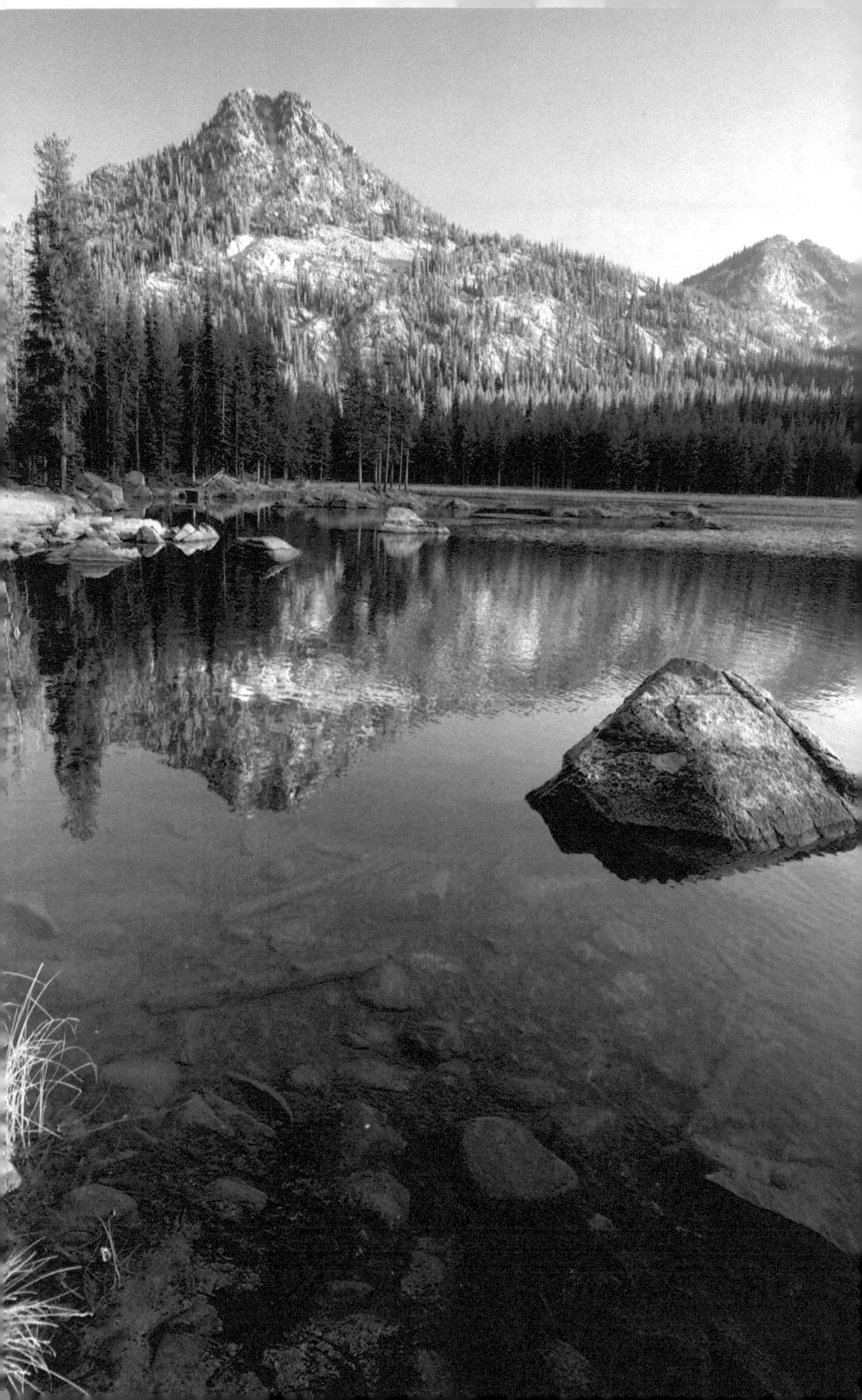

Northeast Oregon

		Distance	EV Gain	Page
103.	North Fork John Day Wilderness	5.6 mi	600 ft	240
104.	Anthony Lake and the Elkhorn Crest	10.8 mi	2,200 ft	242
105.	Twin Lakes and Rock Creek Butte	11.4 mi	2,900 ft	244
106.	Zumwalt Prairie	7.4 mi	1,354 ft	246
107.	Buckhorn Lookout & Eureka Wagon Trail	7.6 mi	1,900 ft	248
108.	Hat Point	1.2 mi	300 ft	250
109.	Summit Ridge via Freezeout Saddle	12.4 mi	3,400 ft	252
110.	BC Falls	2.6 mi	400 ft	254
111.	Ice Lake	16 mi	3,400 ft	256
112.	Hurricane Creek	6.4 mi	1,000 ft	258
113.	Mirror Lake	15.6 mi	2,400 ft	260
114.	Bonny Lakes and Dollar Lake	12 mi	2,200 ft	262
115.	Imnaha Divide	8.6 mi	1,700 ft	264
116.	Summit Point and Pine Lakes Pass	11.6 mi	2,600 ft	266

Northeast Oregon is a land of extremes. Here you have Oregon's highest concentration of tall peaks and two of Oregon's deepest canyons. The Eagle Cap Wilderness is the largest wilderness area in the state, while Hells Canyon is the deepest river gorge in North America; both are worlds unto themselves. Further to the west, the North Fork John Day Wilderness and the Elkhorn Crest are the land of abandoned cabins, mines quiet mountain lakes, and deep forest that are attractive to explore in any season.

The largest caveat to exploring northeast Oregon is that this is an area best explored on extended backpacking trips. Nearly every hike in this section connects to larger trail networks that beckon you deeper into the vast wilderness areas where they are located. This is a guidebook for day hikes, but with a good map, you can use this book to help you create extended adventures of your own. With the Wallowas and Hells Canyon, your itinerary should be limited only by your fitness, preparation, and imagination. Every hike in this section can neverthelsess be completed in one day, and there are even a handful of easy hikes for those days when you don't feel like hiking deep into the wilderness. Many of these hikes also have wonderful short options.

Before you go anywhere, make sure you are as prepared as possible. This is especially important before you visit Hells Canyon, one of the most remote and unforgiving places in Oregon. Always make sure your gas tank is full and that your tires are fully inflated. For more tips to help you prepare for your adventures, see the introduction to this book.

Photo on left: Anthony Lake at dusk (Hike 104)

103. North Fork John Day River

Distance: 5.6 miles out and back
Elevation Gain: 600 feet
Trailhead elevation: 5,192 feet
Trail high point: 5,192 feet
Season: May – October
Best: June – October
Pass: none needed
On the traditional lands of: the Confederated tribes of the Warm Springs

Directions from Baker City:

- There are a variety of ways to get to this trailhead, but the benefit of taking the route described below is the opportunity to explore the beautiful North Fork John Day valley and small mining towns on the way to the trailhead.
- From Baker City, drive OR 7 west for 25.4 miles to a junction with OR 410. Turn right and drive OR 410 for 3.6 miles to the small town of Sumpter, where the highway becomes Granite Hill Road.
- Continue on Granite Hill Road for 16 miles to the town of Granite, population 40.
- Beyond Granite, the Granite Hill Road becomes FR 73. Drive north on this road 8.5 miles to a junction with FR 52, signed for Ukiah. Turn left here.
- Just after you turn left onto FR 52, turn left again into North Fork John Day Campground. Turn into the campground and drive to its far end, where you will find the trailhead. Park in the areas that are designated for the trailhead.
- **Drivetime from Baker City:** 75 minutes

Hike: Mining was the lifeblood of the John Day River canyon, and in some ways, it remains so. Prospectors scoured the canyons and mountainsides all over this part of Oregon looking for gold. Some struck it rich, but many others struck out. What the prospectors certainly found was

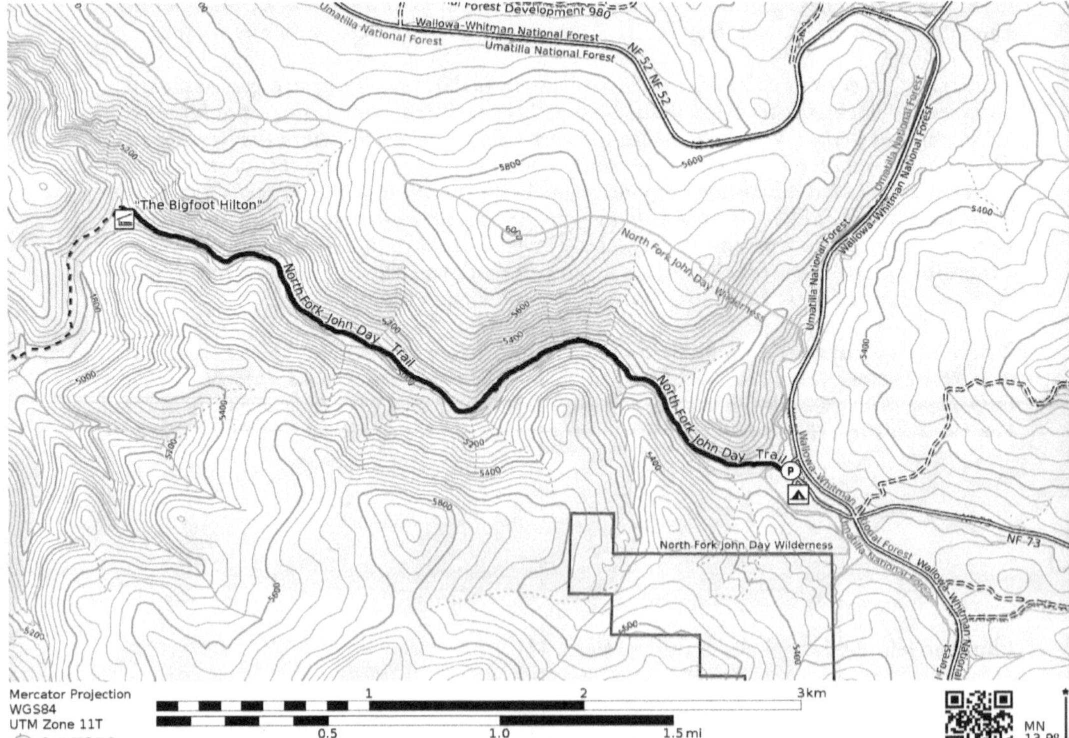

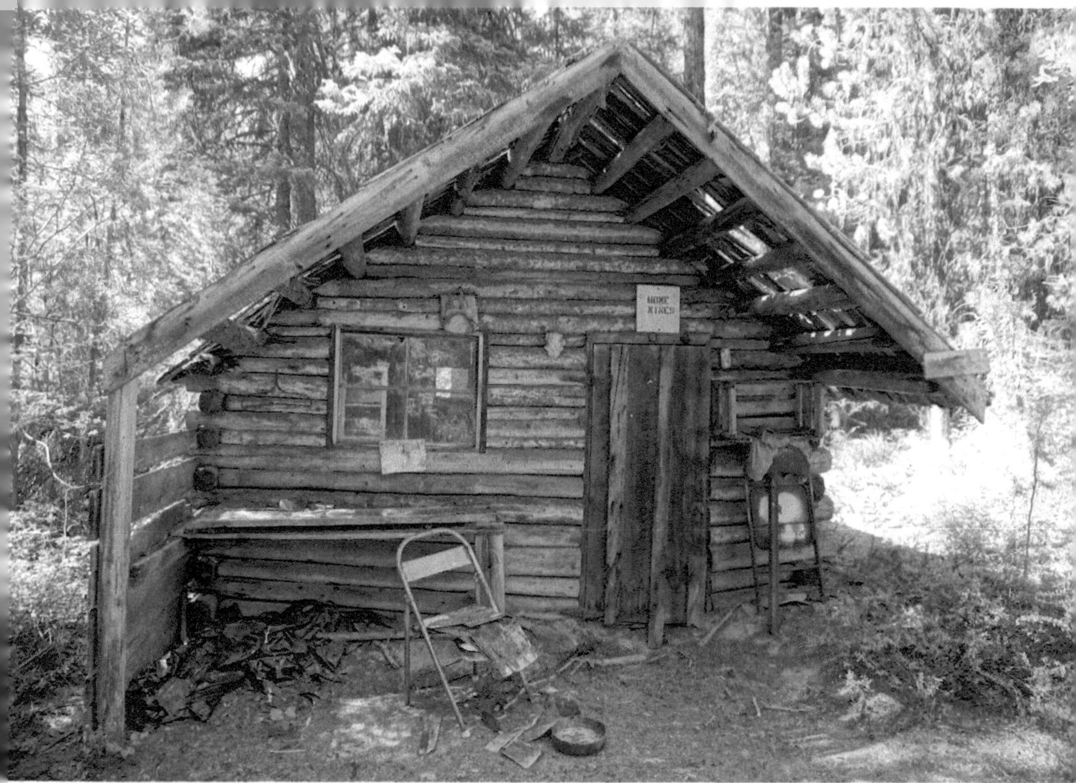

The Home Mines cabin, better known as "The Bigfoot Hilton".

beautiful scenery, and many chose to build cabins in this area to keep digging. You can hardly blame them, as the North Fork John Day River canyon is one of the most beautiful in eastern Oregon. This delightful hike follows the North Fork into the heart of the area's mining country, passing several cabins in a gorgeous rimrock canyon. If you're looking for a fun and beautiful hike, you'll find it here.

From the trailhead signboard, follow the North Fork Trail 100 yards to a fork. Turn right here and cross Trail Creek on a bridge. The trail then proceeds to follow the North Fork down its scenic canyon. Huckleberry bushes line the trail, offering hikers delicious fruit in the summer. In the fall, these bushes turn a brilliant shade of red. Later in the fall, aspens and larch turn various shades of gold and yellow, adding yet more color to the scene. As you hike along, you'll pass a number of mining cabins, all predating the official designation of the North Fork John Day Wilderness in 1984 – meaning that all of them are here legally. Mining does indeed continue on a small scale along the North Fork John Day, and you should adhere to any "No Trespassing" notices you happen to see here. At 2.7 miles, the trail reaches Trout Creek. Do not cross the creek, and instead turn left on a faint trail heading downstream along Trout Creek. In just 100 yards, you'll reach the Home Mines Cabin, better known as "The Bigfoot Hilton". This cabin, now publicly owned, has hosted many hikers over the years but has fallen on hard times as of late due to a lack of maintenance. William L. Sullivan, the dean of Oregon guidebook authors, famously waited out an October snowstorm here in 1985, an episode he recounted in his memoir *Listening for Coyote*. Look for Sullivan's signature on the "Home Mines" sign above the front door. A short trail from the cabin leads to a nice campsite by the river. You should make this the destination of your hike, as the North Fork Trail climbs to the slopes high above the river from here and becomes brushy and boggy. Return the way you came.

Note: If you're looking to combine this hike with a trip to Anthony Lake (Hike 104), drive east on FR 73 from the trailhead for 16 gorgeous, curvy miles to Anthony Lake.

104. Anthony Lake and the Elkhorn Crest

	Hoffer Lakes	Elkhorn Crest Loop
Distance:	2.4 miles out and back	10.8 mile loop
Elevation Gain:	400 feet	2,200 feet
Trailhead Elevation:	7,135 feet	7,135 feet
Trail High Point:	7,483 feet	8,507 feet
Season:	July – October	July – October
Best:	July – October	July – October
Pass:	none needed	none needed
On the traditional lands of:	the Cayuse, Umatilla, and Walla Walla peoples	the Cayuse, Umatilla, and Walla Walla peoples

Directions from La Grande and Baker City:

- Drive to North Powder Exit 285 on Interstate 84. This exit is 24 miles south of La Grande and 19 miles north of Baker City.
- From the North Powder Exit, drive River Lane, following signs for Anthony Lakes.
- Drive 3.9 miles to a junction with Ellis Road. Turn left here and drive 0.7 mile to a junction with the Anthony Lake Highway.
- Turn right here and drive 15.7 miles of winding, curvy pavement to Anthony Lake.
- Ignore the campground and turn left at the next junction.
- After 100 yards, turn right to find the trailhead at the day use area.
- **Drivetime from La Grande and Baker City:** 50 minutes

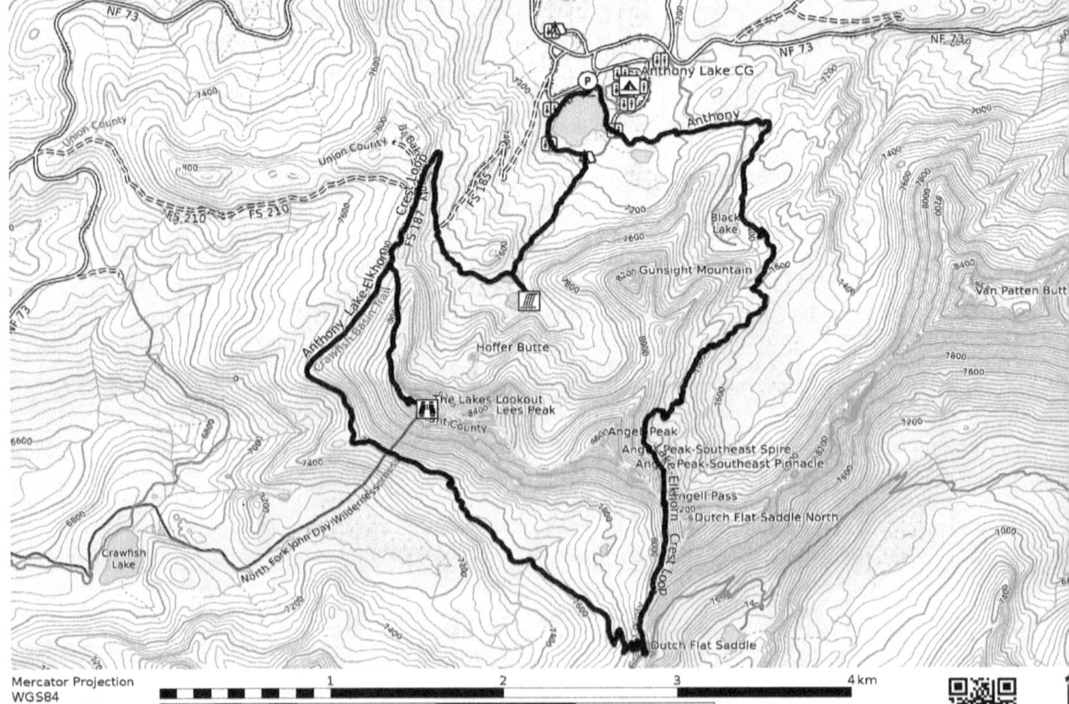

Hike: Every winter, snow-loving Oregonians are lured to Anthony Lakes Ski Area with the promise of exceptional powder and uncrowded slopes. Most Oregonians, if they've heard of Anthony Lakes, associate this area with winter fun. But little do most Oregon hikers know that this is an exceptional place to hike in the summer as well. The short hike up to Hoffer Lakes offers an easy hike with huge rewards, while the long loop around the peaks above Anthony Lake features extraordinary views, several gorgeous lakes, and enough fun to keep hikers enthused for the entire day. If you love hiking, you'll love this area in the summer as much as skiers do in the winter.

From the Day Use area, follow the short trail past the CCC-era shelter to the shore of Anthony Lake, where you turn left. The view of Gunsight Mountain towering over the lake is extraordinary. Follow the lakeshore trail until it dead ends at a junction with a wide trail just beyond the boat ramp. For the easy hike to Hoffer Lakes, turn right here. You'll pass a few walk-in campsites and soon arrive at a junction with the Hoffer Lakes Trail. Turn left here and hike uphill 0.6 mile to the first of the Hoffer Lakes. As soon as you reach the lake, turn left at a junction and follow trails around both of the wildly scenic lakes, which feature a number of excellent campsites. The best of these sites is on the far end of the second Hoffer Lake, set beside a tumbling waterfall in a granite bowl. Expect lots of mosquitoes in July and cold nights in the fall. When you're ready to return, hike back downhill to Anthony Lake and turn left to complete the loop around the lake.

f you're planning on a longer hike you should save Hoffer Lakes for last. From the campground, walk the lakeshore trail around Anthony Lake to the boat ramp, where you turn left. You'll quickly reach the Black Lake Trail at the far end of the campground. Follow the Black Lake Trail through meadows to a junction with the Elkhorn Crest Trail. Turn right here. You'll almost immediately pass another junction with the Black Lake Trail on the right, which continues to its namesake. Keep left. You'll climb up and out of the basin containing Black Lake, and continue up the side of a steep granite ridge to Angell Pass at 3.4 miles, elevation 8,164 feet. Continue downhill another 0.9 mile to Dutch Flat Saddle at 4.3 miles. Here you'll leave the Elkhorn Crest Trail and turn right on the Crawfish Basin Trail.

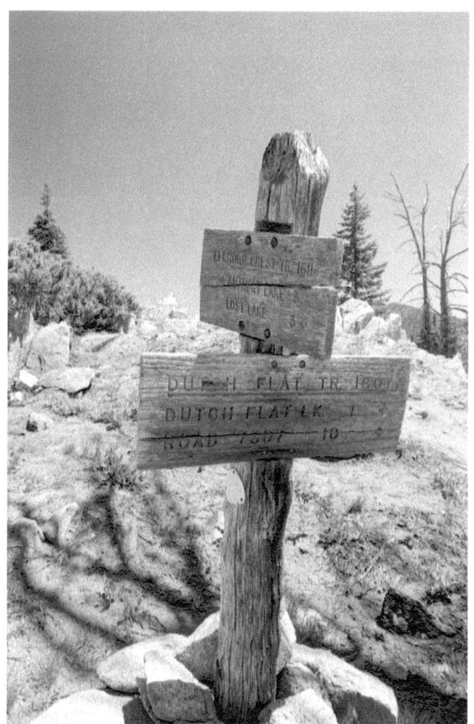

You'll follow the Crawfish Basin Trail for 2.6 rolling miles above its namesake basin. At 6.9 miles, the trail ends at the ski resort's dirt access road. Continue 0.1 mile to a junction with the trail up to the Lakes Lookout. If you're short on time or feeling worn out, you may be tempted to skip this side trip, but it is highly recommended! Turn right here and climb 700 feet in 0.9 mile to the rocky crest of the Lakes Lookout, where you can look across the entirety of the Elkhorn Crest and out to the Wallowas. This might be the single best viewpoint in the entire Elkhorn Range. From here, return to the junction with the dirt access road.

You're in the home stretch now! Follow the dirt access road downhill for 0.7 mile to a junction with the Hoffer Lakes Trail on the right. Turn right here and follow this trail a half-mile to the Hoffer Lakes, where you can take a dip in the lakes or just take a few minutes to soak up the beautiful scenery. From here, follow the Hoffer Lakes Trail downhill 0.6 mile to Anthony Lake, and turn left on the lakeshore trail to return to the trailhead.

105. Twin Lakes and Rock Creek Pass

	Twin Lakes	Rock Creek Pass
Distance:	7.2 miles out and back	11.4 miles out and back
Elevation Gain:	2,300 feet	2,900 feet
Trailhead Elevation:	5,515 feet	5,515 feet
Trail High Point:	7,669 feet	8,298 feet
Season:	July – October	July – October
Best:	July – October	July – October
Pass:	none needed	none needed
On the traditional lands of:	the Cayuse, Umatilla, and Walla Walla peoples	the Cayuse, Umatilla, and Walla Walla peoples

Directions from Baker City:

- From Baker City, drive OR 7 west for approximately 22 miles to a junction on the right with Deer Creek Road. If you're coming from the west, drive east of Sumpter on OR 7 for 3.2 miles to the junction with Deer Creek Rd on the left, between MP 28 and 29.
- Once on the Deer Creek Road, you will immediately reach a fork in the road. Fork left to stay on the Deer Creek Road.
- Drive this gravel road for 3.3 miles to another fork. Turn right here.
- Drive 0.6 mile of narrow gravel road to a four-way intersection. Continue straight, following a sign for "Twin Lakes Tr. 1633", which has a distance of 3 miles on the sign.
- Continue 2.4 miles to a junction with a decommissioned road at 2.4 miles. If you're driving a passenger car, stop here and find a place to park.

Rock Creek Butte looms over Twin Lakes and the Elkhorn Crest.

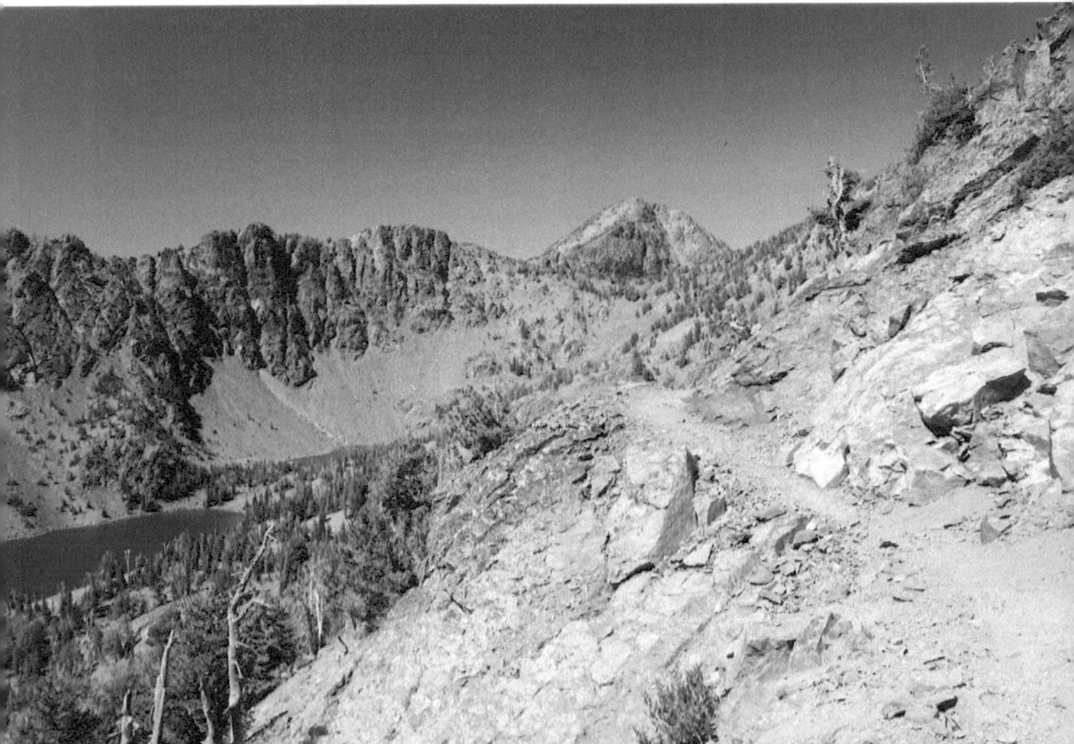

- If you're driving a high-clearance vehicle, continue driving uphill here. The road passes over a pair of deep ruts and charges steeply uphill before leveling out near the trailhead. It's only 0.4 mile from the last junction to the trailhead at a turnaround, and yet it feels like it's much longer. My Subaru Outback barely made it over these ruts, and you might just decide you don't want to deal with it even if you have the clearance to make it.
- **Drivetime from Baker City:** 50 minutes

Hike: Most Oregonians have never heard of the Elkhorn Crest Trail, likely for the simple reason that it's far from the state's most populous cities. Despite this obscurity, this trail is one of a handful in Oregon designated as a National Recreation Trail, and this designation is much deserved. Perhaps the nicest stretch of the trail is its southern end near Rock Creek Butte and Twin Lakes. Unfortunately, the other reason most Oregonians have never visited this area is the awful road access to the trail for much of its length. This hike up to the Elkhorn Crest from Twin Lakes is the most fantastic in the southern Elkhorn Range, and the best access to an amazingly beautiful place few people get to see.

From the trailhead, continue following the road steeply uphill to a fork. Turn right at a sign that says "trail". Once on the trail, you'll hike steeply uphill under towering ponderosa pines until the grade at last begins to ease. You'll descend a bit to cross Lake Creek on a bridge, then commence climbing steadily through the woods above the cascading Lake Fork. At 2.5 miles the trail emerges from the woods into a huge hanging meadow backed by the towering, reddish peaks of the Elkhorn Crest. From here, the trail switchbacks up the open slopes above the meadow and arrives at Lower Twin Lake at 3.8 miles from the trailhead. Look for social trails that lead to the lake, and to campsites in the trees.

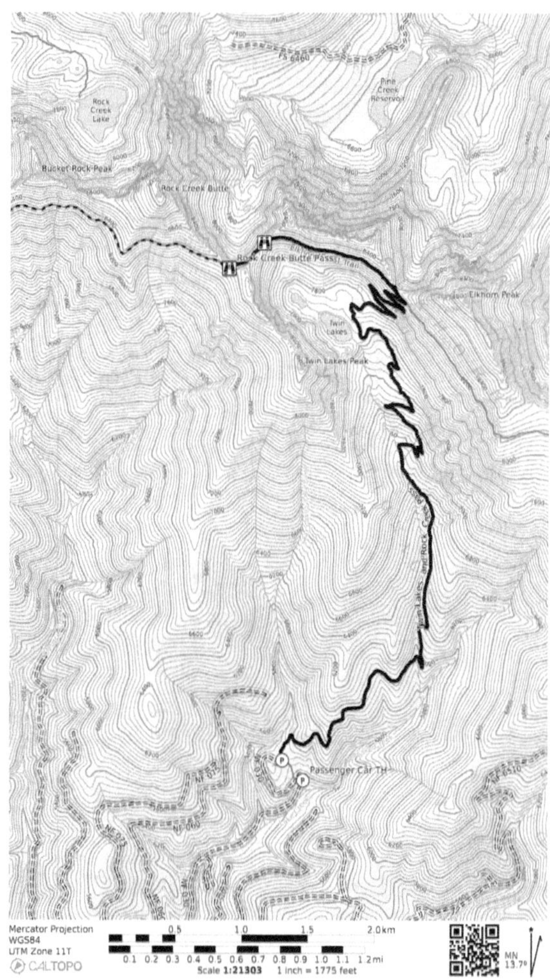

If you're up for the longer hike to Rock Creek Pass, follow the Twin Lakes Trail as it switchbacks uphill away from the lakes. The trail is never steep, and you'll reach the junction with the Elkhorn Crest Trail at a saddle before you know it. You may also be short of breath up here; at an elevation of 8,200 feet, you are now higher than the summit of many Oregon mountains. When you reach the junction, turn left here to hike along the Elkhorn Crest Trail for 0.7 mile to Rock Creek Pass at 5.7 miles from the trailhead. Here you'll find spectacular views to the pyramid-shaped summit of Rock Creek Butte, the highest point in the Elkhorns, as well as views down to Twin Lakes and all along the Elkhorn Crest. It is possible to scramble to the summit of Rock Creek Butte, but you should probably just call it quits here. Return the way you came.

106. Zumwalt Prairie

	Patti's Trail Loop	Harsin Butte	Canyon Vista
Distance:	2.6 mile loop	1.6 miles out & back	3.2 miles out & back
Elevation Gain:	162 feet	692 feet	500 feet
TH Elevation:	4,633 feet	4,829 feet	4,555 feet
Trail High Point:	4,633 feet	5,521 feet	5,022 feet
Season:	April - October	May - October	May - October
Best:	May - June	May - June	May - June
Pass:	None needed	None needed	None needed
On the traditional lands of:	Nez Perce (Nimíipuu)	Nez Perce (Nimíipuu)	Nez Perce (Nimíipuu)

Directions from Enterprise:

- Drive towards Joseph on OR 82. Just before you reach Joseph, turn left onto Crow Creek Road. This road soon becomes Zumwalt Road and changes to excellent gravel.
- Drive this road for 22 miles to a junction on your right with Johnson Road. There is a sign for Zumwalt Prairie.
- Drive 1.4 miles to a pullout by an old barn. This is the trailhead for Patti's Loop Trail. All further directions are listed below in their respective trail descriptions.
- **Drivetime from Enterprise and Joseph:** 40 minutes

Note: Dogs are prohibited on all trails in Zumwalt Preserve.

Hike: Between the Wallowas and Hells Canyon is a vast, rolling plateau known as Zumwalt Prairie. The prairie is a haven for native grasses, flowers, and birds, and contains some of the most serene and extraordinary grasslands in Oregon. The Nature Conservancy bought a 51 square-mile section of this area in separate purchases in 2000 and 2006, and today the prairie is managed as a private nature preserve. There are several trails open to the public, thankfully;

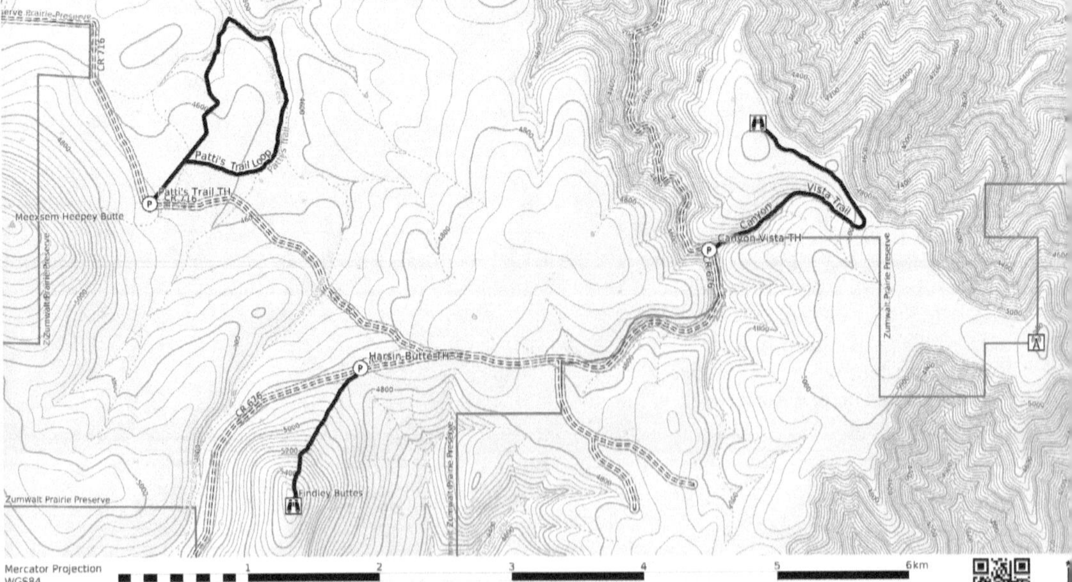

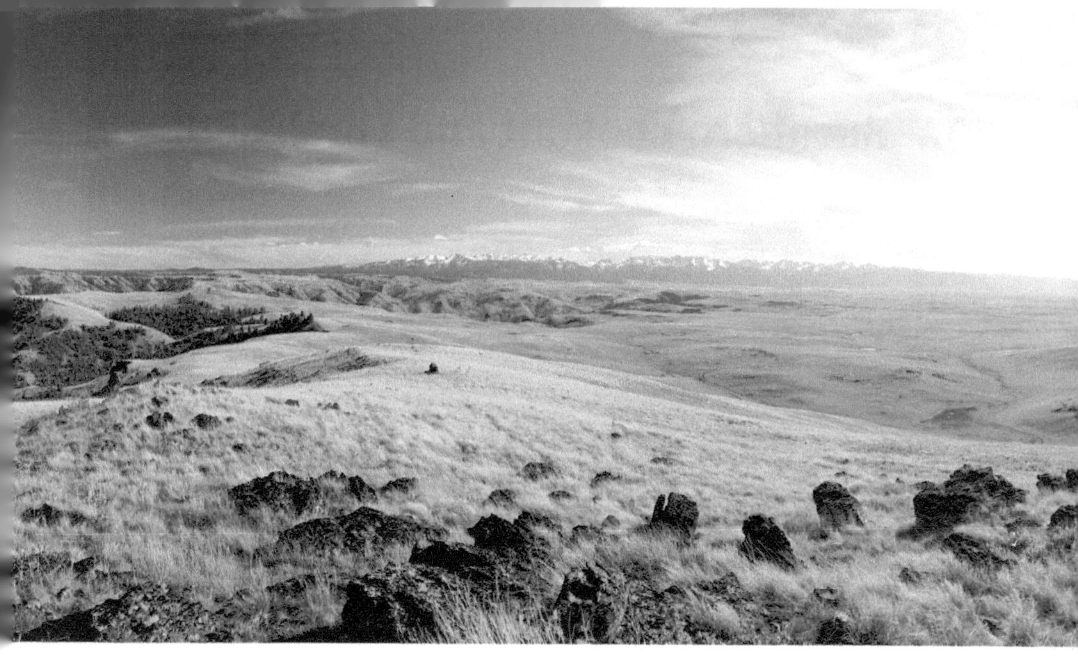

Looking south to the Wallowas from the summit of Harsin Butte.

presented here are the three best and most interesting.

Patti's Trail Loop: This loop explores the heart of Zumwalt Prairie, offering some of the best grassland hiking in Oregon. Start your exploration here. From the trailhead, follow a grassy trail for a quarter mile to the beginning of the loop, where you turn right. You'll pass over several fences with step ladders until the trail descends into a small canyon. The trail passes by a large fence on the right containing a grove of aspen trees. Continue following blue posts to help you navigate this area. The trail then leaves the canyon and traverses gradually uphill. The large hill in front of you is Harsin Butte, the next stop on the itinerary here. When you reach the conclusion of the loop, turn right to return to the trailhead.

Harsin Butte: Once you've hiked the grassland loop on Patti's Trail, drive 1.6 miles of rocky dirt road east on Johnson Lane to a junction. Turn right here and drive 0.3 mile more to a rocky pull-out with a sign for Harsin Butte. The trail up Harsin Butte starts with gradual approach through the prairie, then steepens as it approaches the slopes of the butte. The trail enters the forest and catapults uphill on a trail that becomes steeper as you climb. Be on the lookout for cattle here, as they sometimes hide in the forest to cool off. The trail reaches the summit at 0.8 mile and the views stretch out before you: south across the wide sweep of Zumwalt Prairie to the snowy Wallowa Mountains, east across the depths of Hells Canyon to the Seven Devils Range in Idaho, and north across Zumwalt Prairie into the far southeastern corner of Washington state. For the full dramatic effect, hike this trail in the evening and watch the sun set across the extraordinary views up here. When you're ready, return the way you came.

Canyon View: If you have a lot more time, the Canyon Vista Trail is the hike for you. The road to this trailhead is rough and somewhat tedious but the trail takes you to the very edge of Zumwalt Prairie, allowing hikers to peer into the depths of the Imnaha River's deep canyon while offering views similar to those at Harsin Butte. To locate the trailhead, drive beyond the Harsin Butte turnoff and continue 1.7 miles of rough, rutted, rocky road to the trailhead on the right. From the trailhead, follow the dirt road signed as the Canyon Vista Trail and pass through a gate. The trail enters a peaceful ponderosa pine woods and then enters a grassy plateau. At a little over a mile, the Canyon Vista Trail forks to the left. Turn left here and follow the trail to a spectacular viewpoint into the Imnaha River's rugged canyon. Continuing straight from this fork will take you to an airstrip with similarly excellent views, but this summit is outside of the preserve on private property. Return the way you came.

107. Buckhorn Lookout and Eureka Point

Distance: 7.6 miles out and back
Elevation Gain: 1,900 feet
Trailhead Elevation: 5,231 feet
Trail High Point: 5,231 feet
Season: May – October
Best: May – June
Pass: none needed
On the traditional lands of: Nez Perce (Nimíipuu)

Directions from Enterprise:

- Drive towards Joseph on OR 82. Just before you reach Joseph, turn left onto Crow Creek Road. This road soon becomes Zumwalt Road and changes to excellent gravel.
- Drive this road for 22 miles to a junction on your right with Johnson Road. There is a sign for Zumwalt Prairie.
- Continue straight on Zumwalt Road (which becomes FR 46) another 18.3 miles to a turn-off on the right signed for Buckhorn Overlook.
- Turn right and drive 0.8 mile to a fork in the road. The lookout is 0.2 mile to the right.
- If you have a higher clearance vehicle, turn left at this fork and drive 1.1 miles to a grassy area with a view of Hells Canyon. This is the trailhead. If you're driving a lower clearance vehicle, park at the lookout and walk the road, adding 2.6 miles to the hike.
- **Drivetime from Enterprise and Joseph:** 70 minutes

Hike: Hells Canyon is the deepest canyon in the United States, and even getting a good view into the canyon can be difficult. While the best views are found on long backpacking trips deep into the heart of the canyon, there are good views to be had with far less effort. You can drive directly to Buckhorn Lookout's abandoned cabin, where the view is truly magnificent. But even here, you cannot see the Snake River. For an even better view down into the canyon and to the

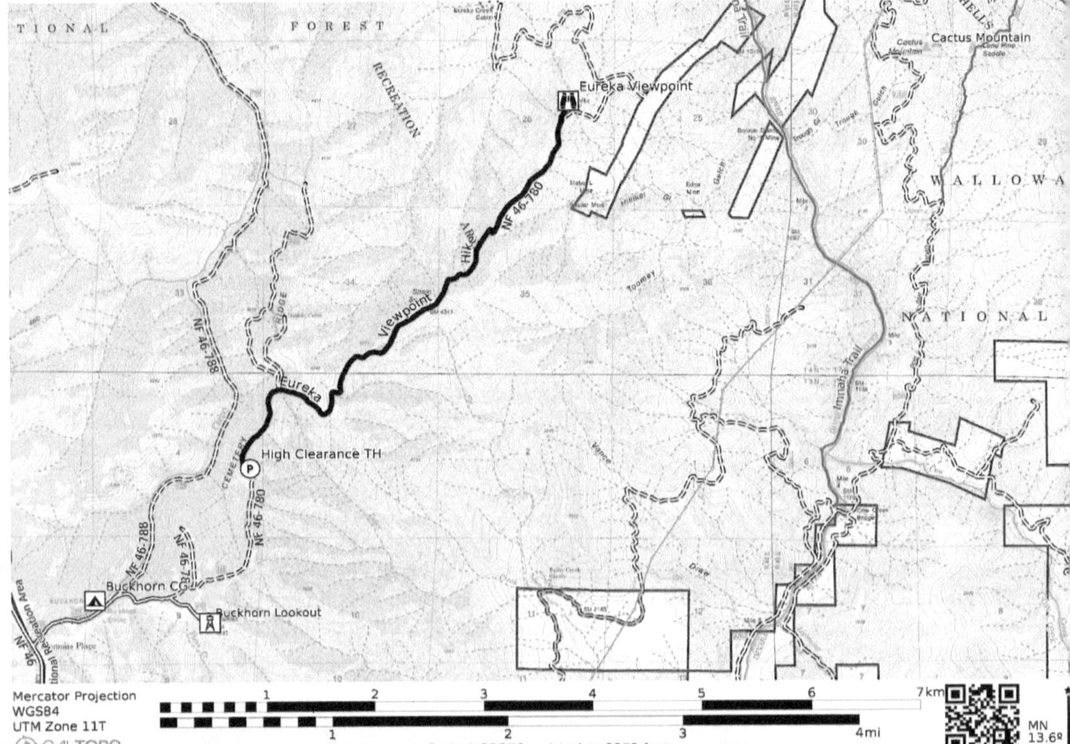

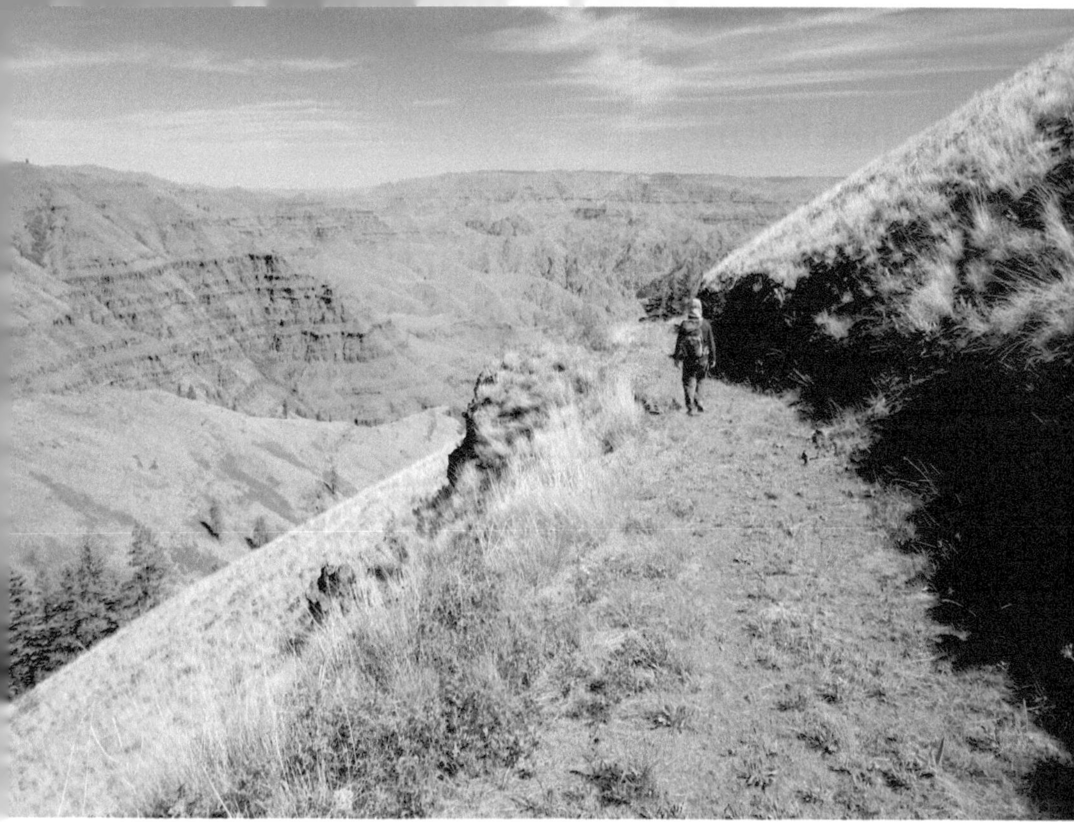

Hiking into Hells Canyon on the Eureka Wagon Road.

elusive Snake River, you can follow the abandoned Eureka Wagon Road into the heart of the canyon, an adventure truly fitting of Hells Canyon.

From the grassy trailhead, follow the road to a gate. Open the gate to walk through, and then close it behind you. The road descends through open forest for 0.6 mile to a junction at a saddle. Keep right to stay on the road, your route for the hike. The road continues its descent along open, steep slopes into the depths of Hells Canyon. Masses of wildflowers adorn these slopes in May and June; look for red and yellow paintbrush, lupine, phlox, larkspur, and so many more. Views open across the canyon to the Seven Devils Mountains in Idaho. At 2.1 miles, you'll reach Spain Saddle. Here the road crosses from the south side of the ridge to the north side. Around the bend you'll get your first view of the Snake River, as well as some of the last shade you'll find on this hike.

Beyond Spain Saddle, the road continues downhill into the canyon, passing through another gate at 2.6 miles. From here, you'll continue descending for another mile until you see some volcanic rocks on your left, just before the road curves to the right. Look here for a cairn and scramble up to the ridge top, which you will follow to its end. This promontory is known as the Eureka Viewpoint. From here, you can see the Snake River in three spots, still some 2,400 feet further down in the canyon. Keen eyes can pick out jet boats on the river below, and you will certainly hear them. Also keep an eye at your feet here, as prickly pear cactus grows on these slope, blooming in April and May. In addition to the cactus, you'll also see golden yellow balsamroot and pale yellow paintbrush. You can, of course, continue further into the canyon towards the Snake River but remember: every step you take downhill is one you'll have to take uphill in the afternoon heat later in the day. Unless this is your plan, you should settle for the Eureka Viewpoint. Return the way you came.

Before you leave, be sure to check out the Buckhorn Lookout nearby; though this historic lookout is abandoned and locked, the view is as good as ever. If you're looking for a place to camp, nearby Buckhorn Campground isn't much but it will do in a pinch.

108. Hat Point

	Hat Point	into Hells Canyon
Distance:	1.2 miles (all trails)	As far as you want to go...
Elevation Gain:	300 feet	but it's all uphill on the return.
Trailhead Elevation:	6,919 feet	6,919 feet
Trail High Point:	6,919 feet	6,919 feet
Season:	June - October	June - October
Best:	June - July	June - July
Pass:	NW Forest Pass	NW Forest Pass
On the traditional lands of:	Nez Perce (Nimíipuu)	Nez Perce (Nimíipuu)

Directions from Joseph:

- From Joseph, drive east on OR 350, following signs for Imnaha.
- Follow this highway downhill for 29 miles to the small town of Imnaha.
- Continue straight through town and onto FR 4240, the Hat Point Road. You will drive 16.4 miles on this narrow, winding gravel road to the Granny Vista Trail on the right side of the road. Beyond this trail, continue 1.3 miles to the Saddle Creek Campground on the right side of the road. If you're planning on camping up here, this is the place. Continue past Saddle Creek another 3.3 miles to a fork in the road.
- Keep right and drive 1.5 miles to the Hat Point Trailhead on the right.
- Note: The first 5 miles beyond Imnaha are extremely steep and exposed, with some enormous drop-offs on the side of the road. Some drivers may get spooked on this stretch of road, and you may also need to stop in the shade to keep your car from overheating. Exercise caution when driving up to Hat Point.
- **Drivetime from Joseph:** 2 hours and 30 minutes

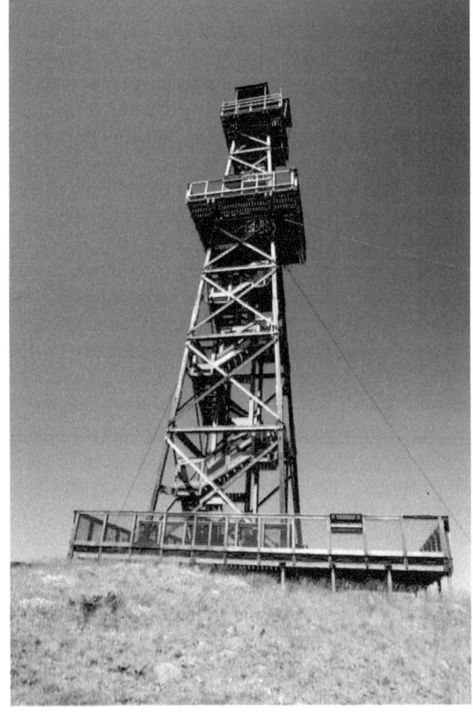

Hike: Hat Point is the highest point on the Oregon side of Hells Canyon and so it makes perfect sense that a lookout tower stands at the summit here. From the lookout you can look down some 5,600 feet to the Snake River, and across the river to the jagged peaks of the Seven Devils Range in Idaho. The Wallowas tower on the western horizon. I remember first reading about Hat Point as a child, and it seemed to me to be as far away as a person could travel from my home in Salem while still being fully in the state of Oregon. When I first visited in the summer of 1993, the viewpoint here took my breath away, and we decided to make Hells Canyon my first-ever backpacking trip. In my opinion, every Oregonian who loves the outdoors should make it to this extraordinary place at least once in their lifetime. The only problem here is where to begin: the best destination is only a few tenths of a mile from the parking lot. The solution here is to hike both short trails described below, then decide if you're up for the adventure of hiking into Hells Canyon. Whatever you do, you need to see this place at least once in a lifetime.

Before you drive to Hat Point, make sure you stop and hike the Granny Vista Loop. This short but gorgeous loop trail takes you to a breathtaking view of the Imnaha River's vast canyon. After the seemingly endless drive on the Hat Point Road, this is more than just a leg stretcher; this is a good chance to catch your breath, only to have it taken away at the viewpoint here. When you're done, get back in the car and drive the last 6 miles to Hat Point.

When you arrive at Hat Point, the first thing to do is to locate the trail to the lookout tower, and follow it to the base of the lookout. From here, walk up 93 steps to the lookout's viewing platform, some 60 feet above the ground. The view here is mind-boggling and defies description. Only the lookout's staffer is allowed to climb the last 30 feet to the cabin, but the staffer may come down to chat with you if they're feeling social. Do not bother them otherwise. When you're ready to head back down, you can follow a pair of very short but scenic loops for additional views and summer wildflowers.

At this point you've only hiked 1.2 miles – or barely a hike at all. You could honestly walk these trails in sandals with no backpack, and only your phone or camera to keep you company. Only very adventurous hikers should continue hiking into Hells Canyon on the Hat Point Trail (or one of the other trails that departs from the Warnock Corral Trailhead nearby, whose access road is narrow and rough). As of summer 2022, both the Hat Point Trail and the Temperance Creek Trail, two traditional routes further into the canyon, were rough and faint and in need of substantial trail maintenance. If you're up to the task, you can follow the Hat Point Trail down into Hells Canyon for 3.4 winding miles to a junction with the High Trail. From here you can follow this long trail to many points north and south, or you can continue on the Hat Point Trail some 4 miles of faint, rough, steep trail down to the Snake River. Whatever you do, only plan on such adventures if you are in shape and prepared for anything – because that's what you should expect.

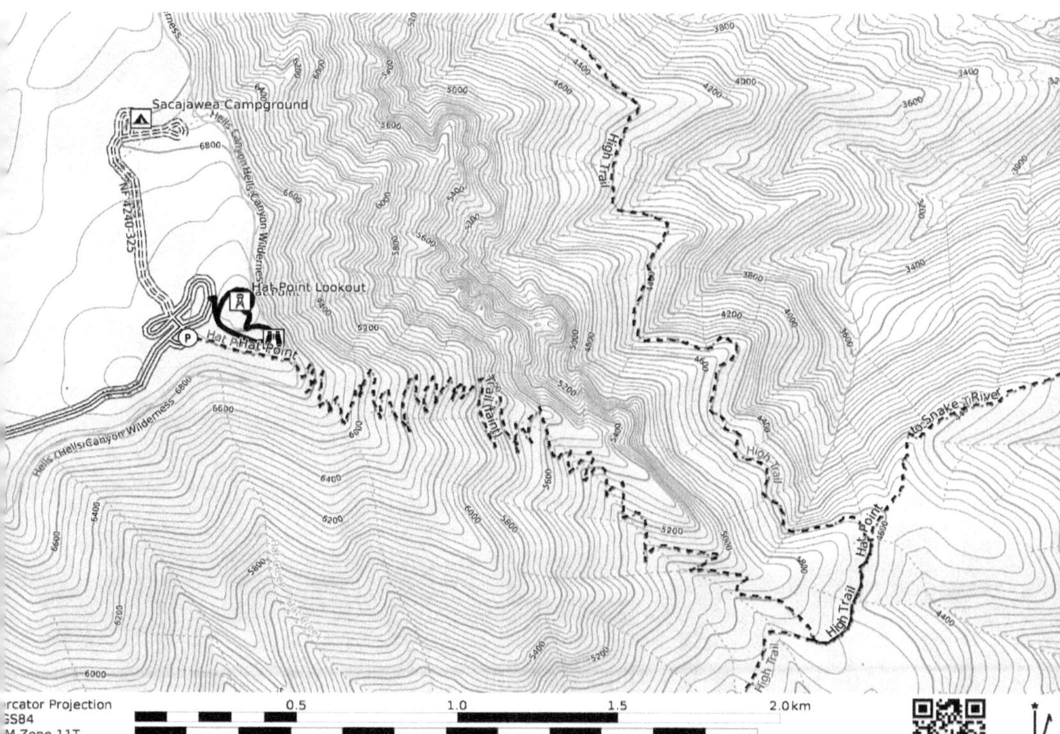

109. Summit Ridge via Freezeout Saddle

	Freezeout Saddle	Summit Ridge
Distance:	6.4 miles out and back	12.4 miles out and back
Elevation Gain:	1,900 feet	3,400 feet
Trailhead Elevation:	3,553 feet	3,553 feet
Trail High Point:	5,442 feet	6,659 feet
Season:	May - October	June - October
Best:	June - July	June - July
Pass:	NW Forest Pass	NW Forest Pass
On the traditional lands of:	Nez Perce (Nimíipuu)	Nez Perce (Nimíipuu)

Directions from Joseph:

- From Joseph, drive east on OR 350, following signs for Imnaha.
- Follow this highway downhill for 29 miles to the small town of Imnaha.
- Just after the bridge over the Imnaha River in the middle of town, turn right on the Upper Imnaha River Road.
- Drive 12.2 miles on this gravel road to a junction with Freezeout Road on the left, just before a bridge.
- Turn left and drive 2.7 narrow gravel miles to road's end at the Freezeout Trailhead.
- **Drivetime from Joseph:** 1 hour and 20 minutes

Hiking on top of the world on Summit Ridge.

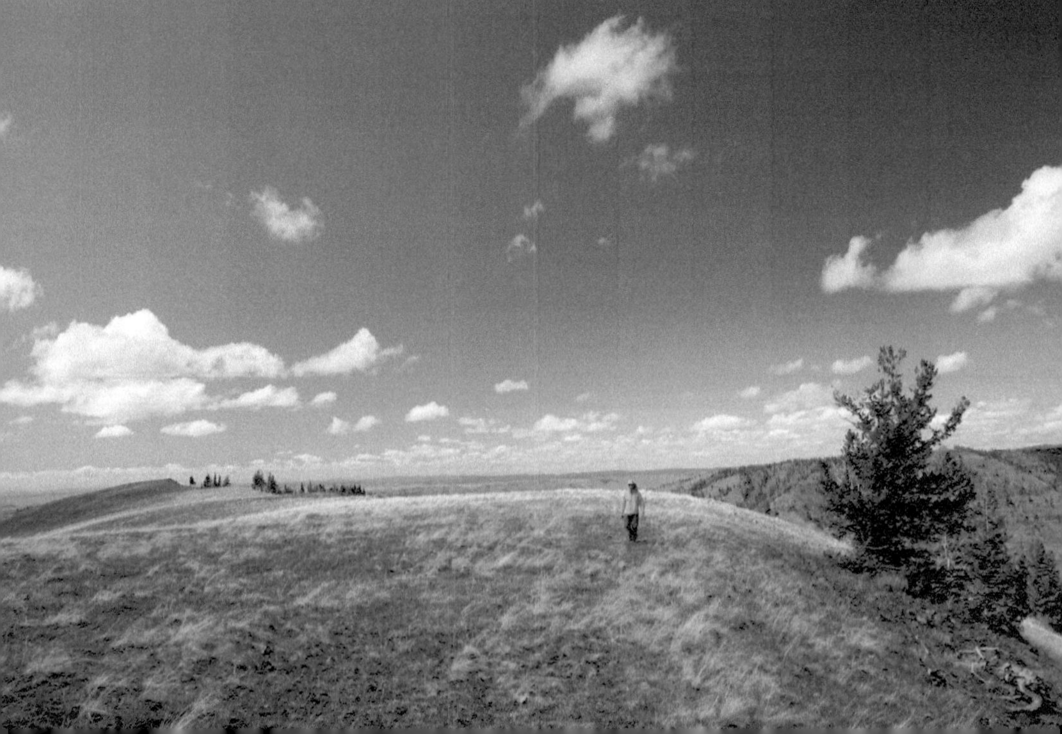

Hike: Hells Canyon is a world unto itself, a vast and mesmerizing place lightly touched by humanity. A vast network of trails helps hikers navigate this immense world, but many of these trails are steep, faint, and unforgiving. There are, thankfully, a few ways to get into this world without planning for a multi-day adventure into this heart of darkness. This hike up to Freezeout Saddle is by far the easiest route to the rim of Hells Canyon, and if you're looking for more adventure, you can follow trails to the edge of Summit Ridge for an extraordinary view across the canyon to the snowy Seven Devils Range in Idaho. Plan on a full day to explore to your heart's desire!

From the Freezeout Trailhead, locate the trail heading uphill under tall ponderosa pines. This well-graded trail climbs out of the woods and onto open slopes full of May and June wildflowers. Look for balsamroot, paintbrush, lupine, pink clarkia, and many others. You should also expect to encounter cattle on this trail, as is so often the case in eastern Oregon. After climbing a long series of switchbacks, you will reach Freezeout Saddle at 3 miles from the trailhead. As mentioned earlier, this is the lowest spot on the rim of Hells Canyon, and the views are spectacular. You can look into the depths of the canyon to the east (though the Snake River remains out of sight), while the Wallowas rise to the west above the prairies and canyonlands between Joseph and Imnaha. For a moderate yet satisfying hike, turn right at the saddle on to the Summit Ridge Trail and follow the trail another 0.2 mile to a series of small knolls above the trail that make excellent rest spots. If this is it for you, return the way you came.

If you're ready for a longer hike, follow the Summit Ridge Trail as it climbs up the side of the ridge, sometimes gradually and sometimes steeply. The wildflowers along this slope are spectacular in June! If you're here early in the season, this is also where you likely will begin to encounter snow. At about 2.5 miles from Freezeout Saddle, the trail parallels the crest of Summit Ridge, some fifty feet or so below the ridgetop. For the amazing views you're looking for, leave the trail here and scramble easily up to the top of the ridge, where the views are truly extraordinary! Look across Hells Canyon to the jagged peaks of the Seven Devils Mountains in Idaho, and look to the west to the full sweep of the Wallowas. Both the Snake and Imnaha Rivers are out of sight in the canyons below you, but chances are you won't care. Make this plateau at the top of the world your destination for this hike unless you're prepared for a longer trip even deeper into Hells Canyon. A loop that continues south and eventually returns to the Freezeout Trailhead does exist, but alas it is rough, confusing and hard to follow in spots, and is thus not recommended; instead, you should return the way you came.

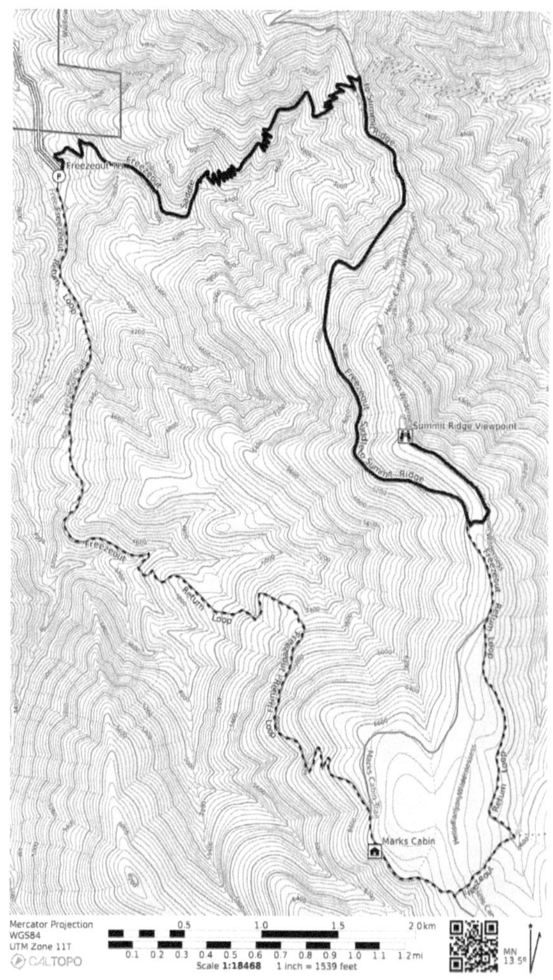

110. BC Falls

Distance: 2.6 miles out and back
Elevation Gain: 400 feet
Trailhead elevation: 4,606 feet
Trail high point: 4,995 feet
Season: June – October
Best: June – October
Pass: none needed
On the traditional lands of: Nez Perce (Nimíipuu)

Directions:

- From Joseph, drive south on OR 82 and continue around Wallowa Lake until you reach Wallowa Lake State Park.
- At a junction on the south side of Wallowa Lake, continue straight for 1 mile to road's end at the Wallowa Lake Trailhead.
- This is the trailhead. Park wherever you can at this busy trailhead.
- **Drivetime from Joseph:** 15 minutes

Hike: Perhaps the only downside of hiking in the Wallowas is the lack of easy options. Most of the best hikes climb for mile after mile to high passes and scenic lakes, and day hikers can often only attain these heights if they are willing to hike all day and then some (or just go backpacking, which is of course the best way to see the Wallowas). Of the few short hikes in this extraordinary wilderness, the ramble to BC Falls is among the best. You'll follow the Chief Joseph Trail to a spectacular waterfall above Wallowa Lake. Adventurous hikers can continue hiking the Chief Joseph Trail up and up, as far as their hearts desire.

From the trailhead, follow the West Fork Wallowa Trail. You'll immediately reach a fork with the East Fork Wallowa Trail, which heads steeply uphill towards Aneroid Lake and eventually

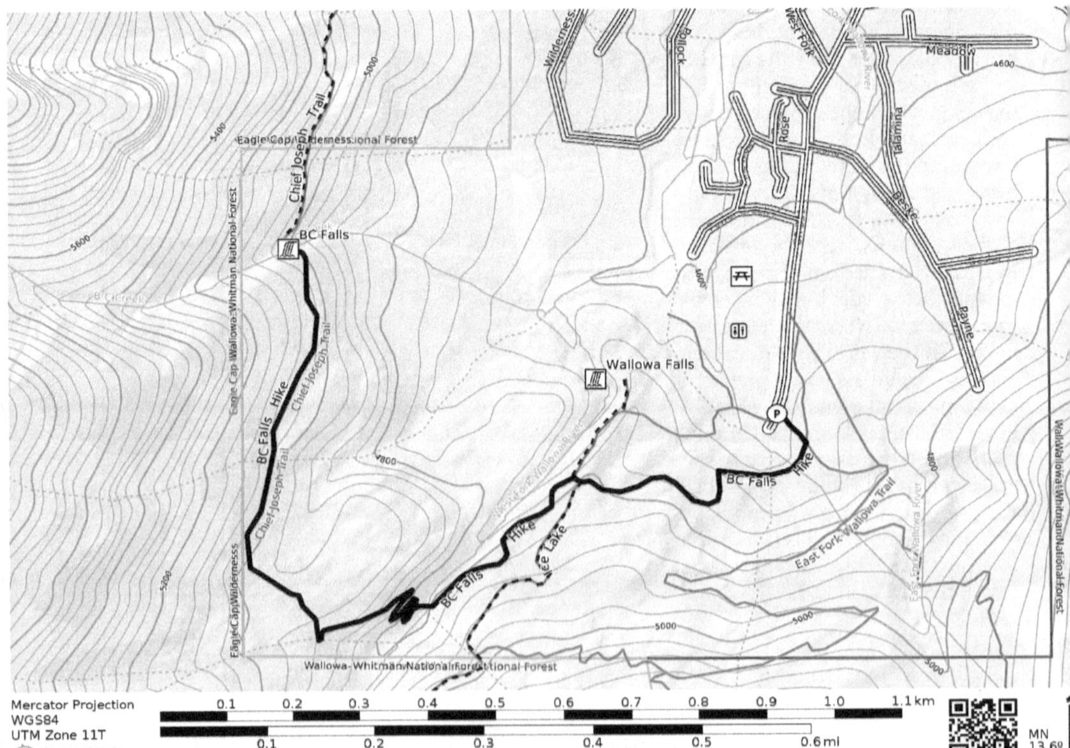

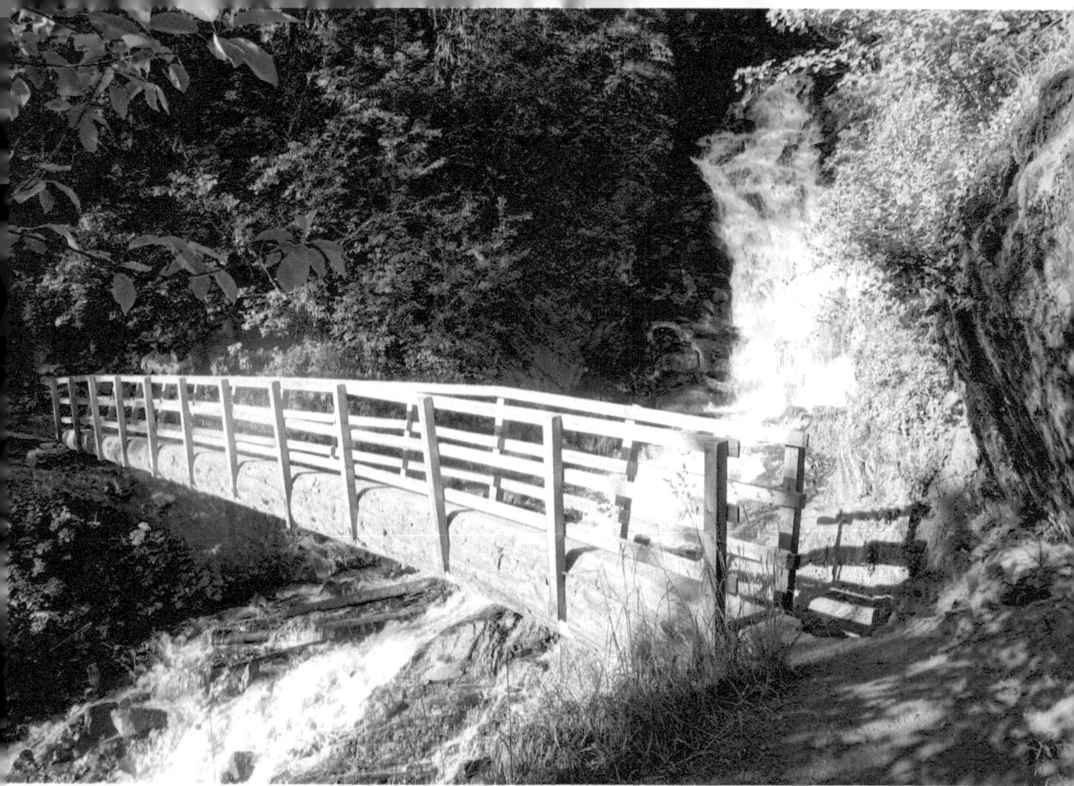

The bridge over BC creek, just below BC Falls.

Dollar Pass (see Hike 114). Keep right. You'll follow the West Fork Trail for 0.4 mile of gradual climbing to another junction. Left continues uphill towards Ice Lake (Hike 111) and the Lakes Basin, while right is another way back to the trailhead. To hike to BC Falls, turn right and then immediately left onto the Chief Joseph Trail. This trail descends to a bridged crossing of the raging West Fork Wallowa River in a scenic, rocky gorge. This is a gorgeous spot and one worthy of a moment to take it all in.

Beyond the bridge, the trail climbs a series of switchbacks before eventually leveling out on a sunny bench above the West Fork's gorge. You'll pass a few rockslides where quaking aspens rise above the trail. The trail reaches a dramatic bridge between two tiers of BC Falls at 1.3 miles. The bridge was installed in 2020, at last offering hikers the ability to cross BC Creek at this extremely exposed spot. This is the destination of your hike. Adventurous hikers can continue following the Chief Joseph Mountain trail uphill for miles and miles to meadows at the base of Chief Joseph Mountain's east face. Along the way you'll gain many thousands of feet of elevation. This is best saved for hikers capable of climbing mountains, even though the trail does not actually reach the summit of Chief Joseph. Return the way you came.

On the way back, you can check out a worthwhile detour. Return to the four-way junction just above the bridge over the West Fork. Continuing straight will take you back to the trailhead, but it's fun to turn left here. This trail will take you above the West Fork's gorge, passing looks down into the river's raging waters. You will also pass an excellent viewpoint out to Wallowa Lake, something the BC Falls hike lacks. If you continue from here, you will gain obstructed views of Wallowa Falls, a 20-foot cataract on the West Fork. From here, you'll need to return the way you came.

111. Ice Lake

Distance: 16 miles out and back
Elevation Gain: 3,400 feet
Trailhead elevation: 4,606 feet
Trail high point: 7,887 feet
Season: July – October
Best: July – October
Pass: none needed
On the traditional lands of: Nez Perce (Nimíipuu)

Directions:

- From Joseph, drive south on OR 82 and continue around Wallowa Lake until you reach Wallowa Lake State Park.
- At a junction on the south side of Wallowa Lake, continue straight for 1 mile to road's end at the Wallowa Lake Trailhead.
- This is the trailhead. Park wherever you can at this busy trailhead.
- **Drivetime from Joseph:** 15 minutes

Hike: The Eagle Cap Wilderness might just be Oregon's best. Here, you have mile after mile of jagged granite peaks and hundreds of deep turquoise lakes. The only catch to visiting the Wallowas is that many of the best destinations are too far away to visit in one day. This long trek to Ice Lake, set at the base of the two tallest mountains in eastern Oregon, might be the best hike in the Wallowas. But it is prohibitively long, and many will opt to carry a full pack in here to spend a night or two. It can be done in a day, but it will kill you to leave.

Begin at the busy West Fork Wallowa Trailhead. Almost immediately you will arrive at a junction. Left leads to Aneroid Lake, but you want to hike to Ice Lake, so keep right. The West Fork Wallowa River Trail follows its namesake for three miles of rolling ups and downs to a

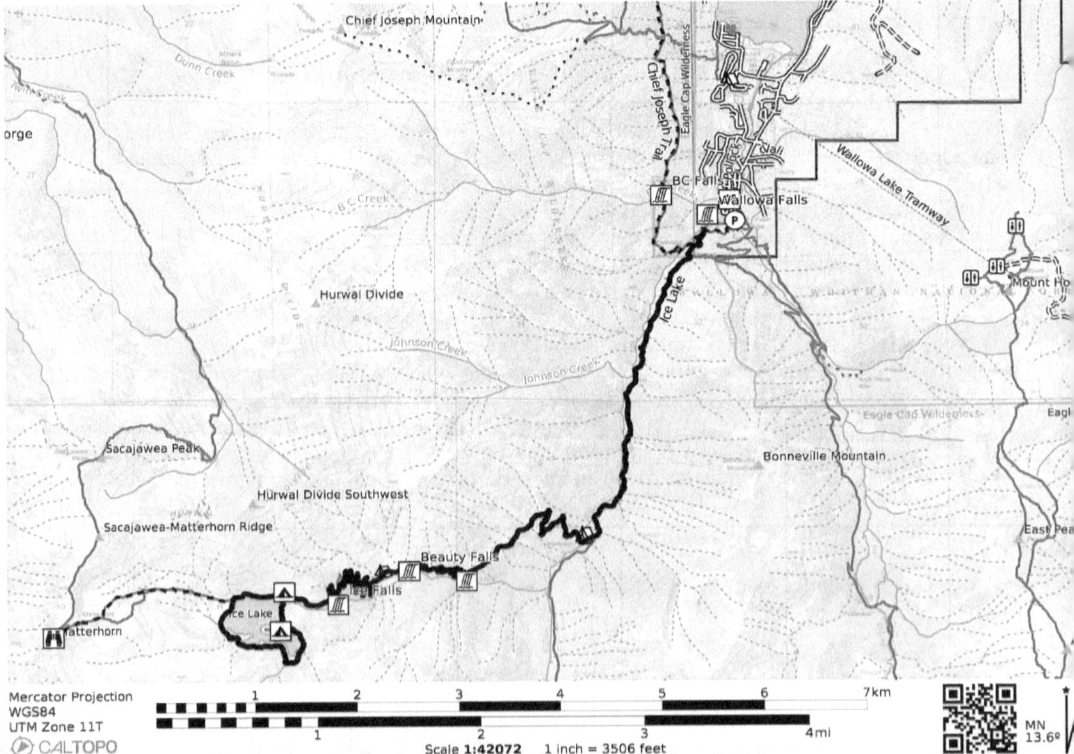

junction with the Ice Lake Trail. Turn right here (continuing straight will eventually take you into the fabled Lakes Basin, a destination firmly out of reach for daytrekkers). Before you go any further, look up and see if you can spot massive Ice Falls tumbling down from the cliffs above; you'll pass by the falls before your hike is done.

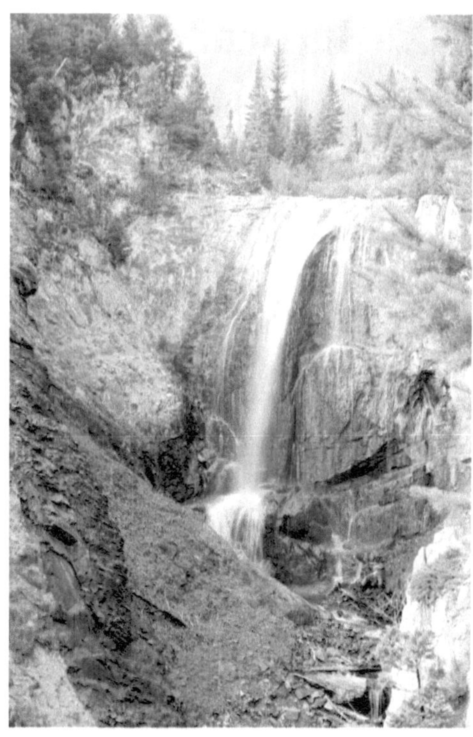

Beauty Falls, just off the trail.

The Ice Lake Trail crosses the West Fork on a log bridge and sets out a meandering course uphill. On your way up, you'll hike under talus slopes and through the woods, generally following Adam Creek. After a couple miles, you'll finally meet up with the creek at a rocky perch along the rushing creek. Take this moment to fill up water or take a break; from here you've got a long ways to go. Another set of switchbacks will bring you to an obstructed view of Adam Creek's middle waterfall, which is sometimes referred to as Beauty Falls. A sketchy side trail offers a better view of the falls but watch your step! Back on the main trail, continue uphill to a sidehill traverse above the falls, where at last Ice Falls comes into view in front of you. From here, the trail relents as it traverses a scenic basin below Ice Falls. After a half-mile of relatively level hiking, you'll begin climbing once more. At this point you've hiked more than six miles from the West Fork Trailhead, and this set of switchbacks is the toughest as a result. Ice Falls tantalizes through the trees, just out of reach. Now, about the falls: there isn't a trail leading to better views of the falls, but many hikers attempt to bash through the brush for a better view of this giant. Better views are possible, but not recommended for most hikers.

After many switchbacks, you'll finally top out at around 7.5 miles from the trailhead. The trail then follows Adam Creek another half-mile until Ice Lake comes into view at last. The many miles of anticipation make the first view of the lake that much sweeter. The rocky crags of the Matterhorn and Sacajawea, the two highest peaks in eastern Oregon, loom across the deep waters of the lake. Swimming is highly recommended, but expect cold water as the name of the lake is no misnomer. At 193 feet deep, this is the deepest lake in the Eagle Cap Wilderness. If you're backpacking, there are many excellent campsites scattered all over this large basin. Mosquitoes are a major nuisance in July.

When you reach the lakeshore, leave the trail here and turn left to cross Adam Creek. The best views, lunch spots, and campsites are across the creek on the bluffs above the lake. Despite the long trek here, this is a popular place; expect to search a little bit for the perfect rest spot (or campsite). Most hikers will be bushed and dreading the many miles back to the trailhead, but if you've got more energy then you've got options here. If you're interested in a loop around the lake, know that at 2 miles long, it's much longer than it seems at first. You'll pass by secluded bays, hike over rocky peninsulas, and pass hidden waterfalls as you work your way around the many nooks and crannies of Ice Lake. If you're superhuman and still have lots of energy, consider the steep climb of 1.5 more miles and 2,000 feet of elevation gain to the summit of the Matterhorn. Follow the Ice Lake Trail and continue hiking up steep slopes until you reach the 9,826-foot summit, where the views are mind-altering. You may want YakTrax or microspikes to help navigate any lingering snow on the trail. Regardless of what you decide to do, return the way you came.

112. Hurricane Creek

Distance: 6.4 miles out and back
Elevation Gain: 1,000 feet
Trailhead Elevation: 5,047 feet
Trail High Point: 5,781 feet
Season: June – October
Best: June – October
Pass: NW Forest Pass
On the traditional lands of: Nez Perce (Nimíipuu)

Directions from Enterprise:

- From Enterprise, drive south on Hurricane Creek Road for 5 miles to a turnoff on the right, signed for Hurricane Creek Campground. Turn right here.
- Drive 3.6 miles of narrow pavement and gravel to the trailhead at road's end. Watch for potholes along the way!
- **Drivetime from Enterprise:** 20 minutes

Hike: Oregon does not generally experience hurricanes, so it may be a surprise to see a place in the Wallowas known as Hurricane Creek. How did this creek get its name? All it takes is a visit to this spectacular canyon to solve the mystery. You'll hike a rolling trail up and down along Hurricane Creek under the tallest peaks in the Wallowas, with views up and down to waterfalls, jagged mountain crests, and the rampaging waters of Hurricane Creek. This dusty trail passes over the granite slopes above the creek, and it can be very hot in the summer; you can cool off at the base of cascading Slick Rock Creek, where the trail passes below a long series of waterfalls. Hikers can continue along this scenic valley to a spectacular view of the Matterhorn above glassy Hurricane Creek.

Hurricane Creek and Sacajawea Peak.

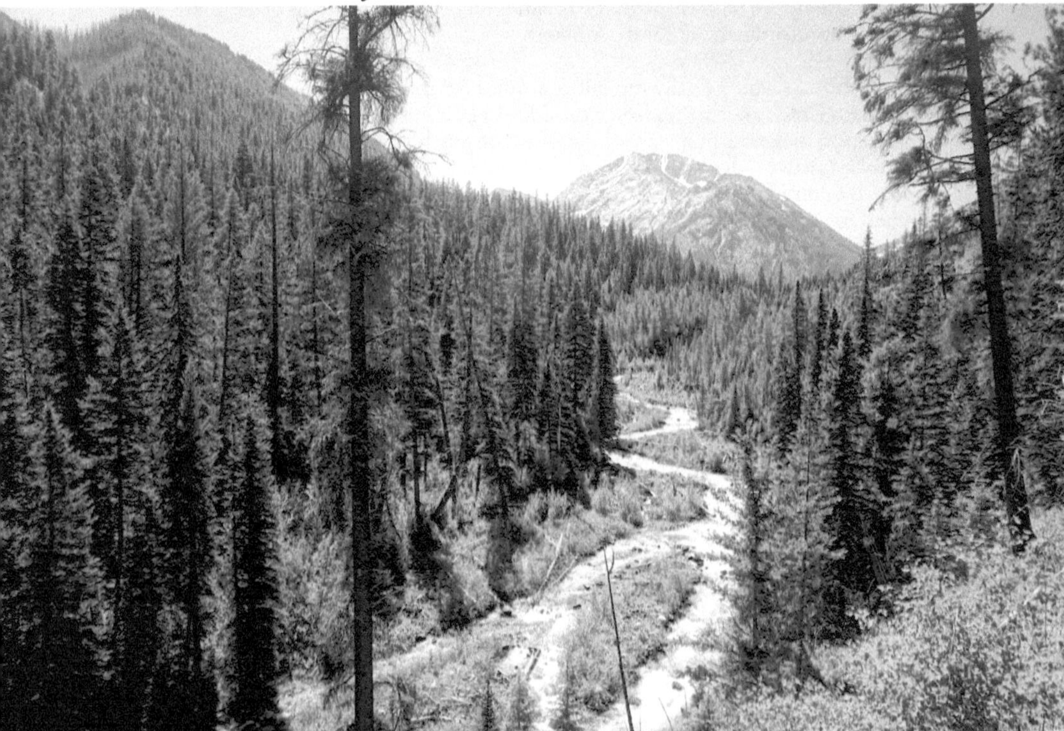

The Hurricane Creek Trail parallels its namesake for the entire hike. At just 0.1 mile from the trailhead, you'll cross wide, multi-channeled Falls Creek. A side trail just before the crossing leads to a better view of this scenic cascade before launching steeply uphill towards the cliffs of Twin Peaks; if you've got the time, this makes for a fun side trip. Beyond the Falls Creek crossing, you'll continue following Hurricane Creek at a distance for the next two miles. As you hike along, look up the slopes of the steep canyon walls, where you'll solve the mystery of how the creek got its name; avalanches are quite common in this canyon, blowing over trees and stripping vegetation off the slopes. Despite the name, the Hurricane Creek Trail is a popular snowshoe in the winter – but make sure you check the avalanche forecast before you come here then! You'll also have excellent views up the canyon walls to the west to Deadman Creek Falls. If you're visiting in the summer, keep an eye out for the vast array of wildflowers that grow along the trail, among them yellow columbine and the intriguing Mountain Lady Slipper Orchid.

At 2.1 miles, the trail reaches an unmarked fork on the left with the abandoned Thorp Creek Trail. This trail descends to a ford of Hurricane Creek and then climbs steeply to meadows at the base of Sacajawea, offering adventurous hikers an alternative destination. There are campsites here, too, should you just be interested in an easy backpacking trip along Hurricane Creek. Return to the main trail and continue following Hurricane Creek upstream. Another mile of hiking will take you first to a spectacular viewpoint down into a narrow gorge on Hurricane Creek, and then to a crossing of Slick Rock Creek just below a waterfall. Unlike with Hurricane Creek, it does not take much imagination to figure out how this creek earned its name – so watch your step crossing the creek. Adventurers love exploring Slick Rock Gorge above the trail, where you can find more waterfalls, even better views, and if you're lucky enough to find it, a natural waterslide. As mentioned previously, the Hurricane Creek Trail can be uncomfortably hot in the summer, and this is the place to cool off.

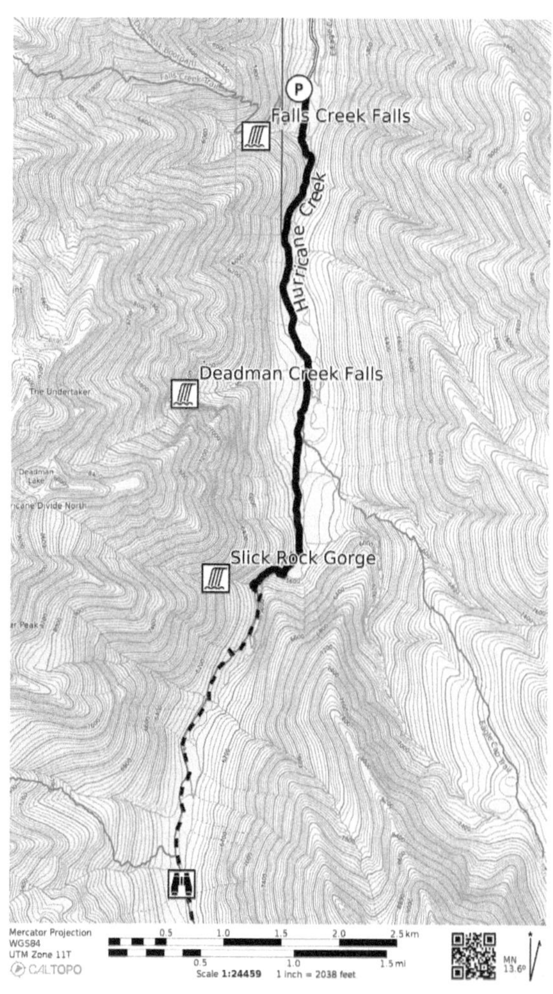

If you're interested in a longer hike, you can follow the Hurricane Creek Trail for many miles upstream into the famed Lakes Basin (see Hike 113), but at a distance of more than ten miles from the trailhead, this is out of reach for most day hikers. For a more reasonable destination you can reach in a day, follow the Hurricane Creek Trail for 2 miles beyond Slick Rock Creek to a vast meadow with a fantastic view of the Matterhorn's imposing west face. The Hurricane Creek Trail crosses its namesake here, in the middle of this scenic meadow. Beyond this point you'll be in the backpacking world, so it's a good idea to return the way you came.

113. Mirror Lake

	Blue Tarn	Mirror Lake
Distance:	7.2 miles out and back	15.6 miles out and back
Elevation Gain:	1,600 feet	2,400 feet
Trailhead Elevation:	5,597 feet	5,597 feet
Trail High Point:	7,090 feet	7,645 feet
Season:	July - October	July - October
Best:	July - October	July - October
Pass:	NW Forest Pass	NW Forest Pass
On the traditional lands of:	Nez Perce (Nimíipuu)	Nez Perce (Nimíipuu)

Directions:

- Make your way to the town of Lostine, some 54 miles northeast of LaGrande or 10 miles northwest of Enterprise.
- From Lostine, drive 6.9 miles of paved road and an additional 10.9 miles of gravel road to the Two Pan Trailhead. The last six miles of gravel are bumpy and rough. A passenger car can make it if driven slowly.
- **Drivetime from Lostine:** 40 minutes

Hike: This gorgeous trek to one of Oregon's most extraordinary places has it all! You'll start in a cool forest and climb gradually through the woods, passing a spectacular waterfall along the way, and then hike through a series of vast meadows to one of the most beautiful alpine lakes in

Mirror Lake and Eagle Cap.

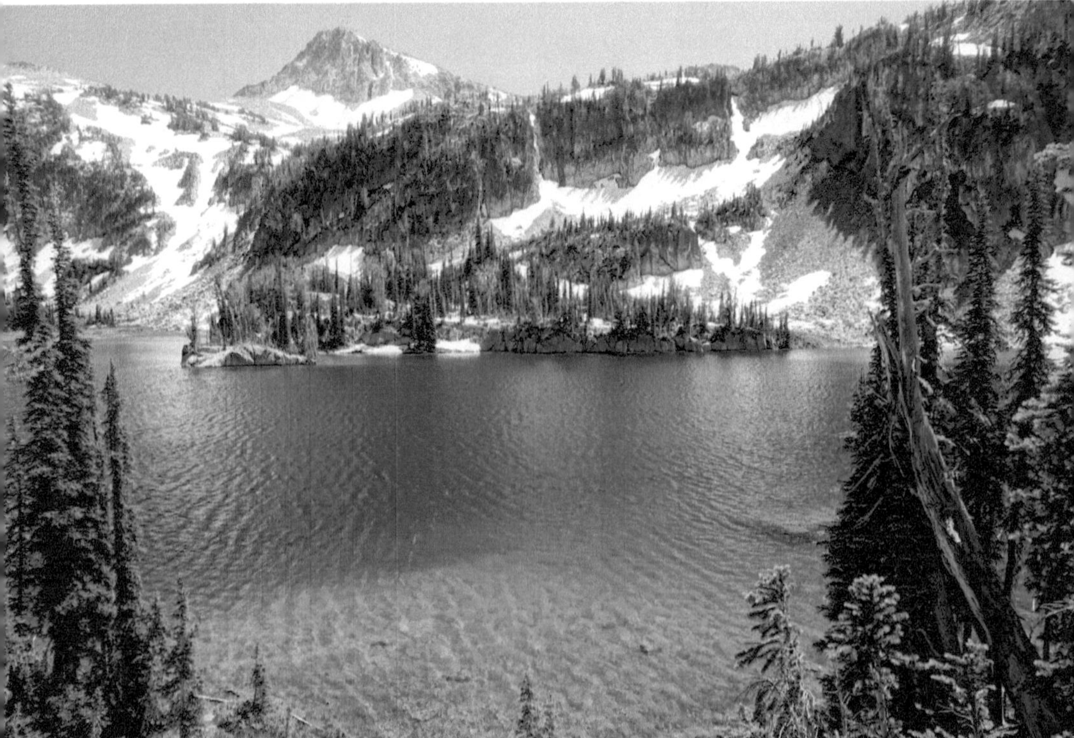

Oregon. Best of all, this hike is easier than it looks. Although you'll hike a distance of nearly 16 miles round-trip, the trail is well-graded and the miles fly by as you take in the beautiful scenery. What are you waiting for?

The hike begins in the woods at the Two Pan Trailhead. You'll soon reach a junction with the West Lostine River Trail, which leads to Minam Lake and other points further in the Eagle Cap Wilderness. Keep left here to follow the East Lostine River Trail. You'll climb 1,000 feet in the first two miles to a vantage point besides a crashing waterfall on the East Fork, a worthwhile place to stop and take a break. Beyond the falls, the trail ascends a few more switchbacks and levels out, entering the long series of vast meadows that make up most of the rest of the hike. Look south to Eagle Cap's snowy summit, looming at the head of the valley. There are campsites just off the trail here as well, should you be needing a place to spend the night. At 3.6 miles, the trail passes above a gorgeous blue tarn with a reflection of Eagle Cap. This makes an ideal destination for a moderate hike. Be kind to the terrain around the tarn and avoid camping nearby.

If you're continuing, the trail continues through the meadows for another 1.8 miles to a broken bridge over the East Fork. The bridge can be crossed with care but you might decide that it's safer to just ford the river, here only knee-deep. From here, you'll continue hiking uphill through the meadows for another 1.5 miles until at last you start climbing again. A half-mile of gentle ascent leads you to a four-way junction, with Mirror Lake in sight to the left. Keep straight here. After more than 7 miles of hiking, you have entered the fabled Lakes Basin. From this point on, the scenery is astounding! The trail follows the north side of this deep alpine pool that lives up to its name: more than anywhere else in the state, this is a place worthy of the name Mirror Lake. There are campsites along the lake but fires are banned, as they should be in this fragile alpine environment. Follow the lakeshore to the east for the best view of Eagle Cap's rocky summit towering above the lake. Make this your destination for this day hike, and unless you're planning on backpacking, return the way you came.

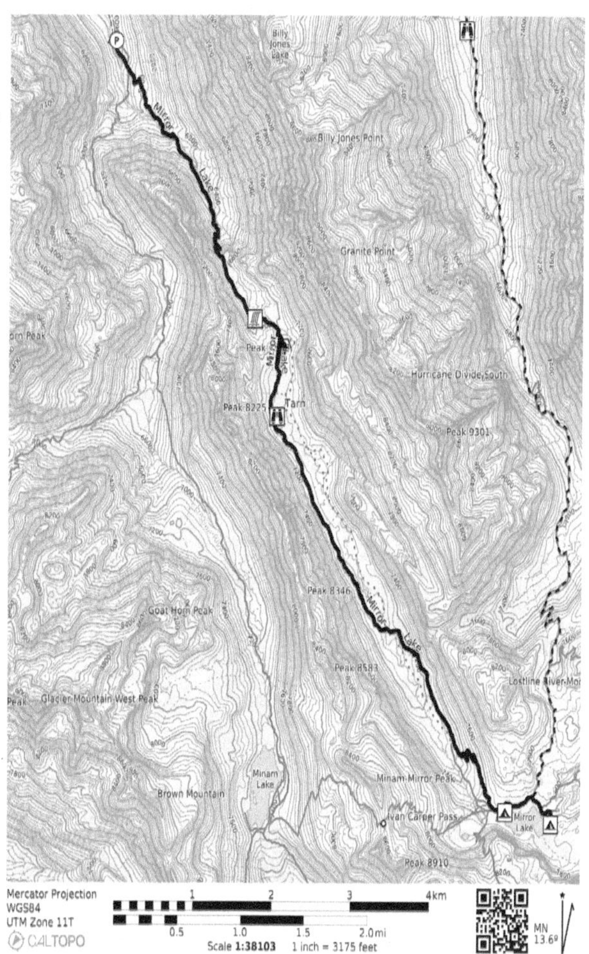

Most people who hike to Mirror Lake do so as part of a longer backpack through the Lakes Basin, deep in the heart of the Eagle Cap Wilderness. If you're planning such an adventure, you've got lots of options. You can continue east less than a mile to Moccasin Lake, you can climb to the summit of Eagle Cap in 2 miles from Mirror Lake, or you can plan an extended backpacking trip to visit either Minam Lake to the west or wildly scenic Glacier Lake to the east, on the other side of the Lakes Basin. Whatever you do here, it is certain to be a blast!

114. Bonny Lakes and Dollar Lake

	Bonny Lakes	Dollar Lake
Distance:	8.2 miles out and back	12 miles out and back
Elevation Gain:	1,300 feet	2,200 feet
Trailhead Elevation:	6,485 feet	6,485 feet
Trail High Point:	7,787 feet feet	8,486 feet
Season:	July - October	July - October
Best:	July - October	July - October
Pass:	none needed	none needed
On the traditional lands of:	Nez Perce (Nimíipuu)	Nez Perce (Nimíipuu)

Directions from Joseph:

- From Joseph, turn left at a sign for Imnaha and Halfway onto OR 350.
- Drive 8 miles towards Imnaha and turn right at a sign for Salt Creek and Hells Canyon.
- Drive 12.5 miles on this road, FR 39, to a junction with 3900-100 on the right, just after a bridge. This junction is about 3 miles beyond Salt Creek Sno-Park.
- Turn right and drive this rocky dirt road for 3.1 miles uphill to the Tenderfoot Trailhead at road's end. Passenger cars can make it if driven very slowly but you'll prefer to have some clearance.
- **Drivetime from Joseph:** 45 minutes

Hike: The east side of the Wallowas are a scenic delight! The forests are more open and reminiscent of Oregon's high desert, the peaks are more rounded and gentler than those in the western Wallowas, and the rocks here are red and grey, adding color to an already lovely scene. This wild

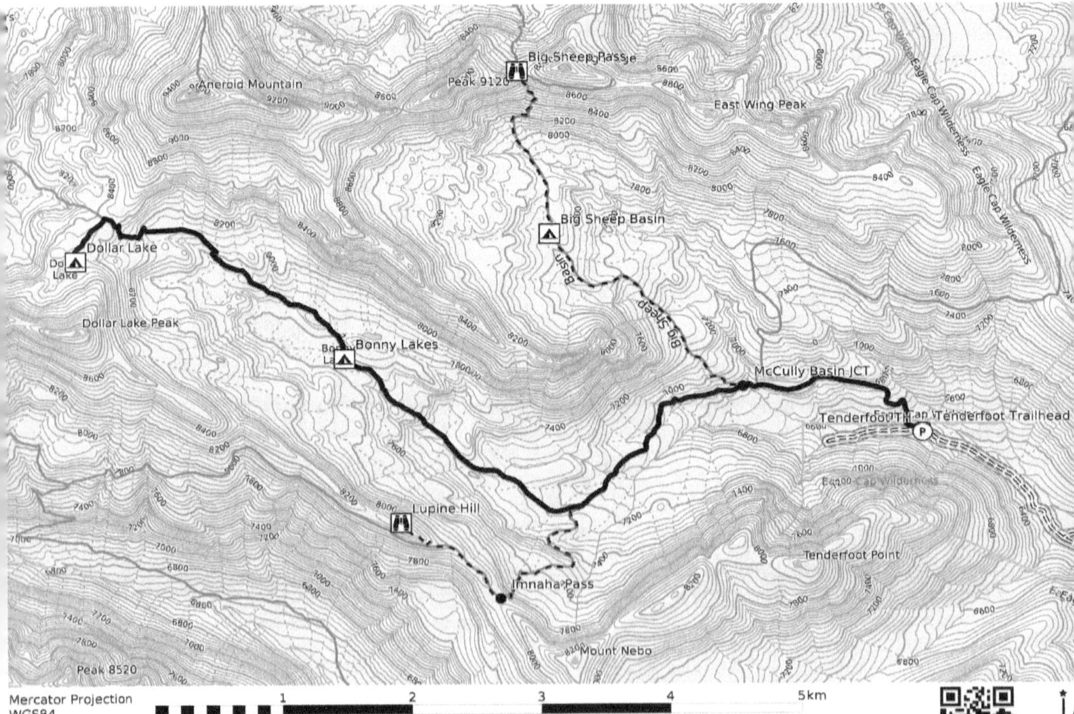

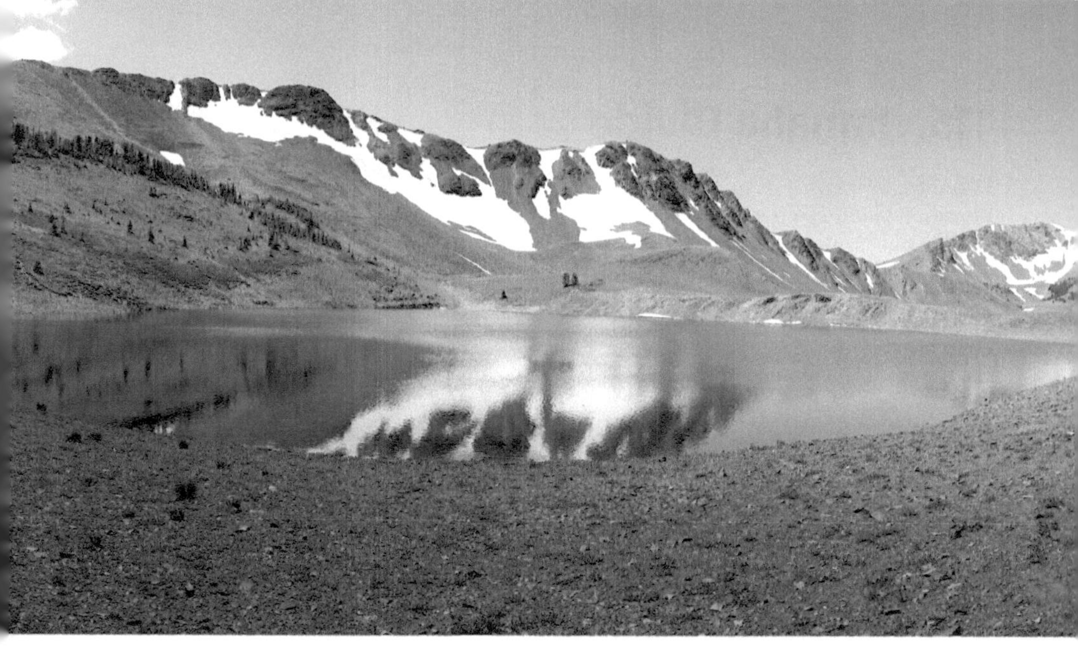

Dollar Lake, deep in the heart of the eastern Wallowas.

and gorgeous hike takes you into the heart of the eastern Wallowas, to a pair of scenic lakes at the base of Aneroid Mountain. Energetic hikers can continue almost 2 more miles to Dollar Lake, an austere gem set at the very crest of the mountains. This hike will stay with you long after you return home, its scenery occupying a place in your heart.

From the Tenderfoot Trailhead, follow what is actually the Tenderfoot Wagon Road to the wilderness boundary, just beyond the trailhead. The trail curves to the right here to cross Big Sheep Creek. Look for a scramble trail that leads down to a bridge, as the main trail leads to the unbridged horse crossing. Once across the creek, the trail begins a gentle ascent through open woods and the occasional hanging meadow full of sagebrush and summer-blooming flowers, among them clarkia, mariposa lilies, and red paintbrush. At 1 mile, the trail crosses a creek at a poorly-marked junction with the Wing Ridge Trail. Continue straight across the creek and soon reach another junction on your right, this time with the McCully Creek Trail at 1.2 miles; this steep trail climbs into beautiful Big Sheep Basin, a rarely-visited place that is worth a hike in its own right. For this hike, however, keep straight on the Tenderfoot Wagon Road. The trail continues for 1.3 miles to a fork in the trail with the North Fork Imnaha Trail. Forking left here takes you to the top of Imnaha Divide, an adventure described in Hike 115. Instead, you'll turn right here and continue hiking gently uphill another 1.6 miles to the first of the beautiful Bonny Lakes. Make these peaceful lakes your destination if you're only looking for a moderate hike.

If you're up for the longer hike to Dollar Lake, continue following the Bonny Lakes Trail another 1.6 miles through increasingly open and rocky terrain. As the trail nears Dollar Pass at 8,486 feet, you may even encounter large snow drifts early in the summer. If you lose the trail, simply heading uphill will take you to the pass. Once you reach Dollar Pass, Sacajawea Peak and the Matterhorn come into view across the valley. At a cairn at the pass, turn left here and follow a faint path to spectacular Dollar Lake. There are a pair of excellent campsites should you wish to spend the night at this beautiful blue pool.

When you're ready, return the way you came.

115. Imnaha Divide

Distance: 8.6 miles out and back
Elevation Gain: 1,700 feet
Trailhead Elevation: 6,485 feet
Trail High Point: 8,181 feet
Season: July – October
Best: July – October
Pass: none needed
On the traditional lands of: Nez Perce (Nimíipuu)

Directions from Joseph:

- From Joseph, turn left at a sign for Imnaha and Halfway onto OR 350.
- Drive 8 miles towards Imnaha and turn right at a sign for Salt Creek and Hells Canyon.
- Drive 12.5 miles on this road, FR 39, to a junction with 3900-100 on the right, just after a bridge. This junction is about 3 miles beyond Salt Creek Sno-Park.
- Turn right and drive this rocky dirt road for 3.1 miles uphill to the Tenderfoot Trailhead at road's end. Passenger cars can make it if driven very slowly but you'll prefer to have some clearance.
- **Drivetime from Joseph:** 45 minutes

Hike: For all of the scenic splendor to be found in the Wallowas, most of the best hikes lead to gorgeous alpine lakes. If you visit the Wallowas regularly, even the most spectacular hikes here can begin to blend together in your mind. For something truly different, consider this moderate hike onto the crest of Imnaha Divide. Although this hike shares its first two miles with the trek to Bonny Lakes and Dollar Lake (Hike 114), the remainder of the hike follows a trail onto a spectacular, flower-spangled ridgeline where views stretch into the far horizon. This is the best ridge hike in the eastern Wallowas, and perhaps the best ridge hike in the entire Wallowa Mountains. Avoid this trail when there is any threat of thunderstorms, as the exposed ridge offers no protection from a summer lightning storm.

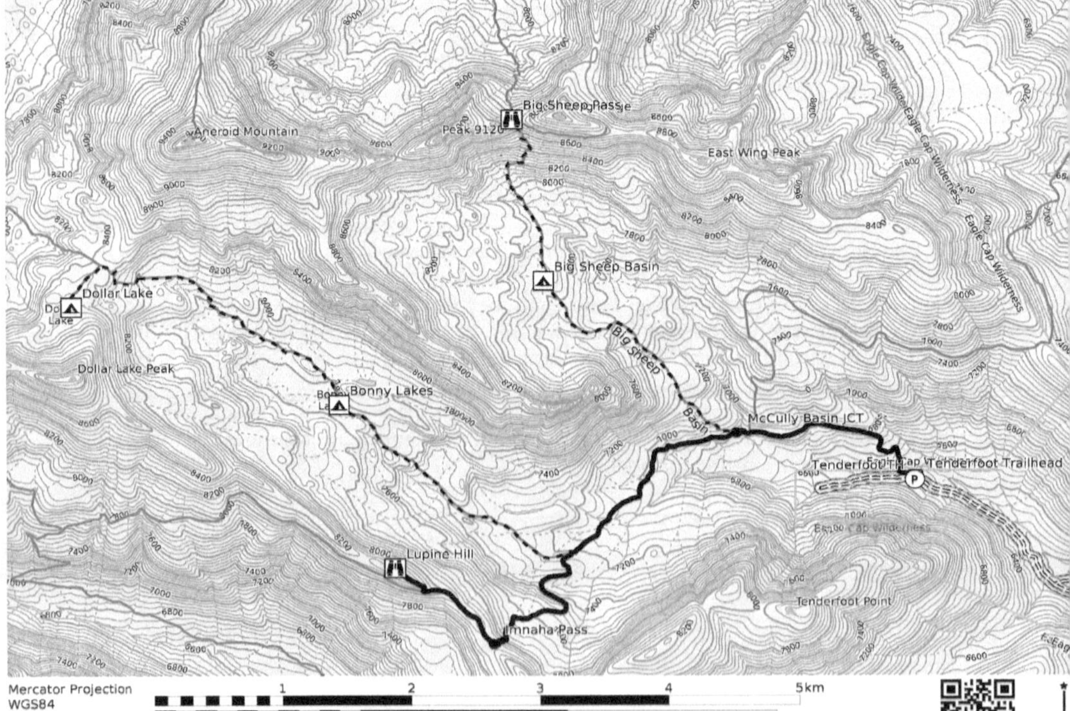

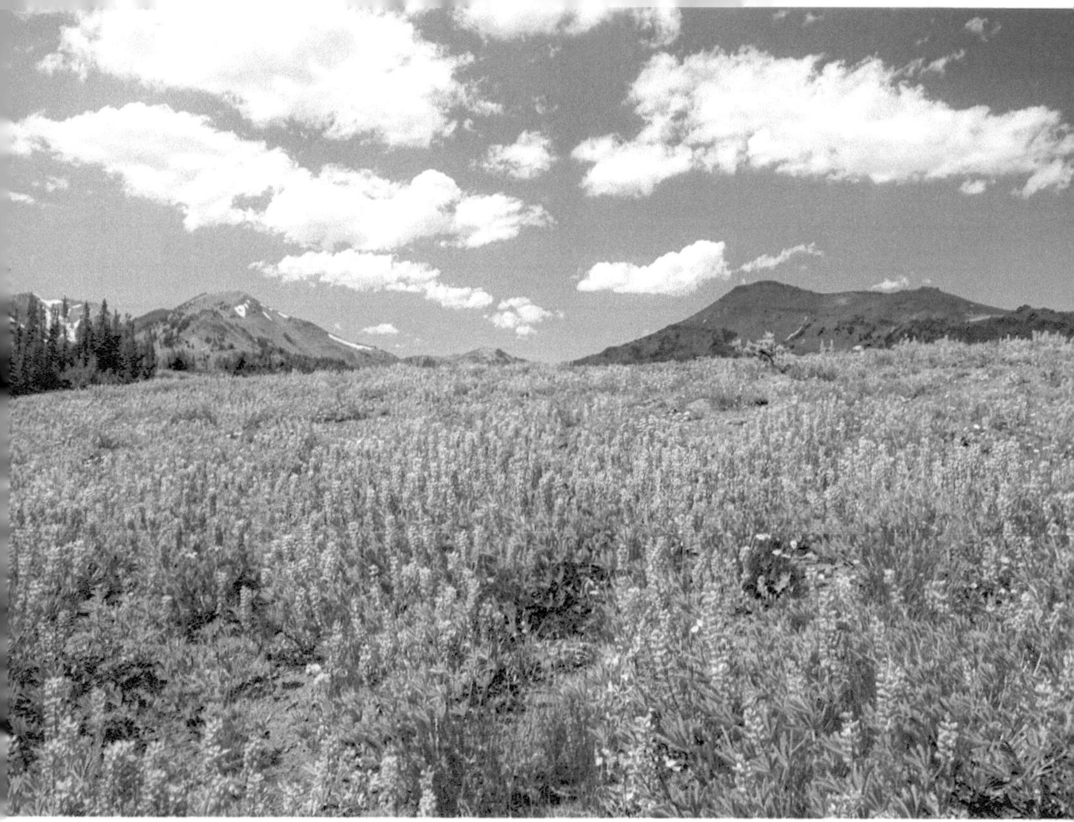

Wildflowers cover Imnaha Divide, a view-packed ridge in the eastern Wallowas.

From the Tenderfoot Trailhead, hike to the wilderness boundary. Notice a scramble trail leading downhill to the right to a bridge over Big Sheep Creek (the main trail leads to an unbridged equestrian crossing). Cross the creek and hike uphill into the open forests and hanging meadows typical of the eastern Wallowas. Just after a creek crossing, the trail meets a junction with the McCully Basin Trail at 1.2 mile from the trailhead. This trail takes hikers steeply uphill to Big Sheep Basin, a beautiful destination in its own right (see the map). For this hike, you'll continue straight on the main trail. The trail climbs gradually for 1.3 mile to a fork. Right leads to Bonny Lakes and Dollar Lake (Hike 114), but here you turn left to hike up to Imnaha Divide.

The trail up to the divide is sometimes gentle and sometimes quite steep, and you'll likely be huffing and puffing by the time you reach Imnaha Pass at an elevation of 7,910 feet, some 3.6 miles from the trailhead. The view here is nice, but there are better views further along the crest. The trail then follows Imnaha Divide's rolling ridge. Below you some 1,300 feet is the North Fork Imnaha River, in a deep and green valley that seems like an oasis. Continue on the North Fork Trail another 0.5 mile from Imnaha Pass until you see a steep green knob above the trail. Leave the trail here and scramble up the knob, following animal trails along the way. When you reach the summit of the knob, the crest of the Wallowas spread out before you. Look for red Aneroid Mountain, the granite profile of the Matterhorn, and many other peaks of the high Wallowas. Lupine blooms profusely on this ridgeline in July, adding color and an intoxicating aroma to the scene. You can ramble along the ridge crest as far as long as you want but remember that the trail is downhill to your left. The further you travel along the ridge, the harder it is to scramble down to the trail.

When you're ready to leave this incredible spot, return the way you came.

116. Summit Point and Pine Lakes Pass

	Summit Point Lookout	Pine Lakes Pass
Distance:	2 miles out and back	11.6 miles out and back
Elevation Gain:	576 feet	2,600 feet
Trailhead Elevation:	6,442 feet	6,442 feet
Trail High Point:	7,018 feet	8,383 feet
Season:	July - October	July - October
Best:	July - October	July - October
Pass:	none needed	none needed
On the traditional lands of:	Nez Perce (Nimíipuu)	Nez Perce (Nimíipuu)

Directions from Baker City:

- From Baker City, drive OR 86 east for 44.6 miles to a junction on the left with FR 77, at a sign for Summit Point Lookout.
- Turn left here and drive 10.6 miles of excellent gravel to a junction on the right with FR 7715, opposite McBride Campground.
- Turn right and drive 1.7 miles to a junction, where you keep right.
- Drive 4.6 miles of steep but mostly good gravel to a turnaround at road's end. This is the trailhead.
- **Drivetime from Baker City:** 1 hour and 45 minutes

Hike: The southern Wallowas are often overlooked by hikers for a variety of reasons: it takes a long time to drive there from almost anywhere, the roads are often quite rough, and most of the best destinations are out of reach of even the most athletic day hikers. This hike on the very southern end of the Wallowas offers you an easy hike to Summit Point's lookout tower, or a more difficult hike to Pine Lakes Pass and its fantastic viewpoint of the southern Wallowa crest. Whatever option you choose, you're sure to love this scenic corner of one of Oregon's greatest wilderness areas.

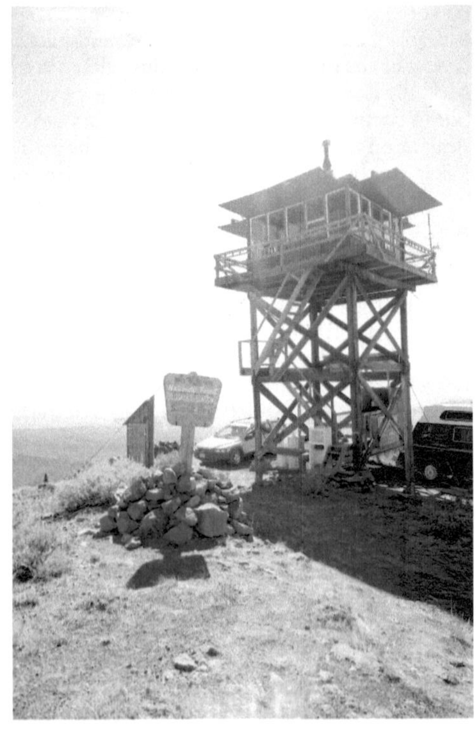

Begin by hiking up the gated road from the trailhead. After 0.7 mile of uphill walking, keep right to continue following the road to the lookout tower. Reach the lookout at 1 mile from the trailhead. Summit Point Lookout, elevation 7,000 feet, is staffed in the summer. The staffer may invite you up for a visit but don't force it, and if invited, don't overstay your welcome. The view here is as fantastic as you would expect, stretching from the Elkhorns to the southern end of Hells Canyon, with the southern Wallowas directly in front of you. As far as easy hikes go, this is about as good as it gets. To return to the trailhead from the lookout, simply walk down the road back 1 mile to your car.

If you're planning on the longer hike to Pine Lakes Pass, walk back down to the last junction and turn right onto the Cliff Creek Trail. You'll climb steadily over a series of knobs for about a mile, eventually emerging at the southern end of enormous Little Eagle Meadow. Follow the trail over a fence and across the vast meadow, where lupine blooms profusely in the summer. The path becomes faint at times due to cattle grazing, but follow cairns and continue hiking in a northernly direction until you reach the junction with the Schneider Cabin Trail at 3.4 mile (including the detour to the lookout). Continue straight here, noting that you will need to fork to the right at the cairn here on your return trip.

Beyond the junction, the trail lurches steeply uphill, gaining 250 feet in short order before leveling out. From here, you'll continue climbing gradually along the western slope of Cornucopia Mountain. Reach a rushing trailside spring at 4.2 miles, where you should absolutely stop and refill your water bottles if you need water; this is some of the most delicious water I've ever tasted in my entire life! Beyond the spring, the trail continues just under a mile to a trail junction at Nip Pass. Turn right here and continue another half-mile of steep downs and ups to Tuck Pass, where you reach yet another trail junction. Turn right at this junction too and climb another 0.8 mile to Pine Lakes Pass at 6.4 miles from the trailhead. Views stretch north to the central Wallowas, west to the Elkhorns, and east to the upper reaches of Hells Canyon. Mountain goats are frequently seen on the slopes up here. Below you here is a spectacular green tarn, and below that the Pine Lakes. The lakes themselves would make an attractive goal but to get there, you'll have to hike another 1.7 miles and lose 900 feet, placing them out of reach of most day hikers. Instead, make this your destination for the day.

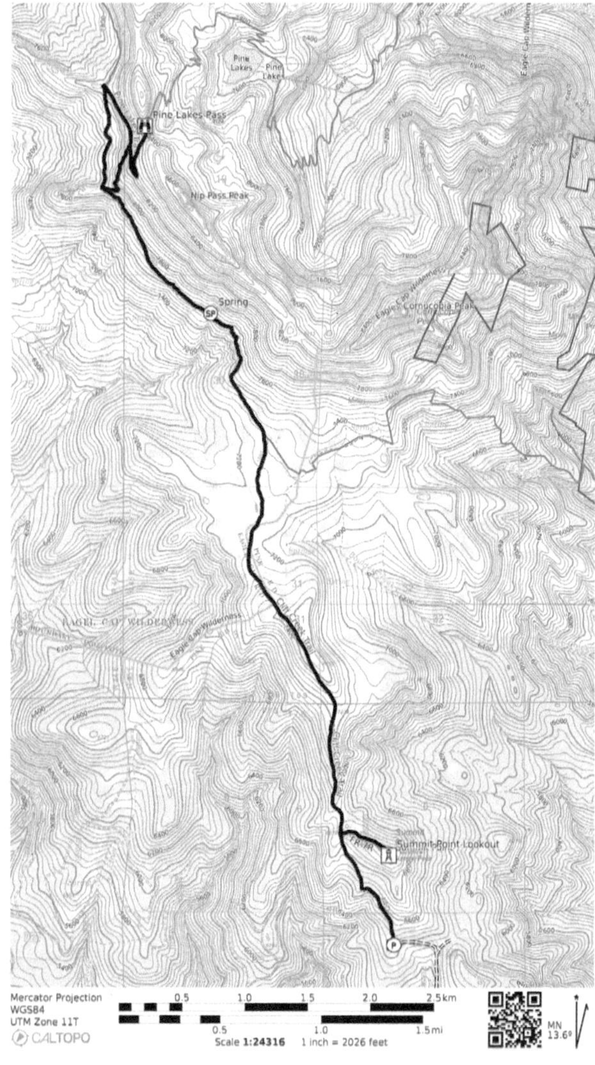

On the return, note the trail junction at a cairn about halfway back to Tuck Pass (some 0.4 mile back from Pine Lakes Pass). To take a scenic detour that shaves more than a mile from your return hike, turn left here and follow this trail steeply downhill. After many switchbacks you'll reunite with the Cliff Creek Trail just below Nip Pass. Turn left here and return the way you came back towards Summit Point and the trailhead.

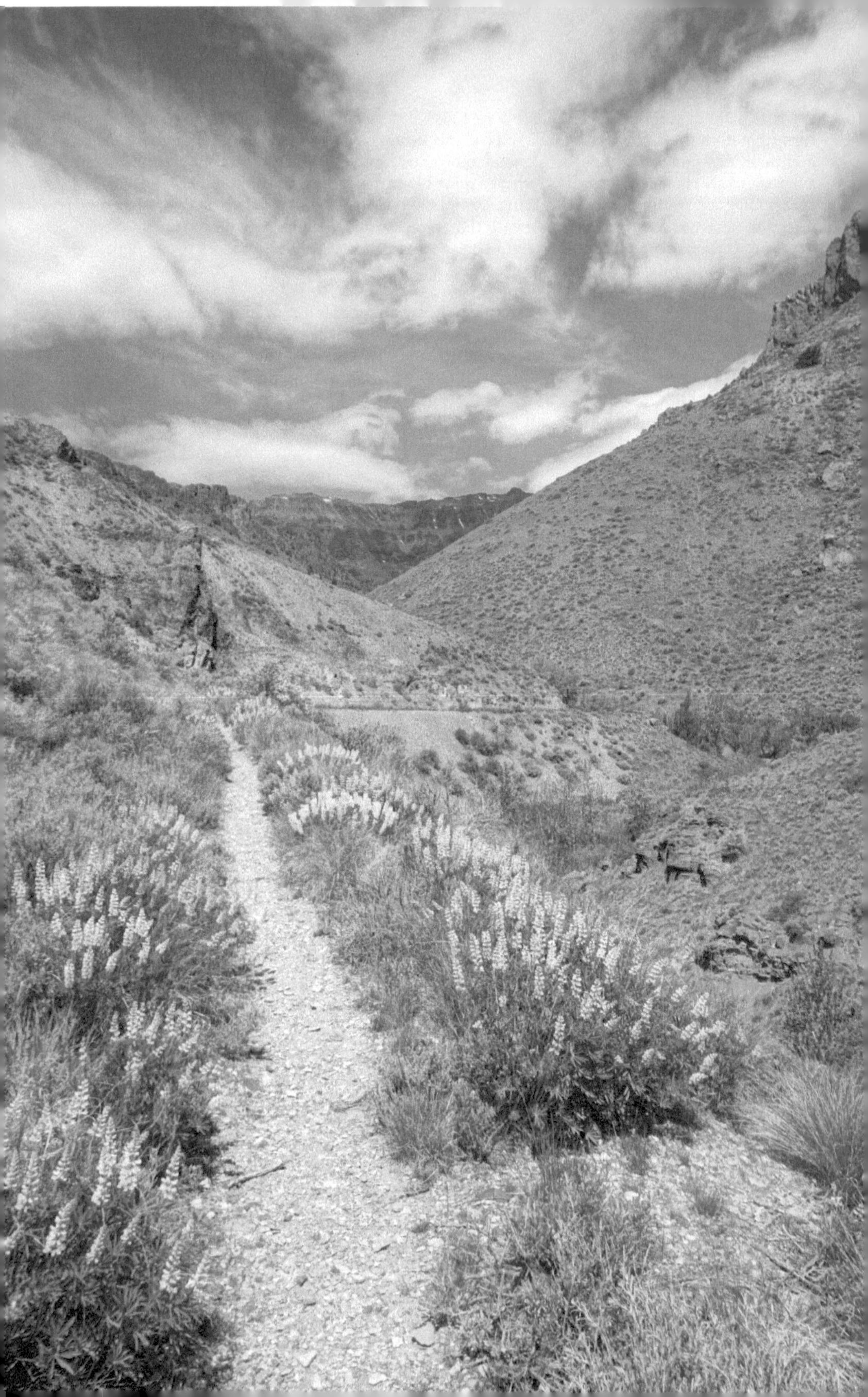

Southeast Oregon

		Distance	EV Gain	Page
117.	Strawberry Mountain	13 mi	3,300 ft	270
118.	Malheur River Trail	10 mi	600 ft	272
119.	North Fork Malheur River	6 mi	200 ft	274
120.	DeGarmo Canyon	1.4 mi	400 ft	276
121.	Barnhardy Basin	5.4 mi	800 ft	278
122.	Little Blitzen Gorge	15.6 mi	1,700 ft	280
123.	Steens Mountain Summit	4.8 mi	1,300 ft	282
124.	Pike Creek	6.6 mi	1,600 ft	284
125.	Leslie Gulch	5.8 mi	1,000 ft	286

Many Oregonians have the impression that Southeast Oregon is all desert and nothing else. While you can certainly find plenty of desert in Southeast Oregon, you'll also find rugged and remote mountains, sprawling forests of ponderosa pine and juniper, and some of the most spectacular red rock canyons this side of Utah. You could spend an entire lifetime and not see even a fraction of this spectacular corner of Oregon.

The greatest challenge in visiting southeast Oregon is the remote nature of the most scenic destinations. While Steens Mountain (Hikes 122-124) is a popular destination with campgrounds and outposts scattered all around the mountain, the rest of the hikes in this section require careful planning. Always make sure to check the weather forecast before you leave for your adventure, and be prepared to change plans if rain, snow, or thunderstorms threaten. Just as importantly, make sure that your gas tank is full and that your tires are fully inflated. Make sure that you have dealt with any and all car issues before you leave for this area. Many southeast Oregon residents bring one or more spare tires and a gas can or two when they explore the area. While this is not always necessary, it isn't a bad idea for any of these hikes. For more tips to help you prepare for your adventures, see the introduction to this book.

The basic premise of this book is that all of these hikes can be completed in a day, and are accessible in almost any vehicle. It is for this reason that there are only nine hikes featured in this section on southeast Oregon. If you plan on exploring Hart Mountain (Hikes 120 and 121), the Alvord Desert (Hike 124), and the Owyhee Canyonlands (Hike 125) further, you should be prepared for rough roads that can only be navigated in completely dry conditions. For more information, consult a good map of the area, inquire locally, and be prepared for the adventure of a lifetime.

Photo on left: Pike Creek Trail on Steens Mountain (Hike 124)

117. Strawberry Mountain

	Little Strawberry Lake	Strawberry Mountain
Distance:	6.8 miles out and back	13 miles out and back
Elevation Gain:	1,400 feet	3,300 feet
Trailhead Elevation:	5,735 feet	5,735 feet
Trail High Point:	6,959 feet	9,038 feet
Season:	July - October	July - October
Best:	July - October	July - October
Pass:	NW Forest Pass	NW Forest Pass
On the traditional lands of:	the Nüümü (Northern Paiute) and Warm Springs peoples	the Nüümü (Northern Paiute) and Warm Springs peoples

Directions:

- From the junction of US 26 and US 395 in John Day, drive 12.6 miles east on US 26 to a junction with Bridge Street in Prairie City. This junction is signed for trailheads and is just after you pass the ranger station in Prairie City.
- Turn right and drive 0.4 mile on Bridge Street to a junction on the right with S. Bridge Street, signed for Strawberry Campground.
- Turn right here and drive 3 miles of paved road and another 8 miles of gravel to road's end at Strawberry Campground, which also serves as the trailhead for this hike. The last 3 miles of this road are steep, bumpy, and narrow but any passenger car should make it just fine if driven with care.
- **Drivetime from John Day:** 40 minutes

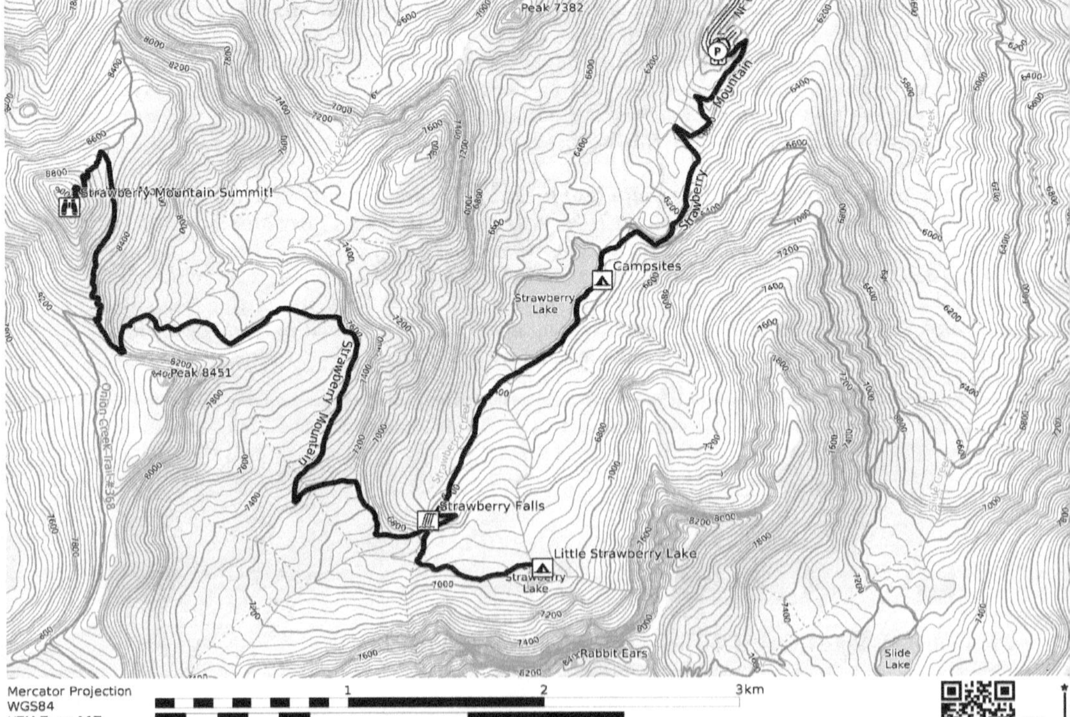

Hike: At the confluence of the high desert and the Blue Mountains, the Strawberry Range is a small slice of mountain paradise that rises over the towns of John Day, Canyon City, and Prairie City. The Strawberries are rarely seen on the bucket lists of Oregon hikers, but virtually everyone who has ever been loves it dearly. This trek to Strawberry Lake and the summit of Strawberry Mountain, the highest point in the range, touches a little bit of everything that makes this corner of eastern Oregon so special.

From the Strawberry Campground Trailhead, locate the trail at the eastern end of the trailhead and follow it gradually uphill. Continue following signs for Strawberry Lake at trail junctions. You will reach scenic Strawberry Lake in 1.4 miles. The trail forks at the lake, so make sure to keep left if you're looking for a longer hike. Strawberry Lake is a fantastic destination for an easy hike, and hikers with children and folks short on time may just decide to stop here. Who could blame you? If you're planning on a longer hike to either Little Strawberry Lake or the summit of Strawberry Mountain, keep left and follow the trail around the lake. There are campsites along the lakeshore as well, should you wish to backpack. The trail stays above the lake all the way to its far end (there are user trails that follow the lakeshore, should you wish to get closer to the lake) and then climbs gradually for more than a mile to scenic Strawberry Falls at about 2.7 miles from the trailhead. Waterfalls are rare in this part of Oregon and this one is a beauty, with a mossy grotto lining the base of the falls. Beyond Strawberry Falls, the trail switchbacks uphill another tenth of a mile to a trail junction just after a bridge over Strawberry Creek. If you're planning on the moderate hike to Little Strawberry Lake, you turn left here. If you're planning on the long trek to the summit of Strawberry Mountain, keep right. Note that the distance listed above does not include the side trip to Little Strawberry Lake; if you're doing both, the round-trip distance is 14.2 miles.

For Little Strawberry Lake, turn left and continue hiking uphill along Strawberry Creek. You'll top out at around 7,000 feet of elevation and drop a short distance to Little Strawberry Lake at 3.4 miles from the trailhead, or 0.6 mile from the trail junction. The lake is a lovely shade of green and blue, and is backed by a huge rockslide and the crags of Rabbit Ears. There are several campsites here should you wish to backpack. Mountain goats are frequently seen at the lake and on the slopes above the lake. If this is your destination, return the way you came. If you're still planning on the longer hike to the summit of Strawberry Mountain, return to the junction and turn left.

From the junction, the trail climbs through several meadows with fantastic displays of summer wildflowers. Sagebrush lines the trail at times, reminding you that you're at the edge of the desert. The trail passes a number of viewpoints down to Strawberry Falls and Strawberry Lake, and before long, Strawberry Mountain's summit pyramid comes into view. After 2.5 miles, huff and puff up to a trail junction with the Onion Trail. Turn right here at a sign for Strawberry Mountain. You'll keep climbing along a shaley slope another 0.7 mile to a junction with the spur trail to the summit. Turn left here and climb up the last 0.4 mile to the summit. The 9,038-foot summit of Strawberry Mountain is the highest point for over 100 miles in every direction, and the views are as extraordinary as you would expect. Below you are the valleys of the John Day and Malheur Rivers. The crest of the Strawberry Range is at your feet. The view stretches north to the Blue Mountains and south to distant Steens Mountain. You should feel proud; you just climbed one of Oregon's most impressive and extraordinary mountains! Spend a few moments to take it all in but beware of summer thunderstorms; if you hear any rumble of thunder, get off the summit as fast as you can. If you're planning on an even longer trip, there are several back-packing routes through the Strawberries that explore more of this beautiful corner of eastern Oregon. Consult a map and plan to your heart's desire. But for this hike, return the way you came.

118. Malheur River Trail

Distance: 10 miles out and back
Elevation Gain: 600 feet
Trailhead elevation: 4,794 feet
Trail High Point: 4,812 feet
Season: May – October
Best: May – June, October
Pass: none needed
On the traditional lands of: the Nüümü (Northern Paiute) people

Directions:

- From the intersection of US 26 and US 395 in John Day, drive south on US 395 for 10 miles to a junction with Canyon Creek Road, just before the road begins a long climb out of the valley. Turn left here. If you drove here from Burns, drive north for 42 miles to the junction on the right, just as the road reaches the bottom of a long descent.
- Drive Canyon Creek Road, which becomes Country Road 65, for 13.5 miles to a junction with FR 16. Turn left here.
- Drive this road for 5 miles to a junction on the right with FR 1643, signed for the Malheur River. Turn right here.
- Drive this curvy gravel road for 8.5 miles and then fork to the left at a sign for the Malheur River onto FR 1651.
- Continue 1.2 miles to the trailhead at Malheur Ford, where FR 1651 crosses the Malheur River. People do sometimes drive across the river here, but thankfully, you won't need to.
- There is one campsite and a pit toilet at the trailhead if you're planning on camping.
- **Drivetime from John Day:** 60 minutes

The Malheur River Trail follows its namesake for 7.6 wildly scenic miles.

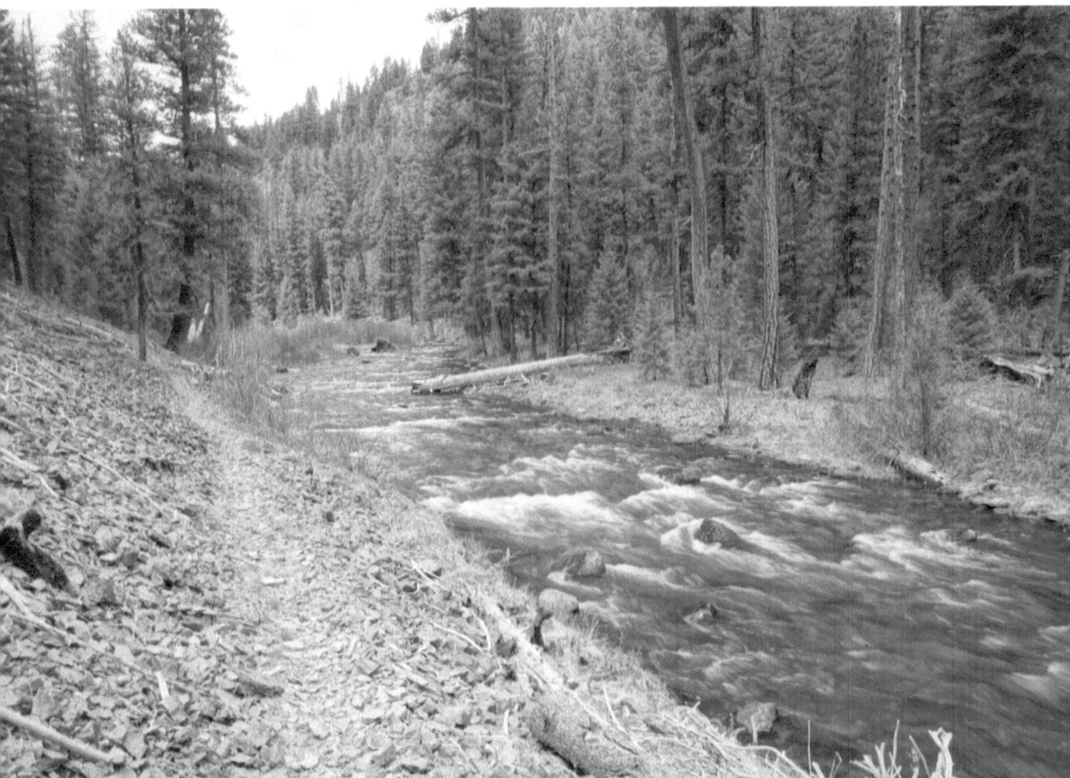

Hike: The Malheur River was named by French trappers for an unpleasant ordeal somewhere in the desert near the river's mouth ("malheur" is best translated as "misfortune" in French), but you'll be all smiles when you hike the Malheur River Trail southeast of John Day. This easy trail follows the wildly scenic Malheur River through a rocky canyon of tall ponderosa pines and spring and summer wildflowers. The easy trail grade, easy access, and plethora of excellent campsites make this a great destination for a relaxed backpacking trip. Whatever you decide to do here, chances are that you'll love it. Quel bonheur!

From the trailhead, locate the Malheur River Trail. You'll follow the river downstream in a forest of stately ponderosa pines and larches. The trail mostly stays close to its namesake but occasionally climbs short distances away from the river to avoid rocky outcrops. Wildflowers line the trail in late spring and early summer, most notably Mule's ears. You should also keep an eye out for ticks, as they are frequently found in this canyon during the warmer months. You may also encounter rattlesnakes here on hot days, but I've never seen one here. Trail markers every mile help you keep track of your progress.

At just under 2 miles from the trailhead, you'll climb to a rocky outcrop above the river, with views to the shaley slopes below. From here, every mile brings a succession of great destinations. At 3 miles, pass a scenic meadow with a nice campsite by the river. This makes the first of many possible turnaround spots, but there are plenty more places downriver to explore if you've still got the energy to continue. If you're spending the night, please resist the temptation to build a fire in this dry canyon.

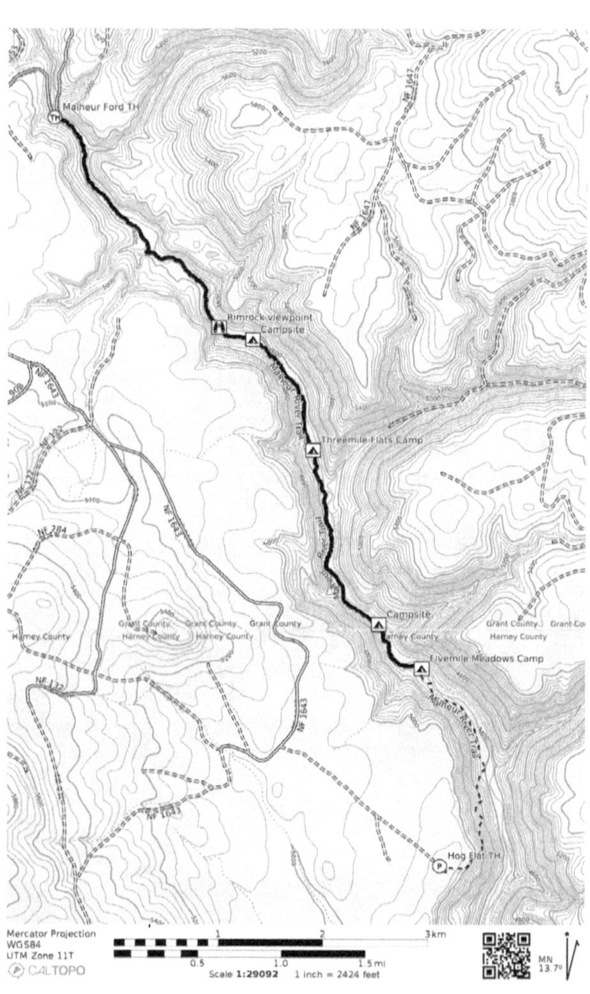

Beyond this point, the Malheur River Trail climbs a little bit to avoid another rocky outcrop above the river, only to return to river level at 4 miles from the trailhead. Very near the 4 mile marker, you'll find a large rock by the river with more than enough room for two people to sit and rest. Beyond this point, you'll continue to follow the river through its scenic canyon. At almost exactly 5 miles from the trailhead, you'll reach another huge meadow by the river with enough room for several people to camp. This would make for a fantastic destination for an overnight backpack, and it is also the recommended destination for a 10 mile day hike.

The Malheur River Trail continues downstream another 2 miles to its lower trailhead at Hog Flat, making a car shuttle possible. To find this lower trailhead, consult the Malheur National Forest for directions. The Malheur River canyon is so gorgeous though that you'll probably just want to return the way you came.

119. North Fork Malheur River

Distance: 6 miles out and back
Elevation Gain: 200 feet
Trailhead elevation: 4,662 feet
Trail high Point: 4,693 feet
Season: May – October
Best: May – June, October
Pass: none needed
On the traditional lands of: the Nüümü (Northern Paiute) people

Directions:

- From the junction of US 26 and US 395 in John Day, drive 12.6 miles east on US 26 to a junction with Bridge Street in Prairie City. This junction is signed for trailheads and is just after you pass the ranger station in Prairie City.
- Turn right and drive 0.4 mile on Bridge Street to a junction on the right with S. Bridge Street, signed for Strawberry Campground. Keep left here, ignoring signs for Strawberry Campground. Bridge Street becomes Country Road 62, Summit Prairie Road.
- Drive 7.8 miles to a junction with FR 13 on the left. Either of these roads will take you to the trailhead, but it's a little faster to turn left here onto FR 13.
- Drive 16.3 miles on this road until you reach road's end at a junction with FR 16, next to Short Creek Guard Station. Turn right here.
- Drive west 2.1 miles to a junction with FR 1675. Turn left here onto this gravel road.
- You'll drive 2.3 miles of mostly good gravel to North Fork Malheur River Campground. If you're driving a low-clearance vehicle, you should park here and walk the rest of the way. It's a beautiful walk! If you have a high-clearance vehicle, continue on a narrow, bumpy dirt road for 1 mile to the trailhead at a fork in the road.
- **Note:** There are many different ways to get to this trailhead, so a good map of the Malheur

The bridge over the North Fork Malheur River at the trailhead.

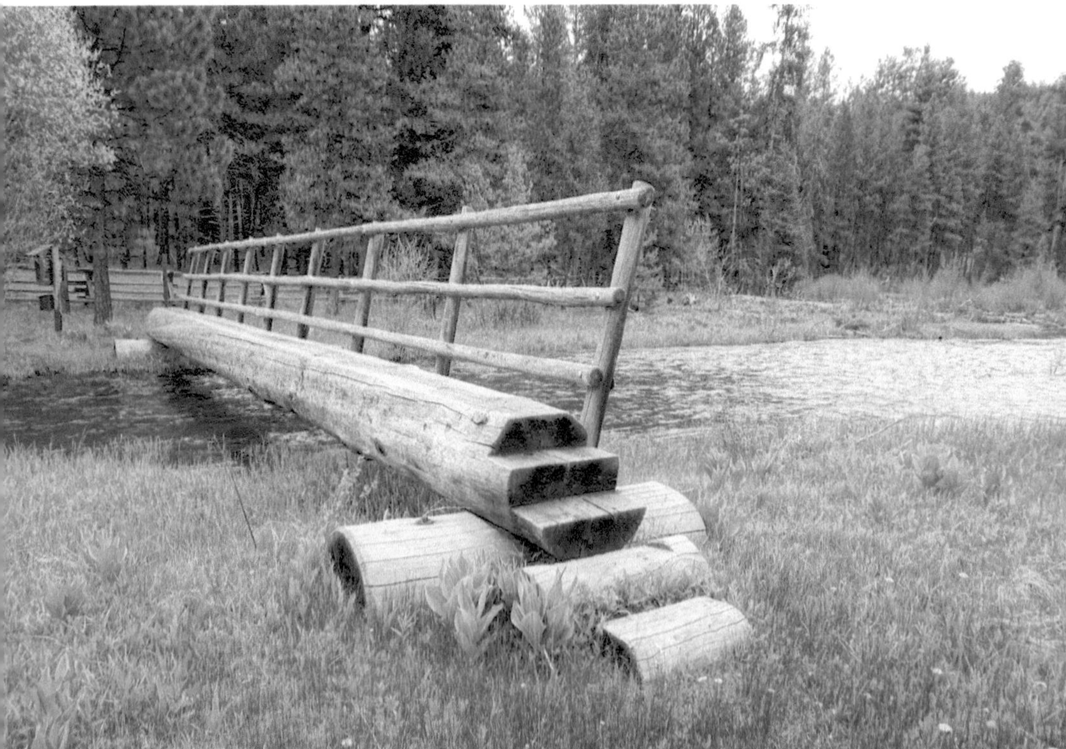

National Forest is a good idea here. This approach is the most direct from the north; if you're coming from the south, your directions will be completely different. When I did this hike, I drove in from the south via Seneca and then drove to Prairie City using the route described above. In any case, it's a long way from anywhere.

- **Drivetime from John Day:** 75 minutes

Hike: Located far, far from any highway, the idyllic canyon of the North Fork Malheur River seems to be a small world of its own. This glassy river flows through a wide meadow of spring and summer wildflowers while huge ponderosa pines and larches provide shade and additional color. This peaceful place was touched by the Black Butte Fire in 2021, but for this recommended hike you'll mostly be hiking in forest that burned at a low severity. One thing you may not enjoy is cows, who roam this canyon on occasion. If you encounter cattle, give them space and let them move off the trail before you continue. Otherwise, plan on hiking this trail slowly to take in the sights and sounds of this pretty little corner of Oregon.

The trail begins by immediately crossing the river on an old log bridge. You'll then cross a secondary channel of the river on a second bridge and begin following the river at a distance. The trail passes through park-like groves of huge ponderosa pines which add a lovely color contrast to the electric green of the river's wide riparian corridor. Signs of the 2021 fire are everywhere here, but mostly at ground level. After about a mile the trail rejoins the river. Follow the river, passing scenic islands full of flowers, especially hellebore. This is one of the prettiest miles of trail in southeast Oregon, even with the noticeable fire damage. Your chances of seeing wildlife are very good if you come in the morning or evening as this trail sees very little use.

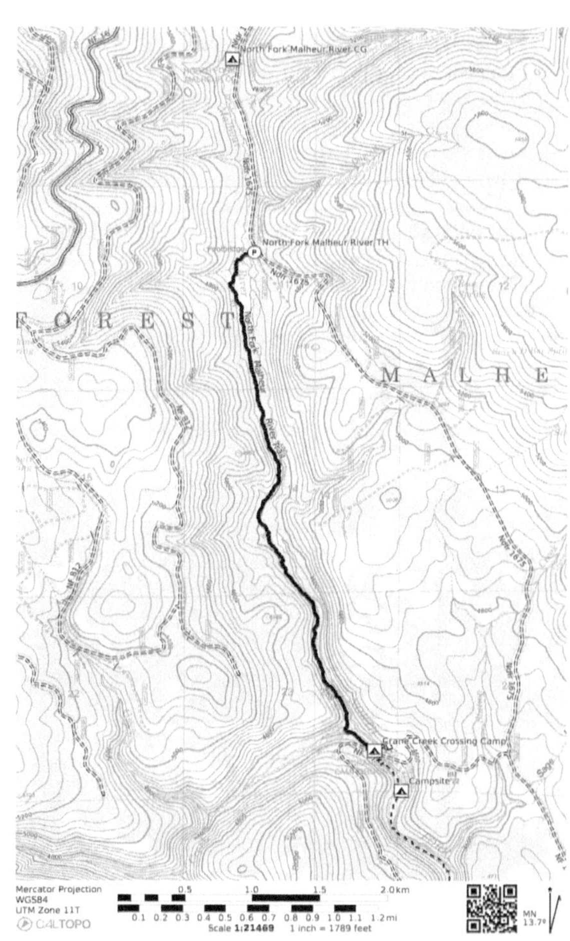

At 2.8 miles, the trail reaches an abandoned trailhead where Crane Creek flows into the North Fork Malheur River. The trail crosses the creek on another wooden bridge. The trail then meets a dirt road, which it follows for 0.2 mile to a large meadow where another road branches off to cross the river at a ford. This meadow is beautiful and features an outstanding campsite; make this your destination for this hike. The North Fork Trail continues for several miles downstream but beyond the campsite the fire damage is severe. If you're continuing downstream, expect to climb over lots of downed trees in a mostly blackened landscape.

Return the way you came instead, taking more time to bask in the beauty of this extraordinary canyon.

120. DeGarmo Canyon

	DeGarmo Falls	DeGarmo Canyon Loop
Distance:	1.4 miles out and back	3 mile loop
Elevation Gain:	400 feet	900 feet
Trailhead Elevation:	4,853 feet	4,853 feet
Trail High Point:	5,273 feet	5,701 feet
Season:	May – October	May – October
Best:	May – October	May – October
Pass:	none needed	none needed
On the traditional lands of:	the Nüümü (Northern Paiute)	the Nüümü (Northern Paiute)

Directions:

- From Lakeview, drive north on US 395 for 5 miles to a junction with OR 140 on the right. Turn right here.
- Drive 15.3 miles to a junction on the left for Plush. Turn left.
- Drive 19.4 miles on this paved road. Just as you leave the small town of Plush, turn right on Hart Mountain Road.
- Drive 8.5 miles of paved road to a junction on the right at a small sign for DeGarmo Canyon. If you're coming from Hart Mountain's headquarters, this junction is on the left, 4.5 miles after the beginning of pavement.
- Turn right and immediately begin looking for places to park. Follow this rough, narrow track for 0.5 mile to the trailhead at road's end. Only high-clearance vehicles will make it to the trailhead; otherwise, you'll have to park along the paved road, or along one of the several side roads that branch off the trailhead road and walk to the trailhead.
- **Drivetime from Lakeview:** 1 hour and 30 minutes

Hike: Hart Mountain is a high desert world of antelope herds, steep slopes, and spring wild-

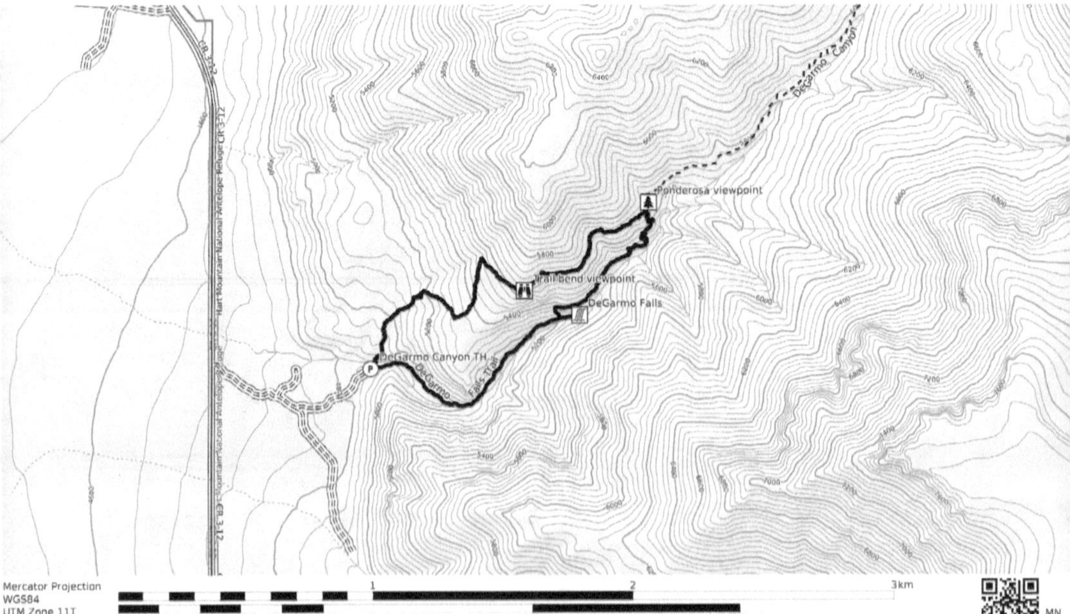

flowers. While there are several wonderful hikes in this faraway outpost, the best introduction to the area is this short but fun hike through a narrow canyon to a secret waterfall. Adventurous hikers who love off-trail scrambling can wander further into this rugged canyon in search of views, spring wildflowers, and the sound of the wind through the aspen trees that line DeGarmo Creek. This hike is not to be missed!

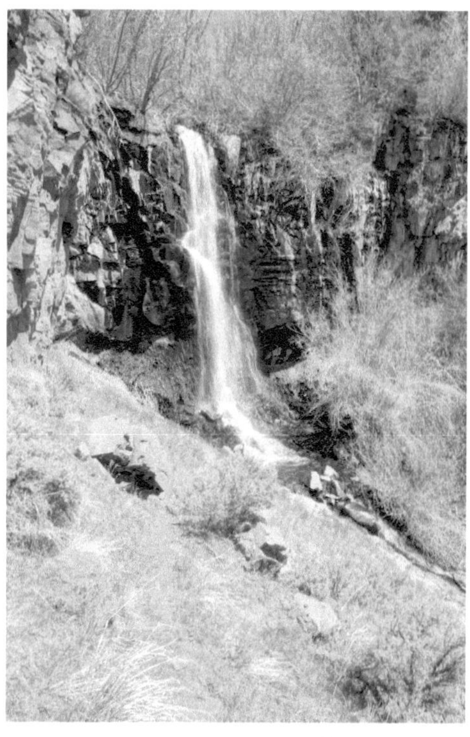

DeGarmo Falls

From the trailhead, locate a path heading uphill into DeGarmo Creek's slot canyon. This trail drops you down to a precarious crossing of the creek just above a small waterfall; at high water you'll need to scramble along a ledge above the right bank of the creek until you reach a wider spot in which to cross. Once you've reached the other side, locate the obvious trail heading uphill along the creek's left bank. You will soon reach a huge rock overhang with a view through the canyon's notch to the valley below. From here, the trail climbs through DeGarmo Canyon's hanging valley another 0.6 mile to the diminutive but lovely DeGarmo Falls. Waterfalls are rare in southeast Oregon, and this one is worth the effort. A cooling spray from the falls cools hikers on a hot day. This is a little slice of paradise! Despite the short distance of this hike, the way is a little rough and most hikers will want to turn around here, content to explore other parts of Hart Mountain as time allows. Adventurous hikers have the option to explore more of this rugged canyon but beware: the slopes beyond are steep and rocky, and trails are faint at best.

If you are up for this adventure, backtrack towards the trailhead some 100 yards to a faint scramble path heading uphill along the cliff band to the left of DeGarmo Falls. Turn here and follow this loose, slippery path steeply uphill along the cliff band. After a few hundred yards of steep scrambling, you will emerge at the slopes above DeGarmo Falls. Follow a faint path through the canyon; cairns help guide your way. When this faint path reaches a large, lonely juniper at a flat some 0.4 mile from DeGarmo Falls, locate the trail on your left heading uphill along a rockslide. Follow this trail uphill, once again using cairns to guide your way. After about ten minutes of steep climbing, you will reach an old cattle drive trail at a viewpoint of a ponderosa pine at the head of DeGarmo Creek's upper canyon. Here you are faced with a choice; do you turn right and continue further into DeGarmo Canyon, or do you turn left for a short but adventurous loop? The exploration of the upper canyon is fun, but the trail is faint and has no obvious destination. For the short but immensely fun loop, turn left at the junction onto the cattle drive trail.

The cattle drive proceeds to climb further above DeGarmo Canyon, offering views across the valley below to Plush and Drake Peak. Delicate white sand lilies line the trail in May and paintbrush is everywhere. After 0.5 mile of dramatic scenery, the trail reaches a bend with a spectacular view up DeGarmo Canyon, and out to Drake Peak. You are almost directly above DeGarmo Falls here. Beyond this point, the trail largely disappears; thankfully, you can see the trailhead some 700 feet below you. To finish the hike, you'll have to ramble down the open slopes towards the trailhead, always keeping the trailhead in view. This is about as easy as off-trail hiking gets. When you reach DeGarmo Creek just across from the trailhead, look for a trail heading down to the creek. As of May 2022, there was a board spanning the creek to help you cross with dry feet. From there, follow the trail uphill 100 feet to the trailhead.

121. Barnhardy Basin

Distance: 5.4 miles out and back
Elevation Gain: 800 feet
Trailhead elevation: 5,945 feet
Trail high Point: 6,592 feet
Season: May – October
Best: May – June, October
Pass: none needed
On the traditional lands of: the Nüümü (Northern Paiute) people

Directions:

- From Lakeview, drive north on US 395 for 5 miles to a junction with OR 140 on the right. Turn right here.
- Drive 15.3 miles to a junction on the left for Plush. Turn left.
- Drive 19.4 miles on this paved road. Just as you leave the small town of Plush, turn right on Hart Mountain Road.
- Drive 13 miles of pavement and 9.6 miles of gravel to the refuge headquarters.
- Just beyond the refuge headquarters, turn right at a sign for Hot Springs Campground.
- Drive 1.5 miles of gravel to a fork, where you keep right.
- Drive 2.5 miles of gravel to another fork. Left leads to the campground, while right leads to the hot springs and the trailhead. Unless you're camping, turn right and drive 100 yards to the hot springs. Park in the lot by the hot springs.
- **Drivetime from Lakeview:** 2 hours

Hike: The Hart Mountain National Antelope Refuge is a long way from anywhere, and once you get there you won't want to leave. The hot springs, mountain views, plentiful wildlife, and beautiful scenery invite a long stay. This easy hike to Barnhardy Basin on the slopes of Warner Peak is a fun introduction to the charms of this oasis. Adventurous hikers can use this hike as a starting point for many off-trail adventures. Whatever your plan is, come prepared for any weather imaginable!

The trail begins at a road closed by boulders. Follow this road past a couple of undeveloped hot springs to the edge of the campground, where you'll turn right on gravel Barnhardy Road. At 0.5

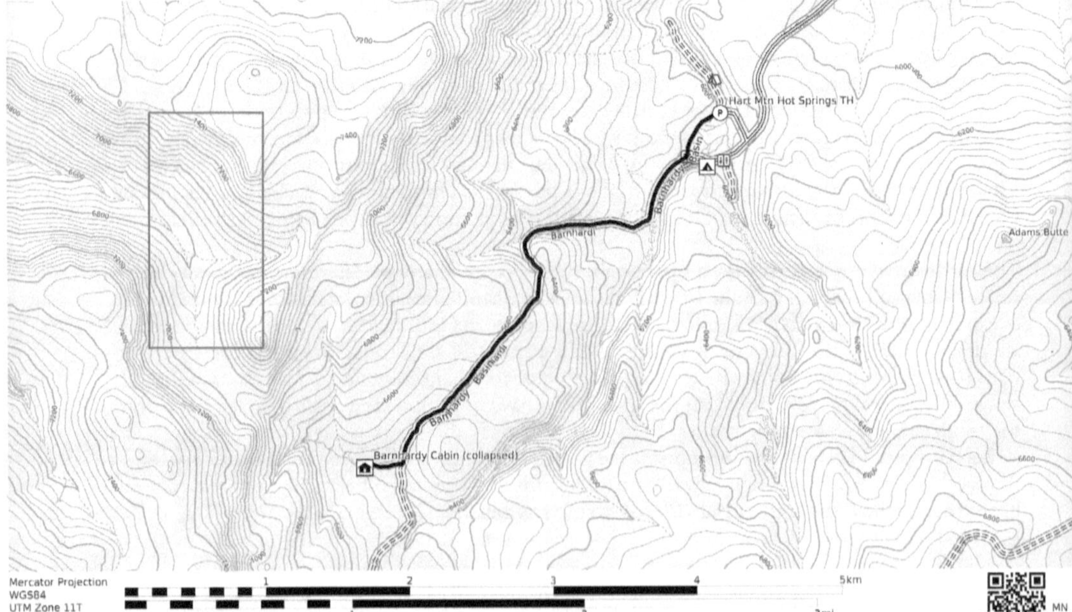

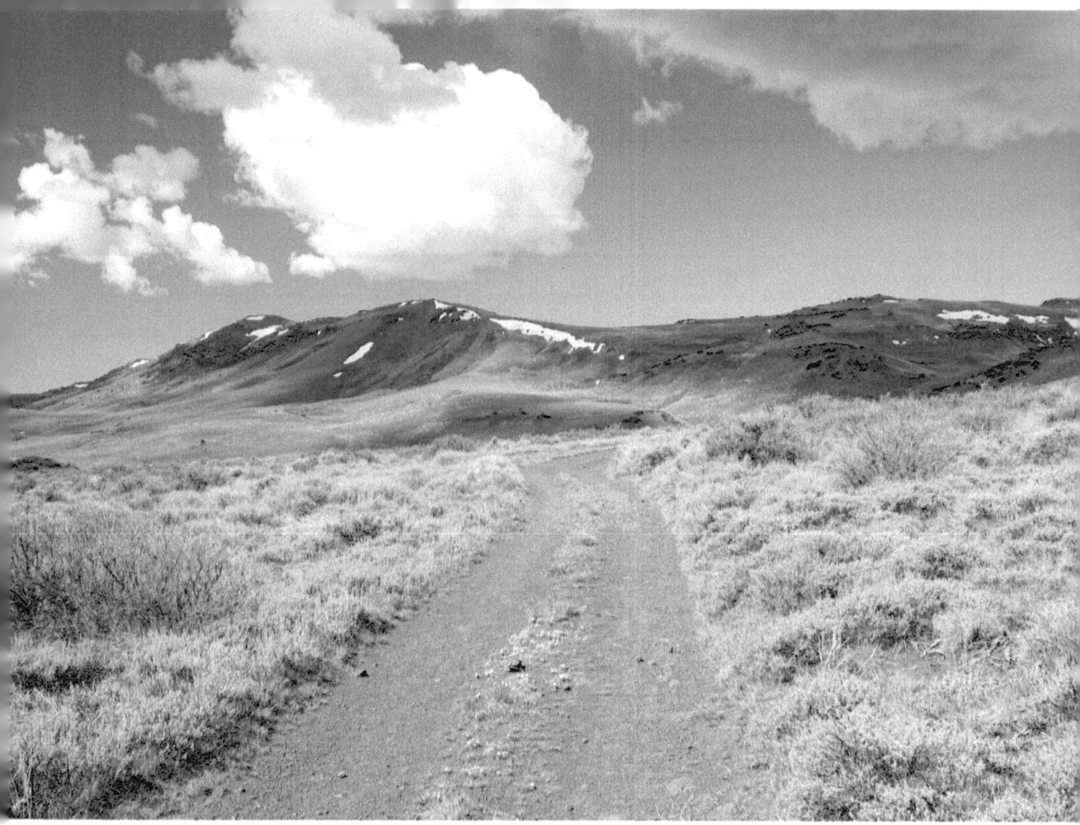

Warner Peak rises above Barnhardy Basin in the Hart Mountain region.

mile from the trailhead, reach a metal gate across the road. This gate is open from August to November, so if you're coming in the fall, you have the option of shortening your hike. In any case, walk around the gate and continue following the road as it ascends gradually through a gully lined with quaking aspen trees. As you hike along, keep your eyes peeled not just for the refuge's native antelope, but for the many other birds, rabbits, and mammals that call the area home. Views open ahead to the slopes of Warner Peak, a destination worthy of an adventurous hike.

At 1.7 miles, reach a fork. A right turn here leads hikers to the slopes above Barnhardy Basin, but for this hike you should continue straight. The road drops a bit as it approaches Barnhardy Basin. At 2.5 miles from the hot springs, you'll see a trail on your right, marked by an orange post, cutting through the meadows towards a tall metal post. The strange metal contraption in the meadow is a SNOTEL site, for monitoring snowpack in the Hart Mountain region. Follow this trail through the meadow until you reach the ruins of Barnhardy Cabin in a grove of aspen at 2.7 miles. The cabin was built during the days when the area was used for livestock grazing. The cabin's roof collapsed sometime in 2020 or 2021 and is no longer safe to enter. Most hikers should make this interesting spot their destination.

If you're up for more adventure, cross-country routes lead up the slopes above to DeGarmo Canyon (See Hike 120) and the summit of Warner Peak. This was my plan when I visited in May 2022, but a surprise snowstorm thwarted my summit attempt. Cross-country travel in the mostly treeless mountains here is limited only by your fitness and imagination; no matter where you go, it will surely be a fun and beautiful adventure.

Return the way you came.

Note: You will see Barnhardy spelled "Barnhardi" sometimes, such as on the map; both spellings are acceptable.

122. Little Blitzen Gorge

	to Moderate Meadow	to Little Blitzen Forks
Distance:	10.2 miles out and back	15.6 miles out and back
Elevation Gain:	1,100 feet	1,700 feet
Trailhead Elevation:	5,339 feet	5,339 feet
Trail High Point:	6,249 feet	6,843 feet
Season:	May - October	May - October
Best:	May - October	May - October
Pass:	none needed	none needed
On the traditional lands of:	the Nüümü (Northern Paiute) people	the Nüümü (Northern Paiute) people

Directions from Burns:

- From downtown Burns, drive east on OR 78 for 1.7 miles to a junction with OR 205 on the right.
- Turn right and drive 68 miles south on this paved highway to a junction with the South Steens Loop Road on the left.
- Turn left here and drive 18.6 miles of winding gravel to South Steens Campground.
- Continue 100 yards to the Little Blitzen Trailhead at a parking area on the right side of the road, complete with pit toilet.
- The trail leaves from the left side of the road
- This trailhead is just before the winter gate across South Steens Road.
- **Drivetime from Burns:** 2 hours and 10 minutes

Hike: Driving towards Steens Mountain on South Steens Road, the mountain's cliffs seem like an impenetrable wall. As you approach the Little Blitzen Trailhead, your eyes are drawn to a huge canyon that pierces Steens Mountain's rugged walls; this is Little Blitzen Gorge. The trek into this huge canyon is surprisingly gentle, with spring and summer wildflowers, quaking aspen

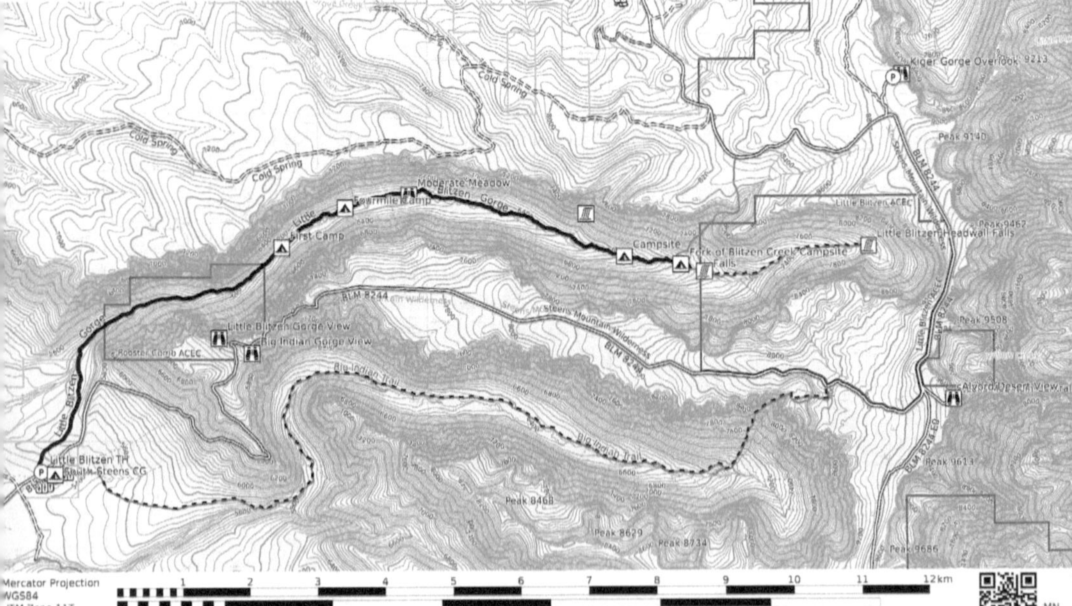

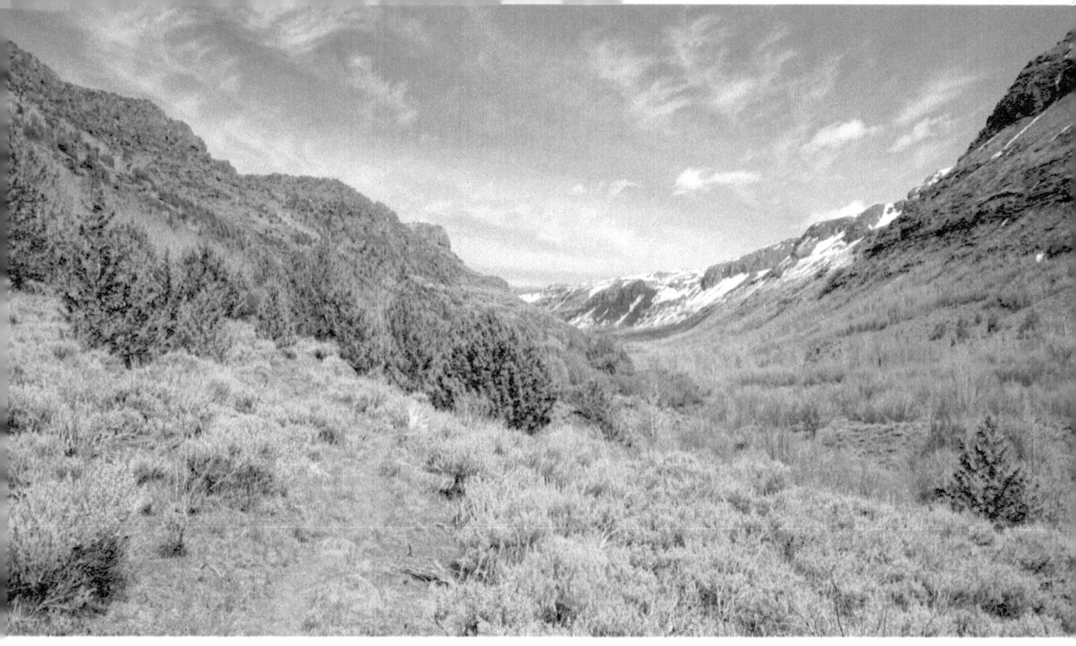

Little Blitzen Gorge on a glorious day in late spring.

trees, and magnificent views up the steep walls of Little Blitzen Gorge to the upper reaches of Steens Mountain. This is one of Oregon's most extraordinary hikes.

From the trailhead parking area, follow the Little Blitzen Trail uphill among juniper trees and spring wildflowers. Views open to the Steens highlands to the south. The trail then descends gradually to a crossing of the Little Blitzen River at 1.4 miles from the trailhead. For most of the year this is an easy ford but in during the spring snowmelt, the crossing is intimidatingly deep and swift. During this time, the easiest crossing is about 100 yards upstream where an island divides the river. In any case, you may want to bring sandals or a spare pair of shoes to ford the river. Once across, you will meet a junction with the Fred Riddle Trail. Turn right here. From here, you will follow the cascading river gradually uphill amid aspens, junipers, and large cottonwoods. The dominant flower here is Brown's peony, which grows profusely along the trail. At a little over 3 miles, pass a large rock at a bend in the river that makes for an excellent rest stop. Once back on the trail, you will soon break out of the woods into a large meadow strewn with huge boulders. Continue another 1.5 miles to another large meadow, where at last Little Blitzen Gorge's headwall comes into sight. This makes for a satisfying destination for those looking for a moderate hike. This location is labeled as "Moderate Meadow" on the map.

Backpackers and energetic day trippers should continue deeper into Little Blitzen Gorge. At 5.3 miles from the trailhead, the Little Blitzen Trail meets the Nye Trail at a cairn. The way from here is increasingly gorgeous. Streaks of snow line the headwall into July, sending seasonal waterfalls down the canyon's steep slopes and adding color and contrast to the beauty of the scene. The trail passes two side creeks with impressive waterfalls on the slopes above, then proceeds to closely follow the river for a spell. The sights, sounds, and scents of the high desert fill the air.

At 7.6 miles from the trailhead, you will meet the Wet Blanket Trail, the path out of Little Blitzen Gorge. Backpackers looking to make a circuit with nearby Big Indian Gorge (another beautiful hike that departs from South Steens Campground) use this trail to reach the slopes above. Unless this is your plan, you should continue another 0.2 mile to a nice campsite under a cluster of mahogany trees near the forks of the Little Blitzen River. Unless you're backpacking, you should stop here. The trail continues another 1.5 miles upriver to a waterfall at the head of Little Blitzen Gorge. The scenery is as good as it gets but remember: every step further into the Gorge you take is another step you'll need to take on the way out. From wherever you decided to stop, return the way you came.

123. Steens Mountain Summit

Distance of all trails: 4.8 miles out and back
Elevation Gain: 1,300 feet
Trailhead elevation: 9,508 feet
Trail high Point: 9,733 feet
Season: July – October
Best: July – October
Pass: none needed
On the traditional lands of: the Nüümü (Northern Paiute) people

Directions:

- From downtown Burns, drive east on OR 78 for 1.7 miles to a junction with OR 205 on the right. Turn right here.
- Drive OR 205 south for 57 miles to the small community of Frenchglen.
- Just past Frenchglen, turn left onto the Steens Mountain Road at a sign for the Steens Mountain Loop. You'll be driving on gravel from here on.
- Drive 22.2 miles to the first stop, the Kiger Gorge Viewpoint. For Kiger Gorge, turn left and drive 0.5 mile to road's end at the viewpoint.
- Back on the Steens Mountain Road, drive another 2.7 miles to a four-way junction. Left leads to the East Rim Viewpoint, straight leads to the summit of Steens Mountain, and right leads downhill on the South Steens end of the Loop Road. Before you do anything else, turn left and drive 0.3 mile to the East Rim Viewpoint.
- Back at the junction, turn left onto the summit access road and drive 1.9 miles to a trailhead at the end of the road. This is the trailhead for the summit of Steens Mountain and for Wildhorse Lake; incidentally, at 9,508 feet of elevation, it is also by far the highest road and trailhead in the state of Oregon. Extraordinary indeed!
- **Note:** As you will be driving in remote areas, do not leave Burns without filling your gas tank and checking your tire pressure. The Steens Mountain area is well-known and you won't have it to yourself but you should absolutely make sure you take care of any potential automobile issues before you leave Burns.
- **Drivetime from Burns:** 110 minutes

Hike: Steens Mountain is not only the tallest mountain in southeast Oregon, it is also the highest point for more than a hundred miles in every direction. From such a lofty vantage you would expect the views to be excellent, and you would be right. But Steens Mountain is about more than just views; as the highest mountain in all of southeast Oregon, this fifty-mile-long fault block is a world unto itself, with its own microclimate and vegetation unlike most of the rest of the state. You'll sample all of this on the long drive up the mountain from Frenchglen, arriving at last in the tundra of the mountain's upper reaches. This hike samples two of the most impressive viewpoints on the mountain, a short and easy trek to the mountain's summit, and a moderately difficult hike down to Wildhorse Lake, a wildly scenic mountain lake tucked into a basin on the mountain's summit flanks. You'll want to stop at each and every one of these spots and take the time to take it all in.

Starting with the Kiger Gorge Viewpoint, leave the car behind and walk the short trail to a viewpoint of Kiger Gorge. If the high elevation doesn't take your breath away, this viewpoint will! Glaciers scoured out five major valleys on Steens Mountain, and Kiger is the deepest and most impressive of these valleys. The trail leads to a signed viewpoint in just a couple hundred yards, but you can follow user trails another few hundred yards to an exposed viewpoint of the valley's upper headwall. When you're ready, return the way you came. From the parking lot, drive to East Rim Viewpoint and walk the short trail to the viewpoint here, down to the Alvord Desert and points east. Watch your step here, as the cliffs are precipitous just past the signed viewpoint. When you're done here, it's time for the main course: the summit of Steens and the gorgeous ramble down to Wildhorse Lake.

From the Steens summit parking lot, walk the gated road a half-mile towards the summit of the mountain, which is covered with radio and communications towers. Along the way you'll have fantastic views down to brilliantly blue Wildhorse Lake in the valley below, and you may have to stop and catch your breath. While this short hike is not at all difficult, it is easy to get winded at this high elevation. You will reach the summit in just a half-mile. where you can reflect on this unusual accomplishment: you just climbed the eight-tallest peak in the state of Oregon, and your vehicle did almost all of the work. When you're ready for dessert, return to the trailhead and locate the Wildhorse Lake Trail heading downhill to the right of the summit.

The Wildhorse Lake Trail drops 0.2 mile to a trail junction at a signboard. Sign your name in the trail register, then fork to the left. You will hike steeply downhill via a series of switchbacks and traverses, passing spectacular displays of alpine wildflowers in July and August. The trail reaches a fork near the lakeshore at 1.2 miles. Turning left here will take you around the lake another 0.3 mile to its far end, where you can look down the rugged canyon of Wildhorse Creek into the Alvord Desert. This is without a doubt one of Oregon's most extraordinary places! You can backpack here but there are not many campsites, and only two parties are allowed to camp at the lake per night. Whether you're here for an hour or a few nights, return the way you came. Remember to save some energy for the climb back out of the lake!

If you've got more time after your hikes, you should plan on returning via the South Steens Road. From the four-way junction, turn left and drive 11 spectacular, thrilling miles of excellent gravel road to South Steens Campground. Drivers with a fear of heights should avoid traveling this section of road, as you will be driving along cliff edges for large stretches of the traverse. Be sure to stop at the viewpoints of Big Indian Gorge and Little Blitzen Gorge (Hike 122), for incredible views into these deep glacial valleys. From South Steens Campground, it's another 19 miles of excellent gravel road back to OR 205.

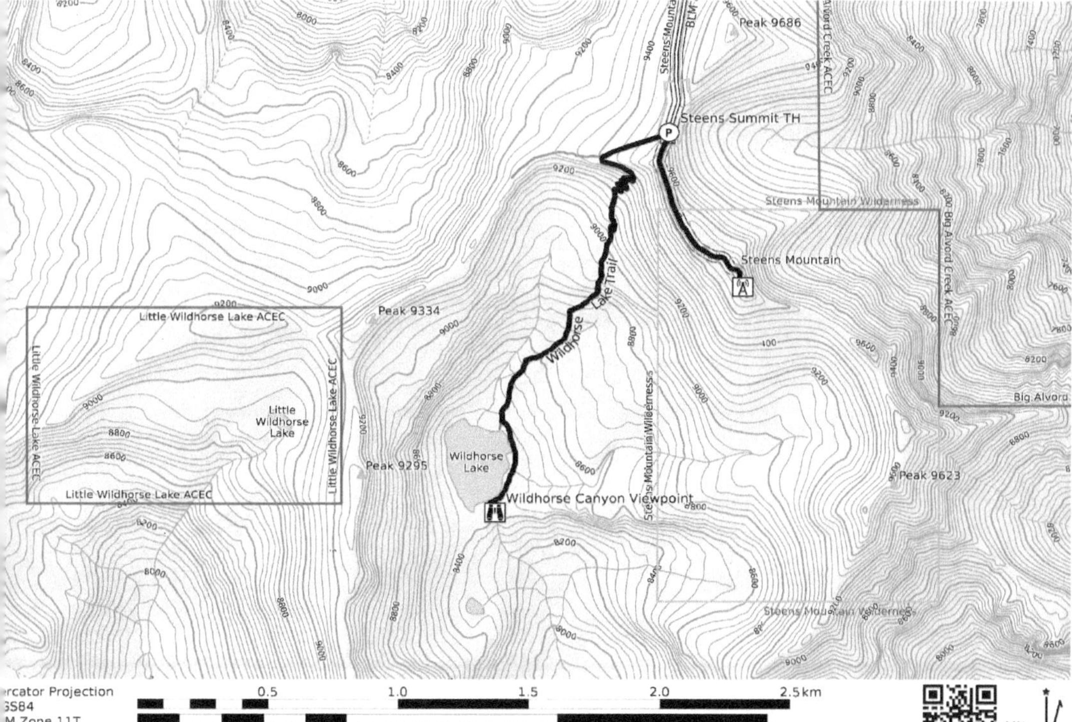

124. Pike Creek

Distance: 6.6 miles out and back
Elevation Gain: 1,600 feet
Trailhead elevation: 4,134 feet
Trail high Point: 5,622 feet
Season: May – October
Best: May – October
Pass: none needed
On the traditional lands of: the Nüümü (Northern Paiute) people

Directions:

- From downtown Burns, drive east on OR 78 for 64.4 miles to a junction with Folly Farm Road. Turn right.
- This road soon becomes Fields-Denio Road as it follows the precipitous eastern face of Steens Mountain.
- Drive 38.7 miles of pavement and excellent gravel to the Pike Creek Trailhead on the right side of the road.
- If you're driving here from Fields, drive north on OR 205 for 1.4 miles to a Y-junction with the East Steens Road. Continue straight to turn onto East Steens Road. Drive north for 11.2 miles of pavement and another 10 miles of gravel to Alvord Hot Springs. Check your odometer here. Continue 2 more miles to the Pike Creek Trailhead on the left.
- **Drivetime from Burns:** 1 hour and 50 minutes

Hike: This spectacular hike into canyon of Pike Creek has an argument for being the best hike in Southeast Oregon, and one of the best hikes in the state of Oregon. You follow an abandoned mining road into a colorful canyon of striated rock formations and May and June wildflowers. The snow-streaked summit cliffs of Steens Mountain tower above you, while Pike Creek and birdsong fill the air. This hike is high desert perfection.

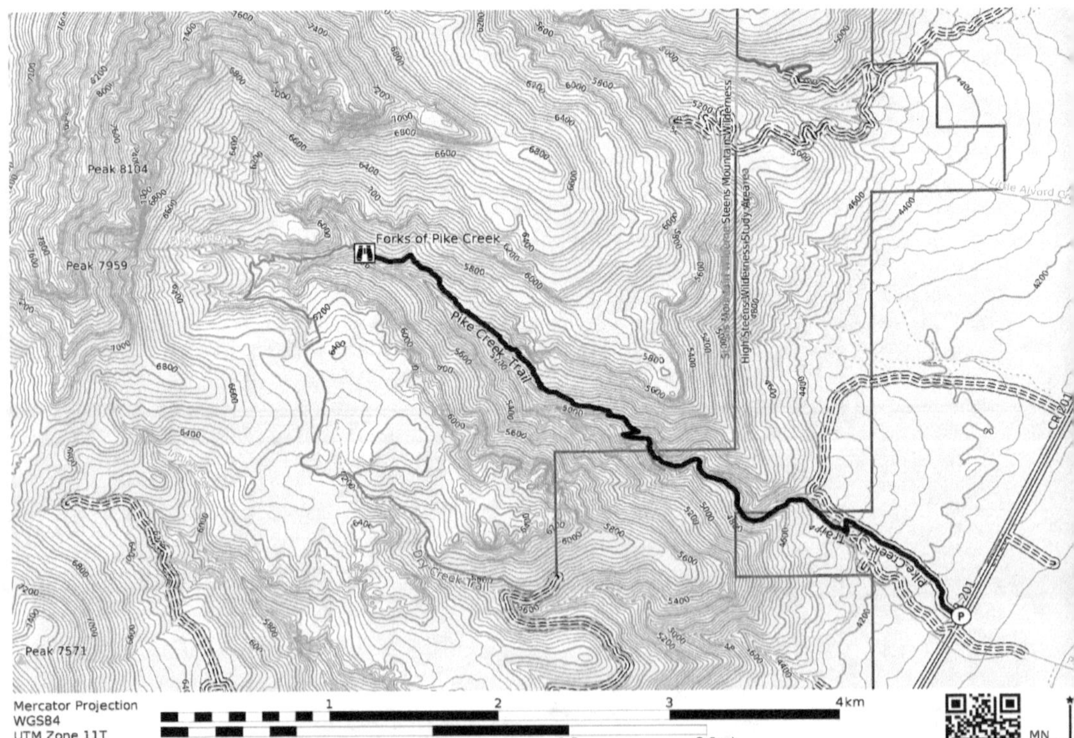

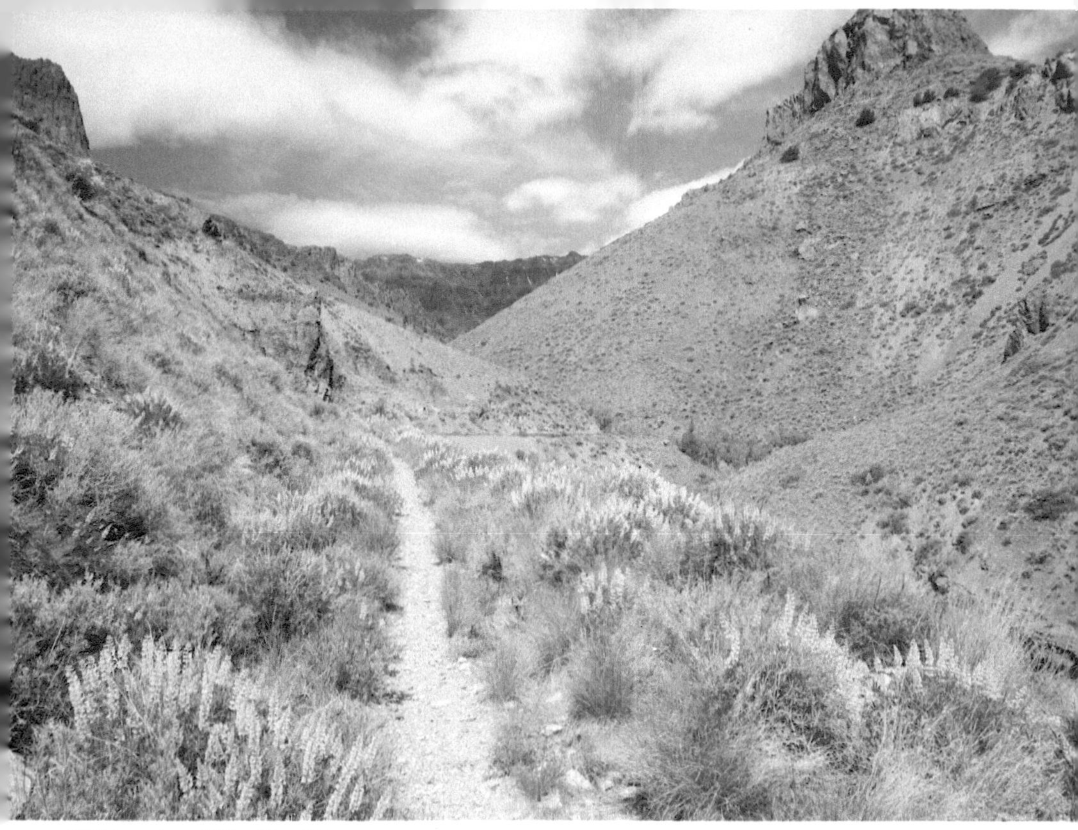

Hiking into Pike Creek's canyon.

Begin by crossing the gate at the trailhead. Follow this now-closed road uphill for 0.6 mile to the hike's former trailhead, now blocked off by boulders. From here, cross Pike Creek and begin hiking uphill into the canyon. You may pass a few cows along the way but soon you'll be climbing into Pike Creek's narrow gorge. In May, masses of fragrant yellow lupine line the trail, spurring hikers along with their intoxicating aroma. As you hike through this canyon, keep your eyes and ears open for rattlesnakes on warm days. The trail drops to cross Pike Creek again, then commences climbing away from the creek at an irregular grade, sometimes quite steeply. Fantastic displays of balsamroot, blue and yellow lupine, red paintbrush, and wild cucumber help hikers take a break, and the steep walls of Steens Mountain's summit crags tower above you. Look behind you for amazing views through Pike Creek's narrow gorge to the Alvord Desert's playa, where you will almost certainly see campers and trucks far out into the sands of this desert mecca.

At 2.5 miles from the trailhead, the forks of Pike Creek come into sight ahead of you. The way there is a rollercoaster of short ups and downs along a bench above the creek. Reach the forks at 3.3 miles, where a large rock tower splits Pike Creek in two. This is an incredibly peaceful place to stop, in a lush desert canyon beneath the towering walls of Steens Canyon. Backpackers will be disappointed to learn that there are few, if any campsites in this beautiful spot. The trail does continue beyond this point but becomes faint and brushy and does not lead to any better views. Instead, most hikers will be content to stop here. Return the way you came.

If you're looking to explore the Alvord Desert after your hike, all you need is to find a place to pull off the road and walk onto the playa. You can even drive across it, but make sure it hasn't rained recently. You can even camp on the playa, as many people do.

If you're driving back through Fields, make sure you stop at Fields Station to top off your gas tank. While you're there, you should order one of their famous milkshakes. They sell dozens of the massive shakes every day, with a wide variety of flavors. They are not to be missed!

125. Leslie Gulch

Distance of all trails: 5.8 miles out and back
Elevation Gain: 1,000 feet
Trailhead elevation: between 3,155 feet and 3,644 feet
Trail high point: 3,936 feet
Season: March – May, September – October
Best: March – May, September – October
Pass: none needed
On the traditional lands of: the Nüümü (Northern Paiute) people

Directions:
- From wherever you live, make your way to the remote community of Jordan Valley, Oregon, just a few miles west of Oregon's eastern border with Idaho. If you're approaching this area from Ontario or Boise, you'll need to drive south on US 95 from that area instead, skipping Jordan Valley.
- Before you leave Jordan Valley, make sure you fill your gas tank and check your tire pressure. You'll see plenty of people between Jordan Valley and Leslie Gulch but you should make sure you take care of any potential automobile issues before you leave town.
- From the Sinclair station in Jordan Valley, drive north for 18 miles to a turnoff on the left signed for Succor Creek and Leslie Gulch.
- Turn left and drive 8 gravel miles to a T-junction at the Rockville School. Turn left here.
- Drive 1.7 miles to a turnoff on the left signed for Leslie Gulch.
- Turn left and drive into the narrow, wildly scenic canyon of Leslie Gulch. You'll reach the trailheads and destinations in the following order, with mileages from the last junction:
- o Dago Gulch: 9.3 miles
- o Juniper Gulch: 10.3 miles
- o Timber Gulch: 11.6 miles
- o Slocum Creek Campground: 13.8 miles
- o Lake Owyhee Reservoir boat ramp and roads end: 14.1 miles
- **Drivetime from Jordan Valley:** 1 hour
- **Note:** If thunderstorms or heavy rain are in the forecast, **DO NOT** plan on visiting Leslie Gulch. Heavy rain can turn the gravel road here to mud, washing out the road and leaving you stuck here until it dries out and somebody comes to fix the road.

Hike: The Owyhee Canyonlands are truly one of Oregon's most extraordinary places, and every Oregonian who loves the outdoors should plan on visiting at least once in their lives. It's not easy, though. Most of this area is a true pain to visit; the roads are long and rocky dirt roads and turn to mud when it rains, rendering them undriveable. The remoteness of the area ensures that anyone who visits needs to take this place seriously, and plan for the worst even when the worst is unlikely. Anything is possible. Leslie Gulch, located on the northern end of this magical canyon, is the only place in the Owyhee Canyonlands that a hiker can visit with an average low-clearance vehicle. It takes a lot of effort to get there, but once you arrive you'll be transported into the depths of this desert splendor. There are five major gulches in the Leslie Gulch area, and three of them make for good, short hikes. The order you hike them in does not matter, but they will be presented here in the order in which I hiked them.

Juniper Gulch: From the Juniper Gulch Trailhead, locate the trail and follow it into the canyon. The trail is quite brushy, so you'll want to make sure you're wearing long pants. If you brought trekking poles (I never leave home without them), leave them in the car for this hike as you'll want the use of your hands here. The trail enters a narrow canyon with red and orange rock walls several hundred feet high; you might think you fell asleep and woke up in one of Utah's magical national parks! At 0.6 mile the canyon splits; left leads to an impassible slot canyon in just a few hundred feet, so instead turn right. The trail splits again in a few hundred yards, where you will head uphill to the right. In just a few minutes, Juniper Gulch's impressive upper headwall comes into view. Continue on this faint trail to the headwall, a spectacular wall of sculpted pinnacles and honeycombed rock formations (see the photo on the next two pages). The trail peters out here but you can make a short loop by following the gully at the base of the honeycombs downhill until you reach the trail again. From here, return to the trailhead the way you came. One quick note about the pit toilet at the Juniper Gulch Trailhead: be on the lookout for black widow spiders in the bathroom, as they like to hide in the corner here. Eeek!

Timber Gulch: Just as with Juniper Gulch, this trail leads into a colorful amphitheater of naturally sculpted red and orange cliffs. Here though the cliffs are even more impressive and the canyon is even narrower than in Juniper Gulch; a more impressive place in southeast Oregon would be hard to find! From the unmarked trailhead, located at a pullout on the right side of the road 1.3 miles west of the Juniper Gulch Trailhead, locate the trail heading downhill into a wash. Follow the wash for a short distance until you reach the continuation on the trail on the left. Pick up the trail here and follow it through brush for 0.2 mile until you reach another trail junction on your right. Turn right here and follow this trail uphill into Timber Gulch's northern amphitheater, which I nicknamed "The Temple" when I visited. At one point on your way up, look to your left to see a huge undercut rock fin that resembles a natural rock arch. The trail then follows the base of a huge cliff for a short distance before ending at the rocky base of this temple. If you love scrambling over boulders and climbing up draws you'll love this spot, so leave yourself time to explore. Return the way you came.

Dago Gulch: This unfortunately-named canyon is quite scenic, but not as much as the first two gulches you visited. Furthermore, the views are better on the return trip and the canyon is quite shady in the afternoon; for these reasons, you should save Dago Gulch for the end of the day. From the trailhead turnaround, follow the road straight into the canyon. After scrambling over rocks and pushing through brush in the first two gulches you visited, the wide road proves a welcome change of pace. As with everywhere else in Leslie Gulch, colorful rock pinnacles tower over the canyon bottom. After 1 mile, you'll reach a cattle gate and a "No Trespassing" sign, which is your clue to turn around. On your way back, take the time to savor the views back into Leslie Gulch's inner sanctum. If you're interested in staying down in this glorious canyon, camping is only permitted at Slocum Creek Campground near the end of the road.

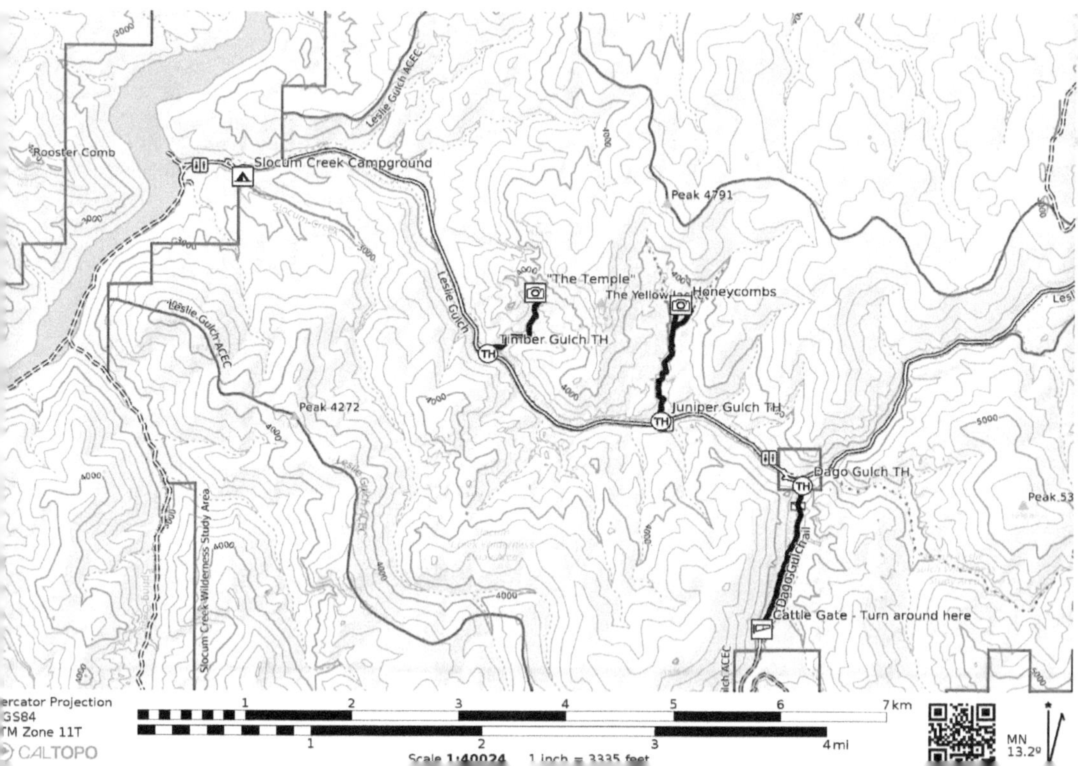

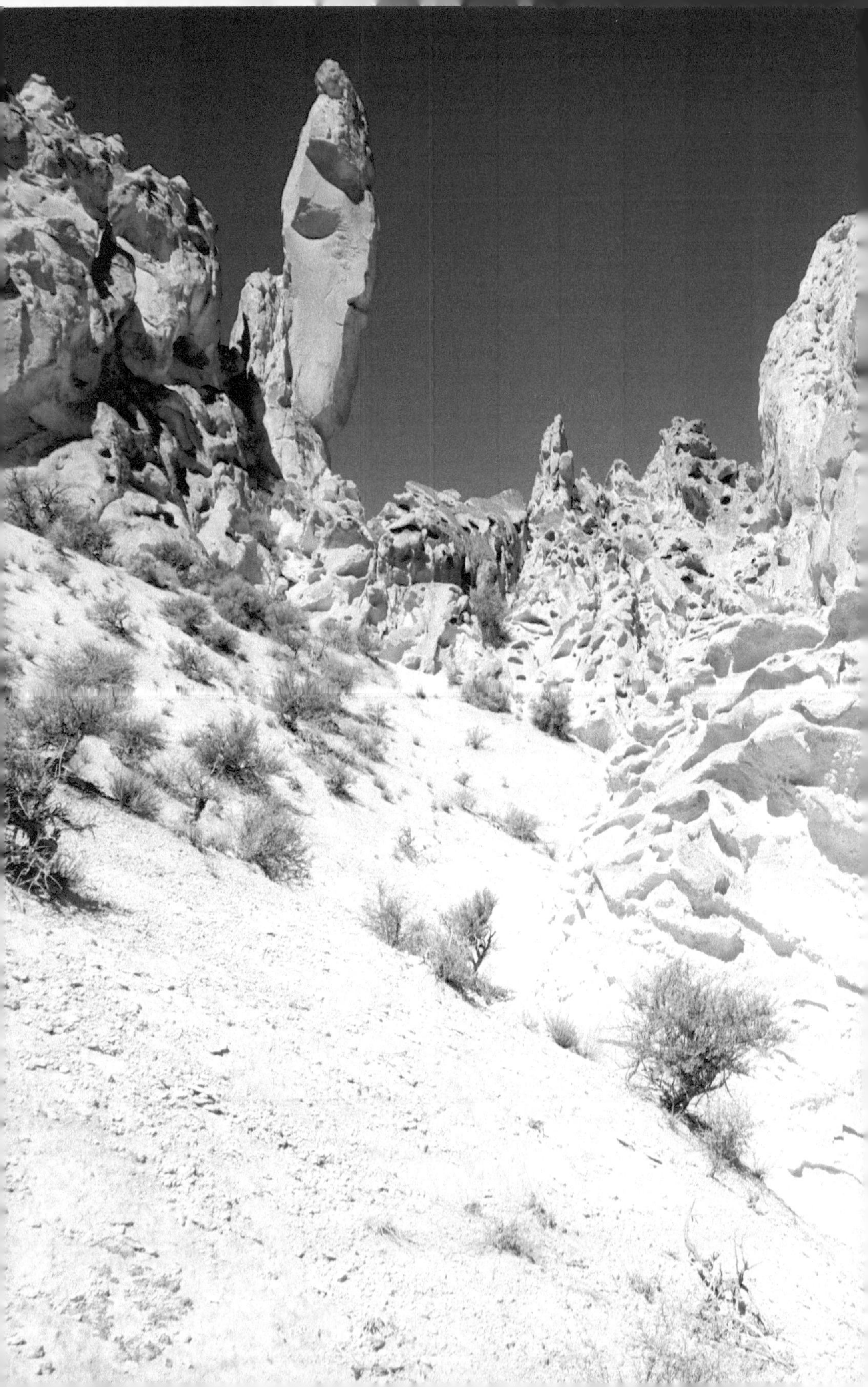

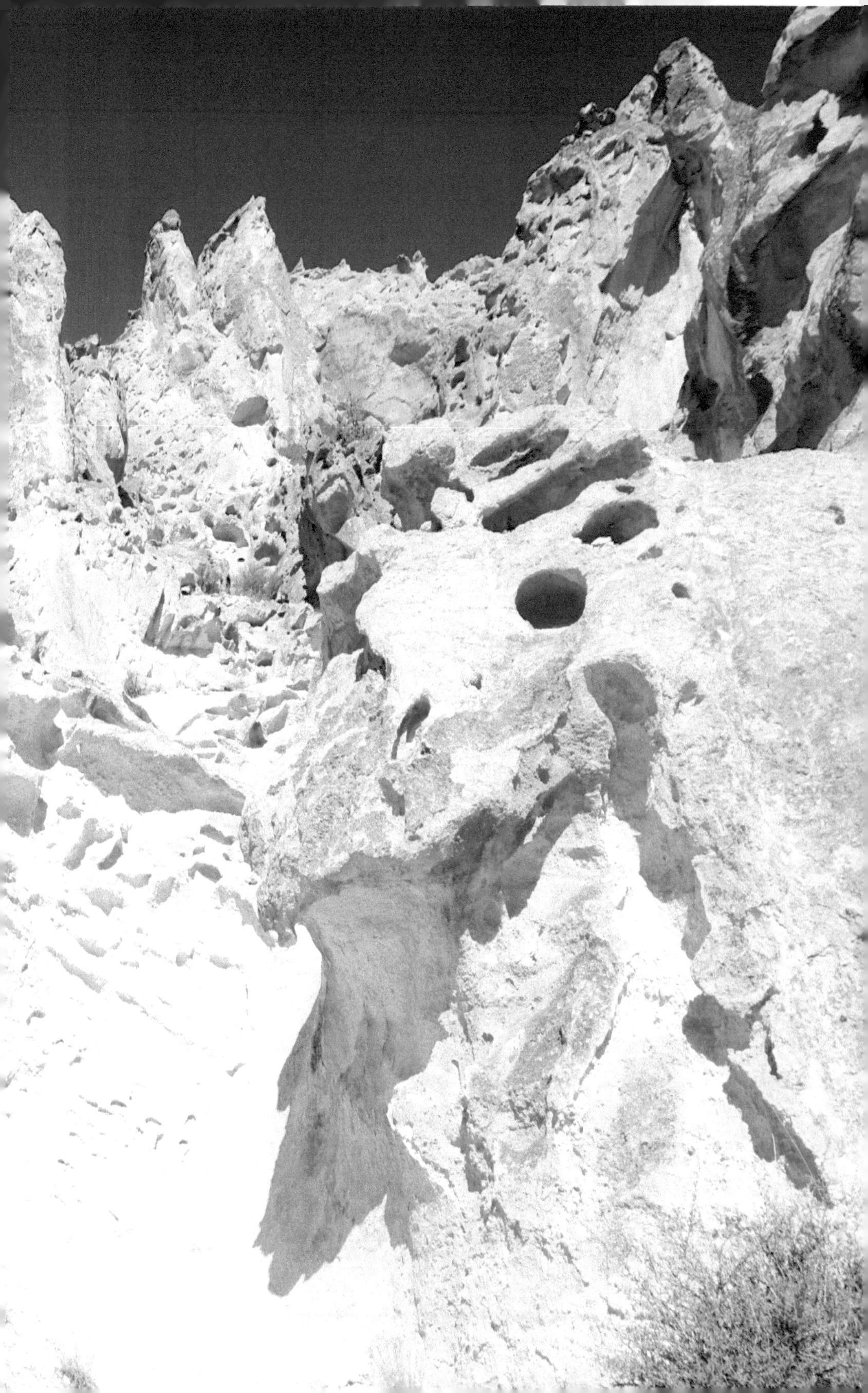

Appendix 1: The Hardest Cuts

While I worked on this book project, I completed more than 200 hikes. Some of these were hikes I had done many times before, and some were hikes that were new to me. As the scope of this project began to take shape, I began to realize that I could not possibly include every hike I researched in this book. I ultimately decided to feature 125 hikes in this book. In honor of the great Texas indie rock band Spoon, I am calling the hikes that did not make it "the hardest cuts". Here is a list of some of my favorites:

Oregon Coast and Coast Range

1. Arch Rock Loop
2. Rockaway Beach Ancient Cedar
3. Netarts Spit
4. Cascade Head
5. Valley of the Giants
6. The Thumb
7. Cape Ferrelo
8. Tincup Trail

Willamette Valley

1. Burlington Creek
2. Camassia Natural Area
3. Molalla River Corridor
4. Horse Rock Ridge

Columbia River Gorge

1. Latourell Falls
2. Larch Mountain
3. Elowah and Upper McCord Falls
4. Indian Mountain
5. Memaloose Hills
6. Sevenmile Hill

Northern Oregon Cascades

1. Laurance Lake Ridge
2. Tamanawas Falls
3. Heather Canyon
4. Burnt Lake
5. Devils Peak
6. Hawk Mountain

Central Oregon Cascades

1. Opal Creek
2. Bachelor Mountain via Bruno Meadows
3. Crescent Mountain
4. Berley Lakes
5. Jefferson Lake Trail
6. Lower Metolius River
7. Whychus Creek Falls
8. Rosary Lakes

Southern Oregon

1. Toketee Falls and North Umpqua Hot Springs
2. Warm Springs Falls
3. Rough Rider Falls

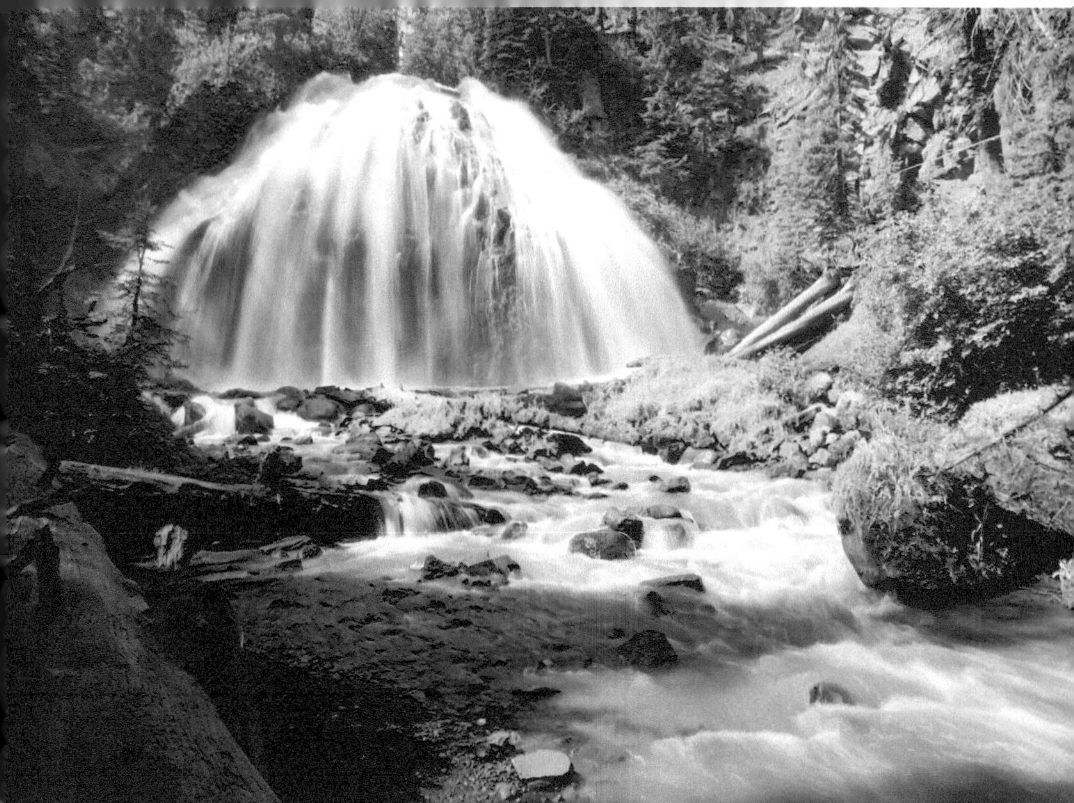

Chush Falls south of Sisters was one of the hardest cuts.

Central Oregon High Desert
1. Spring Basin Wilderness
2. John Day Fossil Beds - Clarno Unit
3. Mecca Flat and Trout Creek
4. Steelhead Falls
5. Oregon Badlands
6. Paulina Creek Waterfalls
7. Black Canyon of Sutton Mountain

Northeast Oregon
1. Ninemile Ridge
2. Temperance Creek
3. Big Sheep Basin
4. Imnaha River and the Blue Hole

Southeast Oregon
1. Craft Cabin Trail
2. Big Indian Gorge

For photos, maps, and more information on these and other hikes, you can check my website at www.offthebeatentrailpdx.com.

Index

N

O

P

R

S

T

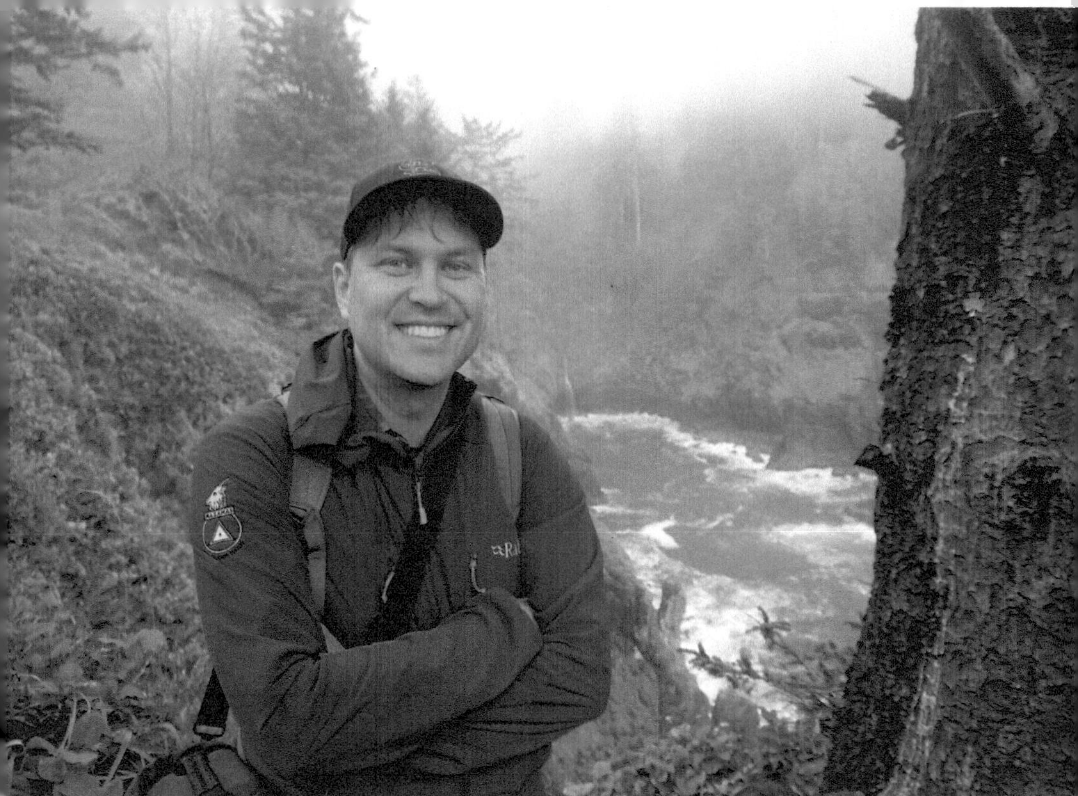

About the author:
Matt Reeder moved from Illinois to Oregon at age 7 with his family. He grew up hiking and camping all over the Pacific Northwest; he never felt more at home than on the trail. He moved back to Illinois at age 16 but returned 8 years later to settle in Portland. Since moving back to Oregon in 2005 he has logged more than 8,000 miles on the trail throughout the Pacific Northwest. *Extraordinary Oregon!* is his first book on the entire state of Oregon.

Matt is also the author of *PDX Hiking 365*, *101 Hikes in the Majestic Mount Jefferson Region* and *Off the Beaten Trail*. He lives in an old farmhouse in southeast Portland with his wife Wendy. When not on the trail or in the classroom, he spends his free time obsessing about music, following the Portland Trail Blazers and reading voraciously. You can usually identify Matt on the trail by his red St. Louis Cardinals hat, a visible sign of his lifelong love of the 11-time World Series Champions.

www.ingramcontent.com/pod-product-compliance
Lightning Source LLC
LaVergne TN
LVHW091112080826
845145LV00008B/1880

* 9 7 8 0 9 8 8 9 1 2 5 4 0 *